Enlarging America

Judaic Traditions in Literature, Music, and Art
Ken Frieden and Harold Bloom, *Series Editors*

Enlarging America

America

The Cultural Work of Jewish Literary Scholars, 1930–1990

Susanne Klingenstein

Syracuse University Press

Copyright © 1998 by Syracuse University Press
Syracuse, New York 13244-5160
All Rights Reserved

First Edition 1998
98 99 00 01 02 03   6 5 4 3 2 1

The paper used in this publication meets the minimum requirements of American National Standard for Information Sciences—Permanence of Paper for Printed Library Materials, ANSI Z39.48-1948. ∞™

Library of Congress Cataloging-in-Publication Data
Klingenstein, Susanne, 1959–
Enlarging America : the cultural work of Jewish literary scholars,
1930–1990 / Susanne Klingenstein.
p.   cm. — (Judaic traditions in literature, music, and art)
Includes bibliographical references and index.
ISBN 0-8156-0540-4 (cloth : alk. paper) —
1. Jewish college teachers—United States—Biography.   2. Jews—
United States—Biography.   3. Critics—United States—Biography.
4. Jews—United States—Intellectual life.   5. United States—
Civilization—Jewish influences.   I. Title.   II. Series.
E184.37.E55   1998
973'.04924—dc21   98-22525

For Jim, with love
and for Rachel, light of my life

What a wee little part of a person's life are his acts and his words! His real life is led in his head, and is known to none but himself. . . . Biographies are but the clothes and buttons of the man—the biography of the man himself cannot be written.

—MARK TWAIN

Whoever turns biographer commits himself to lies, to concealment, to hypocrisy, to embellishment, and even to dissembling his own lack of understanding, for biographical truth is not to be had, and even if one had it, one could not use it.

—SIGMUND FREUD

To write history is so difficult that most historians are forced to make concessions to the techniques of legend.

—ERICH AUERBACH

Susanne Klingenstein is associate professor of writing and humanistic studies at the Massachusetts Institute of Technology. She was educated at Brandeis University, the University of Heidelberg (Germany), and Harvard University. She is the author of *Jews in the American Academy, 1900–1940: The Dynamics of Intellectual Assimilation* (1991) and of numerous articles on Jewish American literature and culture.

Contents

PART ONE | The Harvard Circle

The Spirit of Place

Exploring America

PART TWO | **The Columbia Sphere**

Literary Minds

The Rediscovery of Origins

Illustrations

Preface

THIS BOOK DOCUMENTS not only my subjects' integration into America but my own as well. I fell in love with certain aspects of America: with the intensity and moral seriousness of its intellectual life, and with its thriving Jewish culture, which I had observed longingly from my distant perch at the University of Heidelberg.

Within a few weeks after my arrival in Cambridge in August 1987, I found myself in the embrace of a compelling group of Jewish literary scholars. I began to read their works, to study in their seminars, and to hound them with my tape recorder. It took six years to assemble the basic data for this study and three more years to bring the book into final shape. The difficulty was threefold: First, I was dealing with a moving target. My subjects were alive and steadily producing not only more scholarship but also memoirs and autobiographical writings that continually opened new perspectives on their intellectual lives.

Second, I was struggling with the literary form I had chosen for this book, the writing of history through biography. I did not want to write about Jewish academics as a group. That approach did not seem to me to yield insights beyond the well-documented general pattern of assimilation and dissimilation described, for instance, in Werner Sollors's *Beyond Ethnicity: Consent and Descent in American Culture* (1986). Rather, I was after a history from within. I wanted readers to perceive the integration first of Jewish scholars, then of Jewish issues into American literary academe by following the careers of the most important players. The problem was that once I stopped seeing integration as a group process, it refracted into a myriad of fascinating personal stories governed by chance, individual temperament, and the opportunities of time and place. It was hard not only to select the best players—that is, the most interesting and *representative* witnesses—but also to keep in sight the seemingly well-established history of the group as a whole, which now appeared to be so flat as to seem untrue.

Third, my attitude toward integration, especially toward its first phase, assimilation, became less critical as I grew more familiar with the realities of American life and the dynamics of Jewish American culture. Therefore the early chapters had to be rewritten many times. As a whole, the book has the flaws and virtues (such as they may be) of the unsteady perspective of an outsider to American culture who is herself caught up in a process of integration.

During my long engagement with this book, I have incurred many debts. My deepest gratitude is to my husband, Jim, who has taken my Americanization in hand; to Cynthia Ozick, whose love and friendship first made America a home for me; and to Sacvan Bercovitch, whose story originally inspired this book and who keeps a skeptical distance to America that continues to be a welcome antidote to Jim's unequivocal embrace of this extraordinary country.

I owe an inordinate debt to the scholars who agreed to be interviewed (many of them repeatedly) and who often added more details and anecdotes in subsequent letters and conversations. For their generous gift of time I want to thank Daniel Aaron, M. H. Abrams, Robert Alter, Sylvia Ary, the late Gila Bercovitch, Sacvan Bercovitch, Harold Bloom, Caroline Bloomfield, Jules Chametzky, Dorrit Cohn, Morris Dickstein, Charles Feidelson, Lewis Feuer, Stanley Fish, Leslie Fiedler, the late Alice Fredman, Marjorie Garber, Eugene Goodheart, Gerald Graff, Stephen Greenblatt, Susan Gubar, Allen Guttmann, Geoffrey Hartman, Carolyn G. Heilbrun, John Hollander, the late Irving Howe, Carole Kessner, Lawrence Langer, Elena Zarudnaya Levin, the late Harry Levin, Steven Marcus, Leo Marx, Charles Muscatine, Stephen Orgel, Martin Peretz, Sanford Pinsker, Norman Podhoretz, David Roskies, Barbara Herrnstein Smith, Alan Trachtenberg, and Ruth R. Wisse.

Books cannot be written without friends who pry the struggling author loose from the desk with invitations to concerts, dinners, literary readings, or restorative walks around town. I owe much of my equanimity to Marion Aptroot, Ellen Cooney, Barbara Goldoftas, Jeremy Korzenik, and Shulamit and Hillel Levine.

I also want to thank my colleagues at MIT for their patient support of a newcomer. I am especially grateful to Alan Lightman, Kenneth Manning, and Rosalind Williams for having first given me the opportunity to teach at an exciting and challenging institution, and to Anita

Desai for taking a junior colleague ever so gently under her expansive wing.

For financial assistance I want to thank the German Academic Exchange Service, the American Jewish Historical Society, Brandeis University, Harvard University, the Memorial Foundation for Jewish Culture, and MIT. The most substantial funds I received from Deutsche Forschungsgemeinschaft, which supported this book as a postdoctoral project. For photographs I am indebted to Jill Krementz and Virginia Schendler.

Last but not least I wish to express my gratitude to Robert Mandel, director of Syracuse University Press, for his enthusiastic and unflagging support of this project, to John Fruehwirth and Bettie McDavid Mason for immaculate editing, and to my dear friend Richard Miller, whose astute suggestions and magic red pencil enabled me to shrink the manuscript and to see my way to the end, pursuing only one thought at a time.

Boston, Massachusetts   Susanne Klingenstein
August 1997

Introduction

THIS BOOK IS FIRST AND FOREMOST about a historic phenomenon, namely, the integration of Jewish literary scholars into English departments at American universities. It is the sequel to my earlier study, *Jews in the American Academy, 1900–1940: The Dynamics of Intellectual Assimilation,* in which I examined the opening of American humanities departments, especially philosophy, to the first Jewish academics and analyzed the scholars' strategies of intellectual assimilation. The constant negotiation between the parental culture of Jewish learning and faith and the Christianity-inflected world of American academe shaped the intellectual work of early Jewish academics.

The subjects in this book, though often also the children of immigrants, find themselves at a much greater distance from traditional Jewish culture and faith than their academic predecessors were. With few exceptions, they no longer come from homes where rabbinic learning, familiarity with classical Jewish languages, religious observance, and Jewish community service were thought at least as valuable as the ability to succeed financially or intellectually in modern secular America. Since a life within the confines of the Jewish community was not held out to them by parents, teachers, and peers as a desirable or even viable alternative to life in America at large, the generation of academics portrayed in this book spent much of its intellectual energy on defining its relation to America.

Hence this book is also an account of the intellectual lives of men and women who helped to shape our notion of American culture and its literary traditions. There is, however, very little in it about their personal lives—their loves, marriages, and children—although they too influence the life of the mind and, more importantly, speak incontrovertibly to the central issue of assimilation.

xvii

Until the late 1960s intermarrying, especially if the Gentile partner was the woman, simply meant dropping out of the Jewish people, and it still constitutes a powerful disruption of Jewish identity and communal ties, leading to a closer identification with secular American culture. Intermarriage was quite common in the first generation of Jewish literary scholars, who did not come from families of Jewish learning and who were bent on succeeding in a world dominated by self-possessed white Anglo-Saxon Protestant men. Intermarriage was more frequent in New England than in New York, where WASP dominance of academe was counterbalanced if not overwhelmed by the strong presence of Jews as a socially and culturally familiar and intellectually exciting group.

Despite the indisputably close links between personal life and intellectual preoccupation, very few of the older Jewish literary scholars I interviewed were prepared to talk about their personal lives; those who had intermarried appeared particularly reluctant, and some of them became quite defensive when questions aimed beyond scholarship and toward the construction of their Jewish selves. The strong resistance of most of my subjects to an analysis of the emotional and psychological underpinnings of their academic pursuits swayed me to respect their privacy, to include only the most essential personal information (except when explicitly encouraged to do so), and to refrain from all psychological speculation.

My previous book ended with a detailed portrait of Lionel Trilling, who was hired as an assistant professor in English literature at Columbia University in 1939. Trilling was not the first Jewish professor of English literature in America, but his case was the one most closely watched because his breakthrough occurred at a prominent Ivy League school and because among Trilling's students were many culturally ambitious second-generation American Jews from the New York boroughs for whom Trilling was a role model.

The present study, which retains the focus on Harvard and Columbia, moves on to the next generation of literary academics. It consists of a dozen detailed portraits of Jewish literary scholars, which attempt to delineate the social and intellectual forces that shaped their careers. The amount of detail, for which these portraits may be faulted, and the absence of any theories of ethnicity in this book are partly deliberate and designed to counteract the temptation to think of these Jewish academics in terms of group characteristics and partly the inevitable result of the way in which this book came to be written.

When I first approached my subject, I was filled with theories of American ethnicity. I had absorbed the seminal books by Marcus Klein, Werner Sollors, Ronald Takaki, and many others, and developed a speculative theory of my own about the integration of Jews into American academe. But when I contacted my initial set of interviewees, I discovered that they were not at all intrigued by my theory. In July 1989, Harry Levin wrote to me: "I cannot conceal my reaction of feeling uncomfortable within your present metaphorical scheme, and indeed would rather be left out than fitted into it Procrustes-wise."[1] When I pressed my view of the matter, Levin threatened to withhold his permission for me to quote from interviews and letters, writing me in October 1989 that he felt I "might be distorting the subject by superimposing a framework of preconception which might not accord with the actual experience of those who lived through it."[2] That was a serious charge.

I took my cue from Levin's letter and began to listen to what the scholars were telling me about their careers. It became evident that the resemblance between theories of ethnicity and the reality of the lives lived was a passing one at best, and that what was most fascinating about my interviewees was not the superficial similarity of their shared cultural ambition but the vast differences in their early social circumstances and mature personalities, which more than anything else determined the course of their lives. This book, then, does not examine the careers of Jewish literary scholars through the prism of theory, but instead challenges theorists to hone their constructions on the biographical narratives presented here.

The down side to resisting the conceptualization of these biographical narratives within a theoretical framework is perhaps a seeming innocence in the portrayal of Jews and their relation to America; but what the book may lack in theoretical sophistication it more than makes up in directness and immediacy. Six years of intensive reading and listening diminished the distance between the writer and her subjects (which does not imply that I did not find some scholars more accessible than others or that I did not relate to some better than to others because I found them more attuned to my preferences and commitments). Moreover, for ten years now I have lived in the same sphere as my subjects. I have shared their academic space, studied in their classrooms, sat at their dinner tables, worshiped in their synagogues. Hence, this is in some ways a very personal book. It offers the view of an academic insider with all the advantages and disadvantages such a perspective entails.

An unpleasant consequence of opting for in-depth portraits rather than for a comprehensive series of snapshots was the necessity of being extremely selective. The chosen figures had to be interestingly singular as well as representative, and the series of portraits had to form a consecutive narrative that mirrored in its outline the story of all (or most) Jewish literary scholars in the United States. The most feasible solution was to center the story on two generations of scholars (one born in the 1910s, the other in the 1930s) and on two East Coast universities. This meant ignoring the West Coast, the Midwest, and the South, as well as dropping Princeton and Yale in the East. The latter was done with the greatest regret. But any book sandwiching adequate portraits of the Yale critics Geoffrey Hartman and Harold Bloom between those of their elders and contemporaries would crack at the seams. A study of Jewish literary scholars at Yale, beginning with the educations of Charles Feidelson, Richard Ellmann, and Charles Muscatine, moving on to Hartman, Bloom, and John Hollander, and ending with the rebellious generation of Morris Dickstein, Marjorie Garber, and Stephen Greenblatt, will remain as a future project.

Focusing on Harvard and Columbia makes sense insofar as these are two of America's premier, trendsetting institutions of higher learning and have been especially sought out by Jews—Harvard for its image, Columbia for its location. Moreover, there are many connections between the two institutions (scholars moving as students or faculty from one school to the other), while at the same time the two schools provide an illuminating study in contrast. The pressures encountered by students at Harvard and Columbia were different in kind on account of the institutions' different locations and traditions.

Harvard's setting in the small town of Cambridge, Massachusetts, is provincial. Despite its proximity to MIT, two subway stops away, and the presence of some thirty other colleges and universities in the Boston metropolitan area, Harvard is for anyone affiliated with it, the biggest thing in town. Harvard is an octopus sprawled all over Cambridge with tentacles reaching deep into Boston. There is no escape from it. Even off campus, you are always "there." Once you are inside, however, the Harvard world is, paradoxically, very small, enclosed, and indrawn. It is a cerebral, peaceful place that is happy with itself. Its intellectual forces are centripetal; its student body, especially in the humanities, is, despite Harvard's celebrated love of eccentrics, astonishingly homogeneous. Harvard shapes new arrivals to its needs. The sense of having arrived at the top, of having scaled the Mount Everest of academe, creates in students (after the sophomore slump of self-doubt) and in tenured faculty a soft, fuzzy generosity, a willingness to help the poor devils who are less privileged.

Columbia's challenging urban setting and exciting cosmopolitan environment, by contrast, account for its much tenser atmosphere. Students and faculty seem always wired. The city is crowding the campus. New York, with its tough realities and extraordinary opportunities for stunning careers, is always there, even in a seminar on Shakespeare's sonnets. Columbia is among the smallest things in town, always threatened to be overwhelmed. The students measure who they are against the realities of the city. Hence Columbia's intellectual forces are centrifugal, shattered and refracted by the city, the epitome of the real world. Life in New York shapes the students at Columbia. They are a tough, tense, heterogeneous, adventurous, but pragmatic lot. That the "spirit of place," as D. H. Lawrence termed it, should somehow enter into the literary enterprise, which absorbs and reflects so much of the scholar's personality, taste, and intellect, seems almost a matter of course.

This book is divided into two large parts, "The Harvard Circle" and "The Columbia Sphere." They are each composed of two sections grouping several chapters together. The first section of each part deals with scholars who were immediately and for sustained periods involved with either Harvard or Columbia; the second section presents scholars who left these universities, yet continue to work under their influences. The narrative is roughly chronological, moving from an emphasis on the 1920s and 1930s in chapters 1 and 2, to the 1940s and 1950s in chapters 3 through 5, the 1950s and 1960s in chapters 6 through 8, and the 1970s to 1990s in chapters 9 through 12. The story begins at Harvard in the 1880s and shifts to Columbia only in the 1950s because I already presented much of the material on Columbia in the first half of the twentieth century in my earlier book.

It is quite safe to leave Harvard in the late 1940s because after the appointment of Harry Levin to its English Department in 1939 nothing of interest to historians of Jewish literary scholars happens there until the early 1960s, when the narrative returns to Cambridge to follow the career of Levin's student Robert Alter. During the 1950s the important developments concerning Jewish literary scholars take place all over America, as a huge number of young Jews were being hired as assistant professors of English literature (chap. 6 and 7) and at Columbia University, where Trilling's students reinterpreted his political and literary legacy (chap. 8).

At the time of Trilling's death in 1975, something paradoxical was happening to American culture: it was becoming rapidly diversified and seemingly divided as different social groups clamored for their rights. Yet at the same time the culture was becoming more uniform, more truly national, as the privileges once accorded a particular class, race, and gender were being superseded by everyone's right to be proud of his or her descent. As issues of race, gender, sexual orientation, and so forth were being pushed to the forefront, the activism they engendered forged a new participatory national culture. The paradoxical nature of this development, which dominated the last quarter of the twentieth century, is captured in chapters 9 through 11. The old specificities of locale—Lawrence's spirit of place—are dissolved. It no longer matters whether the story takes place at Harvard or Columbia or elsewhere; universities are now national places participating in the same discussions. In fact, the subjects of chapters 9, 10, and 11 are itinerants moving between Harvard and Columbia, East Coast and West Coast, Canada and the United States. What unites them as a group is their quest for the origins of their community's sense of self.

The book begins with a portrait of Harvard University between the student days of George Santayana in the early 1880s and T. S. Eliot's return to his alma mater in 1933 to deliver the Charles Eliot Norton lectures and to bid farewell to American academe as a homogeneous ("genteel") culture. Harvard Yard from Santayana to Eliot was a place without visible Jews. Chapter 1 describes Harvard's social and intellectual culture and the pressure it put on Jews, especially Santayana's friends Charles Loeser and Bernard Berenson. Coercive as they seemed at the time, these pressures were mild compared to those felt by Jewish Harvard students during the 1920s, when President Abbott Lawrence Lowell thought it his duty to solve Harvard's "Jewish problem" and toughened the administration's stance toward them. Another measure of the changing cultural atmosphere is the difference in attitude toward Catholicism evinced by Santayana and Eliot. The former maintained a comfortable distance from the Church. His "Catholic sympathies" he called "merely sympathies [without] a rational and human backing." But the latter committed himself very seriously to Church doctrine.[3] Concomitantly, Santayana indulged in a teasing dislike of Jews, whereas Eliot concocted a theory of cultural exclusion at the very time of his visit to Harvard University.

Eliot, who was Harry Levin's mentor during Levin's senior year at Harvard, is the ostensible link between the introductory sketch of Harvard Yard (chap. 1) and the first group of three portraits, presenting

Levin and his contemporaries M. H. Abrams and Daniel Aaron (chaps. 2, 3, and 4). Levin and Abrams came to Harvard as freshmen in 1929 and 1930, respectively, while Aaron arrived there as a graduate student in 1933, just as James Bryant Conant took the helm of the university. The portraits of Levin, Abrams, and Aaron (all born in 1912) unfold their strategies of cultural integration as reflected in their scholarly work: Levin's strategy consisted in the mastery of the Western literary tradition, Abrams's in developing a theory of imaginative consent to an "alien" cultural tradition, and Aaron's in a mode of observation that combined inside and outside, distance and daring empathy. Each portrait also highlights one peculiar aspect of study at Harvard. In Levin's case it is the importance of the mentor or tutorial system; in Abrams's it is the impact of study in England, especially at Cambridge University; and in Aaron's it is the rise of American studies as a new field of research.

The social and intellectual life of Harvard during the first half of this century revolved around non-Jewish scholars such as Irving Babbitt, F. O. Matthiessen, or Howard Mumford Jones, who served as important mentors to the earliest Jewish literary academics. Their literary brilliance, wit, and often sheer moral decency, along with the parochial arrogance and smugness of instructors, such as George L. Kittredge and Francis P. Magoun, surrounded Jewish students. Therefore considerable attention is paid in chapters 2 through 4 to these academic giants of the time. Although they too were often outsiders, they represented to their Jewish students the quintessence of Harvard. Only after their decline or passing did the emerging young Jewish scholars grow to full stature.

Continuity in Harvard mentorship is the link between the first and second sections in part 1. The rise of American studies closely connects the portraits of Daniel Aaron and Leo Marx. Section 2, "Exploring America," describes the opening and slow dissolution of the tight-knit circle of Harvard mentors and students in the late 1940s and 1950s. Marx, born in 1919, arrived at Harvard College as a freshman in 1937, when sympathy for radical left-wing causes still ran high among students and faculty. Political rallies, where faculty and students mingled, proved an easy means of integration into one niche of the Harvard community. Marx graduated in 1941 and joined the U.S. Navy. Returning from a tour of duty in the Pacific to his alma mater in 1945, Marx found that the buoyancy of the 1930s had given way to postwar bleakness. His former mentors, F. O. Matthiessen and Perry Miller, were depressed (albeit for very different reasons), and so Marx attached himself to Daniel Aaron's friend and fellow guinea pig in Harvard's American Civilization program, Henry Nash Smith. Through Smith, Marx landed a job in 1949 in the University of Minnesota's pioneering American studies program, which became one of the best in the country. Under Smith's influence, Marx transposed Harvard's idea of American civilization to the Midwest and developed it in new directions before he left Minnesota for Amherst College in 1957.

Although Marx was a novelty as Amherst's first Jewish humanist (rumor had it that one instructor in music was also Jewish), he was unfazed by the standoffishness of the quaint New England town. He had never cared much about being Jewish and was not to be pressured by his WASP fellow townsmen into unearthing what he had so happily buried. Marx's assurance that his Jewishness mattered neither to his being an American nor to his profession as an Americanist was a result not only of his Harvard experience of complete integration but also of his four-year service in the navy, and of the liberal-progressive, universalist orientation of American studies during the 1930s and 1940s that Marx had absorbed.

To Marx's students, however, who came of age during the McCarthy and Civil Rights periods, America wore a different face. The portraits of Allen Guttmann (b. 1932) and Jules Chametzky (b. 1928), two of Marx's students at the University of Minnesota, form a diptych. They show that the rapid opening of the American humanities toward Jewish students and faculty during the 1950s, as well as the increasing prominence of Jews in all aspects of American cultural life, did not necessarily translate into a relaxed, accepting, or positive attitude toward one's own Jewishness. In that generation, attitudes toward Jewishness were determined by such factors as parental influence, neighborhood, class, and so forth; and they could range from indifference (Guttmann) to engagement (Chametzky). What this generation of secular, successfully integrated Jewish humanists shared, however, was disaffection with the universalist idea of America and curiosity about the silenced, neglected Americas of the so-called ethnic cultures. Americanists began to fan out and to discover the "other." During the 1960s they transposed their 1950s sympathy for the alienated individual in the fictions of Franz Kafka or Saul Bellow into empathy for America's disenfranchised minorities, especially African and Native Americans. Academic interest in ethnic literatures also ennobled the Jewish experience in America and, by the late 1960s, elevated it into a subject of serious academic inquiry. The Jewish response to this development remained divided, as the very different studies on the subject by Guttmann and Chametzky demonstrate.

For American Jews a preoccupation with the "other" also triggered interest in what had recently become the ultimate other—the Germans. Scores of Jewish assistant professors flocked to Germany as Fulbright lecturers, but only rarely did the encounter cause them to identify more intensely as Jews or generate interest in the (largely Jewish) literature written in response to the destruction of the European Jews. By the early 1960s, Jewish literature professors raised in the United States were secure in their identities as *American* Jews; and particularly those trained in American studies departments in the early 1950s would define their identities first and foremost in relation to America and not in relation to a now devastated European Jewish culture. Among the exceptions were the pioneers of literary Holocaust studies, men like Lawrence Langer and Alvin Rosenfeld.

In sum, the first section of part 1 examines the beginnings of the integration of Jewish scholars into the fortified bastions of American high culture, while the second section documents its completion. What the first half of this book suggests is that the actual experience of integration into a centrally American community (the Harvard circle), in conjunction with the universalist ideology reigning in literature departments until the late 1960s, created a very strong bond between Jewish literary scholars and America. This tie was not dissolved when the onset of particularism—the rising interest in such fields as ethnic literatures, feminism, and Jewish studies—might have made such dissolution not only easy and feasible but also fashionable. Members of the Harvard circle described themselves as American-Jewish scholars and regarded the hyphen as a connector rather than as a mark of separation.

The second half of this book shifts the focus to Columbia University to investigate whether a different academic setting allowed or enabled other modes of conceptualizing one's identity. Since I have already written extensively about Lionel Trilling (b. 1905) in my first book, and since Alfred Kazin (b. 1915) and Irving Howe (b. 1920), though widely respected New York literary critics, moved outside the Columbia sphere, the three men are not featured in this study.

Part 2 begins therefore with a generation of literary intellectuals who matured under Trilling's sometimes distant mentorship. I chose four individuals (born between 1926 and 1930) whose susceptibility to Trilling's influence differed widely. Chapter 8 is framed by the experiences of two women, Cynthia Ozick and Carolyn Heilbrun, who despite their admiration for Trilling did not feel welcome in his circle of disciples, to which Norman Podhoretz and Steven Marcus unquestionably belonged. Each of the four realized one aspect of Trilling's intellectual ambition.

Ozick became a fiction writer and Podhoretz a magazine editor; Marcus became Trilling's academic successor as cultural critic at Columbia, and Heilbrun, in refashioning Trilling to suit her needs, his successor as opposing self.

No Harvard mentor engendered a comparable variety of responses as did Trilling, although F. O. Matthiessen commanded similar fierce student loyalty. After World War II, Harvard's English department, which had never been (and never would be) a site of emotional exuberance, became a gloomy place whose leading scholars suffered from self-doubt and depression, while Columbia in the 1950s bustled with new life. It seems plausible that the settings of these institutions had something to do with that difference. In a small, encapsulated, self-referential world, the venting of passion disrupts communal harmony and is frowned upon. In a large, open space, where people can get away from each other, passion creates variety and entertainment, and people are more easily induced to act upon impulse, personal taste, and cultural or ideological preference. As section 3, entitled "Literary Minds," demonstrates, Columbia had room for the unfolding of many passionate souls.

Section 4, entitled "The Rediscovery of Origins," deals with scholars who straddle both worlds but got their academic starts at Columbia. In the careers of Robert Alter, Ruth R. Wisse, and Sacvan Bercovitch, courage and opportunity combined to enable inquiry into (and thereby recovery of) lost cultural origins. Their scholarship challenged previously established notions of American-Jewish identity and enlarged the territory of what America encompassed. Alter (b. 1935), who studied with both Lionel Trilling and Harry Levin, became a professor of modern Hebrew literature. His work broadened the understanding of Jewish identity in America to include intellectual and literary traditions outside the Anglophone terrain of the United States.

Wisse (b. 1936), a Canadian who, like Alter, had started out in English literature, became a professor of Yiddish after graduate training at Columbia University. Her work called attention to a neglected non-Anglophone American literature and re-created the intellectual, political, and artistic dimensions of an Eastern European Jewish culture that for most of its descendants had become reduced to knishes, blintzes, and Borscht Belt humor. In her political essays, many of which appeared in Podhoretz's magazine *Commentary,* Wisse draws on her extensive knowledge of prewar European Jewish culture to point out similarities in the social and political pathologies of the European and American Jewish communities. To the displeasure of many, she emphasizes the dangerous continuities in assimilated Jewish culture rather than the comforting notion of American exceptionalism.

Bercovitch (b. 1933), who like Wisse grew up in a Yiddish-speaking home in Montreal, came to America as a graduate student after a peripatetic life that included a prolonged stay on a kibbutz in the brand-new state of Israel. What interested him was precisely the difference between America and Europe. His inquiries into the origins of the American self, into American identity formation through the reinterpretation of hard facts in the light of a mythic master-narrative, illuminated the reasons for America's extraordinary elasticity and explained its capacity for steady enlargement—expansion through integration of territory and people—without any need to abandon or change its original self-definition. Enlargement, Bercovitch declared, was understood by America's earliest thinkers as a process in which the spiritual and material meet; it was part of a redemptive mission in progress and as such the very meaning of America.

The long chapters on Wisse and Bercovitch contain more biographical material than other chapters because the cultural theories of these scholars grew out of their unusual social backgrounds and boundary-crossing lives. Wisse's career as a secular woman scholar moving from English literature into Jewish studies unfolds a pattern not available to an earlier generation and functions in this book as the exact counterpoint to the lives and careers presented in the first part. The chapter on Bercovitch, by contrast, sums up the pressures that led an earlier generation to assimilate to American cultural norms. As a latter-day immigrant, however, Bercovitch moves into America while keeping a skeptical distance from it.

The chapters on Wisse and Bercovitch, then, review the old pressures to assimilate and describe the new freedom to explore the many components that constitute one's American self. They also illustrate the extent to which not only analyses of the cultural past but also prophecies about the future of the Jews are the result of biographical contingencies. Wisse's analysis of Jewish life based on the lessons learned in Europe leads her to bleak conclusions about the future of the Jews as Jews in America unless they become so American as to show initiative on their own behalf. Seen from the perspective of Bercovitch's analysis of America, however, Wisse's fears of yet another abandonment of the Jews do not seem warranted, particularly since America's enlargement now encompasses Israel.

This book ends without resolving the tension between the separatist and the integrationist points of view. Yet in describing the process of the social, intellectual, and professional integration of Jews into American institutions of ideology formation, it confirms Bercovitch's optimistic view of America's expansiveness. But precisely that expansiveness creates worries of another kind. As demographic data indicate, the disappearance of the Jews into America has progressed very far (their share of the population has declined from nearly 4 percent after the Second World War to 2.3 percent today; the rate of intermarriage is currently at 52 percent).[4] Many argue that it has gone too far. Calls for Jewish renewal and reconstitution are issued all over the United States, raising the specter of resegregation in all those glad no longer to be singled out as different. But, as Bercovitch argues, America is large enough for both integrationists and separatists. And Harvard, one of the more conservative yardsticks of American ideology, is a case in point.

Both Bercovitch and Wisse were appointed to named chairs at Harvard University, in 1983 and 1992, respectively. Yet the locale as well as the funding for their chairs suggest that one appointment was regarded as central, the other as more marginal to the school's overall intellectual enterprise. At the end of chapter 10, I analyze the politics of hiring Jewish literary scholars at Harvard from the 1930s to the 1990s. These appointments have always been made along a double track—separatists were relegated to the margins, while integrationists were accommodated at the center of the university (which makes, of course, a certain amount of sense). But as the appointments of Wisse and Bercovitch indicate, margin and center are now beginning to merge.

The epilogue, a final parade of the idols of the tribe, assesses the achievements of Jewish literary scholars at century's end. It concludes with an examination of the fiftieth anniversary session in 1991 of the English Institute, an annual convention of literary scholars founded at Columbia and now held at Harvard. This retrospective confirms my findings on the integration of Jewish literary scholars and brings into view the intellectual chasm that now separates the second and third generations.

Overall, the integration of Jewish scholars into literary academe, beginning symbolically with the striking breakthroughs of Trilling and Levin in 1939 and ending, perhaps, in the intellectual iconoclasm of Harold Bloom and Stanley Fish in the late 1960s, is a history of stunning successes. Jews transformed the study of English literature and the perception of American culture. In the portraits assembled here Jewish literary scholars demonstrate an extraordinary intellectual energy, an astounding optimism, and a highly idealistic belief in the redemptive value of culture. Most notably absent is the idea that one could enter academe simply to make a living. At its most fundamental level, then, this book documents the process of culture formation and, more specifically, the enlarging of the term *America* so that even criticism and dissent become affirmations of America's mission.

By the mid-1970s Jews had become so numerous in literature departments that the situation invited satire. For instance, in A. R. Gurney's very funny novel *Entertaining Strangers* about MIT's beleaguered humanities division, the WASP narrator finds himself surrounded by Jewish colleagues who evoke in him visions of "a long line of dark, bearded Jews, extending across the Atlantic into Europe, across Europe into the heart of Russia." Overwhelmed by the seeming omnipotence of the Jewish chairman of the Appointments Committee "holding on to the written letter of the law," the narrator suddenly realizes what has happened to American literary academe:

> *I* was the outsider. *I* was really the guy standing hat in hand in front of the desk. I alone had escaped *his* pogrom. All my old buddies, all the amateur Wasps who had won the faculty tennis tournaments, and coached the sailing team on the side, and brought flowers to the secretaries around Christmas, and danced the Charleston at departmental parties—all gone from the Humanities. Even the parties were gone. I was the last leaf, the remnant, me, Porter Platt.[5]

Indeed, the broad outlines of the history of Jewish professors in literary academe have become so well known that their eager assimilation, zealous radicalism, avant-garde iconoclasm, and ultimate return to Jewish learning are now stock ingredients in popular university fiction. What is little known, however, is exactly how—person by person—their integration was achieved. This book reconstructs a small slice of a very large development and discovers in the process what historians always discover, which is that the so-called forces of history are really made up of a myriad of actions and decisions by individuals singlemindedly pursuing, amidst the often contradictory claims of love and reason, their calling.

Abbreviations

AJ   Sacvan Bercovitch, *The American Jeremiad*. Madison: University of Wisconsin Press, 1978.

AN   Daniel Aaron, *American Notes: Selected Essays*. Boston: Northeastern University Press, 1994.

ANms   Daniel Aaron, manuscript of *American Notes: Selected Essays*.

API   Sacvan Bercovitch, introduction to *The American Puritan Imagination: Essays in Revaluation,* edited by Sacvan Bercovitch, 1–16. New York: Cambridge University Press, 1974.

AT   Robert Alter, *After the Tradition: Essays on Modern Jewish Writers*. New York: Dutton, 1969.

Au   Howard Mumford Jones, *Howard Mumford Jones: An Autobiography*. Madison: University of Wisconsin Press, 1979.

B   M. H. Abrams, "Belief and the Suspension of Disbelief." In *Literature and Belief,* English Institute Essays 1957, edited by M. H. Abrams, 1–30. New York: Columbia University Press, 1958.

BC   Norman Podhoretz, *The Bloody Crossroads: Where Literature and Politics Meet*. New York: Simon and Schuster, 1986.

BJ   Diana Trilling, *The Beginning of the Journey: The Marriage of Diana and Lionel Trilling*. New York: Harcourt, Brace and Co., 1993.

BP   Abraham Sutzkever, *Burnt Pearls: The Ghetto Poems of Abraham Sutzkever*. Translated by Seymour Mayne. Oakville, Ontario: Mosaic Press, 1981.

BR   Norman Podhoretz, *Breaking Ranks: A Political Memoir*. New York: Harper and Row, 1979.

CM   Sacvan Bercovitch, "Cotton Mather." In *Major Writers of Early American Literature,* edited by Everett Emerson, 93–149. Madison: University of Wisconsin Press, 1972.

CPM   "Culture and the Present Moment: A Round-Table Discussion." *Commentary* 58 (December 1974): 31–50.

CT   Allen Guttmann, *The Conservative Tradition in America.* New York: Oxford University Press, 1967.

D   Steven Marcus, *Dickens: From Pickwick to Dombey.* New York: Basic Books, 1965.

DI   Robert Alter, *Defenses of the Imagination: Jewish Writers and Modern Historical Crisis.* Philadelphia: Jewish Publication Society of America, 1977.

DN   Abraham Sutzkever, *Di nevue fun shvartsaplen: dertseylungn.* Jerusalem: Magnes Press of Hebrew University, 1989.

DR   David Roskies, interview with the author, New York City, February 1992.

FN   Robert Alter, *Fielding and the Nature of the Novel.* Cambridge: Harvard University Press, 1968.

GA   Abraham Sutzkever, *Griner Akvarium.* Introduction by Ruth R. Wisse. Jerusalem: Hebrew University, 1975.

H   M. H. Abrams, "How to Do Things with Texts" (1979). Reprinted in M. H. Abrams, *Doing Things with Texts: Essays in Criticism and Critical Theory,* 269–296. New York: Norton, 1989.

ID   Arthur Crew Inman, *The Inman Diary: A Public and Private Confession.* Edited by Daniel Aaron. Cambridge: Harvard University Press, 1985.

IHP   Robert Alter, *The Invention of Hebrew Prose: Modern Fiction and the Language of Realism.* Seattle: University of Washington Press, 1988.

JSU   Nora Levin, *The Jews in the Soviet Union Since 1917: Paradox of Survival.* 2 vols. London: I. B. Tauris, 1988.

JW   Allen Guttmann, *The Jewish Writer in America: Assimilation and Crisis of Identity.* New York: Oxford University Press, 1971.

LD   Lionel Trilling, *The Last Decade: Essays and Reviews, 1965–1975.* Edited by Diana Trilling. New York: Harcourt Brace Jovanovich, 1981.

LI	Lionel Trilling, *The Liberal Imagination: Essays on Literature and Society.* New York: Viking, 1950.
MG	Leo Marx, *The Machine in the Garden: Technology and the Pastoral Ideal in America.* New York: Oxford University Press, 1964.
MGH	Daniel Aaron, *Men of Good Hope: A Story of American Progressivism.* New York: Oxford University Press, 1951.
MI	Norman Podhoretz, *Making It.* New York: Harper Colophon Books, 1967.
ML	M. H. Abrams, *The Mirror and the Lamp: Romantic Theory and the Critical Tradition.* New York: Oxford University Press, 1953.
N1	"From the Notebooks of Lionel Trilling, Part I." *Partisan Review* 50/51 (1984/85): 496–515.
N2	"From the Notebooks of Lionel Trilling, Part II." *Partisan Review* 54 (1987): 7–17.
OD	Jules Chametzky, *Our Decentralized Literature: Cultural Mediation in Selected Jewish and Southern Writers.* Amherst: University of Massachusetts Press, 1986.
PA	John Lydenberg, ed., *Political Activism and the Academic Conscience: The Harvard Experience, 1936–1941.* Geneva, N. Y.: Hobart and William Smith Colleges, 1977.
PaP	Leo Marx, *The Pilot and the Passenger: Essays on Literature, Technology, and Culture.* New York: Oxford University Press, 1988.
PJ	Carolyn G. Heilbrun, *Poetic Justice.* New York: Avon, 1979.
PO	Sacvan Bercovitch, *The Puritan Origins of the American Self.* New Haven: Yale University Press, 1975.
PP	George Santayana, *Persons and Places: The Background of My Life.* New York: Scribner's, 1944.
PPce	George Santayana, *Persons and Places: Fragments of Autobiography,* Edited by William G. Holzberger and Herman J. Saatkamp, Jr. Cambridge: MIT Press, 1986.
PT	Granville Hicks, *Part of the Truth.* New York: Harcourt, Brace and World, 1965.
RA	Sacvan Bercovitch, *The Rites of Assent: Transformations in the Symbolic Construction of America.* New York: Routledge, 1993.
RALH	Sacvan Bercovitch, ed., *Reconstructing American Literary History.* Cambridge: Harvard University Press, 1986.

RW   Carolyn G. Heilbrun, *Reinventing Womanhood*. New York: Norton, 1979.

SA   Sylvia Ary, interview with the author, Montreal, Quebec, September 17, 1994.

SMH   Ruth R. Wisse, *The Schlemiel as Modern Hero*. Chicago: University of Chicago Press, 1971.

SPP   Abraham Sutzkever, *Selected Prose and Poetry,* trans. Barbara and Benjamin Harshav. Berkeley: University of California Press, 1991.

VL   Henry Nash Smith, *Virgin Land: The American West as Symbol and Myth*. New York: Vintage, 1950.

W   Allen Guttmann, *The Wound in the Heart: America and the Spanish Civil War*. New York: Free Press, 1962.

WL   Daniel Aaron, *Writers on the Left: Episodes in American Literary Communism*. New York: Harcourt, Brace and World, 1961.

PART ONE

The Harvard Circle

The Spirit of Place

1

The Yard from Santayana to T. S. Eliot

TWO DAYS BEFORE GEORGE SANTAYANA sequestered himself in the Blue Nuns' Clinica della Piccola Compagna di Maria in Rome on October 14, 1941, he dispatched the manuscript of the first volume of his autobiography to his publisher, Charles Scribner's Sons, in New York. But because of the war the Italian postal service no longer handled manuscripts and printed matter and returned the package to its sender five days later. The American declaration of war on December 8, 1941, disrupted all communication between Rome and New York, so that Santayana's editor at Scribner's, John Hall Wheelock, had to resort to ingenuity and energetic persistence to obtain the valuable literary property. While trains carrying desperate human cargo crisscrossed Europe, Santayana's manuscript traveled safely in the diplomatic pouch of the Vatican to the American embassy in neutral Madrid and from there to the United States. Finally, on October 22, 1942, Wheelock found on his desk what turned out to be a golden egg—the first part of an extraordinary autobiography. It was the chronicle of a life written in that peculiar genre, so popular in all strata of the American readership, that in capable hands transformed gossip into philosophy. It had been produced by one of America's most private intellectuals.

It was the elegance of the style and Santayana's tone, combining suave gentility with an unnerving asperity, that made *Persons and Places* so extraordinary. When Logan Pearsall Smith, Santayana's former classmate, had published his autobiography, *Unforgotten Years,* in 1938, Santayana found it lacking, as his biographer put it, in "true particularity about the Harvard and Oxford of their youth." Santayana wrote to Smith: "You

5

may say that Henry James has done it once for all, but he, you, all Americans in print, are too gentle, too affectionate, too fulsome. The reality requires a satirist, merciless but just, as you might be if you chose." [1] In his own autobiography Santayana dispensed with all residues of the Victorian reluctance to be frank which, he felt, crippled the social interaction of America's middle and upper classes. He wrote *Persons and Places* during a summer holiday in Fiuggi in 1941 not so much as a satirist panning the foibles of an earlier age, but as a philosopher with an intense distaste for hypocrisy. When the volume was published, however, in January 1944, in an edition of 380,000 copies, it became apparent that it was not possible to say just anything at any time, no matter how true. And it became obvious that Santayana too had not escaped the pieties of his culture, which combined Catholic Spain and Brahmin Boston. But while he succumbed to some of the Brahmins' prejudices, he was also quick to detect and ridicule them. Santayana's disposition and the fact that he had studied and taught at Harvard make him a unique though somewhat tricky source for the reconstruction of the social and intellectual atmosphere there between 1880 and 1930.

Although Santayana was dogged by the post-publication discovery of numerous errors of fact in *Persons and Places,* his editor had to contend with rougher stuff. Readers took exception to passages such as the following, in which Santayana introduces a friend he made in 1882 during his freshman year at Harvard College:

> First in time and very important, was my friendship with Charles Loeser. I came upon him by accident in another man's room, and he immediately took me into his own, which was next door, to show me his books and pictures. Pictures and books! That strikes the keynote to our companion-ship. At once I found that he spoke French well, and German presumably better, since if hurt he would swear in German. He had been at a good international school in Switzerland. He at once told me that he was a Jew, a rare and blessed frankness that cleared away a thousand pitfalls and insincerities. What a privilege there is in that distinction and in that misfortune! If the Jews were not worldly it would raise them above the world; but most of them squirm and fawn and wish to pass for ordinary Christians or ordinary atheists. Not so Loeser: he had no ambition to manage things for other people, or to worm himself into fashionable society. [2]

Wheelock urged Santayana to change at least the sentence about the Jews. Santayana replied:

In regard to your note of Oct. 4, I see that my expressions about the Jews, if taken for exact history or philosophical criticism, are unfair. But they were meant for free satire, and I don't like to yield to the pretension that free satire must be excluded from literature. However, in this case and at this moment [November 12, 1944], when as you say the Jews are super-sensitive, I am glad to remove anything that may sound insulting or be really inaccurate. Now for me to speak of "most" Jews, is inaccurate, since I have known only a few; and "squirm" and "fawn," if not taken for caricature, are insulting words. I propose, then, that you delete those three words and let the passage read as follows: If the Jews were not worldly it would raise them above the world: but many of them court the world and wish to pass for ordinary Christians or ordinary atheists.

This preserves the spirit of what I said: a certain suggestion of vocation missed. For that reason I prefer it to the emendation suggested by you, which concedes too much. The Jews have become of late not only sensitive but exacting. I wish to be just, but I don't want to "squirm and fawn" on my side also.[3]

As in his letter to Smith, Santayana insisted that autobiography was a form of satire in which reality was rendered pointedly. But he conceded that those who did not conceive of the genre in the same way might well feel hurt. In his letter to Wheelock we find him ready to soften the rendition of his memories but not to reconsider their content. While there was indeed a bit of truth in Santayana's observation about Jews at Harvard, his eagerness to expose a friend's weakness in the mode of the merciless satirist tempted him to choose a crass formulation that antici-pated the much crasser phrases in T. S. Eliot's poetry of 1920. Unlike Eliot, however, Santayana had the good sense to take it back. But his annoyance with the "exacting" Jews clearly shows that he had no idea why, in 1944, a satiric presentation of assimilating Jews was inappropri-ate, and why it was not the dignity of the Jews but Santayana's dignity as philosopher and human being that was at stake.

Like T. S. Eliot, Santayana was biased against Jews. Their bias was rooted in the tenets of the Catholic Church, which had castigated the Jews as impervious to spiritual salvation. It was strengthened by the deliberate cultivation of a modern aestheticism whose vulgar antithesis they found in the materialism of the Jews. And it rested, finally, on a genteel disdain for Jews (particularly for those successful in original ways) ingrained in some of the old New England families to which both Santayana and Eliot were connected. The peculiar, snobbish nature of their anti-Jewish prejudice and its rootedness in nineteenth-century Boston can be discerned best in Santayana's only novel, *The Last Puritan* (1936). It was subtitled *A Memoir in the Form of a Novel* and purported to be a recollection of the life of Oliver Alden by his former Harvard philosophy teacher George Santayana, then living in Paris. The early chapters, drafted in the 1890s, satirize the prejudices of an increasingly petrified and anxious elite that felt beleaguered by Boston's new immigrants.

Jews appear infrequently in the novel; but when they do—often in exquisite vignettes of gratuitous viciousness—they represent a variety of ancient and modern stereotypes. They are money-lenders (344), blind to spiritual truth (289), "rowdy company" on board the *Lusitania* (362); they crop up as a poor young doctor in an insane asylum (71), as an athletic "sheeny" on the Columbia football team (395), and as a dubious art dealer, "the very devil of a sharp Jew, who palms off old masters on the American millionaires: and he likes to have a few genuine objects in his shop, to set the tone" (366). And, finally, there is Stephen Boscovitz, a half-Jewish student at Harvard who "isn't liked" because "people can't forget the facts," so he "has to console himself with his books and with his riding" (392).[4]

One of the highlights of Santayana's satire, and one of the most extraordinary examples of sophisticated anti-Semitism in modern writing is his portrait of Stephen's father, old Boscovitz, a jeweler and expert in gems, whose passion is flowers and who finds "religion enough in the love of beautiful things" (435). In a letter to Oliver Alden, Mario van Weyer, a half-Italian, half-American aesthete and classmate of Stephen's, describes old Boscovitz's magnificent greenhouses and then continues:

> And old Boscovitz, with all his Shylock shrewdness and eye for a bargain, has a sort of Biblical poetry in him; shows you about as oily and obsequious as if he were going to sell you something for ten times its value; whereas it's the other way and he loves you for loving his things and treating him with affectionate respect, as a great personage, which indeed he is in his way. Sometimes he picks me a little bunch of the rarest and loveliest flowers for a buttonhole; and it's amusing, when he has chosen his best flower and his best leaf—for the leaves are often the most marvellous part of it—how he wants to stick the thing into my coat with his own hands, like a village lass flirting with her yokel; only his fingers are so thick and clumsy that he can't manage it, and pricks himself with the pin, and I have to come to the rescue, and say, "Oh, Mr. Boscovitz, how awfully kind of you, but let me do it. I don't need a pin; there's a little loop here below the buttonhole on purpose to hold the stems down;

English tailors are so provident." And in a jiffy the flower is in its place; or if there are several and more than you want to wear—because he is ridiculously lavish—I take half or three-quarters of it and in the twinkling of an eye I've stuck it into old Bosco's own buttonhole, before he knows what I'm about; and he's terribly pleased, but shy; because he's very simple in his person, a bit ashamed of himself, perhaps, and would never think of wearing a flower. (433)

Young Mario speaks with the affection of an outsider for an outsider. He sees and understands old Bosco's neediness; yet he cannot resist showing how very much superior, how immensely more cultivated and refined he is than the clumsy old bloke with his sentimental love of flowers. Being slightly better integrated, Mario lords it over the eternal outsider. Boscovitz is unassimilable because "people can't forget the facts" of his racial descent.

Beneath its genial surface Mario's letter to Alden hides a classic anti-Semitic assault. At first Mario seems to dispel the image of a shrewd Shylock by acknowledging that Boscovitz "has a sort of Biblical poetry in him," and by claiming that, unlike the dubious art dealer, Boscovitz does not want "to sell you something for ten times its value," but is courting his visitors so that they may love his collection and by extension the collector. Nevertheless, the image of a shrewd, bargain-driving Jew is evoked and remains in place. "Soft-hearted, but hard-headed" (434), Boscovitz is all the more despicable because the head refuses to be swayed by the heart.

Having established Boscovitz as the wooer and Mario as the wooed, Santayana develops a complex scene of an aborted homosexual seduction around the gift of flowers, which for Boscovitz have the beauty of jewels worthy of a "good woman" (435). Although Mario reverses the gender roles and compares Boscovitz to "a village lass flirting with her yokel," it is clear that Boscovitz is the pursuing male who "wants to stick the thing into my coat with his own hands." Mario assumes the tone of a grand lady rebutting her fumbling suitor, when he says, "Oh, Mr. Boscovitz, . . . I don't need a pin."

At the climax, when Boscovitz pricks himself (rather than Mario) with his pin, our attention is forcefully diverted from the sexual drama by the obvious allusion to Shylock's famous monologue in act three of *The Merchant of Venice,* "If you prick us, do we not bleed?" We accept the diversion all the more readily because the mention of "Shylock's shrewdness" at the beginning of the scene prepared us for it. And so we almost miss the conclusion of the act, when Mario, in a reversal of aggression, takes on old Boscovitz's initiation: " 'There's a little loop here below the buttonhole on purpose to hold the stems down . . . ' And in a jiffy the flower is in its place." The portrait ends in the spirit of Shylock's monologue when Mario is swayed to acknowledge their common humanity, after having reversed the sexual assault, and "in the twinkling of an eye . . . stuck it into old Bosco's buttonhole." Boscovitz "is terribly pleased," and they part with what appears to be an expression of mutual gratitude, but Mario has cleverly extricated his own person from any indebtedness: "The flowers must all wish to say thank you" (433).

At first sight, Mario's portrait of Boscovitz seems to be a warm, albeit ultimately dismissive, assessment of a Jewish businessman turned sentimental horticulturist. But concealed beneath the charming anecdote we find classic anti-Jewish imagery woven into a homosexual encounter between an old suitor and young lover: here is the greedy Jew turned lecher, the rapacious Jew turned effeminate and impotent, the Jew as ineffectual lover who is "terribly pleased" to receive a gift into his own buttonhole. This sophisticated dislike of Jews pervades, almost as a matter of course, the works of both Santayana and T. S. Eliot. And yet both men maintained amicable relationships with Jewish intellectuals. Significantly, most of their Jewish friends and acquaintances were somehow connected to Harvard University.

———

Five decades of extraordinary changes for Harvard as a university and for the humanities as a profession separate the years 1882, when Santayana first met Loeser in Harvard Yard, and 1932, when Eliot returned to his alma mater to deliver the Charles Eliot Norton lectures and to concoct, while he was befriending one of Harvard's brilliant Jewish students, his infamous cultural polemic *After Strange Gods: A Primer of Modern Heresy*. What had not changed by 1932, despite increasing diversity in the student body, was the peculiar Harvard atmosphere—a deliberate exclusiveness that deteriorated often enough into silly snobbery. But that attitude was doomed, and its partisans were aware of losing their significance. Pedigree ceased to be an issue for the new generation of students. T. S. Eliot's tenure as Norton professor in the academic year 1932–1933 was perhaps the last occasion on which the old New England elite presented itself in all its cultural splendor. Eliot knew that it was the final curtain call, and he was wise enough to take his jeremiad about the waning of tradition and the rise of "modern heresy" to the South, to the University of Virginia. The North, where he was worshiped by radicals, liberals, and all sorts of Jewish intellectuals, had to be given up for lost.

With Eliot's return to England and the passing of the Harvard presidency from Abbott Lawrence Lowell to James Bryant Conant in 1933, a new era began that gradually came to prefer merit over ancestry. The humanities, however, were slow to catch on. The old attitudes and prejudices did not disappear completely from campus. They merely retired to a smaller stage: the English department, not only at Harvard but also at other elite universities—Yale, Columbia, and Princeton, for instance. One by one, those bastions of white Anglo-Saxon Protestant culture needed to be challenged and conquered. The non-WASP group to undertake that conquest was the Jews. Hence they were perceived as an immediate threat to the comfortable status quo and were self-defensively blasted as dangerous underminers of the culture's stability and homogeneity. Literature departments, particularly at Ivy League schools, fought hard to keep them out or to accept as few as possible. A description of the social and intellectual atmosphere at Harvard between 1882, when Santayana befriended Loeser, and 1932, when Eliot befriended Levin, shows what Jews wishing to enter literary academe were up against.

The moving depiction of Charles Loeser in Santayana's autobiography conceals a catalogue of the most popular contemporary objections to Jews:

> At Harvard, Loeser was rather friendless. The fact that he was a Jew and that his father kept a "dry-goods store" cut him off, in democratic America, from the ruling society. To me, who was also an outsider, this seemed at first very strange, for Loeser was much more cultivated than the leaders of undergraduate fashion or athletics, and I saw nothing amiss in his person or manners. He was not good-looking, although he had a neat figure, of middle height, and nice hands: but his eyes were dead, his complexion muddy, and his features pinched, though not especially Jewish. On the other hand he was extremely well-spoken, and there was nothing about him in bad taste. To me he was always an agreeable companion, and if our friendship never became intimate, this was due rather to a certain defensive reserve in him than to any withdrawal on my part. Yet in the end, taking imaginatively the point of view of the native leading Americans, I came to see why Loeser could never gain their confidence. His heart was not with them, and his associations and stan-

dards were not theirs. He didn't join in their sports (as rich Jews have learned to do in England), he hadn't their religion, he had no roots in their native places or in their family circles. In America he floated on the surface, and really lived only in the international world of art, literature, and theory. (226–227)

Santayana's portrait of Loeser, which continues in this vein, is an astonishing piece of writing. It is gracious, sympathetic, seemingly indulgent toward a fellow student's quirkiness while actually toying with popular anti-Jewish stereotypes: the dead eyes of the Jew were indicative of his dead soul; the pinched features signified a narrow, commercial spirit; the reserve, rootlessness, and cosmopolitanism suggested the Jew's lack of loyalty and preference for the life of the parasite. Santayana's own objection to Loeser as a Jew was philosophical rather than personal. It rested on a classic argument of the Catholic Church, namely, that the Jews were impervious to spiritual salvation, the root cause of their materialism. Santayana found this view confirmed when during a spring walking tour through Italy in 1895, largely at Loeser's expense, the two friends encountered a Franciscan community:

The monks were evidently peasants, some of them young yokels fresh from the plough, no doubt ignorant and stupid; and Loeser's modern Jewish standards betrayed themselves in his utter scorn of those mere beasts, as he called them. I wondered if St. John the Baptist or Elijah might not also have seemed mere beasts; but I didn't say so. Being at once a beast and a spirit doesn't seem to me a contradiction. On the contrary, it is necessary to be a beast if one is ever to be a spirit. The modern Jew recognizes verbal intelligence, but not simple spirit. He doesn't admit anything deeper or freer than literature, science, and commerce. (*PP* 230)

Santayana's attitude toward material possessions was immensely relaxed. The impoverished Santayana allowed Loeser to support him for years on all outings and travels. To his friend Henry Ward Abbott, Santayana admitted charmingly: "I don't find poverty at all a burden, but rather a stimulant. Besides I sponge systematically and on principle, not feeling my dignity compromised thereby any more than if I were a monk or a soldier." Later, when he could afford it, he permitted others to live off him. He insisted, for instance, that he remain anonymous as the donor of a substantial sum of money that went to the distressed Bertrand Russell.[5]

In 1905, Loeser decided, a bit perversely perhaps, to settle in Florence, where his rival Bernard Berenson, Harvard class of 1887, had set up shop as an art connoisseur. It may have been an obvious choice given the city's treasures and the fact that Henry James's bon mot about Italy in 1894—"all Back Bay was there last year"—was especially true of Florence.[6] But Loeser's choice was also made in defiance of the always successful Berenson. While the wealthy, cultivated Loeser had remained friendless at Harvard, the dirt-poor, sweetly handsome, ingratiating Berenson, born in the depth of Jewish Lithuania and transplanted as a child to the sordid North End of Boston, had been adopted by the ladies of the Brahmin class. When Loeser and Berenson began to acquire reputations as art connoisseurs, bitter rivalry poisoned their once amicable relationship and divided their circle of friends. Their rivalry in the attribution of Italian paintings showing Madonnas, saints, and Crucifixions was about success and recognition in the Gentile world; but its bitterness was fueled by Loeser's resentment of Berenson's betrayal of the Jews—his baptism by a fashionable Episcopalian minister.

Despite Berenson's enormous academic and social efforts at Harvard, he suffered the same hardships as Loeser. As a Jew, Berenson found himself "on the ragged edge of the social body," and perhaps even more so than Loeser, because Loeser had money whereas Berenson had only energy and talent. How Berenson had raised the funds to enter Harvard in the fall of 1884 is unclear. After a year at Boston Latin School, where he had met Santayana, and a year at a private preparatory school, Berenson enrolled at Boston University in 1883. But his mind was set on going to Harvard, his idea of absolute bliss because under the elective system, recently implemented by President Charles William Eliot, he would be able to choose from some two hundred courses.[7]

Having entered the sacred precincts of Harvard Yard in the fall of 1884, Berenson still thought of himself as a future literary critic and novelist and therefore began to study with Barrett Wendell, the future author of the first *Literary History of America* (1900). Wendell's teaching specialty was then the "daily theme," inimitably described in Santayana's novel *The Last Puritan*: "Must be at least one page of specially ruled and prepared paper, and not more than two pages. Automatically teaches you to write good English. Indispensable training for the tabloid press, and for controlling the future thought of humanity" (393). Later scholars would call Wendell "the epitome of Harvard culture at its most self-confident."[8] But Santayana, first his student, later his colleague, found him insufferable, a local yokel whose "books were not worth writing." Wendell, Santayana recalled,

1. George Santayana as an undergraduate at
Harvard. *Courtesy of Harvard University Archives.*

admired the airs of the early nineteenth century, cared for birth and good
breeding, and in literature for mannishness and good form, "rum and
decorum", as he once put it, and for tenderness and distinction of
feeling. . . . He longed for an American aristocracy, not of millionaires,
but of local worthies, sportsmen, scholars, and divines. The New England
literary men and orators of fifty years before would have satisfied him in
respect to their station and manners, but he detested the radical revolutionary turn of their minds. He hated the empty cold self-sufficiency, as
he thought of it, of Emerson and his friends.[9]

From this literary pit Santayana saved Berenson by sponsoring his
election to the newly founded *Harvard Monthly* and to the exclusive
literary society known as the O.K. Club. Unlike Santayana, whose Spanish mother, Josefina Borrás, had been married to a Boston Sturgis,
Berenson "made" no other society. As a Jew he was not clubbable.
Ashamed of his shabby clothes, he rarely socialized. He studied with

2. Bernard Berenson as an undergraduate at Harvard.
Courtesy of Harvard University Archives.

extraordinary energy; he was the spearhead of all those students from the margins of society (many of them Jews from Eastern Europe) who would stream into the colleges two decades later, shock the establishment with their brilliance and determination, and raise academic standards.

But hard work was not Berenson's only resort. Three interlocking events that caused his desertion from literature to art helped his luck. The first was Berenson's conversion to Christianity. He was baptized on November 22, 1885, at Boston's Episcopalian Trinity Church by the famous Phillips Brooks himself. Berenson's biographer Ernest Samuels points out that the young man was then under the influence of Walter Pater's *Marius the Epicurean,* a work that twenty years later, as Van Wyck Brooks testifies, still sent Harvard students spinning into a fake Catholicism in their search for a perfect culture. Christianity undoubtedly had its aesthetic fascination for Berenson. In 1884 he had written: "The church that admits one to the widest range of sympathies is nearest to the ideal. . . . The true and the beautiful are absolutely identical and are that which satisfies every demand of our consciousness." Surely, compulsory chapel at Boston University and Harvard College did not encourage Berenson to remain in the Jewish fold. But opposition to compulsory chapel had been gathering at Harvard for a long time, and attendance was made voluntary in the fall of 1886, with the support of Phillips Brooks, who was then a Harvard overseer. Brooks was not the man to force his flock. What propelled Berenson into the church was perhaps a less honorable motive than aesthetic infatuation.[10]

The "admission" Berenson gained through the church was not only to a wide range of sympathies but also to Back Bay society. One of the most important women of the fashionable set was the unusual Isabella Stewart Gardner, who in the summer of 1885 had returned from a grand tour of the Orient and the Middle East. Berenson probably met her for the first time (event two) when he enrolled in Charles Eliot Norton's fine arts course (event three) in the fall of 1886. Norton (Harvard class of 1846) was truly Old Boston. This meant, as Santayana pointed out, that Norton, like William James, "had seemed at first questionable and irregular. Norton, with ten generations of local magnates behind him, had his inspirations and sympathies far away. He worshipped Greek art, he worshipped Christian art, he loved refined English life. He spoke rarefied English" (PPce 399).

Norton had urged Charles William Eliot to find a place at Harvard for painting, sculpture, and architecture. The president obliged and founded the fine arts department in which his fastidious cousin would lecture for twenty-four years. Norton had snob appeal. His distaste for the vulgarity of the modern world and for American cheapness, which he shared with his younger contemporary Henry Adams, made him immensely attractive to newcomers like Mrs. Gardner. She was originally from New York, and her vocation, Santayana claimed, "was to show Boston what it was missing. Instead of following the fashion, she undertook to set it." When "Boston doggedly stuck to its old ways and its old people" (PPce 364), Mrs. Gardner turned to Norton, whose cult of Dante made her generation crave the possession of Italian works of art. Norton "taught the Proper and Protestant Bostonians to admire the Madonna and Child in a thousand painted versions."[11]

Precisely here, in the newcomer's need for showy cultural refinement, Norton's attentive student Berenson would eventually find his commercial niche. Established as an art connoisseur in Italy after extensive travels through Europe, he became the major purveyor of Italian paintings for Mrs. Gardner's palatial Boston home. In a roundabout way, the cult figure Norton with his exaggerated appreciation of art helped to set the stage, as Ernest Samuels put it, "for the enlightened, if wholesale, plunder of Italian art and for the migration of European masterpieces to the New World on an undreamed-of scale." [12] Paintings were removed from Italian palazzi and churches to adorn a Venetian palace in the Boston Fenway, which the widow Gardner built for herself "as Egyptian monarchs built their tombs" (PPce 364).

Before collecting art, however, Mrs. Gardner had collected protégés, and Berenson, now an Episcopalian and an alleged genius, became part of her circle. When he failed to win one of the four Parker Travelling Fellowships in the spring of 1887, Mrs. Gardner, together with Edward Perry Warren, the son of a wealthy paper manufacturer who had sponsored Berenson's admission to Harvard in 1884, and Ferdinand Bôcher, a professor of French at Harvard, made up a purse of $700, the equivalent of the fellowship, and sent the eager student abroad.

In the galleries, museums, and churches of Europe, the seed of Norton's lectures matured, transforming the leisurely literary critic into an enthusiastic and hardworking connoisseur of art. Berenson began in Paris, sightseeing his way toward Italy and leaving in his wake a trail of admirers. Lionel Johnson, the quintessential product of Walter Pater's tutelage at Oxford, wrote to his friend Santayana in August 1888: "Berenson charmed Oxford for a term, and vanished: leaving behind a memory of exotic epigrams and, so to speak, cynical music. It was a strangely curious time. He is something too misanthropic: but always adorable" (PPce 303).

In the spring of 1895, the thirty-year-old Berenson caused a great scandal in London when he published a short pamphlet assessing the attributions of some one hundred and twenty privately owned Venetian paintings on exhibit at the New Gallery. Of the thirty-three Titians on display, Berenson accepted one as genuine; of nineteen Bellinis he passed three; of the twenty-one paintings attributed to Bonifazio or Veronese, none survived his inspection; seventeen Giorgiones were consigned to oblivion. The British aristocracy was in shock: Berenson's forty-two-page essay had not only reduced their collective worth by several million pounds but also unsentimentally eclipsed the glory that comes with having a Titian in one's palace. The practical Mrs. Gardner, however, remained unfazed by the overthrow of tradition and in 1895 accelerated her acquisition of paintings through Berenson. The benefit was mutual, since Berenson, always low on funds, charged only 5 percent commission rather than the usual 10 percent. Mrs. Gardner's purchasing power and her intention to assemble the finest privately owned art collection in Boston assured Berenson of an income that set him free to read and write.

In 1900 Berenson married Mary Logan Costelloe, and acquired I Tatti, a villa just outside Florence, which he made his permanent residence. Upon his death in 1959, I Tatti with its art collection and huge library became the Harvard University Center of Italian Renaissance Studies.[13] Berenson's achievements became an asset of the very institution that had distrusted his reliability in matters of taste and judgment at a crucial moment.

The main instigator of this distrust had been Charles Eliot Norton, whose recommendation was conspicuously missing in Berenson's application for the traveling fellowship. Years earlier Norton had come across Berenson in Harvard Yard studying Walter Pater's *Renaissance*. He borrowed the book and upon returning it remarked, "My dear boy, it won't do." As an admirer of medieval austerity, Norton thought lusciousness vulgar, particularly in art. It was whispered in the Yard that Norton on entering heaven exclaimed, "Oh, oh! so overdone! So Renaissance!"[14] In Berenson's dazzling, exuberant, cocky application, Norton had perhaps missed the element of restraint, the elegant English understatement mastered by true Harvard men. It was a conventional sort of modesty but indicative of the self-confidence instilled by a secure place in society. In his portrait of the fine arts professor, John Jay Chapman (Harvard class of 1884) located the source of Norton's imperturbability in the "family feeling of class and county" from which Norton derived his "aristocratic manner."[15] Of course, family feeling of class and county, at least of Norton's, was precisely what Berenson lacked. And Norton, amply warned about Berenson's lapses in taste, refrained from recommending him as one of the best men Harvard could send abroad. What Norton did not realize in 1887 (nor did Chapman in 1915) was that the days were numbered when Harvard College could be considered the domain of New England families like the Adamses, the Eliots, and the Lowells. Santayana, Loeser, Berenson, and a handful of other exotic characters, among them a few African Americans, were the avant-garde of a host of non–Anglo-Saxons that would help transform a passable provincial college into a superb national university.

By 1905, when Henry Adams described his class of 1858, the student body he once knew had ceased to exist, although its spirit would haunt the Yard for many more decades:

The Class of 1858, to which Henry Adams belonged, was a typical collection of young New Englanders, quietly penetrating and aggressively commonplace; free from meannesses, jealousies, intrigues, enthusiasms, and passions; not exceptionally quick; not consciously sceptical [sic]; singularly indifferent to display, artifice, florid expression, but not hostile to it when it amused them; distrustful of themselves, but little disposed to trust any one else; with not much humor of their own but full of readiness to enjoy the humor of others; negative to a degree that in the long run became positive and triumphant. Not harsh in manners or judgment, rather liberal and open-minded, they were still as a body the most formidable critics one would care to meet, in a long life exposed to criticism.

As much as Henry Adams hated the college, it is obvious from his description that he loved his Harvard class, which was then still synonymous with social class.[16] Consequently, he considered it "the mark of all intelligent Jews," as he wrote in a letter to Elizabeth Cameron in 1901, to despise their own crowd or, as he put it, to be "in a state of antisemite rebellion". About his first encounter with Berenson in Washington in 1904, Adams confided to Cameron:

At last—Barenson [sic] and his wife! Well, you know, you see, you know, I *can't* bear it. There is, in the Jew deprecation, something that no weary sinner ought to stand. I rarely murder. By nature I am humane. Life, to such people, is perhaps dear, or at least worth living, and I hate to take it. Yet I did murder Barenson [sic]. I cut his throat first, and chopped him into small bits afterwards, and rolled the fragments into the fire. In my own house I ought not to have done so. I tried to do it gently, without apparent temper or violence of manner. Alas! murder will out![17]

What exactly irritated Adams so much about Berenson, whose main foible—an excessive aesthetic fastidiousness—invites mockery rather than murderous ferocity, is hard to ascertain. Most likely, Adams's rage is a resurgence of the all-consuming anger he began to nurse in the wake of the economic panic of 1893, which threatened to destroy his wealth. By 1895 he was concentrating his ire on the Jews. Although Adams's anti-Semitism is a complex matter, it is striking that it arose, as in less sophisticated people, at the very moment when his own financial and social security seemed imperiled. Adams later revised his view of Berenson and gained in him a learned friend and compelling correspondent; yet he never quite overcame his uneasiness about Berenson's being a Jew.[18]

In Charles William Eliot, however, who, like Adams, was a member of Boston's social and intellectual elite, the Jews had a reliable friend. Like Adams, Eliot had attended Harvard (class of 1853) and thought the college in need of reform. During his forty years as Harvard's president (1869–1909), the small institution for gentlemen of the upper crust blossomed into a modern university. Eliot succeeded because he was a practical man with a vision of America that did not focus on the past achievements of his class and culture. In his inaugural speech he noted that "it is very hard to find competent professors for the university. Very few Americans of eminent ability are attracted to this profession." Eliot set out to change that. He raised tuition in order to raise faculty salaries, which in turn increased the prestige of the profession, and he doubled the number of instructors within his first decade in office. When he retired, the faculty had grown from 32 (in 1870) to 169, and the number of courses had increased from 73 to over 400. Eliot called for the creation of a graduate school of arts and sciences after the model developed by Daniel Coit Gilman at Johns Hopkins. He strengthened existing professional schools and established new ones in medicine, law, and business. He abolished Greek as an entrance requirement to Harvard College and introduced the system of free electives because he believed that a young man of eighteen could choose his own course, even when given a confusing wealth of options; and he contended that all nonvocational subjects, if they were well taught and studied, had an equal cultural or disciplinary value.[19]

The opposition mounted by traditionalist educators to Eliot's abolition of the Greek requirement and to his introduction of free electives was enormous. But the traditionalists were steadily losing ground, and their last resort was ridicule. In 1885, James McCosh, president of Princeton University, amused a New York audience by describing the Harvard training of future clergymen, doctors, and lawyers as consisting of dilettante readings of French novels (F. Bôcher's French 8), dabbling in watercolor (C. H. Moore's Fine Arts 1), listening to lectures on English drama (F. J. Child's Shakespeare), and piano playing (J. K. Paine's five music courses). What McCosh neglected to say was that despite Eliot's refusal to recognize an "antagonism between literature and science," Harvard's president boosted separate technical schools for those interested in vocational skills only. Four years after McCosh's speech in New York, responses to a survey showed that in the minds of students Eliot's new system was clearly carrying the day. Asked to identify what made Harvard so attractive, one student wrote: "the spirit of a universal learning and development, as distinguished from the intent and temper of a sectarian college." [20]

This, however, did not mean that Eliot, the son of a Unitarian minister and one-time mayor of Boston, had given up on the idea that there was an intimate connection between Harvard and Christianity. In his inaugural speech Eliot acknowledged this connection with a rhetorical flourish: "Let [Harvard] be devoted to Christ, the great teacher of truth, and to his Church, the great means of human education." Yet he risked this clarification: "The worthy fruit of academic culture is an open mind, trained to careful thinking, instructed in the methods of philosophic investigation, acquainted in a general way with the accumulated thought of past generations, and penetrated with humility. It is thus that the university in our day serves Christ and the church." [21] As Harvard's president, Eliot's primary concern was the excellence of the institution committed to his care, and he recognized that old hats had to go. He did away with compulsory chapel and had no qualms about telling a student who woke him in the middle of the night because he had just had a vision that the president was prepared to accept Jesus Christ as his personal savior that the student had been misinformed. [22]

In America's increasingly diverse society, disdained by Chapman as a "jumble of nationalities," [23] Eliot saw an untapped source of strength, not least of all for his school. He did not hesitate to enlist the best of those who set no stock in Jesus Christ as their personal savior. He hired a number of Jewish professors: Frank Taussig in economics (1882), Charles Gross in history (1888), Hugo Münsterberg in philosophy (1892), and Leo Wiener in Slavic languages and literature (1896). After three years Wiener surprised his employer with a *History of Yiddish Literature* (1899) that achieved for Yiddish what Wendell undertook for American literature a year later. In 1903 the Harvard Semitic Museum opened, made possible by a gift from Eliot's personal friend Jacob Schiff. Almost two decades later, in 1921, when the United States lowered its immigration quota for Jews from Eastern Europe and the discussion of a *numerus clausus* for Jews was in the air at Harvard and elsewhere, President Emeritus Eliot, then eighty-seven years old, wrote an appreciation of Jacob Schiff for the *Menorah Journal*.

The question of a quota for Jews at Harvard came up partly in response to Eliot's liberal admissions policy. He had quadrupled the student body from 563 in 1869 (3 or 4 of whom were Jews) to 2,265 in 1909, and as Jews became interested in higher education, they started coming to Harvard. The presence of Jewish freshmen at Harvard increased from 4.6 percent in 1908 to 21.5 percent in 1922. Despite this spectacular numerical growth during the Lowell presidency (1909–1933), the real change for Jews at Harvard had come during Eliot's reign. With the founding of the Menorah Society in 1906, Jews became an organized cultural presence and increased their visibility on campus. Furthermore, the type of Jewish student changed. German Jews, who had assimilated into America's upper and upper-middle classes, were soon outnumbered by Eastern European Jews, many of whom were recent immigrants. In 1908, 71 of the 95 Jews at Harvard were from Russia. Among them was a freshman, Harry A. Wolfson, who had completed a traditional course of Jewish studies at famous *yeshivot* [Talmud academies] in Eastern Europe. Seventeen years later, in 1925, Wolfson became Harvard's first professor of Hebrew literature and philosophy.[24]

This development was in part a result of Eliot's respect for people as individuals. He believed that Harvard's task was to educate qualified young men. His conviction led to an astonishing diversification of the student body. Yet any assembly of individuals—even if it is, as Eliot thought of Harvard's students, the nation's elite—will tend to subdivide and coalesce in little groups, according to academic and extracurricular interests, religion, descent, culture, and class. Among the most exclusive of these groups at Harvard was the small crowd of the socially acceptable who congregated in such "waiting" and "final" clubs as the D.K.E., the Institute of 1770, or the Porcellian. Jews, even when rich, charming and refined, were usually not clubbable, as Walter Lippmann (class of 1910) was to learn, much to his chagrin. But diversification meant that one need not care about exclusion; one could go out and find or found a group that was congenial. Eliot, unlike his successor, saw no reason to interfere with the groupings. Even so, he conceded, "one could wish that the University did not offer the same contrast between the rich man's mode of life and the poor man's that the outer world offers, but it does, and it is not certain that the presence of this contrast is unwholesome or injurious."[25]

What was injurious, however, was the exclusivity or, rather, impenetrability of the English department, which the "Angry Saxons" (Berenson's term) ran like a social club. The department had evolved slowly. Eliot's class of 1853 had been offered only one course in English literature, an introduction to Chaucer. The first professorship in English was established in 1876. The appointee was Francis James Child, the son of a Boston sail maker's large family of modest means and a Harvard tutor since his graduation in 1846. He tutored first in mathematics, then in history, political economy, and finally in English composition, when he succeeded Edward T. Channing as Boylston Professor of Rhetoric. Child was unhappy about his new assignment. Johns Hopkins University, the emerging leader in hard philological research, recognized in the remarkable "Stubby" Child a neglected treasure and made him an offer. Harvard reacted quickly by creating a chair in English literature, and in 1876, Child gladly gave up teaching rhetoric for courses in Anglo-Saxon, Chaucer, and Shakespeare. He trained George Lyman Kittredge (class of 1882), who after a stint at Phillips Exeter joined the Harvard faculty in 1888 to become the quintessential philologist and "one of the glories of the University." [26]

The research positivism of "Stubby" and "Kitty," their teaching of sources and parallel references, was counterpoised by courses in composition and literary appreciation that were taught by the more or less distinguished sons of old New England families. Student favorites were Charles Townsend Copeland and LeBaron Russell Briggs; the even more popular Barrett Wendell introduced American literature into the curriculum, and the mild Bliss Perry taught the first course on Emerson (1908–1909). The career of Lewis E. Gates was regrettably cut short by a nervous collapse in 1902, "his health having been seriously impaired by his excessive devotion to his studies and his work as instructor and professor." [27] All in all, the presence of these men during the first decade of the twentieth century gave Harvard the appearance of a literary college. Quite possibly the literary glamour sparkled even more brightly because of what Bliss Perry dubbed the "irresponsible individualism" of the scholars and critics who formed its English department. "Here was a brilliant array of prima-donnas," Perry recalled in 1935, "each supreme in a chosen role: men like Briggs, Wendell, Copeland, [Fred N.] Robinson, [George P.] Baker, and the famous Kittredge, with younger scholars like [William A.] Neilson and [Chester N.] Greenough coming on. But it was difficult for a stranger to discover any common denominator in their activities. What was the underlying philosophy of the Department, its ideal aim, its relation with liberal studies as a whole?" [28]

The complete absence of rigorous theoretical self-reflection created a certain "literary" haze. When Van Wyck Brooks was looking for a school to nurse his gifts ("I knew I was a writer born"), he came to Cambridge because he supposed that "Harvard was the college for writers. It was intensely literary." The student body certainly contained a liberal sprinkling of stunning literary talent: Robert Frost spent the years

3. T. S. Eliot as an undergraduate at Harvard in 1907. *Courtesy of Harvard University Archives.*

1897–1899 at Harvard; Wallace Stevens left the school in 1900; Brooks arrived in 1904, as did the poet John Hall Wheelock; in 1906, T. S. Eliot, John Reed, and Walter Lippmann enrolled in the class of 1910; Conrad Aiken was a year behind them and became Eliot's close friend. In 1915 the Harvard Poetry Society was created by a new crop of literary men. Among its most notable founders were e. e. cummings (class of 1915), John Dos Passos (class of 1916), and Robert Hillyer (class of 1917). All in all, however, there were too few of the really gifted in the Yard before World War I to satisfy its thirst for literary glory. Hence Brooks complained that "the cultivation of taste at Harvard was not only occasionally mistaken for talent but sometimes went far to stultify it." [29]

There was indeed something sterile about Harvard's literary men, which was partly the result of being condemned to dabble in the shadow of outstanding philosophers. The 1890s have been called the golden age of Harvard's philosophy department. Gold gave way to brass after the death of William James in 1910. He had tried to retire in 1903 but continued to have students until 1908, when Horace Kallen completed his doctoral thesis. George Herbert Palmer retired in 1913 at the age of seventy-one. Josiah Royce was fifty-seven when he suffered a stroke triggered perhaps by severe grief over the deaths of his son and his friend William James within a few weeks of each other. Although Royce recovered physically, he declined intellectually. With the outbreak of the World War I he poured his remaining energies into a bitter anti-German campaign. This hurt his German-born colleague Hugo Münsterberg, who energetically defended the kaiser. The two philosophers did not live to see the end of the war. Both men died in 1916, Münsterberg at age fifty. Santayana had resigned from his professorship in 1912, refusing to belong any longer to that "anonymous concourse of coral insects, each secreting one cell, and leaving that fossil legacy to enlarge the earth" (PPce 397).[30] He had given his academic regalia to his former teaching assistant Horace Kallen, the son of a rabbi, and left for Europe.

With the waning of the philosophy department and the passing of the presidency from Eliot—whom Santayana considered an antihumanist because Eliot had once said to him that "we should teach *the facts*, not merely convey *ideas*" (PPce 392)—to Lowell in 1909, the path seemed clear for the unobstructed growth of Harvard's men of letters. But what had been mediocre remained so. The man of the hour proved to be an outsider, Irving Babbitt, and the man of the future his student T. S. Eliot. Both deplored the intellectual laxity that had crept into the Yard with President Eliot's elective system, and snubbed what was popular with the crowd. Babbitt scorned Wendell as a dilettante, and T. S. Eliot thought Santayana's lectures "soporific." In later years, Eliot, an Anglo-Catholic by choice, and Santayana, a born Catholic turned atheist, kept enough distance between them to avoid an exchange that would have made their disapproval of each other public. Yet Santayana shared with Eliot and Babbitt a deep distaste for romantic individualism, and a disdain for uncontrolled outbursts of emotion that in 1900 led Santayana to say of poets that "the glorious emotions with which he bubbles over must at all hazards find or feign their *correlative objects.*" This statement came two decades before Eliot proposed his theory of the "objective correlative" in his essay "Hamlet and His Problems."[31]

Eliot never referred publicly to Santayana. He found it easier to acknowledge his debt to Babbitt, adding, however, that if Babbitt had taken his humanism a bit further into the direction of Christianity as embodied by the Catholic Church, he might have developed a durable theory of cultural salvation. But as Babbitt refused to accept "any dogma or revelation," the task was Eliot's to complete. By the time Eliot returned to Harvard as the Charles Eliot Norton Professor in 1932, a year before Babbitt's death, he had begun to develop a cultural theory so rigid and exclusive that it would have caused his old mentors to gasp for breath. In part, this theory had its American origin in Babbitt's provocative first book, *Literature and the American College* (1908), published some months before Eliot took Babbitt's course. Peter Ackroyd has rightly cautioned that "a teacher does not dominate a young man as clever as Eliot—he simply provides the framework, or language, in which he can develop and serves to confirm the direction which he is already instinctively taking." [32] The framework Babbitt provided for Eliot bears examining.

With the changing of the guard at Harvard around 1910, the relaxed tolerance of the genteel elite, exemplified by such men as Norton and Charles William Eliot, was replaced by a new mode of exclusivist thinking then arising in the United States. Fast economic expansion and mass immigration threatened the cultural and economic security of New England's old governing class and even more so the always elusive security of those who were not quite members of the elite, because these changes allowed and encouraged new groups to rise to power. The calls for Jewish quotas at Harvard and other Ivy League schools were an expression of growing social insecurity. This fear of displacement is also reflected in Barrett Wendell's regret over the emancipation of the slaves. Wendell, who despite his pretension to gentility was never part of the Brahmin class, maintained that the antislavery movement in Massachusetts had permanently "lowered the personal dignity of public life, by substituting for the traditional rule of the conservative gentry the obvious dominance of the less educated classes." The truly genteel Norton, by contrast, had staunchly and unequivocally advocated the education of blacks. [33]

Of course, T. S. Eliot's theory was not born whole from the spirit of Babbitt's humanism. Rather, it was shaped by the social and cultural anxieties of the intermediary generation (of Wendell, Babbitt, and Santayana) that congealed into fear and a defensive exclusivism in the generation of the Brahmins' epigones. As Santayana wrote, Eliot hoped "to set up barriers of custom and barriers of taste." [34] These barriers dominated literary academe until Jewish critics insisted that they were irrelevant to the cultivation of intellectual excellence.

At Harvard, Babbitt's New Humanism prepared the ground for the development of Eliot's cultural theory. In 1908, the year of Norton's death, Irving Babbitt published his first book, a collection of interconnected essays entitled *Literature and the American College*. Babbitt, then forty-three years old, was a Midwesterner who had been deeply and lastingly influenced by Norton's notion of culture. After his graduation from Harvard in 1889, he had gone to Paris to study Sanskrit and Pali under Sylvain Lévi. He returned to his alma mater to continue oriental studies with Charles R. Lanman. His only classmate in the fall of 1892 was Paul Elmer More, who became his lifelong friend.[35] Except for a brief teaching stint at Williams College in 1893, Babbitt spent the rest of his life at Harvard,—not in the classics department, as he had hoped, but as a teacher of French literature.

He was still an assistant professor, untenured and married, when he launched his double-pronged attack on the rigidity and narrowness of German-style "scientific" philological research and on the unrestricted liberty permitted to students within Eliot's elective system that had too rashly done away with obligatory training in the classics. Eliot, then retiring as president, took Babbitt's outbursts calmly, but Kittredge and his philological colleagues were up in arms. The trouble with both, Babbitt argued, was an overemphasis on the individual, resulting too often in a cultivation of the purely eccentric, be that the little pellets of research deposited by the philologist in some dusty corner of the library or the indulgence of a student's private tastes and sentiments. "This outcry about originality" in research, Babbitt wrote, "is simply the scientific form of that pedantry of individualism, so rampant at the present hour, which, in its sentimental form, leads . . . to an exaggerated respect for temperament and idiosyncrasy." A decade after he had studied with Babbitt, T. S. Eliot sharpened his teacher's argument, while limiting it to poetry, when he wrote in "Tradition and the Individual Talent" (1919) that the "search for novelty in the wrong place," by which he meant the merely personal and experiential, "discovers the perverse."[36] Eliot would express precisely this view, now widened toward a cultural theory, in the Page-Barbour lectures delivered at the University of Virginia in April 1933 and published infamously in 1934 under the title *After Strange Gods*.

Babbitt perceived yet another detrimental effect of individualism as practiced by Harvard's president. "The elective system, so far as it is inspired by the desire of the sentimental humanitarian to set up a pure and unrestricted liberty, to make selection wholly individual, evidently denies the principle on which the college rests." It was, however, a rather small group whose communality—the basis for tradition—Babbitt saw endangered. "As formerly conceived, the college might have been defined as a careful selection of studies for the creation of a social élite. In its present tendency, it might be defined as something of everything for everybody." Babbitt took care not to condemn President Eliot's democratic impulse, since it had been to his own benefit. As a youngster he had worked as a newsboy and farmhand. "Evidently the college should be democratic in the sense that it should get rid of all distinctions of family and rank. . . . In a few of our Eastern colleges the snobbishness of family exists, but not to a dangerous degree." In his gratitude to Harvard, Babbitt was willing to overlook that his social isolation there, even as a professor, was largely due to his ancestral marginality. At most he conceded that "some of the more luxurious of our college dormitories and clubhouses testify to an extravagant and foolish use of money." But this was negligible given "a laudable desire in our colleges to give everybody a chance. Indeed the more humanitarian members of our faculties are ready to waste their energies in trying to elevate youths above the level to which they belong, not only by their birth, but by their capacity." [37]

Less than two decades later, college administrators began to worry about the long-term effects of Eliot's broadening of Harvard's student body and the notion in Babbitt's last sentence was translated into code phrases (such as "above their level", "beyond their capacity") identifying hard-working Jewish students ("grinds"). Their academic achievements gradually raised college standards and threatened to marginalize the old student population that had scraped by on gentlemen's Cs. Feeling beleaguered by an army of grinds, college administrators resorted to selective admissions. In 1922, the new dean of Columbia College, Herbert Hawkes, defended the recently adopted measures in a letter to Columbia's president, Nicholas Murray Butler, against the charge that they were particularly hard on Jews. His letter puts Babbitt's notion to practical use: "We have honestly attempted," Hawkes wrote, "to eliminate the lowest grade of applicant and it turns out that a good many of the low grade men are New York City Jews. It is a fact that boys of foreign parentage who have no background in many cases attempt to educate themselves beyond their intelligence. Their accomplishment is over 100% of their ability on account of their tremendous energy and ambition. I do not believe however that a College would do well to admit too many men of low mentality who have ambition but no brains" [38]

Times had changed. In the 1880s, studiousness had simply been one of Berenson's eccentricities. A decade later, Santayana noted that the presence of Jews in his courses had become stronger. As their numbers rose, group characteristics were noted by those who felt their space infringed upon by the newcomers. In 1915, T. S. Eliot perceived a certain Jewish type that he found amusing rather than threatening. In a letter to Eleanor Hinckley, he compared the students in Cambridge, England, to their American counterparts: "the men impressed me by their resemblance to Harvard graduate school types; serious, industrious, narrow and plebeian. The more *brilliant* ones (one or two) more like the clever Jew undergraduate mind at Harvard; wide but disorderly reading, intense but confused thinking, and utter absence of background and balance and proportion." [39] In the early 1920s, confronted with the ever rising number of clever Jews, amusement turned into hostility.

In *Literature and the American College,* Babbitt did not mention Jews. He was more concerned with "the eager efforts of our philanthropists to do something for the negro and the newsboy." Babbitt's attitude did not betray that he too had once sold newspapers in a rough section of New York City. He felt that "a society that hopes to be saved by what it does for its negroes and its newsboys is a society that is trying to lift itself by its own boot-straps." In his essays he proposed that American education could not be saved by the humanitarian, "a person who has sympathy for mankind in the lump," but only by the humanist, who is "interested in the perfecting of the individual rather than in schemes for the elevation of mankind as a whole," and whose sympathy is "disciplined and tempered by judgment." Citing the Latin writer Aulus Gellius, Babbitt pointed out that the word *humanitas* was "incorrectly used to denote a 'promiscuous benevolence, what the Greeks call philanthropy,' whereas the word really implies doctrine and discipline, and is applicable not to men in general but only to a select few,—it is, in short, aristocratic and not democratic in its implication." Instead of broad knowledge and sympathy, Babbitt wanted discipline and selection as embodied in the idea of the English gentleman scholar who, Babbitt claimed, resembled most closely the cultivated man in the intensely aristocratic democracy of Athens.

Vis-à-vis Christianity, Babbitt found himself in a fix. He thought it quite nonsensical, but in a society as thoroughly Christian as New England he had to make concessions. Typically, his compliment turned into yet another reproach. We suppose, he argued, that an "unselective and universal sympathy, the sense of the brotherhood of man," was introduced by Christianity when, in fact, Christians have been quite selective. "Historically, Christians have always inclined to reserve their sympathies for those who had the same doctrine and discipline as themselves, and only too often have joined to a sympathy for their own kind a fanatical hatred for everybody else." To Babbitt the Christian tradition represented the worst possible combination of sympathy and selection and was therefore of no use whatsoever in the proper education of the humanist.[40] Here Eliot parted company with his teacher.

Just as Babbitt's views had been shaped by Norton (who had been a skeptic in matters of religion), Eliot's were influenced by Babbitt—not exclusively, not even fundamentally, but significantly. Eliot acknowledged as much in 1941 when he wrote:

> I do not believe that any pupil who was ever deeply impressed by Babbitt, can ever speak of him with that mild tenderness one feels toward something one has outgrown or grown out of. If one has once had that relationship with Babbitt, he remains permanently an active influence; his ideas are permanently with one, as a measurement and test of one's own. I cannot imagine anyone coming to react *against* Babbitt. Even in the convictions one may feel, the views one may hold, that seem to contradict most important convictions of Babbitt's own, one is aware that he himself was very largely the cause of them.[41]

In 1916, a year after Eliot had finished his dissertation and decided to remain in Europe and not to return to Harvard for his defense, he taught a course in modern French literature at the Oxford University Extension School. In their reaction against romanticism, Eliot's lectures indicated his indebtedness to Babbitt. But other influences too made themselves felt. Eliot's intense religious experiences at Harvard in 1914, for instance, were beginning to ferment, activated by his encounter with the ideas of T. E. Hulme. In his lecture "The Reaction Against Romanticism," Eliot alluded to a theory of Hulme's: "The classicist point of view has been defined as essentially a belief in Original Sin—the necessity for austere discipline."[42] By the time he published "Tradition and the Individual Talent" in *The Egoist,* there were, he would claim in 1961, two influences at work on him: that of Irving Babbitt and that of Ezra Pound. "The influence of Babbitt (with an infusion later of T. E. Hulme and of the more literary essays of Charles Maurras) is apparent in my recurrent theme of Classicism versus Romanticism." In *After Strange Gods,* Eliot explicitly replaced this dichotomy with the terms "orthodoxy" and "heresy," because in these lectures he attempted to rewrite "Tradition and the Individual Talent" or, as Eliot put it, "to outline the matter as I now conceive it."[43]

Between the essay (1919), which still reflected Babbitt's freethinking views on the relation of originality to tradition, and the Virginia lectures (1933), which revised these views by giving "tradition" a specific meaning, Eliot published an essay entitled "The Humanism of Irving Babbitt" (1927). It proposed a general critique of Babbitt's humanism. Eliot had reached a turning point, indicated not so much by his change of citizenship or even his conversion on June 29, 1927, but, rather, by his readiness to go public with his Anglo-Catholic views. The premise of his essay on Babbitt was simple: "The problem of humanism is undoubtedly related to the problem of religion." What he took issue with was equally simple: "Mr. Babbitt makes it very clear . . . that he is unable to take the religious view—that is to say that he cannot accept any dogma or revelation; and that humanism is the *alternative* to religion." Eliot then set out to prove that humanism was not an alternative to religion (meaning Christianity), but instead was ancillary to it. His three arguments were that Christianity was continuous whereas humanism was sporadic; that humanism's doctrine of the "inner check" replacing the disintegrating "outer check" ("the outer restraints of kingship, aristocracy, and class") was inefficient, whereas "the idea of religion is the *inner* control"; and that Babbitt was mistaken in his fear that organized religion "should cramp and deform the free operations of his own mind." Eliot's reasoning led him to conclude "that the humanistic point of view is auxiliary to and dependent upon the religious point of view. For us, religion is Christianity; and Christianity implies, I think, the conception of the Church."[44] This was a strong statement, but Babbitt himself may have provoked it.

In the summer of 1927, Babbitt stopped in London on his way back to Cambridge from Paris, where he had lectured at the Sorbonne, to have dinner with his former student. "I had not seen Babbitt for some years," Eliot recalled, "and I felt obliged to acquaint him with a fact as yet unknown to my small circle of readers, . . . that I had recently been baptized and confirmed into the Church of England. I knew that it would come as a shock to him to learn that any disciple of his had so turned his coat, though he had already what must have been a much greater shock when his close friend and ally Paul Elmer More defected from Humanism to Christianity. But all Babbitt said was: 'I think you should come out into the open.'" Eliot was nettled by this remark. "I had not been conscious of skulking, having been more concerned with making up my own mind than with making any public use of it when made. But Babbitt's words gnawed on my conscience, and provoked, for my next volume of essays [*For Lancelot Andrewes*], a preface that perhaps went to the opposite extreme from that of which I had felt myself accused." The preface contained a sentence to the effect that the author was "a classicist in literature, a royalist in politics, and an Anglo-Catholic in religion. I ought to have foreseen that so quotable a sentence would follow me through life." [45]

Small wonder, perhaps, because the statement itself contained a memorable quotation. In 1913 the *Nouvelle Revue Française,* a magazine Eliot continued to read after his post-graduate year in France, described Charles Maurras as the embodiment of three traditions—*classique, catholique, monarchique.* That sounds quite civilized and in tune with Eliot's admission to being influenced by "the more literary essays of Charles Maurras." But, in fact, Maurras was a fascist who later teamed up with the Vichy government. Cynthia Ozick put it succinctly: "When Eliot first encountered him, Maurras was the founder of an anti-democratic organization called Action Française, which specialized in student riots and open assaults on free-thinking Jews. Eliot, an onlooker on one of these occasions, did not shrink from the violence." [46] The wild yet disciplined activism of the chauvinist Maurras gradually supplanted in Eliot the influence of Babbitt's tough yet free-roaming cosmopolitan intellect. [47]

Five years after Eliot had first explained himself to Babbitt, he was invited to deliver the Norton lectures at Harvard. It was an opportunity to air his views. Eliot looked forward to his visit, "to engaging Babbitt in some of the perambulatory conversations that his pupils know so well." But Babbitt was already a sick man, and Eliot saw him only twice, in November 1932; "thereafter his illness made communication impossible." [48] Babbitt died on July 15, 1933. Eliot had already returned to England.

Eliot decided to play it safe at Harvard, which, like America at large, had been perceptibly "invaded by foreign races" and as a result was, like much of American society, "worm-eaten with Liberalism." In Cambridge he gave the lectures collected in *The Use of Poetry and the Use of Criticism.* He reserved the presentation of his "strong convictions" for the students at the University of Virginia, "one of the older, smaller and most gracious of American educational institutions, one of those in which some vestiges of a traditional education seem to survive." [49]

At the center of his strong convictions was a new and precise understanding of tradition. It was that of the Catholic Church, and it required that Eliot substitute for the pagan and secular literary terms *classicism* and *romanticism* the Christian and theological terms *orthodoxy* and *heresy*. In Virginia, Eliot no longer spoke as a literary critic, as he had at Harvard, but "ascended the platform of these lectures only in the role of moralist." Speaking indeed ex cathedra, he felt free to say, "I believe that a right tradition for us must be also a Christian tradition." Truly new here was his insistence on a "right" tradition for a very specific American "us." Eliot was beginning to connect social criteria and Christianity. The ideology of "unselective and universal sympathy" was matched to a constituency that recalled the small social enclaves created by the medieval feudal system. Within that system Christianity worked so well precisely because it was an ideology of hierarchical control and social subordination. Although Babbitt might not have objected to the feudal, vaguely aristocratic element in Eliot's notion of the Christian tradition, he would have greatly resisted Eliot's attempt to graft it onto the American people. Virginians, however, albeit at Jefferson's university, may have liked what they heard. "What I mean by tradition," Eliot said, "involves all those habitual actions, habits and customs, from the most significant religious rite to our conventional way of greeting a stranger, which represent the blood kinship of 'the same people living in the same place.' " If a tradition was limited to "a particular people in a particular place" (which was the opposite of what St. Paul had had in mind for Christianity), it could not be expansive or imperialist (as America was). Eliot admonished, however, that we should not "cling to traditions as a way of asserting our superiority over less favoured peoples." He then continued to outline the preconditions for the recovery of tradition in America:

> Stability is obviously necessary. You are hardly likely to develop tradition except where the bulk of the population is relatively so well off where it is that it has no incentive or pressure to move about. The population should be homogeneous; where two or more cultures exist in the same place they are likely either to be fiercely self-conscious or both to become adulterate. What is still more important is unity of religious background; and reasons of race and religion combine to make any large number of free-thinking Jews undesirable. There must be a proper balance between urban and rural, industrial and agricultural development. And a spirit of excessive tolerance is to be deprecated.[50]

Eliot had come a long way in his cultural thinking since asserting in "Tradition and the Individual Talent" that tradition "cannot be inherited, and if you want it you must obtain it by great labour." This implied that tradition could be acquired intellectually, by an exertion of intelligence and imagination, and not by social osmosis, by living continuously in one place. What Eliot described in "Tradition and the Individual Talent" was applicable not only to his own life but equally to the lives of thousands of immigrants to America. It was this early Eliot, the "American" Eliot who enacted the American experience of acquiring tradition through his journey to England and conversion to Anglo-Catholicism, who was taken seriously by liberal intellectuals. Jewish admirers of his poetry preferred to ignore Eliot's nasty lines, although, as George Steiner pointed out, "Eliot's uglier touches tend to occur at the heart of very good poetry." They occur most notably in the poems of 1920: "Gerontion," "Burbank with a Baedecker: Bleistein with a Cigar," and "Sweeney among the Nightingales." His early Jewish admirers wanted to remain unenlightened about the direction of Eliot's cultural theories; or, if they suspected them, they found it difficult to criticize Eliot.[51] After all, he was central to the culture, and they were not—or so they thought.

At the time, it would have required a courage bordering on foolishness for Jews to point out that there was too much Christianity in Eliot's prose. Harry Levin dared to say as much in 1934, but only in a private letter to F. O. Matthiessen. Santayana could have taken Eliot to task, but he too preferred to bury his observations in a private "Note on T. S. Eliot," written in the mid-1930s. "The thought of T. S. Eliot," Santayana mused, "is subterranean without being profound. . . . [His] peep-and-run intuition appears . . . even in his Anglo-Catholicism: he likes this in Christianity and he dislikes that, and feels a general dismay at the natural course of the world. He dreads and does not understand the radical forces at work in the world and in the church; but he is beautifully sensitive to the cross-lights that traverse the middle distance; and he hopes to set up barriers of custom and barriers of taste, to keep mankind from touching bottom or from quite seeing the light."[52]

Santayana perceived in Eliot an anxious narrowness that Eliot had detected in Babbitt.[53] Eliot's fearful dogmatism may have kept him, in Santayana's view, from becoming a master in his adopted tradition, but it also kept him from doing greater harm. Witnessing from Rome the steady decline of the genteel tradition that came to an end at Harvard with Eliot's tenure as Norton professor, Santayana assumed a pose of indifference. In his farewell to that tradition, published in 1931, he wrote:

aristocratic people, who are sure of their own taste and manners, are indifferent, except for a general curiosity, to the disputes of critics and pedants, and perhaps to the maxims of preachers; such things are imposing only to those who are inwardly wondering what they ought to do, and how they ought to feel. A truly enlightened mind is all the simpler for being enlightened and thinks, not without a modest sort of irony, that art and life exist to be enjoyed and not to be estimated.[54]

By 1930, the genteel tradition had declined in dignity and largesse, but it had lost little strength as a social force. In the early 1930s, Harvard was still riddled with large pockets of exclusive groups that were fortified by the new fad of an elitist Christianity, which also infected Warren House, the home of the English department. In the course of the 1930s, three young Jews—Harry Levin, Daniel Aaron, and Meyer Abrams, all born in 1912—emerged from under its roof as serious literary scholars bent on careers in academe. Their eventual ascension to professorships took a great deal of luck, much courage and social perspicacity, and, most important of all, critical verve and scholarly brilliance.

2

*Portrait of a Scholar
as a Young Man:
Harry Levin*

TOWARD THE FALL OF 1929, Harry Levin left his hometown of
Minneapolis for Boston. There he would cross the Charles River to
reach Cambridge and his ultimate destination, Harvard University. Levin
made his first journey east in a Model T, but for all subsequent travel he
took the train. Thinking back, some four decades later, on his trips
between his old and his new home, Levin recalled that the thirty-six-
hour train ride marked "a transition from one way of life to another, and
all but induced in the passenger a state of cultural schizophrenia." Levin,
then barely seventeen years old, was in search of history and culture. He
had enrolled with alacrity in what he perceived to be the most traditional
of American colleges, and he was propelled eastward by the peculiar
sense of despair that descends on the intellectually ambitious when they
realize that the pleasant environs of their youth are a cultural desert.
Years later, these beginnings would enable Harry Levin to relate Perry
Miller's "immense avidity" for history and culture to his colleague's
Midwestern origins and to the fact that in the middle of America culture
"was not to be taken for granted at any point." His own youthful ennui
Levin attributed to his feeling then that in the Midwest he was outside
history. History, he thought, was something that happened in Europe
and perhaps on the East Coast. In Minnesota he felt marginal to the
culture he had begun to care for.[1]

But there was something else that increased his desire to move on.
Levin was Jewish, and as his much younger fellow townsman, the poet

Allen Grossman, was still compelled to acknowledge two decades after Levin's departure, "Jews in Minnesota weren't going anywhere. There was no future for the mind in Midwestern Jewish culture, at least not in Minneapolis. If you wanted to grow, you had to leave." Grossman went east in 1950, "because Harvard was the only place I had ever heard of." Levin had heard of others. He had also applied to Yale and had been accepted there. With a little effort, however, he might have found out that locally, at the University of Minnesota, he could have learned more about Shakespeare from Elmer Edgar Stoll than at the feet of Kittredge in Cambridge. But Levin, though in his own assessment "shy, awkward, and socially backward," was determined to leave his home town for the great "world elsewhere." The lure of Harvard was irresistible. Encouraged by one of his favorite teachers, Hannah Griffith, a Radcliffe-trained Quaker, and with the blessings of his parents, Levin had applied to Harvard and gotten in. Whatever awaited him there could not be worse than what Minneapolis, later called "the capitol of anti-Semitism in the United States," had in store for him.[2]

Under the circumstances, Levin's father, Isadore Henry Levin, had done very well for himself. He had come to America as a boy from rural East Prussia and settled with his family in Minnesota, where eventually he enjoyed a fair amount of success as a furniture manufacturer in partnership with two brothers. He married Beatrice Tuchman, whose grandparents had emigrated from Germany in the mid-nineteenth century. As was typical for German Jews of that period and background, Beatrice was brought up with barely a touch of Reform Judaism. The emptiness of her religious education and the anti-Jewish snobbery of her environment made her the willing convert of an aunt who had become a Christian Scientist. As a new religion that rejected "the validity of the testimony of the senses" and focused instead on the will to be healed, Christian Science provided an escape from the aches of being Jewish for ill-adjusted but socially ambitious women. Beatrice's son Harry, born on July 18, 1912, was sent to Christian Science and Jewish Reform Sunday school and thus saw, as he put it, "the two religions at their thinnest."[3] Like his mentor, Irving Babbitt, Levin would always find religion unappealing.

Beatrice's Christian Science and Isadore's affluence made it possible for the Levins to move into a prosperous Gentile neighborhood. Levin recalled that their presence there "often produced little bits of social snobbery on the part of socially climbing neighbors" (interview). The problem was in fact quite serious. When Harry Levin was ten, Jews were excluded from virtually all social organizations in Minneapolis. In 1922, the remarkable year that saw the publication of *Ulysses* and *The Waste Land* (from which Ezra Pound had successfully excised Eliot's Bleistein), and that witnessed the assassination of Germany's Jewish foreign minister, Walter Rathenau, Maurice Lefkovits wrote in the Rosh Hashanah number of a Minneapolis Jewish weekly: "There is not, to my knowledge, a single Jewish member in any of the numerous city and country clubs; nor are Jews solicited in the Boat Club or Automobile Club; and even the Athletic Club, I understand, has raised the barriers against any further Jewish accessions above those who were permitted to enter when its sacred precincts were first opened some years ago." [4]

Isadore Levin, who had no college education, was a member of the Athletic Club. Fondly nicknamed "Busy Izzy" in the community, he was the only Jew in the Chamber of Commerce, a director of the Northwestern National Bank, and, very briefly, a member of the State Republican Committee. The Levins belonged to the upper middle class of Minneapolis, and it was precisely there that the city's anti-Semitism made itself most felt. A Jewish homeowner in a fashionable section of the city had his windows shot out with buckshot to make him move, and elsewhere prospective Jewish buyers were approached by neighborhood committees urging them not to purchase in their particular area because it was "a Christian neighborhood." [5] The Levins knew that such things could happen to them too. Choosing a school for their oldest son was not easy. Their social status and affluence would have made it possible to send Harry to a good private school, perhaps to the one country day school nearby. But partly fearing that Harry might experience anti-Semitism in that exclusive environment and partly clinging to their belief in the rationality and soundness of the American people, they chose a public school.

It was a good decision. Harry was happy there. He became editor of the weekly newspaper as well as president of two clubs. It was evident to all that he was bright and a bit bookish. When he was eleven, the only book he took along to camp was a volume of Shakespeare's plays; at fourteen he was an avid reader of the *Dial,* an avowedly "aesthetic" magazine, and at seventeen he was on his way to Harvard. His father was hoping that he would return to enter the family business. But the apprentice jobs he had assigned his son during vacations convinced Harry that he would never be a businessman. Five decades later Levin wrote that he was glad to have had those assignments "since they gave me a clearer impression of how most Americans pass their lives," an impression that probably strengthened his resolve not to return to his parental home but to enter for good the world of culture and scholarship.[6]

Abbott Lawrence Lowell and the Jews

A few short summer months before Harry Levin arrived in Boston, Harvard's president, Abbott Lawrence Lowell, had preached his twentieth baccalaureate sermon to the graduating class of 1929. He had taken his text from Deuteronomy: "And when the Lord your God brings you into the land which he swore to your fathers . . . to give you, with great and goodly cities, which you did not build, . . . with vineyards and olive trees, which you did not plant, and when you eat and are full, then take heed lest you forget the Lord, who brought you out of Egypt, out of the house of bondage" (Deut. 6: 10–12). In keeping with the tradition of the university, the president interpreted this text typologically. He spoke about the American mission, the "noble future" arising from a "worthy past"; about America's responsibilities as a preeminent nation; about self-control, discipline, and energy; and about the obligation to make cautious use of America's bounties "so that all mankind may be the better because America is inhabited by Americans."[7] One of the scandals of the Lowell administration had revolved precisely around the question *who* was an American and thus chosen to participate in the noble and ennobling enterprise. In Lowell's view the people to whom the American mission was entrusted were outstanding individuals assimilated to each other and transformed into a homogeneous group by a singular experience. The Israelites' preparatory sojourn in the Sinai desert, one of the types of the Pilgrim Fathers' preparatory crossing of the Atlantic, became in Lowell's sermon a type of the preparatory years spent at Harvard before these young men entered the promised land, America, and dealt responsibly with its bounties.

It is not surprising, then, to find that Lowell opposed large-scale immigration of "alien races." He believed that American social and political institutions could not survive in a heterogeneous society. While his predecessor at Harvard, Charles W. Eliot, had made countless statements on behalf of the National Liberal Immigration League, and had not only expressed his belief in the ability of the United States to assimilate immigrants without stripping them of their individuality but had proven his faith by opening Harvard to a diverse student body, Lowell was terrified of what the ever-swelling flood of immigrants might bring.

In 1912, three years after succeeding Eliot, Lowell assumed the national vice-presidency of the Immigration Restriction League, founded in Boston in 1894. He had come to the conclusion "that no democracy could be successful unless it was tolerably homogeneous," and he was certain, as Marcia Synnott put it, "that some Europeans could not be easily assimilated into American life." He also thought this true of Asians, blacks, and Jews. In a letter to George F. Moore written in 1922, Lowell wished, a little paradoxically, that "the Jews who come to Harvard College should retain their characteristics, but on admission be overcome with an oblivion of the fact that they were Jews, even though all the Gentiles were perfectly aware that they were Jews." [8]

For Lowell, a former professor of government, Harvard College was not simply an institution for the education of American leaders; rather, it represented the goals and ideals of American society. Foremost among them was the idea that America provided a unifying experience and was an undertaking of a community of men. The self-segregation of Jews at Harvard, more imagined by Lowell than real, was only one disruptive factor. Another was Eliot's elective system, which Lowell deplored because it gave free reign to the whims of the individual. He replaced it with a more systematic plan of undergraduate study to be supervised by tutors. They brought coherence into their students' course work, which was to terminate in general examinations at the end of the senior year. The "intellectual cohesion" Lowell hoped for was to be paralleled and supported by a new "social cohesion" fostered by collegiate living in the original sense of the word. Lowell, who as a student had not accepted his election to a final club—a club for the social elite among college seniors—was disturbed by the increasing social polarization and snobbery at Harvard that had been tolerated by Eliot. The poor commuted or huddled together in Cambridge digs, while the rich resided in the clubs or residential buildings along the Gold Coast of Mount Auburn Street; the Jews congregated in "Little Jerusalem," Hastings Hall, and a handful of African American students were hiding wherever they could. This had to end. "I fear," the professor of government had written to President Eliot in 1902, "that with the loss of that democratic feeling which ought to lie at the basis of university life, we are liable to lose our moral hold upon a large part of the students, and that this feeling can be maintained only when a considerable proportion of every section of students is living within the walls of the *collegium*." [9]

In 1914 the freshman halls opened. African Americans were excluded; but the president had high hopes that the dormitories would encourage democratic life by breaking down segregation based on schools and geographic distribution. Living together in freshman halls, he had predicted in his report for the year 1909–10, "would give far greater opportunity for men from different schools and from different parts of the country, to mix together and find their natural affinities unfettered by the associations of early education, of locality and of wealth; and above all it would tend to make the college more truly national in spirit." [10]

Fifteen years later, a generous gift from Edward S. Harkness, a Yale graduate, allowed Lowell to realize his long-cherished "House Plan." It was to provide relatively inexpensive rooms in communal dormitories for the men of the three upper classes. "The Houses are a social device for a moral purpose," Lowell claimed. But when the houses opened, (the first two in 1930, the other five in 1931), Lowell had a hard time convincing the fashionable social set that "democracy" was good for them. Eventually, with the Depression in full swing, most students moved in and immediately resegregated. In March 1933, Kenneth B. Murdock, a professor of American literature and master of Leverett House, wrote to the dean of Harvard College that "there is growing up a marked social classification among the Houses, and the result we must anticipate is, I think, that . . . some of our most 'fashionable' and 'successful' students will refuse to enter the Houses at all unless they gain admission to one of the two or three 'socially eminent' ones." [11] Two years into Lowell's democratic experiment, it threatened to fail.

One of the reasons why residency in the houses was unpalatable to the fashionable set, the administration surmised, was the large number of Jews admitted to the dormitories. A memorandum on "Suggested Procedure for Assignment to Houses," circulated in 1934, advised all masters that "care must be taken at this point to see that the total number of Jews does not exceed what 'the traffic will bear.' By this method, the racial problem can be squarely met and we shall avoid last year's situation, in which, because of racial difficulties arising in some particular House, superior Jews were vetoed by some Master too late for them to be given an opportunity in another House in which Jews with inferior claims had been accepted." [12] The problem was that as long as the main criterion for admission to the houses was scholastic achievement, Jews, and particularly those with no other means to live by than their wits, would continue to do well. Between 1933 and 1942, 32 percent of the students who made the dean's list were Jews, compared to only 11 percent of the students from "selected private schools," Harvard's social cream.

Conversely, 7 percent of the Jewish freshmen had unsatisfactory records, compared to 20 percent of freshmen belonging to the social elite; the class average was 16 percent. Marcia Synnott summarized these figures aptly when she wrote, "as a student's social standing rose, his academic standing often declined." [13]

There was really no way of controlling the number of Jewish students in the houses unless the admissions criteria were changed. This is exactly what happened. Consequently, the percentage of Jewish resident freshmen plummeted to 10 percent in 1934 and recovered only one percentage point in 1935. Obviously, Lowell's "moral purpose" was not the creation of a democratic community based on individual merit. In 1933, Lowell was succeeded in office by James Bryant Conant. Lowell's administration, however, was still in place, and many officers remembered his attempt in the early 1920s to regulate the number of Jews admitted to Harvard. Where Lowell had failed, his administrators succeeded. Concealed from the public eye, they began to apply subjective categories to keep at least the number of resident Jews to an attractive minimum.

Ever since Lowell's plan to establish a *numerus clausus* for Jews admitted to Harvard College had been defeated by a faculty vote in 1923, the president was haunted by the idea that Harvard had a "Jew problem." His nightmare had begun in February 1920, when during a $15 million fundraising campaign a letter from an alumnus arrived inquiring into the exact number of Jewish undergraduates. Although the inquiry had no further consequences at the time, the president was put on the alert. In April 1922 research brought to light that the number of Jewish students at Harvard had risen from 7 percent in 1900 to 21.5 percent in 1922. Lowell blew the whistle. He sent a proposition to the Committee on Admission aimed at limiting the number of successful Jewish applicants. The committee refused to adopt the measures without the consent of the faculty. The issue was brought before the faculty and hotly debated during four meetings in May and June of 1922. [14]

Demanding clarification in writing, William Ernest Hocking, a professor of philosophy, asked Lowell "whether our concern is on account of the increase of Jews as Jews, or on account of the increase of 'undesirable Jews'. . . . It seems clear to me that if the 'undesirable Jews' were eliminated the question of the proportion of Jews would automatically disappear. The presence of the undesirable Jew casts a spot-light on all his compatriots and makes them conspicuous." Hocking suggested taking advantage of a split in the Jewish community and letting the acculturated and successful (German) Jews do the sifting of Jewish applicants. This would reduce the number of undesirable (poor Eastern European) Jews "without raising the cry of racial discrimination." But Lowell saw through Hocking's clever maneuver to avoid the taint of racism at the eleventh hour by granting the Jews autonomy on the issue. A sort of *Judenrat* was to do the dirty work and leave the WASP establishment unblemished. Lowell hated hypocrisy. If any measure was taken, he wrote to Langdon P. Marvin, senior partner in Franklin D. Roosevelt's law firm, one had to be direct and open about it. To Hocking, Lowell replied that "the main problem caused by the increase in the number of Jews comes . . . not from the fact that they are individually undesirable, but from the fact that they form a very distinct body, and cling, or are driven, together, apart from the great mass of the undergraduates. . . . We must take as many as we can benefit [read: assimilate], but if we take more, we shall not benefit them and shall ruin the college." To save the college, Lowell wanted to establish, as he wrote to Rufus Tucker, a clear Jewish quota of 15 or 16 percent. What Lowell really resented, as so many had before him, was that the Jews resisted assimilation—a position not unrelated to resenting the very existence of Jews. In Lowell's case, however, the resentment was limited and clearly linked to his frustration that his idea of a homogeneous America was not to be. Hocking eventually understood that the issue debated by the Harvard faculty was not just the composition of the student body of some college, but ultimately, as he wrote in a letter to Felix Frankfurter, "the constituency of the nation." Seeing that the *idea* of America was at stake, Hocking, although he was clearly no friend of the Jews, voted consistently against any measure that could lead to a quota.[15]

Most faculty members, however, were so confused that a motion was carried on May 23, 1922, which instructed the Committee on Admission, in deciding on admissions of transfers from other colleges and of candidates with unsatisfactory requirements, "to take into account the resulting proportionate size of racial and national groups in the membership of Harvard College." Five days later, two petitions circulated, pointing out that the recent decision "relating to controlling the percentage of Jews in Harvard College is a radical departure from the spirit and practice of the College." The thirty-one signers—among them very few of the famous humanities professors—believed "that racial discrimination should not be an element in the conditions of admission to Harvard College before a careful and deliberate study of the whole question of the Jews shall have been made by the Faculty." A special faculty meeting, convened on June 2, rescinded its vote of the previous week and recommended that a special committee look into the matter but that publicity be avoided. Lowell was displeased. The next morning he dictated an addition to the minutes of the meeting: "The President stated that there should be no doubt that the primary object in appointing a special Committee was to consider the question of the Jews and that if any member of the Faculty doubted this, let him now speak or forever after hold his peace." [16]

The Committee on Methods of Sifting Candidates for Admission submitted its report in April 1923. It objected to racial and religious discrimination, recommended the rejection of academically weaker candidates, and suggested that the college make an effort to attract more applicants from the South and West. The latter was to be achieved through the so-called "highest seventh": the top seventh of good high schools was offered admission without examination. The stricter scholastic requirements were meant to block transfers from New York and Boston colleges as well as students with weak secondary preparation, for instance, in English composition. If Lowell had hoped that this would decrease Jewish enrollment he was in for a surprise. While the stricter requirements designed to block transfers may have prevented the admission of a few Jewish students, the "highest seventh" ruling increased it. In 1923, 32 percent of those admitted without examination were Jews; the figure rose to 42 percent in 1925, bringing the total of Jewish freshmen to almost 28 percent. The administration, which by and large supported restrictions, was getting desperate. It planned to resort to selective admissions without the explicit consent of the faculty. In December 1926, the chairman of Harvard's Committee on Admission, Henry Pennypacker, informed the dean of Yale College, Clarence W. Mendell, that Harvard's admissions officers were "now going to limit the Freshman Class to 1,000 including dropped and rated which means about 850 new men. After this year they are going to discontinue—for the East at least—the 'first seventh' arrangement which is bringing in as high as 40% Jews. They are also going to reduce their 25% Hebrew total to 15% or less by simply rejecting without detailed explanation. They are giving no details to any candidate any longer. They are getting small representation from the West and none from the South and have no plan for improving the situation." In the following years Jewish enrollment at Harvard dropped. Selective admission continued into the Conant years. Between 1933 and 1942, Jews made up about 14 percent of each freshman class. The informal quota limiting Jewish enrollment was not given up until after World War II.[17]

Freshman Levin

Levin experienced the much vaunted "Harvard indifference" as a "liberation." That catchphrase of his student days reveals a truth about the college: once you were in, you were a Harvard man like everybody else. Anti-Jewish sentiment was limited to a specific kind of social snobbery and could be easily ignored. Levin was lucky. Not only had his Midwestern origin almost certainly been an advantage during the admissions process, but at the beginning of his sophomore year he was accepted as a resident by the master of the newly opened Lowell House, Julian Lowell Coolidge. Levin remembered him as a "rather snobbish professor" who used to refer to anyone from outside New England as an "Ohioan." Coolidge (Harvard class of 1895), whom Levin described as "a pudgy little character with a speech defect," was a professor of mathematics and an amateur astronomer, and a Boston Brahmin of the old kind. Fit in mind and body, the former track star and notorious cyclist, who had taught Military Science I in the fall of 1916, took an active interest in the selection of his residents. Oddly enough, scholarship was most important to him; hence athletes and final club men were scarce in Lowell House. Levin was reasonably happy there. "There were a number of Jews in Lowell House," Levin recalled, "some of whom were my good friends. I would have said that in associating together we recognized that we were Jews. But it meant not much more than recognizing a number of other Midwesterners."[18] At the time, when Harvard was still very much perceived as an upper-crust New England institution, being Jewish or from the Midwest could produce the same sense of marginality.

Compared to the crass discrimination practiced in Minneapolis, whatever social snobbery surfaced at Harvard must have seemed a negligible problem to Levin. The "Harvard indifference" left him free to pursue what he really cared for—the world of literature and ideas. "To leave Minneapolis for Cambridge," Levin wrote some sixty years later, "was to immerse oneself in a live tradition, a central concern for intellectual matters which might elsewhere have been regarded as on the fringe." At Harvard, Levin felt liberated from "the middle-class conformities of the business-world (as satirized by [Sinclair] Lewis and Mencken)."[19] He was fascinated by the world of literature. It suited his temperament and soothed his soul. The more deeply he immersed himself in it, the more intense would be his participation in a "central concern," and the greater his distance from the world of his parents ("elsewhere"). Moreover, mastery of the intellectual tradition of America's dominant culture would surely put an end, if not to discrimination, then at least to his sense of being an outsider. Harvard, as not only the oldest college in the nation, but, one that valued individual excellence, was in Levin's eyes an ideal locale to achieve immersion in his world of choice. Choosing to acquire a tradition meant to assert a freedom that only America, and never Europe, had been willing to grant as a right to all, including the Jews.

There was a happy confluence between Levin's intellectual passions and his social needs. His intense love of literature and history made study an exhilarating pleasure. At the same time academic achievement was a possible ticket to acceptance and integration in the new world Levin had entered. Mastery of the Gentile and genteel literary tradition could indeed be achieved. Tradition, T. S. Eliot had famously propounded in 1919, "cannot be inherited, and if you want it you must obtain it by great labour. It involves, in the first place, the historical sense, which . . . involves a perception, not only of the pastness of the past, but of its presence." Levin set out to make Eliot's cultural tradition, "the whole of the literature of Europe from Homer and within it the whole of the literature of his own country," his own.[20] "My years as an undergraduate, 1929–1933, registered not a growth but a lag in my awareness of the twentieth century," Levin remembered. "Possibly I was too busy finding my way back to traditions barely glimpsed on an earlier and then more distant horizon. . . ."[21]

Levin studied everything the English department had to offer. He was, in his own description, "a good boy, *un bon élève*" (interview). Levin worked so hard that the incoming freshmen class perceived the junior as a legendary figure. Yet while he was acquiring "an old-fashioned education in the humanities," in the seminars of Kittredge and his nemesis Babbitt, he made close friends in the other camp, especially with F. O. Matthiessen and Theodore Spencer, the modernizers in the department. Such antithetical moves had been and would remain typical for Harry Levin. They suggest that his periods as *bon élève* repressed energies that needed to be released on the fringe, in areas of mischief tolerated by the central groups. Levin's great delight in being fondly called a "Young Turk" by the established poet and critic Allen Tate can serve as an emblem for the psychological structure of Levin's antithetical moves. This inner disposition may explain why the very beginning of his scholarly career is split between Elizabethan drama and the "aberration" James Joyce.[22] One might contend of course that passions for Renaissance and modernist literature are perfectly compatible, as T. S. Eliot demonstrated and F. O. Matthiessen argued. But the adversarial stance Levin signaled to the elders in his department by his early dedication to Joyce was of utmost importance to the young man. His exploration of the not-yet-canonical balanced his immersion in an established tradition and demonstrated to himself a good measure of intellectual independence.

This precarious balance of sympathy and opposition also characterized Levin's relationship to the three men who, more than his other teachers, eased him into the Harvard world. F. O. Matthiessen, Irving Babbitt, and T. S. Eliot, were ideal as initiating mentors because they were centrally Harvard and yet thought of themselves as on the fringe. Levin's relationship to these teachers was amicable and adversarial at the same time. The sympathy between student and teachers arose from social similarities Levin perceived, while opposition to his mentors was provoked by the exclusive intellectual positions they held. A reconstruction of Levin's critical dialogue with Matthiessen, Babbitt, and Eliot reveals the dynamics at work in the transformation of a precocious Jewish boy from the American hinterland into one of Harvard's outstanding professors and a kingmaker in literary academe. I acknowledge readily that such a reconstruction is highly speculative, yet it may illuminate why Levin insisted on historical accuracy and avoided partisanship in his critical work. It may also indicate the enormous costs of Levin's achievement.

The Example of F. O. Matthiessen

Levin considered it his "great good luck" that he had been a freshman in the fall of 1929 and attended the very first course Matthiessen ever taught at Harvard. As Levin put it years later, Matthiessen was associated with the "shift from the philological to the critical approach and from a historical to a contemporary emphasis." His mind was "richly associative rather than strictly logical," as was Levin's, and he had a "special feeling for the relations between the arts and above all for the interrelationship between social problems and cultural developments."[23] Matthiessen's critical practice indicated new directions and possibilities in literary academe and helped to shape Levin's own critical approach. The fields of their major academic pursuits did not really overlap. But the two men shared one intellectual passion that had deep personal reverberations for both of them—the poetry of T. S. Eliot.

Matthiessen's presence in Levin's freshman year was in many ways powerful and enabling. It was also fortunate for entirely personal reasons: Matthiessen was simultaneously so completely inside Harvard while his private life with his companion Russell Cheney on Beacon Hill and in Kittery, Maine, was so hopelessly outside that he could serve as role model for a Midwestern Jew who perceived Harvard as "a rich man's New England gentleman's institution" (interview) and had little hope of becoming an integral part of it. Matthiessen showed Levin that it was possible to negotiate being inside and outside, although the cost of doing so might be very high. Levin believed that he and Matthiessen faced a similar problem. Levin's visit to McLean Hospital in January 1939, where Matthiessen weathered a severe depression, was an expression of his connectedness with his former teacher, a gesture of solidarity. Matthiessen may have sensed as much when he noted about Levin's incongruous appearance at McLean: "I wonder what went through Harry's head at coming to a place like this." But he was clearly uneasy about the visit, as was Levin, who wrote, somewhat defensively, fifty years later that "it might have been callous if I had not paid that visit." What may have gone through Levin's mind and informed "the simple directness of gesture" with which he gave the suffering man a book on Daumier was perhaps the thought that Matthiessen, too, was conscious of "belonging to a harassed minority."[24]

The example of Matthiessen's painfully split life helped Levin to relax about his own situation as a social outsider at Harvard and not to feel hurt by the fact that certain doors there remained closed to him. Matthiessen, ten years Levin's senior, was born in Pasadena, California, in 1902. Because of his father's unsettled life he spent a good deal of time in the house of his grandfather Friedrich Wilhelm in La Salle, Illinois. Like Levin's father, F. W. Matthiessen was an immigrant from Germany who became a wealthy businessman. Because of his time in Illinois, Francis Otto considered himself a "small town boy" from the Midwest.[25] He prepared at Hackley School in Tarrytown, New York, and after a short period of service in the Canadian Air Force entered Yale in the fall of 1919. At Yale Matthiessen developed the interests, views, and tendencies that would set him apart from the majority of his colleagues at Harvard. His emotional, undogmatic Christianity intensified; his political opinions formed, propelling him far to the left; and his homosexuality emerged as an unavoidable and upsetting fact in his life. After graduating from Yale in 1923, he went to Oxford as a Rhodes scholar. There, in the spring of 1924, he read *Sexual Inversion* (1897) by Havelock Ellis and John A. Symonds and was very disturbed: "Then for the first time it was completely brought home to me that I was what I was by *nature*." Some months later, on the boat to England, where he was to begin his second year at Oxford, he met the painter Russell Cheney (Yale class of 1904). The prospect of loving Cheney healed the shock of "coming face to face with the fact that I could probably never marry." Life with Cheney was the unexpected escape from the bleak alternatives Matthiessen had envisioned: repression, self-abuse, and promiscuity.[26]

Matthiessen returned to America in 1925. He had earned an Oxford B. Litt. with a thesis on Oliver Goldsmith and decided to pursue a graduate degree at Harvard. In Cambridge he met a set of teachers unlike any he had studied with so far. "By far the most living experience in my graduate study at Harvard," Matthiessen recalled in 1947, "came through the lectures of Irving Babbitt, with whose neo-humanistic attack upon the modern world I disagreed at nearly every point. The vigor with which he objected to almost every author since the eighteenth century forced me to fight for my tastes, which grew stronger by the exercise." William Cain pointed out that despite ideological differences Matthiessen admired Babbitt's prophetic intensity, his advocacy of educational reform, and his commitment to the idea of a university that was not just a Ph.D. mill.[27] But what appealed to Matthiessen above all was a social similarity, Babbitt's isolation and stance as an outsider within the institution.

Matthiessen received his M.A. in 1926 and his Ph.D. in 1927. He had planned to write his dissertation on Walt Whitman, an indication, perhaps, that through his relationship with Cheney, Whitman's poetry had taken on a new glow, and that he may have felt strong enough to engage in his criticism the aspect of homosexuality in Whitman's poetry. Matthiessen was then already moving toward Eliot's theory, expounded in the Norton lectures, that the enjoyment of a poem is the basis for the critical process. However, Harvard authorities disallowed the topic with the argument that nothing new could be said about Whitman.[28] Matthiessen wrote his thesis under John Livingston Lowes on the art of Elizabethan prose translations, took his degree in June of 1927, established a household with Cheney in Maine the same month, and left for his first teaching job at Yale in the fall. Two years later he was back in Cambridge as a tutor in History and Literature, Harvard's new under-

graduate honors program. Houghton Mifflin in Boston had just published his mannered, slightly sentimental book on Sarah Orne Jewett, a
relative of his beloved mother. This study, together with a graduate
seminar on early American historiography taken with Kenneth Murdock
at Harvard, were Matthiessen's only credentials as an Americanist. But
Murdock knew a good man when he saw one, and entrusted to his
former student a course on the "Literature of the West and South
centering around Whitman, Poe, and Mark Twain." Matthiessen was
thrilled: "The prospects of what I am to give are so exciting as to send
shivers through my already too stimulated body." In the following spring,
he changed the title of his course to "American Literature outside New
England" so as to feel "no absurdity in including Melville." [29]

Levin, however, was more interested in his tutor's Elizabethan learning than in his Americanist adventures, because Levin had come to
Harvard "largely in quest for links with the past." And the past for him
was classical and European—if at all American, it was not likely to be
found outside New England. Inevitably, Levin passed on (or, better
perhaps, regressed) to Matthiessen's own mentor, Irving Babbitt. Nevertheless, Matthiessen had been ideal as initiator. His critical stance, striv-
ing to combine broadly cultural, political, and aesthetic concerns; his
Ivy League credentials yet social marginality; and his origins in the
Midwest, yet easy acquisition of New England culture all eroded for
Levin the imagined monolithic quality of Harvard, making it appear
permeable and accepting of those who thought they did not belong.
After one of his first teas with the Murdocks, Matthiessen had written
jubilantly to Cheney: "[it] was really great fun; pleasant and easy and
giving me the sense of belonging." [30] In turn, Matthiessen made Levin
feel at ease and at home through the way he taught literature. His trick
was to pretend in class that the question of belonging, the problem of
inside and outside, did not exist. What mattered was literature alone,
and it belonged to anybody who cared enough about it. A passage from
one of Trilling's essays comes to mind wherein he defines snobbery as a
set of questions: "Do I belong—do I really belong? And does he belong?
And if I am observed talking to him, will it make me seem to belong or
not to belong?" To the extent that these questions meant nothing to
Matthiessen, he represented the new Harvard that emerged from the
demise of the genteel tradition. This new indifference to pedigree was
connected to the single most important aspect of Matthiessen as a
teacher of ideas. "Matty," John Rackliffe wrote, "was in many ways as
American as they come. . . . Yet he was always somewhat rootless, he

had no province, no *'pays.'* "[31] Herein he was like Babbitt and unlike T. S. Eliot.

Under the Influence of Irving Babbitt

Levin took Babbitt's course on Romanticism as a sophomore in just about the last year he gave it. Babbitt was exactly the kind of teacher Levin needed: fully in command of the universe of literature, classical, biblical, scholastic, humanistic, oriental. He was demanding, challenging, committed and expecting commitment, intellectually shaped by Harvard yet clearly not of it in speech and manners. "I was very devoted to him," Levin remembered; "he was a very inspiring teacher. Often he inspired you to react, especially if you were committed, as I was, to the moderns."[32] The encounter with Babbitt resulted in Levin's first academic laurels. His paper for Babbitt's course won the Bowdoin Prize and was published under the title *The Broken Column: A Study in Romantic Hellenism* by Harvard University Press in 1931. It was dedicated to Matthiessen; its theme and attitude were inspired by Babbitt; but its style was Levin's, an ironic preciousness that later yielded to a graver mode. The speaker of the opening lines falls gracefully into the pose of an epigone of Walter Pater's but veers around suddenly to expose the luscious scenery as stage props.

> Archaeology is a sentimental science. It indulges our modern fondness for the fragmentary; we strike postures before its ruins, reconstruct vanished golden ages from corroded copper coins, and soliloquize on the transiency of time in accents of exquisite melancholy. Mention of Greece calls to our minds the vision of a cypress grove, a heap of shattered marble, clear sunlight and cool shade, a wooded hillside, and the blue Mediterranean below. The solitary figure who invariably stands in the corner of the picture may appear, from this distance, to be Ajax, but closer inspection is certain to reveal the spectacles and side-whiskers of Herr Schliemann.

Levin's topic was "the changes which affected the classical tradition in the romantic age, and, perhaps, through an examination of the conception of Greece held by two or three representative romantic poets [Byron, Shelley, and Keats], to discover, in the discrepant points of view, certain fundamental distinctions between the two ways of thought." The tension between devotion to and reaction against Babbitt was fully played out in the essay and remained unresolved. Levin actually liked the poetry of Byron, Shelley, and Keats, who were among the favorites of Babbitt's academic antagonist, John Livingston Lowes. But when Levin spoke of the Romantics in general, he descended into satire. "The romanticists," Levin wrote, "have discovered that the supposed simplicity of Greek life disagrees with their own experience of life. Rather than change their interpretation, they conclude that they are undergoing a phase of experience which the Greeks did not know."[33]

Echoing Babbitt (who was echoing the French critics Pierre Lasserre and Charles Maurras), Levin deplored the decline of classical education beginning with the Romantics and ending with Harvard's elective system. Wittily, Levin made his point in French, a language Babbitt considered "only a cheap and nasty substitute for Latin," by quoting Stendhal: "Vous n'avez à la bouche que les noms de Sophocle, d'Euripide, et d'Homère, et vous ne les avez seulement pas lus." Levin demonstrated that he had, and in Greek, too, by quoting from Sappho and Thucydides in the original. Adding a liberal sprinkling of Latin quotations for good measure, he showed that the classics were not Greek to him, as they had been to "poor Keats."[34] In the course of his sixty-three-page essay, he mentions some one hundred and forty names, from Abbé Barthélmy, Aeschylus, and Alcman to Vico, Villemain, Villoisin, Winckelmann, and Wordsworth. He did it with elegant nonchalance; yet the endless name-dropping seems to be a habit acquired from Babbitt, whose more enterprising students used to pool their pennies and bet on how many exponents of this or that literary theory Babbitt would mention during his lecture. The winning number was usually around seventy. In the course of his career, Levin learned to control his wealth of information, yet an abundance of names, quotations, and references remained a hallmark of his writing. Like Babbitt, Levin had mastered "the tradition" and became its guardian.[35]

Unlike Babbitt, however, Levin would develop two critical approaches, the comparative and the contextual methods, that turned the mastery of mass, at which Babbitt had excelled, into an asset. During the 1950s, Levin learned to weave the pearls that Babbitt scattered at random into a complicated texture. "The comparative method," Levin wrote in 1950, "enables us to follow an individual process of development by bringing together different manifestations which have taken similar forms."[36] The contextual method, first mentioned in a 1934 letter to Matthiessen, reflected Levin's view of history as a complex yet describable set of events. As Burton Pike explained, history for Levin was "a succession of constantly changing constellations of people, conventions, values, fashions, and ideas. He takes history as the fluid collective form of a society as it moves forward in time. He marks out certain thematic constants in this variable succession of steady states, constants of development and change in social and literary convention, and examines individual works and authors against this background." [37]

It is possible to claim Matthew Arnold as an ancestor of Levin's comparative and contextual methods, since the Englishman had argued in his inaugural lecture at Oxford in 1857, that "no single event, no single literature, is adequately comprehended except in its relation to other events, to other literatures." Levin quoted this sentence in his own inaugural lecture as Irving Babbitt Professor in 1960. Yet it is more realistic to suspect that Levin was under the more immediate influence of Babbitt. To master the tradition of European and American letters was for both Babbitt and Levin a source of pleasure. At the same time this achievement propelled them from the social margin to the intellectual center of the university. It worked for Levin because with the election of a new president in 1933, Harvard was ready to shift its focus from social standing to academic merit and began to retain young Jewish scholars. The premise from which both Babbitt and Levin operated was that those belonged who "owned" the place intellectually. This view also shaped their understanding of the critic and his task. Babbitt was quite perplexed, for instance, when Levin told him that his course paper would be published; Babbitt considered Levin not old enough to practice as a critic. "It was a question of gaining a critic's license," Levin wrote about Babbitt's reaction, "by getting to know one's business, so to speak, by mastering a complex and voluminous body of material. How could one judge or discriminate or generalize or trace relevant connections or, in short, make valid interpretations without such groundwork?" Levin and Babbitt both spurned the mere acquisition of knowledge without critical evaluation. For them "scholarship was the precondition of criticism, . . . as criticism was the consummation of scholarship." [38]

How important Babbitt's beginnings as Midwestern outsider were to his student became evident in Levin's 1960 inaugural lecture as the first incumbent of the Irving Babbitt Professorship of Comparative Literature. The occasion canonized Babbitt and provided Levin with a pedigree. Sub rosa Levin's lecture was about new kinds of pedigrees. Levin began lightly, recounting a line of notable Harvard professors: James Russell Lowell, Francis James Child, and Irving Babbitt, counterpoised by a line of intellectuals who had turned down or left their Harvard appointments, George Ticknor, John Fiske, Charles Sanders Peirce, and Henry Adams. Like Adams, Babbitt was opinionated and doctrinaire, but unlike Adams he never thought of leaving Harvard. The reason was Babbitt's sense of mission. President Eliot, "who represented the Puritan temperament at its best," had relaxed educational standards, in Babbitt's view: "Hence it required a maverick to present the case for tradition." Babbitt's intellectual pedigree was of Harvard's finest. Levin mentioned "that the two portraits [Babbitt] placed in his Widener study were those of Sainte-Beuve and Charles Eliot Norton." Sainte-Beuve's picture also hung in Emerson's study in Concord; Emerson had been Norton's mentor, and Norton had been Babbitt's. Levin described Norton as "highly cultivated and many-minded yet somewhat amateurish and provincial." But Norton the scholar was less important for Babbitt as "rugged young Middle-Westerner" than Norton the gentleman, a role that Levin considered "so very strategic in Babbitt's thought." The appearance of Emerson in Babbitt's intellectual lineage left his eulogist somewhat at a loss, because Babbitt, who knew intimately what life west of Concord was all about, had no patience for Emerson's optimism. Despite a shared reverence for Sainte-Beuve, Emerson and Babbitt did not make a pair. Levin settled for the safest common denominator and opened the section about Babbitt's rough childhood with the sentence: "Ralph Waldo Emerson was a strikingly untraditional thinker; but his conception of the American scholar is by now a tradition in itself, to be saluted in passing on these occasions, and emulated all the more earnestly by outlanders migrating from the Middle West to New England." [39] The last phrase, incidentally, describes both Babbitt's and Levin's provenance. As the first incumbent of the Babbitt professorship and as his former student, Levin "inherited" Babbitt's Harvard lineage. But politely adversarial, Levin clung to his own. He preferred a series of Midwestern boys who, by way of New England, managed to enter the mainstream of literary culture— Babbitt, T. S. Eliot, and Matthiessen.

But there was something else about Babbitt. Like Matthiessen, and Levin himself, he had a social blemish. Levin revealed it with the gesture of the detached researcher: "Though [Babbitt] was suspicious of the quest for origins, and too proud to welcome an intimate scrutiny of his background, it is always illuminating to find latent sources of inspiration more profound than the entries in a *curriculum vitae.*" Levin had come across two letters whose revelation, he felt, "cannot embarrass [Babbitt's] inherent dignity at this stage." They were by Babbitt's father. The first had been written in 1847 by a lad of nineteen teaching in a country

school in Missouri. It was addressed to Longfellow and asked him to
support his application to Harvard. The enclosed writing sample consisted of two cantos of a long romantic poem, "Gem of the Sea." The
second letter had been sent from Los Angeles by Edwin Dwight Babbitt,
M.D., to William James in 1898 along with a volume from "a set
of books titled *Human Culture and Cure,* replete with testimonials and
illustrations, including a diagram of the author's brain." Letter and literature revealed that the sender, "who could be consulted by mail, practised
in the light of hypnotism, spiritualism, phrenology, clairvoyance, mas-
sages, sun-baths, electrical treatments, inhabited planets, and utopian
socialism. . . . As author, publisher, and bookseller, he brought out such
items as *Babbitt's Health Guide; Vital Magnetism, the Fountain of Life;* and
Marriage, with Sexual and Social Up-Building." [40]

William James had acquired the reputation of being precisely the right
address for that sort of thing. As Santayana observed, James had "kept
his mind and heart wide open to all that might seem, to polite minds,
odd, personal, or visionary in religion and philosophy. He gave a sincerely respectful hearing to sentimentalists, mystics, spiritualists, wizards,
cranks, quacks, and impostors—for it is hard to draw the line, and James
was not willing to draw it prematurely." Santayana, who was very fond
of James, called him a "genuine and vigorous romanticist." [41] That was
exactly what Irving Babbitt thought wrong with him. James's *Varieties of
Religious Experience* he retitled "Wild Religions I have Known." Having
grown up under the tutelage of an eccentric father and suffered the
attendant social and economic hardships, Babbitt developed an intense
distrust of all ideologies promising comprehensive salvation, including
Christianity. It speaks for T. S. Eliot's astuteness when he remarked about
Babbitt: "His attitude towards Christianity seems to me that of a man
who had no *emotional* acquaintance with any but some debased and
uncultured form: I judge entirely on his public pronouncements and not
at all on any information about his upbringing." Alfred Kazin was
equally perceptive when he claimed that Babbitt's conservatism, "from
earliest youth, was not a philosophy but an emotion." [42] It was the *sauve
qui peut* of a terrified child who had witnessed "breaking up housekeep-
ing" too often.

The Levin household in Minneapolis had, of course, been eminently
stable despite the fact that one parent oddly combined science and
religion. Levin's secret blemish was of a different sort from those of
Babbitt and Matthiessen but equally determining (in the peculiar way of
blemishes that touch on social acceptability) of the direction and inten-

sity that came to characterize the young man's scholarship. Levin was Jewish in a world where Jewishness was still perceived as a stigma. Slowly that view had become unacceptable in the course of Levin's academic career. By the time Levin gave his inaugural speech in 1960, his audience felt not in the least compelled to look "for latent sources of inspiration more profound than the entries in a *curriculum vitae*" that may have shaped Babbitt's successor. But the incumbent was aware of the importance and power of those subterranean social forces. His own "blemish" he thought quite visible. He had never tried "to pass," as it was then called. "I have known such [Jews]," Levin remembered; "we never had any great respect for them, those of us who knew about them. I was always grateful that my name and physiognomy put that temptation out of the way." [43]

In one instance Levin may have welcomed what he imagined to be his Jewish visibility because it relieved him of the explanation Charles Loeser had once so frankly offered to his fellow student Santayana. The occasion was Levin's first visit to the rooms of T. S. Eliot in Eliot House, where he was to have tea with the poet in the fall of 1932. In the long friendship between Eliot and Levin "the matter of my Jewishness never came up, of course," Levin reported. Eliot's tenure as Charles Eliot Norton Professor of Poetry was the highlight of Levin's senior year and the encounter with the famous poet completed Levin's initiation. [44]

T. S. Eliot and the Harvard Circle

For Levin's slightly younger contemporaries, who would congregate around *Partisan Review* in the 1940s and 1950s, Eliot was "a commanding literary figure who had no successful rivals and whose formulations were in fact revered." [45] Jewish intellectuals, too, were under Eliot's spell; those among them who knew about the tough life in the big cities found Eliot's poetry particularly appealing. Eliot was, as Irving Howe explained, "a central figure in modern culture, a writer of the highest literary intelligence. Eliot wrote poetry that seemed thrilling in its apprehensions of the spirit of the time, poetry vibrant with images of alienation, moral dislocation, and historical breakdown. If his vocabulary came to draw upon unacceptable doctrine, his sensibility remained intensely familiar. It is very possible that the power and the charm of Eliot's poetry, which touched me closely as a young man, kept me and others from acknowledging the streak of bigotry in his work." The key point is that Eliot was perceived as central to a culture to which Jews

4. T. S. Eliot, passport photograph of 1932. *By permission of Houghton Library, Harvard University.*

considered themselves newcomers. Overstating the case but bringing out a truth, Leslie Fiedler confessed in an interview that he accepted the anti-Semitism of James, Pound, and Eliot to "establish my credentials as a full fledged up-to-date citizen of the Republic of Letters." [46]

Levin, Fiedler's senior by five years, read Eliot's poetry in high school and fell prey to its magic. "It was the most exciting thing in the world. . . . We admired his poetry tremendously; we used to chant it—a few of us, who read poetry—in the Poetry Club." For Levin's generation, Eliot became the "poetic revolutionary as well as the critical arbiter." And if Irving Howe, eight years younger than Levin, thought that Eliot's "journey from provincial St. Louis to cosmopolitan London" could help New York Jews "negotiate a somewhat similar journey from Brooklyn or the Bronx to Manhattan," we may imagine the excitement of a Minneapolis public high school graduate at the discovery that "this American, with so strong a sense of the past, had also come from the Middle West and gone to Harvard seventeen years before." If Eliot was not exactly a god for Levin, he certainly was a giant. He became the most eminent figure

5. Class album photograph of Harry Levin in
1933. *Courtesy of Harvard University Archives.*

in Levin's pedigree when he reappeared at Harvard to deliver the Norton
lectures. In a retrospective essay Levin summed up Eliot's significance
for him in 1932: "And here was a legend become a reality before our
very eyes—the legendary reality of a middlewestern boy who, by way of
New England, had somehow managed to enter the mainstream of English literature. It was quite improbable and, obviously, inimitable." [47]

Levin stopped well short of imitation. He had done work on the
Metaphysical poets, and Theodore Spencer showed Levin's paper on
John Cleveland to Eliot. Although, as Levin recalled, it "took issue with
some of Eliot's views, his generous response was to accept it for publication in his *Criterion*," where it appeared in October 1934. And so their
acquaintance began. Levin attended Eliot's public lectures but not his
course. Late in the spring of 1933, Eliot returned to England and Levin
graduated. He received a traveling fellowship (on recommendations
from Babbitt and Matthiessen) and decided to divide his year of leisure
between London and Paris, between the British Museum and the Sorbonne. Eliot had graciously invited the young man to come see him in

London and had furnished Levin with a letter of introduction to James Joyce, then living in Paris, whom Eliot considered "the greatest master of the English language since Milton." [48]

His sojourn in Europe left Levin in doubt as to what to do next. "I was sure I did not want to go back to Harvard in order to take the doctorate in English." He was not even sure that English would remain the focus of his literary studies. A cablegram from Kenneth Murdock, then dean of the Harvard faculty, ended his indecision. Murdock invited Levin to join the newly established Society of Fellows. Founding this society had been one of Lowell's pet projects. Modeled on the Fondation Thiers in Paris and on the Prize Fellows at Trinity College in Cambridge, England, the Harvard Society of Fellows offered three-year fellowships to some two dozen superb college graduates. They were encouraged to pursue whatever research they liked, but could not work on a Ph.D. Lowell wanted to offset the mass production of Ph.D.'s and the ever greater conformity of doctoral candidates by creating a nest for the hatching of "the rare and independent genius." The plan had been worked out and rooms in Eliot House left empty, but no donors could be found. It did not diminish Lowell's enthusiasm for his dream. "To be thoroughly effective," he stated in one of his last presidential reports, "the Society should be well endowed, but where conviction of value is strong and enduring the means of execution are sometimes forthcoming." Soon afterward the university received an anonymous gift to get the society off the ground. It had come from Lowell. The president emeritus had pledged two million dollars, nearly all the money he had. On September 25, 1933, the new fellows sat down to the first of their ritual Monday night dinners. In the fall of 1934, Harry Levin joined the hand-picked group. [49]

But before he could begin this new period of his life, old issues demanded clarification. Levin spent the summer of 1934 in Minnesota. He was disappointed that Matthiessen had not been more encouraging in the matter of his academic career. "Matthiessen had a misleading idea of my family's affluence," Levin recalled; "he felt I could afford to be an independent scholar." Since Matthiessen knew that it could be tough for a Jew, even of Levin's accomplishments, to obtain a position at a first-rate institution, he may have been more protective of his student's feelings than Levin wishes to acknowledge. Matthiessen himself had no doubts about Levin's academic abilities. He sent him a copy of his recently completed manuscript, *The Achievement of T. S. Eliot,* and asked for his response. Exiled in Minneapolis, Levin "clung to it deliberately, as tangible evidence of the existence of interests that are not cultivated and values that have never been recognized hereabouts, or as the only experience of the summer that I should like to remember." [50]

What Levin had in hand was Matthiessen's first sustained attempt at a critical study, for which neither his impressionist essay on Sarah Orne Jewett (1929) nor his scholarly dissertation on Elizabethan translations (1931) had prepared him. He had chosen a confoundingly difficult subject. It was obvious that Eliot had been moving rapidly into a political direction contrary to Matthiessen's own and that this direction informed his poetry. Matthiessen himself observed that "Eliot dwells repeatedly on the integral relation of any poet's work to the society of which he is a part, to the climate of thought and feeling which give rise to his expression. In line with such reflections Eliot can say: 'The great poet, in writing himself, writes his time.' " Yet in his study Matthiessen deliberately ignored Eliot's politics: "In my evaluation of Eliot's poetry I have not been concerned with tracing the development of his thought. . . ." Thus Matthiessen accepted willy-nilly an axiom that Paul Elmer More had called "heretical" in a letter to Austin Warren in 1929 and for which he had scolded Eliot, namely, "that ethics and aesthetics are to be kept rigorously separate." Matthiessen quoted approvingly from *After Strange Gods* and considered "Gerontion"—the poem he cites most frequently in his study—"the most mature, balanced work of art among Eliot's earlier poems [because] he hit upon a situation in the sombre brooding of the old man that enabled him to set down a particular statement of life in concrete objectified form." [51] This reading indicated why Matthiessen was not concerned about the poem's anti-Semitism and bigotry: the prejudices were the made-up views of Gerontion and not convictions held by the poet.

In Matthiessen's further explanation of the poem, we get a glimpse of the ties that bound Matthiessen to Eliot despite their political differences, and of the deep accord in their views of life. Eliot, Matthiessen wrote, "can project into the thoughts of Gerontion an expression of one of his most moving, recurrent themes: the horror of a life without faith, its disillusioned weariness of knowledge, its agonized slow drying up of the springs of emotion." Matthiessen shared Eliot's Christian sense of evil as arid; the dry rot of evil perverted the world into a bleak and hopeless wasteland. William Cain argued that "this dimension of [Matthiessen's] Christian belief leads him in the final analysis to be deeply skeptical about the potential of socialism to convert minds and reorder society and its institutions." But this is not necessarily so, because Matthiessen's view of socialism was neither Marxist nor Leninist, but inspired by Whitman. Matthiessen thought of social democracy as originating in fellow-feeling and producing in turn a sense of brotherhood; the same was true for Christianity. The liquid exuberance of Whitman's "Democratic Vistas" and his *Leaves of Grass* or the luscious *fluidum* of Melville's "A Squeeze of the Hand" chapter in *Moby-Dick* were very much part of Matthiessen's utopia. Fellow-feeling and brotherhood (be it homosexual or socialist or Christian) redeemed the individual from the arid wasteland of evil. Evil—religiously, socially, and politically—was a drying up of the springs of emotion. Matthiessen perceived this thought in Eliot's poetry and found in it a reflection of his own anxiety: "The dry intellectualized distrusting of the emotions, which Emerson recognized as the worst blight that had been left by waning Puritanism, still prevails in the vestiges of the genteel tradition, and thus produces distorted lives in which thought and feeling find no harmony. And the jagged cleavage that separates such lives from that of Sweeney and the mass of the populace is sufficient measure of our continued failure to establish anything like a balanced social order." [52] To remedy with love was, of course, an impossible program, yet it was one in which the writers of the American Renaissance and their scholarly critic firmly believed.

Matthiessen argued that "the prevailing theme of Eliot's poems is the emptiness of life without belief, an emptiness that finally resounds with sickening fear and desperation in 'The Hollow Men.' " This summary sounds too facile, too neatly put. Matthiessen chose to conceal (in order to protect himself) how close Eliot had come to touching a raw nerve in his life. But we get a glimpse of his troubled soul in one of the most convincing passages of his book: when Matthiessen speaks about the interconnectedness of sexuality, religion, and suffering, about the penance of the lustful, his sentences reverberate with a deep, physical awareness of pain. [53]

Although Matthiessen's readings of Eliot still reflected his early conviction "that the enjoyment of poetry cannot be wholly divorced from the beliefs it expresses," Matthiessen took great care to emphasize "that for an appreciation of Eliot's poetry the question of our own acceptance or rejection of his doctrine remains irrelevant. The point is fundamental to any understanding of the nature of art, and hence is one of the cruxes of my interpretation of Eliot." Matthiessen's approach makes possible the separation of content and form, thought and aesthetics. Consequently, an anti-Semitic, misogynist, or racist poem can still be a good *poem*. Matthiessen explained that this is also Eliot's later position. In the course of his study of Dante, Eliot came to the conclusion "which is similar to what [I. A.] Richards has reached from a very different angle, that it is perfectly possible 'to have full literary or poetic appreciation without sharing the beliefs of the poet.' "[54] This view split aesthetics from religion. And while it was opposed by humanists like Paul Elmer More, who regretted the rigorous separation of ethics and aesthetics, this belated acknowledgment of Enlightenment thought was the precondition for the full acceptance of non-Christians as interpreters of English and American literature. It enabled, for instance (albeit via Richards rather than Matthiessen), the development of M. H. Abrams's concept of imaginative consent. The strict separation of religion and aesthetics, which Matthiessen's interpretation of Eliot affirmed and which Eliot's later work tried to undo, made Jews acceptable as teachers of a literature whose intellectual and spiritual basis had been, until quite recently, largely Christian. The first significant books of American literary criticism written with precisely that split in mind were Abrams's study of English Romanticism, *The Mirror and the Lamp* (1953), and Charles Feidelson's *Symbolism and American Literature* (1953). The latter was specifically directed against Matthiessen's Christianity-inspired views in *American Renaissance*.

Levin returned the manuscript of *The Achievement of T. S. Eliot* on the last day of July 1934. In his lengthy comments Levin made it very clear that despite its problems, the separatist stance was the only tenable one. It meant that one would have to accept that bigoted minds could produce exquisite poems; but it meant also that Jews could be interpreters of Christian literature. Levin was not to be excluded from the world he loved by an admired modernist turned reactionary. He was shocked to discover that Eliot had "transferred his intellectual burdens to the church." Levin was understandably upset. He was back in provincial Minneapolis; his hopes of embarking eventually on an academic career had been dampened by the teacher he most trusted; in Europe he had discovered that the recent direction of Eliot's political thought indicated the wave of the future, that reaction was on the advance in France, to say nothing of Germany; and to top it all, Matthiessen had written a book that did not shout No! but, to use Irving Howe's formulation, mewed like a pussycat under the strokes of Eliot's new orthodoxy.[55] Levin was disappointed and angry.

Graciously, deferentially, Levin set out to attack both Matthiessen and Eliot. He praised Matthiessen's detachment but found his literary analyses inexact and insufficient. "An epigraph from Charles Maurras is not, in my opinion, sufficient recompense for the half-dozen pages you might have devoted to a concrete technical analysis of Eliot's style." He deplored Matthiessen's failure to reconstruct fully Eliot's context, since "the habit of literary reminiscence . . . is Eliot's most characteristic and, in a sense, most original trait." Failing to grasp Eliot's literary and historical context, Matthiessen was either unable or unwilling "to distinguish style from thought." Furthermore, Levin accused Matthiessen of complicity in the construction of Eliot's exclusive (literary) pedigree: "Eliot, no doubt, will be pleased with the austere and discriminating taste you have shown in selecting his influences. Latterly he has revealed an increasing disposition to cover his tracks. . . . A man cannot choose his own ancestors, after all: and if we ignore Eliot's immediate literary environment in favor of more remote ones, we put him in the awkward situation of a rich costermonger who leases a place in Surrey and fills it with spurious portraits."[56]

Eliot's fastidiousness in choosing his pedigree of poetic influence was counterbalanced by his air of complete control over European culture between 1300 and 1850, which Levin exposed as hollow pomposity. To be effective, the technique of the "objective correlative" depended on the recognizability of the object, on the fact that the correlative triggered vaguely the same response in reader and poet. That presupposed a shared frame of reference. Taking the figure of Coriolan as his example, Levin demonstrated with wit and brilliance that Eliot could not "control an inference, once he has touched it off." He could not control the web of associations that constituted intellectual culture. Was Eliot able, then, to avoid "associative anarchy"? Levin had his doubts. "If the system of poetic suggestion that Eliot employs is to be regulated by anything stronger and more universal than personal caprice, the poet must not only be sensitive, erudite, and precise; he must be omniscient." If Eliot had hoped that Christianity, "the only milieu broad enough to envelop both Dante and Baudelaire," would hold it all together, he was mistaken, because "a background stretched out so thin loses its uniformity and continuity, and becomes too vague for critical purposes." Eliot's actual joining of the Church of England Levin found a bit peculiar, because he regarded Eliot's religion as a purely "literary conception." But the act had encouraged Eliot to pontificate. "His penchant for citing the titles of books approved by himself I find a trifle irritating," Levin complained. Eliot did not realize, perhaps, that his authority was rather limited and in fact dwindling to the degree that "the traditions to which Eliot attaches himself have become fragile and tenuous." He did not control the culture, neither did Christianity; and any hope to the contrary would be disappointed. "In the last analysis," Levin wrote, "Eliot's critical technique is impressionistic, his dogma based on nothing less ephemeral than good taste, and his authority a personal authority."[57] The idol had fallen; Levin was free as Matthiessen was not.

When Levin returned to Harvard in the fall of 1934 to begin his first three-year term as junior fellow, he had great doubts about his future. He knew that although Jews were occasionally hired to teach in junior positions, they rarely attained senior faculty status. A classic case in the English department was Theodore Silverstein, a medievalist, who could not find a job for years. John Livingston Lowes kept rehiring him as his assistant, partly because Lowes had become quite forgetful and at one point had had to teach his course from Silverstein's notes. At one of the Society's Monday night dinners, Levin took the bull by the horns and asked Lowes, then a senior fellow, why he thought Silverstein could not find a job. "He praised him to the skies," Levin recalled, "what a wonderful man he was, so intelligent, so few people had his scholarly learning, his knowledge of the Middle Ages, and skill." But Lowes professed himself ignorant of the reasons why Silverstein had such trouble finding employment. When Levin pushed the matter and suggested that anti-Semitism might be a factor, Lowes replied, " 'I can't believe it.' And after a pause he added, 'Of course, it might be, because he retains certain objectionable Jewish traits.' "[58]

The Beginnings of an Academic Career

During his five years as junior fellow, Levin became briefly active in the Harvard Teacher's Union, for which he claimed to have recruited F. O. Matthiessen. Otherwise he concentrated on his research, building up a store of knowledge that served him for decades to come. Although he continued to stay in touch with modern French and English literature, he made Elizabethan drama his academic field. During his second tenure as junior fellow, he was invited by John Tucker Murray to teach a graduate seminar in that area. When Murray went blind over the summer of 1939 and was forced to retire, Levin, who had published a few articles and edited a selection of Ben Jonson's works in 1938, was appointed to a junior faculty position.[59] Nobody objected to the appointment on the grounds that Levin was Jewish. Howard Mumford Jones, however, who had recently arrived from the University of Michigan, was not enthusiastic about the appointee and only grumbled his consent, as Levin learned later. But Jones was above suspicion; not only was his wife, Bessie Zaban Jones, Jewish, he had also brought along a Jewish assistant, Daniel Aaron.

In the spring of 1939, Levin married a beautiful young Russian emigrée, Elena Zarudnaya. The couple moved into a house on Memorial Drive. There Delmore Schwartz and his wife, Gertrude, were their neighbors from 1940 to 1942. Although Levin and Schwartz would often sit out on the front steps together, "talking pessimistic," they were an ill-matched pair. Schwartz held an insecure appointment as Briggs-Copeland instructor, while Levin had just joined the regular faculty. Schwartz was self-conscious and abrasive, and very unsure of his creative and critical powers, while Levin was smooth and gracious, and not only in the process of building a career as a brilliant scholar of Renaissance drama, but also increasing his reputation as a learned critic of modernist prose, which was the area that meant most to Schwartz. While Levin sailed through Harvard with an unperturbed air, Schwartz was always hyperconscious of his Jewishness. He regarded Harvard as "enemy territory" and thought modernist literature riddled with anti-Jewish bigots. The overt anti-Semitism of Pound and Eliot disturbed him profoundly, and, as his biographer put it, he "felt personally slighted whenever his literary heroes expressed distaste for Jews, for it fed his self-hatred and cast doubt on his self-chosen identity as their cultural heir." Pound's *Guide to Kulchur* infuriated Schwartz so much that he wrote a letter to the author that ended with the sentence: "I want to resign as one of your most studious and faithful admirers." [60]

Levin seemed to have made peace with it all. Schwartz observed his neighbor and was simultaneously fascinated and repelled. His portrait of Levin in the story "Modern Romance" was unsparing and ungenerous. Yet another sketch of Levin is concealed in Schwartz's later fiction, "The World Is a Wedding." Here one of the characters tells an anecdote about Mortimer London, a young teacher and critic reputed to be brilliant: "London told me (keep in mind the fact that London himself tells this story about himself) that when he was in England last year, he had paid a visit to T. S. Eliot who had given him a letter of introduction to James Joyce, since he was going to Paris also. Now London says that he was confronted with a cruel choice, whether to use the letter and converse with the author of *Ulysses* or to keep the letter in which a great author commends him to a great author. He decided to keep the letter!" Levin took the gibe in good humor. It was only when asked by the *Harvard Advocate,* some time after Schwartz's death in 1966, to explore his memories of the poet that he offered a few sentences in his own defense.

> Well, I must confess that I had happened into that situation, and had talked about it with Delmore. . . . I had been embarrassed by the letter of introduction, since I could not think that such an encounter would be anything more than an importunity. Yet I felt obliged to forward it, together with a covering note which suggested that no answer was necessarily expected. To my great relief, Joyce never answered. I was later told that he would have, one way or another, if only out of courtesy to Eliot, had it not arrived during a crisis precipitated by his daughter's breakdown. Five years afterward [in 1939], when we had something to talk about (namely *Finnegans Wake),* he voluntarily sent a postcard.[61]

Joyce's postcard to James Laughlin, in which he declared that Levin was the only man who understood what he (Joyce) wrote,[62] had been sent in response to Levin's essay "On First Looking into *Finnegans Wake."* The young scholar had been invited to contribute this essay to Laughlin's *New Directions,* after Levin's bold review of Joyce's novel had appeared in John Crowe Ransom's *Kenyon Review* in the fall of 1939. Laughlin then encouraged Levin to write a longer work on Joyce.[63] In 1941, Levin published *James Joyce: A Critical Introduction* with Laughlin's press. It marked the beginning of an enormously fruitful academic career that peaked in the 1960s. Levin published some twenty-seven books and over two hundred and fifty articles covering the Renaissance and Shakespeare, theoretical aspects of realism and comedy, nineteenth-century French and American novels, and twentieth-century English and American literature. His favorite fields, however, remained Shakespeare and the modernists, particularly Proust, Eliot, and Joyce. About Pound, Levin always had reservations. To the Renaissance and modernist poets Levin returned again and again, confirming Matthiessen's observation that "it is not accidental that the same people who respond to Proust and Joyce have also found something important in Donne."[64] Among Levin's best-known works are *The Overreacher: A Study of Christopher Marlowe* (1952), *The Power of Blackness: Hawthorne, Poe, Melville* (1958), *The Question of Hamlet* (1959), *The Gates of Horn: A Study of Five French Realists* (1963), *The Myth of the Golden Age in the Renaissance* (1969), *Shakespeare and the Revolution of the Times* (1976), and his last book, *Playboys and Killjoys: An Essay on the Theory and Practice of Comedy* (1987).

At Harvard, Levin advanced quickly. He was promoted to associate professor of English in 1944 and to full professor in 1948. From 1955 on, he served as professor of English and comparative literature. In 1960 he was named Irving Babbitt Professor. His visiting appointments were numerous and included the Eastman chair at Oxford. More important, however, than the accumulation of published scholarship and academic honors is the fact that Levin's work was actually read. It entered and informed the culture so that in an article in the *New Republic,* for instance, Nadine Gordimer could refer with natural ease to what Harry Levin had once written about the whale Moby-Dick. Asked more specifically about the respect commanded by Levin's work in Renaissance literature, Stephen Greenblatt and Stephen Orgel agreed in their assessment: Levin's scholarship is "what we know," and all later research is based on that knowledge.[65]

One of the constants in Harry Levin's career as a critic was his effort to maintain a stance of Arnoldian disinterestedness. Literary criticism, he believed, "should stand by in sympathetic detachment, and set its sights by an ultimate prospect of understanding, rather than engage in the fluctuating traffic of revaluation." Levin emphasized repeatedly that he had gone out of his way "to avoid identification with any particular school or coterie or set of dogmas." We may suspect that his effort not to take sides was inspired less by Matthew Arnold than by the "monitory examples" of Levin's partisan teachers Babbitt, Eliot, and Matthiessen. The ideal of objectivity Levin encountered as the first literary appointee in a Society of Fellows composed of scientists he found very soothing. That environment, Levin said, influenced him a great deal. But the desire to remain neutral, detached, invisible as a critic also reflected the wish not to stand out, not to become a target. An undercurrent of fear connects that wish to Delmore Schwartz's epigram about the Jewish source of brilliance: "Antisemitism ever / Sharpens Jews to be more clever." Years later Levin wrote about Schwartz as if replying to his epigram: "Delmore's peculiar gift was his *Angst,* his unreassuring certainty that discomfort is a basic component of our psychological condition, his accusation leveled against all who are complacent enough to feel at home in the universe he rejected."[66]

Schwartz did suffer from a severe case of paranoia, as Levin recognized early on. Yet it is difficult to see how American Jews could not experience extreme discomfort during the late 1930s and early 1940s when the Jews of Europe were systematically being reduced to stench and ash. By the fall of 1942, Americans knew about the German atrocities in

Eastern Europe. The news had broken in England during the summer. Given that historical context, a remark in the preface to Levin's book *The Power of Blackness* (1958) might strike one as an instance of the complacency against which Schwartz so vehemently rebelled. There Levin acknowledged the generosity of the Guggenheim Foundation which "during the year 1943–44 provided me with the leisure to accumulate a backlog of reading upon which I have been subsequently relying." Anyone familiar with the cataclysm in Europe, even to the extent that it was known in the early forties, must find the juxtaposition of "the year 1943–44" and "leisure to accumulate a backlog of reading" painfully jarring. One owes it to a man of Levin's intellectual stature and moral seriousness to ask what indeed was going on in his mind and soul (if one may still use such an old-fashioned word) when he sat down to read fiction in those catastrophic years.

Levin was never a man who spoke about his feelings in public; he was diffident where his own person was concerned. Therefore one has to arrive at his soul by indirection. The opening chapter to *The Power of Blackness,* the book Levin was working on as a Guggenheim fellow, is titled "The American Nightmare" and begins with the story of Peter Rugg, a homespun American version of the Wandering Jew. When after a nightmarish journey the weary traveler finally reaches home, he arrives just in time to see his ruined estate being auctioned off. A voice in the crowd proclaims, "Time, which destroys and renews all things, has dilapidated your house and placed us here. . . . You were cut off from the last age, and you can never be fitted to the present. Your home is gone, and you can never have another home in this world." [67]

One is tempted to speculate that Levin, a master of allusion and indirection, began his study of Hawthorne, Poe, and Melville with a story that could very well have summed up his own cultural situation in the mid-1940s. The home he had come from, by way of his father, was lost to the barbarian onslaught, his culture destroyed. One of his father's sisters perished in Germany. Indirectly, perhaps, Levin's worry and concern at the time found their way into the book that dealt with the despair of American intellectuals a century earlier. But such speculation obviously grants Levin a great deal.

What could Levin do? His brother Jack, Harvard class of 1940, had joined the navy and was serving on a destroyer in the Atlantic. Like his brother, Levin would have applied for officer's training but didn't, because he was told by his doctor that he would probably fail the physical exam and would then be inducted into the army as a private rather than an officer. He was classified 3A, married with child, and as a teacher was thought to contribute to the war effort on the home front. Accepting the Guggenheim fellowship meant that he would be reclassified 1A and could be drafted any day. All through the Guggenheim year the Levins lived in a state of great uncertainty. But Levin was too deeply committed to his literary scholarship to play it safe. More than anything he wanted to write his book.

Moreover, the argument could be made that humanity had to be saved from the barbarians, and that the way to do it was to contribute to the intellectual life.[68] There had been a famous precedent for that argument. In 1941, E. M. Forster delivered a speech at the 17th International PEN Congress, which, he wrote later, had been politely dismissed. The issue he had chosen to raise before this prominent gathering was this: "Art for Art's sake? I should just think so, and more so than ever at the present time. It is the one orderly product which our muddling race has produced." He offered history as proof: "Ancient Athens made a mess," he declared, "but Antigone stands up. Renaissance Rome made a mess —but the ceiling of the Sistine Chapel got painted," and so on. He ended by citing Shelley's famous assessment of poets as unacknowledged legislators. In a lecture about the responsibility of intellectuals, Cynthia Ozick inquired: "How do we know when a thinker formulates an issue badly? In just this way: When an ideal, however comely, fails to accord with deep necessity. In 1941, 'blood, sweat, and tears,' is apropos, a dream of the 'possibility of aesthetic order' is not. It is not sufficient to have beautiful thoughts while the barbarians rage on. . . . People who are privileged to be thinkers are obliged to respect exigency and to admit to crisis."[69]

It is perhaps just such an explicit admission of crisis, of confusion about the collapse of the moral foundation of European high culture, that one misses in Levin's published works, although a keen eye may occasionally catch glimpses of Levin's confusion, pain, and anger. In 1942, between finishing his book on Joyce and becoming a Guggenheim fellow, Levin edited one of the most damning poems ever written about the human race, "A Satyr Against Mankind" by John Wilmot, earl of Rochester (1647–80). In his introduction to the poem, Levin, then thirty years old, wrote: "No other age except our own, perhaps, has been so painfully conscious of those extremes [virtue and vice], or so bent upon realizing their conflicting possibilities." What, exactly, in our age Levin was thinking of is not clear. It is striking, however, how closely the world views of John Wilmot and Levin's neighbor in those years,

6. Harry Levin in his office at Harvard in 1944. *Courtesy of Harvard University Archives.*

Delmore Schwartz, resemble each other. Schwartz scorned bigots, but in his bitterness turned against the Jews and finally against himself. Wilmot scorned all mankind. Thus his satiric poem had a certain appeal in 1942. Among the many horrible things Wilmot had to say against man there is what one might call a more catholic rendition of Schwartz's scathing epigram about the source of Jewish cleverness.

> The Good he acts, the Ill he does endure,
> 'Tis all from Fear, to make himself secure.
> Merely for Safety, after Fame they thirst;
> For all Men would be Cowards if they durst:[70]

One of the copies of Wilmot's poem, shelved in Harvard's Widener Library, once belonged to Karl Viëtor, Harvard's Kuno Francke Professor of German Art and Culture from 1935 to 1952. It bears an inscription by Levin, dated September 1945. At first glance, Levin's gift to Viëtor looks like one of the unsettling, ironic gestures Levin was capable of that reveal their barb long after the pleasantries have passed. But in this case,

Levin's wife assured me, the present conveyed straightforward admiration. Viëtor, who had a Jewish wife, had left Germany in 1934 and come to Cambridge. During the war, when students flocked to hear Levin, Viëtor's classes were tiny. Hardly anyone was taking German apart from a handful of European refugees, over whom Viëtor would cast his spell. One of his most devoted students at that time was an emigrant from Vienna, an accomplished young lady from an upper-class Jewish family who had been educated on the run.

Dorrit Cohn had left Vienna and her Gymnasium at the age of thirteen, a few days before the Anschluss, the Nazi takeover of Austria in March 1938. Subsequently she attended, in steady flight further west, the Zugdorf Schule near Zurich; St. George's, a British boarding school in Montreux; the American school in Paris; and finally, from 1939 to 1942, the French lycée on East 95th Street in Manhattan, where she received a *baccalauréat* in both the sciences and the humanities. Cohn went up to Radcliffe, because some of her classmates did, and majored in physics, because "the sciences were non-linguistic territory. The sciences to me were a kind of escape hatch from my linguistic confusions," Cohn remembered.[71]

She learned about Viëtor's courses from another emigrant, a girl from a Prague family, who belonged to her circle of friends. With Viëtor's course on the second part of Goethe's *Faust,* German came back into Cohn's life. Three decades later, in 1971, she was offered a professorship in Harvard's Comparative Literature department, which had been completely revamped by Harry Levin during the 1950s. She accepted because she recalled Harvard as a vibrant, interesting place—and because, as she confessed, she was just a bit of an Ivy League snob. She had left Harvard after taking her master's degree in 1946, when Harry Levin was stirring up the English department with his course on Joyce, Proust, and Mann that "prompted students to plan their entire course load around it."[72] While at Radcliffe, Cohn had sat in on Levin's "enormous course on the European novel. People were hanging from the rafters for that course. It was the glamorous event of the week that one went to Levin's course." Levin was then barely thirty years old. When Cohn returned three decades later, in 1971, as one of the first five women hired to tenure at Harvard, she was quite surprised. "My Ivy League snobbishness had a rude awakening. I had the sense of having come into a backwater intellectually. I had the sense of being back in the nineteenth century."[73]

Levin's innovations of the 1940s, such as the introduction of the troubling "moderns" into the Harvard curriculum, were now part of the tradition. The moderns' dissent had been completely assimilated. Levin's protest against the old fogies of his time, such as it was, had been tied up with the rise of the moderns; and as they passed and became canonized, so did he. Like his mentors, Babbitt, Eliot, and Matthiessen, the Young Turks of their age, Levin became a custodian of culture, a remembrancer and preserver of the great tradition, which, he had once feared in the 1920s, was not a fate conceivable for a boy from a Midwestern immigrant Jewish household. Harry Levin died in Cambridge, Massachusetts, on May 29, 1994. To his students and colleagues he left not only his impeccable scholarship but, as his former student Donald Fanger declared, "standards of intellectual curiosity, commitment, and seriousness that we could try to make our own."[74]

3

Man of
Imaginative Consent:
M. H. Abrams

WHEN MEYER ABRAMS went up to Harvard in the fall of 1930, he had a rather curious notion of that college. He looked at it "through the perspective of the more or less sentimental novels" he had read about athletics at Harvard and Yale. One of them was called *Stover at Yale* (1911), by Owen Johnson, author of *The Varmint* and *The Tennessee Shad*. Its hero is one Dink Stover, an acclaimed football player at Lawrenceville, who comes up to Yale with the desire to excel and become a leader of his class. His enthusiasm is quickly dampened when he learns that leadership at Yale begins with submission not only to the team spirit but to the authority of upper classmen who would eventually select the leaders of the lower class on the infamous Tap Day. According to one of Stover's classmates, the goal of an Ivy League education was "First, a pretty fine type of gentleman, with good, clear, honest standards; second, a spirit of ambition and a determination not to be beaten; third, the belief in democracy." [1]

By "democracy" Johnson and his characters mean something quite similar to what Harvard's president Abbott Lawrence Lowell had had in mind for his school, namely, that all "elements" at the college were to be given equal opportunity to become Yale men or Harvard men and thus future leaders of the nation. Stover's induction into Yale democracy begins when

he suddenly realized the stern discipline of it all—unnecessary and stamping out individuality, it seemed to him at first, but subordinating every-

73

thing to the one purpose, eliminating the individual factor, demanding absolute subordination to the whole, submerging everything into the machine—that was not a machine only, when once accomplished, but an immense idea of sacrifice and self-abnegation. Directly, clearly visualized, he perceived, for the first time, what he was to perceive in every side of his college career, that a standard had been fashioned to which, irresistibly, subtly, he would have to conform.[2]

Taken out of context, it would be uncertain whether this was the attitude of a German youth in a Nazi elite school, say, or of a young man in the society of ancient Sparta. We no longer recognize the sentiment of this passage as democratic. Rather, we might be inclined to call it proto-fascist. But early in this century the term *democratic,* spoken in an Ivy League context, actually meant aristocratic, which is "the rule of the best" over the uneducated many, a concept deeply embedded in the political thinking of the early American republic and reflected in the structure of the American government.

Abrams found out very quickly that nothing could have been further from the reality at Harvard in the 1930s than Johnson's view of Yale in 1910. Despite President Lowell's efforts to turn the college into a "machine" for the production of Harvard men, the school had remained committed to President Eliot's individualism, meritocratic ideals, and love of brilliant eccentrics. Abrams's high school principal, the scion of an old American family and himself a Harvard graduate, trusted his alma mater as much as his students, when in the fall of 1930 he sent three Jewish freshmen from Long Branch, New Jersey, up to Cambridge. "He decided we were the bright ones," Abrams recalled, "and that we ought to go on. It was a remarkable thing for a man of his background. He wrote to Harvard and got us some financial aid. So we all went."[3]

Had it not been for his enlightened principal, Harvard might not have been in the cards for Meyer ("Mike") Abrams. His parents were immigrants from the Eastern European town of Grodno, who came to the United States as young adults at the beginning of the century. Joseph Abrams had been conscripted into the Russian army, and therefore had received little or no education, Jewish or Russian. He had attended *heder* (Jewish elementary school), where he learned to read Hebrew and to read and write Yiddish. He spoke both Polish and Russian but had little facility in reading or writing these languages. According to his son, he was a rather vain young man who went to a tailor and had a uniform made that resembled an officer's. In this new outfit and shining cavalry boots, he had his picture taken. Life was hard for Jews in Russia and harder still for Jews in the Russian army. In 1906 a pogrom ravaged Bialystok, a largely Jewish town not far from Grodno. When Joseph Abrams realized that in his shining cavalry boots he might one day be marched to a parricide rather than a parade, he escaped from the army with the help of a white lie and a sympathetic officer, and made his way to New York. There he befriended a *landsman* (compatriot), who ran a paint and wallpaper shop, learned the trade, sent for his fiancée, married her upon arrival, and moved to Long Branch, New Jersey, where their son Meyer was born in 1912. Joseph Abrams soon became a painting contractor and was regularly called on to paint some of the largest resort hotels in town. When Meyer was a young child, his father was able to give up contracting and to establish instead a paint and wallpaper shop on Broadway, the main business street of Long Branch.

The language of the Abrams household was largely Yiddish until Meyer was six years old and attended the first grade. Meyer and his brother switched the family language to English, in which their father was not literate. During his early days in New York City, he had usually worked two jobs, one by day and another in the evening. As a result, he had had no time to attend one of the night schools for immigrants and therefore never mastered the reading and writing of English. His wife had been more fortunate. Her father had owned a cigarette factory in Eastern Europe and had been solidly middle class. Like so many female immigrants, Sarah Shanes Abrams adapted better and more quickly than her husband to the new environment. She read and wrote English, and though remaining "a genuine believer and observant, she was willing to temporize and was open to Gentile mores and food" (interview). Her husband, however, who had been rather casually observant as a young man, became more orthodox as he matured. By the time he moved to Long Branch, he was ready to deepen his sense of allegiance to Judaism. "He became deeply involved with the ritualistic and social life of the synagogue, and as a result, inevitably in that institution, with synagogue politics as well" (letter). While this involvement represented to him an American freedom (to be what he was or chose to be), it also grounded him in a stable enclave of familiar faces, minds, and sensibilities. Sarah and Joseph Abrams sent their two sons to a Hebrew school run by old-fashioned and usually aged teachers. Meyer obliged his father until his bar mitzvah, but he went reluctantly and without great joy:

It was a rough schedule. You went all day to public school, and when school was over you went next door and spent another couple of hours there. By the time you were finished, during the winter, it was cold and dark and too late to play outdoors. We would learn Hebrew by rote, the old-fashioned way, without studying the grammar. I don't think some of our old teachers ever heard of grammar, and that made our studies as dull as dishwater. (interview)

Abrams preferred to roam the streets of Long Branch, a seashore community of some twelve thousand people that was sharply divided between WASPs, Italians, and Jews. Ethnic tension existed, but was casual and informal rather than a matter of street gangs. An Italian kid got his nose bloodied when he startled Meyer on his way home from Hebrew school with an anti-Semitic insult. Even in the mid-twenties, when the Ku Klux Klan was fairly strong in New Jersey, as elsewhere in the United States, ethnic tension did not erupt into violence. Together with a WASP friend, Abrams stumbled across a pile of sheets and hoods in an empty shed near a holiday racetrack outside town. But no cross burnings ever materialized.

All in all, Abrams spent an unspectacular small-town childhood in the fond embrace of parents who were Jewish in an uncomplicated way. The guests at their poker and pinochle evenings were mainly Jews of their own kind. In such communities the lives of the sons were determined without much ado. Of course they would go to college and become lawyers and doctors. The parental goal, to provide the next generation with a good education, was identical throughout the community. "It was never discussed," Abrams recalled, "it was simply taken for granted. My father was willing to make any sacrifice to send me to college" (interview). Principal Cate caught on to the drift of that community, and he proved himself a man of the future when he sent his three Jewish boys up to Harvard because they were "the bright ones."

Abrams's initial awe before the antiquity and prestige of the college vanished quickly. As President Lowell had foreseen, the house plan made it easy for students to become integrated. During his first year, Abrams lived in one of the dormitories along the Charles River. In the fall of 1931, he moved into the newly opened Kirkland House. Although the Great Depression continued with unabated force, the outside world dropped away for the young men in the houses. "It was curious," Abrams recalled, "my undergraduate years were in the absolute Depression, but we lived high on the hog at Harvard. We had lots of space in our living quarters. We ate our meals in the houses; we had white tablecloths and waitress service. It was a very plush time in which we were insulated from the Depression outside, not by intention, but in fact" (interview). But America's economic nadir did impress itself upon the students; they were aware of an "awful world out there where you could not get jobs" (interview).

The collapse of the job market allowed Abrams to drift and to pursue the subjects he liked. He majored in English because he enjoyed reading. "I figured I could read lots of good things. Unlike Harry Levin, who knew what his goal was, I think, almost from the time he was born and very deliberately planned his academic career as a man of letters, I just blundered into it." Abrams and his classmate Daniel Boorstin would occasionally run into Levin, who was a year ahead of them. "He was obviously brilliant and having an effect" (interview).

Abrams, by contrast, pursued his course leisurely. He developed a cunning system to study German more efficiently, wrote a near-perfect and prize-winning exam in the first-year German course, and in his senior year achieved his bachelor's degree *summa cum laude*. He won both a Henry Fellowship for a year of study in England and a Bowdoin Prize for his thesis *The Milk of Paradise: The Effect of Opium Visions on the Works of De Quincey, Crabbe, Francis Thompson, and Coleridge,* which was published by Harvard University Press in 1934. Abrams's choice of a Romantic topic indicates that he did not conform to the views of T. S. Eliot and other modernists, for whom the Romantics represented a deplorable fall from the classic literary tradition.

Abrams kept his own counsel. He studied with John Livingston Lowes and listened to some of the lectures by Arthur O. Lovejoy, who spent the year 1932–33 as a visiting professor at Harvard and delivered what became *The Great Chain of Being* as the William James Lectures in the spring semester. Lowes and Lovejoy were men near the apex of their fame. Although Lowes was developing a memory loss, he was still an effectual and sonorous lecturer. His book on Coleridge, *The Road to Xanadu* (1927), retained its high repute among critics as well as scholars well into the era of the New Criticism. Yet within the critical avant-garde Lowes's method of interpreting authors against their specific literary backgrounds, a method employed by Abrams with some modification in his senior thesis, would soon be replaced, first by Marxist criticism and then by its opposite, the New Criticism. While the fame of Lowes had just peaked (in 1927), Lovejoy's was to reach its zenith in 1936 with the publication of *The Great Chain of Being.* Abrams explained that "through the 1930s, among advanced graduate students, and in the judgment of vanguard young teachers such as F. O. Matthiessen and Perry Miller, the must-read books setting the standards for scholarship and criticism were headed by Lovejoy's *Great Chain,* Whitehead's *Science and the Modern World,* E. A. Burke's *The Metaphysical Foundations of Modern Science*—all these were exemplars of intellectual and literary history—as well as two early formers of the New-Critical standards, I. A. Richards' *Principles of Literary Criticism* and T. S. Eliot's *Selected Essays"* (letter). But while Lovejoy was still at the height of his intellectual power and influence, the views that would eventually supplant his own were already fermenting among his young listeners and readers. Lovejoy's critical realism, for instance, once formed in opposition to Josiah Royce's absolute idealism, was about to be superseded by the views of behaviorists, physicalists, and logical positivists developed by graduate students who were just then returning from studies with Wittgenstein in Cambridge and their encounter with the philosophy of the Vienna Circle. In an essay on Lovejoy at Harvard, his student Lewis Feuer grasped the drama well when he pointed to Einstein's view that "the greatest tragedy that can befall a teacher . . . is when he finds that his language, method, and problems have ceased to be those of the new generation of students, whose presuppositions he may find not only alien but willfully irrational." [4]

Although Abrams too would soon come under the transforming influence of I. A. Richards, who supervised his work at Cambridge University, he would retain in his scholarly work significant elements of the methods of his early teachers. [5] Abrams continued to value knowledge of an author's literary background, and in his first book, *The Mirror and the Lamp* (1953), he presented a history of ideas that was couched in an analysis of the shift in key metaphors in literary criticism from the Neoclassical age to Romanticism. Abrams's critical work matured slowly. One of its hallmarks was the author's imperviousness to critical fads. Throughout his career Abrams endorsed a pragmatic approach to literary method. "The test of the validity of a theory," he wrote in 1972, "is what it proves capable of doing when it is put to work." He acknowledged that there were limits to the rigidity with which a method could be applied. Critical discourse, Abrams claimed, "is controlled in considerable part by norms that we call good sense, sagacity, tact, sensibility, taste." [6] Obviously this left a great deal to the discretion of the critic. And it meant that every essay took the measure of its author's character.

In the spring of 1934, when Abrams won the Bowdoin Prize for his essay on Romantic poets, he was still drifting. He considered becoming a lawyer. The economy was still depressed and job prospects were bleak in all professions. Abrams thought he would lose nothing by accepting the Henry Fellowship and went to England. He attended Cambridge University for a year and came back to Harvard in 1935, thoroughly, but not fanatically, committed to the pursuit of literary criticism and theory. He received his master's degree in 1937, completed his Ph.D. in 1940 while an instructor and tutor in the English department (1938–42). In 1942 he was invited to join the Psycho-Acoustic Laboratory at Harvard as a research associate by its director, S. S. Stevens.

"The laboratory," Abrams explained,

> was established in 1942 by the Defense Department in order to work, experimentally, on the problem of voice-communications (over interphones and radio telephone, as well as orally-aurally) in noisy military environments. Since I was already in my thirties when the U.S. went to war [Abrams had turned twenty-nine a few months before the Japanese attacked Pearl Harbor in December 1941], I was getting too old for standard military service. Professor Stevens invited me to join his new laboratory because he knew me as a co-teacher (with the young psychologist Donald McGranahan) of a course, "The Psychology of Literature," taught under the auspices of the Harvard Psychology Department. Smitty Stevens hired me in part because I knew something about phonetics, from my work in the old philology-centered curriculum in English graduate studies, but mainly, he told me, because although a student of literature, I "thought like a scientist."
>
> During my three years at the Laboratory, I helped test communications equipment and also helped to develop highly audible vocabularies and codes for military use, as well as standard tests for selecting the most able operators of voice-communications stations in various armed services. In the last days of the war the Psycho-Acoustic Laboratory was asked to turn its attention to the problem of redesigning the equipment and operations of the Combat Information Centers of warships, in order to adapt these nerve centers of the ship to meet the deadly threat of Japanese kamikaze (suicide) attackers. For years after 1945, my publications in the practical science of military communications (although all classified) greatly exceeded my publications about literature. (letter)

In the fall of 1945, when the war was over, Abrams joined the faculty of the English department at Cornell University as its first Jewish professor. In an era when the usual beginning rank was that of instructor, Abrams was appointed right away to an assistant professorship. Within

7. M. H. Abrams in 1945. *Photograph by Morris Peck. Courtesy of Division of Rare and Manuscript Collections, Cornell University Library.*

two years he was given tenure as an associate professor. He became full professor in 1953 and was given his first chair in 1960. Abrams felt welcome at Cornell. "By the end of the war, in part as a result of growing information about the Holocaust and of Jewish participation in the armed forces, the earlier animus against adding Jews to college faculties had greatly weakened. In addition, a number of the older, more hidebound university teachers and administrators had retired or lost much of their clout. I never felt any prejudice at Cornell—hardly ever any awareness—that I am Jewish. (That does not entail, of course, that there was no prejudice outside my personal ken.)" (letter).

Abrams had not planned to become a professor of English literature; indeed, he claimed that his whole career "was a matter of accident rather than vocation" (interview). It is fairly certain, however, that one of the turning points in his life was his year in Cambridge, and, more specifically, his studies with I. A. Richards, whose *Principles of Literary Criticism* opened his eyes to new ways of thinking about literary texts. Almost as important to Abrams were the writings of C. K. Ogden, which seemed to provide him with a key that unlocked the English literary tradition. Having such a key was a first step toward deeper involvement. Two books in particular acted as catalysts in Abrams's process of discovery: *The Meaning of Meaning* (1923) by I. A. Richards and C. K. Ogden, and the latter's book on the empirical utilitarian Jeremy Bentham, entitled *Bentham's Theory of Fictions* (1932). Bentham, who among other things was trained as a lawyer, dealt with fictions primarily in the legal realm. Indebted to the tradition of Locke, which distrusts metaphors and searches for literal language as the only way to approximate truth, Bentham's basic procedure was to show that legal and moral terminology was metaphorical, in the sense that its central terms could be traced back to Latin roots that are metaphors. The word *obligation,* for instance, goes back to a root meaning "tied to."[7] "It was Bentham," says Abrams, "who first got me interested in the role of unrecognized metaphors in discourse in general, and especially in philosophy and literary criticism" (letter).

In Jewish readers, Abrams's play with the etymology of *obligation* evokes Abraham's tying his son Isaac to a stack of firewood. The incident in Genesis 22, referred to by Christians as the "sacrifice" and by Jews as the "binding" of Isaac, is of course about the conflicts created by equally valid ties or obligations to God and kin, about the clash between one's commitment to vision (the life of idea and intellect) and one's family bonds. Abrams did feel tied to and by his father's tradition; he was bound by a sense of obligation that he did not feel free to disregard. By temperament and conviction, however, Abrams was a rationalist. His sympathies lay with the Enlightenment, which he identified as "the period of rational triumph over superstition and over accepting things by authority and tradition" (interview). Abrams wanted to be free of his father's orthodoxy without having to espouse something else instead, say, the poetry of T. S. Eliot. Abrams wanted no other gods in the place of the one he dethroned. He wished to be free without being cut loose.

It was important, therefore, to establish a relationship to Gentile culture[8] that permitted Abrams access to its inner sanctum, to its chain of ideas and ideological mechanisms, without demanding an investment of emotion or belief. Abrams did not wish to transfer his obligations from one culture to another. The possibility, pointed to by Bentham, Ogden, and Richards, of reading the literature of Christian Europe not as an immediate appeal to one's identity, but as a series of metaphors, offered a distancing mechanism that allowed Abrams to speak analytically rather than appreciatively about it. In the course of his career as a critic, Abrams developed his own literary method, which, inadvertently, made a case against the exclusion of Jews or any other non-Christian group from the study of Christian writers, who contributed the majority of texts to the Western literary tradition. Abrams was determined, as he wrote in 1957, to "stand as an infidel *in partibus fidelium.*"[9]

Before Abrams's seminal study *The Mirror and The Lamp: Romantic Theory and the Critical Tradition* appeared in 1953, he had published only two critical articles. "Unconscious Expectations in the Reading of Poetry" came out in 1942 and was signed Meyer Howard Abrams; "Archetypal Analogies in the Language of Criticism," a trial run for the history-by-metaphor method of *The Mirror and the Lamp,* appeared in 1949 and was signed, as were all subsequent publications, M. H. Abrams.

The early articles focused on the psychology of reading and of literary invention; Abrams's book combined these two interests in a comprehensive analysis of the dynamics of aesthetic theory. *The Mirror and the Lamp* opened with a spectacular introduction modestly titled "Orientation of Critical Theories." It claimed that the history of literary criticism could be written by tracing the gradual shift in the alignment of the literary work to each of the three elements in the literary world: the external universe, the audience, and the artist.

Abrams's introduction accomplished three things. First, it ordered the chaos of aesthetic theories with the help of a simple but elastic analytic framework that has proved very useful indeed in introducing students to this field; second, it provided a historic basis for the espousal of critical pluralism; and third, it argued implicitly for the flexible and pragmatic application of theory. Unafraid of the opposition his views might arouse, Abrams formulated them explicitly near the beginning of his book. The criterion for a good critical theory, Abrams claimed, was "not the scientific verifiability of its single propositions, but the scope, precision, and coherence of the insights that it yields into the properties of single works of art and the adequacy with which it accounts for diverse kinds of art."[10] Abrams's pragmatic critical pluralism did not come under fire until the rise of deconstruction in the early 1970s.

In the remainder—that is, the bulk—of his book, Abrams analyzed the transition from Neoclassicism to Romanticism with the help of "submerged conceptual models" (metaphors and similes), which he also called "archetypal analogies." When poets spoke of art as a mirror, they were still thinking in mimetic, which is to say, pre-Romantic terms.

According to Abrams, Romantics preferred metaphors for art that were not reflective but expressive or projective (such as a lamp). "In the generation of Wordsworth and Coleridge, the transformation of the key images by which critics pictured the process and product of art is a convenient index to a comprehensive revolution in the theory of poetry, and of all the arts" (*ML* 53). By taking the poets' metaphors for art seriously (in a pragmatic fashion), Abrams could write an analysis of Romanticism without recourse to external reality (historic events, political and social change, and so forth). He combined the goals of intellectual history with the text-focused analytic methods of the New Criticism. *The Mirror and the Lamp* made perfectly clear that it was quite possible for a "freethinking Jew" (T. S. Eliot) to penetrate the intricacies of the Romantics' "high argument" (Wordsworth) without necessarily sharing any of their beliefs.

Four years later, Abrams was called upon to explain how that worked. The occasion was the 1957 English Institute, convened to throw light on the issue of "Literature and Belief" in one of its sessions. Abrams was the only Jewish speaker on that panel. The paper he delivered spelled out the theoretical underpinnings for the integration of Jews and other infidels into an academic priesthood that still expounded largely the Christian literary canon. Picking up on his 1942 theme of unconscious expectations in the reading of poetry, Abrams argued that poetry "depends for its efficacy upon evoking a great number of beliefs" (*B* 5). Literary works, Abrams claimed, were not experienced in an act of disinterested contemplation "free from any reference to desire, will, or the reality and utility of the object," (*B* 7) as adherents to objective theories from Kant to the New Critics would have it. Rather, poems were for and about people and hence intimately connected to them (*B* 12). Their interpretation "engages the whole mind, including the complex of common sense and moral beliefs and values deriving from our experience in this world" (*B* 11). In short, we bring "beliefs and dispositions . . . to the poem from life" (*B* 17). Abrams was ready to confirm his claim with examples taken from Keats, Shakespeare, and Dante. His implicit argument was that most of the time encountering a poem means having to overcome more or less serious cultural differences, but that experienced readers are demonstrably able to do so and to arrive at an adequate understanding of and response to a specific literary work. It is important, however, that the reader suspend his or her disbelief in the creed expressed or implied by the author of the work or by a character in that work. In reading a lyric poem, for example, it is only by suspending disbelief in the opinions expressed by the lyric speaker that clash with our own that we are able to recognize our lot in the lyrical I, and "to consent imaginatively to [the speaker's] experience until it is resolved, in both artistic and human terms" (*B* 18). The reader's "imaginative consent," however, is yielded only for the duration of the poem, drama, or novel, and does not constitute intellectual consent.

Abrams showed that this flexible response by an experienced reader can overcome even vast religious differences. He chose as his example Piccarda's assertion to Dante, "In His will is our peace; it is that sea to which all moves" in the *Divine Comedy* (Book 3, Canto 3, ll. 85–86). When read in its context the utterance served to render "in the most efficacious possible way—as a truth achieved through error—a universal doctrine which is one aspect of the total theological truth propagated by the poem" (*B* 22). Abrams then explained that we do not have to feel excluded from Dante's Catholic universe, because we are in fact able to read his poem with adequate understanding and engagement:

> For the first time in our discussion . . . it becomes relevant to consider the relation of the reader's beliefs to his apprehension of an isolated poetic statement, offered for his assent. And the testimony of innumerable readers demonstrates that the passage can certainly be appreciated, and appreciated profoundly, independently of assent to its propositional truth. It touches sufficiently on universal experience—since all of us, whether Catholic, Protestant, or agnostic, know the heavy burden of individual decision—to enable us all to realize in imagination the relief that might come from saying to an infallible Providence, "Not my will, but Thine be done." This ability to take an assertion hypothetically, as a ground for imaginative experience, is one we in fact possess.(*B* 22)

Having established the principle of imaginative consent in order to put an end to the exclusion of anyone from the pursuit of English literature on the grounds that he or she does not share its intellectual or religious tradition (note that Abrams does not list Jews, and presumably subsumes himself in the rubric agnostic) Abrams turned again to the Romantic period to undertake in earnest an analysis of the continuity of religious thoughts and concepts in secular literature.

In 1971 he published to great acclaim *Natural Supernaturalism: Tradition and Revolution in Romantic Literature*. In it Abrams demonstrated inadvertently that Eliot had been right when he maintained that English society and culture, "so far as it is positive" had not ceased to be Christian.[11] English literature was the product of a Christian culture. Abrams's argument of 1957, however, that critics were capable of "imaginative consent," made it perfectly clear that the Christian nature of Western culture was no reason why Jews, Muslims, Hindus, or anyone else should not be able to speak about it intelligently, or to analyze it adequately. Abrams then proceeded to do so. In *Natural Supernaturalism,* Abrams wrote in 1976, "I tried, by an effort of imagination, to understand a great Romantic enterprise by looking at it from within." [12]

In 1972, J. Hillis Miller published a thorough deconstructive review of *Natural Supernaturalism* in *Diacritics,* which, according to Vincent B. Leitch, was "drawing up the first battle lines in America between deconstructors and orthodox literary historians." [13] Moreover, the battle began on Abram's own turf, since *Diacritics* was published at Cornell, where he had taught since 1945. At the apex of his fame—he would become Class of 1916 Professor of English in 1973—Abrams suddenly found himself in the position Lovejoy and Lowes had been in forty years earlier. Decades of thorough research and careful thinking afforded him adequate certainty about what could and could not plausibly be done with literary texts. From this stable position he could observe new ideas fermenting in the minds of the young, whose presuppositions he found not only alien but willfully irrational.

Against the deconstructors' "disregard of auctorial intention, the voiding of referentiality, and the renunciation of criteria of interpretative correctness," [14] Abrams pitted the interpretative assumptions that had guided the writing of *Natural Supernaturalism:* Romantic poets and critics wrote to be understood; they obeyed communal norms of language; their texts had a core of determinate meanings that could be understood by a competent reader (a critic), who made his interpretations public to test their validity. Against the nihilism and despair of deconstruction, Abrams pitted the "Romantic positives" of life, love, liberty, hope, and joy, which he thought "deliberately reaffirmed the elementary values of the Western past." [15] Of course, Abrams did so, he said, "with a good deal of Socratic irony. I love to present myself as an all-out traditionalist and unreconstructed backward-looking person, and to a certain extent that is true; but don't be misled by any of that" (interview). In fact, he accepted the position of the deconstructors

that there *is* no ultimate foundation on which the Romantic positives can rest; whether that foundation is religious, or the primal presence of God, or an absolute which exists by some means or other in the universe. But

this does not entail that our human selves and our cultural inheritance
do not provide adequate assurance about the central values of western
civilization. It seemed to me, on my initial acquaintance with deconstruction, that its widespread triumph would be ominous. The initiators of
the deconstructive theory—the master unbuilders—are humane people
who have already absorbed these values, can take them for granted, and
so continue to live by these values, even as they "undermine" or "decon-
struct" their grounds and claim, as a consequence, that all meaning and
all values, since they lack a ground, are "undecidable." But what would
be the cultural and moral result if such a view were to be widely accepted,
including by people who lack philosophical sophistication? Who can tell?
(letter)

Since the early 1970s, Abrams has taken a firm but unfanatical stance
against deconstruction in a number of essays for which he was praised
by that theory's archdebunker David Lehman.[16] However, there was
never any glee, triumph, or animosity in Abrams's critiques of poststructuralist theory. Instead, his attitude toward these inventive theorists,
many of whom belong to the next generation of Jewish literary critics,
seemed compounded of admiration and concern and, sometimes,
amusement. This is particularly evident in an essay about the theories of
Jacques Derrida, Stanley Fish, and Harold Bloom, published in *Partisan
Review* in 1979. Against Derrida's playful deconstruction of the supposi-
tion that language had an absolute foundation, Abrams held that we
did not need one, because, as Wittgenstein had already argued in his
Philosophical Investigations, language was not a metaphysics but a practice.
"One of Wittgenstein's liberating insights," Abrams had written elsewhere, "is that the validity of language consists in the way it is in fact
used to some purpose, rather than in its accordance with logical models
of how it should be used; and another is his view that meanings do not
consist in what expressions name and describe but in how they are used."
As in his espousal of critical pluralism, Abrams's attitude is essentially
pragmatic: we should use what is serviceable.[17]

Turning his attention to Stanley Fish, Abrams noted that "Fish's rehu-
manization of reading is only a half-humanism, for it begins by diminish-
ing, and ends by deleting, the part played by the author." Abrams
examined Fish's reader-response theory and found it to be "an extreme
form of methodological relativism, in which the initial choice of a
method of reading is 'arbitrary,' and the particular method that the reader
elects creates the text and meanings that he mistakenly thinks he finds."[18]

To disarm his critics, Fish readily admitted that his own reading "strategy" was no less arbitrary than any other, and that, like other modes of reading, it produced "fictions." But Abrams could not help being somewhat put out by the flippancy of Fish's famous assertion: "My fiction is liberating. It relieves me of the obligation to be right (a standard that simply drops out) and demands only that I be interesting (a standard that can be met without any reference at all to an illusory objectivity). Rather than restoring or recovering texts, I am in the business of making texts and of teaching others to make them by adding to their repertoire of strategies."[19] Abrams pointed out that many of Fish's close readings were not only interesting but right: "They are interesting because they are bravura critical performances by a learned, resourceful, and witty intelligence, and not least, because the new readings never entirely depart from implicit reliance on the old ways of reading texts" (H 286).

Abrams clearly enjoyed the compelling brilliance of Fish's mind; but he seems to be a bit sorry to see such dazzling talent employed toward what he would consider dubious ends. Abrams and his generation of Jewish scholars had fought too hard for the privilege to participate in the shaping of the country's moral and aesthetic standards not to protest vigorously the wholesale abolition of all standards whose mastery had not only ensured their own academic success but provided the basis on which their rebellious sons set up their business of making texts.[20]

As Abrams turned to his former student, Harold Bloom, he found a much darker depiction of the "scene of literature." Unlike Fish, Abrams wrote, "Bloom restores the human writer as well as reader to an effective role in the literary transaction. But if Fish's theory is a half-humanism, Bloom's is all too human, for it screens out from both the writing and the reading of 'strong' literature all motives except self-concern" (H 287–288). Analyzing Bloom's theory of poetry, he concluded that Bloom "compels us to face up to aspects of the motivation to write and misread poems—self-assertiveness, lust for power and precedence, malice, envy, revenge—which canonical critics have largely ignored" (H 293). Abrams added a strong testimonial to the power of Bloom's revisionary criticism: "To those of us who yield ourselves to Bloom's dark and powerful eloquence, the Scene of Literature will never look the same again; such a result is probably the most that any writer compelled by an antithetical vision can hope to achieve" (H 293).

Having spoken in an interview critically but with cautious admiration about the acrobatic acts of reading by the next generation of Jewish critics, about their brainteasing somersaults turned high up in the thin air of language, Abrams was moved unexpectedly to reflect about his own rootedness. He was not a *luftmensch* (a man who lives on air), who could make his home in language alone. He was tied to Jewish culture. "This is a very deep attachment," he said, "it vibrates internally. I have never broken away from it, and I never wanted to break away" (interview). These ties were the source of Abrams's strength, of the adequate assurance he needed to pursue his work on the tightrope of language suspended over Derrida's abyss. From there, too, he derived the assurance needed for his mission. In 1975, Abrams had stated his pedagogical credo clearly:

> What we need to get our students to recognize is that the stance of the liberal humanist is a very difficult one, which takes poise and courage to maintain. It takes a secure balance and a firm will to conduct, rationally, a discipline in which many of the premises, procedures, and conclusions are essentially contestable, without surrendering either to an all-dissolving skepticism or to the inviting dogmatism of the visionary and the fanatic.[21]

Abrams's equanimity and pragmatic rationality helped him to weather the storms of deconstruction while being deeply involved in the discussion surrounding it. His own solid scholarly work has withstood the test of time. Like Harry Levin's books on Renaissance drama and French realism, Abrams's studies of English Romanticism became part of "what we know." Abrams and Levin were both men who, while being friendly and collegial, steered their own course. As students at Harvard they had kept their own counsel—the latter because of a great shyness that he never quite overcame, the former because he rested calmly in himself.

Their exact contemporary, Daniel Aaron, the third Jewish literary scholar to emerge from Harvard in that generation, was quite different from his two fellow pioneers in personal temperament and intellectual interest. Aaron arrived at Harvard as a graduate student from the Midwest and after a lengthy period of adjustment, during which he actually gave up on the school as too provincial, too self-enclosed, and too hard for an outsider to warm to, he was suddenly pulled into the New England swing of things. His political curiosity about the left and his scholarly interests in American history and culture introduced him to an aspect of Harvard culture and Cambridge society that had not opened up for Abrams and Levin.

4

The Lure of
Literary Stewardship:
Daniel Aaron

Years of Migration

IN THE FALL OF 1933, Daniel Aaron, a recent graduate of the University of Michigan but still green as duckweed, set out for Harvard University to complete his education. He had spent a frustrating summer in Chicago looking for a job as a newspaperman. When his name was finally put down behind four hundred others on the waiting list of the Chicago City News Bureau, he remembered the words of the chairman of the English department at Ann Arbor. "We do not usually encourage students of Jewish extraction to go on for a master's degree in English," O. J. Campbell had told Aaron, "but in your case we strongly hope you will do so." [1] There was little else to do in 1933.

America was still living in the pit of the Great Depression, which had also affected Europe on a massive scale. Hitler came to power in Germany against weak opposition and began to implement his racial politics while the world looked on. "Hitler is certainly a sensible bird to drive the German Jews out of Germany, provided he is clever enough to do it without wrecking German business," wrote the American diarist Arthur Inman on May 11, 1933.[2] Inman would enter Aaron's life forty-five years later. Outright expulsions from Germany were rare in 1933, and few migrations were directly caused by Hitler's impending regime of terror. Yet nationalism moved people about in other parts of the world. Hans Kohn, a later colleague of Aaron's and a native of Prague who became a scholar of nationalism and an authority on the problems connected with its rise, left Palestine for America in 1933 because the chauvinism of the Zionists disappointed him and the United States "with its open, pluralistic society . . . promised a greater measure of freedom and diversity than was possible in Europe."[3] The poet Abraham Regelson, by contrast, a native of Hlusk, near Minsk, left America for Palestine because he felt that his Hebrew poetry of redemption should grow out of that land and its returning settlers. Nor would T. S. Eliot and the Southern Agrarians have altogether disagreed with Regelson. In the spring of 1933, Eliot spoke approvingly of the "re-establishment of a native culture" to students at the University of Virginia: "It is not necessarily those lands which are the most fertile or most favoured in climate that seem to me the happiest, but those in which a long struggle of adaptation between man and his environment has brought out the best qualities of both; in which the landscape has been moulded by numerous generations of one race, and in which the landscape in turn has modified the race to its own character."[4]

What seemed oppressive to the political thinker Kohn—restoration through the creation of homogeneity—appeared desirable to the poets. It should be noted, however, that in their countries of choice, England and Palestine, both Eliot and Regelson remained what Thorstein Veblen called "aliens of the uneasy feet." The freedom from "traditional and conventional verities" and "nationally binding convictions" that comes with exile Veblen had considered a precondition of intellectual achievement. The poets disagreed; they preferred to put down roots in reclaimed territory and to worship at the altar of tradition. Unlike Eliot, however, James Joyce in Paris had not been induced by his release from the confines of Ireland and the Catholic Church "to set up a new line of idols," as Veblen had put it.[5] And it was Joyce more than Eliot, we remember, whom Harry Levin wanted (yet failed) to see when he crossed the Atlantic in the summer of 1933. The world Levin was then leaving behind, a world Aaron was soon to enter, was a tiny academic enclave that was changing as rapidly as the world around it.

A new guard came to power. Roosevelt took office in January 1933, and former president Calvin Coolidge died on the sixth of that month, mourned only by rare birds like Arthur Inman, who now saw America "adrift, leaderless," because Coolidge, always on hand "in case of dire necessity, . . . is no longer available" (*ID* 520). Another president, A. Lawrence Lowell of Harvard, retired and was succeeded by James B. Conant, a New England blue blood like Lowell, but a modern man and a chemist like Lowell's own predecessor, Charles W. Eliot. Irving Babbitt, too, retired in 1933, and died that summer; and new men began to brighten the horizon of literary studies. Granville Hicks published *The Great Tradition,* a Marxist interpretation of American literature since the Civil War, and Harvard University Press brought out Perry Miller's brilliant first book, *Orthodoxy in Massachusetts: A Genetic Study.* In the fall of that busy year, when the university was caught up in the transition from Lowell to Conant and the English department struggled to appear modern with a crew of old fogie and a few young instructors, Daniel Aaron, barely twenty-one years old, drifted onto the Harvard scene. Aaron went to Harvard, he recalled, because it seemed to be the most suitable place after his application to study at the University of London had been denied. At this time he felt half-educated and lacking in the essential skills of scholarship. His only interest was English literature (interview).

The faculty of Harvard's English department, then inhabiting Warren House, ranged from old-style philologists like George Lyman Kittredge, who retired in 1936, to young instructors like Theodore Spencer and F. O. Matthiessen, who began to absorb New Critical methods. I. A. Richards, after all, had spent a term as visiting lecturer at Harvard in 1931. All in all, the faculty appeared sufficiently equipped to illuminate even a well-read, Anglophile youth about the delights and intricacies of English literature. One graduate student, however, who took his Ph.D. in 1935, professed himself "disappointed in the quality of intellectual labors in the English Department." To Robert B. Heilman "it seemed hard to imagine grown men preoccupied with the kinds of problems that came up in seminars."[6]

Aaron liked his courses in Anglo-Saxon, Beowulf, Chaucer (where Theodore Silverstein substituted for John Livingston Lowes), and drama before Shakespeare, but he was put off by the dictatorial manner of the faculty, who thought of graduate students as interlopers. "The graduate students," Aaron recalled, "were simply gypsies that arrived and were not terribly welcome" (interview). Graduate students who came to Warren House to register were processed without ceremony. They did not choose their courses; they were assigned them. Aaron had envisioned a community of scholars bound by a love of literature and eager to exchange ideas. Instead he found that a good many of his fellow students were leery of divulging their discoveries lest someone snitch them.

Moreover, in reserved and reticent Cambridge he felt like an outsider, not because he was a Jew, but because he was a Midwesterner. Not

having gone to the right schools and being without the right antecedents, he was not so much discriminated against as simply ignored: "It
was hard as an outsider to be taken into New England" (interview).
Aaron felt relegated to the margins of campus life but refused to be
discouraged. He managed to find kindred spirits in John Finch, with
whom he roomed, and Finch's friend, the poet Charles Olson. The
three lived happily on the Harvard fringe. Scornful of the dry-as-dust
scholars, they thought of themselves as artistic and literary. They spent
their talents as lavishly on pranks and clever mischief as on romance and
serious scholarship. In fact it was Olson, who while beginning to work
on his book *Call Me Ishmael* (1947), got the Anglophile Aaron interested
in Melville. An accidental find in the vast stores of Widener Library
resulted in Aaron's first publications, two scholarly notes written in the
witty, carefully irreverent style of the beginner who does not want to let
on that he is indeed quite pleased with the opportunity to demonstrate
his skills. The notes, concerning Melville's sojourn in the Pacific and the
ways in which he aroused the animus of the local missionaries, appeared
in the *New England Quarterly* in September and December of 1935.
These pieces inaugurated a valuable and much-appreciated friendship
with the *Quarterly*'s editor, Stewart Mitchell, himself a historian, biographer, and man of letters.

The connection with the *Quarterly* and Mitchell, the scion of an old
Boston family, would eventually prove to be important, but in 1935 it
came too late to keep Aaron in New England. After two years at Harvard, still displeased with his situation and uncertain what to do, Aaron
accepted happily when his old mentor from the University of Michigan,
Eric Walters, offered him a job teaching freshman composition in Ann
Arbor during the academic year 1935–36. "I was damn glad to leave. I
had never been so homesick in my life" (interview).

Aaron once compared his first two years at Harvard to his college
experience in Michigan, which he likened to being "thrown into a
great, big sea, and you would sink or swim" (interview). This is a
startling image of abandonment. We see Pip abandoned by the crew of
the *Pequod*, while Ishmael, Pip's sensible double, repeats the image,
surviving afloat in the ocean on Queequeg's coffin, and ends his narrative with the word "orphan." I am not suggesting that Aaron took to
Melville's work, or to the story of the author marooned on a Pacific
island, because of an abandonment trauma. What I suggest is, rather,
that a trauma of that sort can generate a keen desire to make friends in
new places, to establish connections that turn into a semblance of roots.

The pleasure of sharing cultural interests and intellectual pursuits with kindred spirits was an important force propelling Aaron's academic work. It was aided by an intense curiosity and a passion to know America in all its facets. These attributes made Aaron into a meticulous historian whose field is the almost-contemporary literary culture of the United States. Aaron's scholarship created connectedness to his country and its culture and thus partly made up for the loss Aaron had suffered in the breakup of his family.

———

Daniel Aaron was born in Chicago in August 1912. His parents, Henry Aaron and Rose Weinstein, had come to America as small children. Henry went to law school at night and eventually founded a law firm. In 1916 he moved his wife and five children (Daniel was the middle son and next-to-youngest child) to Los Angeles into a large house off of Wilshire Boulevard, for which a housekeeper, a cook, and a chauffeur were hired. A manservant looked after Henry Aaron, who had developed multiple sclerosis and was confined to a wheelchair. Household help became indispensable when his wife contracted tuberculosis. Aaron remembered periodic visits to the nearby Monrovia sanitarium, where he talked to his mother through a screened porch. She died in 1919; a year later her husband succumbed to his illness. Henry's unmarried brother Charles, a senior partner in the law firm, became the children's guardian. Since Charles continued to live in Chicago, Henry's sister Rose came to live with her five orphaned nieces and nephews in Los Angeles. Aaron was alarmed when he was told that the family's rather elaborate household would have to be dismantled. The five siblings moved from the big house into more modest quarters, and Aaron's anxieties gradually subsided. "The great shock," Aaron recollected, "was coming back to Chicago in 1924" (interview).

Daniel Aaron was ten when the siblings' household finally broke up. His sister Ruth went off to the University of Wisconsin and then to medical school. His younger brother Benjamin left for San Francisco to live there with a recently married aunt. Daniel's elder brother David and sister Judith returned to Chicago where both enrolled in the University of Chicago. Two years later, Daniel was installed in his sister's apartment near the university and committed to the care of an elderly housekeeper. He finished grammar school and entered Hyde Park High School. "Those were miserable years," Aaron remembered. He disliked his school and found Chicago ugly and its inhabitants aggressive. In California he had known few material worries and had taken no notice of class or ethnic differences. In Chicago, however, these differences were forced on his attention. His movements were restricted because some of the city's neighborhoods were dangerous.

It hardly consoled Aaron that his sister, who kept a sharp eye on her kid brother, allowed him to buy one book a week at a large bookstore on Michigan Avenue. Aaron was not stinted for books; his parents had been avid readers and owned a library "well stocked with sets of standard authors." Reading had been a family pastime, so Aaron simply read whatever came along, from *Famous Men of Greece* to Zane Grey's *The Lone Star Ranger*. The authors of novels he devoured, referred to as "trash" by his elders, presented a nasty underside of America that Aaron thought as unreal as the Emerald City: "Most of these writers were shameless racists, inveterate glorifiers of Anglo-Saxon blood. To them all Mexicans were 'greasers,' Jews invariably 'little' and abominable, any persons east of Calais 'niggers.' But I can't say their ugly biases affected me in the slightest."[7]

Despite the indications of loss and sadness, Aaron asserts that he grew up comfortably, fitting into his "local brier patch as naturally as Brer Rabbit did into his. I remember thinking, 'You are Daniel Aaron, a character in the neighborhood' " (*AN* x). In Chicago he enjoyed the pastimes and endured the pains of adolescence, spent summers in boys' camps or taking canoe trips in northern Wisconsin. He befriended the curator of prints at the Art Institute and an employee at the bookstore on Michigan Avenue, where he would go once a week for his book.

Although Aaron and his older siblings lived on their own during the second half of the Roaring Twenties, their uncle Charles tried not to neglect his duties as guardian. He hired their housekeeper and himself lived near their place with his mother. She led an observant Jewish life, having retained the ritual practices of her youth; since these had never been explained to Aaron, his grandmother seemed "bizarre and strange" to the boy (interview). Aaron had no feelings at all for her Judaism, but he tried to please her. He was more assertive vis-à-vis his uncle, whose criticism of his lackluster high school performance he rather resented. His uncle's influence was curbed somewhat when Aaron's eldest sister drove out the housekeeper and took over the management of the Aaron family ménage. She was about to complete her bachelor's degree, and since everyone was absorbed in social life or work, there was no one to monitor Aaron's schoolwork. He did pretty much as he pleased. Through his sister he encountered many free spirits from the university.

One of them, a young medical intern, took him in hand, after Aaron had expressed an interest in becoming a doctor. Together they went to the anatomy lab, where cadavers were being dissected, and watched a series of operations in Cook County Hospital. What Aaron saw did not entice him to enter medicine, but that he went along was typical for him: Aaron would never be one to say no when an experience was to be had. He became an observer and connoisseur of American life early on.

Although the University of Chicago was a good place for Jews during the 1920s, Aaron chose not to attend his sister's school.[8] Instead, he enrolled at the University of Michigan and moved to Ann Arbor in September 1929, when he had just turned seventeen. His tuition was paid for by his guardian, and he received an allowance that permitted him to indulge his tastes and curiosities. He barely noticed the Great Crash in October. "I can remember asking one of my younger uncles, does it look bad? And he said, yes it does. But it didn't affect me at all" (interview). The young man was practiced at building defenses. His uncle Charles lost heavily in the Depression. On the other side of the tracks, in the Jewish Chicago evoked in Meyer Levin's classic novel *The Old Bunch,* things looked grim indeed:

> The Sixteenth Street Savings Bank was a cheesy little neighborhood bank where a lot of old Jews, actually old Yids with beards, kept their few dollars; and when it went bust, of course Droopy Meisel had to have his total savings there. It was only about eighteen dollars in an Xmas Savings Account, but he felt as if the whole thing had been done against him.
>
> What was the use of scroining away his lunch and carfare money when the bank lost it for him? He could just as well lose it for himself.[9]

That was the sort of world Aaron had little knowledge of. He continued to live a sheltered life. At the University of Michigan he withdrew into an imaginative realm of his own construction, "literary England, and the 'Europe' evoked by James Gibbons Huneker. Huneker, Mencken's mentor, had long been out of fashion when I first read him in 1929 . . . and became his acolyte. His enthusiasm for what he called the 'soul wreckers' infected me. I stuccoed my secret journal with quotations from Schopenhauer, Leopardi, Strindberg, Huysmans, Nietzsche, and Dostoevsky" (*AN* x). Huneker offered a comprehensive if not always entirely reliable guide to the literature of the European *décadence* that had enthralled the young of the leisure class around the turn of the century. Although it was a bit late in the day for a new crop of dandies, a "group of bohemian types, very contemptuous of the kind of middle-class respectability that Michigan students had" did emerge on the Ann Arbor campus (interview). To divert themselves, the young men went slumming in Detroit. The city was racked by poverty and violence. "Detroit was a ghastly place. It was a huge factory. People had to scramble around to survive" (interview). For the middle class there was the Detroit Symphony Orchestra, which Daniel Aaron would go to hear. Its conductor at the time was Ossip Gabrilowitsch, whose wife was the daughter of Mark Twain. But even the kindly disposed Howard Mumford Jones, soon to be Aaron's mentor, found Gabrilowitsch to be "a conductor with a timid beat and utterly conventional tastes." [10]

There was very little in Michigan to draw Aaron out. "Still self-cocooned" (AN x), he graduated in 1933 and went back to Chicago. Coming home to a city marred with breadlines and ravaged by years of economic decline upset him greatly. In fact, returning to Chicago in the summer of 1933 repeated the shock of 1924. It caused the first cracks to appear in the protective shell Aaron had been constructing around himself since childhood. His wish, at that point, to become a newspaperman, whose job it was to find out as much as he could about real life, indicated an awakening, and perhaps a desire to move on from voyeurism to investigation. For the time being, however, Aaron was forced to remain a spectator. He took scientific German at the University of Chicago and went to radical meetings of various kinds in the city. "I thought it was very outlandish. I had nothing in common with the people that went there. All kinds of odd people came that I never associated with socially. I think throughout my so-called radical days there seemed to me something strange and almost comical about radicals" (interview). When no job materialized in Chicago, Aaron went off to Harvard knowing little about America and its societal structure and even less about himself.

His first two years at Harvard taught him a surprising fact, that "my name and ancestry stamped me as a hyphenate" (ANms). Aaron was never one to react immediately to a disturbance; even as a child he tended "to conceal and cover up" (interview), while as an adult he developed "an inclination to register emotional perturbations through political symbols" (AN xii). What this means, Aaron explains, is "that you don't directly face what's troubling you; you project it onto something else" (interview). Upon his return from Harvard to the University of Michigan in the fall of 1935, Aaron, who had been proud of not having read an American book in college, began to study American history and took a course on American literature with Howard Mumford Jones. The encounter with Jones and his subject turned out to be Aaron's great good fortune.

Howard Mumford Jones, a native of Michigan, had become an Americanist by accident rather than intent. He had graduated from the University of Wisconsin in 1914 and then gone on to the University of Chicago, where he received his master's degree in 1915 for a translation of Heinrich Heine's epic cycle *Die Nordsee*. For the next nine years Jones taught comparative literature (including English and American fiction) at southern and western universities, was married to a difficult Montana girl (from 1918 to 1925), and struggled to write his dissertation. Since he was still "in the grip of the conventional Ph.D. syndrome," he did not realize "the vast potentialities latent in the story of Western development, or, for that matter, in American development as a whole" (*Au* 113). He focused instead on "the slow adaptation of Old World assumptions to a New World setting." [11]

Jones presented his dissertation to the University of Chicago in 1924 and was told, much to his dismay, that he would have to do more course work to earn his degree. Jones was then thirty-two years old, with a wife and child to look after, and could hardly afford to go back to school. He revised his thesis and offered it to the University of North Carolina Press, which published it in 1927 as *America and French Culture*. A year later Jones contributed translations to *The Romanesque Lyric: Studies in Its Background and Development from Petronius to the Cambridge Songs, 50–1050,* and wrote "The European Background" for *The Reinterpretation of American Literature* (1928), one of the founding documents of American studies, urging scholars to overcome the fragmentation of academic disciplines. In 1929, Jones edited a volume of Poe's poetry and received a job offer from the University of Michigan, which he happily accepted. He began to teach there in the fall of 1930, offering courses on British and American literature. But gradually he realized, as he said before the National Council of Teachers of English in 1935, that the English literary tradition may not be of such great interest to American students whose ancestry reached back to countries other than England. His words fell on deaf ears. Jones was fifty years ahead of his colleagues.

Divorced in 1925, Jones remarried in 1927. His second wife, Bessie Zaban, born in Atlanta, Georgia, was the daughter of Jewish immigrants. She had graduated from the University of Chicago in 1923 and introduced her husband to what he called "the glorious and generous-hearted Jewish community that in the twenties occupied apartment houses in the Hyde Park district of Chicago. For me, at least, the life of this community was a revelation of what civilized behavior could demand and be." Jones marveled at his being taken in by that community "without a shadow of discrimination" (*Au* 130). This remark, like his presentation to the English teachers, showed Jones's ability to imagine the "other's" point of view.

With his tenure at Michigan, Jones moved deeper into American history and literature. Although the Guggenheim Fellowship he received in 1932 was for research on the Irishman Thomes Moore, Jones did not pass up the opportunity to examine a vast collection of pamphlets about seventeenth-and eighteenth-century America he discovered at the Huntington Library in California. He used his notes to prepare a number of articles, such as "The Drift to Liberalism in the American Eighteenth Century" (1936). Jones could hardly know that this was the best preparation for an encounter with his formidable future colleagues Kenneth Murdock, F. O. Matthiessen, and Perry Miller. It was this man, Jones, a seasoned but kind-hearted scholar of enormous learning, whom Aaron adopted as his "surrogate father" in 1935 (interview). Aaron had put his bet on the right man. In 1936, Jones received an honorary doctorate from Harvard University. The citation, read at the Harvard Tercentenary celebration, was not only apt, it also contained the rationale for a new humanities program that President Conant was about to announce. The Harvard worthies called Jones "an American writer and scholar whose critical study of our literature assists the country to appraise justly its own culture" (*Au* 183). In order to help Harvard students to do precisely that, and so to increase their resistance to fascist and communist agitators, Conant offered Jones a professorship at a staggering ten thousand dollars a year, and a share in the responsibility of building up an interdepartmental American Civilization program. Jones accepted, and Aaron, who wanted to go with Jones, volunteered as guinea pig in the program. In the fall of 1936, Aaron was back at Harvard and roomed again with Finch. But everything else was different. The next three years, possibly the most important years in Aaron's life, were filled to the brim with people and events. In those years the foundation for all of Aaron's future scholarship was being laid.

Graduate Studies at Harvard

Between 1936 and 1939 the atmosphere in Harvard Yard changed profoundly. The "large contingent of Old Harvard and Old Boston" (interview), whose unostentatious but firm dominance Aaron had still felt in 1933, was, if not quite dethroned, at least displaced from the center of Harvard life. Carl Schorske, who graduated from Columbia College in 1936 and came to Harvard as a graduate student in history that fall, described how what remained of Old Harvard was perceived by outsiders:

> On the one hand . . . we knew it was a rich man's school. From my own high school in Scarsdale . . . people who wanted to go to Harvard went away to prep school to be sure they got in, even during the depression. The sense we had of it was that this was . . . where the *real* social upper crust went. When I visited the place . . . I found [that] Harvard was indeed as socially tony as our mythology had had it. . . . On the other hand, we thought of Harvard as a place where tremendously serious work was done by students. If they wanted to do it, they were protected. There were no noon rallies to distract them. There was none of that political excitement which . . . I so loved at Columbia; but then as a Harvard student, one would not be continually interfered with in one's studies. It just didn't seem from the outside that much politics was going on there.[12]

Schorske noted three forces of change at Harvard: the professionalization of academic studies in the humanities by a new crop of scholars not trained at Harvard; the influx of a new type of student, often descended from immigrant parents, raised unequivocally as American, but without regional allegiances; and the politicization of campus life, which attracted and affected old New Englanders as much as newcomers and created a common ground between old-stock and new-stock Americans in a shared concern for the improvement of America and world society. These three elements—professionalization, diversification, and a brief period of radicalization—caused changes in the style of social interaction, classroom behavior, and self-perception of faculty and students in the humanities in general, but particularly in English literary studies.

The new interdepartmental program in American Civilization, which was symptomatic of that change, was considered a "disturber of the peace" by old-style English professors. They thought the program "diffuse and sentimental, or chauvinistic and grandiose in its expectations, or simply 'unsound' " (*AN* xi). Perhaps it was all of the above, but it proved ideal for Daniel Aaron.

In the summer of 1936, Jones had suggested a dissertation topic to Aaron: a cultural history of the Ohio Valley in the 1830s and 1840s.

Jones advised Aaron that such a study would have to touch on "the coming in of schools and lyceums, of architecture and painting, of the introduction of religion and politics in that region" (*AN* xiii). Aaron balked; he knew that Jones loved surveys of that kind and that his perspective on America was in a peculiar way European, not so much because Jones followed too closely Tocqueville's lead but because, like many early Americanists, he tended to derive his categories of evaluation from Europe. Jones's point of view was that of a cultural comparatist rather than that of an Americanist, as Aaron very well knew, since he and Jones had cooperated on a paper called "Notes on the Napoleonic Legend in America," published in the *Franco-American Review* in the summer of 1937. If Aaron wanted to come to grips with his country, which would include making an effort to understand the rebuff he had suffered during his first stay at Harvard, he would have to focus his research more closely than Jones had done on America and embark on "a coordinated study of American history and literature, of American religion, education, and political thought" (*AN* x).

Harvard was a good place to begin at the beginning. With Kenneth Murdock, Aaron read the sermons of seventeenth- and eighteenth-century New England divines, and with Perry Miller he explored the world of Puritan concepts and doctrines that went into the making of the peculiar Boston world Aaron had encountered in 1933. He began to see connections between the style and dignity he had observed in the offices of the *New England Quarterly,* and in its editor Stewart Mitchell, and the principled discipline in the literature of the local forebears. "I began to have a feeling for certain qualities of the New England mind, particularly for the idea of responsibility and stewardship. I learned it as much from Murdock and Miller as from the general ambience here" (interview). With greater knowledge came greater self-esteem and the insight that one could become a steward only if one had taken possession of a region. Under the tutelage of Jones and Harvard's younger scholars, Aaron started the process of acquisition. "Digging for ore in the Americana mine gave me, son of immigrants, a proprietorial feeling toward my country and its institutions" *(ANms)*.

Aaron's efforts were rewarded by his appointment to an unexpected "stewardship" that opened the doors of Harvard to him. As he recalled it, a message came from the office of President Conant on Quincy Street, summoning him. Conant greeted him in the most genteel New England manner, "Mr. Aaron, how kind of you to come see me." Handling the conversation as if president and graduate student were simply meeting to chat as gentlemen, Conant told Aaron that Harvard was embarking on a new extracurricular experiment. Harvard undergraduates were deplorably ignorant of American history and culture and the basic institutions of their country. Hence the university wanted to appoint a counselor for the freshman class who would not only be available for consultation, but would also conduct meetings, invite speakers, and preside over an American Civilization table in the Freshman Union dining room. It would please him very much, Conant said, if Aaron accepted the counselorship. "Needless to say, I accepted this offer with alacrity" (interview). His new position integrated Aaron into the world of the college. As counselor in American Civilization, Aaron moved from the fringe, to which he had found himself relegated as a graduate student, into the center of the university.

Aaron's task was to instruct Harvard freshmen about the history, literature, and destiny of their country, a subject that only three years earlier he had known nothing about. But by the time of his appointment in 1937, Aaron had mastered enough of the material to be able to make specific choices among the traditions America had to offer. In opposition to the leftist cosmopolitan ideologies that began to float around on campus in the 1930s, Aaron sketched his own social and political model in a 1937 journal entry. "It would be America-centered, at once ethical and pragmatic, disciplined and free. It would fuse the discrete and often mutually repellent strains in American political thought" (*AN* xii). In a recent essay Aaron marveled at his youthful eclecticism. "How I intended to amalgamate and reconcile the Puritan concept of stewardship, Franklin's civic spirit, Tom Paine's anticlericalism, the conservatism of Madison, Tocqueville, and James Fenimore Cooper, the social theories of communitarian experimenters, Thoreau's principled anarchism, Whitman's universalism, industrial unionism, and Vernon L. Parrington's progressivism I have no idea" (*AN* xii).

Although Aaron taught nothing outlandish and held views that combined various elements of the American mainstream, his office in the Yard "turned out to be a place where all the misfits came; none or very few of them had gone to private schools." Harvard people, Aaron observed, "would not be caught dead [in American studies]. They made a great distinction between greasy people who did that sort of thing and themselves" (interview). Aaron noticed that many of the students he counseled came from the Midwest, sometimes from modest backgrounds. While his table in the Freshman Union was slighted by the established and select, "the lost, the people who didn't fit in, just found it a place to go" (interview). At Harvard Aaron himself occupied an odd social position; he was poised on the outside of the inside. This perch agreed with him and he would re-create it with relish throughout his professional life.

Aaron's involvement in American Civilization also propelled him into Harvard's academic circles. He began to write reviews for the *New England Quarterly* and the *Boston Evening Transcript;* he visited with the Murdocks and spent weekends with Perry Miller, with whom he shared a tenuous Chicago connection. In addition, Aaron hosted a serious Marxist study group in his apartment that attracted all sorts of people, among them Harry Levin and Daniel Boorstin. At the same time, however, he was poking fun at the Communists and their party jargon with his friend John Finch. By 1938, Aaron, now married to a young woman who had been born and bred in Cambridge, was securely part of Harvard life. "You begin to write," Aaron explained, "you begin to be invited to talk, and you get into the general swim of things" (interview).

Meanwhile Aaron worked hard toward his degree. In 1937 he was joined by Henry Nash Smith, his senior by five years. Smith had graduated from Southern Methodist University in 1925 and then pursued a year of graduate work at Harvard. He had returned to Dallas in 1927 and subsequently taught at SMU for ten years. But the American Civilization program drew him back to Harvard. He enrolled in 1937 and took his degree as the first graduate of the program in 1940. During the academic year 1938–39, Aaron and Smith met once a day to work together in preparation for their final exams in the summer of 1939. A fascinating result of their labors was a coauthored article entitled "Recent Works on the Social History of the United States, 1935–1939." It documented crisply the impending shift of American studies from an excessive indebtedness to Parrington toward historians and critics who were, as Jones put it, less "blind to aesthetic charm." [13]

Parrington's *Main Currents in American Thought* had dominated American studies since its publication in 1927. The first two volumes won the Pulitzer Prize in 1928; Parrington died in 1929, and a third volume appeared posthumously in 1930. It was a passionate retort to the German notion that a historian ought to be an impartial collector of data; and it was, as the native Midwesterner cheerfully confessed, intended as a "calculated revolt against the intellectual dominion so long exercised by Harvard College." Parrington had disliked Harvard intensely during his two years of graduate work there (1891–93). He conceived *Main Currents in American Thought* during his tenure at the University of Oklahoma, which ended when he was dismissed in 1908 on the grounds of being a morally permissive instructor who condoned smoking and dancing. Parrington moved on to the University of Washington, where he felt very much at home and began productive work on his magnum opus, savoring the notion, as Henry Commager put it, that "Cambridge was as far from Seattle as Seattle from Cambridge." *Main Currents* was a fiery though neatly dialectical work in which Parrington reviewed the major battles of American intellectual history and gleefully took sides. In his narrative, Puritan theocracy lost to Independence, Old World tyranny to New World liberty; federalism was pitted against republicanism, slavery against freedom, frontier against seaboard, agrarianism against capitalism, and labor against industry.[14]

As a student of Murdock, Miller, and Matthiessen, Aaron naturally did not care for "Parrington's reductive anti-Puritanism" or his "arbitrary separation of American writers into good Jeffersonian sheep and bad Hamiltonian goats;" yet he subscribed "wholeheartedly to his political philosophy and contextualizing of literature" (*AN* xv–xvi). Although Aaron eventually rejected Parrington's simplistic dichotomies, he retained two of Parrington's ideas throughout his career. One was the view that literature (understood to include not only belles lettres but also theology, economics, law, politics, and journalism) mirrored the American mind; the other was the conviction that America had a native radical tradition (made up of Protestants, rebels, and progressives) that provided a more relevant analysis of the ills of American society than the imported ideas of Marx and Lenin. The latter view provided the seed for Aaron's first published book, *Men of Good Hope* (1951).

In their 1939 review, Aaron and Smith praised Frederick Jackson Turner's "study of sectional tensions, and Charles A. Beard's analysis of class struggles" because their works "had the effect of directing attention to a wide range of materials that historians of an earlier day had neglected. . . . The common man, whether on a Midwestern farm or a city streetcorner, was recognized as a factor to be reckoned with. . . ." Parrington, by contrast, they found appealing because he demonstrated "the close relation between literary expression and social and economic conditions." In the same vein they commended Newton Arvin's *Whitman* (1938) because "brilliantly written, and by no means devoid of critical judgments, this book is nevertheless symptomatic of the recent tendency in American literary studies to abandon an exclusively esthetic emphasis in order to consider American writers in terms of the social environments in which they moved."[15]

Although Aaron and Smith applauded the new trend, their attitude toward the aesthetic was much more complicated than they were willing to admit. In F. O. Matthiessen's lectures, for instance, Aaron witnessed, as he observed in his 1942 review of *American Renaissance,* how "Mr. Matthiessen's comments on language and style, in addition to being discerning as criticism, become finally profound reflections on 19th Century American society." It was Matthiessen's gift of enhancing the historical and social import of a text by bringing into play its aesthetic dimension that made Parrington's shortcomings so obvious. Aaron's review of *American Renaissance,* aptly entitled "Parrington Plus," marked the passing of the old master. "Parrington's neat but cut-and-dried pronouncements," Aaron conceded, "were enormously stimulating; he could portray with brilliance and force a Tom Paine or a Daniel Webster, but in deliberately minimizing aesthetic judgments, he coarsened many of his literary evaluations and blinded himself to less obvious but equally important aspects of our culture." In an exuberant postscript to his review, Aaron suggested that Matthiessen's book epitomized the rationale for Harvard's American Civilization program. He wrote that *American Renaissance* "ought to convince the critic that a knowledge of America, or perhaps I should say, a sympathetic awareness of the American experience, is indispensable for the elucidation of our literary culture, a culture, in Mr. Matthiessen's words, 'whose greatest weakness has continued to be that the so-called educated class knows so little of the country and the people of which it is nominally part.' " While the clubbable elite continued to scoff at the new program, Aaron intensified his commitment to "America and its people." [16]

This was all the more remarkable since the program, paradoxically, attracted all sorts of radical instructors whose orientation was internationalist rather than American. The best known of them was Granville Hicks. He was a member of the Communist Party (1933–39), the literary editor of the *New Masses* since 1934, and the author of a biography of John Reed (1936). Hicks was a Harvard graduate (1923), the recipient of a Guggenheim Fellowship (1935–36), and an astute critic of American literature. These things cut little ice, however, with the outraged local newspapers when they learned in April 1937 that Harvard had the audacity to offer Hicks a position as "Counsellor in the extracurricular reading of American history." [17] But as always when attacked from the outside, Harvard stuck to its candidate, and Hicks arrived on campus in the fall of 1937. The Harvard counsellorship in American Civilization was Hicks's first academic position in three years. The time of his appointment coincided with the period of his deepest commitment to communism. Hicks was then at work on a book entitled *I Like America* (1938), which Daniel Aaron described as "a soft-spoken and amiable declaration of independence in the old reformist vein; it is grass-roots Marxism, an argument for the progressive verities: justice, equality, opportunity"; and it was the "only book [by Hicks] the party made a serious effort to circulate." [18]

For Aaron the arrival of Hicks in Cambridge meant an addition to his circle of personal friends and led to a crystallization of his radical activities. Aaron was intrigued by Hicks. He accompanied him to a debate with Father Francis Curran, Boston's version of Detroit's fascist radio-priest, Father Coughlin, invited him to guide the "ad hoc Sumner Road seminar through the mysteries of the Marxist Handbook," [19] and visited Hicks in his home in Grafton, New York. In his autobiography Hicks recorded such a visit in December 1937:

> Robert [Gorham] Davis arrived with Dan and Janet Aaron, and then John Strachey [author of *The Coming Struggle for Power* and a well-known British Marxist] came from New York. . . . The evening before Strachey was to leave Ollie [Birk], deciding that there should be a special entertainment, volunteered to do a strip tease. . . . Dan was instructed to prepare a poem to accompany the process of disrobing. Robert, John, and I were banished to the study. . . . [t]owards midnight we were summoned. [Ollie] stood in front of the fireplace, slowly removing her clothes while Dan chanted a mock heroic ode on the class struggle. She was a doll, and when at last she was reduced to an approximation of what would today be called a bikini, Strachey cried, "Oh my God!" (*PT* 168–169)

Aaron liked sophisticated horseplay and had indulged in it as a student with his friends John Finch and Charles Olson. "The Harvard atmosphere, in my case at least," Aaron confessed, "was not conducive to the making of revolutionists. Rather it fostered irreverence." He developed a taste for the writings of e. e. cummings and Nathanael West and a disrespect for the Communist Party. "I realized even then, for I was studying American church history, that to join the Party was the equivalent of joining a church." Heywood Broun, who at the invitation of Archibald MacLeish came up to Harvard to give a talk to the Nieman Fellows, had noticed much the same thing and converted to Catholicism. The choice, he said in Hicks's report of the evening, was between the Communist Party and the Catholic Church, "And the Church has always been easier on backsliders" (*PT* 165). Aaron, by contrast, "felt no doctrinal commitment and wasn't prepared to make a metaphysical leap into faith. So when Granville Hicks hesitantly suggested I do just that, I declined." Hicks was not displeased, as Aaron found out later, since "he himself was trembling on the edge of apostasy." Shortly after the nonaggression and trade pacts between the Soviet Union and Nazi Germany were announced on August 23, 1939, Hicks resigned from the Communist Party. A wave of disillusionment was sweeping through the American radical scene and transformed it thoroughly.[20]

In the fall of 1939 having passed his exams in American Civilization but not yet written his dissertation, Aaron left Harvard for a teaching position at Smith College, his academic base for the next thirty years. It was at Smith, really, that Aaron honed his writing skills and developed into an "observer and reporter, something of a social historian and literary critic, and academic scholar and journalist but not an originator or spearheader of movements or hot activist" *(ANms)*.

Scholarship

Although written over a period of five decades, Daniel Aaron's work shows a remarkable intellectual consistency, which is not a euphemism for narrowness or high specialization. On the contrary, Aaron's books, essays, and reviews cover a vast number of American writers from the eighteenth to the twentieth century and tackle a broad array of issues. Aaron produced one book at the beginning of each decade, which one might be tempted to regard as his programmatic statement about the tasks of the intellectual in the period ahead. His numerous shorter works are not only scholarly contributions to American literary history, but also a running commentary on the contemporary political and intellectual scene.[21]

Aaron's style is lucid and swift, even crisp and journalistic at times. Aaron rarely uses metaphors, and when he does, they surprise. In 1953 he wrote about Emerson and Henry Adams: "Both men are splendid and formidable Goliaths struck down by the stone of principle." What Aaron had liked about Parrington, the art of portraiture in words, he perfected and took one step further by making many of his sketches double portraits. In 1963 he observed Walt Whitman through the eyes of Paul Elmer More: "How testily he approaches this (to More) dirty, garrulous, half-educated loafer, touched with insincerity and 'speaking in the patois of the pavement.' Yet despite his irritation and even disgust with Whitmanism, the critic triumphs over the prig." And in 1967, Aaron tartly depicted James Russell Lowell: "An exact contemporary of Melville (whom he missed entirely despite friendships they had in common) and of Whitman (whose muse he mistook for a strumpet), Lowell is often presented as their stuffy antithesis, nurtured by an indulgent society, applauded by uncritical friends and rewarded far beyond his deserts." [22]

The example concerning Whitman and More conveys yet another quality of Aaron's writing. It is seldom judgmental, but Aaron loves to take on men of strong (preferably unfashionable) opinions, slip into their minds, and sketch the world from their vantage points. This method is a variant of Aaron's favored perspective, that of an observer perched on the outskirts of the inside. This position allows him to illuminate the absurdities of a world that appears all too reasonable when seen from within the whirl of the mainstream, and to tint with an appealing glow the weirdest men, whom we might otherwise have written off as cranks. Throughout his career, but particularly during the 1940s, Aaron was "alert to the signs of social and intellectual disorder and fascinated by writers who concealed cheerless messages in harshly comic wrappings" (*AN* xv). In later decades he could dispense with the comedy. It is not accidental, Aaron wrote in 1993, "that so much of my writing is about rebels, reformers, and dissenters" (*AN* xi). He had made a similar observation some thirty years earlier but had not bothered to look into the reasons. "What drives [a historian] to choose a man, a period, an event is an inner necessity of which he may very likely be unaware." [23] Aaron's essays are not overtly self-reflective in the manner of academic criticism today; hence they are rarely self-conscious.

Aaron's unselfconsciousness squared well with his notion of the historian. "Ideally," Aaron wrote in 1965, "the historian should always be *in* history, so steeped and soaked in it that for short periods he loses his own identity" (*AN* 15). This technique of immersion—which ends orphanhood and starts the process of sprouting roots—became Aaron's favored "expository method." It was a way of inserting himself into American culture. Immersion creates a home for the mind. In 1972, Aaron conceded that William Phillips had been right when he had criticized *Writers on the Left* for reliving rather than reexamining or rethinking the period of literary communism. This was due to his expository method, Aaron explained, his "trick of paraphrasing the views of his subjects, major and minor, as if he had entered into their minds and was speaking in their behalf. Hence ideological and literary fatuities

were set down most of the time without explicit authorial comment." [24]
A good example of Aaron's method is the portrait of Whitman perceived
through the eyes of Paul Elmer More. Aaron, we know from other
essays, did not think of Whitman as a dirty, garrulous loafer; More
did. Without the parenthesis, added as an afterthought, perhaps at the
suggestion of an editor, the reader could not be sure whose point of
view Aaron is presenting, whether More's or his own. Aaron simply
disappears inside More, whose voice cloaks and muffles Aaron's.

It is tempting but too pat to call this expository method assimilationist
or integrationist. Although Aaron considered the integration of diverse
elements America's supreme social goal, he himself did not like to be
swallowed up so easily. He wanted his writings to be fishbones in America's throat. Aaron's technique reflects a deliberate commitment to and a
conscious investment of himself in America (preferably via men who
kept a critical distance from the mainstream). The word *investment* here
is chosen carefully because its etymological root reminds us of the fact
that authority was conferred by enveloping a person in the cloak *(vestis)*
of his office. That is, the individual was effaced in the execution of the
task for which he or she had been appointed. Similarly Aaron slipped
into the cloak of his office by enveloping himself in the voices of the
American intellectuals who speak in and through his essays. Increasingly
familiar with the American literary scene, Aaron intensified his expository method over the years. It reached its climax and fulfillment in his
edition of the Inman diary in 1985. "This is really my novel," he remarked in a conversation. And a bizarre novel it is—part elegy, part
tragicomedy. That Aaron never pushed his expository method over the
critical edge, say, into the realm of fiction, was due to what he called his
"greed for facts" (interview). He began his career uncharacteristically,
with a book not focused on people but on a city—a city, moreover, that
he had never visited and that, biographically, meant nothing to him.

Cincinnati, Queen of the West was published fifty years after the manuscript was presented to a committee of Harvard professors as a dissertation in the American Civilization program in 1942. The thesis was
accepted without enthusiasm, and one professor, Aaron suspected, "regarded it as an object lesson of what can happen when disciplinary
frontiers are willfully breached" (*AN* xiii). For his thesis Aaron had pared
down Jones's first suggestion to study "the inter-action of indigenous
seaboard and European elements in the Ohio Valley region in the 1830's
and 1840's" to a study of Cincinnati between 1819 and 1838, dates that
marked the onset of financial panics. Aaron's approach is pro-Tocqueville

in its emphasis on the cooperative spirit and on the pragmatic aspects of democracy, and anti-Turner in its emphasis on the similarities between frontier Midwesterners and other Americans. Far more significant, however, than the difference between East and West, in Aaron's view, was the difference between city and countryside. "Indeed, as early as the 1820s many Cincinnati citizens resembled Philadelphians or Bostonians more closely than they did the farmers in the neighboring counties—and rejoiced in the fact." The gap between East and Midwest was narrowed by a self-conscious effort on the part of Cincinnatians that contrasted sharply with the exodus of the young elite from Chicago a century later as described by William McNeill. "Men and women in this so-called assertive and unconventional western city," Aaron wrote, "had eyes cocked toward the East; aped eastern manners, culture, and ideas; and were keenly sensitive to any criticism which suggested an absence of gentility and decorum." Migration from East to West facilitated the leveling of differences so that eventually "the Cincinnati merchant or lawyer transplanted to Boston would have felt only slightly out of place, even less out of place in Philadelphia. His politics and his religion, his tastes and aversions were not materially different from those of his eastern countrymen." [25] Given the cultural context in which Aaron wrote his dissertation and the substantial evidence of New England snobbery toward men from the Midwest, keenly felt on first coming to Harvard by Babbitt and Levin, Jones and Aaron, the minimizing of cultural difference between East and West in Aaron's thesis was a bold counterstatement. [26] It also reflected Aaron's dislike of splitting the country into regions, a dislike that extended equally to the self-segregation of ethnic groups and cultures within the United States.

Reading one's way through Aaron's Cincinnati, re-created compellingly from nineteenth-century documents, has a curious effect. In the end one discovers that one actually loves this city just as one loves Leopold Bloom's Dublin, which likewise one may have never seen. It was this study of Cincinnati, the intensive engagement with one particular city and its inhabitants, that sealed Aaron's unequivocal commitment to America. With the possession of knowledge, a proprietary attitude toward his country took hold of him, and with appropriation came a sense of responsibility. It is hardly surprising, then, that Aaron ended his dissertation with a chapter on the men and women who considered the status quo intolerable and reforms necessary. At political meetings in Chicago in 1933, Aaron had been struck by the fact that there was something quite outlandish and almost comical about radicals; in his dissertation he re-created the sense of amazement, alienation, and undisguised horror that traditional Cincinnati citizens must have felt at the sight of reformers descending in swarms upon the Queen City.

Aaron had a good deal of sympathy for "the wicked sorcerers," as John P. Foote called them, "the men and women who sought to crack the cornerstones of the state: private property, the home, and the church; who imputed social evils to environment rather than to the human heart; and who supported organizations of laborers." They were strong, independent, interestingly nutty, and they "caught a glimpse of the reality behind the appearances and were not beguiled by the myth of economic equality." To Aaron the appeal of the nineteenth-century reformers increased to the degree that the radical movement in his own time disintegrated. Aaron had never liked the idea of a dictatorship of the proletariat and was looking for an alternative model, a communitarian-minded grass-roots movement composed of individual reformers and radical idealists that would point precisely and insistently to the areas in American life that needed mending. "I had a great desire," Aaron wrote, "to locate in American social history the roots of a national radical tradition." [27]

That desire had its origins neither in discontent nor in youthful radicalism, but in a principle that Aaron had first encountered in the world of the Boston Brahmins and traced back to the Puritans: the concept of stewardship. It derived from a passage in Genesis (1:26–28) that describes God's appointment of Adam as steward over the earth, the plants and animals, but also indicates that dominion is granted temporarily and provisionally. The privilege of possession comes with the obligation to treat well what has been entrusted to one's care, since all possession is only a loan. Among Boston Brahmins privilege ideally entailed responsibility for the underprivileged. To this tradition Aaron responded. As a new proprietor of a share in America he was concerned, in the ways available to a scholar, about the country's flaws and interested in righting the imbalance of social injustice. The last chapter of his thesis presented the views and causes of social reformers as well as a description of the dire situation of African Americans and the struggle of Cincinnati's abolitionists. This double focus pointed to the future direction of Aaron's work: the discovery of an indigenous radical tradition and, enacting that tradition, the uncovering of America's darkest spots, the wounds inflicted by lack of proper stewardship.

In 1951, Aaron published a description of what he believed to be America's very own radical tradition. He wrote *Men of Good Hope: A Story of American Progressivism* "in the belief that the idealistic and ethical concerns of the old progressives are essential to any liberal movement." [28] He was convinced that the liberal community either disdained or had forgotten its roots. Aaron's undertaking was less a resurrection of neglected idealists than a re-creation of a movement never known. His book put progressivism on the map and made it available as a cultural phenomenon. Aaron's definition of the key term is fundamental to perceiving the unity of the book, which consisted of nine separate portraits.

> By "progressivism" I mean a social philosophy that derived in part from Jeffersonian ideas about popular government, the pursuit of happiness, and the fulfillment of human potentialities, and in part from an unorthodox Protestant Christianity more urgent and more fiercely evangelical than the bland reasonableness of the Enlightenment. As I see it, progressivism was born at that moment in our history when a moral and righteous minority began to observe the social ravages produced by the industrial age and to protest against what they felt was the betrayal of the republican ideal.
>
> What distinguished the progressives from the extremists was their unwillingness to detach themselves from those elements in society they wished to reform. Their program was conservative in the sense that it sought to retain the social patterns of an agrarian democracy with its emphasis upon equality and human worth. The prospect of a stratified society alarmed them. Throughout their lives they envisaged a kind of democracy in which a man would not be snared by institutions and where, to quote one of them, "the least individual shall have his rights acknowledged, and the means and opportunities for the fullest expansion of his faculties guaranteed." They differed widely in their policies and attitudes (their political and economic views ranged from the moderate to the radical), but all agreed that whatever form society took, the proper concern of government, as Emerson said, was the care and culture of men. (*MGH* xi–xii)

In Aaron's view the progressives were people who took the stewardship principle seriously and understood it to confer on the privileged a responsibility for the welfare of the less fortunate. The progressives assembled in Aaron's book were indeed a motley lot. Emerson and Theodore Parker were included as precursors; Henry George, Edward

Bellamy, Henry Demarest Lloyd, William Dean Howells, and Thorstein Veblen made up the bulk of "prophetic agitators"; while Theodore Roosevelt and Brooks Adams brought up the rear as latter-day progressives.

Aaron presents these men as precursors of contemporary liberals but some of them profoundly and vociferously despised certain segments of humanity. Aaron knew that but he did not give it much play. About the antislavery agitator Theodore Parker Aaron wrote: "[H]is provincialism in no sense invalidates his charges against slavery as a system any more than does his personal, almost physical distaste of Negroes as individuals. It was typical of Parker that he could risk his life and liberty to rescue a fugitive slave and at the same time refer to the Negro as an 'equatorial grasshopper' " (*MGH* 47). This happens to be one of Parker's more printable pronouncements. Parker disliked Jews just as much as African Americans, and what he had to say about Jews makes Santayana's insinuations look pale in comparison.[29]

Another interesting case is Brooks Adams. He was preoccupied with America's past and future economic development. It did not prove conducive to level-headed analysis that Brooks, like his brother Henry, "attributed to international finance an almost occult energy and pervasiveness that hardly differed from the fantasies of the primitive Populists they ridiculed." One is not surprised to find "the Jew" implicated in Brooks Adams's economic world conspiracy. He developed the concept of the "gold-bug," an amalgam of plutocrats, bankers, and Jews. It was "the quintessence of everything vile and rotten in his generation." After a thorough study of economic history, Brooks wrote to Henry in 1896: "I tell you Rome was a blessed garden of paradise beside the rotten, unsexed, swindling, lying Jews, represented by J. P. Morgan and the gang who have been manipulating our country for the last four years" (*MGH* 259–260). Only the Jews, it seems, could accomplish the feat of being both lecherous (Santayana) and unsexed (B. Adams).[30]

On the other end of the progressive spectrum is Thorstein Veblen, a man Aaron liked and identified with. Born into a consciously Norwegian-American family in 1857, he became an early faculty member of the University of Chicago. But, Aaron claimed, Veblen "remained, in a spiritual sense at least, a hyphenate and a renegade, separated from the place of his origin physically and mentally and yet not at home in the world of the gentile" (*MGH* 211). Aaron read Veblen's famous 1919 essay, "The Intellectual Pre-Eminence of Jews in Modern Europe," autobiographically. Later writings make it clear that Aaron saw aspects of himself in the Jew Veblen described both as the ideal type to propel scientific research and as the epitome of the modern age. Veblen's observations are a far cry from the gold-bug nightmare that haunted Brooks Adams:

> The intellectually gifted Jew is in a peculiarly fortunate position in respect of [the] requisite immunity from the inhibitions of intellectual quietism. But he can come in for such immunity only at the cost of losing his secure place in the scheme of conventions into which he has been born, and at the cost, also, of finding no similarly secure place in that scheme of gentile conventions into which he is thrown. For him as for other men in the like case, the skepticism that goes to make him an effectual factor in the increase and diffusion of knowledge among men involves a loss of that peace of mind that is the birthright of the safe and sane quietist. He becomes a disturber of the intellectual peace, but only at the cost of becoming an intellectual wayfaring man, a wanderer in the intellectual no-man's-land, seeking another place to rest, farther along the road, somewhere over the horizon. They are neither a complaisant nor a contented lot, these aliens of the uneasy feet; but that is, after all, not the point in question.[31]

Veblen's Jews were neither rooted nor religious; this state of intellectual, spiritual, and social orphanhood Veblen considered the precondition for their achievements. He predicted that if the Zionists were granted their wish and established a Jewish homeland, it would mark the end of Jewish preeminence in the world of science. Rootlessness—that is, having escaped the conventions of the tribe and its culture (so Aaron read Veblen)—was conducive to radicalism. This train of thought allowed Aaron to conclude in his 1947 essay on Veblen that "all radicals, in one sense, are out of step with their times" (*MGH* 214). Similarly, Aaron would say about his book: "*Men of Good Hope* was out of tune with the times" (*AN* xix). But, so Aaron's reading of Veblen continued, "the psycho-neurotic or racial factors that alienate a man from the majority will sometimes clarify his vision" (*MGH* 214). And while Veblen had a cranky sort of lucidity, Aaron thought himself clear-eyed about America's problems. Being a lesser satirist than Veblen, however, Aaron contented himself with the resurrection of men he cared for rather than developing reformist schemes of his own.

What had attracted him to the visionary company assembled in *Men of Good Hope* were their literary gifts as much as their moral seriousness and utopian blueprints. As the manuscript was nearing completion,

Aaron noticed that his own radicalism was changing. He was moving away from the bourgeois-baiting of the 1930s and the business-bashing he had indulged in immediately after the war.[32] By the late 1940s, Aaron was "trying to make the case for the Middle Way and its enlightened middle-class promulgators . . . who had written powerfully and wittily on capitalist enterprise" (AN xviii). Esteem for the middle-class was, of course, the American mood during the boom years; and "the middle way," originally a Puritan concept, became a phrase associated in critical circles with Lionel Trilling. Although Trilling was perceived as having sold out to conservatism, Aaron called him an "intelligent and discriminating antiprogressive" and conceded that Trilling's criticism of the progressives had a "real basis" (MGH 302). Despite the changing mood of the times, Aaron still considered himself sufficiently radical to offer his book as a "brief for a liberal politics both pragmatic and visionary" (AN xvii). For its author the book was nothing less than the "native middle-class equivalent" (MGH 297) of an international-minded communism that had fallen into disrepair:

> Today progressivism, properly interpreted, provides a philosophy for America that is deeply radical in its implications, thoroughly rooted in the American experience, and irreconcilably antitotalitarian. It is a humanist philosophy, undisguisedly ethical, riveted to principles. It is not a creed for opportunists, for the politically ambitious, . . . but it is a satisfactory faith . . . for a person who wants to stay on good terms with himself. (MGH 306–307).

Despite this passionate credo, Aaron's appreciation for American conservatism increased, particularly after a year spent as visiting professor in Finland in 1951–52. In Helsinki, Aaron learned to value the bravery of the Finns, and became disgusted with the Soviet Union and its officials after a run-in with a Soviet recruiter.[33] Yet when he returned to the United States, Aaron spoke out against Sen. Joseph McCarthy. In 1954, Clinton Rossiter, a professor of government at Cornell University, invited him to participate in a research project that attempted to measure the extent and clarify the nature of Communist influence on American life. One of the areas to be explored was communism and American literature. Men of Good Hope had demonstrated that Aaron never subscribed to communism but was otherwise perfectly perched to investigate and describe its effects on the intellectual and literary community. In fact, a passage toward the end of Men of Good Hope already contained the findings of Aaron's next book in a nutshell: "The propagation of Marxist ideas invigorated our universities, stimulated scholarship and teaching. If the results were not always good, a large number, if not all, of the novelists, poets, historians, and critics who passed through and out of the communist phase were none the worse for their experiment" (*MGH* 296–297).

Writers on the Left: Episodes in Literary Communism (1961), dedicated to Howard Mumford Jones, became an instant classic. Like *Men of Good Hope,* it put a radical movement on the intellectual map of America and made it available to scholars as a literary phenomenon that had a beginning, a middle, and an end. But unlike progressivism, presented to Americans at a time when they thought they were living in the best possible society, communism contained a set of radical ideas that a new generation of intellectuals wanted to hear about.

Despite its immediate elevation to the status of a classic in literary historiography, *Writers on the Left* is probably the most personal book Aaron would ever write. This is not to say that it was overtly autobiographical in any way. Rather, it was personal in the fashion of Matthiessen's *American Renaissance.* Both studies carved out and defined a literary period, and the ways in which Matthiessen and Aaron re-created and structured their slice of time, whom they chose as representative men and whom they left out, reflected their personal tastes, prejudices, and experiences. In the introduction to a new edition of the book, published in 1992, Alan Wald indicated the shortcomings of *Writers on the Left;* its narrow focus, for instance, that failed to illuminate the participation of women and African Americans in the radical movement. But Wald did not dispute the book's preeminence and right to classical status. Wald, who was born in 1946, was a good judge of the matter, since his own groundbreaking study of the rise and decline of the anti-Stalinist left was enabled by Aaron's book. The difference between Wald and Aaron as historians of the literary left was significant and not purely generational. It is pithily revealed in a sentence in Wald's introduction. Speaking about Aaron's analysis of Granville Hicks, Wald concluded: "Aaron made a convincing case that excessive Soviet influence on U.S. radicals was among the primary causes of the failure of the leftwing literary movement."[34] As a matter of fact, Aaron never believed, as Wald clearly does, that the literary left had a mission or a cause (similar to the progressives) in which it could succeed or fail. Aaron saw the "movement" not as a community but as a motley crowd of individuals. Reflecting on his research for *Writers on the Left,* Aaron wrote in 1966, "my interviews and reading lead me at the same time to a conclusion I cannot document, but which I nevertheless strongly believe, that some writers joined or broke from the movement because of their wives, or for careerist reasons, or because they read their own inner disturbances into the realities of social dislocation. To put it another way, the subject matter of politics (left-wing politics in this case) was often simply the vehicle for nonpolitical emotions and compulsions" (*AN* 13–14).

Moreover, Aaron was not interested in the ideas of communism in the same way that he was interested in the ideas of the progressives. The agonies of the left were to him a kind of theatrical display. Having spent time with literary radicals in the 1930s, he concluded that the espousal of communism by American writers was not anything that would translate into political action and affect domestic social reality; rather, it was an infatuation with a set of powerful ideas enjoyed while it lasted and barely mourned when it came to an end. "From the start," Aaron recalled, "I was less absorbed in the niceties of literary Communism than in the human spectacle—the mix of idealism, dedication, courage, religiosity, self-deception, vanity, and damn foolishness exhibited by the radical brotherhood" (*AN* xxiv).

Writers on the Left was a book about Aaron's elders, about men he knew or almost knew or had gotten to know during his research. Its narrative begins in 1912, the year Aaron was born, and touches on occasions and events Aaron was old enough to remember but had no personal responsibility for, "strikes, trials, elections, marches, riots, the publication of a book, the performance of a play, the disputes of literary factions" (*AN* xxv). In a sense, *Writers on the Left* was an inquiry into a world of possible intellectual fathers. Understandably, then, Aaron was more intrigued by the men themselves than by their ideas. During his research he became "personally involved in the ancient feuds of some of the principal actors," but as was typical for him, he remained perched on the outskirts of the inside. "I did my best to maintain the manner of the detached witness and cultural historian of tragicomic events whose function was to describe and explain, not to take sides and pass judgment" (*AN* xxiv–xxv).

Apart from its unconventional structure and its transgression of the boundaries of traditional scholarship, perhaps the most important and idiosyncratic aspect of *Writers on the Left* was Aaron's effort to locate literary radicalism within the tradition of American dissent. Aaron's second book commenced precisely at the point where the first had ended, with the presidency of Woodrow Wilson. Literary communism was not an un-American activity, but like progressivism it embodied the quintessence of an American tradition: "American literature, for all of its affirmative spirit, is the most searching and unabashed criticism of our national limitations that exists, the product of one hundred and fifty years of quarreling between the writer and his society. . . . Paradoxically, the American writer's running quarrel with his society, his natural inclination to admonish and to castigate in the guise of entertainment, may have sprung as much or more from his identity with that society as from his alienation" (*WL* 1–2).

Writers on the Left was widely reviewed when it came out and triggered an avalanche of mail from readers who had lived through the thirties. Overnight, Aaron became "an expert on the 'Red Decade' and in fact on every aspect of the American dissenting tradition. That I was nothing of the sort didn't stop me from writing about radicals and reformers of all periods and persuasions" (*AN* xxvi). The 1920s and 1930s became Aaron's favorite period. It was populated by men he knew and filled with sentimental associations. Those were also the decades when it was still possible to make a living as a man of letters, unencumbered by an academic post. Had not professionalization and academicization intervened, this would almost certainly have been Aaron's life-style of choice. Among the men he sincerely admired was Edmund Wilson. He, if anyone, was Aaron's critical model. In one of many essays that touch on Wilson and mourn the passing of the man of letters as an institution, Aaron presented a sketch of him that came close to being the portrait of a man Aaron would not have minded being:

His principal concern then was an art "become increasingly private and privileged at the expense of its responsibility." This Arnoldian concern persisted. It derived in part, I think, from something akin to a Puritan sense of stewardship, for although Wilson . . . rejected Puritanism in the Menckenian sense of that misunderstood term, his self-appointed role of culture-bearer had a ministerial aura. . . . [he] was not so different from Emerson who embraced letters and scholarship as a vocation. In his own way he was consecrated to his calling of "critic." He refused to flatter or cajole or soothe his readers. Rather, he lectured to them, diverted them, corrected and set them straight, tried to make them intellectually regenerate.[35]

Apart from Wilson, Aaron cared particularly about Theodore Dreiser and John Dos Passos. While Dreiser was clearly no friend of the Jews, as

Aaron did not hesitate to point out (*WL* 277–278), Dos Passos, emerging from Harvard in 1916 and exploding with rebellious energy, considered Harvard graduates, including himself, "a pretty milky lot," and placed his hopes for change in the Jews:

> All the thrust and advance and courage in the country now lies in the East Side Jews and in a few of the isolated "foreigners" whose opinions so shock the New York Times. They're so much more real and alive than we are anyway. . . .
>
> And what are we fit for when they turn us out of Harvard? We're too intelligent to be successful business men and we haven't the sand or the energy to be anything else.
>
> Until Widener [Library] is blown up and A. Lawrence Lowell assassinated and the Business School destroyed and its site sowed with salt—no good will come out of Cambridge. (*WL* 346)

Dos Passos vented some of his fury by roaming through France and Italy in the last year of the Great War as a vagabond ambulance driver in the company of a future Harvard professor. "With Robert Hillyer," Aaron reported, "he repaired broken engines, scavenged for wine and omelets, and collaborated on a novel" (*WL* 347). Twenty years later, when Jones arrived at Harvard, all the newcomer could find to say about the wartime companion of Dos Passos was that "Hillyer was Boylston Professor of Rhetoric and Oratory, but taught neither subject, preferring to write his own poetry and supervise the writings of others" (*Au* 204). To top things off, Hicks made fun of Hillyer's verse in the *New Republic* (*PT* 149–150)—such were the Harvard revolutionaries.

Dos Passos's fiery remarks, however, point to an issue that Aaron did not address in *Writers on the Left,* and that is the role of the Jews. It would have been a difficult thing to do, first, because Aaron cultivated no awareness of who was or was not Jewish; and second, because he was trying to connect left radicalism with an American tradition of reformers, rebels, and dissenters who were motivated, in his view, by the obligations of the stewardship principle. Although that principle was derived from a book fundamental to Jewish thought, it was evident that the radicalism of the Jews did not derive from an American tradition and that its goal was not the desire to improve just *American* society. More often than not, Jews were fierce internationalists, and their radicalism was less manageable and genteel, less middle class, than the progressivism of the New England scions. Aaron's confusion on the subject

of left-wing radicalism and the Jews shows in his introduction to Harvey
Swados's novel *On the Line,* a classic of radical fiction. Aaron had this to
say about Swados, who was born in Buffalo, New York, in 1920, to
Russian-Jewish parents: "That he happened to be a Jew and a socialist
did not make him feel marginal or alienated, according to his testimony,
for by the time of his coming of age, Jewish Americans had already
pretty well merged with the rest of the nation and the 'socialist attitude'
was 'firmly in the American grain.' "[36]

In 1936, the year Swados entered the University of Michigan, Lionel
Trilling was dismissed from the staff of the English department at Columbia University. "The reason for my dismissal," Trilling recorded in
his journal on April 20, "is that as a Jew, a Marxian, a Freudian I am
uneasy. This hampers my work and makes me unhappy." How far Jews
had merged with the rest of the nation, in that nation's perception, is
less certain than Aaron's "pretty well" suggests. Moreover, most Americans would also have disagreed vehemently with the notion that the
kind of socialism important to Swados was firmly in the American
grain.[37] Obviously, some groups of American Jews had indeed "merged,"
and some aspects of socialism had indigenous counterparts. But the fact
remains that throughout the 1930s a socialist Jew was an unsettling
specter to much of the nation west of the Hudson River. There were
very few socialist Jews, if any, who were not aware of that effect.

In the mid-1960s, when Americans were interested in "ethnics,"
Aaron finally took the difficult bull by the horns and wrote an essay
entitled "Some Reflections on Communism and the Jewish Writer."
Compared to the cautious, fact-based article on "Richard Wright and
the Communist Party" he undertook a few years later, Aaron's essay on
the Jews assumed much and proved little, because Aaron was unfamiliar
with the Jewish radicals' social and cultural milieux. Aaron began with
the interesting observation, however, that "the key writers among the
literary radicals of the 1920's . . . were not Jews," but that "the literary
historian of the 1930's, while acknowledging that the names of non-
Jewish writers and artists are discoverable and important, can scarcely
fail to take notice of the high number, if not the preponderance, of Jews
in radical literary circles." Aaron then set out to investigate the reasons.
He discovered two sets of reasons for the attraction of Jews to left
radicalism, one set for immigrants and another for their sons and daughters. The two sets differed in appearance but not in their basic assumptions, so it will suffice to examine the first set. Aaron described the
motivations and hopes of "the ghetto Jews," who, "although intensely

intellectual . . . had not much interest in American culture" but who "might have read 'The Raven' or 'Hiawatha' in translation." These "segregated Jews seldom or never had the chance to become intimate friends with non-Jews of the middle class." But there was hope:

> In Communism they find a composite answer to pressing social, psychological, and intellectual needs: (1) a company of associates with whom they can relax and be themselves without fear of social discrimination . . . ; (2) the promise of a classless world where Christian and Jew are brothers and in which they might escape from gentile snubs—particularly in the highly stratified and snobbish college and university campuses; (3) a doctrine that appeals to their latent religiosity, to their humanitarianism, and to their rationality, and one that offers a future when the Egyptians will be humbled and the righteous assume their rightful places; (4) a Party that provides opportunities for the Talmudic theoreticians (the lay rabbis contemptuous of business and consecrated to higher speculations) to refine and resolve the ambiguities of the Marxist scriptures; (5) a cause that enables the ambitiously gifted to acquire reputations and power; (6) a movement that offers a cloak of anonymity to people whose origins and background bar them from the gentile community.[38]

Aaron's checklist presents what until recently has been the standard analysis of the reasons for the continued attractiveness of Communism to Jews settling in America. Aaron's tone seems patronizing and his ascription of motives a bit disdainful. He is conscious of the vast distance between himself—Chicago-born and Harvard-bred—and the new immigrants laboring in sweatshops, yet still insecure enough, as new-stock American, to need to emphasize that distance by tinting his quite conventional observations with just the slightest hue of condescension and ridicule. Aaron's expository method, his complete immersion in the minds of his subjects, fails him in the case of the Jews, perhaps because they are too close for comfort to a man who has not really worked out his relationship to them. For that reason Aaron also relies rather heavily on an article by John Higham instead of undertaking his own research. Even within the narrow confines of academe Aaron might have turned up some pertinent facts regarding his first and second points. While it is true that Jewish immigrants tended to spend much time with *landslayt* (other immigrants speaking the same language), they did not do so because they feared discrimination in the company of Gentiles. On the contrary, Jewish immigrants faced discrimination squarely; even their offspring deliberately entered areas (medicine, law, literary academe) where competition was stiff.[39] In college, the vast majority of immigrant Jews became "grinds" rather than Communists, because what mattered was to make it in America, to provide social stability and economic security for one's family.

Aaron's analysis of communism and the Jewish writer boils down to the observation that Jews were attracted to communism and left-wing causes in order to improve their own lot, an objective that—as in the case of Aaron's own family—was much more easily achieved within a capitalist democracy. Yet Aaron's essay culminated in a declaration of Jewish self-centeredness and setimentality: "And so the Jewish intellectual identified himself with a group that defends the rights of all ethnic minorities in the United States. No one more vehemently upholds the privileges of Negroes or any other suppressed minority or weeps more sincerely for the wrongs of the toiling masses. Because the Jew weeps for himself." [40] While Aaron is right about the fundamental sentimentality of Jewish idealism, what he fails to recognize in 1965 is the genuinely selfless (and thus, some argue, self-destructive) nature of the idealism of the old Jewish left, which laid the foundation for the radical politics of the then nascent new Jewish left.[41]

Of course Aaron never denied being Jewish himself. At the Chicago World's Fair he volunteered along with hundreds of others to have his picture taken for a Harvard laboratory unaware of the purpose for which the photograph might be used. It was eventually included in Carleton Coon's strange book *The Races of Europe* (1939). In the photograph, reproduced on a page depicting seven Russian Jews, Aaron looks out at the reader, seemingly bemused by the enterprise. Coon described him as a "tall, blond, dolichocephalic Jew from Illinois, whose parents were born in Russia. Metrically Nordic, only the morphology of the nasal tip suggests non-Nordic ancestry. Like many American Jews, this young man has not acquired the 'Jewish' facial expression more common among the generation born in Europe."

The " 'Jewish' facial expression" was a bizarre phenomenon indeed. "There is [a] quality of looking Jewish," Coon maintained, "and its existence cannot be denied. . . . There is, however, no known physical criterion or set of criteria by which this quality can be measured." An examination of the physical features of Ashkenazi Jews led Coon to conclude that "the deciding factor may not be so much physical, as social and psychological." He assured his readers that "the possession of a national or ethnic facial expression" was not necessarily a bad thing. Good people had it too: "The English Public School man of standard type, trained in a social tradition as definite in its own way as that of the Jew, has a look that can be recognized almost anywhere, and one which is just as easy prey to cartoonist as is that of the Jew." Such a "look" then, Coon seemed to say, is part of a group's cultural heritage, produced and fostered by cultural solidarity. "And since the ethnic solidarity of the Jews is remarkable for its strength and constancy," Coon wrapped up his discussion, "so the Jewish look seems to be one of the most noticeable and most easily distinguished of characteristic facial expressions found within the racial family of white people." [42] Coon's peculiar observations illuminate a preoccupation of the time. His discussion sums up what was then understood to be one of the missions of America, namely, to make that look disappear. Just as America had expanded the "inferior chest diameters of the East European Jews, once considered a racial character," so it could heal the ethnic look. In Coon's view, not having the "Jewish look" indicated that Aaron had already been "healed." [43]

Aaron's fundamental attitude toward religious, ethnic, or cultural minorities in the United States was integrationist. Segregation of any kind, whether voluntary or enforced, was not to his taste; it was contrary to the enlightened idea of America that Aaron cherished. He articulated his integrationist stance clearly in a 1964 essay entitled "The Hyphenate Writer and American Letters." In Aaron's view, the hyphen (as in "Mexican-American") "symbolized the reluctance of 'other' or older North Americans to grant complete acceptance to the late-comer." For Veblen, hyphenation had been a precondition of intellectual preeminence; but Aaron called attention to the danger when hyphenation was not chosen but ascribed: "The hyphen that separates two words is also mentally disjunctive. It signifies a tentative but unmistakable withdrawal on the part of the user; it means that mere geographical proximity does not entitle the newcomer or outsider to full and unqualified national membership despite his legal qualifications and despite official disclaimers to the contrary." [44]

The cultural context for this essay was the emergence of "ethnic" American writers during the 1960s and the celebration of America's literary and social "reethnicization." In academe this mood swing of the 1960s developed into a full-blown backlash against the reign of T. S. Eliot and the New Critics—against Eliot's cultural exclusiveness and the New Critics' emphasis on text rather than context. Suspecting the new separatist mood to be a continuation of exclusion by other means, Aaron remained a fervent integrationist. The ultimate goal, he maintained, was "dehyphenation," a three-stage process at the end of which "the minor-

8. Daniel Aaron in 1974. *Photograph by Virginia Schendler.*

ity writer passes from the periphery to the center of his society." This was achieved through education. The writer lost his sense of hyphenation when he had "appropriated [American] culture and linked himself with his illustrious literary predecessors to the degree that he can now speak out uninhibitedly as an American, as a deserving beneficiary of his country's intellectual heritage." [45] One may wonder, of course, whether clinging to one's descent culture—say, to the ethics of Confucius or the Talmud—would make one somehow less deserving. More important than Aaron's vision of a nonsegregated America was the fact that the bulk of his essay dealt with Jewish and African American writers and had the courage to comment on the beginnings of their troubled relationship.

Thinking about African American writers had been an important subtheme in Aaron's work all along. Eventually it led him to the topic of his fourth book, published in 1973. The book had an extraordinary jacket. It showed an overturned inkwell spilling black ink from the upper left to the lower right corner. In the huge black blot, red letters announced the title *The Unwritten War* and white letters the subtitle *American Writers and the Civil War*. The name of the author appeared in red (that is, neither white nor black letters) in the upper right corner. It was an ingenious cover since Aaron located one of the reasons that American men of letters had revealed so little about the meaning, if not the causes, of the Civil War in the racial fears of American intellectuals. In his introduction Aaron wrote:

> The "emotional resistance" blurring literary insight, I suspect, has been race. Without the long presence of chattel slavery, Americans would not have allowed the usual animosities springing from cultural differences to boil up into murderous hatreds. Without the Negro, there would have been no Civil War, yet he figured only peripherally in the War literature. Often presented sympathetically (which ordinarily meant sentimentally and patronizingly), he remained even in the midst of his literary well-wishers an object of contempt or dread, or an uncomfortable reminder of abandoned obligations, or a pestiferous shadow, emblematic of guilt and retribution.[46]

Aaron's investigation into the attitude of American literati and intellectuals toward the Civil War was also an investigation into one of the most blatant failures of stewardship. Two of the book's seven parts were concerned with New Englanders. But Aaron's own cultural context had as much to do with the writing and direction of this book as had the skeletons in the closets of his "illustrious literary predecessors." In the preface to the 1987 edition, Aaron surmised that "the agitation for civil rights in the 1960s and 1970s and the Vietnam war must have thrust before me analogies to the Civil War. . . . The former underscored the invisibility of black Americans in Civil War literature; the latter pointed back to a war no less savage, divisive, frustrating, and mismanaged."[47] But more important even was that the Vietnam War and the continued discrimination against people of color in American society illuminated the complete disintegration of the stewardship principle that had once inspired the progressives in whom Aaron had put his hope.

Like Aaron's previous books, *The Unwritten War* had been commissioned. In 1965, during a time of national upheaval, Aaron had been asked to document and assess the impact of a crisis of equal or greater proportion on the American literary mind. It was a difficult task. "It took several years of concentrated work," Aaron recalls, "before I began to appreciate the ways in which the Civil War had engaged the American literary imagination, why Whitman thought the 'real war' would never 'get in the books,' and how few writers squarely faced their racial fears and antipathies in recounting it" *(ANms)*. The intensive research, however, allowed Aaron to reenter nineteenth-century American history and to lose himself in it as his expository method required. But more than three decades as a professor had taken their toll. *The Unwritten War* is Aaron's most academic and seemingly most disengaged book. The daring of his earlier work, his technique of presenting a person's views as if speaking from inside his or her head, had given way to a more conventional historiographic mode that interspersed phrases like "Melville argued," "James hinted," "Howells intimated," and so forth. Nevertheless, the book still managed to give the impression that Aaron had actually been on the scene, present at the moment when the words were spoken and action was taken.

In reality, however, Aaron was back at Harvard. After thirty years and much soul-searching, he had left Smith College in 1971 to accept a professorship at his alma mater. "The best thing that ever happened to me," Aaron said in retrospect. And a good thing it was indeed. Residency in Cambridge made Aaron a natural candidate for a job of truly monstrous proportion, namely, to prepare an edition of the diary of Arthur Crew Inman, a chronicle that contained some seventeen million words. Aaron accepted the task. It meant intensive exposure to the day-by-day record of a "warped and deeply troubled man" over a period of six years *(ID* 4). The editing work began in the late 1970s. *The Inman Diary* appeared in 1985. In this masterpiece of an edition, Aaron's expository method, his ability to enter another person's mind fully and selflessly, came to full fruition. Ninety percent of the diary needed to be cut, while the published 10 percent, still some sixteen hundred pages, had to preserve the integrity of the writer's personality as well as the "honesty" of the work. Obviously the editor faced a formidable task. "I had to decide," Aaron wrote, "what to emphasize and what to play down, how to balance Inman's outrageous thoughts and deeds with his mitigating decencies and curious genius—in short, how to represent fairly the contents of a many-layered and strikingly original work . . . and the convoluted personality of its vulnerable and perverse creator" *(ID* 1).

Arthur Crew Inman, born in Atlanta on May 11, 1895, was the only child of wealthy and prominent parents. His school years in Pennsylvania were unhappy and his two years at Haverford College miserable. He terminated his formal education at the age of twenty when he developed

9. Daniel Aaron in 1991. *Photograph by Virginia Schendler.*

a mysterious illness that would not respond to conventional medical treatment ("my whole nervous system went on strike"). Inman married in 1923, settled in Boston, and cultivated his semi-invalid state for the next forty years. "A comfortable allowance enabled him to foot his medical bills and support an expensive establishment at Garrison Hall, then a somewhat seedy but respectable apartment hotel in Boston's Back Bay. In that snug burrow a succession of paid helpers (men and women, but mostly women) catered to his needs. Since he required around-the-clock attention, the cooking and cleaning, the airing and curtaining of rooms, the driving of automobiles, the secretarial duties, and the negotiations with the outside world were parceled out among a fluctuating personnel—which included his wife, Evelyn Yates Inman, the heroine of the Diary" (*ID* 2).

Inman conceived the idea of writing an extensive diary in the early 1920s. It was to be a diary unlike any other ever written, "an absolutely honest record of himself, and his age" (*ID* 1). And it was meant to win him fame. On July 21, 1930, Inman recorded his hopes and doubts:

> Will this diary make me illustrious one of these days? If so, it will do its doing only after I am a long time dead. I wish I knew whether it were worth the nervous perseverance with which I have striven to hold up quality, honesty and virility. When I put down a tide of words, do they carry sense to another mind than my own? Are the ideas callow? Am I not of a conceited turn of mind to deem anything I write of merit? Or am I, as in my hopeful moments I like to conjecture, inscribing upon these pages a human document which may be of incalculable interest and assistance to the scholars and to the romanticists of the future.
>
> I want to picture myself. I want to picture America.
>
> . . . If I am to be tortured, let me never neglect to see to it that I make constructive use of each new sensation and experience with which I am harassed. Who knows but one day this jagged document may lend succor of spirit to some poor devil of a soul? Fame or no fame, I hope that. (*ID* 416–417)

Like Thomas Mann, Inman was a minute observer of himself; but he also stayed in touch with life in ordinary America through an ingenious device. In late December 1924 he placed an advertisement in the *Boston Evening Transcript* that read, "Wanted: Persons who have had interesting experiences and who can tell them interestingly to talk to an invalid, $1 an evening. Telephone . . ." (*ID* 259). The people who responded "served as his principal windows to the world," as his editor put it (*ID* 3). Some of these paid talkers became friendly visitors, intimates, or correspondents. Although Inman enjoyed listening to men, he clearly preferred women, as his editor observed:

> Young women in particular fascinated him, not only because he loved to fondle and, in some cases, have sex with them but because he could identify with their anxieties and sympathize with their resistance to parental restraints. He was in every sense an explorer of women. He studied their moods and vagaries, bought them clothes, corrected their speech, and counseled them on their love affairs. He took down the life histories of his female talkers and relished their chitchat. The Diary among other things is an offbeat and unconventional study of American women. (*ID* 3)

This is certainly true. But Inman was not a nice man; he had spells of being perfectly nasty to his wife, who could not pick up and leave when the evening talk was over. On May 15, 1924, Inman wrote:

> At bedtime Evelyn came in. She will not make an effort to talk in a way which does not irritate me. Either whines or sounds like back alley. Her voice annoys me to desperation. Last night I was tired. She commenced to whine. I told her to talk humanly or else get out. One thing led to another. I talked to her in a manner no self-respecting rat would have listened to. If she protested, her empty words were as chaff to fire. God, what a spiritless worm! (*ID* 245)

There was talk of divorce, but the marriage lasted until Inman shot himself at the age of sixty-eight, on December 5, 1963. Aaron did well to dedicate his edition to "Evelyn Yates Inman, who lived it." The diary concealed nothing—no crudeness toward Evelyn, no grossness toward the world. One of Inman's women visitors had had an operation that left her sterile. Inman noted on August 6, 1930:

> Evelyn and I are wondering how Johnny Garsoyan, Syrian, will look upon this sterility outcome of the matter. He wanted children. All the dirty races want them. . . . When all is looked at calmly, are not the anti-Nordics colonizing and appropriating America for themselves as surely and as unremittingly as did our Nordic ancestors take over this continent from the Indians? (*ID* 417)

The diary registered the fears of the middle class; it kept track of immigration, economics, national and international politics. Inman loathed the filthy Irish, despised the unspeakable Jews, admired Hitler, referred to FDR as "the Rat," praised Coolidge and Nixon, and wept when Joseph McCarthy died. Inman's diary offers a minute social history of the United States between 1919 and 1963 from the perspective of an apartment hotel in Boston.

There may not have been other diaries like Inman's, but there certainly were novels that shared Inman's desire to "picture America," and to present its *comédie humaine* ("I trust to do in nonfiction what Balzac did in fiction," *ID* 8). Dos Passos's *Manhattan Transfer* was such a novel, as was his *U.S.A.*, which had influenced the structure of Aaron's *Writers on the Left*.[48] If there was ever a perfect match between critic-historian-editor and subject, it was that between Inman and Aaron, passionate

Americans both, each in his own way; inveterate observers of American life, in print and out of it; tireless readers and chroniclers, one a recorder, the other an interpreter. Attuned to American fiction composed of facts, Aaron caught on to the novelist in Inman. Aaron called the diary a nonfiction novel whose author "becomes in effect his own literary creation, the hero or antihero of a novel-autobiography" (*ID* 8). In this postmodern age there is little to stop us from thinking that Inman may actually be the invention of his editor, who is himself a character in the *Diary*. It opens, as lengthy novels of the *War and Peace* sort do, with a "cast of characters." Under the fifth letter of the alphabet we find the entry "Editor":

> Unknown person Arthur addresses throughout the Diary who will bear responsibility of shaping and preparing the manuscript for publication. Arthur furnishes him with a running series of directives and admonishes him not to cut out shocking or indecorous details lest the "honesty" of the work (its most essential ingredient) be impaired. At once insider and outsider, the Editor in headnotes and concluding section gradually changes from detached observer to engaged commentator to one-man chorus. (*ID* xvii–xviii)

There is a double irony involved in the perfecting of Aaron's expository method during his work on the Inman diary. The first irony lies in the ease with which Aaron slips into the mind of an inveterate anti-Semite, producing in a communal effort—the diarist riding piggyback on the editor—Aaron's most American book. The second irony lies in the inadvertent closeness of the diary editor's literary theme—impersonation and the dissolution of history in language—to an all-consuming obsession in postmodern Jewish literature, namely, the uncertainty of what and who is real. Harold Bloom (re)created the author of *Genesis* and parts of *Exodus* in an intellectual novel called *The Book of J*. In Cynthia Ozick's novel *The Messiah of Stockholm*, a made-up character is looking for his father, a real author by the name of Bruno Schulz; and in her story "Puttermesser Paired" a real author, George Eliot, takes over the life of the invented character Ruth Puttermesser. In the novels of Philip Roth that claim to be autobiographies (*My Life as a Man*, for instance) or confessions (say, *Operation Shylock*,) the usurpers find cover in a jungle woven of fiction and reality. When the reader is done with the sorting out, he or she will not find it altogether unreasonable to assume that Philip Roth is a character in a novel by Moishe Pipik. The great theme in literature written by Jews two generations after their ancestors stepped off the boat into American modernity is, quite appropriately, impersonation. The chameleon-man in Woody Allen's *Zelig* is a harmless precursor of the usurpers in Roth's latter-day novels. Leonard Zelig impersonated whomever he met in America; in Roth's confidently American novels, the Jews impersonate themselves. Regarding his skills of impersonation, we can place Daniel Aaron safely between Leonard Zelig and Moishe Pipik and are thus led to conclude that the author told us the truth. *The Inman Diary: A Public and Private Confession* is indeed a novel by Daniel Aaron. At long last Aaron had written a Jewish book.

———

Literary impersonations are most dazzling and successful when their authors are themselves quite certain of their own identities. This was surely the case with Bloom, Ozick, and Roth, all born around 1930. An earlier generation of literary Jews, however, entering the colleges and universities during the 1930s, was at a disadvantage because at that time the ability to impersonate was not play but dire necessity. It was considered a matter of course among Jews, with the exception perhaps of the religious fringe, that one wanted to "merge with the rest of the nation"; but the nation was not always ready to make room. In 1945 social pressures and constraints began to ease. Colleges and universities expanded and prepared themselves to face grown men returning from a war in which many of them had seen active combat. Among those released from the U.S. Navy in 1945 was a Harvard graduate (class of 1941) by the name of Leo Marx. In the general disorientation immediately after the war, Marx floated back to his alma mater to find out in which direction he should take his life. By chance rather than design, he threw in his lot with the Harvard English department. Marx's life and career is representative of an interim generation of Jewish literary scholars, suspended between the strong, assimilationist precursor generation of Aaron, Abrams, and Levin and the rebellious dissimilationist generation of their students, who would begin to ask uncomfortable questions about the factual reality of the integrationist image of America their teachers had constructed. While Marx shared the later generation's critical stance, he also shared the former generation's desire to disappear as Jews in America's open culture. It was all right for others to be ethnic, but Marx did not wish to be an "other."

Exploring America

5

Leaving the Yard:
Leo Marx

IN OCTOBER 1945, a young sailor traveled from New York to Cambridge to find out whether he could still enroll in the Harvard Law School. He had served with the U.S. Navy for four years and continued to be on active duty near New York. The navy had offered to take care of him and his wife, who was then expecting their first child, for another year or two. But Leo Marx needed better prospects. Unsure of his vocation, Marx crossed the Yard from the Law School to Widener Library and went looking for the man who had meant much to him during his undergraduate years at Harvard in the late 1930s. He found F. O. Matthiessen, who had been rejected from the Marine Corps as too short, in his library study.

Little seemed to have changed there, except perhaps that Matthiessen was a shade more intense, the spring in him more tightly coiled. Marx had seen him last in the summer of 1941, when he had graduated from Harvard College, and Matthiessen's *American Renaissance* had just become available in the bookstores. Since then Matthiessen had been promoted to a full professorship; he had written a study of T. S. Eliot's *Four Quartets* and finished his book on *Henry James: The Major Phase.* The life of the mind had continued throughout and despite the war. It was reassuring to Marx, as well as tempting, to hear Matthiessen speak of Harvard's need for graduate students and teaching assistants in American Civilization.

Matthiessen, too, was trying to reorder his life. In July 1945 his companion Russell Cheney had died and left Matthiessen wondering, not for the first time, whether he could face life without him. The

133

answer was no. At Harvard, Matthiessen became increasingly isolated as left-wing radicalism disintegrated and the political climate changed.[1] Postwar students were politically cautious and reserved; and the administration was more determined than ever to broaden and professionalize college and graduate education. Harvard's men of letters, central to the educational ideals of Charles William Eliot and Abbott Lawrence Lowell, were, if not quite forgotten, certainly marginalized. "Gentlemen," Harvard president James Bryant Conant had said to students leaving for the war in January 1943, "with anxious pride, Harvard awaits the day of your return."[2] In October 1945, Marx had indeed returned and was sitting again in his professor's library study. Could Matthiessen recommend in all honesty that Marx return to a world that he (Matthiessen) regarded as politically doomed? Of course it would be splendid to have Marx back on campus. He had been an ardent student activist; but . . . A knock on the door announced Henry Nash Smith, who, at loggerheads with the University of Texas, had found refuge as a visiting professor at Harvard while Perry Miller was on leave. Matthiessen must have welcomed Smith's arrival in his study as a heaven-sent solution.

Smith and Marx had never met, although both had come to Harvard in 1937—Marx as a freshman, Smith as a graduate student—and pursued similar interests. Matthiessen performed the introductions and suggested that Marx discuss his situation with Smith. It was a unique moment. Marx, still undecided about his path, was in the presence of the two men whose scholarship was to shape his own thinking profoundly. Born just five years apart—Matthiessen in 1902, Smith in 1907 —the two Americanists belonged nevertheless to two different generations. This had as much to do with regional identity (New England versus Texas) and time of graduate training (mid-1920s versus late 1930s) as with personal disposition, taste, and interests shaped by the culture of the period. When Matthiessen suggested that Marx confer with Smith, he passed on his former student to a man he thought of as having a future. Smith would indeed become a founder of the so-called myth and symbol school, to which Leo Marx and his work are linked.[3]

The moment of decision passed when Smith and Marx turned to go, closing the office door on their old teacher and starting to talk to each other. "Within a few minutes," Marx recalled forty-one years later, "Smith had begun to change my life." Perhaps men of Matthiessen's intense and troubled originality do not want disciples. Smith's open, affable nature left others room to unfold. Smith had written to Aaron that Matthiessen's *American Renaissance* was a slow book. "You can see the imprint of Matty's personality on every page." The book required him to be passive as a reader and thinker, and to put himself into the mood of Matthiessen's prose. "It is, I discover, a very refined mood: this may be what you mean by pedantic: sort of T. S. Eliotish." Smith, by contrast, wanted his readers and interlocutors to be active, to bring themselves and their needs into play. Marx recalls his "uncommon interest in such practical student concerns as income, housing, and child care." In retrospect, Marx recognized that when he made his decision in October 1945 to enroll in Harvard's American Civilization program "it had a lot to do with . . . Henry's unusual empathetic interest in students as whole persons, . . . the concentrated interest he directed toward me and my problems."[4] Smith made discipleship easy. Marx, however, never relinquished his deep attachment to Matthiessen. One of the reasons, perhaps, for Marx's continued loyalty was that Matthiessen had demanded of his student a fierce commitment to America at a time when Marx was still what one might call a cultural orphan.

———

Leo Marx was born in New York in 1919. Both of his parents had been born in America, but all four of his grandparents had immigrated: his mother's parents perhaps from Poland, his father's from Germany and Alsace-Lorraine. Leo Marx senior was the youngest of fourteen children. The Marxes were energetic people. A family legend preserved the suspicion that they were somehow related to Karl; but nobody ever cared enough to ascertain the facts, and it certainly did not keep family members from making profitable investments in business and politics. Leo Marx senior married in 1908; had two children, born a decade apart; and had built a successful business when he died in 1925. His wife was devastated by his death. Theresa Rubinstein Marx came from a complicated family with an intense emotional life, not all of it happy. The family was ruled by a tyrannical father. Isaac Rubinstein preferred his two sons to his five daughters and thought nothing of it. The girls asked for more education or training of their musical talents, but Rubinstein would not hear of it. Instead the girls were to marry in the order of their age. They did it to get out of the house, except for the youngest. Blanche ran off to Paris, where she married Claude Auzello, a relatively poor World War I veteran, who became manager of the Ritz Hotel. Blanche lived vicariously but happily in a world of elegance and wealth until 1963, when she was shot by her husband of almost fifty years. He was desperate because Blanche refused to believe that a new management had displaced him and that she would have to leave the world of glamour and deceptive courtesy where she had found refuge for so many years.[5]

Like Auzello's retirement from the Ritz, the death of Theresa's husband caused a great crisis because it shattered a world of security and much-needed emotional comfort. Although Leo Marx senior left his family financially well-off, Theresa felt deprived of her protective shell and vulnerable once more to her father's tyranny. "She really hated the man," Leo Marx reminisced, "she was scared of him and just kept out of his way" (interview). The child perceived his grandfather through his mother's eyes. "She made me remember him as a mean-spirited man." But Isaac Rubinstein was also Leo Marx's only source of Jewish information and experience. He was observant in the manner of Jews from rural Eastern Europe. Marx remembered going to what he called "the holy Jewish Sabbath ceremony" on Friday nights; and he recalled "these occasions when [his grandfather] wore his yarmulke and did some of these more extreme things . . . with a chicken." It is possible that Rubinstein performed the ritual of *kapparot* (expiation) on the day before Yom Kippur, during which the sins of a person are symbolically transferred to a live chicken—a cock for a male, a hen for a female. As it is swung around the head three times, the following words are said: "This is my substitute, my vicarious offering, my atonement; this hen (cock) shall meet death, but I shall find a long and pleasant life." Happening as it did on New York's Upper West Side, in the midst of what seemed civilization, the boy was understandably frightened. At home these scenes were not explained to the child or put into a religious perspective. Marx's mother, having equated her father's intolerance and tyranny with orthodox Judaism, maintained a hostile distance from Jewish matters, religious and secular. This hostility communicated itself to her son, at least to the extent of stifling all curiosity about the world of the Jews.[6] Throughout his life Marx would have no interest in Jewish issues or communal affairs. The result was a certain homelessness. When the family lived in New York City and most of Leo's friends were suffering through their bar mitzvah preparations, the boy had a sense of "being left out." By that time, Marx was not sure anymore which world was really his. Soon after his father's death, his mother had moved the family to Paris to be near her sister but without quite settling there. Her depression kept the family on the move. From 1926 to 1928 and again from 1929 to 1931, Marx lived in Paris and attended French schools in Passy and on the Champs Elysées. He lived in a decidedly non-Jewish world and formed a deep emotional attachment to his nanny, a stylish young Catholic woman from the Vendée, who became a second mother to him. Then the family moved back to New York.

It was not until his last years in high school that structures of belonging began to establish themselves, hesitantly and tentatively, under the influence of Marx's much older sister, who worked as a book reviewer in New York for the *World, World-Telegram,* and *Time*. She was friends with other book critics, moved in left-wing literary circles, and was soon involved in the activities of the American Newspaper Guild. A senior colleague of hers on the *World* and the *World-Telegram* was Heywood Broun, the first president of that union, and coauthor of a remarkable book on discrimination in America, *Christians Only* (1931). She met her future husband on the picket line of the first strike the Newspaper Guild ever conducted. Her mother and brother participated vicariously in her exciting New York life and she introduced them to sophisticated political ideas. Pragmatic and utopian schemes were discussed around the kitchen table. With the rise of the Nazis to power, Theresa Marx began to identify more closely with the fate of the Jews, perhaps because she recognized the pattern of terror and empathized with people in fear of a tyrant.[7] She never conquered her childhood traumas and eventually took her own life.

Theresa Marx had surprisingly conventional thoughts about being Jewish in America. They may have masked feelings that were more difficult to express. "She had these little clichés," Leo Marx remembered; "if you are a Jew, you always have to work harder, because people will discriminate against you." Her words had the desired effect. "She made me aware that there was discrimination," Marx said. But his mother's premonitions were counterpoised by his sister's daily experiences of shared concern over workers' conditions and by the egalitarian ideals of the left. When the Moscow purge trials confirmed some of his mother's misgivings, Marx was on his way to college. Many of his friends were going to the University of North Carolina; so he applied there too. But urged by his sister's fiancé, he also applied to Harvard and was accepted. He was the first in his family to go to college.

In the fall of 1937 the politicization of Harvard Yard was reaching its peak. It was almost a matter of course that freshmen were attracted to radical ideas and became involved in left-wing activities. Marx made friends with people who shared his point of view. He joined the Harvard Student Union, which in 1938–39 had its largest membership with some five hundred to six hundred souls, and immediately found himself in the midst of great excitement. He was constantly circulating petitions concerning the civil war in Spain or workers' causes, teasing professors like Harry Levin who "agonized so about signing these things" (interview). Marx contributed to the *Harvard Progressive,* a magazine modeled on the *Nation* and the *New Republic,* and eventually became its editor. He was elected to the Signet Society, a literary club that did not bar Jews, and was asked to serve on a Student Council committee that examined admissions to the houses and the question of quotas there.

Marx still recalls "Harvard's vague formula of student admission: 25 percent of the freshmen came from the St. Grotlesex schools [Episcopal boarding schools, cf. p. 438n. 13]; 25 percent from Andover and Exeter; and then 25 percent from public schools. That was the general notion of the Conant administration" (interview). The remaining quarter probably came from other private schools. Since there were not enough places in the houses to accommodate all students, the question of allocation arose. After an initial phase of rejection in the early 1930s, the houses were favored by the fashionable set, and students observed that "obviously there was a higher percentage of Jews who didn't get in." Much to his surprise, Marx found the administration prepared to discuss quotas "not publicly but frankly. The justification was that they did not want any of the houses to become a ghetto. Kirkland House, for instance [where M. H. Abrams had lived], was considered a Jewish house. The administration wanted to do everything they could to preempt such developments. That was the justification for some allocation" (interview). Marx had noticed, however, that he had been assigned three Jewish roommates for his freshman year. He did not mind, but he was "very conscious of the fact that they had done this deliberately." The year after, when he got to pick his roommate before entering Winthrop House, he picked a Jewish friend. "It would not have been unheard of but still somewhat unusual," Marx recollected, if he had not chosen a Jew.

Like many students, Marx focused his attention on fighting injustice and inequality on a larger scale and in the "real" world. The students were exhilarated not only because they felt that their words and deeds counted but also because the involvement of faculty members in some of the same social and political causes created an unprecedented sense of community that emphasized the urgency of action. Naturally, there was considerable disagreement about how to improve the world and the workers' lot.

Daniel Boorstin happened to be Marx's sophomore tutor. He had just returned from Oxford, where he had studied as a Rhodes scholar. Late in 1938 he asked Marx to come to tea. On that occasion he disclosed to his baffled student that he was a member of the Communist Party. He did not wish to influence Marx secretly but rather desired that his tutee be aware of any bias that might result from the tutor's political outlook (interview). Boorstin was to change political direction very soon, but by that time Marx had passed on to another instructor.

Perry Miller, an ardent interventionist who disdained political waffling as much as secrecy, was Marx's tutor during his junior and senior years (1939–41). He seemed to share some of the qualities of the seventeenth-century divines who dominated his scholarly life. He combined fierceness with forthrightness and gave the altogether believable appearance of a man grimly poised for immediate action. He had once envied his older contemporaries, to whom the boon of "adventure" had been offered by the First World War, and he jumped at the chance to participate in the Second. He returned to campus as Major Miller, former officer in the OSS (which later became the CIA), who had accompanied General Leclerc during the liberation of Alsace. One knew exactly where Miller stood without having to come to tea; and Miller in turn was not inclined to take too much cognizance of his students' sensitivities. In 1946, David Levin, a future biographer of Cotton Mather, reported to Perry Miller's suite in Leverett House to inform him that he, Miller, had been assigned to him as tutor in history and literature.

> He invited me to sit in a black wooden chair with cherry arms and the Harvard seal on the back. As I took my seat I had to notice that a German battle flag, with an immense swastika, hung on the wall behind me and that a pair of knee-high boots gleamed beside the left rear leg of my chair. "I got the flag and the boots when I liberated Strasbourg with Leclerc," Miller said, . . . "Where were you?"
>
> That was the simplest question he ever asked me. For the next fourteen weeks I often felt as if, having been captured by the Germans after all, I were under interrogation in front of that flag. Miller was not unkind; he was simply relentless.[8]

Levin could afford to take Miller's question literally. Deeply upset by the successes of the German army, Levin had enlisted in the Army Air Corps in 1943. Miller believed in personal commitment to a task, course of action, or set of ideas, not as a result of some conditioning circumstance (say, Levin's strong Jewish identity leading him to enlist), but as a result of reasoning from principle so that any action could be charged fully to the account of the agent. "The achievement of a personality," Miller wrote in *Errand into the Wilderness,* "is not so much the presence of this or that environmental element—no matter how pressing, how terrifying—as the way in which a given personality responds." Applied to American literary historiography, Miller's principle of full personal responsibility seemed to amount to nothing less than a refutation of Frederick Jackson Turner's frontier hypothesis, or of his theory, as Miller put it, that "democracy came out of the forest." [9]

During his last two years in college, however, Marx was less concerned with precisely what kind of historiographic approach Miller preferred and more interested in the freedom of choice Miller's tenet of conscious commitment seemed to signal. Miller, born on Chicago's West Side in 1905, had famously determined to expound what he "took to be the innermost propulsion of the United States" during a sojourn in the Belgian Congo in the mid-1920s. His resolution then to "begin at the beginning" had led him to become a scholar of Puritan literature. Neither descent nor "personal predilection" had predetermined such a course or prepared Miller for it. [10] Rather, Miller's quirky choice was an assertion of freedom. Cultural orphanhood, Marx saw, could be terminated at any time.

In the late 1930s, the direction of Marx's own commitment was not yet clear. He was fascinated by the economist Paul Sweezy, who persuaded him "to adopt a radical view of American society, to recognize that the great contradictions of American society are deeply systemic or structural and probably cannot be resolved by piecemeal reform." [11] But it was Matthiessen, a demanding presence in Marx's senior year, who had his unqualified admiration. Matthiessen combined passionate scholarship with passionate politics, but did not mix the two. He was openly a socialist; a practicing Christian among agnostics; an intense, challenging teacher but without a trace of Miller's militarism; and, most important, he was known to be a fighter, one who opposed "Conant's relentlessly mechanical slide ruler autocracy." [12]

Marx was aware of his teachers' complicated personalities despite the fact that Miller and Matthiessen were men who kept a tight lid on their inner turmoils as long as possible. [13] Moreover, the late 1930s were a fast-moving, troubled, but highly idealistic time, at least in academe. The rise of fascism, the Spanish Civil War, and the Stalinist purges, as well as national strikes, excited the minds and hearts of a large part of the campus community. There was little time and less patience for the troubled souls of "privileged" individuals—quite apart from the fact that it would have been presumptuous on the part of an undergraduate to inquire into a professor's personal life. Shared political and social interests made student-teacher relations slightly less formal than they had been, but the chasms separating undergraduates, graduate students, and faculty were as deep as always. The bustle of world events on campus concealed the emotional and psychological suffering of individuals. With the end of the Second World War, the bustle subsided and individuals came into view again. But then the returning students were caught up in their own lives; new wives and children needed to be taken care of on very little money. The political idealism of the exciting 1930s became a casualty of the battlefields of everyday life; and whatever enthusiasm for left-wing causes survived was dampened by the McCarthy inquisitions and by the trials of Alger Hiss and of Ethel and Julius Rosenberg. The disintegration of those who had invested themselves in radical politics and who needed the bond of a common political purpose proceeded quietly.

F. O. Matthiessen's suicide on April 1, 1950, was a shock to the literary community in general and to Matthiessen's friends in particular. It recalled them to the principle of personal responsibility. Preoccupied with their own lives, Matthiessen's friends had been much less available to him after the war. During the last five years of his life, Matthiessen tried to resurrect the spirit of the 1930s by endorsing the progressivism of Henry Wallace and the socialism of Czechoslovakia. By 1948 both causes were dead and Matthiessen's idealism defeated. In 1950 friends and students were tempted to conclude that their exchange of radical ideals for more modest and pragmatic goals amounted in the end to an abandonment of Matthiessen. This was certainly the tenor of May Sarton's novel *Faithful Are the Wounds* (1955), which re-created Matthiessen's last years and the soul-searching of his friends after his death. Leo Marx's sharply critical assessment of his own generation also betrayed a sense of guilt. Somehow one had failed to fulfill a promise:

> Most of us, particularly the students whom I knew in the thirties' radical movement, were highly motivated, ambitious children of the lower middle class for whom going to the university and launching academic careers was (among other things) a convenient channel toward a higher status and security and position. . . . [W]e were all performers in the sense of being obedient to the performance principle. . . . We all got along well —much too well to suggest that the radicals were very radical. . . . [We] were chiefly cerebral radicals. . . . [Y]ou probably can't be a very effective

radical if your goal is professional advancement and preferment. . . . Almost none of us has fulfilled the role that one might set forth for a radical intellectual—which is to provide the indispensable thinking necessary to establish a genuine Left politics in the United States. (*PA* 38, 41) [14]

The immediate goal of returning student GIs was indeed professional advancement. It was a legitimate concern for married men not independently wealthy and yet dedicated to the pursuit of academic careers. In the late 1940s, the nation, like many of its citizens, needed to rethink and reconceive itself. The economic boom of the 1920s, followed by the Crash, the Great Depression, the Red Decade, and the exertions of the Second World War had left the country breathless. Moreover, in 1945 the United States was somewhat nonplussed to find itself transformed into a superpower. At the beginning of the Cold War, America concealed uncertainty behind a posture of invincibility. If Marx wanted to accuse his generation of anything, it ought not to have been the betrayal of radical ideals, but perhaps the invention of a too simple, too easily graspable image of America.

Books like Henry Nash Smith's *Virgin Land* (1950), R. W. B. Lewis's *American Adam* (1955), Richard Chase's *American Novel and Its Tradition* (1957), Leslie Fiedler's *Love and Death in the American Novel* (1960), Charles Sandford's *Quest for Paradise* (1961), Leo Marx's *Machine in the Garden* (1964), Alan Trachtenberg's *Brooklyn Bridge: Fact and Symbol* (1965), Richard Slotkin's *Regeneration Through Violence* (1973), and many others translated the complexities of American history into smooth stories built on accessible dichotomies. The so-called myth and symbol school to which some of these writers belong later came under fire as much for what John Higham terms its "appeal to homogeneity, continuity, and national character" as for the particular characteristics that Bruce Kuklick decries: its "crude Cartesian view of mind," its covert Platonism, and its simplistic way of using " 'collective' images and symbols . . . to explain the behavior of people in the United States." [15]

But the fact of the matter is that the thinking of the myth and symbol school did not constitute a sudden departure from more radical forefathers. Rather, it was a direct outgrowth of the strictly dichotomic thinking and narrative mode of precursors such as Parrington and Beard, with whom Marx, for example, also shared a commitment to the political left.[16] Marx's disappointment with himself in 1975 because he had relinquished some of his radicalism during the 1940s and 1950s may have also concealed a regret that his magnum opus, *The Machine in the*

Garden, had been less a trenchant critique of American reality than the reconstruction of a fantasy about America. Paradoxically, this was partly due to his personal and intellectual loyalty to Matthiessen and Smith. He never quite freed himself of their influence. It is difficult to trace irrefutably a scholar's intellectual debts to a multitude of friends, colleagues, and forebears. In the case of Leo Marx, however, it is possible to isolate some plausible and illuminating strands in the tangle of indebtedness.

Perry Miller, Marx's tutor in college, became his dissertation adviser after the war. Miller was a loner, an autodidact, a self-made scholar. When he returned to the University of Chicago from the Congo jungle in 1926, his decision "to commence with the Puritan migration" was regarded as yet another of Miller's eccentricities since Puritan studies were thought to be the pastime of upper-crust amateurs and patriotic obscurantists. It was considered an exhausted field in which scholarly talent would almost certainly go to waste. Miller's adviser, Perry Holmes Boynton, however, "held that a boy should be allowed to do what the boy genuinely, even if misguidedly, is convinced should be done." The University of Chicago proved flexible and permitted Miller to take the majority of his courses at Harvard with Samuel Eliot Morison and Kenneth Murdock. Miller received his Ph.D. in 1931 from Chicago, dedicated his dissertation *Orthodoxy in Massachusetts* (1933) to Boynton, and returned to Harvard to teach.

Miller maintained that "history itself is part of the life of the mind," or, more clearly, that "the mind of man is the basic factor in history." With one sweep Miller set himself in opposition to Turner and to the economic and social historiography of Beard, Parrington, and Charles Truslow Adams. In 1931, at the callow age of twenty-six, Miller announced his opposition to these men and to Marxists of all persuasions in the pages of the *New England Quarterly* in an essay on Thomas Hooker. Miller's "historical conscience was outraged" by the irresponsible statements of Parrington and Adams. His own historiography was an attempt, as Gene Wise put it, "to impose form upon experience." [17] For Miller, mind dominated matter, even though matter shaped mind. In Miller's work Marx could observe how physical data became metaphors or stories (which are metaphors-in-progress). Miller perceived that the rhetoric of seventeenth-century folk had created the New England mind. Marx was on hand when Miller began to write the sequel to *The New England Mind* and was in search of a metaphor that might capture the ability of mind to transform matter and thus to shape history.

In the prefatory note to his essay "Errand into the Wilderness," Miller described how he found his most successful metaphor. Rethinking the title of Samuel Danforth's election sermon, Miller discovered that "Danforth was trying to do what I too am attempting: To make out some deeper configuration in the story than a mere modification, by obvious and natural necessity, of an imported European culture in an adjustment to a frontier." Miller recognized the frontier—that is, the proximity of the wilderness—as a basic conditioning factor, but he asserted that the process of history, which he also called "the achievement of personality," consisted of transforming the elemental fact of the frontier into a mental construct. The Puritans subjected nature to mind (and not, as Turner had it, mind to nature). At that moment the "errand into the wilderness," however much a physical reality, became a metaphor capable of conveying Danforth's message. The factual wilderness could be endured because of the metaphor's power to transcend it. As a result, the errand was more important than the wilderness.

It was a short step from Miller's interest in the "achievement of personality," the triumph over nature and environment, to perceiving history as a series of "mental constructs." [18] And it was an even shorter step from "mental constructs" to "myths and symbols." Henry Nash Smith, too, had been Miller's student. Miller knew, however, that Danforth's metaphor was a simplification. In his view a historiography that relied on the analysis of "collective representations" could hardly be fruitful. The reason was that the complexity of matter defied the power of mind, that collective representations (metaphors, myths, and symbols) never adequately captured and stored history as it unfolded. Reality was always larger and more complex than mankind's imaginative faculty. "This ostentatiously simple and monolithic America," Miller wrote, "is in fact a congeries of inner tensions. . . . Confronted with so gigantic a riddle, the analyst becomes wary of generalizations, though incessantly he strives to comprehend." [19]

Miller's readiness to acknowledge the complexity of cultural processes squared with the mind-set Marx had encountered in Matthiessen. "Perhaps the most profound and elusive lesson he taught," Marx wrote, "was that a smooth and absolutely logical structure of ideas is not necessarily a sign of the greatest intellectual maturity" (PaP 238). Matthiessen was even more finely attuned than Miller to the intellectual tensions and contrarieties in New England culture. In a 1983 essay on Matthiessen, Marx argued that the tacit theme of American Renaissance was "the debilitating sense of disunity engendered by the double consciousness" (PaP 249). Marx saw that it was quite possible to write literary history as a series of unresolved conflicts. He claimed that "Matthiessen's emphasis upon the contradictions rather than the harmonies of meaning, value and purpose . . . signaled the virtual disappearance of the older, complacent idea of our national culture as an essentially homogeneous, unified whole" (*PaP* 245). That complacency had actually already died with Barrett Wendell. All subsequent American (literary) histories of note (the works of Parrington, Beard, Calverton, Hicks, even Ludwig Lewisohn's *Expression in America* of 1932) were full of strife. Most interesting to students during the late 1930s and 1940s, however, was the fact that literary historians seemed to respond to each other in their works.

It is possible, for example, to see in *American Renaissance* Matthiessen's answer to Miller. *American Renaissance* could be read as an alternative to Miller's construct; it presented another way of getting to know the American mind.[20] Matthiessen's writers may have been divided against themselves, but they belonged to a society he perceived, despite his awareness of class divisions, as culturally homogeneous. Like Miller's, this society was beset by "congeries of inner tensions," and an individual's "double consciousness" became almost a badge of group membership in that society. To Matthiessen's students, moreover, the fact that their teacher set "little store by logical consistency" (*PaP* 247) placed Matthiessen himself in "the tradition which runs from Emerson to the open universe of William James" (*PaP* 238). In the eyes of their students, Miller and Matthiessen were part of the culture their works (re)created and whose most outstanding attribute was a divided, double, or conflicted self (a feature with which many Jewish students could identify). When Marx came to analyze the troubled response of "our serious writers" to the onset of industrialization in *The Machine in the Garden,* he was mainly interested in the response of the writers dealt with in Matthiessen's *American Renaissance.* His most important addition to Matthiessen's roster, Mark Twain, had been brought into academic culture by Henry Nash Smith.

———

Marx took his first class with Smith in 1946. It was a lecture course on "Literature of the American West." Smith was then still focused on turning his dissertation into a book. He had received his Ph.D. in 1940 as the first graduate of Harvard's American Civilization program with a thesis on "American Emotional and Imaginative Attitudes Toward the Great Plains and the Rocky Mountains, 1803–1850." His aim had been to chart "the superstructure of the Westward Movement." This phrase from Smith's 1939 prospectus indicates the residues of a Marxist approach. Daniel Aaron, too, had used the word "superstructure" in describing the content of his thesis. Unlike Aaron, however, Smith was less interested in the material reality of the westward movement than in the mental constructs associated with it, although, as Marx pointed out, "Smith had a firm grasp of that material reality and its interplay with ideas."[21] And unlike Miller, Smith was not primarily interested in the individual and the genesis of metaphors, the "personal achievement" of transforming nature into mind, but rather in the collective imagination and the genesis of myths. And again unlike Miller, who recognized that metaphors simplified reality, Smith slowly came to believe that collective mental constructs existed independently, beyond reality, and had a life of their own in the American cultural memory. The structure of *Virgin Land*, Smith wrote shortly before his death in 1986, "is basically a conflict between an assumed historical reality and the ideology, myths, and symbols generated in American culture by contemplation of the moving frontier of settlement and the territory beyond."[22] Karl Marx had turned Hegel upside down; Smith put Marx back on his feet and arrived, as Bruce Kuklick demonstrated, at the dualisms of the philosophical idealists.

The best account of the genesis of *Virgin Land* is buried in the letters exchanged by Smith and Daniel Aaron over an eleven-year period (1939–50). In a letter to Aaron written in October 1939, Smith recorded the point at which he perceived the split between reality and imaginative construct.

> The fiction is turning out to be more important than I thought. . . . I think something interesting will develop when I start to make a list of themes which recur in the nonfiction and are taken up in the novels (I think almost none of the American novelists had actually been in the mountains, and they were almost certainly getting what small information they had from books). I believe I can separate themes in the novels which are merely literary conventions of the fiction of the times, and themes derived from explorers, etc., that make the books about the Far West different from other novels. This will give me something to trace and demonstrate instead of merely classifying and describing materials.

Smith was somewhat at a loss about how to proceed. His only option was to pursue his topic by sifting huge amounts of material, making lists, sorting, classifying, and accidentally hitting on something. "Believing that I was operating without hypotheses, I set about reading all published descriptions of or comments on the Great Plains and the Rocky Mountains—all the narratives of travel and residence in these areas, articles in magazines, poems and stories and novels that I could lay my hands on. Of course, this proved to be an impossibly ambitious project, especially as my roughly chronological approach revealed an increasing proliferation of such materials with every passing decade." [23]

Smith was swamped with literature and felt compelled to read his way through all of it. Part of his problem was that he did not (yet) have an adequate literary or cultural theory that would have allowed him to conceptualize his topic and to argue by way of example rather than from the totality of evidence. Nor did Smith observe that anyone at Harvard working on similar themes in literary history had any useful theory to speak of. On the contrary, Smith noted that the faculty's attitude toward literature "was anti-theoretical to the point of being anti-intellectual" (PA 49).

In his need to find an organizing central metaphor, Smith fell back on Turner's easily graspable frontier hypothesis, despite the fact that Smith, better than anyone, knew that Turner's thesis was the culmination of a long tradition of popular misconceptions about the American westward movement. Turner's central contention had been that "the existence of an area of free land, its continuous recession, and the advance of American settlement westward explain American development" (quoted in VL 291). From this contention Smith derived his central metaphor, the virgin land, which was both an empty space waiting to be transformed into a garden paradise and a blank surface ready to reflect Europe's fantasies. The frontier moving westward into a "vacant continent" (VL 4) had been summarily defined by Turner as the battleground between savagery and civilization. Not until years later did Smith realize that despite his ideological distance from Turner, he had not paid enough attention to the tragedies Turner's hypothesis concealed: the destruction of the wilderness and the murder of Native Americans. Crestfallen, Smith wrote in 1986:

> I recognized that "civilization" brought with it the theory of a fixed typology of social stages through which every society must pass as it develops from a state of nature upward toward the level of . . . Europe and the eastern United States. But I did not realize to what extent the notion of civilization embodied a doctrine of inevitable progress so deeply buried it was almost inaccessible to critical examination. Thus I took over

from Turner . . . a refusal to acknowledge the guilt intrinsic to the national errand into the wilderness. Like my teachers and academic colleagues, I had in this fashion lost the capacity for facing up to the tragic dimensions of the Westward Movement.

I had acquired an even more important contagion from Turner's conception of the wilderness beyond the frontier as free land: the tendency to assume that this area was in effect devoid of human inhabitants.[24]

Only two academic generations after Smith did Native Americans gradually come into view. Among the many books of quiet protest by Leo Marx's student Allen Guttmann there is an early volume coedited with Louis Filler, entitled *The Removal of the Cherokee Nation: Manifest Destiny or National Dishonor?* (1962).

In May 1947, after his visiting appointment at Harvard and a year of writing and research at the Huntington Library, Smith could report to Daniel Aaron that *Virgin Land* was two-thirds done. Smith had finally conquered the material and found three myths "growing out" of the westward movement. In a letter to Aaron he outlined *Virgin Land* in its final form. In April 1948 the manuscript was ready for publication. Houghton Mifflin wanted substantial revisions and so did Knopf. Smith revised the first six chapters; Knopf thought the revisions splendid and then rejected the book. Howard Mumford Jones and Perry Miller urged Harvard University Press to take it.[25] And this is where *Virgin Land* appeared in 1950.

———

Smith's "master symbol of the garden" (*VL* 138) became the starting point for Leo Marx's analysis of America's reaction to the onset of industrialization. The gestation period for Marx's major work, *The Machine in the Garden,* equaled that of *Virgin Land.* Marx received his Ph.D. in 1950 with a thesis on the responses of Emerson and Hawthorne to industrialization. In late winter 1948 he had been offered an assistant professorship in the new American Studies program at the University of Minnesota, where he began to teach in the fall of 1949. The program had been started by Tremaine McDowell in 1945 together with his dissertation advisee, Mary C. Turpie, who upon graduation in 1943 (with a thesis on "The Growth of Emerson's Thought") had been appointed to the faculty of the English department. In 1947, McDowell

hired Smith, who brought in Leo Marx and Bernard Bowron in 1949.
J. C. Levenson followed a few years later.[26]

Marx's interest in the transformative power of technology derived
from his experience in the U.S. Navy during the Second World War.
The earliest record of Marx's preoccupation with the American response
to the beginning of industrialization is an essay, extracted from his thesis
and entitled "The Steamfiend," which Marx submitted under the pseudonym Ralph Heidegger to a Harvard essay contest in 1949. But it was
not until 1956, after having published articles on Melville and Mark
Twain, that the main theme of his academic career came into focus.
"My aim," Marx wrote in 1956, "is to demonstrate one of the ways in
which a sense of the transformation of life by the machine has contributed to the temper of our literature" (*PaP* 113–114). In order to do so
successfully, Marx, like Smith before him, needed to find a central metaphor, concept, or myth that could help him organize the enormous mass
of material on his subject. Marx took his cue from Smith, who had
claimed that "one of the most significant facts of American intellectual
history is the slow and inadequate fashion in which the momentum of
the new [technological] forces was appreciated, or, to put the matter
another way, the astonishing longevity of the agrarian ideal as the accepted view of Western society" (*VL* 182–183). It is the idea and ideal
of the land, "the master symbol of the garden . . . expressing fecundity,
growth, increase, and blissful labor in the earth" (*VL* 138) that holds
Americans back and informs their response to the appearance of mechanical means of production and transportation. In 1956, as Marx was
rereading writers who responded forcefully to technology, he found that

> as [. . .] statements of Emerson, Adams, and Hawthorne suggest, the
> evocative power of the imagery of industrialism is not to be attributed to
> any intrinsic feature of machines. What gives rise to the emotion is not
> the machine, but rather its presence against the felt background of the
> older historic landscape. The American landscape, in fact, accounts for
> another singular feature of the response to our Industrial Revolution. In
> this country mechanization had been arrested, among other things, by
> space—the sheer extent of the land itself. (*PaP* 117–118)

Unlike Smith, Marx was more interested in the changing physical
American landscape than in the persistent myths about it. Taking his cue
from Smith's material that suggested that "the myth [of the garden] may

have taken shape, or at least reached its fullest development, under pressure from industrialization" (*PaP* 118), Marx observed that the myth intensified at the very moment the landscape changed and open (garden) space began to disappear by being occupied, developed, industrialized. Idea and reality, which, as Smith had argued, had concurred for a time, parted company. With the onset of mechanization, the American landscape no longer conformed to descriptions of it, and the idea of a garden in the middle of America became a "myth." Smith too had pointed to the split between idea and reality, but was only interested in it as a fait accompli. "When the new economic and technological forces, especially the power of steam working through river boats and locomotives, had done their work, the garden was no longer a garden" (*VL* 139). And here the matter rested for Smith. Marx, by contrast, was interested in the moments when dream and reality, garden and machine, clashed with the greatest force.

One of these moments was the first appearance of the machine in the garden. It became Marx's organizing conceit. He listened to the shrill whistle of the locomotive in numerous rural scenes that crop up throughout American literature. The locomotive disturbed the peace in Hawthorne's Sleepy Hollow, at Thoreau's Walden Pond, and in the forest of Faulkner's "The Bear." Marx's questions concerned the dreams and thoughts the whistle had disrupted. Smith had suggested that despite the destruction of the garden, "the image of an agricultural paradise in the West, embodying group memories of an earlier, a simpler and, it was believed, a happier state of society, long survived as a force in American thought and politics" (*VL* 139). This implied that the bucolic image was a substantial and culturally productive (mythogenic) memory rather than simply a lingering afterglow enchanting people in the wake of industrialization. Did that memory even predate American reality? It was clear to Marx that his investigations were to go beyond Turner and Smith back to Europe. He needed to look at the impact of the land on the American mind in a different way—not as an impression of reality upon the imagination, as Turner and Smith had seen it, but as the superimposition of an imported idea upon a landscape (a variant of Miller's approach). In Europe thinking about land and cultivated landscapes had generated a complex tradition, of which one strand, pastoralism, dated back to antiquity. Marx put it to striking use in his major work, *The Machine in the Garden: Technology and the Pastoral Ideal in America,* published in 1964.

Among the significant features of pastoralism Marx chose to emphasize was naturally the figure of the shepherd (pastor). He mediates between the realm of organized society and the realm of nature, between
the city and the wilderness. As Marx put it, "to mediate in this context
means, quite literally, to resolve the root tension between civilization
and nature by living in the borderland between them." [27] The mediator
is a person of "double consciousness," capable of imagining two separate
worlds. Matthiessen's legacy resurfaced in Marx's book.

The Machine in the Garden had a deceptively simple structure. It
opened with a contemplative figure in a pastoral landscape disturbed by
the whistle of a locomotive. Marx's analysis of Hawthorne's sketch
"Sleepy Hollow" allowed him to introduce his theme and the "trope of
the interrupted idyll" (*MG* 27). The second chapter examined the pastoral ideal in Shakespeare's *Tempest* and prepared the ground for the argument that a distinctive trait of American pastoral was "the identification
of America . . . as a place where arcadia could be literalized." [28] In the
third chapter, "The Garden," Marx traced the pastoral tradition in
America in the writings of eighteenth-century men who hoped to establish on the newly settled continent "a home for rural virtue" (*MG* 104).
In chapter 4, titled "The Machine," Marx showed that mechanization
was welcomed by Americans; machines were equated with fast and
unencumbered progress. The ebullient rhetoric of optimism that accompanied the humming, screeching, and whistling of machines became the
dominant force in public discourse. Positive responses to the arrival of
the machine formed the "undertone for the serious writing of the
period."

But as Marx explained in the next chapter, "Two Kingdoms of Force,"
which was really the heart of his book, Emerson, Thoreau, and Hawthorne as well as Mark Twain and Henry Adams discovered very quickly
that the machines threatened their cherished way of life with destruction. They dug in their heels and became a "dissident minority" beset
with feelings of dislocation, anxiety, alienation, and foreboding. In the
pastoral mode, Marx claimed, they found a tradition of thought that
focused and empowered their diffuse resistance.

In retrospect, however, Marx thought his explanation for the close
affinity between the American response to industrialism and pastoralism
"parochial and finally misleading." Accepting invitations extended by
Sacvan Bercovitch and Myra Jehlen in 1986 to review their work, Smith
and Marx bemoaned their failure to be more inclusive—always an inevitable shortcoming—but did not analyze the academic as well as cultural

and political pressures that had shaped their theories. In 1961, Marx had written that "to possess the past . . . the true scholar should attack it with questions arising from his sense of present realities—including political realities." [29] It would have been fascinating to learn what precisely Smith and Marx perceived the political realities of their time to be and how they thought those realities determined the questions with which they tackled the past. Reviewing his work, Marx offered instead an excellent summary of his main contentions in *The Machine in the Garden*.

> If American artists and intellectuals were attracted to the pastoral mode, I argued, it was because of the compelling similarity between the unusually promising geopolitical situation in which they had found themselves— the actual and potential conditions of life they enjoyed—and the ideal vision embodied in the classic, Virgilian pastoral.
>
> In the New World, in other words, it actually seemed possible, as never before, for migrating Europeans to establish a society that might realize the ancient pastoral dream of harmony: a *via media* between decadence and wildness, too much and too little civilization. [30]

Marx had ended his book with a passionate epilogue, entitled "The Garden of Ashes." It presented a reading of *The Great Gatsby* that reflected Marx's ambivalences and his heartache at finding the green fields gone. Like Jefferson, Fitzgerald conveyed the appeal of the pastoral ideal but knew that it was never to be realized; at best it afforded an adversarial point of view in a world of materialism. "That is why we are asked to believe that Gatsby, for all his fatal limitations, turned out all right in the end. The pastoral hope is indicted for its deadly falsity, but the man who clings to it is exonerated." [31]

Three decades later, Marx's construction of American pastoralism became itself the subject of an indictment. In a reappraisal of American pastoralism, Lawrence Buell reviewed newer scholarship growing out of a "hermeneutics of skepticism." Its assessment of myth-symbol Americanist scholarship, indulging in a "hermeneutics of empathy," was nothing if not critical. Buell wrote that Marx invited a debunking interpretation of American pastoral by younger critics partly because of his exclusive roster of authors. "Although Marx saw American pastoral vision as antioligarchical in spirit, from the same bibliography it could also be argued that American pastoral continued, as in the Old World, to be the elegant recreation of the elite: southern planters and canonized authors. Here *The Machine in the Garden* played into the reading of classic American pastoral as a patriarchal reflex." [32]

But this was not how Marx had concluded his book. He had written off American pastoralism altogether, declared it finished and obsolete as a mode of mediation as well as dissent. A few weeks after his book was published, the student revolt at Berkeley began in earnest, and Marx witnessed, much to his surprise, that pastoral ideals continued to inspire radical dissent. "The manifest continuity between the extremist rhetoric of the rebellious students' leader, Mario Savio . . . and that of Henry Thoreau . . . turned out to be the mere surface expression of a much deeper ideological continuity between our nineteenth-century pastoralism and the radical movement (or counterculture) of the 1960s." But a closer look at the new left pastoralism revealed that the green ideology did not stoke revolutionary fires. It was, after all, an ideology for a stable, concerned middle class. In an era of high technology, Marx concluded, pastoralism "may be particularly well suited to the ideological needs of a large, educated, relatively affluent, mobile, yet morally and spiritually troubled segment of the white middle class." [33] In short, pastoralism was a good vehicle for the global, national, and domestic worries of professionals and academics. Before the rise of the serious eco–criticism of the 1990s, pastoralism was fundamentally a conservative ideology because it left the labor-capital relationship untouched. It combined various traditions of nonrevolutionary dissent, ranging from Thoreau's civil disobedience to Brooks Adams's "education of conservation." [34] It was in fact a version of the Puritan-Brahmin stewardship principle. The American ideology Marx chose to shape his academic identity turned out to be not fundamentally different from the one that Daniel Aaron had chosen as his guideline for responsible citizenship. In both cases it helped to anchor these sons of new-stock Americans firmly in the culture that was their unequivocal home.

Did it matter that they were Jews? Yes and no. It mattered very little to themselves and was of no importance in their scholarship. Their works do not deal with Jews or touch upon Jewish subjects. They deal with America as it was envisioned then by the academic custodians of its history and culture. It was an America where Jews (or other non–Anglo-Saxons) were not much in evidence. Similarly the European tradition that engaged Abrams and Levin was exclusively Christian. And this is precisely the point to be made here: the first Jewish literary scholars were integrated into East Coast literary academe as facsimile WASPs; had they been visible as Jews or written on Jewish topics, they would not have had academic careers.

Having grown up in assimilated, rather well-off, nonreligious households, they never lived intellectually or culturally as Jews. Hence they had nothing to give up or to deny or to suppress when they entered Ivy League academe and when they married non-Jews.[35] In that generation of literary scholars, men like Abrams—reared in fairly religious, small-town, lower-middle-class families with strong ties to the local Jewish community—are the exception. What men like Aaron, Levin, and Marx retained as Jews was their genetic endowment and their names. That they were Jews was invisible. Unlike African Americans, Jews could pass as facsimile WASPs, especially if they had, as did Aaron and Levin, a Midwestern speech pattern, which during the 1940s became the accepted speech pattern in New England and New York City. In the absence of overt cultural identification and markedly Jewish appearance, only the Jewish names could alert students and colleagues that something unprecedented was going on in American academe: Veblen's aliens of the uneasy feet had settled down and were explaining their country to the descendants of old-stock Americans. The experiment was successful. The intellectual assimilation of that first generation of scholars, whose minds were shaped before knowledge of the Holocaust made American Jews self-conscious, established the basis for the rapid integration of Jewish scholars into literary academe.

This is not to say that Jews and WASPs, especially outside the urban centers, always had an easy time with each other. In 1958, Marx was appointed to a tenured position at Amherst College in bucolic New England to replace Alfred Kazin, who had not been happy at Amherst, nor Amherst with him. There was little love lost between the two. "It was not a matter of race but of class," Daniel Aaron said about a similarly difficult situation at Smith College, where Kazin taught in the academic year 1954–55. Kazin begs to differ.[36] In the mid-1950s the quaint New England college towns were not yet ready for the intensity and mannerisms of a New York intellectual. The Harvard-trained Marx, accompanied by his Yankee wife, posed a much lesser challenge to town and gown despite his left-leaning political views. When the Marxes arrived at Amherst in the fall of 1958, they were surprised by the prevailing tone and "patrician habits." Faculty wives wearing gloves came to call or left calling cards when the Marxes were out. Dinner parties were

10. Leo Marx in 1976. *Photograph by Calvin Campbell. Courtesy of MIT News Office.*

given with the help of servants in white jackets. The Marxes settled in well and stayed for almost twenty years. In 1976, Marx received an offer from the Massachusetts Institute of Technology in Cambridge to help organize a program that "was to insinuate a critical point of view into the course of studies at MIT" (interview). Marx accepted, teaching in the belly of the beast until his retirement in 1991.

Marx's career illuminates some of the major steps in the history of Jewish literary scholars: the opening of Ivy League English departments to Jewish graduate students, their fanning out into the Midwest as young faculty, and the opening of New England's elite colleges to Jewish professors. The measure of the immense distance traveled by Jewish literary critics in academe between Harry Levin's departure from Minneapolis in 1929 and Leo Marx's arrival there in 1949 was taken inadvertently in an essay Marx published in 1953, entitled "Mr. Eliot, Mr. Trilling, and *Huckleberry Finn*." The essay was a declaration of independence from the theological coercion of Eliot and the moral coercion of Trilling. It accused the two of betraying the cause of freedom by using formalist criteria to justify the farcical, "faint-hearted" ending of *Huckleberry Finn,* in which Huck betrays his friendship with the runaway slave Jim by giving in to Tom Sawyer's wish to play at liberating the recaptured man. Supported by Santayana, Marx charged Clemens with having only "half-escaped" the genteel tradition (*PaP* 45), and indicted both Eliot and Trilling for having succumbed to "that absolutist impulse of our critics to find reasons, once a work has been admitted to the highest canon of literary reputability, for admiring every bit of it." In short, like Huck, Eliot and Trilling bowed to authority at the expense of "social or political morality" (*PaP* 48).

Only a few years earlier, the lumping together of Eliot and Trilling would have struck anyone as rather strange, not least of all because Eliot's exclusive view of culture had no room for people like Trilling. In fact, their interpretations of *Huckleberry Finn* were rather dissimilar; they reflected Eliot's religious and Trilling's moral notion that man was very much in need of restraints.[37] But since neither of the two believed that man's primary need was the realization of freedom, which for Marx was the novel's chief issue, Eliot and Trilling failed equally to measure up to the novel's moral and political challenge. "The main thing is freedom," Marx wrote; and "freedom in this book specifically means freedom from society and its imperatives" (*PaP* 45, 49). What the mastery of convention and tradition had been to Levin in 1929, the realization of freedom for all Americans was to Marx in 1949. In the twenty years separating 1929 and 1949, the constraints of gentility had lost their luster and their lure. Marx left Harvard Yard without regrets (even if he could not quite free himself from the intellectual grip of Miller and Matthiessen). "I was offered a chance to stay at Harvard. But Perry Miller said, don't be crazy. It is terrible for people to hang around here. So I got out" (interview).

———————

Harvard Yard had changed and so had literary academe. Men of letters were professionals now. Barriers against Jews seemed to have all but disappeared. That was a start. Of course, the academy's tolerance was not being too severely tested, because the Jews who cared to go into literary studies during the 1920s, 1930s, and 1940s had no intellectual interest in their Jewish heritage, and they certainly were not religious.[38] But this would change when the first Jewish students fully trained by the prewar generation had secured reasonably stable positions in academe.

Occasionally and surprisingly these instructors (born around 1930) turned to Jewish topics. More often than not, this was neither an easy nor a natural thing to do. The careers of Allen Guttmann and Jules Chametzky, students of Leo Marx's at the University of Minnesota, are examples of this new development.

6

The Meaning of Freedom: Allen Guttmann

LEO MARX'S OUTBURST "the main thing is freedom" was a cri de coeur. His influential 1953 essay indicting Samuel Clemens, T. S. Eliot, and Lionel Trilling for the betrayal of freedom by endorsing the ending of *Huckleberry Finn* was written against a new conservatism that was gaining ground in literary academe in the early 1950s.[1] It became the unassigned task of Leo Marx's student Allen Guttmann to conceptualize his mentor's passionate outcry and to determine precisely its political and, oddly enough, Jewish coordinates. Guttmann cared as little about being Jewish as Marx; but he belonged to a generation for which it became possible, and sometimes necessary, to speak of Jewishness in the university.

Allen Guttmann was born in Chicago in 1932. He grew up on the South Side, in a Catholic working-class neighborhood. His playmates came from Italian and Irish families. Occasionally these Catholic boys, accusing him of having killed Christ, assaulted their puzzled victim. Guttmann's parents were nonreligious, poorly educated second-generation American Jews. His father, Emile Jacob, was raised by a French-speaking mother of Sephardic origin (from New Orleans) and a German-speaking father who was an immigrant. Since cultural difference was little valued in American society around 1900, enormous pressure was put on Emile to assimilate. He grew up speaking only English, but eventually married a woman who, like him, had one German-speaking immigrant parent. His prospects for happiness withered in 1936, in the depths of the Depression, when the birth of a daughter left his wife partially paralyzed.

In 1942, when Allen Guttmann was ten years old, the family moved from Chicago to Miami, where Emile hoped a milder climate might improve his wife's health. Here the elder Guttmann made a fundamental mistake that turned his son against him and became a source of substantial emotional and psychological stress. In Miami, Guttmann recalled,

> my father tried to pass as a Methodist because it was very difficult for Jews to get jobs in certain areas. I was very upset by that even as a child. Because they would say to me in school, you are Jewish, aren't you? And my father ordered me to say no. I was really upset about that. My father was too ignorant even to claim to be a Lutheran, which might have been plausible. When my mother died [in 1947], my father had her buried with a Jewish ceremony. By that time, I think, he had a job in Miami Beach, which was mostly Jewish. Then it was okay to be Jewish again. But I was angry at the humiliation, at having to lie to my friends for years, and then admitting the truth.[2]

Emile Guttmann's sister had moved to Florida in 1941, passed as a Gentile, and married a Gentile. She had asked her brother not to reveal that they were Jews. "But he might have tried to hide it anyway," Guttmann suspected. "I am afraid that he was a coward in many ways" (interview). Cowardice in public was, unfortunately, compensated for by petty tyranny at home, and at age seventeen Allen ran away.

This difficult legacy produced in Guttmann an intense dislike of definitions of identity based on nationalism, tribalism, peoplehood, ethnicity, and so forth. To him, the only acceptable basis of identification was an individual's actions and abilities. "Each person," he held, "should at least attempt to choose his or her own life." The right to create one's self and to choose that self-made identity over a fated primary identity represented to Guttmann the fulfillment of the Emersonian promise of freedom. He observed, however, that this was not a notion shared by the majority of Americans. "In America," he realized, "you are identified—as you are in other societies—on the basis of your parents and grandparents, that is, by ascription rather than achievement." This put Guttmann in an awkward position. While he felt that *he* knew who he was, he found it difficult to come up with a descriptive category that would satisfy others:

> I was very unsure what to say about myself because I was not observant. I had never been bar mitzvahed; I had no belief whatever in Judaism. I

didn't even know anything about it. When people asked: are you Jewish? I didn't know what to say. I said yes, because that's the answer they expected. I used to say at one point, well, my parents are. Then you are, they said. So I gave in. If you say I am, I am. It was an identification that did not mean much to me in those days; and, to tell the truth, it still doesn't. (interview)

Ironically, the problem of how to define Jewishness—biologically, ethnically, religiously, culturally, or, intellectually—became a major issue at one point in Guttmann's academic career. That he insisted on thinking about the problem of Jewish identity in America and pursuing it to what appeared to him its logical and inevitable end—the disappearance of the Jews—speaks for his moral seriousness. The fact that Guttmann did not seem to mourn such an end embittered some American Jews and had rabbis up in arms.

As a student Guttmann's chief concern was to find people with whom he could communicate. He enrolled at the University of Florida, which was, financially, his only option. He was quickly disillusioned about the students there. "They were racists," Guttmann remembered, "they seemed vehemently anti-intellectual and full of all kinds of prejudices. I hated them. By the end of my freshman year, I was really in bad shape psychologically" (interview). When he did find a group of friends who were interested in ideas, the question of Jewishness was not salient. Guttmann graduated in 1953. Although he had earned an "A" in all eleven of his English courses, he was refused a chance to continue as a graduate student. Uncertain of his future, he volunteered for military service.

Nine years after World War II and the demise of the Nazi regime, Allen Guttmann arrived in Frankfurt, Germany, as a member of the U.S. Army. He started to learn German from the moment he set foot in the airport. He was not deterred by the fact that the first sign he saw there, "Trink Coca-Cola eiskalt," sounded more like an order than an invitation. Nor was he bothered by the temporal proximity of the Nazi period. "Of course I wondered what the older people had done," but in keeping with his belief in individual responsibility, he was not ready to think about Germans collectively, or to reject all of German culture. "I said to myself that German culture is larger than Hitler; and I am not going to give up Mozart and Beethoven just because of the Nazis. I felt that very strongly; and I still feel that way. You can't hate an entire group on the basis of some members. That means imposing collective guilt. It's not right" (interview).

11. Allen Guttmann in New York City
in 1955. *Courtesy of Allen Guttmann.*

Guttmann's attitude toward Germany was not shaped in response to
the merits of German culture, but in opposition to the attitude of the
majority of American Jews who throughout the 1950s and 1960s tended
to ostracize Germany. Guttmann refused to be coerced into subscribing
to attitudes that reflected group membership rather than personal experience. Unlike his father, he would not submit to any pressure connected
with his Jewish descent. His attitude toward Germany was a deliberate
declaration of independence in the face of a historical event that unified
American Jews like no other until the Six-Day War of 1967. When
Guttmann's children were born in the early 1960s, he called them Hans
and Erika. "I gave them very German names partly because that goes
with my own last name and partly because there were a lot of Jewish
academics at the time who said, I can't buy a Volkswagen because of the
Holocaust, I can't eat Wiener Schnitzel because of the Holocaust. I
thought that was wrong and I got into terrible arguments with them."
A few years later, in 1967, he planned to apply for a Fulbright position
in Germany. The same arguments flared up in Guttmann's circle of

friends and colleagues about Jews helping Germany to restore a semblance of normality and the impossibility of any Jew speaking on behalf of the dead. Those arguments, Guttmann recalls, made him even more determined to go (interview).

Guttmann was fairly fluent in German when he left the army in 1955. He moved to New York, married, and pursued a graduate degree in comparative literature at Columbia University. But, once again, he was unhappy with his school. "The university was very cynical about its students. You had to chase professors, beg for a chance to talk to them. I was very distressed with the place. I remember trying to talk to Richard Chase. He was not quite running, but he was walking very fast because he did not want to be bothered by a student" (interview). When Guttmann received his master's degree in 1956, he transferred to the University of Minnesota and instantly fell in love with it. He liked Minneapolis, loved his fellow students (among them Jules Chametzky and Alan Trachtenberg), and found the faculty exciting and accessible. His anger subsided and he threw himself into his work.

In the fall of 1958, two years after Guttmann's arrival at the University of Minnesota, Leo Marx took up his post at Amherst College. And a good thing it was. When a temporary position in English and American Studies opened in 1959, Marx upset the Amherst routine, which was to get somebody from Harvard. "They didn't recruit," Guttmann explained. "Harvard would send somebody, picked by Amherst people there. But this time Leo said, wait a minute; there are other schools. Why don't you look at candidates from Yale, Berkeley, or Minnesota? And they thought this a wonderful, new, radical idea" (interview). Guttmann interviewed, got the job, and has been at Amherst College ever since. He was tenured in 1965 and promoted to professor in 1971, the year his third book appeared.

Guttmann's early work reads like an attempt to reconstruct the historical context for the emotional battles of his mentors' generation. He was beginning to connect himself to American traditions that could appeal to someone who had always felt "something of an outsider to American society" (interview). His first book, *The Wound in the Heart: America and the Spanish Civil War* (1962), examined the reflections of a war that had galvanized the generation of Daniel Aaron and Leo Marx. "No public event of the years between 1919 and 1939," Guttmann wrote, "excepting the Great Depression itself—moved Americans as did this Spanish conflict."[3] Contrary to conventional wisdom, he argued, "the extraordinarily passionate concern that great numbers of Americans felt for the fate of the Spanish Republic was not—for the most part—the result of a movement toward radicalism" (*W* 3). Spain was not a "Communist cause." Rather, it was "one more manifestation of the liberal tradition in America." In a Europe crawling with fascists, Americans supported Spain's Loyalist government "because it was thought to be legal, constitutional, republican, liberal, democratic" (*W* 3). To absolve volunteers for Spain of the taint of communism and "to relate the Spanish Civil War to the liberal democratic tradition in America" (*W* vi) was the chief concern of the book.

In *The Wound in the Heart* Guttmann measured the responses of Americans to the war in Spain, slowly moving his focus from the political right to the left. Particularly fascinating is the last third of the book, where Guttmann's analysis of the liberal response to the Spanish Civil War culminates in his exposé of an absurd situation. Despite the general popularity of the Spanish Loyalists' cause among liberal Democrats and left radicals, American foreign policy steered a course that eventually harmed the Loyalist side. Fear of becoming involved in another European war swayed Roosevelt to uphold the Neutrality Act of 1935 and to supplement it with legislation that prohibited the sale of arms to the Spanish Republic. This embargo hurt the Loyalists more than the rebels because the latter were supplied illegally by Europe's fascist governments. This created an imbalance of machine power (bombers, tanks, trucks) between Loyalists and rebels and produced a curious reversal in American liberal thinking.

Among the fundamental assumptions of the liberal movement had been a "belief in a universe where laws are discoverable by human reason and a belief in progress based on a more and more complete discovery of those laws" (*W* 82). In *The Machine in the Garden,* Leo Marx had demonstrated how the advent of technology, an embodiment of rationality, had reinforced the liberal belief in progress. Machines were good because they made life easier and increased productivity. That faith, Guttmann argued, "weakened as it was by Darwin, Marx, and Freud," had been threatened by World War I, when technology had visibly inflicted suffering on a massive scale for the first time. "Much of the intensity of the support given the Loyalist government," he concluded, "was, therefore, the intensity of fear" of machines (*W* 114). After the bombing of Guernica and Barcelona, and with the arms embargo still in place, the Spanish conflict came to be seen by many Americans as a conflict between man (Loyalists) and machine (fascists). Unexpectedly, liberals found themselves on the side that opposed machines and wondered about "the implications and the actualities of technological society" (*W* 191). The war dampened the liberals' enthusiasm about machines but left them unwilling to give up on the idea of mechanization altogether. "Nevertheless," wrote Guttmann, "to say that most men were willing to mechanize or to condone mechanization . . . is *not* to say that they were untouched by the fear of mechanization or . . . by a desire for the spontaneity and the freedom from repression that we associate with an organic relationship to the natural landscape" (*W* 191). One can easily recognize the concerns of Leo Marx and Henry Nash Smith in these thoughts.

Guttmann contended that at the core of American fiction about the Spanish Civil War—in particular, Ernest Hemingway's novels—was the conflict between man and machine, the Spanish earth and fascist weaponry, primitivism and progress:

> In other words, there was in Spain as in nineteenth-century America the dilemma and the paradox of primitivism and progress that Henry Nash Smith has assayed in *Virgin Land*. Just as the dream of America as an industrial Titan contradicted the dream of America as a new Garden of Eden, so the attempt to discipline and organize and mechanize "feudal" Spain [i.e., to arm the Loyalists] contradicted the desire to preserve a spontaneous, organic, archaic relationship of man and nature. (*W* 193)

At this point liberals shake hands with conservatives. Regarding man's rootedness in the "soil," there was little that distinguished Hemingway's vision from that of T. S. Eliot and the Southern Agrarians. Guttmann did not comment on that disquieting confluence, but contented himself with the remark that "one need not be a primitivist today to feel that technological mass-society is both repressive and frighteningly unstable" (*W* 194). Today this assertion strikes Guttmann as rather feckless. In short, Guttmann described the perception of Spain in American fiction as an imaginative extension of American concerns onto foreign territory, just as Marx and Smith had once argued that America's presumably virgin soil had served as a mirror for Europe's utopian fantasies:

> Hemingway's vision of the Spanish war has its roots in a very *American* tradition of thought and feeling. The Spanish war was, among other things, a fight against the desecration of that relationship between man and nature that Natty Bumppo sought in forest and prairie, that Thoreau found while floating quietly on Walden Pond, that Herman Melville

pursued in his quest for an "authentic Eden in a pagan sea," that Walt Whitman contemplated in a blade of summer grass, that Huck and Jim discovered while drifting down the Mississippi on a raft. . . . Here, as elsewhere, we found in the Spanish war a mirror reflecting the image of our own unquiet desperation. (*W*194–195)

What bothered Guttmann more than the imaginative imperialism of American writers, however, was the fact that the Spanish cause exposed so clearly the limitations of the liberal tradition in America. "The liberal consensus in the United States," Guttmann complained, "has led, in a sense, to the ideological equivalent of the one-party system and to the emotional and intellectual stagnation of a tradition that does not constantly define itself against an opposing tradition" (*W* 211). In order to stave off complacency, liberalism needed a worthy antagonist. He found himself agreeing with Lionel Trilling that "in the United States . . . liberalism is not only the dominant but even the sole intellectual tradition. For it is the plain fact that nowadays there are no conservative or reactionary ideas in general circulation." [4] But when Trilling pushed on and claimed that conservative impulses "express themselves not in ideas but in 'irritable mental gestures which seek to resemble ideas' " (*W* 211– 212), Guttmann demurred.

Out of the demurral grew Guttmann's next book, *The Conservative Tradition in America* (1967), which traced the influence of Edmund Burke and like-minded European Conservatives on American political and intellectual life. Guttmann's central contention was that in the realm of politics the ideas of Burke had been successfully and lastingly displaced by the liberal tradition derived from the philosophy of John Locke, but that Burkean philosophy lived on as a literary phenomenon: "Pushed in disarray from the battlefield of political activity, Conservatism has taken refuge in the citadel of ideas." [5] Guttmann supported this claim by examining the literary tradition from the disillusioned liberalism of Henry Adams to the agrarianism of Allen Tate, with lingering stops at the humanism of Irving Babbitt and Paul Elmer More and the materialism of George Santayana.

Guttmann's chapter on Conservative American men of letters was an important signpost in the history of the integration of Jews into American literary academe because it analyzed unselfconsciously precisely the tradition that had put up the barriers against non-WASPs. Harry Levin had had to contend with that tradition when he arrived at Harvard in 1929. Leo Marx left Harvard for Levin's native city in 1949, and Marx's student Guttmann, untouched by the Harvard magic, reconstructed the ideological framework that linked Adams, Santayana, Babbitt, Eliot, and the Southern Agrarians, and described the walls that had to be scaled by the generation of Lionel Trilling and Harry Levin. That they succeeded against the formidable phalanx marshaled in Guttmann's book continues to amaze.

For Guttmann the issue at stake was the tension between individual freedom and social restraint that Marx had elucidated in his essay on the critical responses to the ending of *Huckleberry Finn*. Marx's own view was founded in Rousseau, whereas the views of Eliot and Trilling, as Marx saw them, were firmly rooted in the tradition of Edmund Burke. Guttmann's book gave Eliot and Trilling their due but concluded that Marx's faith in individualism was preferable. Teacher and student, who had escaped from the Jewish version of Mark Twain's shore society, believed fervently in the right of the individual to choose his own destiny. Guttmann pointed out that the crucial distinction between liberals and conservatives was found in their definitions of freedom. Far from expressing itself merely in "irritable mental gestures," as Trilling would have it, Conservatism, Guttmann explained, was in fact a tradition with precise ideological contours derived from Edmund Burke's definition of freedom. Burke's response to the French Revolution had not been jubilant. In October 1789, Burke had written that real liberty "is not solitary, unconnected, individual, selfish liberty, as if every man was to regulate the whole of his conduct by his own will. The liberty I mean is *social* freedom. It is that state of things in which liberty is secured by the equality of restraint." Elsewhere Burke had admonished that the "inclinations of men should frequently be thwarted, their will controlled, and their passions brought into subjection. . . . The restraints on men, as well as their liberties, are to be reckoned among their rights" (quoted in *CT* 7–8).

These views are not alien to Mark Twain's novel. Huck's willfulness, for example, is famously checked by Jim.[6] The happy life on the raft is indeed secured by the equality of restraint, as Eliot and Trilling but not Marx realized. In his book Guttmann demonstrated how Burke's views lived on in one strand of the American literary tradition. He detected Burke's philosophy of restraint in Irving Babbitt's "inner check" and Paul Elmer More's "external checks in the form of government" (*CT* 139). He saw it reflected in Eliot's and More's espousal of Christianity and in Santayana's insights that "liberty follows from the recognition of necessity" (*CT* 143) and "true liberty is bound up with an institution, a corporate scientific discipline, necessary to set free the perfect man, or the god within us" (*CT* 144). Finally, Guttmann turned to the Southern Agrarians, analyzing the views of John Crowe Ransom, Allen Tate (his teacher at the University of Minnesota), and Robert Penn Warren. He traced the influence of T. S. Eliot and outlined the development of the New Criticism. He indicted this critical approach as an insidious form of Conservatism because its hermeneutics of textual analysis were intimately tied to a reactionary, repressive world view (*CT* 156–157). Guttmann did not quite come down on the side of Leo Marx and his unequivocal embrace of freedom but rather on the side of Karl Marx, who had been ready to give up liberty for equality. "Socialism with a sense of the past," Guttmann wrote, "is the name of my desire" (*CT* 180). It seemed that Guttmann was theoretically willing to give up a measure of his personal freedom if the collectivity in question was freely chosen rather than imposed. Guttmann's desire was not put to the test.

———

What was tested, however, was his sense of the past. "It seems unlikely," Guttmann had pronounced, "that a people uninterested in its origins—however inglorious they may be—can respond fully to its present, or worry intelligently about its future" (*CT* 179–180). Guttman was soon called on to think about the conflict between origins and destiny, between a legacy of Jewish obligations and the enticing prospect of escaping from this burden into America's freedom of choice, a tempting invitation that he, like so many American Jews, had happily accepted.

In 1962, while working on *The Conservative Tradition in America*, Guttmann was invited to give a talk on Jewish literature at the Jewish student organization of the University of Massachusetts at Amherst. He accepted and went to one of the talks in the series to find out what was expected of him. He was put off by the speaker's adulation of Bernard Malamud and Philip Roth. "It was a very positive presentation: how wonderful these writers were; these are our writers, and aren't they wonderful! That approach didn't appeal to me. It seemed uncritical, as if the purpose were not to understand Roth and Malamud but to celebrate Jewishness." Guttmann sensed group coercion and dug in his heels. Research for his own presentation revealed "what minimal identification most American Jewish writers had with Judaism." Guttmann did not hesitate to point out that unwelcome fact (interview).

In his talk "Jewish Radicals, Jewish Writers," Guttmann asserted that the political radicalism of the American Jew had been misunderstood. He claimed that it was "an unrecognized fact that American Jews who rejected the political *status quo* have also rejected Jehovah and Torah and Talmud. Their radicalism has involved the abandonment rather than the intensification of their faith in Judaism as a religion. . . . The radicalism of Emma Goldman and a host of others is actually the exodus of those who rejected both Judaism and the political, economic and religious orthodoxies of the society in which they lived." [7] With the collapse of political radicalism in the United States, the speed of that exodus slowed down, but Jews continued to voice their dissent: "Daniel Aaron, Daniel Bell, Saul Bellow, Herbert Gold, Paul Goodman, Irving Howe, Alfred Kazin, Norman Mailer, Leo Marx, Philip Rahv, David Riesman, Philip Roth, J. D. Salinger, Morris Schappes, Harvey Swados and Lionel Trilling—to name a mixed handful—are among the foremost and often the angriest critics of American minds, morals, and possibilities. Despite their Jewish backgrounds, none of these men is noted for affirmation of Judaism as a religion." [8]

Since their radical and political values could hardly be redefined as Jewish values, Guttmann asked by what right and reason these men were pressed into service as Jews. If one wanted to see them within a specific tradition, he said, it must be the tradition of dissent and alienation outlined in Veblen's essay "The Intellectual Pre-eminence of Jews in Modern Europe." All other efforts to enlist these intellectuals as Jews were doomed to fail. Judging the future by the past, Guttmann wrote, "it is plain, even to a very timid Jeremiah, that the extraordinary postwar outburst of literary dissent will, as an identifiably *Jewish* renaissance, be as short-lived as the now defunct tradition of foreign-language political radicalism." [9] Guttmann serenely predicted the disappearance of the Jews into America. He upheld the right to personal freedom and individual choice over the restraints imposed by a sense of an inherited communal past.

It cannot have come as much of a surprise to him that he made many of his listeners angry. His thesis and tone were deliberately adversarial. His stance resembled the defiance of Ozzie Freedman in Roth's story "The Conversion of the Jews." Ozzie, freed from tribal constraints and superstitions, forces the community of Jews to avow their faith in Christ by threatening to jump off a roof. Much to Guttmann's amusement, the Amherst rabbi attending his talk rose to the occasion. "He was furious," Guttmann recalls, "and he began to denounce me as a friend of the Nazis. That really fascinated me" (interview). When the *Massachusetts*

12. Allen Guttmann c. 1985. *Courtesy of Allen Guttmann.*

Review, which had been receptive to Guttmann's earlier work, declined to print a revised version of his presentation, he turned to the *American Scholar,* then edited by Hiram Haydn, who was Jewish and had been a student of Marjorie Nicolson's at Columbia twenty years earlier. Haydn gave the essay to Alfred Kazin, who recommended it for immediate publication. Its appearance in the fall issue of 1963 provoked a torrent of angry letters. "By this time," Guttmann remembered, "I was really interested in this reaction" (interview). As always, resistance made him even more determined to pursue his course.

When *The Conservative Tradition* had gone to press, Guttmann immersed himself in fiction and autobiographies by American Jews. Four years later he published his third book, *The Jewish Writer in America: Assimilation and Crisis of Identity* (1971). It is Guttmann's most sustained effort to come to terms with a tradition to which others said he belonged. The book was an attempt to be fair; but its findings were nevertheless predetermined, not least of all because Guttmann, despite months of reading books on Jewish thought and Jewish history, did not

really gain intellectual access to the complex and, at times, difficult body
of literary texts written in several languages and over many centuries
that constitute Jewish knowledge. The French philosopher Emmanuel
Levinas had argued in 1954 that to remain Jewish in the modern world
required intense study, amounting in fact to the resolve "to follow a new
discipline." Yet doing so, Levinas continued, "is impossible unless we
return to Hebrew." [10] I suspect, however, that ignorance of Hebrew was a
lesser factor in Guttmann's failure to achieve an intimate and sympathetic
understanding of the Jewish intellectual tradition than his profound inner
resistance to the subject. His distance to what he had been able to
uncover was reflected in his book's final sentence. It predicted that "the
survival in America of a significant and identifiable Jewish literature
depends upon the unlikely conversion to Judaism of a stiff-necked, in-
tractable, irreverent, attractive generation that no longer chooses to be
chosen." [11] He declared his abdication as a Jew, or, as he preferred to put
it, his "own refusal to acquire an authentic Jewish identity." [12]

Guttmann's book opened ominously with Aaron's defiant apostasy at
the foot of Mount Sinai. While Moses conferred with God on the
mountain top, Aaron fashioned the golden calf. Guttmann is only half-
joking when he asks whether Aaron was still a Jew. The underlying
question was serious: At what point *did* one stop being a Jew? Was it not
enough to violate the central tenets of Judaism? How and why did one
remain tied to other Jews? It was with some relief that Guttmann noted
the temporal nature of these ties in America. In the freedom of the
promised land, religious, ethnic, and sociocultural ties were dissolved
through acculturation and assimilation, a process that frequently led to
the abandonment of Jewish law a generation after an observant ancestor
had set foot on the American shore.

Guttmann's first concern in the book was the process of assimilation,
from Mary Antin and Abraham Cahan to Philip Roth and Alfred Kazin.
His central thesis emerges most clearly in his reading of a fascinating
novel by Myron Kaufmann, titled *Remember Me to God* (1957). It depicts
the cowardly behavior of a third-generation American Jew, Richard
Amsterdam, at Harvard College from 1938 to 1942. Richard is a
"greaseball," an epithet invented for Jews at Harvard. His aspirations are
noble—to become a worthy American modeled on the image of the
Boston Brahmins—but his means betray incompetence, pettiness, and
envy. Richard pushes his way into the *Lampoon* as a stepping-stone for
election into one of Harvard's social clubs, preferably the Hasty Pudding.
He believes that only conversion and marriage to an American blue

blood can assure his acceptance by the high society he wishes to cultivate and make his own. Richard's father, Adam Amsterdam, is shocked when he learns of his son's intention to convert to Christianity. He tries to dissuade him by explaining the importance and meaning of Judaism as bequeathed to him by his immigrant father. But much to his dismay, Adam finds himself unable to conceptualize the meaning of Judaism or to defend its importance. He had clung instinctively to inherited notions while fighting to secure for his family a life in Boston's middle class. Guttmann concluded, "Adam Amsterdam has gone too far along the path of assimilation to prevent his son from going further" (*JW* 61). Guttmann blamed the father for the son's decision to drop out, as if the principle of individual responsibility, otherwise a mainstay in Guttmann's weltanschauung, were not applicable here.

Guttmann then turned to writers who endorse the principle of peoplehood, from Horace Kallen to Chaim Potok, reserving his highest praise for Ludwig Lewisohn's novel *The Island Within* (1928). It is surprising that Guttmann should like this novel because its protagonist, an assimilated Jewish doctor whose marriage to a Gentile is disintegrating, comes to accept views that are close to those held by Kallen, views that Guttmann thought passionate but illogical (*JW* 94). Lewisohn's protagonist Arthur Levy shuts down his practice to join the staff of the hospital, symbolically named Beth Yehuda (House of the Jew), because he had come to the conclusion that to declare oneself human was not enough: "What is it to be human? Nothing abstract. Show me a human being who isn't outwardly and inwardly some *kind* of a human being, dependent, though he were the most austere philosopher, in his human life on others of more or less the same *kind*. There is no place for *kindless* people in the world. . . . In a word, this vague cry, let us be human—it's a favorite cry among Jews—means nothing and gets you nowhere."

Kallen had argued that one was most human by being most particular, most American by being most ethnic.[13] The resolution of Lewisohn's novel, a conflicted return to ethnicity, brings to mind Philip Roth's story "Eli, the Fanatic." The moral forces to which Lewisohn's Arthur Levy and Roth's Eli Peck succumb are very similar. In Roth's story the modern American's *tshuvah* (return, repentance) is brought about by a hasid, a survivor of the gas chambers, who needs a place for his school and its refugee pupils. In Lewisohn's pre-Holocaust novel the moral imperative is also represented by a hasid who has preserved the memory of medieval pogroms in the form of a manuscript documenting the slaughter of Jews during the Crusades, and who needs help to relieve the suffering of Jews persecuted in Eastern Europe. The appeal for help by the two hasidim is not directed at free and prosperous Americans. Rather, it is addressed to the Jews hiding behind the façade of their American freedom and middle-class prosperity. It is an appeal to what Morris R. Cohen called "tribal consciousness" and to family feeling. The guilt feelings induced by the two messengers from history represent precisely the kind of coercion Guttmann cannot abide because it sorts people into groups: If you don't help us, you help them and acquiesce in the murder of your family.

Arthur Levy needs the moral cudgel less than Eli Peck because, embroiled in a mid-life crisis, Levy is ready to exchange the emptiness of American middle-class life for the heavy burden of history. But even the young suburbanite Eli Peck eventually succumbs and picks up his *pekl* (burden). He puts on the hasidic garments left on his doorstep by the hasid's helper. In this attire Eli walks to the hospital to welcome his newborn son. To relinquish America's freedom for medieval Jewish bondage is considered insane by Eli's friends, and they have his caftan replaced by a straitjacket. Roth's message seems clear: you may survive the death camps in hasidic garb (that is, with the help of faith), but if you don it in free America, you imprison yourself. The tone of Roth's story indicates that Eli has done right by trying to take the hasid's point of view. Guttmann, however, concluded that Eli was driven insane "by the hardness of the zealots who have treated him as a fanatic" (*JW* 71). Guttmann did not comment on the similarities between Lewisohn's novel and Roth's story; they may have struck him as less persuasive than Roth's denial, at a *Commentary* symposium in the early sixties, of owing any special allegiance to the Jews.

The third section of Guttmann's book, "The Revolutionary Messiah," examines the works of Jewish radicals. This substantially enlarged version of Guttmann's 1963 paper broadened the term *radical* to include Norman Mailer and Allen Ginsberg. Mailer received extensive treatment, and Guttmann captured nicely his preferred state of permanent adolescence. "In the explosive and protean variety of his literary and political postures," Guttmann wrote, "he can be taken to represent the extraordinary energy of the gifted Jew described in Veblen's essay. He is the Jew released from his ethnic identity and invited to act out whatever roles are now within reach of his imagination" (*JW* 154). Mailer's flights of fancy were constrained neither by a sense of social obligations nor by a sense of the past. Being self-invented, Mailer disproved to Guttmann's mind Morris Cohen's stark admonition that "no change of ideology—

no matter how radical—can make a man cease to be the son of his parents. It is not only vain but also incompatible with self-respect to try to appear other than what we are" (*JW* 94). Guttmann knew what Cohen meant but preferred to misread him along with Kallen as advocating that a child become "a replica of his parents and grandparents" (*JW* 94). Nothing could be more nonsensical, since both Kallen and Cohen had deliberately turned away from the religious observance practiced by their fathers to become secular professors of philosophy. What Guttmann's book finally illuminates is that unlike Kallen and Cohen, Mailer had very little to turn away from; nor was his vacuity, one might add, altogether his parents' fault.

The final section of Guttmann's book was devoted to Saul Bellow, who at that time had already produced seven novels. In Guttmann's analysis of *Dangling Man* (1944), the theme of freedom versus captivity (or commitment), which had been at issue in Leo Marx's essay "Mr. Eliot, Mr. Trilling, and Huckleberry Finn," came unexpectedly into sharper focus. Joseph, the dangling man of the novel's title, finds himself "unable to take advantage of the dreadful freedom offered by marginality" (*JW* 182). Bellow's termination of Joseph's dangling state placed the author squarely in the Conservative tradition as outlined in Guttmann's previous book. Guttmann explained that

> Joseph turns—within the time of the novel—from a position that is markedly Protestant and Romantic [focused on individual freedom] to one that is shared by Judaism [Trilling's principle of personal responsibility] and Catholicism [Eliot's submission to the Divine]. He gives up the quest for freedom and accepts the strictures of institutional commitment [by joining the army; Roth's hasidic garb or straitjacket]. It is certainly arguable that Joseph has returned metaphorically from the empty wilderness within in order to surrender himself to a secular equivalent of *Chalakah* [*sic*], the Law. Within the emotional economy of the novel, it is nonetheless a defeat. (*JW* 183)

For Guttmann, as for Marx, submission to a set of laws, to the constraints of society, spelled defeat. Guttmann chose freedom from communal obligations. When he turned to writing his next books—they would be on sports—it was to enter a world "where theoretically at least, individual merit is what matters. Success in sports is based on your achievement and not on an ascription. Not what you were born is important, but what you can do" (interview). But even in the world of sports, Guttmann realized, the issue of freedom was not so simple.

His first book on sports, *From Ritual to Record: The Nature of Modern Sports* (1978), ended with a contemplation of two forms of freedom. One was complete autonomy, as epitomized in the long-distance runner; the other was voluntary conformity, as demanded by any team sport. Guttmann linked these forms of individualism and conformity to the notions of "freedom from" and "freedom to," both part of the liberal tradition. Guttmann confessed that he had grown skeptical about the former. He now had misgivings about "the individualism which flourishes under a kind of negative freedom when a man is unbound by the restraints and trammels of institutional order."[14]

The second notion, to which Guttmann now subscribed, was a form of democratic socialism stressing "the individualism which thrives under positive freedom, when a man is free to choose among alternatives and to act upon his choice." It was precisely the freedom to choose that Guttmann felt had been denied him by the tendency of Jews to perceive themselves as a *Schicksalsgemeinschaft,* a community knitted together by fate, and by their expectation that each Jew act as if the survival of all depended on his or her particular behavior. Guttmann opted to exercise an American right, available in no other culture, when he minimized his natal identity and replaced it with a fate of his own choosing. America, after all, offered refuge from history.

To Guttmann's friend Jules Chametzky, American meant the exact opposite: it offered refuge *to* history. It was a place that allowed Jews to recollect themselves.

7

A Jew from Brooklyn: Jules Chametzky

TO A CASUAL OBSERVER Allen Guttmann and Jules Chametzky may look very much alike: Both are secular urban Jews, born around 1930 (give or take two years), who attended commuter colleges (as the first in their families to go beyond high school), became radicalized in the 1940s, never rid themselves of left-wing sympathies, went to the Midwest for graduate school, and then landed jobs in bucolic Amherst, where they spent the rest of their professional lives, excepting a few teaching stints overseas, lecturing and writing and passing on their ideas about America.

In truth, however, these two Jewish professors are cut from very different cloths. Their perceptions of their country and of themselves as Jews differ widely, and so does their writing on American literature. For Guttmann the basic unit is the individual on his or her way into an America capable of realizing its motto, *e pluribus unum*, and of producing a literature that remains committed to a cosmopolitan ideal. Walt Whitman is Guttmann's favorite example. For Chametzky, by contrast, the basic unit of self-definition is the group or community into which one was born. He sees America as a mosaic of different groups working within one society, where each group has the rights only of *unus inter plurimum*.

While Guttmann emphasizes consent, cooperation, freedom of choice, and the individual's right to self-fashioning, Chametzky stresses descent, the utilization of the particulars of gender, race, ethnicity, and class as a path to knowledge, and the American freedom to remain whoever one is. He finds it liberating and empowering to say, "I take

175

my stand as a Jew from Brooklyn because this is what I am" and to use his particularity to read the fiction of African American writers. The connecting bridge is built of empathy and of what M. H. Abrams called "imaginative consent."

However, Chametzky's approach to Jewish American literature is, like Guttmann's, accommodationist. He has his eyes trained on the movement of Jewish writers toward and into America rather than on the persistence of Jewish cultural ideals and traditions within America. In the early 1970s the two professors, who are friends, arrived at the same conclusion about literature written by American Jews—it was going to disappear—a judgment predetermined by the starting points of their investigations. At the time, Guttmann and Chametzky claimed that contemporary Jewish writers in America had fully mastered the nuances of the English language and the literary skills of the Gentile world. They had liberated themselves from their native material as well as from the literary dictatorship of T. S. Eliot, and were "now free to bend the materials of [their] experience to [their] independent vision." [1]

The paths by which the two scholars arrived at their conclusions were very different. While Guttmann's had the advantage of logical coherence, Chametzky's gained support from the fact that little about Jews is strictly logical, their strengths being the ability to live with contradiction and paradox. "In other words," Chametzky summed up, "I am more dialectical, while Guttmann is a Lockeian, bound by logical coherence; it excludes, I include." [2] Writing about Philip Roth's first book, *Goodbye, Columbus* (1959), for instance, Guttmann held that when Roth disparaged the Jews, he really meant it; while Chametzky blithely asserted that to denigrate an ethnic past was to affirm its strength. The need to denigrate proved that the past endured and continued to affect the writer. Self-deprecation was an asset, and a funny one to boot. More seriously, Chametzky argued that despite Roth's efforts "to liberate himself from its smothering effects upon his creative imagination," Roth did not, could not, and would not evade "the particularities of his experience," because they formed the very basis of his career as a writer (*OD* 12). It was by way of the particular, Chametzky claimed, that Roth attracted an *American* urban audience. Despite some common denominators, then, the two liberal Jewish literature professors represent very different attitudes toward Jewish identity and culture in America, which seemed to be given a new lease on life in the early 1960s. Unlike Guttmann, Chametzky reveled in the revival.

Jules Chametzky was born in Brooklyn, New York, in 1928. His parents were immigrants from Eastern Europe. His father was born in the Russian province of Volhynia in 1896 and arrived in New York in 1913; his mother, a native of Lublin, came to the United States as a child around 1903. Her father had been a cattle dealer in Poland and dreamed of having land on which to raise his own cows. Maurice de Hirsch made it possible. Realizing that more Russian Jews were willing to emigrate to the United States than to the wilds of Argentina or arid Palestine, the German-born banker let himself be persuaded by Jewish American philanthropists and officials of the Hebrew Emigrant Aid Society (HEAS) to donate almost $2.5 million to settle Jews on American farmland. Among the agricultural schools and colonies established with the help of the Baron de Hirsch Fund was Woodbine, New Jersey, where shortly after the turn of the century Chametzky's grandfather found himself milking cows.[3] His farm prospered until his daughters decided to marry and brought on a severe shortage of labor.

Chametzky's parents settled in Brooklyn. They were fairly observant, Yiddish-speaking, and working-class. After years of sweating in a clothing factory, Chametzky's father found employment in a butcher's shop. His wife worked two days a week in a sweater factory. In the midst of the Depression, they brought home $35 a week. Their older son Leslie graduated from high school in 1936 and made $9 a week working on a truck. Thus the family had enough of a financial margin to allow Jules a more elaborate education. The Chametzkys were down-to-earth Jewish folk. Yiddish continued to be spoken at home, although Leslie and Jules spoke English to each other; and Yiddish newspapers served as the parents' windows onto a larger world.

In Chametzky's family three Yiddish dailies were consumed. His father read *Der Tog* (The Day). Founded in 1914, *Der Tog* was a liberal, nonparty paper, respectful toward religion but not pious, and sympathetic to Zionism without endorsing any particular faction. A sign of both its traditionalism and its openness toward new needs was the fact that from 1922 to 1927, *Der Tog* undertook the monumental serial publication of the Bible rendered in Yiddish by the poet Yehoash.

Even more popular than *Der Tog* was the *Forverts* (Forward), which was read by one of Chametzky's uncles, who was a factory worker. The *Forverts,* founded in 1897, was a social-democratic paper that printed anything from cheap sensationalism to high culture. Under the distinguished editorship of Abraham Cahan, the subject of Chametzky's monograph *From the Ghetto* (1977), the paper gradually became adviser, guide, and comforter to immigrants on their way into American society. Cahan, as Chametzky saw him, was a mediator, an enabler of transitions. His task, Irving Howe wrote, was "to educate [immigrants] in Yiddish culture and tear them away from it in behalf of American fulfillment."

The latter goal was anathema to *Die Freiheit* (Liberty), a Communist daily that started publication in 1922. It was read by another of Chametzky's uncles, who was a presser in a garment factory. As the German-Russian nonaggression pact of 1939 was announced and Nazi troops invaded Poland, the readership of *Die Freiheit* began to dwindle. The paper tried to salvage what it could from the ruins of the pact and the beginning of the war. It did not print the statement of the Communist Party that it was not in favor of boycotting German goods; but when it became known that *Die Freiheit* endorsed the party line, "a kind of pall fell upon the Yiddish-speaking community; it all seemed beyond credence."[4]

In Chametzky's family the ties to Eastern Europe were strong. Small checks were sent "home" to help support the parents of Chametzky's father and several aunts, whose photographs were displayed in the Brooklyn living room. These relatives did not survive the Nazi occupation.[5] Newsreels about the victorious German army overrunning Europe in all directions terrified the American Chametzkys. In 1940, when Jules was twelve, the Germans took Paris. Chametzky conveyed some of the anxiety his family felt at the time when he wrote in 1983, "I daresay no Jew, however attenuated his or her connection with Judaism, could feel that those German troops photographed by Movietone News marching down the Champs Elysées in the spring of 1940 were not coming directly after him/her" (*OD* 92). In 1940, Leslie enlisted in the infantry, in the famous First Division. "He was a Hemingwayesque character," Chametzky recalled. "He saw a lot of action and escaped death by a hair many times. He participated in the invasion of North Africa, was captured by Rommel's Afrika Korps in Tunisia early in 1943, escaped after ten days of captivity, and then took part in the invasion of Sicily beginning in July 1943" (interview).

Chametzky was thrilled by his brother's adventures but thought that one adventurous character in the family was enough. If the war dragged on, he figured, he had to avoid being drafted into the infantry. Therefore he decided to enroll in the engineering curriculum at Brooklyn Tech in

1942, an elite high school, which would increase his chances for an officer's career. A more immediate reason for Chametzky's choice was that his junior high school was located in a rough Brooklyn neighborhood where, after school, street fights with black and Italian kids were the rule. If you made it into Brooklyn Tech, you could get out of junior high school a year early. To his dismay, however, Chametzky soon discovered that "engineering was not for Jews" (interview). Some of his teachers made life difficult for Jewish students; but with the threat of the infantry hanging over his head, Chametzky toughed it out and graduated just as the war was coming to an end.

Since his parents had achieved financial stability, having bought in 1939 the butcher shop Chametzky's father worked in, Chametzky could go on to college. He had become interested in the humanities and would have liked to study at City College, but his engineering curriculum had not included the foreign languages required there. So Chametzky enrolled in Brooklyn College, where he could make up the requirement in a year of intensive study. Its campus was closer to home and seemed idyllic. "It looked like a little pastoral island in the middle of Brooklyn" (interview). Years earlier, Chametzky had become sensitized to his surroundings. "When I saw *Dead End* as a kid in Williamsburg, I remember the jolt at realizing that I lived in a slum! My first response was to be alarmed in ways I had never thought to be."[6] But the child discovered a pleasant compensation that offset his discovery of the slums and anti-Semitism. "We were in the movies: not bad. We were certainly not outside of the human experience of our times" (*OD* 66).

The student body at Brooklyn College was overwhelmingly Jewish; there was a sprinkling of Catholics and African Americans. Most of the administrators, however, were white Protestants from the Midwest. Because the school was mainly a commuter college, integration was not imposed from above by assignments to dormitories. One of the consequences was that student societies, houses, social and athletic clubs, fraternities, and so on were organized along ethnic lines, with the possible exception of socialist and communist groups. Orthodox students who came from Yeshiva University High School or Flatbush Yeshiva did not participate in the extracurricular life of the college until Alan Dershowitz, Chametzky's junior by ten years, established the first Orthodox Jewish house plan at Brooklyn College.[7] Chametzky, of course, had long lapsed from faith. His only brush with orthodoxy was during the afternoons when he taught English at a Brooklyn yeshiva for $30 a week. In his sophomore year, however, Chametzky gave Jewish learning another shot. At the urging of a neighborhood friend, Norman Podhoretz, he took a couple of evening classes on "Comparative Religion" and "Jewish Literature" at the Jewish Theological Seminary; but they did not excite him.

His passion during college was writing plays. It was a possible road to either Broadway or Hollywood. Some of Chametzky's fellow hopefuls actually got there. Howard Sackler, the author of *The Great White Hope,* made it, as did Morty Gunty, who starred in one of Chametzky's plays and appears in Woody Allen's *Broadway Danny Rose.* A neighbor, Irwin Mazursky, better known as Paul Mazursky, made films about Jewish themes as early as 1953 *(Next Stop Greenwich Village).* His 1989 film *Enemies, A Love Story,* based on Isaac Bashevis Singer's 1972 novel about a man arriving in America after the Holocaust and his attempts to deal with the traumas in his life, presented a subject close to the heart of Brooklyn's Jewish residents. The influx of displaced persons into the neighborhood during the 1940s had been a visible sign of the tragedy that had occurred in Europe; but the Holocaust itself was not discussed in any significant way until the trial of Adolf Eichmann in Jerusalem in 1961.

In the late 1940s, the anguish and excitement surrounding the founding of the state of Israel displaced the sorrow over the catastrophe in Europe. It was an opportunity for American Jews, who had remained largely passive during the war, to become active on behalf of Hitler's victims. They did not think of Israel as a place for themselves. The first political action in which Chametzky ever participated was picketing the White House in support of the state of Israel. That Chametzky's commitment was otherwise to the left was no contradiction at the time. Israel was thought of as a socialist experiment: a new kind of Jew, bronzed athletic kibbutz youths, would transform a desert into a garden paradise.

Chametzky had been brought into the left by a college friend, Gene Bluestein, who was an editor of the college newspaper and a "bit-actor and stage hand with the leftwing Yiddish Theater Ensemble, a remnant of ARTEF, the classic Yiddish theater of the thirties."[8] Chametzky had been radicalized during his last years in high school when he read antifascist literature in powerless rebellion against his harassment by profascist teachers. But it was not until 1948 that he joined the American Labor Party. Two years later he graduated from Brooklyn College and joined the Labor Youth League, an offshoot of the Young Communist League of the 1930s. Although not every member was a Communist, most members were solid Marxists. The reason for the continued attractiveness of the far left to American Jews was not, as Daniel Aaron speculated, that "they were barred (or at least felt excluded) from the economic, cultural, and social opportunities available to non-Jewish segments of the population," or that "the heterodoxy [of the left] answered their psychological needs and released damned up energies and aspirations." [9] Young men like Chametzky did not know enough of the world to feel excluded from anything. Rather, the pull of the left was partly a function of the social environment: if you were Jewish, working-class, educated, upwardly mobile, and had a social conscience, your world would be full of people on the left. Chametzky and his peers did witness discrimination. They saw the exclusion of others, mainly black Americans, from opportunities that were open to whites—to Protestants, Catholics, and Jews (in that order). Contrary to Daniel Aaron's surmise that "the Jew weeps for himself," it was in fact much easier, as Irving Howe wrote, "to feel sorry for others." [10]

In 1950, Chametzky followed the lead of many other Jews and joined the NAACP. Shortly afterward, when he had left Brooklyn College for the University of Minnesota, he was put in charge of the committee on fair employment practices. He was intensely involved in Minnesota's passing of the first American Fair Employment Practices Act. Joining the Communist Party, however, was out of the question. In 1951, Chametzky was approached by a recruiter who suggested that he become a party member. "I thought very hard about it," he remembered; but finally he declined for three reasons. He thought the CP's position on literature was too simplistic; he was upset about its treatment of political opposition; and he disagreed with its views on the "national question, the ethnic question, and the Jewish question" (interview).

These were legitimate concerns. The "Jewish question," in particular, had begun to plague left-leaning Americans with strong Jewish identities. After a brief period of ardent support for Israel, the Soviet Union, led by a paranoid, physically and mentally declining dictator, changed its policy. The years between 1948 and 1953 are known as the "black years" in Soviet Jewish history. On the stage of world politics, the Soviet Union embarked on a course of fundamental realignment. Perceiving Israel as firmly in the grip of Anglo-American imperialists, it declared that the Zionists were no longer interested in abolishing imperialist oppression in Palestine. The "progressive workers in Palestine," under the leadership of various communist organizations, would now lead the struggle for national liberation. The new Soviet line in Middle Eastern foreign policy, first discussed publicly in June 1949, took up the cause of Arab national liberation movements. By stimulating these movements, the Soviet Union hoped to enable indigenous people to bring about "changes in the entrenched regimes and the expulsion of the British from their military position in the Arab world." [11]

Although the Soviet Union increased its attacks on the alleged imperialist objectives of Great Britain and the United States in the Middle East during the early 1950s, it remained silent in a number of UN debates touching on issues that concerned Israel directly. Important at that point was the revaluation of the word *Zionism* to connote a stance, policy, and objective inimical to the outlook and goals of the Soviet Union. Behind the scenes, the meaning of the term *Zionist* was further refined. In the late 1940s, the internal power struggle between Stalin's possible heirs intensified and spilled over into the satellite states. It triggered a ferocious anti–Semitic campaign that served as a vent for general discontent about deteriorating social conditions and as a cover-up for fractious Communist infighting. Leading Jewish functionaries in Romania, Poland, and Hungary were dismissed or indicted as imperialist spies and Zionist conspirators; and Jews were arrested "who had never had any sympathy with Zionism or the state of Israel, as well as Zionists in Romania and Czechoslovakia, where Zionist activity and emigration to Israel had been quite legal" (*JSU* 517). One of the most prominent incidents was the trial of Rudolf Slansky, a Czech Jew, and thirteen other "conspirators" (eleven of whom were Jewish), which opened in Prague on November 20, 1952.

Slansky had been dismissed as secretary-general of the Czechoslovak Communist Party, after a sensational "conspiracy" had been uncovered in Prague in the summer of 1951. He was arrested in September 1951, tried in November 1952, and executed along with seven of his Jewish codefendants on December 3, 1952. Slansky was charged, writes the historian Nora Levin, "with shielding Zionist criminals, with heading a 'Central Organization for Plotting Against the State,' and with making contact with David Ben-Gurion, Henry Morgenthau, and other prominent Jews involved in an espionage chain which included Harry Truman, Dean Acheson, and others symbolizing American imperialism and the enslavement of Israel to the United States" (*JSU* 522). It was a classic show trial patterned on the Moscow show trials of the 1930s, complete with "confessions" of monstrous crimes and tortured "witnesses." One of the trial's insidious elements was its blurring of the terms "Zionist" and "Jew." In his study of the trial, Otto Arie wrote in 1969: "While

13. Jules Chametzky in 1987. *Photograph by Stephen Long. Courtesy of* Contact *magazine.*

the terms cosmopolitanism or Zionism might have been too difficult or too general for some people, the term 'of Jewish origin' used in the trials, was clear to everyone" (quoted in *JSU* 524).

When news of the Slansky trial hit American newspapers in November 1952, Jules Chametzky had enough. "I thought the trial was just a display of Russian anti-Semitism." He broke with the left. "It had already been over in 1951. But the Slansky affair was my break" (interview). Chametzky was dumbfounded when he was "named as a subversive element" in the testimony of a witness before the Subversive Activities Control Board of the U.S. Justice Department in January 1954. "[Gene] Bluestein and I were singled out. There was a big to-do in Minneapolis. I was a case, and so was Bluestein" (interview). Chametzky and Bluestein were written up in the local paper and called before a special Investigating Committee appointed by the president of the University of Minnesota in February 1954.[12]

Bluestein was Chametzky's friend from Brooklyn College. It was due to him that Chametzky found himself pursuing graduate studies at the

University of Minnesota. Chametzky had received his degree in mid-year (late 1949) and was happy writing plays and making $30 a week teaching English at a yeshiva. But when the Korean War broke out in 1950, he recalled the threat of the infantry. Hence he did not have to think long when Bluestein, excited by the glowing reports of a mutual friend, said he was going to Minnesota. Chametzky simply said, "All right, I am coming too" (interview). He hoped to study with Robert Penn Warren, whose novel *All the King's Men* had been made into a play, and with Eric Bentley, whose book *The Playwright as Thinker* had profoundly impressed him. But when Chametzky arrived on the scene, Warren had left for Yale and Bentley for Columbia.

Chametzky's disappointment over their departure was soon dwarfed by other issues. Chametzky had arrived in Minneapolis with "the notion abroad in my circle that ten years earlier it had been found to be the most anti-Semitic city in the country." Naturally, this notion, picked up in an article by Carey McWilliams,[13] and "developed around the cafeteria tables of Brooklyn College," filled Chametzky with apprehension. But it was the nation's political climate rather than the city's anti-Semitic past that would become a problem for him.

While the pursuit of literary studies in English transported him into a rarefied world, his involvement in the NAACP exposed him to the raw underside of contemporary America. When he was "named" in 1954 along with Bluestein, he knew the fight was on. Senator Joseph McCarthy had unleashed a witch-hunt that to Chametzky had clear anti-Semitic overtones. "It was the era of the Rosenberg case; that was an important element," he remembered; "a lot of Jews were scurrying for cover. Anybody who was in the least tainted with political leftism was frightened to death" (interview). Intellectuals close to the Communist Party argued that anti-Semitism played a role in the public persecution of the Rosenbergs, whereas the anti-Stalinist left, among them the New York intellectuals congregated around *Partisan Review,* vigorously denied the charge. To Chametzky the connections between anti-Jewish prejudice and the vilification of the Rosenbergs were obvious. He found them confirmed as he observed that many of his friends, who were largely Jewish and working-class, went into hiding during the McCarthy period. Lionel Trilling too saw the connection. In his 1955 essay on Freud, as David Suchoff pointed out, Trilling "quite originally draws a parallel between Freud's Jewish identity in anti-Semitic Vienna and the experience of McCarthyism in America."[14]

But literary subtleties were of little help to Chametzky, who was caught up in the melee as a Jew and a man of the left. When he was finally cleared in late 1954, after half a year of harassment, Chametzky wrote a story about his emotions during that period. He called it "Rites of Passage" and set it in Brooklyn in the late 1930s. On his way home from a victorious marble game, a Jewish boy is waylaid by a gang of Italian kids. They corner him and demand to know his name. Too terrified to speak, he is assisted in his confession by one of the Italian boys who offers: "The drip's name is Charlie Russo." The gang leader, expecting a Jewish name, is "caught between disbelief and rage." His confusion owes to "a harried immigration official on Ellis Island [who] had not bothered to ask the frightened Jew standing before him to repeat a mumbled name. A slip of the pen, an association with the immigrant's homeland, and Leb Reiserwitz became Louis Russo. It had been a matter of indifference to them, for they both knew exactly who he was, but for Louis Russo's heirs and descendants in the new land an issue had been born that had to be resolved. Charlie braced himself for the question which had been unnecessary a moment before."

Since external markers, including names, have become ambiguous, and the Italian boys do not think of making Charlie drop his pants, clarification can be obtained only through self-ascription, or (given the fact that this hearing in the street is a cipher for the McCarthy investigations) through self-incrimination. The leader, furious at Charlie "for making him break the rule of the game," for making him violate the *rites* of passage, finally snarls: "All right, snotnose, are you a Jew or a Cath'lic?" The means of escape, so enticing to American Jews from Bernard Berenson to Emile Guttmann, are presented to Charlie. It is a moment Charlie had envisioned in his dreams; it would be easy to obtain the *right* of passage with a simple lie. Instead he tells the truth: " 'A Jew!' he said; and then he ran." When he reaches his apartment building, he comes to a house of communal mourning. One of his cousins has died of a long illness shortly before his bar mitzvah, the rite of passage that initiates a thirteen-year-old boy into the religious obligations of an adult Jewish man. The death of his cousin in an American hospital is obviously meant to contrast with Charlie's safe arrival home. The hospitable world of America seems to spell death for the Jews. The cousin's disappearance, "which almost every family felt [as] a personal loss," signifies the dropping out of second-generation American Jews, their failure to come back home.[15]

Charlie's refusal to take the easy way out encapsulated basic decisions in Chametzky's life. It represented, for instance, his refusal to name names before the university's Investigating Committee in 1954 as well as his standing firm at crucial moments during his academic career. But most clearly Charlie's fessing up to being Jewish reflects Chametzky's own commitment:

> For various reasons I thought you had to take a stand where you are. There came a very non-political, non-ideological gut-feeling that you are what you are. In the academic profession at that time a lot of people were becoming Episcopalians, Presbyterians, New Critics. They were just stripping themselves of their personal and ethnic identities. And I said, to hell with all that. I am a Jew from Brooklyn, and that's where I take my stand. . . . I found a certain bedrock reality for myself. (interview)

He made his own experiences the basis for understanding the experiences of others; like Horace Kallen, Ludwig Lewisohn, or Cynthia Ozick in Chametzky's own generation, he meant to arrive at the universal by starting with the particular. Chametzky felt encouraged in this approach by the writers, critics, and teachers he admired. When Isaac Rosenfeld came to the University of Minnesota for a brief teaching stint in 1952, Chametzky told him that a phrase in one of his essays had been a "key experience" for him. Rosenfeld had written that a certain measure to improve social conditions was like cupping the dead. Chametzky recognized in the unusual English phrase a Yiddish expression for ineffectiveness: *es vet helfn vi a toitn bankes,* meaning something was as useless as cupping a corpse.[16] Rosenfeld's phrase signaled to Chametzky that one could use one's inherited language and culture fruitfully and without shame even in the pages of a journal as high-minded as *Partisan Review.* When the opening chapters of Saul Bellow's novel *The Adventures of Augie March* (1953) appeared in that journal, Chametzky was thrilled. He recognized that in this novel Rosenfeld's attempts to draw on his first language, vernacular Yiddish, had been transformed into an art. Obviously, the language Bellow had fashioned drew also on Mark Twain's literary vernacular in *The Adventures of Huckleberry Finn* and on the high style of T. S. Eliot's essays and poetry. It was an unprecedented combination that took one's breath away right from the opening sentence: "I am an American, Chicago born—Chicago, that somber city —and go at things as I have taught myself, free-style, and will make the record in my own way: first to knock, first admitted; sometimes an innocent knock, sometimes a not so innocent."

Augie was street-wise, not quite a tough, certainly not a thug, because he had a heart for his idiot brother Georgie (Bellow's nod to Faulkner). Humming along in Bellow's chorus of voices borrowed from Mark Twain, T. S. Eliot, Faulkner, and other American moderns were the voices of Montreal and Chicago Jewish street-smarts. Bellow's new language was an extraordinary aesthetic experience for Chametzky, who was then in his mid-twenties and involved in an academic struggle with Samuel Johnson. "Bellow was a liberation and an empowerment for a whole generation," Chametzky recalled, "the way Rosenfeld was for me personally. *Augie March* was enabling because it legitimated an experience which in the academy was somehow not appropriate" (interview). John Berryman, who began teaching at the University of Minnesota in 1955, would occasionally meet Chametzky for coffee. His response to the young man's excitement was a deep sigh: "Oh Saul!" When pressed for an explanation, Berryman sent Chametzky home to read Bellow's earlier novels, *Dangling Man* (1944) and *The Victim* (1947).

Berryman, like Bellow, Rosenfeld, and Delmore Schwartz, was part of the crowd connected to *Partisan Review,* but with a difference. Not being Jewish, he was not always clued into the code (which hardly ever mattered), but he admired Jews. In the early 1940s, while teaching as Briggs-Copeland Lecturer at Harvard, an appointment for which Delmore Schwartz had strongly agitated, Berryman was an intimate witness to Schwartz's defiance of the Gentile establishment, literary and academic. Ten years later, members of the *Partisan Review* crowd flocked to Princeton. Its community, James Atlas wrote, "was to the 1950s what Harvard had been to the 1940s, a place where eminent American writers gathered." In the fall of 1952, Bellow and Schwartz were both at Princeton and found consolation in each other's company. It was a place Bellow described in *Humboldt's Gift* (1975) as "a sanctuary, a zoo, a spa, with its own choochoo and elms and lovely green cages"—in short, not a place for urban Jews. According to Atlas, Schwartz "saw himself and Bellow as 'blood brothers,' intellectuals, writers, Jews, banded together in academic exile." When *Augie March* was published a year later, Schwartz, who hardly ever liked anything, gave it a rave review in *Partisan Review,* calling it "a new kind of book." He declared that "the only other American novels to which it can be compared with any profit are *Huckleberry Finn* and [Dos Passos's] *U.S.A.,* and it is superior to the first by virtue of its subject matter and to the second by virtue of a realized unity of composition." [17]

Berryman, "notorious for his fanatical jealousy," had observed these developments closely. He was waiting to see what the neophyte Chametzky would make of Bellow after he had read all of his books. Chametzky returned flushed with excitement and confessed that *The Victim* "had blown him away." He was not prepared for Berryman's reply: " 'It is too neurotic,' he said. 'If the editorial board of *Partisan Review* could write a collective novel, that would be it.' When I got to know the editorial of *Partisan Review,* in the late 60s and early 70s, I realized that he may have been right" (interview).

Not long after Berryman and Chametzky had this conversation, William Phillips, the editor of *Partisan Review,* came out to Minneapolis to teach there for a semester. Things did not go as well as he had expected. His students, Phillips complained to Chametzky, "sit there with blank faces and I can't get through to them." Chametzky, quite sensibly, asked Phillips what he was teaching. When the reply was Kafka, Chametzky was flabbergasted. "You are teaching them about alienation? These are kids from the cornfields. They are not alienated" (interview). It was through encounters with people like Rosenfeld, Berryman, and Phillips, and by exposure to Bellow's novels and magazines like *Partisan Review,* that Chametzky began to notice a new literary atmosphere. There was a Jewish notion abroad; a Jewish (self-)consciousness was stirring. People began to tell Jewish stories to each other, and even academics began to feel more secure. "Nevertheless," Chametzky said, "the Jews in the English Department did feel marginal" (interview). But Chametzky was lucky; he met an outstanding scholar who encouraged him by way of example to stay in touch with his "bedrock reality." That teacher was Henry Nash Smith.

Although Chametzky was also strongly influenced by the political theorist Mulford Quickert Sibley, a Quaker, pacifist, and socialist who weaned him away from Marxism, and by Leo Marx, whose course on writers of the American Renaissance he attended with enthusiasm, it was Henry Nash Smith who transformed the dabbling playwright into a serious literary critic. Chametzky thought that Smith was "the best mind I had ever encountered" and felt that studying with him was an intellectual turning point (interview).

Two other things about Smith appealed to Chametzky. First, Smith had always liked Jewish students, and he liked Chametzky for being precisely the way he was. "He used to laugh because I was so irreverent and brash and quirky." Smith was the director of graduate studies when Chametzky arrived there in 1950. "He was so very nice and interesting," Chametzky recalled, "and he liked me." It was part of Smith's extraordinary personality that he cared about his students, including the Jews. In

June 1941, for example, Smith had recommended one of his students, who was going on to Harvard, to Daniel Aaron despite the young man's annoying intellectual tics:

> He's frightfully adolescent and of course that is a disease, but I have observed that all men destined for greatness . . . are particularly painful to everyone including themselves when they are eighteen or twenty. The lad—Eric Axilrod—is hipped on symbolic logic (he may go into philosophy) and used to infuriate me by demanding that I formulate everything I wanted to say in lectures in terms acceptable to students of Principia Mathematica. Remember his name and look him up when you are in Cambridge.[18]

Smith's second endearing feature was related to his unreserved acceptance of Chametzky as a Brooklyn Jew: Smith was a Texan with passion and conviction. He was a committed regionalist who pointedly distinguished the Southwest from the South and who believed that first-rate literature was waiting to be discovered in regions distant from the eastern seaboard. For most Americanists, New England was the center of the American literary universe—certainly until the time of William Dean Howells; and very few academics had scholarly interests in fiction written after Howells.

Smith, however, isolated as he was at Southern Methodist University, where he taught from 1927 to 1937 and again from 1940 to 1941, pursued his own path. In 1929 he praised Faulkner's novel *The Sound and the Fury.* He claimed that some of its pages were "very near great literature" and emphasized that the "book has shown unguessed possibilities in the treatment of provincial life without loss of universality." This was, of course, a particular concern of the regionalist Smith, who thought the same could be said about Mark Twain, and not only in regard to *The Adventures of Huckleberry Finn.* Not everyone agreed. "When Henry Nash Smith left Minnesota in 1953 to go to Berkeley to become the Curator of the Mark Twain Papers," Chametzky wrote, "many people in the English department bemoaned the wasting of such a fine mind and scholar upon such a sub-literary and unworthy subject."[19]

Chametzky was lastingly influenced by Smith's views. In his critical work he considers indebtedness to a region as important a social and literary determinant as class, gender, race, and ethnicity (*OD* 4). Chametzky argued in his essay collection *Our Decentralized Literature* that taken seriously, these specifics have a "decentering" effect in the way we view literature. They invalidate the ordering perspective imposed by seminal works such as Matthiessen's *American Renaissance* with its roster of white male eastern seaboard writers. Chametzky's counterperspective was that of a "decentralized literature," a phrase coined by William Dean Howells in 1899. Yet for Howells as well as for Chametzky, it was important that the adjective *decentralized* be prefaced by *our.* In their view that pronoun kept the nation from breaking apart no matter how decentralized its literature. The kind of literary history Chametzky had in mind as suitable for the America he envisioned emerged best in his 1972 essay "Our Decentralized Literature: The Significance of Regional, Ethnic, Racial and Sexual Factors." (The last term connotes issues of gender rather than sexual orientation.) Here Chametzky declared the works of George Washington Cable, Abraham Cahan, Charles Chestnutt, and Kate Chopin to be of equal importance in the constitution of "our" national literature (*OD* 21–45). What was a pioneering feat twenty years ago has now become commonplace and serves as a starting point for further decentering by today's critics.

While emphasizing the particularities that contributed to the making of a writer, Chametzky had not given up on Smith's idea, expressed in the review of *The Sound and the Fury,* that in great literature the provincial contained the universal. Faulkner was also Chametzky's premier example. He had initially discovered him through Smith. During a chance meeting on campus just before Smith was to leave for Berkeley in 1953, Smith asked Chametzky whether he would like to be an editor for the journal *Faulkner Studies.* Chametzky went home, read four of Faulkner's novels, and said yes. For two years Chametzky engaged in what his friend Norman Podhoretz called "Talmudic Faulknerism," and it was during this period that his "interest in how the provincial and regional may be transformed into the major and the universal began" (*OD* 18).

Chametzky's preoccupation with Faulkner led him to discover other "Southern" authors (Mark Twain, Thomas Wolfe, William Styron), but it also induced him to inquire into the "black situation" and to read African American writers. In this area Chametzky's scholarly and political interests coalesced. As editor (1963–74) of the *Massachusetts Review,* he accepted essays on African American culture, history, literature, music, and art. He encouraged emerging black authors; published the first stories by Mike Thelwell, Julius Lester, Shirley Ann Williams, Toni Cade Bambara, and others; and reprinted classical pieces of African

American writing, like W. E. B. Du Bois's description of his difficult student days at Harvard in the 1880s.[20] Chametzky went about his work with energy and enthusiasm. To provide a forum for unheard voices was an imperative derived from the political convictions that had led Chametzky to work for the NAACP; but his editorial work also concealed an academic program directed against the conservative trends of the New Criticism. "We wanted to break the logjam of ideas represented by the New Criticism and formalism," Chametzky said about the editorial board of the *Massachusetts Review*. To publish "ethnic" and "marginal" voices (which then included Jewish as well as black and women's voices) "was important as a way of breaking that formalist kind of High Church dominance of the 1950s and of letting in fresh political and ideological currents" (interview).

In *The Conservative Tradition in America,* Allen Guttmann postulated an intellectual genealogy that ran from Irving Babbitt and Paul Elmer More to T. S. Eliot and the Southern Agrarians to the New Critics. Jules Chametzky received his training as a scholar by exponents of that tradition. He immersed himself in New Critical readings of Faulkner, studied with Allen Tate, and after some deliberation chose to write his dissertation on the plays of John Marston, a Renaissance dramatist he had discovered in a footnote to one of T. S. Eliot's essays. His adviser, Leonard Unger, who was Jewish and a follower of John Crowe Ransom, had trained with Cleanth Brooks and Robert Penn Warren. To have mastered the tradition outlined by Eliot as well as the New Critical techniques of interpretation was de rigueur for anyone aspiring to a job in academe in the 1950s, but particularly for Jewish candidates. Suddenly the market was glutted, Chametzky observed, "with Jews doing close readings of John Donne and Anglican poetry" (interview).

With credentials in Metaphysical poetry as well as in Elizabethan and Jacobean drama, Chametzky entered the job market in the mid-1950s and was interviewed by the University of Montana, where Leslie Fiedler had become a full professor in 1954. Fiedler, Chametzky knew, had written his dissertation on John Donne, and he was notorious for the hiring of "unusual" instructors. "I had begun soft and easy," Fiedler wrote in 1969, "by appointing new staff members [two of them were Jewish] with degrees from Harvard, Yale, and Princeton, figuring that their Ivy League associations would appeal especially to that hunger for and innocence about the traditional which I knew our new [university] President must surely share with all other Montanans." By 1958, Fiedler was getting bolder. "I began to make offers to young instructors who had quarreled with their administrators, or had asked their students to read *Catcher in the Rye,* or had themselves written poetry containing dirty words, or were flagrantly Jewish or simply Black—and had not, to redeem any or all of these faults, gone to Harvard or Yale or Princeton."[21]

When Chametzky showed up for his interview at the 1954 convention of the Modern Language Association, Fiedler took him aside and told him that he could not hire any more Jews for now without risking upheaval in Montana. Chametzky stayed on at the University of Minnesota for two more years as an instructor and then accepted a job at Boston University teaching basic literature classes and general education. "Five classes, fifteen hours, one hundred and twenty-five students every semester. It paid well, but you worked like a dog" (interview). Chametzky stayed for two years (1956–58). He received his Ph.D. in 1958 and, supported by Leo Marx, applied for a job at the University of Massachusetts at Amherst. During a visit to its campus, Chametzky stopped by the office of Max Goldberg, a scholar of eighteenth-century literature with a side interest in the writer and critic Ludwig Lewisohn. Goldberg shuffled his visitor's job application from a high pile to a stack that was only slightly shorter, and Chametzky's heart sank.

The University of Massachusetts was a new but rapidly developing place. By the late 1950s, Amherst College was still recruiting heavily through the old-boys' network at Ivy League schools, while the university had begun to look for a different kind of instructor. At the university "they were recruiting second-generation Jews," Allen Guttmann remembered, "and maybe third-generation Jews whose parents were city people" (interview). As a result, Amherst College began to feel very uneasy about the changing neighborhood. From their perch, down the road from the fancy college, Chametzky and his colleagues did not notice the growing anxiety of the college (naturally, since they were not the ones feeling threatened). In fact, Fiedler's hiring strategy at the University of Montana was duplicated at the University of Massachusetts: Jews with Ivy League degrees were the first "outsiders" to come in. Max Goldberg had graduated from the respected Boston Latin School and then gone to Yale. Sidney Kaplan held a Ph.D. in American Civilization from Harvard. Goldberg and Kaplan favored appointments of non-WASP graduates of state universities. One might argue that hiring at Amherst College developed similarly when Leo Marx brought in Allen Guttmann. But there was a significant difference. Marx (who had replaced the abrasive Alfred Kazin) and Guttmann had deliberately fashioned non-ethnic selves, whereas Chametzky was hired precisely because he was proud to be a Jew from Brooklyn and could therefore broaden the ethnic spectrum of courses offered at the university.

In 1959, Chametzky taught his first course on Jewish American fiction. In 1961, at the age of thirty-three, he was tenured and became managing editor of the *Massachusetts Review,* which he had cofounded with F. C. Elbert, Sidney Kaplan, and others. Kaplan encouraged Chametzky to intensify his interests in African American culture. Kaplan's own preoccupation with African American history and culture, and its representation in white society, dated back to the 1930s, when he was deeply involved in left–wing politics at City College and Harvard University. As an army officer attached to the Advocate General's office in England during World War II, Kaplan defended soldiers, frequently African Americans, in court-martials. He came to the University of Massachusetts in 1947 and succeeded in translating his social and liberal political interests into a scholarly career by becoming a pioneer in African American studies. He organized a seminal exhibit on the portrayal of blacks in American painting (in 1963), wrote ground-breaking studies on Africans in America, and cofounded the African American Studies department at the University of Massachusetts. Many Jews, securely integrated into literary academe, continued to be firmly on the left and actively engaged in making African American voices heard in America. Of the forty contributions assembled in *Black and White in America: An Anthology from "The Massachusetts Review,"* edited by Chametzky and Kaplan in 1969, sixteen (or 40 percent) were written by Jews during a period (1959–69) when Jews constituted about 7 percent of the faculty in American English departments.[22]

Chametzky's task as editor of the *Massachusetts Review* was to drop the Metaphysicals for what was then called the "marginals." In the 1960s this term referred to Jews as well as African Americans and other minority writers. In his capacity as managing editor, he advised the chief editor of the magazine against publishing Allen Guttmann's 1962 essay "Jewish Radicals, Jewish Writers." Chametzky argued that Guttmann's definition of Jewishness was much too narrow. Obviously, the radicalism of Emma Goldman and Alexander Berkman "involved the abandonment rather than the intensification of their faith in Judaism as a religion." But it did not follow, as Guttmann claimed, that if one rejected the Jewish God and rejected "Torah and Talmud,"[23] one stopped being a Jew or wanted to drop out of the Jewish people. "Isn't Sidney Kaplan a Jew? Isn't Jules Chametzky a Jew?" Chametzky asked the chief editor. We may look like apostates, but "we surely are conscious Jews" (interview). Religion, Chametzky argued, had little or nothing to do with being Jewish. The editor said that made sense and rejected the essay. Guttmann took the rejection to mean that he had been too controversial. The issues at stake, however—what defines a secular Jew as Jewish, and can one stop being Jewish—were hotly debated by American Jews throughout the 1960s and 1970s. When Chametzky assumed the editorship of the *Massachusetts Review*, he did not allow himself to be drawn into a debate that was as aggravating as it was parochial. Instead he pursued a policy that one might call broadening the canon through gentle mediation. His model was William Dean Howells and his strategists Mark Twain, Abraham Cahan, and Saul Bellow.

What Babbitt and Eliot had been to Harry Levin, William Dean Howells was to Chametzky. Howells, a "midwestern commoner," had risen to prominence in Boston's intellectual society. But Chametzky believed, following Henry Nash Smith's argument, that Howells remained ambivalent "toward the *official* culture . . . on a deeply disguised level." Some former outsiders refuse to sacrifice their social conscience on the altar of social ascent. Or, as Larzer Ziff put it, Howells "was of the establishment, yet keenly aware of its shortcomings." Chametzky argued that Howells resolved the tension between descent and ascent by becoming a mediator between inside and outside, between the ignorant and the educated, between margin and center. "Howells did heroic and priceless work," Chametzky wrote, "in using his position to introduce fresh, dissident talent to frequently indifferent or philistine audiences" (*OD* 31).

Chametzky's characterization of Howells could serve as a description of his own editorship at the *Massachusetts Review*. He made the magazine into a forum for fresh, dissident talent. Moreover, Howells's sponsorship of Mark Twain and Abraham Cahan prefigured in some ways Chametzky's dedication to the early Saul Bellow, who combined elements of both. Mark Twain, Chametzky argued, was "using the energy and concreteness of the vernacular to undercut the lofty pretentiousness of the all but official culture. . . . Twain's task was to mediate between the worlds of the vernacular and the official or high culture, sometimes uneasily, sometimes triumphantly" (*OD* 116). It was this tradition Chametzky saw at work in Bellow's *Augie March*, which fused "the energy of the vernacular" with "knowledge of the high style" (*OD* 64). The inspiration of Bellow's vernacular was Yiddish, a language with an in-built mechanism to deflate pretentiousness. By contrast, Abraham Cahan's fiction in English, Chametzky pointed out, failed to make use of Yiddish as a creative resource. Howells liked Cahan because the latter's "treatment of the immigrant problem—as largely one of the immigrant's accommodation to American values, rather than of his impact upon those values—was basically reassuring to someone like Howells" (OD 34). In turn, Howells reassured his readers that Cahan, despite his Jewish stories, was really one of "us" and that the center held.

Bellow fulfilled and perfected what Howells and Cahan had promised. The voice of Augie March was a Jewish voice in the middle of America, Chicago-born, but no more subversive or radical than the all-American Huck Finn. Bellow reassured Americans that no revolution (other than literary) was afoot and signaled to Jews that all exclusion had come to an end. "Those of us who grew up through the forties and began to read Bellow in the fifties," Chametzky wrote, "felt that here indeed, with absolute authority, someone was also writing for us. But we were insiders now, we were all Augie Marches who could handle the Harvard five-foot shelf *and* the lessons of the streets, achieving the kind of urban intensity and brilliance we learned and taught others to value" (OD 66).

———

The integration of Jews into literary academe, which began tentatively in the late 1920s, was successfully completed forty years later. During the period that spans the early careers of Allen Guttmann and Jules Chametzky, Jews moved into all of the established fields of inquiry in English and American studies where they did more or less conventional work during the 1950s and 1960s. For that generation the great intellectual shake-up came in the late 1960s, when in response to the social and political upheaval in the wake of the civil rights movement and the Vietnam War, literary academe finally threw off the shackles of the New Criticism and discovered social markers such as class, gender, race, and ethnicity as a subject and the basis for a new approach toward literature. For Jewish professors, especially for those in American studies, it became possible then to rediscover and explore the Jewish dimension of their Americanness. As the contrasting portraits of Guttmann and Chametzky showed, however, not all Jews wanted to be "ethnics." The long decades of assimilation had left their mark on the generation born in the 1930s. The reorientation of literary academe during the 1960s revolution made clear that there were two ways of thinking about oneself as American. One could conceive of oneself either as an Emersonian, self-made individual or as a member of a group. It was Chametzky's group-based, rather than Guttmann's individual-based thinking that carried the day in literary academe, first in American studies, then in other fields, and it is still going strong today.

Chametzky's path led into new and fruitful areas of inquiry. Having discovered themselves as members of a group, Jewish literary scholars began to compare their collective experience with that of other American minorities, especially with that of African Americans. Their plight touched a raw nerve in assimilated American Jews who were just then trying to come to grips with their history of persecution and dehumanization from Czarist Russia to Nazi Germany. The outpouring of books and articles by Jewish literary scholars on African American subjects during the 1960s and 1970s is truly astonishing. To a certain extent, it can be understood as an attempt to work off a deep-seated sense of guilt for having so luckily escaped persecution and death in Europe and achieved safety, prosperity, and positions of social status in America. The overwhelming gratitude arising from that realization is translated into empathy for those less fortunate and into the determination and energy to help others to achieve similar advantages.

For Jewish literary scholars, academe's new emphasis on particularity and ethnicity, which led to the discovery of the new holy trinity of class, race, and gender, and to the discovery of the "other" as a critical category, had yet another dimension that meant little to non-Jewish scholars. For Jews, Germans were the ultimate "other." Right after the end of World War II, Germans had been ostracized as having morally and intellectually discredited themselves. Jewish literary scholars of Guttmann's and Chametzky's generation set out to explore what the monstrous Germans were really about. They accepted Fulbright professorships to Germany and, once there, decided that the new generation ought to be given a chance.

When Chametzky arrived in Tübingen, a small but distinguished university town in southern West Germany, in 1962, only seventeen years after the end of the war, he considered himself on a twofold mission: "One was to learn more about postwar Germany and about what was going on there; and the other was to figure out what to do with the new generation. The students were eighteen, nineteen, twenty years old. They were not guilty, they were not responsible." But teaching in Germany was not easy. The awareness of working in a country that had slaughtered millions of Jews just two decades ago was painful (interview).

Chametzky returned to Germany in 1970 to teach as a guest professor in Berlin. There he met Werner Sollors, who would become one of his most successful students. As in America, the late 1960s were watershed years in Germany. Students rebelled against the "establishment," and the issue, deep down, was their parents' involvement in the Nazi regime. German students began to discover the "other" in order to atone for the guilt of their parents and to escape from the isolation and sense of cultural claustrophobia produced by their artificially homogeneous society, Hitler's only lasting achievement. The craving of young Germans for "others" and of German officials for imported Jews, whose presence would testify to the world that the Federal Republic was a new kind of Germany, was met in some sections of the American Jewish community by a great curiosity about Germany, its culture and inhabitants, and by a willingness to participate in the reconstitution of a strong, liberal, and democratic culture in that country.

All of these elements came into play, along with his expertise on African American culture, in 1975, when Chametzky found himself on a German dissertation committee as first reader of Werner Sollors's doctoral thesis on the African American poet Amiri Baraka/LeRoi Jones, which he recommended to be approved summa cum laude. Sollors went on to build a distinguished academic career in the United States, where his specialty was the study of ethnicity in American culture.[24]

A German Legacy: Holocaust Literature

Not all Jewish literary scholars took as easily to postwar Germany as did Guttmann and Chametzky. The rediscovery of themselves as members of a group to whom unimaginable atrocities had happened in Europe led other Jewish scholars on Fulbright stays in Germany, foremost among them Lawrence Langer (b. 1929) and Alvin Rosenfeld (b. 1938), in a very different direction, namely, toward the discovery of Holocaust literature as a subject to be included in English literary studies. Langer and Rosenfeld were pioneers in this area.

Langer, Chametzky's junior by one year, had attended City College and gone on to pursue a graduate degree in English at Harvard, where he studied with Howard Mumford Jones. Perry Miller directed Langer's dissertation on the American Civil War. In 1963, Langer received a Fulbright lecturership and was chosen by the narratologist Franz Stanzl to come teach at the University of Graz, because Miller and Stanzl were friends. Langer had been to Germany in 1955 and had passed Dachau on his way to Munich. Not knowing that Dachau was a bucolic Bavarian village, he had been wondering why the Germans would mark a concentration camp on their map. He decided to visit the site and found that ten years after the war the camp was still inhabited by so-called displaced persons. The SS barracks were still standing, and the camp had not yet become a tourist stop.

Eight years later, when Langer and his wife traveled to Austria, the Holocaust was still rarely on the public mind. Langer was puzzled by an odd pattern of continuity and discontinuity. While getting a haircut in a Graz barbershop, he saw in the local paper that a war criminal who had been interned in Italy had been released and was welcomed back by his fellow citizens. The camp of Mauthausen near Graz was unvisited. But Schloß Leopoldstein, where Langer gave a talk, was marked with a plaque identifying it as a former hunting resort of Hermann Göring. A nearby cemetery had only a plaque in Hebrew. Langer, who knew German but not Hebrew, found out that on this site Jewish inmates of a small labor camp had been shot when the Germans moved out in 1945 to flee from the approaching Russians. Langer began to make cautious inquiries into what the Austrians he met had been doing during the war. He was surprised by the answers he obtained— either they had been prisoners of war or didn't know anything. Embarrassment and shame were not among the emotions Langer encountered.

During an excursion to the town where the composer Joseph Haydn was buried, a tour guide showed the visitors around, saying in passing, "Und hier ist unsere Judengasse" [and this is our Jews' Lane]. Langer was stunned. "He spoke about the Jews of the town as if he were speaking about the seventeenth century." [25] In the spring of 1964, Marion Rapp, a Fulbright professor in Vienna, suggested that they travel to Auschwitz near Cracow. Langer agreed. They visited the camp on a warm day in May 1964. Rapp fell ill afterward and did not leave his bed for twenty-four hours. Langer would be haunted by the camp, its history, its survivors, the literature and memories connected with it, for the next thirty years. In the preface to his first book on the Shoah (Holocaust), *The Holocaust and the Literary Imagination* (1975), Langer wrote about his visit to Auschwitz,

I still recall my astonishment upon seeing Polish children playing beneath bright sunshine in sandboxes no more than twenty yards from the entrance to the camp. They lived in neat brick buildings adjoining the site of the former camp, SS barracks that had been converted into apartments after the war and whose windows looked out on the barbed wire that still surrounded the area. The disparity between expectation and reality which that image inspired lay like a constant weight on my consciousness for several weeks, until it suddenly resurfaced later that summer as I sat in a courtroom in Munich at the war-crimes trial of Karl Wolff, Heinrich Himmler's adjutant and liaison officer to Hitler during part of World War II.

By 1964 Wolff was a mild-mannered businessman with silvery hair and a vague memory. . . . Again I was unable to connect the appearance of the man with the crimes he was accused of, as if some vital link joining normalcy and horror had dissolved. . . . The dilemma achieved a more concrete focus a few days later, as I stood before a [late nineteenth-century pastoral] painting [entitled Dachau] in the Neue Pinakothek art museum in Munich and once more experienced that uncanny sensation of discontinuity, of a fact inaccessible to the imagination in any coherent or familiar form.[26]

In his subsequent work Langer tackled the question of "whether the artistic vision of the literary intelligence could ever devise a technique and form adequate to convey what the concentration camp experience implied for the contemporary mind."[27]

After two more books, *The Age of Atrocity: Death in Modern Literature* (1978) and *Versions of Survival: The Holocaust and the Human Spirit* (1982), Langer produced his most astonishing work. *Holocaust Testimonies: The Ruins of Memory* (1991) was based on the author's analysis of videotaped oral testimonies by victims of Nazi violence. These he found in a collection at Yale, the Fortunoff Video Archive for Holocaust Testimonies. Working with hundreds of testimonies, Langer, through his years of emotionally draining labor, began to understand the haunting nature of Holocaust memory. In his 1991 book he spelled out his findings, finally bridging a divide of which he had first become aware when he had stood uncomprehending at the gates of Auschwitz in 1964. Almost thirty years later Langer wrote: "A main effect of these testimonies . . . is to begin to undo a negation—the principle of discontinuity which argues that an impassable chasm permanently separates the seriously interested auditor and observer from the experiences of the former Holocaust victim."[28] Although many of the survivors greatly doubted in their testimonies that those who had not shared their experiences in the camps would ever be able to understand them, Langer found that he was enabled to do so—to close the gap between the incommensurable worlds of the survivor and the safe American—through "the sympathetic power of the imagination" (xv). Interestingly, Langer's scholarship was an unintended application of M. H. Abrams's principle of "imaginative consent."

With the completion of their integration into American society and its high cultural bastion, literary academe, Jews became more self-confident and, concomitantly, more interested in reestablishing ties with their descent culture. Gradually, they also became less satisfied with secondhand knowledge. When interest in Yiddish and Hebrew texts began to arise (the latter boosted by the existence of Israel), Jewish literary scholars who had gotten doctorates in English in the late 1960s but had acquired knowledge of Hebrew and Yiddish as children or adolescents moved in the early 1970s into comparative literature, and then in the late 1970s and early 1980s into newly established Jewish studies programs. There they proceeded to apply modern critical methods to the interpretation of Jewish texts, ranging from the Bible to Yiddish drama to Israeli poetry. How, when, and why this happened, is the subject of the second part of the book.

While the Harvard circle remained largely focused on America and the relation of individuals or groups to American culture, the Jewish literary intellectuals orbiting in Columbia University's cosmopolitan sphere were much less impressed with America's achievements. At first this was perhaps an expression of cultural insecurity that was foreign to Harvardians, who rested securely in America's historical bosom. But Jewish literary scholars at Columbia turned that cultural insecurity into an asset. When literary academics discovered themselves as ethnics, Jewish scholars trained at New York City institutions (in the overwhelming presence of a city continuously replenished with immigrants and populated by three million Jews) were encouraged to take their inquiries abroad, back to the Old Countries and to the non-Anglophone languages of the Jews. To move from English studies to Hebrew and Yiddish literary scholarship, as Robert Alter and Ruth Wisse did, was a much less outlandish thing to do in crazy New York, where these languages had a real-life presence, than it was in the culturally conformist atmosphere of Harvard.

Although the career paths of scholars in the Harvard circle and the Columbia sphere seem to spell the same journey from assimilation to dissimilation, or from an emphasis on consent to an emphasis on descent, the ways in which this journey was undertaken by Harvardians and Columbians—by scholars whose focus remains America and by scholars whose focus is on the Jews as Jews—are so immensely different as to be hardly the same journey. The following chapters, then, narrate an alternate route toward Jewish identity.

PART TWO

The Columbia Sphere

Literary Minds

8

Refractions of Lionel Trilling

FROM 1939, WHEN HE PUBLISHED HIS DISSERTATION on Matthew Arnold and was appointed to an assistant professorship in the English department at Columbia University, until his death at the age of seventy in 1975, Lionel Trilling represented in academe the possibility of a literary criticism responsive to the cultural and political moment. His essays were considered gems. In person he appeared poised, graceful, and gentle; his circumspection, one assumed, produced not only his refined style but also that peculiar hesitancy in his essays that made one think of his writing as affected. Trilling kept himself opaque, and opacity increasingly came to characterize his essays. Friends and critics usually spoke with appreciation of Trilling's moderation and his manners. But since the posthumous publication of excerpts from Trilling's notebooks and of Diana Trilling's memoirs, we know about the terrifying abyss of melancholy and self-doubt that the mask of poise and graciousness helped to conceal.

Trilling's Jewishness was of no importance to his Gentile students, because they did not notice in his speech or gestures, in his teaching or writing, any trace of what used to be mocked as Jewish style. Jewish topics certainly were rare in Trilling's essays and seminars. In fact, Trilling had famously insisted on the separation of his life as a Jewish citizen, which "exists as a point of honor," and his professional life in the world of letters. In 1944 he wrote,

It is clear to me that my existence as a Jew is one of the shaping conditions of my temperament, and therefore I suppose it must have its effect on my intellect. Yet I cannot discover anything in my professional intellectual life which I can specifically trace back to my Jewish birth and rearing. I

207

do not think of myself as a "Jewish writer." I do not have it in mind to serve by my writing any Jewish purpose. I should resent it if a critic of my work were to discover in it either faults or virtues which he called Jewish.[1]

To Trilling's Jewish students, however, his being Jewish mattered enormously, because at a time when Jewishness connoted loudness, brashness, vulgarity, and Yiddish accents, Trilling personified elegance and understatement. He was a gentleman. "His speech was filled with practiced hesitation," Eugene Goodheart remembered, "and there was a sort of Jamesian fineness about him and his sentences."[2] That Trilling had mastered Columbia's gentility mattered to his Jewish students so much that some of them got angry when Jewish subjects threatened to surface in his prose. Their anger expressed itself in mockery. John Hollander, born in 1929 and Goodheart's senior by two years, recalled the student response when the first version of "Wordsworth and the Rabbis" was published in 1950: "Some of us felt a little funny about it. The concept of coming out of the closet had not yet emerged. But it was as if this were happening a bit. It caused one man, Robert Gottlieb, who became the editor of *The New Yorker* and whose background was totally assimilated, having read the essay, to come in the next day and just before Trilling came to class, post himself outside the room and recite 'Tintern Abbey' with a Yiddish accent."[3]

What Trilling did, said, and wrote was important to his Jewish students in a way that students of Harry Levin would have found puzzling. In part this was due to the fact that acceptance to Harvard meant being safe socially. Entering Harvard offered an escape from the stigma of Jewishness whereas entering Columbia did not. While the percentage of Jewish students at Columbia and Harvard was roughly the same after the Second World War, there were differences between the two groups. Jewish students at Columbia tended to have grown up close to the world of Jewish immigrants (often their parents or grandparents), and to maintain stronger social and emotional ties to that world than their Harvard counterparts did. Many Jewish students at Columbia continued to live at home while attending college. While Harvard worked actively toward the integration of its fairly small population of commuters into its student body, no such effort was made at Columbia. In fact, severe shortage of dormitory space resulted in Columbia's policy that rooms on campus would not be given to freshmen who were residents of New York City. Very often, bright Jewish students would get accepted to both Harvard and Columbia and receive tuition scholarships, but be compelled to choose Columbia because their parents were too poor to come up with the money for room and board at Harvard.[4] Students who stayed in New York City for that reason would often have one foot in the crowded, intense, and anguished world of Brooklyn or the Bronx, and the other on a ladder whose steps were composed of the masterpieces of English literature. Trilling, they imagined, had accomplished such an ascent. His Jewishness was important *ex negativo,* as something that no longer obstructed the path to stature and eminence. However, the tidy academic world that eventually engulfed many of Trilling's students differed markedly from the world that mattered most to Trilling —the messy, emotional, close-circuited world of the literary magazines and journals to which he and his friends contributed; a world that in a secular way was intensely Jewish. It was the polar opposite of the socially homogeneous and politically unruffled world in which Trilling's near-contemporary Harry Levin had cocooned himself. The Harvard scholar and the Columbia critic did not see eye to eye on their tasks as literary intellectuals. Levin was tremendously piqued by the indifference of literary New York to Harvard scholarship; he could not know that the very seriousness of Harvard scholars gave Trilling the willies.

Trilling and Levin

Harry Levin once argued that his appointment at Harvard and Trilling's at Columbia were parallel cases. It is true, of course, that both Trilling and Levin were appointed as the first Jewish faculty members in the departments that had trained them and remained the only Jews there until such tokenism became untenable. But a closer look reveals that the cases of Trilling and Levin are very different.[5] The differences arose as much from their idiosyncratic temperaments and dispositions as from the peculiar social conditions and academic environments in which they found themselves. Levin, cloistered at Harvard far away from his parents, could reinvent himself during the 1930s; while Trilling, hanging on at Columbia by his fingernails during the Depression years, lived in close contact with his own and his wife Diana's parents and remained enmeshed in a network of New York literary friends.

Unlike the monastic existence offered to Harvard scholars, life in New York City did not permit seclusion. One was always confronted with real, not literary, crises involving jobs, politics, money, or friendships. The city's openness, aggressiveness, and excitement enforced the

14. Lionel Trilling in 1964. *Courtesy of Columbia University.*

notion that the task of the literary intellectual was not to tease poems, dramas, and novels for their "thematics" and conventions, but to take to "the dark and bloody crossroads where literature and politics meet." One did not go there gladly, Trilling wrote, "but nowadays it is not exactly a matter of free choice whether one does or does not go."[6] That much was obvious to Trilling in 1946; and he ventured into those crossroads as Levin never did. The difference between Harvard and Columbia, between a culture of professors and a culture of literary critics, is illuminated in an entry Trilling made in one of his "untidy notebooks"[7] in 1951:

Harry Levin sends me a paper on The Tradition of Tradition with the inscription "forgive the gibe"—he refers to a "sly" association of the phrase "the liberal imagination" with conservatism or reaction: he is ever forward. And with this paper I know that I could never go to Harvard— for they would take me *seriously*, with that seriousness of men who have no real sense of reality, but who believe they should have. Here at Columbia I am of my own kind—if there is any hostility and dislike there is no slightest attempt to meet me on my own ground, at best a secret inner *flounce*. But at Harvard, nothing is beyond a Harvard professor. I should not be allowed to make my writing cancel their scholarship as here— they too are critics; and if not critics then serious men who would hold me *to account* for what I say. Here no one tries to understand except E[mery] N[eff] and I am left in peace.[8]

Less than twenty years later, in the spring of 1970, Trilling did go to Harvard to deliver the Charles Eliot Norton lectures, which were published as *Sincerity and Authenticity* (1971). Trilling's claim that he was not taken seriously at Columbia was obviously exaggerated. But he was right in detecting a different, nit-picking kind of seriousness in Harvard's literary academics. Their lives, after all, were devoted to scholarship, and it was hard on them to countenance a critic who combined an interest in belles lettres and politics with teaching literature at a university. Columbia's supposed frivolity stood over and against Harvard's scholarship. In the war between the scholars and the critics, which Gerald Graff dates from 1940 to 1965, the self-esteem of scholars was at stake.[9] If, in terms of conveying knowledge and insight, a critic's essay, written in the course of a few weeks or months, could accomplish as much as an entire book and its footnotes, what then justified the monastic, self-sacrificing life of scholarship? Worse even, scholarship might turn out to be mere self-indulgence. The rise of the Columbia critics was perceived as a threat by the men invested in pure scholarship.

But Trilling also encroached on the turf staked out by the pioneers of cultural criticism. In 1940, for example, anticipating by one year Matthiessen's presentation of the intellectuals' "double consciousness" in *American Renaissance,* Trilling described the very phenomenon compellingly in his essay "Reality in America":

A culture is not a flow, nor even a confluence; the form of its existence is struggle, or at least debate—it is nothing if not a dialectic. And in any culture there are likely to be certain artists who contain a large part of the dialectic within themselves, their meaning and power lying in their contradictions; they contain within themselves, it may be said, the very essence of the culture, and the sign of this is that they do not submit to serve the ends of any one ideological group or tendency. It is a significant circumstance of American culture, and one which is susceptible of explanation, that an unusually large proportion of its notable writers of the nineteenth century were such repositories of the dialectic of their times

—they contained both the yes and the no of their culture, and by that token they were prophetic of the future. (*LI* 9)

Matthiessen's *American Renaissance* made precisely Trilling's point over some 650 pages. The remarkable similarities between Trilling's essay and Matthiessen's book have to do with the fact that both were written against the kind of literary historiography launched by V. L. Parrington in *Main Currents in American Thought* and against what Trilling called Parrington's "errors of aesthetic judgment" (*LI* 4). This does not mean that Trilling found himself in complete agreement with Matthiessen. They differed vastly in their assessment of Theodore Dreiser, for instance, for reasons that had to do with their personalities, politics, and self-definitions as cultural critics. When Trilling appended his 1946 critique of Dreiser to his 1940 critique of Parrington, calling the combination "Reality in America" and placing the essay at the beginning of *The Liberal Imagination,* he intended it to define his position as a critic in academe.

Trilling and Liberal Literary Academe

Trilling's goal was "scholarship without pedantry, university teaching without academicism." To this remark in his notebooks he added enigmatically, "living in N.Y.—a N.Y. continuity" (*N1* 509), indicating that he remained connected to the world of his literary friends and their magazines and to the tough reality of New York City life. He was determined not to fall prey to "that seriousness of men who have no real sense of reality" that characterized Harvard professors. Trilling knew that acceptance to Columbia, unlike acceptance to Harvard, Yale, and Princeton, did not signify ascent into a social elite, and that the social and cultural situation of his upwardly mobile Jewish students continued to be precarious. The anxieties caused by their commute between the seemingly incompatible worlds of Brooklyn and Morningside Heights and the students' need for guidance and mentorship became burdensome to him. Eventually, Trilling withdrew from teaching in the graduate school. In 1951 he observed in his notebook: "I was a free man when I taught in the college and ceased to be free when I taught in the Grad. school. . . . The relation with the students who worked under me was unpleasant, although sometimes seductive—most of them were badly prepared, poorly endowed. One was led to 'reject' them, and then because of their personal situations, to become terribly partisan with them. And the time one had to give, and the personal involvement, almost worse than the time!" (*N1* 515). As he often is in his notebooks, Trilling here is somewhat uncharitable toward himself. He willingly made time for students, as Steven Marcus put it, "when he was interested in you." [10] That was the case when Trilling detected in a student what he called "the electrical qualities of mind" (*LI* 14).

This was Trilling's phrase for Henry James, who throughout "Reality in America" served as his spokesman to define his own aesthetic preferences as a critic in opposition to the literary historians inspired by Parrington and trained in American Civilization programs, and the cultural critics *avant la lettre,* like Matthiessen. Trilling was of course familiar with Matthiessen's work on Henry James, and he qualified his disagreement with the Harvard scholar by saying that Matthiessen "certainly cannot be accused of any lack of feeling for mind as Henry James represents it" (*LI* 15). Their disagreement was largely political; and Trilling undertook to demonstrate in *The Liberal Imagination* how literary appreciation was linked not simply to one's political ideas but to one's apprehension of reality.

In the opening essay Trilling showed himself profoundly irritated by Parrington, who embodied for Trilling all that was wrong with liberal or progressive thinking about American culture, because "he expresses the chronic American belief that there exists an opposition between reality and mind and that one must enlist oneself in the party of reality" (*LI* 10). [11] Its partisans in the university made up "what might be called the literary academicism of liberalism" (*LI* 10). Their belief in the incompatibility of mind and reality, Trilling declared, was "exemplified by the doctrinaire indulgence which liberal intellectuals have always displayed toward Theodore Dreiser, an indulgence which becomes the worthier of remark when it is contrasted with the liberal severity toward Henry James" (*LI* 10). James's creativity showed the "electrical qualities of mind," whereas Dreiser's books had "the awkwardness, the chaos, the heaviness which we associate with 'reality.' In the American metaphysic, reality is always material reality, hard, resistant, unformed, impenetrable, and unpleasant. And that mind is alone felt to be trustworthy which most resembles this reality by most nearly reproducing the sensations it affords" (*LI* 13). Trilling found the liberal view of Dreiser best summed up in Matthiessen's review of Dreiser's novel *The Bulwark.* Although well aware that Matthiessen had stated in the preface to *American Renaissance* that his concern was "the opposite" of Parrington's, Trilling still accused him of bad thinking, of accepting "the liberal cliché which opposes

crude experience to mind and establishes Dreiser's value by implying
that the mind which Dreiser's crude experience is presumed to confront
and refute is the mind of gentility" (*LI* 15). Liberal critics took the
ungainliness of Dreiser's style to be a reflection of the ungainliness of
the reality that was Dreiser's subject. And once Dreiser's style became
defensible, so too became his thought, including his vulgar anti-
Semitism. "It is much to the point of his intellectual vulgarity," Trilling
observed, "that Dreiser's anti-Semitism was not merely a social prejudice
but an idea, a way of dealing with difficulties" (*LI* 18).

Trilling found Dreiser's religious affirmation in *The Bulwark* similarly
offensive. He called it not a failure of nerve, as Matthiessen had done,
but a failure of heart and mind. "The offense lies in the vulgar ease of
its formulation," Trilling wrote, "as well as in the comfortable untrou-
bled way in which Dreiser moved from nihilism to pietism" (*LI* 20).
What Dreiser's work negated was literature as the locus of moral seriousness, a negation continued, in Trilling's view, by the "liberal criticism, in the direct line of Parrington, which establishes the social
responsibility of the writer and then goes on to say that, apart from his
duty of resembling reality as much as possible, he is not really responsible
for anything, not even for his ideas" (*LI* 21).[12]

Two years later, in 1948, Trilling answered a query from *Partisan
Review* concerning the state of American writing. More clearly than in
the essays combined in "Reality in America," Trilling explained in his
reply to *Partisan Review* that Parrington's thrust against a literature endowed with moral imagination and the electrical qualities of mind represented "the suppositions about our culture which are held by the
American middle class so far as that class is at all liberal in its social
thought." (*LI* 3). Trilling then unfolded the meaning of the word *liberal*
as he never would throughout all of *The Liberal Imagination.* Summing
up the cultural suppositions of the middle class, its love of the literal (or
"real") and rejection of the "method of imagination, of symbol and
fantasy," Trilling noted,

> what I have been describing is simply Philistinism. . . . It is also possible
> to call it Stalinism, for Stalinism becomes endemic in the American
> middle class as soon as that class begins to think; it is a cultural Stalinism,
> independent of any political belief. . . . Parrington is the essential arbiter
> of the literary views of our more-or-less intellectual middle class, Parring-
> ton who so well plows the ground for the negation of literature.[13]

Lionel Trilling had not always been so angry at the American middle class. In 1939, for instance, he had replied in a more hopeful way to another set of questions posed by *Partisan Review* about the situation in American writing:

> My own literary interest . . . is in the tradition of humanistic thought and in the intellectual middle class which believes that it continues this tradition. . . . What for me is so interesting in the intellectual middle class is the dramatic contradiction of its living with the greatest possibility (call it illusion) of conscious choice, its believing itself the inheritor of the great humanist and rationalist tradition, and the badness and stupidity of its action.
>
> By and large, it is for this intellectual class that I suppose I write.[14]

By the late 1940s, however, Trilling's patience with the imaginative limitations of the middle class began to wear thin. In 1951, Trilling confided to his notebook, "If one defends the bourgeois, philistine virtues, one does not defend them merely from the demonism or bohemianism of the artist but from the present bourgeoisie itself, which is exactly no longer a bourgeoisie itself . . . but rather a highly politicized group, extravagantly sensitive to trends, tendencies, demands, ideals— which it does not have the mental equipment to deal with" (*N1* 513).

Nevertheless, Trilling remained loyal to the middle class. His goal was its education—urging it to make room in its mind for the difficult and complex, warning it of the herd instinct and the stupidity of the merely fashionable, coaxing it into accepting the variousness of human expression, and hoping that, in the end, it would broaden its notion of reality to include the life of the mind, by which he meant the realm of the imagination that comprised both the emotions and the intellect.

Trilling's goal, spelled out in the preface to *The Liberal Imagination,* was immensely appealing to his impoverished, culture-starved Jewish students, who thought of themselves as breaking out of worlds that did not seem to allow for the "variousness, possibility, complexity, and difficulty" (*LI* xv) that Trilling ascribed to literature. Setting out on the path Trilling delineated held out the promise of one's ascent from poor Jewish neighborhoods into an American middle class without having to subscribe to the narrow, "bourgeois" hopes and aspirations of one's immigrant parents. Second-generation Jews born in the New York boroughs in the Depression era who came to study with Trilling recognized that their parents' dreams of one day having a son (more rarely a daughter) who was a doctor or a lawyer were ennobled by a wish to arrive at material success by way of acquiring humanistic and scientific knowledge. But many Jewish children quickly abandoned not only their family's pragmatic approach to learning but also all thought of home when they heard Trilling's siren song of culture and the life of the mind.

———

Trilling's Jewish students responded strongly and variously to his ideas, his style, and his stature as a critic in the university. Each of them created the Trilling he or she needed and desired. That Trilling lent himself so easily to refraction, and later to the recollection of many different Trillings, is now part of his mystique. The forty-odd portraits so far written by friends, students, colleagues, scholars, and his wife testify that what Cynthia Ozick once wrote about the novels of E. M. Forster is also true of Trilling: he excites "competitive passions—possessive rivalries, in fact —among serious readers, each of whom feels uniquely chosen to perceive [his] inner life." [15] But Trilling was also subject to refraction in that the intellectual and professional possibilities that combined in his person were sundered in the next generation. The four portraits of Trilling assembled in this chapter reflect that disintegration. His person appears refracted through the minds of a fiction writer (Cynthia Ozick), a magazine editor (Norman Podhoretz), an academic literary critic (Steven Marcus), and a feminist literary scholar (Carolyn G. Heilbrun). The combined effect of these portraits, I hope, will illuminate the ways in which Trilling facilitated the integration of Jews into American literary academe and made their presence there a matter of course.

Cynthia Ozick, Writer

On January 4, 1952, a twenty-three-year-old aspiring novelist wrote to a friend in the Midwest about a man who two years earlier had risen to a position of preeminence in the glutted world of New York's literary intellectuals:

> Lionel Trilling (perhaps you know that I am in his seminar at Columbia) is a man I do not much like. Every week I leave his presence with a sense of humiliation. He has the strangest ability to create tension in the classroom, to stir up rivalries, to project the scornful smile. He is a liberal,

but a dogmatic one. He is a Deweyan pragmatist; he has not yet escaped the particular atmosphere of the thirties, and lacks totally, I think, the mystic prowess that can jump into another's mind and know it. He is an egotist, smug, but undeniably right and bright. I can barely wait till the end of the semester to escape him, or at least his ideals for graduate students, which are Prosiness, Research, Tenacity. Tedium.

This sketch is certainly among the more unusual portraits of Trilling. In 1990, when Cynthia Ozick recovered the letter she had written to Judson Jerome almost four decades earlier, she confessed surprise: "That sounds not at all like the Trilling I came to know later on!" [16] Her shrewd formulation allows for the possibility that there were different Trillings whom one could get to know, like a novel, at different ages, and who would appear changed in different times and different settings. It also suggests that one's perception of Trilling was shaped by those circumstances in one's life that were relevant in an encounter with him. Foremost among them, perhaps, was one's achievement as a literary intellectual.

When Trilling and his former student met again, more than twenty years later, as copanelists at a symposium in September 1973, Ozick had established herself as a writer. She had published a long Jamesian novel entitled *Trust* (1966) and a collection of short stories called *The Pagan Rabbi* (1971) that dissected the dilemmas of modern Jews in a Gentile culture with the sharp pen of the moral satirist. In addition, she had written a dozen literary essays, on topics ranging from the novels of Arthur A. Cohen to the classic feminism of Virginia Woolf. These essays had their intellectual roots in the critical tradition devised by Trilling as a combination of the imperatives of Matthew Arnold and John Erskine. It hardly needed the 1973 Award in Literature from the Academy of Arts and Letters to confirm that Ozick had used her talents well and become a literary voice that had to be taken into account. Walking together to the subway after the symposium, at which Trilling had been melancholy and pessimistic and Ozick almost silent, the two talked of their love for the novelist E. M. Forster. He had been the subject of Trilling's second book, published in 1943, and more recently, in 1971, of an essay by Ozick, boldly titled "Forster as Homosexual." Trilling had responded with a letter expressing his admiration for the essay and his astonishment that he himself should have been so blind to Forster's homosexuality. The Trilling whom Ozick came to know in that exchange was one who acknowledged intellectual parity; and while at the time there was no equality of achievement, Ozick recognized that Trilling regarded her as an ally in his opposition to the current direction of modern culture. Their shared concern about the decline of literary culture produced in Trilling and Ozick a feeling of being in the same sinking boat. Ozick's "overall sense of Trilling" derived from that late encounter. In a letter written in 1989, she spoke of Trilling as someone "whom I came to feel absolute affection for: in later years, when he noticed my work (and having no recollection of my having sat in his seminar), he was exceedingly kind to me, and humorously open about himself (on the subject of E. M. Forster)." [17]

Trilling and Ozick walked off together from a symposium that had been organized and orchestrated by Norman Podhoretz as the editor of *Commentary*. The participants included six men, among them Trilling and his former students Podhoretz and Hilton Kramer, and one woman, Cynthia Ozick. The panelists were to speak to the "state of high culture in America at the present time," a topic one would have expected *Commentary* to leave to its then less political rival, *Partisan Review*.[18] The lasting significance of the symposium for two of its participants, Ozick and Podhoretz, lay in the fact that it re-created the classroom situation of Trilling's seminars and allowed them to relive their roles, possibly undo their earlier defeats, and so heal long-festering wounds. It was only natural that Podhoretz, as the organizer of the symposium, dominated the discussion. But the transcript, which appeared in *Commentary* fifteen months after the event, reveals that the panel discussion amounted to more than a simple reversal of classroom roles. The symposium included a showdown between Trilling and Podhoretz.

At first, Trilling refused to play. He ignored baiting and provocation until Podhoretz finally managed to put him on the spot. Discussing the disastrous effects of the counterculture on high culture, Podhoretz sent out a probe:

> The counterrevolution of the 60's, with its repudiation of the modernist canon, and indeed of rationality itself, posed as a further development of the modernist revolution but was in actuality a resurgence of philistinism, very often of simple cultural barbarism. We don't want any of that stuff, it said, and not only don't we want it but we wish to be congratulated on our rejection of it; our rejection is a sign of superiority.

Trilling replied, somewhat put out by Podhoretz's extreme formulation and thus pushed into defending the counterculture.

REFRACTIONS OF LIONEL TRILLING

But that has to be understood not as we generally understand philistinism. I think if we look at it objectively, we have to see that it is a counterculture undertaking to assume a moralized position in relation both to bourgeois life and to the high cultural life. We can criticize it adversely, but we can't, as it were, assimilate it to mere vulgarity. (CPM 44)

This was precisely where Podhoretz wanted to have him. He had forced Trilling to repeat the betrayal that festered like a wound at the heart of their relationship. Trilling's hesitation to "dissociate himself from the radicalism of the sixties," [19] his unwillingness to speak out clearly against the political ideas and actions of the New Left, constituted for Podhoretz a betrayal of the values Trilling had undertaken to teach and thus an abandonment of his student. The symposium was an opportunity to have it out, to remind Trilling of his obligations, and to hear what he had to say in his defense. Podhoretz spoke impersonally, but he could be sure that his reproach was heard:

Now, there was, and is, a class of people in this society who are neither self-appointed nor appointed by God but who commit themselves to artistic and intellectual enterprises, and who are therefore obligated to defend those enterprises when they are under attack, out of elementary self-respect if nothing else; if that class of persons suffers a failure of nerve, it is hardly to be wondered at that no one else will speak for those values.

As for why such a failure of nerve took place, my explanation would be expressed in moral language: there was an epidemic of cowardice, together with an enormous panic to get on the right side of what looked like a triumphant revolution. (CPM 45)

At this moment Hilton Kramer piped up to soften the sting of Podhoretz's words. But Trilling knew that he was called upon to explain, as Podhoretz put it in his memoir *Breaking Ranks*, "why he could never summon up the will to go into 'opposition' . . . even at those moments when he was tempted to do so" (*BR* 302). Trilling replied:

There is a reason to say cowardice in individual cases, but as a general explanation of the situation Norman Podhoretz refers to I think the word "cowardice" might lead us astray. One has to conceive of it rather in terms of fatigue and of, as it were, alienation. Subjects and problems got presented in a way that made one's spirits fail. It wasn't that one was afraid to go into it, or afraid of being in opposition—I suppose I am speaking personally—but rather that in looking at the matter one's reaction was likely to be a despairing shrug. The terms weren't what one was used to, they didn't come at one in a way that would elicit a positive response. (CPM 46)

This was an extraordinary and unprecedented admission of defeat. Culture had developed in a way that Trilling found alien. He could no longer identify with its concerns, and he was compelled to perceive the culture's "subjects and problems" as so distant from, if not hostile to, his own thinking that he despaired of being able to oppose them. But there was more to Trilling's admission of fatigue than a failure of spirit. Trilling came to recognize that the cautious intellectual—who did not deal in extremes, in fashions and fads—could not lastingly influence the culture. Ideas were born, snatched up by the savvy dabbler, and marketed before they had been thought through, tested, and their impact on the culture apprehended.

Trilling had always been aware of the American trend to rush in droves, like lemmings to the sea, toward the new and different in hope of redemption. He would have preferred it if his fellow citizens had begun their search for answers in a reexamination of the past. In his 1942 essay "The Sense of the Past," which became part of *The Liberal Imagination,* Trilling wrote,

> The educated classes are learning to blame ideas for our troubles, rather than blaming what is a very different thing—our own bad thinking. This is the great vice of academicism, that is concerned with ideas rather than with thinking, and nowadays the errors of academicism do not stay in the academy; they make their way into the world, and what begins as a failure of perception among intellectual specialists finds its fulfillment in policy and action. (*LI* 192)

Podhoretz's critique of Trilling at the symposium had been based precisely on this train of thought. But Trilling was now ready to acknowledge that the continued failure of perception among his own intellectual class had exhausted him. He had made the life of the mind, by which he meant the critical examination of ideas in literature and politics, the central obligation of the privileged class of intellectuals to which he belonged. The counterculture of the 1960s forced him to realize that he had failed to make his case for the values of the middle class, for moderation and moral seriousness; that he was being rejected by the young; and that his books would be consigned to the dustbin of history.

Hilton Kramer tried to mitigate again: "There was something else, too: the enormous promise implicit in the countercultural position, the promise of being able to start one's life over again from the beginning, the promise of youth, of eternal possibility, of escape from complexity" (CPM 45). But Kramer's statement served only to reinforce Trilling's insight that he had failed in his task as an intellectual, which was to demonstrate that the promise of newness, of eternal renewal, of infinite recommencement—the most beloved of American dreams—was an illusion. If you wanted to mend society, you had to develop a sense of the past and move forward from there to face the complexity of the present. The "promise" Kramer spoke of produced only "bad thinking" and demagoguery; the rhetoric of promise allowed that a "lie is established in society" (CPM 42). Kramer's enticing description of the counterculture reminded Trilling of the Stalinist "lie" that had ensnared so many of his friends forty years earlier: "Like this promise, that one entailed a rejection of the notion of society and all the strains, difficulties, contradictions, of living a social life" (CPM 46).

Only now did Trilling turn to Podhoretz, and throw in the towel. "Something has happened to make cowardice a possibility," Trilling conceded. "Not that anyone is exempted from fulfilling his duties as an intellectual, but something has been going on for a sizable number of years, which is the disaffection of the middle class" (CPM 46). Surprisingly, Podhoretz let Trilling get away with this attempt to shift responsibility from the intellectuals to the middle class at large. Trilling did not say very much after that. The sense of intellectual defeat that pervaded much of the symposium was overwhelming. Podhoretz cared too much about Trilling, whom he had gotten to know at the height of his power, not to be moved by it. A sign of his loyalty and affection was that years later, in the second volume of his autobiography entitled *Breaking Ranks,* he accepted Trilling's explanation of fatigue for his "failure of nerve" (*BR* 296, 302). Podhoretz's reversal of the classroom situation was successful; but his demand that the great man justify himself was a Pyrrhic victory, because Podhoretz still loved the fallen king.

Cynthia Ozick had said almost nothing during the panel discussion at the symposium. Her silence had as much to do with her great personal shyness as with the circumstance that the symposium had re-created a classroom situation, in which she had been quite unhappy, when she had been one of two women attending Trilling's graduate seminar in 1951–52 at Columbia University.

In the summer of 1951, Ozick completed her graduate work at Ohio

15. Cynthia Ozick and her future husband Bernard Hallote in New York City's Central Park in 1951. *Courtesy of Cynthia Ozick.*

State University with a master's thesis on parable in Henry James. She had no intention of becoming a critic, having made up her mind to become a writer of fiction. But she applied to Columbia's Ph.D. program so as to be allowed to attend Trilling's seminar. "To get into this seminar," Ozick wrote in 1972, "you had to submit to a grilling wherein you renounced all former allegiance to the then-current literary religion, New Criticism, which considered that only the text existed, not the world. I passed the interview by lying—cunningly, and against my real convictions, I said that probably the world *did* exist and walked triumphantly into the seminar room." [20] At the time, Ozick "was preoccupied wholly" with the writing of a philosophical novel. Referring to the late 1940s and early 1950s, she explained in a letter that "for those few years . . . it was regarded as a disgrace to have a Ph.D. if you were serious about writing." [21] Although Trilling did not put it as starkly, he had been thinking along the same lines. In his notes toward an autobiographical lecture, he observed

I did not ever undertake to be a critic—being a critic was not, in Words-worth's phrase, part of the plan that pleased my boyish thought, or my adolescent thought, or even my thought as a young man. The plan that did please my thought was certainly literary, but what it envisaged was the career of a novelist. To this intention, criticism, when eventually I began to practice it, was always secondary, an afterthought: in short, not a vocation but an avocation.[22]

When his future wife, Diana, asked him during their courtship why he was pursuing a Ph.D. if he intended to be a novelist, "he replied that fiction had altered in our century and that the novelist had now to be a man of learning." She did not quite believe him. "His seemingly neutral response had for me a tone of personal problem. I felt that he was revealing an uncertainty about himself as a novelist, recognizing the greater pull which criticism had for him" (*BJ* 90). But Trilling remained plagued by his ever-increasing distance from a life as a fiction writer. Coming across a letter written with self-abandon by a drunk Ernest Hemingway to Clifton Fadiman, Trilling confided to his notebook in 1933: "how far—far—far I am going from being a writer—how less and less I have the material and the mind and the will. A few—very few —more years and the last chance will be gone" (*N1* 498). It is this entry that disclosed to Diana Trilling the origin of her husband's curious high regard for Hemingway. He thought of him as having achieved what was essential for a novelist—"inner freedom" (*BJ* 371). He envied Hem-ingway the recklessness with which he lived his life. "[H]ow right such a man is compared to the 'good minds' of my university life," Tril-ling noted in 1933, "how he will produce and mean something to the world . . . how his life . . . is a better life than anyone I know could live, and right for his job." But not only did a novelist's life have to be filled with "life," it also had to be exposed "without dignity" (*N1* 498). This was a problem for Trilling. Haunted by Hemingway—"he was the only writer of our time I envied"[23]—Trilling became the very opposite: a gentleman critic, who was considered by his colleagues and students the embodiment of dignity and grace. *That,* to Trilling, was a failure of nerve.

When Ozick attended Trilling's seminar, he had published his disser-tation, "a biography of Arnold's mind" (1939); a study of E. M. Forster (1943); his novel *The Middle of the Journey* (1947); *The Liberal Imagination* (1950); and a handful of short stories, the last of which had appeared in *Partisan Review* and *Harper's Bazaar* in 1945. In 1948, with most of the essays that would constitute *The Liberal Imagination* written, Trilling recorded in his notebook that his blossoming career as a critic was likely to absorb the strength he needed as a novelist:

> My being a professor and a much respected and even admired one is a great hoax. But sometimes I feel that I pay for the position not with learning but with my talent—that I draw off from my own work what should remain with it. Yet this is really only a conventional notion, picked up from my downtown friends, used to denigrate myself and my position, to placate the friends. . . . Suppose I were to dare to believe that one could be a professor and a man! and a writer!—what arrogance and defiance of convention. Yet deeply I dare to believe that—and must learn to believe it on the surface. (*N1* 511)

Trilling was quite ambivalent about teaching. He had felt a flurry of enthusiasm for it in the late 1930s, and he continued to care about college teaching. But he detested graduate seminars. Late in 1951, he entered in his notebook, "all graduate students trouble & in a way repel me and I must put down here the sensation of liberation I experienced when I arranged for my withdrawal from the graduate school, from seminars and the direction of dissertations" (*N1* 515). Trilling's aversion communicated itself to his students and produced a furtive aggressiveness. When Ozick described to her Ohio friend Trilling's "ability to create tension in the classroom, to stir up rivalries, to project the scornful smile," she was not overreacting to the high anxiety level that is normal at Columbia University. Rather, she was recording accurately, as someone not involved in the graduate studies rat race, the effect Trilling produced:

> There were four big tables arranged in a square, with everyone's feet sticking out into the open middle of the square. You could tell who was nervous, and how much, by watching the pairs of feet twist around each other. The Great Man presided awesomely from the high bar of the square. His head was a majestic granite-gray, like a centurion in command; he *looked* famous. His clean shoes twitched only slightly, and only when he was angry.
> It turned out that he was angry at me a lot of the time. He was angry because he thought me a disrupter, a rioter, a provocateur, and a fool; also crazy.[24]

Later in the essay we learn that Trilling was actually not angry at Ozick, who was too intimidated to speak up. "In those days I was bone-skinny, small, sallow and myopic, and . . . scared. . . ." Trilling was irritated by the only other woman in the seminar, who, unlike Ozick, did speak up. She became the other students' free, outspoken, outraged alter ego. Ozick did not speculate about the sources of the "Crazy Lady's" anger. She wanted to make another point. When Trilling returned the students' papers, he addressed Ozick, who had been quiet and orderly, by the name of the Crazy Lady, rebuking her for "starting an essay with a parenthesis in the first sentence, a habit he took to be a continuing sign of that unruly and unfocused mentality so often exhibited in class." Ozick understood immediately; "because the Crazy Lady and I sat side by side, because we were a connected blur of Woman, the Famous Critic, master of ultimate distinctions, couldn't tell us apart." Because of her gender, Ozick had been deprived of her individuality as an intellectual. "Even among intellectual humanists," Ozick commented, "every woman has a *Doppelgänger*—every other woman." [25]

Trilling's enlightened humanism had its limits. Ozick withdrew from the seminar. It could not teach her anything she would need as a writer. Trilling's criticism produced a small gesture of defiance. "Ever since then," Ozick confessed, "I've made a point of starting out with a parenthesis in the first sentence." But years later, after Trilling's commendation of her article on Forster and their encounter at the *Commentary* symposium, came a time for closure: "Trilling was cordial and very kind to me, and I felt redeemed, though it took two decades to earn his approval." [26] At the symposium Podhoretz played the part of the Crazy Lady to Ozick's silent onlooker. In the end, Ozick was left with the choices facing Hawthorne's Robin Molineux: she could join the crowd or walk off with the fallen king.

The perception of Trilling that distinguishes Ozick's portrait from those of her male counterparts was her recognition of Trilling's anger. It was part of his depression, which he usually controlled well in public. Diana Trilling explained: "For no perceptible reason he would suddenly fall into an extreme bleakness of mood and be unable to function with appropriate spirit. At these times he regarded me as his enemy and acted toward me as if it were I who were the cause of his despondency—there was always anger at the heart of his depression. Yet no one of his acquaintance and no one with whom he worked outside the home was aware that he was subject to these alterations of mood" (*BJ* 162). Ozick discerned Trilling's capacity for anger, perhaps because she felt particularly vulnerable in Trilling's class. Not only was she a woman graduate student; she also lacked, she thought, the armor of sophistication and

16. Cynthia Ozick in 1997. *Photograph by
Jill Krementz.*

the shield of indifference (especially toward Jewish matters) that the male
students at Columbia seemed to possess. One day she inadvertently
touched off Trilling's anger. She described the incident in 1989:

> It's humiliating for me to remember how I stuck up my hand and won-
> dered out loud whether the fact that Freud, Marx, and [Einstein were
> Jewish] *signified* something. Surely it did? It was a babyish thing to say,
> blatant, foolish, unsophisticated above all. But Trilling's reaction was out
> of proportion even to such gaucherie. He blew up at me, was enraged,
> *out*raged: I don't remember his words anymore (but I was able to recall
> them for a good long while afterward)—still, I definitely saw that I had
> committed an *affront:* I had mentioned, in an atmosphere of intellectual
> respectability, the one taboo: the idea that there might be some intellec-
> tual element or connection, or actuality of perspective or content or
> evocation, in *Jewishness.* I had made him *furious;* I had sullied—*vulgarized*
> is closer to his response—his class. . . . It's not much of an anecdote; but
> it shook me at the time; it shocked me, because I was made to feel

SHAME over having introduced the idea of Jewishness as a contributing force.[27]

To explain this incident to herself, Ozick drew on what was public knowledge: Trilling's difficulties in establishing himself at Columbia and the downplaying of his Jewishness, which many considered to be causally related matters. Yet Trilling remained connected to the Jews. Most of his literary friends were Jews; he had written stories and reviews for the *Menorah Journal,* and, when pushed, would contribute to *Commentary;* he took note throughout his work of what had happened to the Jews; and he wrote stories about their creativity and their suffering even in such unlikely places as his short piece on Tacitus (*LI* 202).

And what about Ozick's question? Did it matter that Freud, for example, was Jewish? No! was the answer Jewish intellectuals gave during the 1950s, 1960s, and 1970s. Freud's Jewishness was insignificant, and that was one of the reasons why Freud mattered so deeply to Jewish literary intellectuals at Columbia and elsewhere. Freud (along with Marx and Einstein) signified that the Jews were not parochial and selfish but contributed to mankind's enlightenment and to the universal improvement of the human lot. At most, the New York Jewish intellectuals might concede that Freud's Jewishness had induced him, as the member of a beleaguered minority in the capital of a strife-ridden, multiethnic empire, to develop theories that minimized religion, ethnicity, and class; for whenever those elements asserted themselves in European politics, Jews were in peril.

Freud's theories tied neatly into Columbia's educational goal of ethnic disembodiment. They provided an escape from the social circumstances of descent since they pared the self down to its psychosexual core. And they confirmed the Enlightenment proposition that mankind was created equal (except for the little matter of gender, which mattered little enough at the Columbia of Trilling's days). Jews have remained ardent believers in all theories proposed, in the wake of the Enlightenment, that proclaimed them no different from anybody else. In Freud's universe of human sameness, the bad Jew was merely a metaphor for the bad father.[28] In the world of Freud's theories, the burden of communal history seemed to melt away. Trilling sometimes forced himself to an awareness of that burden, as in his painful essay on Isaac Babel; but it was a burden of which he did not like to be reminded, least of all by a young Jewish woman.

Our commonly accepted, pious image of Trilling barely accommodates a man who would lose his temper at the unapologetic mention of Jewishness. Was he embarrassed, offended, annoyed, exasperated? Was he angry that something he had thought tamed and overcome was suddenly offered to him as a great virtue? Was he upset that parochial pride could make its way into his classroom? Or did his anger have nothing at all to do with Ozick's question but with some other, private unhappiness? We cannot know. Whatever answer we choose will reflect the Trilling we need. The great merit of Ozick's impious portrait is that it makes us a bit more uncertain about the Trilling we thought we knew so well.

Norman Podhoretz, Editor

For Norman Podhoretz, who was two years younger than Cynthia Ozick and was never beset by the idea of becoming a novelist, Trilling was the great enabler. He was the cultural eminence who held out to all students, but particularly to gifted Jews from the poor neighborhoods, the possibility of pursuing the life of the mind. Podhoretz, who entered Columbia College in 1946 at the age of sixteen, worked hard to duplicate Trilling's success. Indeed, the argument could be made that Podhoretz replicated Trilling's career but reversed Trilling's decision, made in 1930 at the age of twenty-five, to leave the *Menorah Journal* and move into academe. It had been no easy thing at the time to leave Greenwich Village for the derided, dry-as-dust world of academe. In 1953, Podhoretz decided to quit his pursuit of an academic career for a position at *Commentary,* which was edited by the same man, Elliot Cohen, whom Trilling had deserted at the *Menorah Journal* in 1930. From his mid-twenties on, Podhoretz lived out an unrealized aspect of Trilling's self.

Their relationship combined supportiveness and antagonism, and was complicated by Podhoretz's grim outspokenness and ardent political partisanship. Podhoretz perhaps best summed up the relationship in the acknowledgments to his memoir *Making It* (1967): "I wish, finally, to acknowledge," Podhoretz wrote, "my immense debt to Lionel Trilling, who has taught me more than he or I ever realized—though not, I fear, precisely what he would have wanted me to learn." Trilling had urgently advised his student not to publish the book, "warning that it would take me ten years to live it down" (*BR* 220). But Podhoretz, bent upon upsetting the apple cart, went ahead anyway.

What Trilling had objected to was the publication of an autobiography that focused on the journey from Brooklyn to Manhattan, from being the son of an immigrant workman to sitting at the feet of F. R. Leavis, from craving publication as a hapless graduate student to becoming editor of *Commentary* at the age of thirty. There was nothing unusual in the structure of Podhoretz's rags-to-riches story. What was new about the memoir was that it spoke of a career in the world of art and intellect as if it were a career in business. All hell broke loose. "From the reviews one might have supposed that he had written *Mein Kampf*," Diana Trilling recalled (*BJ* 91–92). Indeed, the highbrow literary establishment was, as Norman Mailer put it, "scandalized, shocked, livid, revolted, appalled, disheartened and enraged" (*BR* 221). The reason was that *Making It* had brilliantly exposed its hypocrisies.

The people to whom *Making It* mattered, the New York Intellectuals, most of whom were associated at one time or another with *Partisan Review,* could be thought of as a Jewish family. Although several core members (Mary McCarthy, Richard Chase, Dwight MacDonald, F. W. Dupee, and Elizabeth Hardwick, among others) were not Jewish, the term *Jewish,* Podhoretz wrote, "can be allowed to stand by clear majority rule and by various peculiarities of temper."[29] Those who were Jewish (Lionel Abel, Daniel Bell, Nathan Glazer, Paul Goodman, Clement Greenberg, Sidney Hook, Irving Howe, Alfred Kazin, William Phillips, Philip Rahv, Harold Rosenberg, Meyer Schapiro, Robert Warshow, and many others) came from immigrant worlds. Podhoretz explained that "these were people who by virtue of their tastes, ideas, and general concerns found themselves stuck with one another against the rest of the world whether they liked it or not (and most did not), preoccupied with one another to the point of obsession, and intense in their attachments and hostilities as only a family is capable of being" (*MI* 110). Their pursuit was the criticism of art, literature, music, film, society, and politics. They celebrated the great masters, believed in the sublime nature of a work of art, yet were committed to "view all phenomena, including the arts, in their historical and social context" (*MI* 115). They were contemptuous of the middlebrow and philistine, which is why they thought America hopeless and turned their attention to Europe. They were intellectual elitists whose style was hypercritical, learned, and allusive. In short, they were men (mostly) of the world, and their living in America was as accidental to their cultural ideals as their Jewish backgrounds were irrelevant to their appreciation of works of high art, literary and pictorial. They considered their escape from what they deemed the narrow, impoverished, unenlightened "world of their fathers" through instant mastery of Western high culture an achievement; they

17. Norman Podhoretz. *Photograph by Leslie Jean-Bart.*

valued it as an intellectual liberation; and they were not going to let that *pisherl* Podhoretz tell them there was something wrong with it.

Making It attacked on three levels. First, by writing his memoirs in the Horatio Alger tradition, Podhoretz implied that the ascent "out of the ghetto" necessitated a change of class. He charged that those on the rise were induced to think of their parents' culture with contempt. His teacher had informed him that because "I was a talented boy, a better class of people stood ready to admit me into their ranks. But only on one condition: I had to signify by my general deportment that I acknowledged them as *superior* to the class of people among whom I happened to have been born" (*MI* 20).

Second, by designing his story as a meditation on American attitudes toward success, Podhoretz illuminated the feature that distinguished the intellectuals from every other professional group, namely, their "cult of failure" (*MI* xv). Trilling once described that cult precisely when he spoke of an "old feeling, which was the feeling of my youth, that if you made a success you were a fraud" (*CPM* 47). Podhoretz contended that the cult of failure was a far cry from the feeling that prevailed in the Jewish immigrant milieu, a culture notorious for its ambition and esteem of worldly success. There was a vague sense among Jewish immigrants that poverty was the noble lot of the seriously learned man because of a rabbinic injunction against taking payment for the teaching of Torah. But in America one did not have to choose that lot. If you had a golden head, you made the most of golden opportunities. The cult of failure and the feeling that Trilling spoke of were nursed in the rarefied air of Columbia College, where the word " 'successful' glided automatically into the judgment 'corrupt' " (MI xv). In that atmosphere budding Jewish intellectuals were cleansed of any grossness and crudity. Podhoretz wrote that

> a system of manners existed at Columbia which prohibited any expression of worldly ambitiousness. To yearn for the applause of posterity may have been legitimate, but it was thought contemptible to dream of the rewards contemporary society had to offer, and altogether despicable to admit to so low a hunger, except in tones of irony that revealed one's consciousness of how naughty a thing one was doing. (MI xv)

In short, Columbia in the 1950s cultivated a modernized version of Harvard's genteel code that despised the greaseball and the grind. Podhoretz conceded that it was all right to be silly in college; but when grown-ups pretended to be fastidious about success, he charged, when they professed disinterest in the pursuit of money, fame, or power, they were either hypocrites or fools—because not to want success in a world that played hardball left one sitting on the bench.

Third, by presenting his rags-to-riches story as a "confessional work" (MI xvii) and interpreting it along the way as a "spiritual" autobiography, Podhoretz meant to convey what had actually been taking place in American high culture: the conversion of the Jews. His preferred term for the intellectuals' newly attained faith, the "gospel of anti-success," pointed to the origins of the notion that the artist, who was a modern saint, ought not to be tainted by worldly aspirations. Poor was pure; great art didn't sell. The superiority (or saintliness) of a poet, painter, or critic was reflected in the inadequate material conditions of his or her life. Podhoretz presented the first half of his story of ascent as a narrative of his conversion from the crass materialism of the Jews to the pure spirituality of Gentile high culture. What he had called "the two warring American attitudes toward the the pursuit of success" (MI xvi) turned out to be, where the "family" was concerned, a hot conflict between the Jewish need for safety (best achieved through the acquisition of money and power) and the Gentile notion of being cultured, which derived from the Christian dualism of body and soul, and the idea that the true devotee of the life of the mind had to overcome the corrupting desire to possess the goods of this world. If you wished to achieve purity, your best shot was obviously to live in a Thoreauvian wood shack and to "keep your accounts on your thumb nail." [30] Yet for Jews to devote their lives to a notion of culture that would perpetuate their own power-lessness struck Podhoretz as a singularly perverse thing to do. It violated the survival instinct of history-conscious Jews and required them to believe that America was different from Europe. During the 1950s there was of course little reason to think that America would turn on the Jews. What stopped Podhoretz in his tracks (and made him record the second half of his story as a fall from grace) was the realization that subscribing to gentility demanded that as a sign of his conversion he pass judgment on the world he had left behind and think of the Jews as crude, vulgar, loud, pushy, materialist, and crass. That he could not do.

In 1953, Podhoretz began to reverse the assimilationist direction of his life. *Making It* was written in 1967 from the perspective of one who regretted his conversion and was trying to make amends. Fifty years earlier, Abraham Cahan had introduced the theme of regret at the end of his novel *The Rise of David Levinsky* (1917). Although Podhoretz was less nostalgic than Levinsky, he was equally bitten by guilt: "It appalls me to think what an immense transformation I had to work on myself in order to become what I have become: if I had known what I was doing I would surely not have been able to do it, I would surely not have wanted to. No wonder the choice had to be blind; there was a kind of treason in it: treason toward my family, treason toward my friends" (*MI* 4).

When *Making It* appeared, the "family" around *Partisan Review* was furious on two counts. They resented that Podhoretz implicated them in his "betrayal." He accused them of having converted, albeit less for-mally than Bernard Berenson, to the faith of high art. That faith spelled, if not always the condemnation of the Jews as a people, certainly the repudiation of their ideals, manners, and forms of social interaction. What Podhoretz perceived was that New York Jewish Trotskyists wor-shiped side by side with Southern Agrarians in the church of high art. That is why *Partisan Review* published T. S. Eliot's "East Coker" despite the poet's antithetical politics and racial views. The New York intellectuals stuck together to protect themselves, Podhoretz explained, "against contaminating influences from the surrounding American world: from *Kitsch*, from middlebrowism, from commercialism, from mass culture, from academicism, from populism, from liberalism, from Stalinism, from Louis B. Mayer, from John Steinbeck, from George S. Kaufman," and so on (*MI* 118). The worship of high art produced snobs; and a Jewish snob was someone who did not like to think back to the Bronx, who winced at the Yiddish-accented English of his parents and thought their apartments tawdry (*MI* 51). "The dominant emotions of snobbery," Trilling had written, "are uneasiness, self-consciousness, self-defensiveness, the sense that one is not quite real but can in some way acquire reality" (*LI* 209–210). He was right on the money, as was Podhoretz, and the "family" knew it.

The other objection the "family" had to *Making It* concerned form. New York literati were annoyed by the unabashed style of Podhoretz's confession and atonement. That he had teamed up with *Commentary*, whose grand plan was to arrange "a marriage between the intellectuals (that is, the family) and American culture, and at the same time a reconciliation between them and the Jewish community" (*MI* 207), was strictly his business. But it was another matter altogether to publish an autobiography that reverted to immigrant manners, that applied to the life of the mind the notion of "making it" to the top of the pile. Podhoretz had scrambled to the top, sounded the fanfare, and announced that regarding "the hunger for worldly success . . . as low, ignoble and ugly" (*MI* 55) was bunk. Influence counted, and it wasn't to be had in the stacks of the library or as assistant editor of a high-culture magazine read by literary types in the dim corners of the Hungarian Pastry Shop across from the Cathedral of St. John the Divine. *Making It* was brash, cocky, tasteless, and self-inflating. Its purpose was to undo Podhoretz's conversion to "taste" and hypocrisy; it was a "frank, Mailer-like bid for literary distinction, fame, and money," but it was also a trenchant critique of the guardians of American high culture.

It was part of Trilling's greatness that he perceived the validity of Podhoretz's philippic and recognized that his former student attempted to act on the principles that informed the teacher's cultural essays. First among these principles was the intellectual's obligation to remain responsive to reality. Beneath its swagger *Making It* admonished intellectuals not to contribute to their own marginalization by ignoring the importance of power and influence. The place of the mind was at the "bloody crossroads where literature and politics meet." And what led there was the intellectual's awareness that he or she was in some measure responsible for the shape of reality. In Trilling's work that responsibility expressed itself in a "highly developed sense of context." Trilling had no tolerance for the New Critical withdrawal from the world. "[A]lmost everything he ever wrote," Podhoretz explained, "emerged from and was directed back into the surrounding atmosphere—a prevailing idea, a current attitude, a fashionable taste that needed correction or modification or qualification" (BR 279). This "political resonance" of Trilling's writings excited Podhoretz. "In the case of Trilling's critical essays, the political charge was strong enough to electrify the mind and yet so subtle and muted that it never overwhelmed their independent value as literary criticism" (BR 280). Podhoretz admired Trilling's tightrope act so much that years later he called a collection of his critical essays *The Bloody Crossroads* (1986). Yet Podhoretz knew that he had long ago jumped back to the ground. He had chosen a life of political commentary.

Norman Podhoretz, born in Brooklyn, New York, in 1930, came to Columbia College from Brooklyn Boys' High. He had won a scholarship to Harvard but was unable to accept it because it did not cover all expenses and his parents were too poor to make up the difference (*MI* 18). He attended Columbia as a commuter. A Pulitzer scholarship covered his tuition and paid a small stipend. His father, who had come to America from Galicia in 1912, believed that "the way to be a Jew was to get a Jewish education" (*MI* 30), and accordingly had extorted from his son the promise to attend Seminary College, the undergraduate liberal arts division of the Jewish Theological Seminary, located a few blocks north of Columbia. Like Robert Alter and Morris Dickstein after him, Podhoretz experienced life at the seminary as "perfectly continuous with the life I had always known," while Columbia "represented an almost total break with the familiar, not only in the kind of people who studied and taught there, but also in the curriculum and the way in which it was treated" (*MI* 32). The seminary's expectations were concrete, explicit, and unambiguous: Become a good Jew. Columbia's goal, by contrast, was seductively abstract and idealized: Become a gentleman, someone of enlightened and gracious mind who comported himself like an upper-class WASP. Ambition was frowned upon. The Columbia code was similar to the one Harry Levin had encountered when he first came to Harvard: "It was a code which forbade one to work too hard or to make any effort to impress a professor or to display the slightest concern over grades" (*MI* 36). One studied in order to refine one's sensibility and to partake of Western culture, which was not thought of as the creation of a particular group of people but considered to be the "repository of the universal, existing not in space or time but rather in some transcendent realm of the spirit" (*MI* 43). Trilling's courses offered a slight corrective, but it was not strong enough to call that notion into question.

Podhoretz graduated in 1950. As the recipient of Kellett and Fulbright fellowships, he left for Cambridge University, where he lived at Clare College. It did not take him long to discover that F. R. and Q. D. Leavis held court at Downing College. His encounter with the Leavises was, if not a exactly a meeting of minds, a perfect match of intensities. Podhoretz, for whom in disregard of the genteel code the "frenetic pursuit of 'brilliance' " had become habitual at Columbia (*MI* 72), responded without reservation to the fierce seriousness of the Leavises, to their "puritanical ferocity" (*MI* 79) and their single-minded dedication to literary criticism, which entailed nothing less than "the common pursuit of true judgement and the correction of taste." The phrase was that of T. S. Eliot, with whom the Leavises concurred in their redrawing of the map of English literature. Their goal was to safeguard Englishness, the homespun alternative to the public school ethos that reigned at Oxford and Cambridge. Englishness resided in the robust vitality of Shakespearean English and was preserved in the poetic tradition that ran from Shakespeare through Ben Jonson, the Metaphysical poets, the Jacobeans, Bunyan, Pope, Johnson, Blake, Wordsworth (with reservations), Keats, and Hopkins, and ended with T. S. Eliot.[31] A countertradition of Latinate or verbally attenuated writers began with Spenser, continued through Milton—a literary disaster who anesthetized the English language—and comprised Dryden, Shelley, Byron, Tennyson, and Browning.

Two years before Podhoretz found his way to Downing College, F. R. Leavis had published *The Great Tradition* (1948), in which he had argued that in the nineteenth century, despite Wordsworth, Keats, and Hopkins, Englishness was best preserved in the novels of Jane Austen, George Eliot, Henry James, and Joseph Conrad. The Leavises' revaluation of D. H. Lawrence and Charles Dickens followed in 1955 and 1970, respectively. Defoe, Fielding, Richardson, Sterne, most Victorian novelists, Joyce, Woolf, the Bloomsbury writers, and in fact most authors after D. H. Lawrence "constituted a network of 'B' roads interspersed with a good few cul-de-sacs."[32]

Podhoretz was struck by the uncanny similarities between *The Great Tradition* and the authors preferred by his American mentor, Trilling. Podhoretz saw his studies at Downing College as an intensification of his studies at Columbia. He was spellbound by the close readings Leavis performed for his students:

> He brought to bear on these analyses a knowledge of the literary, cultural, and social history of England frightening in its intimacy, a sensitivity to the nuances of English style phenomenal in its range, and a sense of the relations between tradition and the individual talent—to use a phrase of the prelapsarian Eliot to which Leavis was very devoted—that was breath-taking in its inwardness. (*MI* 78)

Podhoretz had witnessed similar feats at Columbia College in Andrew Chiappe's lectures on Shakespeare; F. W. Dupee's classes on Joyce, Yeats, and Proust; and Trilling's course on the Romantic poets and Victorian novelists, where Podhoretz had earned a rare "A-plus" (*MI* 42, 78). "Trilling, indeed, had the same power Leavis displayed for exposing the filaments which connect a great work of literature to all the life around it, energizing and vitalizing it; and like Leavis, he understood literature as an act of moral imagination and as an agent of social and political health" (*MI* 78–79). The common source from which both Leavis and Trilling derived their critical approach was Matthew Arnold, and Podhoretz used this commonality to reconcile "the conflict of loyalties I felt toward my two godfathers in culture on either side of the Atlantic" (*MI* 80–81). When *The Liberal Imagination* appeared in England in 1951, Leavis invited Podhoretz to review it for *Scrutiny,* the critical magazine Leavis had founded in 1932. To write for *Scrutiny* was an accolade that marked the neophyte's assumption into the circle of the elect, the Scrutineers. Podhoretz was flattered but did not wish to surrender completely to the English. His solution was to read *The Liberal Imagination* as a work of criticism firmly rooted in the tradition of Arnold and to imply that "as the most significant American critic now writing" Trilling was in fact the Leavis of the New World.[33]

While Trilling would not have denied that he shared certain views with Leavis, he had his reservations about the English critic. In an essay on the controversy involving C. P. Snow and Leavis, which Podhoretz persuaded Trilling to write (*BR* 116), Trilling was gracious but firm in his criticism of Leavis. He pointed to "Dr. Leavis's belief that the human faculty above all others to which literature addresses itself is the moral consciousness, which is also the source of all successful creation, the very root of poetic genius. The extent of his commitment to this idea results in what I believe to be a fault in his critical thought—he does not give anything like adequate recognition to those aspects of art which are gratuitous, which arise from high spirits and the impulse of play." [34]

It took Podhoretz another year to discover that there was something too narrow about an intellectual who made his students feel that "literature was of the supremest importance" (*MI* 79) and that the literature of certain English men and women was the best of all. Moreover, it seemed as if Leavis derived no pleasure from literature and was not receptive to the exuberance that was the best feature of certain literary works. A year after his appearance in *Scrutiny*, Podhoretz realized that it was time for him to quit the dour court. In the summer of 1952, having received a B.A. from Cambridge University and a First on the English Tripos, Podhoretz returned to New York. The Trillings invited him to come see them at their summer home in Connecticut.

This visit proved to be a turning point in Podhoretz's life. Trilling listened patiently to his visitor's long and rapid disquisition about his reservations concerning a life in academe, and instead of being shocked, as Podhoretz had expected, he replied that he understood exactly:

> [H]e asked me what I really wanted to do with myself, what kind of power I was after, this ensuring that if anyone was to be shocked that afternoon, it would be me. Power? Who ever said anything about power? What did I have to do with power, or it with me? "Don't be silly," he said, "everyone wants power. The only question is what kind. What kind do you want?" Well, I asked slyly, what kinds were there to choose from? Money, he said, was a form of power, so was fame, so was eminence in a given profession. Oh in *that* case, I replied, greatly relieved, the answer was fame, no doubt about it; I wanted to be a famous critic. (*MI* 96)

Not long afterward Podhoretz received a phone call from Elliot Cohen, the editor of *Commentary*, who had heard about Podhoretz from Trilling and read his piece in *Scrutiny*. Cohen invited Podhoretz to his office for a talk. Podhoretz knew next-to-nothing about *Commentary* and so it surprised him to see "that it was possible to be an avant-garde intellectual and at the same time to be interested in things Jewish" (*MI* 99). His disjointed education at the seminary and Columbia and his familiarity with *Partisan Review* had led him to think of "universal" and Jewish culture as radical opposites. When he mentioned this notion to Cohen, the editor grinned and said: "The main difference between *Partisan Review* and *Commentary* . . . is that we admit to being a Jewish magazine and they don't" (*MI* 99–100).

In Elliot Cohen, Podhoretz had met his match in outspokenness, brilliance, and intensity. Born in Des Moines, Iowa, in 1899 as the son of immigrants from Russia, Cohen grew up in Mobile, Alabama. His father, who had been educated to be a rabbi, had opened a clothing store in nearby Tama. Cohen was a prodigy who could read the headlines of the local newspaper at the age of two or three. He entered Yale College at the age of fifteen, specializing in philosophy and English literature. He received his B.A. in 1918 and went on to do graduate work at Yale. But he realized soon that as a Jew he would not get an academic post, and so he looked around for something else to do. He had been president of the Menorah Society at Yale and in his junior year had won a national contest for outstanding writing on a Jewish topic with an essay called "The Promise of the American Synagogue," in which he had declared that American rabbis knew little about contemporary Jewish life. In October 1923, Cohen began to write for the *Menorah Journal,* and two years later, at the age of twenty-six, he became the editor of the magazine. He recruited for its pages the up-and-coming second generation of New York Intellectuals, Anita Brenner, Clifton (Kip) Fadiman, Felix Morrow, Henry Rosenthal, Herbert Solow, Tess Slesinger, and Lionel Trilling. Trilling's first story appeared in the June-July 1925 issue. All in all, Trilling contributed twenty-four pieces to Cohen's magazine, the last of which, a review of Lion Feuchtwanger's novel *Success,* appeared in June 1931.[35]

In his eulogy for Cohen, who died in the spring of 1959, Trilling spoke of the depressed, edgy, and difficult man as "the greatest teacher I have ever known." Trilling added, "If I may speak of my own particular case, I would wish to acknowledge him as the only great teacher I have ever had." Cohen had firmly believed in the Menorah program, which had set itself the task "to normalize the American Jew's sense of himself" or, as Robert Alter put it, "to validate Jewish cultural phenomena by assimilating them to Western analogues."[36] Cohen had pushed the young Trilling toward thinking of and about himself as a Jew, forcing him to produce the very few pieces in which he addressed the question head-on. Even more important was the fact that Cohen insisted that Trilling *write,* and that he do so clearly and gracefully. "He believed that no idea was so difficult and complex but that it could be expressed in a way that would make it understood by anyone to whom it might conceivably be of interest. He was able to instill this belief in many, and he painstakingly demonstrated how it could be implemented."[37]

In the summer of 1952, when Podhoretz went to meet Cohen, *Com-*

mentary was barely seven years old. Its editor was eager to ferret out fresh talent and train them as writers. Having been fired from the *Menorah Journal* for political radicalism in 1931, Cohen had spent fourteen bitter years as a fundraiser for a Jewish organization until the founding of *Commentary* in 1945 enabled him to return to a job he loved. Cohen had what it took to create a Jewish magazine that skirted parochialism and appealed to a broad but smart audience that included non-Jews. As Trilling recalled, "he taught the younger men around him that nothing in human life need be alien to their thought, and nothing in American life, whether it be baseball, or vaudeville, or college tradition, or elementary education, or fashions in speech, or food, or dress, or manners." [38] Simply put, Cohen was no snob.

This was the insight Podhoretz came away with from his first interview with Cohen. The young man's notion of the gulf between high art, Jewish culture, and the world at large must have amused Cohen. It is easy to imagine with what secret delight Cohen hurdled his interviewee from criticism to politics, from politics to Jewish scholarship, from Jewish scholarship to motion pictures, from the movies to sports, only to settle into an extensive discussion of baseball. The puzzled look on Podhoretz's face finally moved Cohen to interrupt himself "in the midst of a highly intricate analysis of Casey Stengel's managerial style" (*MI* 100) to ask Podhoretz whether he thought Stengel was an unworthy object for the critical intelligence to dwell upon and whether that faculty should be reserved exclusively for the contemplation of Henry James? Podhoretz suddenly understood that there was another way of looking at the world. It connected elements that had seemed at odds with each other in the course of his education, and it forced him to rethink himself not so much as a Jew but as an American. The interview with Cohen ended unexpectedly:

> Abruptly he handed me a book. It was a review copy of a first novel, *The Natural,* by a writer named Bernard Malamud, whose stories Cohen had been publishing. "Well," he said, "you seem to know something about novels, you know something about symbolism, you know something about Jews, and you know something about baseball. Here's a symbolic novel by a Jewish writer about a baseball player. I guess you're qualified to review it. (*MI* 101)

Podhoretz's inordinately long review did not appear until March 1953. By that time he was back at Cambridge University working on a dissertation. He had chosen the novels of Disraeli as his topic because their author was a Jew "who had made it to 'the top of the greasy pole' (his phrase)" (*MI* 104). Moreover, writing about Disraeli would force him to learn more about politics, a field in which, thanks to *Commentary,* he had become more interested. But Podhoretz was becoming bored with England, the English literary heritage (including Leavis's idea of Englishness), and the academic life, so in the summer of 1953 he returned to America to immerse himself in the "jittery excitement" of contemporary intellectual life.

Podhoretz's ascent at *Commentary,* described in *Making It,* was both facilitated and complicated by the death of Robert Warshow in 1955 and by Elliot Cohen's subsequent depression, which terminated his work at the magazine (although he nominally remained its editor) and eventually led to his suicide in May 1959. After his return from England, Podhoretz began to write regularly for *Commentary.* Under the benign tutelage of Warshow he produced one long piece a month, condemning *The Adventures of Augie March,* analyzing American television, reflecting on the revival of religion among literati, artists, and academics. In December 1953, Podhoretz was drafted into the army for two years. Upon his discharge in December 1955, he joined *Commentary* as assistant editor, filling the seat left open for him after Warshow's untimely death in the spring of 1955. Podhoretz had greatly looked forward to working on the magazine, but he discovered that the tone in the editorial offices had changed, and he debated whether he should stay on. In August 1956, Trilling recorded in his notebook, "Speaking with [Diana] of Norman Podhoretz's dilemma about E[lliot] E. C[ohen].—he has no real connection with E., saw him only a very few times before going to work for *Commentary* and not at all since then, and yet he feels that he should remain until some time after E's return to sustain him against the Greenberg brothers [Clement and Martin, who were editing the magazine in Cohen's absence]" (*N2* 8). In 1958, Podhoretz could not bear the tension any longer and left, only to be asked by the American Jewish Committee, which sponsored the magazine, to take over the editorship in late 1959 after Cohen's death.

In 1960, at the age of thirty, Podhoretz occupied a position of intellectual influence. It was a different kind of power than he had envisioned in his conversation with Trilling in 1952, and Podhoretz was very much aware of the fact that he was not going to become a "famous critic." In another way, however, he was still connected to a part of Trilling's life, since at *Commentary* "Lionel's student [was] succeeding Lionel's teacher" (*BR* 174). Almost immediately Podhoretz began to revamp the magazine. It became more political, and while it remained explicitly Jewish, the new *Commentary* "bespoke, and reflected, a more advanced stage of acculturation than the old, and was accordingly more general than Jewish in emphasis" (*MI* 309).

At the same time, Podhoretz reconceived his political position in a complicated way. He was gradually turning against the hard-line anti-Communist liberalism that reigned in the "family." Podhoretz did not think that the anti-Communist position shared by the editors of *Partisan Review* and the Trillings had been proven wrong. "What I did begin to question was whether these ideas were still applicable to the Soviet Union under Khrushchev" (*BR* 172). Such doubts brought him into sharp conflict not only with "everything [he] had been educated to believe as a young intellectual" (*BR* 172) but also with his elders, mentors, and friends. He speculated that his desertion of the anti-Communist line seemed to Trilling an "act of political betrayal" (*BR* 173). It is indicative of the extent to which Podhoretz considered himself an heir to (at least a part of) Trilling's legacy that in his political memoirs of 1979, written shortly after Trilling's death, he took his speculation a step further. The betrayal, Podhoretz wrote, "was also personal," or so his elders "must have felt": "Here was I, Lionel Trilling's student and protégé and friend. Had he taken the trouble to teach me so much in the classroom and out, had he encouraged and helped me along in so many different ways, that I should wind up sponsoring the resurgence of ideas and attitudes he had spent most of his adult life battling against?" (*BR* 173–174).

Moreover, Podhoretz was slowly turning against the liberal consensus on domestic issues that had been established by his elders and radicalized by his contemporaries. "I was finding my way toward a political position that was in some essential respects more consistent with everything I had been educated to believe as a student of literature," which was "authenticity in the expression of feeling and honesty in the exploration of ideas" (*BR* 171, 172). The piece that best exemplified Podhoretz's defiance of the "established liberal opinion" and the sentimental values of "polite liberal society" of the early 1960s (*BR* 170, 171) was an essay entitled "My Negro Problem—And Ours," which appeared in *Commentary* in February 1963. It opened with a discrepancy Podhoretz had noticed as a child growing up in a Jewish-Italian-black working-class neighborhood:

> Two ideas puzzled me deeply as a child growing up in Brooklyn during the 1930's. . . . One of them was that all Jews were rich; the other was that all Negroes were persecuted. These ideas had appeared in print; therefore they must be true. My own experience and the evidence of my senses told they were not true, . . . especially such evidence of the senses as comes from being repeatedly beaten up, robbed, and in general hated, terrorized, and humiliated.
>
> And so for a long time I was puzzled to think that Jews were supposed to be rich when the only Jews I knew were poor, and that Negroes were supposed to be persecuted when it was the Negroes who were doing the only persecuting I knew about—and doing it, moreover, to *me.*

Podhoretz went on to describe incidents of assault and battery by black boys, whose victim he was, and the strategies of physical intimidation and violence by means of which black youths ruled the streets. The enmity between blacks and whites was not comparable to the more casual animosity between Italians and Jews.

Podhoretz's efforts to understand the violent hatred of African Americans toward whites in the 1930s and 1960s led him to James Baldwin, whom he had met in Paris in 1951. From Baldwin he learned about the "sense of entrapment that poisons the soul of the Negro with hatred for the white man whom he knows to be his jailer." But again, idea and reality did not square: "How could the Negroes in my neighborhood have regarded the whites across the street and around the corner as jailers? On the whole, the whites were not so poor as the Negroes, but they were quite poor enough, and the years were years of Depression. As for white hatred of the Negro, how could guilt have had anything to do with it? What share had these Italian and Jewish immigrants in the enslavement of the Negro? What share had they—downtrodden people themselves breaking their own necks to eke out a living—in the exploitation of the Negro?"

Podhoretz answered Baldwin's notion that "one of the reasons Negroes hate the white man is that . . . in white eyes all Negroes are alike" by asserting that the reverse was also true: whites are faceless to blacks. "To the Negroes, my white skin was enough to define me as the enemy, and in a war it is only the uniform that counts and not the person." Furthermore, he saw the hatred between black and white arise from fear and envy, and he attributed the increasing distance between the two groups to pointless theorizing and refusal to look at the facts, a continuation of facelessness by other means. His solution, the unmaking of color through miscegenation, did not happen.[39] What was new about

Podhoretz's essay and anathema to liberal opinion at the time was the observation that the violence of urban blacks was not an innocent expression of despair but a deliberate articulation of bigotry and prejudice.

As the 1960s drew to a close, Podhoretz grew less sure that the "new radicals" on the left to whom he had felt attracted were capable of putting an end to the racial nightmare. He observed on the contrary, that in order to rectify past injustice, a new system of injustice, was created, replacing one kind of discrimination with another. It was then, in the early 1970s, that Podhoretz felt betrayed by Trilling. He had expected him, as a classical (or paleo-) liberal, to speak out against the implementation of affirmative-action quotas in universities and colleges, which in the eyes of Podhoretz undermined the liberal principles and middle-class values Trilling had upheld in his critical work.

By the early 1970s, intellectuals were greatly confused as to who was or was not liberal, and what was or was not liberal politics. Podhoretz's strand of liberalism, which accepted the New Deal but rejected the political and cultural developments of the late 1960s, began to be called "neoconservatism" by his opponents, and the label stuck. But they, Podhoretz argued, deserved the appellation "liberal" even less because

> the new "liberals," in direct violation of traditional liberal principles, supported quota systems rather than individual merit—or equality of result rather than equality of opportunity—as the road to social justice. But this brand of egalitarianism was not simply antiliberal; it also contributed to the undermining of middle-class values by making rewards contingent upon membership in a group favored for one reason or another by the government, rather than upon individual effort and achievement. It could be understood, then, as an extension into concrete policy of the adversary culture's assault on the "Protestant ethic." (BC 133–134)

Against this assault Podhoretz expected Trilling to protest with all the authority that his achievements conferred upon him. The opportunity presented itself in 1972, when Trilling was chosen to deliver the first Jefferson Lecture, sponsored by the National Endowment for the Humanities. Trilling did address the recent directive of the Department of Health, Education, and Welfare requiring that "institutions of higher education which receive government funds shall move at once toward bringing about a statistically adequate representation on their faculties of ethnic minority groups." And he did warn his audience that "there will be serious adverse consequences for the academic profession if it is required to surrender an essential element of its traditional best sense of itself, its belief that no considerations extraneous to those of professional excellence should bear upon the selection of its personnel" (*LD* 117, 118). But to Podhoretz, Trilling's protest appeared to be altogether ineffectual. "[S]o long did he spend in getting to the point, and so heavily did he load it with academic baggage, that its power to impress—and to offend—was almost entirely dissipated" (*BR* 301).

It was clear to Trilling's former student that he had to take over from his teacher the defense of what he had been taught by him to value. That same year Podhoretz received an invitation from the dean of admissions at Harvard College to talk to his staff about affirmative action in student admissions. He accepted with alacrity. Here was an opportunity to articulate in the realm of action, before admissions officers, all that Trilling had failed to say from the lectern:

> Sitting around a table in an informal session, I told the group of admissions officers that I supported special efforts to recruit qualified blacks and that I also supported special efforts to help unqualified blacks compete on an equal footing. What I opposed was the admission of unqualified persons in order to fill a predetermined quota. Such a system, meant to fight racism, was itself implicitly racist in assuming that blacks would never be able to compete with whites on an equal footing. I myself did not believe this, and if I were black, I would feel insulted by it. But I was not a black and I would not presume to talk to them as one. I would talk rather as what I was—a liberal, a Jew, and an intellectual. In each of these capacities, I said, I had a strong reason for opposing quotas. As a liberal I believed in the traditional principle of treating individuals as individuals and not as members of a group; as a Jew, I feared that a quota system designed to overcome discrimination against blacks would almost certainly result in discrimination against Jews—and I could not bring myself to believe that the only way to achieve social justice in the United States was to discriminate against my own children; and as an intellectual, I worried about the lowering and erosion of standards entailed by any system of reverse discrimination. (BR 301–302)

Podhoretz's listeners were incensed. Their questions, Podhoretz remembered, were so hostile "that I found myself wondering whether even a public reading from *Mein Kampf* could have elicited greater outrage" (*BR* 302). This inimical response was not a reaction to Podhoretz's bluntness. Rather, it was the result of a widening gap between old-style and new-style liberals. Podhoretz compared notes with friends. "Almost everyone who took the antiquota position in those days had similar tales to tell, and yet neither when he delivered his Jefferson Lecture nor when he published it in a small bound volume did Trilling elicit more than a polite yawn" (*BR* 302). It was evident, and barely needed Trilling's admission of "fatigue" in 1973, that the mighty lion had grown old. But he had heirs. Podhoretz stood ready to defend in the bloody arena of politics what he perceived to be Trilling's values, while on Morningside Heights the mantle of academic succession descended on Podhoretz's friend and rival Steven Marcus.

Steven Marcus, Literary Critic

The dreams that Lionel Trilling's mother nourished for her son were somewhat uncharacteristic of Jewish middle-class families of the time. "From earliest boyhood," Diana Trilling claimed, "Lionel's life had been directed to an intellectual and literary career. He was only six when his mother told him that he would go to Oxford for a Ph.D." To Fanny Trilling, née Cohen, who had grown up in London's East End, Oxford seemed the university attended by the choicest minds, and what these minds would eventually apply themselves to was the task of culture. "No one," Diana Trilling continued in her memoir, "had ever supposed that he might become a doctor or a lawyer, an engineer or a physicist, an explorer, anything but what he did become, a teacher of English literature and a writer" (*BJ* 18).

No one taking a peek into the cradle of the newborn Steven Marcus imagined that he would grow up to write books about English culture and teach literature at Columbia College. Marcus's parents were the American-born offspring of immigrants who had come to New York from the countryside near Vilna around the turn of the century. Adeline Gordon and Nathan Marcus grew up on the Lower East Side. Both attended high school, and Nathan Marcus went on to business school for two years to become an accountant. They met, married, and like so many Jewish newlyweds, settled in the Bronx, in a neighborhood that went up overnight at the end of World War I. Ten months after Steven was born (in December 1928) the stock market crashed, and the lives of the Marcuses changed profoundly. Nathan Marcus lost his job and remained unemployed for five or six years. The family lost its tenuous hold on the middle class and slid into poverty. They gave up their Bronx apartment and went to live with a relative in Mount Vernon, New York. Once the job market began to stabilize, the Marcuses, now a family of

four, moved back to the Bronx, into a lower-class neighborhood called
Highbridge, near Yankee Stadium. Although Marcus's parents regained
their financial balance, their sudden fall into poverty remained the crucial event in their lives:

> The trauma was such that it spread to all their interests; they were inter-
> ested in nothing; they were only interested in staying alive. . . . My par-
> ents existed in a state of terror about money. It might all disappear again
> tomorrow. They were literally panic-stricken about the idea of not having
> enough money. Especially my mother developed a phobia about spending
> money. She could not even buy dresses for herself. She virtually went
> around in rags for the rest of her life. Although my father never really
> had a good job, it was not as if the wolf was always at the door; but it
> was as if the Depression could always happen again. They never really got
> over it.[40]

His parents' experience of sudden, undeserved, irreparable economic
deprivation was to shape the son's direction and sympathies as a literary
critic. As a boy, Marcus attended P.S. 11 at Highbridge. The neighborhood was populated by Irish, Italian, and Jewish families. Most of the
Catholics attended the local parochial school, so the students at P.S. 11
were mainly Jewish. Marcus also went to Hebrew school in the afternoon for a few years, but he found it a complete bore and continued
only to please his father. His parents were minimally observant, going to
services on the High Holidays and using a separate set of dishes during
Passover.

In the street Marcus identified more often with the Irish than with
the Jews. The neighborhood was stratified socioeconomically as well as
ethnically. The Jews belonged largely to the "regular middle class,"
whereas the Irish and a few of the Jewish families, like the Marcuses,
belonged to the lower middle class. Marcus perceived the Jews in his
neighborhood as "people who did not suffer in the Depression as much
as we did. They had more money because their fathers had better jobs"
(interview). But Marcus shared the aspirations of the Jews rather than
the strange dreams of the Irish. The general sense in his neighborhood
was that the Bronx was a way station; everybody wanted to get out.
"The aim of the Irish kids," Marcus remembered, "was to get into the
FBI, or to become a policeman, or a politician, if you were very, very
lucky. The ambition of the Jewish kids, by contrast, was either to go
into business, if your parents were in the cloak or suit business or some-

thing of that sort, or to go to college and to become a doctor or a lawyer, if you were lucky and good." Nathan Marcus wanted his son to go to college. "My parents wanted me to be a doctor," Marcus recalled, "that was my father's idea of heaven" (interview).

Marcus attended William Howard Taft and De Witt Clinton High School, from which Lionel Trilling had graduated in 1921. Marcus graduated in 1944, at the age of fifteen, and was admitted to Harvard and Columbia. Both schools offered him scholarships. But as in the case of Norman Podhoretz, his parents could not afford to pay for room and board at Harvard, so Marcus entered Columbia College. When he arrived there, he was completely stunned. "I felt like I was on Mars," Marcus recalled. "It was a completely new world, and I was absolutely knocked over. I fell in love with it. It was marvelous. There were all these books to read and all these things to learn that I had no idea about. I was overwhelmed by it, by how much I had to read and by the foreignness of the material. Homer, Aeschylus, Euripides; I had never heard of half these people. It was an extraordinary experience. It changed my life" (interview).

Books, however, had always been essential to Marcus. "Books were all my life. They were an escape from the life I lived in the Bronx. I used to go to the Public Library all the time; and I would read continually. It was a way of imaginatively escaping from the world I was living in" (interview). Columbia not only allowed but urged Marcus to transform his passion for books into a way of life, to make books his reality. Although he continued to live at home and brought his lunch to school in a paper bag, the only world that counted was the one whose doors were now being thrown open to him by Richard Chase, Andrew Chiappa, F. W. Dupee, and Trilling. With his complete immersion in reading and writing came a new exhilaration: "I suddenly found that that was what I was good at" (interview).

Marcus graduated from college in 1948 and enrolled in Columbia's graduate school, whose faculty "was full of old-fashioned historical scholars" (interview). But Marcus did not mind. He was going to be on his own and find out whether he had the stuff it took to become like the men of letters and literary critics he had studied with in college. In that frenzied summer, dedicated to literary self-discovery, Marcus encountered the novels of Charles Dickens and thought that he was "the greatest novelist I had ever read." Nevertheless, he decided to write his master's thesis on Henry James. "It was important to me," Marcus explained, "to master Henry James before I could do Dickens" (interview).

Trilling's lectures, as well as his essays in *The Liberal Imagination,* most of which Marcus read as they were appearing in literary magazines during the 1940s, convinced him that there was no way around Henry James. Certain of his novels also had an immediate appeal for Marcus insofar as their heroes allowed him to come to terms with himself as a young man from the margins of American culture. About the "line of novels" that encompassed *The Princess Casamassima,* Trilling had written:

> The defining hero may be known as the Young Man from the Provinces. He need not come from the provinces in literal fact, his social class may constitute his province. But a provincial birth and rearing suggest the simplicity and the high hopes he begins with—he starts with a great demand upon life and a great wonder about its complexity and promise. He may be of good family but he must be poor. He is intelligent, or at least aware, but not at all shrewd in worldly matters. He must have acquired a certain amount of education, should have learned something about life from books, although not the truth. (*LI* 61)

Marcus knew that the tradition Trilling outlined was not confined to fiction. It had its counterpart in reality, where the theme played itself out in the lives of Trilling himself, Harry Levin and M. H. Abrams, Podhoretz and Marcus, Eugene Goodhart and Morris Dickstein, and many others. At Columbia in the 1940s the young men from the provinces were Jewish boys arriving from Queens, Brooklyn, and the Bronx. It was thought then that education, the movement from the province into the city, from simplicity to sophistication, constituted the European theme par excellence. The original American theme was its opposite, the move from civilization into the wilderness. Trilling, for one, argued that James's adaptation of the European theme made his a rather singular appearance on the American literary scene. "In America in the nineteenth century," Trilling wrote, " Henry James was alone in knowing that to scale the moral and aesthetic heights in the novel one had to use the ladder of social observation" (*LI* 212).

It was largely due to Trilling's praise of James in such essays as "Reality in America" (1940/1946) and "Manners, Morals, and the Novel" (1947/1948), and in his assessment of *The Princess Casamassima* (1948) that Marcus decided to make James the starting point for refining his literary education. In fact, a James renaissance had been under way since the mid-1940s, associated largely with academics such as F. O. Matthiessen and Kenneth Murdock. But they had little influence on

Marcus, who was completely focused on his teachers at Columbia. His early mentor there was Frederick Dupee, whose collection of critical essays, *The Question of Henry James* (1945), was the first book that surveyed the enormous disagreement on James among men of letters, writers, and critics. Dupee's own response in the classroom and in his subsequent book on James (1951) was admiration for the novelist's psychological subtlety. Yet it mattered more to Marcus that Trilling considered James, in the "masterpieces" of his late years, an exceedingly difficult writer. "This is the fact," Trilling wrote, "and nothing is gained for James by denying it. He himself knew that these late works were difficult; he wished them to be dealt with as if they were difficult" (*LI* 59). Hence, choosing to write a master's thesis on Henry James and his critics implied that Marcus was serious about the literary profession and ready to test his skills. He undertook a rather complicated rite of passage; but after he accomplished it, his credentials could not be questioned. He was on his way to becoming a critic with authority.

Trilling had smuggled a surprising caveat into his praise for James. Speaking about two of the less difficult novels, *The Bostonians* and *The Princess Casamassima,* Trilling declared that James's prose, although idiosyncratic enough, was perfectly in the tradition of the nineteenth-century novel. "It is warm, fluent, and on the whole rather less elaborate and virtuose than Dickens' prose" (*LI* 59). Marcus noted with delight and some astonishment that one could progress from James to Dickens; and so he decided to write his dissertation on Dickens.

Before he could give the dissertation much thought, however, life intruded in the form of an instructorship at Indiana University. Having received his master's degree in 1949, Marcus spent the next academic year living on a pig farm, a mile from town, and teaching freshman English to what Jules Chametzky called "kids from the cornfields." Marcus loved it, but in 1950 *The Liberal Imagination* came out, and he yearned to be back in New York City. He managed to get appointed to a lectureship at Baruch College (of the City College of New York). "It was a return to familiar people," Marcus remembered. "They were mostly adults who were working during the day. So it was a much easier group of people to deal with than the kids from Indiana" (interview). He taught at Baruch College for two years because he needed the money, having recently gotten married, and completed his graduate work at Columbia. In 1952 he won a fellowship to Cambridge University. Marcus was only now beginning to focus on his dissertation. His determination that it be on Dickens was strengthened by the opportunity to study in England and "to hear what the people in Dickens were sounding like." One of the attractions Dickens held for Marcus was his language: "It was like Shakespeare, it was poetry" (interview).

That same year, Trilling's first essay on Dickens appeared in the *Griffin* (the monthly magazine of an intellectual book club, the Readers' Subscription), which Trilling coedited with W. H. Auden and Jacques Barzun. In his essay Trilling declared Dickens to be "one of the two greatest novelists of England, Jane Austen being the other." He explained that this was not the received opinion in his student days at Columbia. When John Erskine told an undergraduate class that *Bleak House* was "a very good novel indeed," Trilling passed it off as "at best a lively paradox of Erskine's, intended to shock his young listeners, at worst an aberration of his critical intellect." [41]

Yet Trilling held that "the literary sophistication of one day is the literary obscurantism of the next" and set out to explain the ways in which "our contemporary literature has had the effect of bringing to light . . . the importance and profundity and accuracy of Dickens." He discounted, for instance, Henry James's dismissal of *Our Mutual Friend,* arguing that "it was necessary for him to reject what he thought to be Dickens's extravagances in order to make room for his own"; and he added that "James's extravagances have in turn helped us in our own acceptance of Dickens's." [42]

At Cambridge University, F. R. Leavis did not share Trilling's reassessment of Dickens. In the early 1950s, the only work by Dickens that Leavis grudgingly admitted into the great tradition was *Hard Times.* Marcus, like Podhoretz, was drawn into the orbit of the literary polemicist at Downing College; but unlike Podhoretz, he resisted Leavis's influence entirely and stuck to working on Dickens during his years at Cambridge. In the fall of 1953, when Marcus had just become a supervisor at one of the Cambridge colleges, *Kenyon Review* published Trilling's introduction to *Little Dorrit,* which Trilling called "one of the most profound of Dickens' novels and one of the most significant works of the nineteenth century." Trilling was not known to make such pronouncements lightly. He added that *Little Dorrit* would "not fail to be thought of as speaking with a peculiar and passionate intimacy to our time." [43] When Marcus finally published his book on Dickens a dozen years later, in 1965, he confessed to preferring the later novels, like *Little Dorrit,* to the earlier ones that were in fact the subject of his book, "for not only do his later novels constitute his major achievement, but they speak to the present time with special force and cogency, and in a language, an idiom of the emotions, often unmistakably related to the idiom of our own literature." [44]

Marcus's first book, *Dickens: From Pickwick to Dombey* (1965), showed the influence of Trilling very clearly in its context-conscious approach to Dickens's novels as well as in certain minutiae of interpretation, such as the sparing but sophisticated use of Freudian theory. At the same time, Marcus's *Dickens* was an independent, mature, and moving book. It had few of the flaws of a first book, not only because of its long gestation but also because Marcus had been able to serve his apprenticeship as a writer elsewhere. In 1952 he had told Trilling that he believed himself ready to write, and Trilling had sent him downtown to see Elliot Cohen, whose cultural interests were more catholic than Marcus's.

> His first question to me was did I like baseball. And I said what are you talking about? Do I like baseball? I was raised within a stone's throw of the Yankee Stadium in the Bronx. What do you want to know about the Yankees? He gave me a long lecture about how important baseball was for American culture. I listened to that for about an hour. And then suddenly he said now you go see Robert Warshow, he will give you something to write. It was like sitting through a crazy test. (interview)

Marcus began to write for both *Commentary* and *Partisan Review* about the time he left for England; his first pieces appeared in December 1952 and March 1953 while he was studying at Cambridge. When Marcus returned to America in 1954, he was drafted into the army, went through basic training at Fort Dix, and then was stationed in northern Greenland. Discharged in 1956, Marcus returned to Columbia, where he was hired as an instructor. Five years later, in 1961, he defended his dissertation and was appointed to an assistant professorship. When he was tenured in 1967, he had published two books, his study of Dickens and *The Other Victorians: A Study of Sexuality and Pornography in Mid-Nineteenth Century England* (1966); and he had received a Guggenheim Fellowship for the academic year 1967–68, which he spent doing research in England, France, and Germany.

The power of Marcus's book on Dickens to move the reader is the result of the author's deep engagement with his subject. When he was reading Dickens, books began to take on another quality for Marcus; they were no longer a means of escape, but became a mirror of his own life. It is no coincidence that Marcus thought of the summer of 1948, when he first read Dickens, as a time of self-discovery. He recognized in

Dickens's depiction of lower-class life in England in the 1830s and 1840s the social circumstances of his own childhood in the Bronx. The resemblance lay not so much in the experience of material deprivation, which was of course different enough for the English characters and their American critic, but in the emotions that poverty induced: "an extreme and ineradicable feeling of humiliation, of having been violated, degraded and declassed" (*D* 82). Most uncanny of all, however, was the similarity in the traumatization caused by the fate of the fathers, John Dickens and Nathan Marcus: their sudden and complete impoverishment and prolonged period of helplessness (through imprisonment for debt in the case of Dickens, unemployment in the case of Marcus).

An analysis of Dickens's career as a novelist permitted Marcus to work through his childhood in the Bronx and to "surmount," as Marcus wrote about Dickens, "his feelings of bitterness against [his father] and act as if the relationship had always been quite unexceptionable" (*D* 33). Writing about Dickens allowed Marcus to do what he surmised "without doubt" Dickens had done in his second novel *Oliver Twist,* which was to record his "memory of the central episode in his own childhood and the neglect he suffered at the hands of his parents" (*D* 82). The evenhandedness of Marcus's book, its compassion without sentimentality and directness without sensationalism or ideological zeal, was the result of a long analytic engagement with Marcus's own childhood that had been turned into literature in the novels of Dickens. It was an extraordinary process from which Marcus emerged in fully conscious possession of his past.

It is no surprise, then, that it took Marcus more than ten years to complete his "analysis." His uses of Freud's theories suggest submerged self-reflection, as does his emphasis on the father-son relationship as a leitmotiv in Dickens's work. If Marcus's book on Dickens was a work of self-clarification, it is obvious why Marcus never redeemed the pledge he gave at the end of his preface. "This volume, he announced, "is planned to be the first of two" (*D* 11). He had intended to move on to the second half of Dickens's career and to the novels preferred by the critical taste of the early 1960s: *Bleak House, Hard Times, Our Mutual Friend.* But he never did. Marcus desisted not because Trilling had written on these later novels but because his "analysis" was finished, the core problem that had attracted Marcus to Dickens recognized and worked through. It was fitting that Marcus should move on from a book that focused so much of its attention on the fate and portrayal of children to one whose theme was of overwhelming importance in adolescence and adulthood: sexuality and pornography.

A small but essential part of the psychic labor Marcus performed in the Dickens study consisted of tying his childhood in the Bronx to his adult life at Columbia. He attempted to create coherence between his experiences as a child and his outlook as an adult. Many small details in the Dickens study register Marcus's social discoveries at Columbia as well as his efforts to square his life and views with those of the people around him. He did not want the Bronx to become a discarded part of himself.

Despite some socioeconomic similarities, the childhoods of Trilling and Marcus were psychologically very different. Before the Depression, Trilling's parents (like Marcus's) were solidly in the middle class. David Trilling manufactured fur-lined coats; his household employed a full-time maid, and it was a matter of course that both children, Lionel and Harriet, were to go to college. The Depression destroyed David Trilling's business and caused him to sink into paranoia, while his wife tried desperately to maintain middle-class appearances until Harriet could be safely married. During the 1930s, the Trillings were quite poor and depended throughout the Depression on financial support from their son. Lionel, newly married after his return from a teaching stint at the University of Wisconsin in 1929, was eking out a living first as part-time instructor in the evening sessions at Hunter College, then as assistant editor of the *Menorah Journal*. He received a fellowship from Columbia and finally, beginning in the fall of 1932, was hired as an instructor in the Columbia English department, a job that paid an astonishing $2,400 a year. Trilling's support of his parents was unwavering (*BJ* 166–171). In part, he was giving back what he had received in his childhood. The boy had been the center of his family's attention. "No child was ever more cherished than Lionel," Diana Trilling wrote. "His parents did everything they knew how to do to ensure his happiness." She marveled that "the constant fuss and nervous attention directed to him" had no visibly damaging effect. "Raised like a princeling, he was the least royal of people, the least self-imposing" (*BJ* 36, 38). Trilling was brought up with a sense that there were higher callings than the mercantile life and that he was destined and entitled to achieve eminence.

In the Podhoretz household, too, the son was the shining star. Podhoretz recalled the emotional exuberance of his destitute family. "I was quite blatantly the favorite at home," Podhoretz recalled.

[A]s a precocious, eager, affectionate, chattering child, I was also the special pet of numerous relatives, neighbors, and teachers. . . . [T]he adult world, and especially the female part of it, was one vast congregation of worshipers at the shrine of my diminutive godhead. They praised, they kissed, they pinched, they pulled, they hugged, they smothered me in their bosoms. . . . They called me adorable, they called me delicious, they called me a genius, and predicted a great future for me: a doctor at the very least I would be. (*MI*56–57)

Smothering love has become a stereotype in the portrayal of Jewish and Italian families, but it was real enough and of enormous psychological importance. As Ruth Wisse wrote about Saul Bellow's novel *Herzog* (1964), the abundance of love the family lavished on the young protagonist "blesses the child with a secure sense of self even as it bedevils his later abilities to 'get along.' "[45] In *Making It*, published three years after *Herzog*, Podhoretz rightly established a connection between his sense of entitlement to love and adoration experienced as a child and his expectation as an adult of breezing through life on the wings of success (*MI* 57).

In the American Jewish family this sense of entitlement to success, which often produced real success, was not a matter of class but rather the result of the emotional dynamics of functional families. Adeline and Nathan Marcus had very fragile selves that had been severely shaken by the Depression. As parents they were unable to provide a supportive environment. Although the Podhoretzes in Brooklyn and the Marcuses in the Bronx were members of the same socioeconomic class, the former were more confident and had greater self-esteem. Julius Podhoretz was financially not more successful than Nathan Marcus, but like most immigrants he believed in American opportunity and placed his hopes in his American-born son;[46] for the second-generation Marcuses, however, the American dream had worn thin and collapsed entirely in the Depression, leaving them with the simple desire of "just staying alive."

It was the energy and confidence exuded in college by young men like Podhoretz that swept up students like Marcus and carried them along. Marcus's amazement at the *chutzpah* of entitlement emerged in his discussion of *Oliver Twist*, one of the few novels by Dickens in which poverty does not traumatize the child. "Only success," Marcus wrote, speaking of Oliver Twist as much as of a briefly self-assured Dickens, "only the achievement of one's birthright—whether that involved becoming a famous writer, or a gentleman, or both—was the conclusive judgment on one's being" (*D* 84).

Marcus's reading of Oliver's character seems to make very little sense within the fixed hierarchical structure of English society. The notion of *achieving* one's birthright or *becoming* a gentleman were contradictions in terms. Moreover, as Podhoretz observed about the Cambridge society of the early 1950s into which he and Marcus were thrown as students, "so long as one was a member of the upper class, one could behave as one damn well pleased without fear that one's patent of nobility would be taken away; and if one were not a member of the upper class, there was no way to behave that would bring one any of its benefits" (*MI* 67).

This was precisely *not* the case in *Oliver Twist,* Marcus argued. "For the style of the gentleman, Oliver Twist asserts, rests not on birth but on behavior, not on legal privilege but on the incorruptibility of character" (*D* 86). This idea presupposes a society in flux, ready to admit the worthy outsider if only the "declassed, disinherited" conducted themselves like gentlemen. Nowhere had Marcus observed a more convincing enactment of this idea than in the Columbia English department. It was Trilling, Podhoretz claimed, who had substituted the notion of admirable social *conduct* for upper-class *origins* in Columbia's concept of the gentleman (*MI* 48). But Trilling pointed to John Erskine and his notion "that men who were in any degree responsible for the welfare of the polity and for the quality of life that characterized it must be large-minded men, committed to great ends, devoted to virtue, assured of the dignity of the human estate and dedicated to enhancing and preserving it; and that great works of the imagination could foster and even institute this large-mindedness, this *magnanimity*" (*LD* 234). In other words, it was possible to become a gentleman at Columbia, to escape from the limitations of one's middle-class or lower-class upbringing by having before one's eyes "great models of thought, feeling, and imagination" (*LD* 234). Nobility could be achieved. If it was only a matter of moral behavior, anyone could rise in the world and be "acquitted" (*D* 86) of his parents. This reading of *Oliver Twist* allowed Marcus to connect his impoverished childhood in the Bronx to his ascent at Columbia. "What a person is," Marcus wrote as much about himself as about Oliver Twist, "rather than where he begins has become the absolute test of character. . . . [C]onduct has become the only means of deliverance: if someone behaves like a gentleman, some day he can hope to awaken and find he has been one all along" (*D* 87).

Marcus's reading of *Oliver Twist* was inspired by his own hopes and experiences within an American society in flux. At Cambridge University, where Marcus worked on his Dickens book from 1952 to 1954, he could observe, within the academic setting familiar to him, that the rigidity of the English class structure could not be overcome by gentlemanly conduct or by the emulation of the great models of thought, feeling, and imagination. F. R. Leavis was in fact a victim of that rigidity.

As young men both Leavis and Trilling came to the university and academic literary studies as outsiders. As a Jew, Trilling represented the ethnically other and undesirable whose unchecked infiltration threatened the values and stability of American society. In 1939, when Trilling had finally been appointed to an assistant professorship, his former dissertation adviser Emery E. Neff came to visit him at home. Diana Trilling remembered that "what Emery Neff came to say was that now that Lionel was a member of the department, he hoped that he would not use it as a wedge to open the English department to more Jews." [47]

The otherness of Leavis, by contrast, was largely a matter of class. He was the son of a piano dealer and had grown up in the provincial lower middle class. Nonconformist, hard-working, morally serious, Leavis found himself opposed to "the frivolous amateurism of the upper-class English gentlemen who filled the early Chairs of Literature at the ancient Universities" and to the "leisurely and expansive connoisseurism personified by Saintsbury and Quiller-Couch." [48] On the other hand, he was put off by the literary coterie of Bloomsbury, London's classy version of New York's "family." This smallish group of writers and intellectuals "addressed themselves . . . to the elite who had been educated at public schools and at Oxbridge, together with any who had climbed the educational and social ladder and had assimilated to the upper middle class." [49] Leavis could not abide the urbanity, pretentiousness, and literary tastes of either group. His adversarial court at Downing College, on the margins of Cambridge University, attracted the English equivalent of students from Brooklyn and the Bronx: they were graduates of provincial grammar schools whose learning was focused rather than broad and who lacked the social confidence and literary knowledge to play in Bloomsbury's elysian fields. "Such people," Noel Annan claimed, "were apt to be scared or depressed by the vast area of reading that seemed to be expected from them before they were thought fit to utter a word about the literature of their own country. Now [under Leavis's tutelage] they felt able to turn their backs on foreign literature, on the grounds that the critic cannot profitably deal with a work unless he can unravel every strand of the texture of its language." [50]

Trilling and Leavis entered the university as men whose descent cultures were considered marginal by the intellectual establishment. Nevertheless, they managed to become part of the university through the study of literature and then began to attract students of their own otherness, partly because the students regarded them as role models and partly because they taught literature in a way that allowed their students to overcome their otherness and to move toward the class and culture they aspired to. Yet Leavis's model was not working very well. While Trilling became a man of national renown, Leavis became a figure of notoriety. While Trilling moved into the center of his academic institution, replacing his precursors, Leavis succeeded at most in offering a third way of thinking, on the fringe of his university, as an alternative to the Cambridge literary faculty and Bloomsbury. The literary establishment of Frank and Queenie Leavis—whose Jewishness mattered less to the English educated class than her descent from a draper and hosier—remained a "marginal anti-salon" even though it became the "vanguard of 'the highbrow front' in culture." [51]

The reasons for Trilling's social success and Leavis's relative social failure are complex, because they are tied in with the social dynamics of their countries of residence as well as with the personalities and ideologies of both men. Trilling's chances to succeed were certainly enhanced by his grace and moderation, by his appreciation of psychological complexity and emotional depth. Leavis, by contrast, was a contentious, angry, scornful elitist whose tone, as in his attack on C. P. Snow, even Trilling had to call "impossible." [52] At the same time, it is fair to say that the fundamental classlessness of American society enabled Trilling to ascend, on condition that he behave like a gentleman and acquire the appearance of a WASP; whereas noble behavior would have gotten Leavis exactly nowhere within English upper-class and Oxbridge society between the World Wars. One could downplay ethnicity in America; but one could not live down class in England, at least not yet. Marcus's assertion apropos of *Oliver Twist* that "the style of the gentleman . . . rests not on birth but on behavior, not on legal privilege but on incorruptibility of character" (*D* 86) expressed the ideals not of Cambridge but of Columbia.

One of the most intriguing sections in Marcus's book on Dickens is an appendix entitled "Who Is Fagin?" Marcus played down Fagin's Jewishness and presented a biographical and psychoanalytic interpretation of the villain. It turned on Dickens's ambivalent feelings about his father. The appended chapter, an extraordinary piece of literary and psychological detection, was also an essay in which Marcus demonstrated that he was not partial, that he was neither compelled by nor confined to Jewish issues, but committed to a comprehensive vision of humankind as mandated by the Columbia code. The path to such a vision was education. Ascent required assent to the cultural norm.

One sentence in the appendix on Fagin aptly illustrates the transcending move from the particular to the universal. At a specific point in the novel, "Fagin, the terrible, frightening old Jew, becomes relevant. For the traditional popular mythology of the Jew as Devil and Anti-Christ, as the castrator and murderer of good little Christian boys, corresponds itself to this image of the terrible father of infancy and of our primal fantasies, and is indeed one of western culture's chief expressions of it." Transformed into humanity's traumatizing nightmare and all-purpose bogeyman, Dickens's vicious portrait of a Jew lost its sting. In Marcus's psychoanalytic reading there was indeed "nothing particularly Jewish" about Fagin. Marcus's book demonstrated that the author had understood and converted to Columbia's educational goal.

Nevertheless, the Columbia faculty did not accept Marcus without a struggle. Alice Green Fredman, who attended Marcus's dissertation defense in 1961, described it as a fascinating event. The committee, she said, was full of "anti-Trilling people. They attacked Steven's dissertation as a means of attacking Trilling. I was enormously offended by all the sniping, because that dissertation was so clearly superior to most of the manuscripts that we had." [53] There was very little Trilling's opponents could do. Marcus had already published a number of articles on English and American literature and culture, and in the previous year (1960) had collaborated with Trilling on an abridgment of Ernest Jones's *Life and Work of Sigmund Freud* (1961). Marcus was uniquely qualified for an appointment at Columbia, which he received immediately after his defense. He had already taken over some of Trilling's courses, including the senior survey of Romantic and Victorian literature. Morris Dickstein took the course with Marcus but felt strongly that he "inherited" his view of nineteenth-century English literature "from Trilling through Marcus." [54]

To say that Marcus followed in Trilling's footsteps is not to say that his work is imitative. On the contrary, Marcus developed his own style. His essays were starker and closer to reality than Trilling's, and he was more interested in history than his mentor had been. He also placed greater emphasis on "the study of literature as modes of knowledge." [55] Yet what Marcus chose to write about remained within Trilling's ken. "Upon my work in criticism, upon my intellectual life in general," Trilling observed in an autobiographical lecture of 1971, "the systems of

18. Steven Marcus. *Courtesy of Columbia University Office of Public Affairs.*

Marx and Freud had, I have never doubted, a decisive influence." Trilling did not wish to acknowledge any "doctrinal authority" on their part, but rather their power of enforcing "the sense of the actuality and intimacy of history, of society, of culture" (*LD* 237). Marcus became heir to this perception.

Of course it was too late in the day for Marx to have a decisive influence on Marcus. But when Marcus returned from his Guggenheim Fellowship to Columbia University in 1968, he found the campus radicalized, his colleagues either shell-shocked or thrown back to their Marxist youth. Only Trilling seemed to be "essentially unchanged." Marcus felt confronted by a new generation of students.

I came back and started to teach a graduate lecture course in Victorian literature; and I suddenly realized that the graduate students had changed; they all said they were very radical. It took me a few weeks to figure out what they were radical about. It was mostly the Vietnam War. Their radicalization resembled the German radicalization at the time. They demanded that the university give a voice to the cleaning ladies and stop the Vietnam War. After a certain point I began to get very annoyed, because I thought this was inappropriate behavior for graduate students in literature who were supposed to understand something about history. So I decided to assign to them Engels's book *The Condition of the Working Class in England in 1844.* But I realized very soon that they didn't understand Engels any more than they understood anything at the time. At this point I thought, I am going to show them. I am going to write a book about what a young radical is really like. (interview)

That book, *Engels, Manchester, and the Working Class,* appeared in 1974 and was dedicated to Lionel Trilling. Marcus's first book, the Dickens study, which was so much about fathers and sons, had no dedication, neither to his parents nor to his mentor. In fact, Marcus's parents are not mentioned anywhere in his publications. *The Other Victorians* (1966), published a year after *Dickens,* was dedicated to Marcus's second wife. That his various interests should lead him to write a book on Victorian pornography, Marcus explained, was obvious enough: "It did not require a dialectician's cunning to make out that Dickens plus Freud might conceivably add up to an interest in sex and sexuality in mid-nineteenth century England." [56]

To date, Marcus has published two more books: *Representations* (1975), a collection of literary and cultural essays; and *Freud and the Culture of Psychoanalysis* (1984). The latter contained Marcus's essay "Freud and Dora: Story, History, Case History." While the essay was conceived as a tribute to Freud's case history as a work of modern literature, Marcus did not hesitate to expose Freud's "fantasies of omniscience," which propelled him not only from interpretation into "demented and delusional science" but led to his abuse and victimization of Dora.[57] It took a certain courage at the time to write about the case from Dora's perspective. That Marcus did so testifies to his intellectual honesty. It cannot have been easy for him, because Freud was still very much his cultural hero—a hero he shared with Trilling. "The figure of Freud," Marcus wrote shortly after Trilling's death in 1975, "was for him very close to a moral ideal, or to an ideal of personal character and conduct." [58] To point to some of the flaws in Freud's character was not to denigrate but to humanize him. With the rise of feminism, a reexamination of Freud became inevitable, and Marcus's essay on Freud and Dora was a start. It signaled that he had accepted the obligation of the critic that had been most important to Trilling: "readiness to confront and deal with difficulty and complexity" (*LD* 230).

Carolyn G. Heilbrun, Feminist Scholar

There was little doubt among Columbia faculty and students during the 1960s that Marcus was the one "upon whom the mantle had descended."[59] But by 1970 another voice that claimed successorship to Trilling was asking to be heard. Carolyn G. Heilbrun argued, first hesitantly in her mystery *Poetic Justice* (1970), and then with increasing fervor in essays and speeches, that the essence of Trilling's legacy was not what was being passed on through his male heirs at the center of the university but rather an element in his work that instilled in those on the margins the "powers of indignant perception."[60] Women in academe, Heilbrun claimed, were the true heirs of Trilling's notion of the opposing self. As a woman who had had to fight to be accepted as a full member of the Columbia community, Heilbrun perceived more clearly than Trilling's male disciples that the idea of an opposing self was not limited to Trilling's description of a conflict between the necessary constraints of civilization and the disruptive desire of the self to transcend those constraints. During the 1980s, Heilbrun espoused a more active reading of Trilling's concept and attempted to use it in her effort to remake the views women had of themselves. About Trilling himself she regretted, as did his wife Diana, that he always chose to come down on the side of civilization and constraint thus avoiding the free flight of "impulse, pleasure, and imagination."[61]

There had been a short period in Trilling's life when he had openly opposed the social constraints of culture. In April and May of 1936, the Columbia English department tried to discontinue his appointment as instructor. Summarizing what had been said to him in the department, Trilling recorded on April 20, 1936: "The reason for dismissal is that as a Jew, a Marxist, a Freudian I am uneasy. This hampers my work and makes me unhappy" (*N1* 498). Trilling felt that he needed to confront his established colleagues who wanted him out before he had his Ph.D. and could ask for a more secure position. He got feverishly busy, spoke to the department members one by one, and forced them to voice their complaints about him to his face or otherwise to admit that he did good work. He became furious when he thought he detected duplicity, as in his dissertation adviser, Emery E. Neff, who complained about Trilling to Irwin Edman, a philosophy professor at Columbia who happened to be Jewish, but unnoticeably so. Edman telephoned Trilling to report Neff's objections, which were that Trilling had "involved himself with Ideas," that he was "too sensitive," that he did not "fit because he [was] a Jew" (*N1* 500), and that he had been appointed against the will of the department in 1932. Trilling's reaction was swift and decisive. "Called E. E. N.," he noted in his journal, "and made date to annihilate him on Thursday" (*N1* 500). After a long struggle for reappointment, Trilling prevailed. In the process he exposed his colleagues' vague antipathies toward him as untenable prejudices since they could not point to any evidence of Jewish, Marxist, or Freudian thought in his work. In the end, the Columbia English professors lacked the nerve to say they simply did not want a Jew no matter how good his work, and Trilling prevailed on account of his merits as a teacher and scholar.

It is this incident that Heilbrun took to be the immediate experiential source of Trilling's notion of the opposing self, to which she considered herself the heir. Jewishness, however, was a weak link between Heilbrun and Trilling, since Heilbrun's parents had cut themselves off from the Jewish world. Heilbrun's father, Archibald Gold, came to America from Russia around 1900, when he was still a child, to join his adolescent sisters, Fanny and Molly, who had earned the money for his passage in a New York sweatshop.[62] Gold went to work early and put himself through night school to become a certified public accountant. In 1926, at the age of thirty, when his only child, Carolyn, was born, he had ascended to a partnership in a brokerage firm and made a million dollars. He lost this fortune in the Depression, and the family's move from East Orange, New Jersey, to Manhattan's Upper West Side in 1932 was made on borrowed money. In time Gold would regain his wealth, but his wife remained deeply disturbed by the family's sudden poverty, and their loss of social status and security. The experience of having a traumatized parent was a legacy of the Depression that Heilbrun shared with Lionel Trilling and Steven Marcus.

The Golds, however, were even less Jewish-identified than the Trillings and Marcuses. "Like Gatsby," Heilbrun wrote, "my father had been his own creation" (*RW* 19); but unlike Gatsby, he had a weakness for American religion and during the 1930s began attending the "Divine Science Church of the Healing Christ" in Manhattan every Sunday (*RW* 60). He could afford to send his daughter to the Birch Wathen School, a private girls' school in Manhattan. Its "tone was distinctly high Episcopalian" but it was enlightened enough to admit Jews (*RW* 60). Carolyn

Gold went on to Wellesley College in the fall of 1943. In February 1945 she married James Heilbrun, a Harvard undergraduate, who was about to leave for active duty in the Pacific.[63]

At Wellesley, Heilbrun was completely unaware that she was being perceived as Jewish, because the WASP milieu felt entirely congenial to her. It was only when she recalled her college years on the occasion of her thirtieth reunion in 1977 that it became clear to her "that Wellesley had always been, in the nicest way, anti-Semitic" (*RW* 18). She realized then that she had been and still was an outsider. "I had assumed that Wellesley ignored me because I was a feminist. Now, I discovered, Wellesley had ignored me because I was a Jew" (*RW* 18). For Heilbrun this discovery brought together the terms *feminist* and *Jew* (*RW* 19) and induced her to think about the possibility of a causal relationship between the two. "I began to understand that having been a Jew, however unobserved that identification was, however fiercely I had denied the adamant anti-Semitism all around me as I grew up—still, having been a Jew had made me an outsider. It had permitted me to be a feminist" (*RW* 20). It was a strange thought because it is difficult to see how her educational experience at an all-girls prep school and an elite college as an entirely assimilated upper-crust Jewish girl would have made her feel marginal on account of her gender or her ethnicity. Swept up in the feminist movement, Heilbrun was rereading her childhood and adolescence from a new perspective; and since she had not been disadvantaged as a girl, she used her Jewish descent to construct an experience of marginalization that was an important community-building element in the feminist movement.

The linking of the terms *feminist* and *Jew,* however, served another purpose as well. Gender and ethnicity were of inverse significance to Heilbrun and Trilling in their relation to Columbia University. While Trilling found himself an outsider there as a Jew, he was an insider as a man; whereas Heilbrun considered herself on the margins as a woman, yet at the center as a "facsimile WASP" (Podhoretz's term). Heilbrun's linkage of feminism and Jewishness suggested that one might compare the experiences of marginality to which both women and Jews were subjected at elite schools in different decades. That in turn opened the possibility of establishing a commonality with Trilling despite the fact that Heilbrun thought of him as adversarial to women at Columbia.[64] Yet his early difficulties as a Jew at the university could be considered comparable to the difficulties experienced by women in academe. And so Heilbrun came to argue in *Reinventing Womanhood* (1979) that "in speaking of the self, and particularly of the 'opposing self,' [Trilling] spoke in a way . . . particularly meaningful to women" (*RW* 131). In adopting Trilling's notion of the opposing self for her literary and cultural criticism, Heilbrun declared herself one of his rare female heirs.

By her own admission, Heilbrun admired Trilling tremendously when she began to attend Columbia's graduate school in 1947. She read everything he wrote, and even joined the Readers' Subscription because of his connection with it. In an essay devoted to the analysis of Trilling's influence on her mind, Heilbrun remarked that he "taught me most of what I was to learn about the connection between literary ideas and culture" (*RW* 127). She called him the teacher who placed his finger upon her soul. It was Heilbrun's misfortune that she came to study with Trilling as a graduate student (Columbia College was not coeducational until 1983), since Trilling so utterly disliked teaching in the graduate school. It was dominated by scholarly types and given to the cranking out of specialists in this or that period, whereas Trilling did not believe "that a high incidence of conscious professional intellect in a society necessarily makes for a good culture." [65] Nevertheless, Heilbrun became Trilling's disciple. Like Cynthia Ozick, she was ignored and felt that Trilling was only comfortable with his male students, most of whom he had known as undergraduates. She explained: "Trilling had no sense of my discipleship. The word disciple was his, and the role was filled by several men, some of whom became my colleagues and, in interpretations of the process of the moral life, my adversaries. They are the ones whom Trilling confirmed until his death. Yet I think it was a more profound tribute to a teacher and writer that he touched the life of someone whose cultural attitudes he could not admire" (*RW* 126).

Heilbrun's awareness of her differences with Trilling was counterbalanced by a desire to be close to him. She received her master's degree in 1951 and her doctorate in 1959, while teaching freshman composition at Columbia and taking care, with the help of sufficient personnel, of three children, a husband, a dog, and a large Upper West Side apartment. [66] With her Ph.D. completed and her dissertation well on the way to becoming her first book, *The Garnett Family* (1961), Heilbrun was looking for a job. She was appointed to a position at Brooklyn College, which paid better than Columbia. The job was considered by her fellow instructors at Columbia a "very nice plum." [67] But Heilbrun did not like it there. She wanted to return to Columbia. In 1960 she accepted a position in the School of General Studies, Columbia's adult extension program. Rising through the ranks to an endowed chair, Heilbrun stayed at Columbia University for all of her professional life.

For the first fifteen years of her career at Columbia, she taught in close proximity to the critic and teacher she most admired. He personified to Heilbrun the university's opposition to women by resisting their integration into the English literature faculty of the college. Heilbrun never resolved her fundamental ambivalence toward Trilling; and it was not necessary that she do so. In fact, most of Trilling's students are slightly illogical when they describe their relation to this complicated and immensely private man. In 1970, Heilbrun tried to pin down what irked her about Trilling in her mystery *Poetic Justice.* It is a fantasy about a healed relationship with Trilling.

Under the pseudonym Amanda Cross, Heilbrun had created her amateur detective Kate Fansler in 1961 as a fancy alter ego, liberated from all social and economic constraints (including Jewishness). The wealthy, patrician Fansler, who is single and childless yet anchored in a secure relationship with a younger man, was an individual, Heilbrun wrote, "whose destiny offered more possibility than I could comfortably imagine for myself." [68] Yet Fansler, like Heilbrun, is a professor of English at a university strongly resembling Columbia, an upper-class New Yorker whose left-leaning views concur with Heilbrun's own. It is Fansler whom Heilbrun sends forth to do battle with Trilling in a novel that dispenses not only with logic but also with what Trilling's scrupulous scholarly colleague Marjorie Nicolson called "an Hebraic insistence upon justice as the measure of all things." [69] Fansler's encounter with Columbia's éminence grise presents a refraction of Trilling through the prism of fantasy.

Poetic Justice, set at Columbia University in 1968, opens with a wish fulfillment. "I used to fantasize," Heilbrun wrote in 1979 about Trilling and herself, "that we would one day engage in dialogue" (*RW* 127). The fantastic is easily achieved in fiction, and so it is that on the second page of the mystery's prologue an avatar of Trilling stops (or stoops) to speak to his colleague Fansler. He is aptly named Frederick Clemance, combining allusions both to an absolutist Prussian king who thought of himself as the highest servant of his people—Kate, indeed, thinks of her colleague as "Frederick the Great " [70]—and to a series of rather inclement popes. In Heilbrun's novel Trilling/Clemance is notable for both his mildness and his manners. When he first appears, emerging like a startled owl from the dark recesses of a campus building into the spring sunshine, he announces that he has just been evicted from his office by rebellious students. His dialogue with Fansler, whom he finds admiring the first tulips and damning the students who "were trampling thoughtlessly across the new grass" (*PJ* 11), leads to a further abdication. When Clemance learns of Fansler's interest in Auden, he asks her to relieve him of the burden of directing a dissertation on the poet, already in its final stages, and to take his chair on the examination committee.

Clemance's choice of Fansler to replace him is an anointment of sorts, a gesture in the direction of successorship, which had its uncanny counterpart in real life five years later. In November 1975, Heilbrun was asked to replace Trilling, who was gravely ill, as a speaker before the Friends of the Columbia Libraries. She agreed, though reluctantly, preferring that one of his disciples be asked to serve as stand-in. But she gave the talk. "My only prayer was that Trilling would not actually die on the day of the dinner. But of course he did. . . . My gentle revenge consisted in talking of women, and, moreover, in ending with a quotation from Trilling that could be used to declare a new dispensation for feminine endeavors" (*RW* 127–128).

Poetic Justice was written before Heilbrun was fully swept up in the feminist movement. Its main plot concerns the antagonism between Columbia College and the School of General Studies (called University College in the mystery), which grants bachelor and advanced degrees to adults. Some members of the elitist college faculty want to kill off the School of General Studies because they fear that its existence and granting of degrees cheapen their own institution. But just before significant steps can be taken by the dean of the college—together with one of Clemance's disciples, tellingly named O'Toole—it is the dean himself who is killed. Obviously, all members of the General Studies faculty are under suspicion. Fansler, who belongs to the neutral graduate school faculty, is called on to investigate.

The real-life underpinning to the power struggle depicted in Heilbrun's mystery had to do with the pressure to admit women to Columbia College and to appoint women to its faculty. The college fought very hard to preserve its identity. Trilling was perceived as being particularly invested in the preservation of the college as an elite male institution devoted to the pursuit of literary and cultural criticism (rather than the narrow scholarship cultivated in the graduate school). It comes as a complete surprise, therefore, that Clemance turns out to be the one who killed the dean. This solution fulfills Heilbrun's wish that, just once, Trilling would show himself enlightened and progressive and actively

19. Carolyn G. Heilbrun. *Courtesy of Columbia University Office of Public Affairs.*

support her side. And because the murder is committed for the sake of a good cause, against the elitist college and for the democratic, all-inclusive School of General Studies, the murderer is not brought to justice. He is absolved and let go by no less a personage than Kate Fansler's new husband, Reed Amhearst, who works for the New York district attorney's office. He declares the murder an accident since Clemance is properly contrite.[71]

In her earlier mysteries Heilbrun demonstrated that she assigned little significance to the murder itself. For her the perpetrator's motivation is the center of a mystery. The absurdity of Trilling/Clemance as murderer focuses the reader's attention on the motive—his sympathy for Fansler's/Heilbrun's adversarial camp. The School of General Studies had been Heilbrun's gateway to Columbia; in the late 1960s it was still something of a refuge for those who were not part of New York's financial, social, and cultural elite. And to these outsiders, Heilbrun thought, the sympathies and support of the Trilling *she* cherished ought rightly to belong.

Throughout her career as a distinguished feminist literary scholar,

Heilbrun frequently referred to Trilling both critically and admiringly. While he supported and enforced the social structures Heilbrun sought to change, she detected in this complicated man enough resistance to the social, cultural, and moral norms to allow her to reinterpret Trilling's concept of the opposing self as encompassing active political opposition. One could argue, as Susan Kress does, that "Heilbrun wanted to reinvent Trilling, to put him to the service of women."[72]

Moreover, Heilbrun thought of the barriers against Jews in Trilling's time as the same barriers that now hampered the professional progress of women. And she considered the discrimination Jews in literary academe experienced in the 1920s and early 1930s comparable to the discrimination that women continued to suffer in academe and elsewhere. Relegated to the margins, women found themselves in the same opposition to the dominant culture that Trilling had lived through in his brave moments in 1936. If that comparison held, Heilbrun could think of herself as Trilling's true heir. In her 1986 University Lecture, modeled on Trilling's Jefferson lecture of 1972, Heilbrun declared: "I have been a member of the Columbia University community for more than thirty-five years, and I can only consider myself to be speaking as what Lionel Trilling called an opposing self, opposed to culture, in this case the culture of the university."[73] Heilbrun served at Columbia for another six years before taking early retirement in 1992 to protest the university's continued discrimination against women.

———

Ozick, Podhoretz, Marcus, and Heilbrun entered college in the heyday of the so-called Age of Criticism. The teachers who thrilled and inspired them, apart from Trilling, tended to be critics who published evaluative essays in *Partisan Review* or *Kenyon Review,* rather than the old-fashioned scholars who sent pellets of knowledge to the *Philosophical Review* or the *Publications of the Modern Language Association of America.* The critics brought to academe not only their urgent concern with high modernism and contemporary culture but also an extraordinary liveliness and, as Robert Alter put it, "a sense of vital engagement in the experiential dynamics of reading." Moreover, Alter argued, the critics of the 1940s and 1950s created "a moment of optimal closeness between the academic scrutiny of literature and the kind of attention devoted to serious literature by an educated public outside the academy."[74] Since many of these critics were also poets, novelists, or dramatists, there was a sense of dissolving boundaries in the intellectual realm.

This was all the more exciting as new and rigid borders began to emerge and assert themselves in domestic and international politics. As the question of who was and was not a Communist gained importance in the public domain, so the question of who was or was not a Jew began to lose its nasty edge in academe. Some Jewish intellectuals who had grown up in left-leaning homes and had involved themselves in left-wing politics feared that "Communist" was really a code word for "Jew"; but their fears were dispelled within a few years. In fact, the immediate postwar period, until the radicalization of student protest in the late 1960s, was a safe and productive time for American Jews, who moved into all niches of American public, social, professional, and intellectual life. Those two decades of almost cocky self-assurance also saw the rise of Jewish authors in what came to be called the American Jewish literary renaissance. It began with the publication of Saul Bellow's novel *The Adventures of Augie March* in 1953 and peaked in 1964 with Bellow's *Herzog* and the reissue in paperback of Henry Roth's 1934 novel *Call It Sleep.* But while this renaissance turned out to be an "illusion,"[75] another development proved to be an amazing realization of a dream.

The period of American Jewish cultural self-confidence coincided with the founding of a secular democratic Jewish state in 1948 and with Israel's gradual assertion of its role as a major (armed) player in the Middle East. More clearly than the 1948 War of Independence, the wars of 1967 and 1973 demonstrated to the world community that the Jews living in Israel were determined not to become victims again. It was around that time that a new kind of scholarly Jew obtained professorships in American academe—one whose relation to Jewishness was not based on bagels, lox, and dusty memories of the immigrant experience, but on an immersion in the Jewish intellectual heritage.

The Rediscovery of Origins

9

Unfolding Hebrew Prose:
Robert Alter

IN 1961, AS THE EICHMANN TRIAL moved the Holocaust and its survivors into the Israeli consciousness and riveted the attention of American Jews, there appeared in *Commentary* an article by a twenty-six-year-old American entitled "The Genius of S. Y. Agnon."[1] Its author, Robert Alter, could be sure that the majority of his readers had barely heard of the Israeli writer and were even less likely to have read his work in the Hebrew original. Alter was captivated by Agnon's brilliance and attempted to attract more readers by linking him with Franz Kafka, then the single most important European writer on the American Jewish scene, a Czech Jew of undisputed genius writing in German about man's spiritual and social isolation in a modern universe that had disposed of God.

After reviewing the social connections as well as the literary similarities between Kafka and Agnon, Alter announced that Agnon was "much more than a Hebrew Kafka" (*AT* 136). Not only was Agnon annoyed by his critics' insistence on Kafka's influence on his work, there was indeed, Alter asserted, "one radical difference between the two writers: While Kafka exemplifies the distress of rootlessness that has characterized so many Jews in modern times, Agnon's uniqueness derives from the fact that he is so deeply rooted in a tradition. Agnon is in many ways the most profoundly Jewish writer to have appeared in modern Hebrew literature, and it is in his role as heir to a Jewish religion and cultural heritage that much of his artistic distinctiveness is to be sought" (*AT* 136). Agnon, whom Alter had met in Jerusalem in the winter of 1960, was intimately familiar with the Jewish literary canon: "Agnon continues

273

the tradition of the illustrious rabbinic line from which he is descended, and possesses a voluminous knowledge of traditional Hebrew and Aramaic source materials—the Bible with all its rabbinic commentaries, the Talmud, the Midrash, Maimonides and the medieval Jewish philosophers, legal codifiers, and poets, the Kabbalah, the literature of the *Musar* movement and of the Hasidic tradition of more modern times" (*AT* 138).

That anything resembling literary high modernism on a par with Kafka's artistic anguish had emerged from the assimilation of these sources was a notion as shocking as it was novel to Alter's former teachers and fellow students at Columbia University. Trilling, who was not insensitive to possible connections between the Jewish experience (notably persecution, displacement, and alienation) and modernist high art, had undertaken an essay on Isaac Babel in 1955, whose stories, however, had not been accessible to him in the Russian original. Alter went beyond Trilling's observations when he argued, taking Agnon as his example, for a link between modernist vision and Jewish literacy. For Alter, the latter term stood for nothing less than the mastery of Jewish canonical texts. He pushed his argument even further. Agnon's creative genius, Alter maintained, could best be examined and appreciated in Hebrew because he had created "a Hebrew of his own that . . . is about as different from the Hebrew spoken in Israel today as Elizabethan English [is] from modern colloquial American" (*AT* 140). This idiosyncratic linguistic medium, Alter declared, reflected Agnon's adaptation of classic Jewish texts, while the "motifs and symbols he employs [disclose] the recurrent ideas and concerns of Jewish tradition" (*AT* 139).

It was evident that Alter had not only read Agnon in Hebrew but was also familiar with some of his intellectual and linguistic sources in their original languages. Alter's talk of symbols and motifs reflected his academic literary training and, most notably, the concerns of his teacher at the time, Harry Levin, with whom he was then writing his dissertation. But in the literary argument Alter unfolded about Agnon, his emphasis was on the importance of the critic's mastery of Hebrew, ancient and modern. Alter's own competence in this area clearly gave him an edge in his work on Jewish literature over the Columbia crowd of fledgling literary critics and even over older hands such as Trilling, Marcus, and Podhoretz, with whom Alter was competing for space and attention in the literary magazines. It turned out later that the Columbia critics, who had nurtured Alter in the 1950s, winced at his suggestion that the qualities that made Agnon so remarkable were not to be found in resemblances to European writers but "in the characteristics unique to him as an individual artist, as a user of the Hebrew language, and as a Jew" (*AT* 133). Alter in turn was no less unhappy with the inadequate, sentimental ways in which Jewish writers, active in Europe, Israel, or America, were dealt with by American critics, who for the most part had no access to the original texts. They rarely read European languages with ease and were even further removed from the Hebrew and Aramaic texts of the Jewish tradition.

Alter's essay on Agnon delineated the minimal requirements for critical competence in dealing seriously with Jewish writers: adequate command of at least one major Jewish language (Hebrew, Aramaic, or Yiddish) in order to assess stylistic independence as well as creative innovations; familiarity with the main works of the Jewish intellectual tradition in order to recognize allusions, leitmotifs, and symbols, and to discern the writer's distance from, or proximity to, his or her legacy; and knowledge of Jewish history in Europe and the Middle East to allow for the evaluation of Jewish writing within the cultural context of its production. Over the next thirty years, Alter's demands regarding the minimal intellectual equipment of anyone wishing to write about Jewish literature fairly and competently developed into a full-scale educational program, which Alter embarked on as a teacher at the University of California, Berkeley, in the late 1960s.

Back in 1961, Alter's intention was to put an end to the sentimental criticism produced during "that false springtime from the 1950s through the early 60s," subsequently known as the Jewish literary renaissance.[2] Alter's attempts to tie critical pronouncements on Jewish literary works to tough intellectual prerequisites were aimed at ennobling those works by demanding that they be treated with the same intellectual scrupulousness brought to the interpretation of Swift, Yeats, or Joyce, for whom no serious American critic would claim critical competence on the strength of having Irish grandparents. Moreover, Alter's stringent demands implicitly criticized the intellectual slackness of assimilated American Jews vis-à-vis things Jewish and took the literary elite to task for their lazy neglect of one of the most stunning literary phenomena in twentieth-century culture, the invention of modern Hebrew prose. That Alter had put his money on the right horse became apparent to his colleagues when Agnon was awarded the Nobel Prize for literature in 1966. Agnon was then seventy-eight, his American champion thirty-one.

Robert Alter was born in the Bronx in April 1935. His father, Harry

Alter, had come to America from Romania as a teenager before World War I. His mother, Tillie Zimmerman, was born in a small town in Lithuania in 1903 and had been brought to America as an infant. Harry Alter owned a small fleet of taxis in New York City, which he lost in the last years of the Depression. The family then moved to Albany, where Alter spent his formative years. Harry Alter, who had secured a factory job in war production, settled his family in a working-class neighborhood populated by Catholics and Jews. Although Robert Alter's closest friends were Jewish, he also had playmates among the Irish, Polish, and Italian children in the neighborhood. Interethnic hostilities were limited to occasional fights with the kids from St. Patrick's parochial school, a few blocks away from the little synagogue where Alter attended Hebrew school. "I never grew up feeling either disadvantaged being a Jew or discriminated against because I was a Jew," Alter recalled.[3]

Alter was very athletic and played many sports in a large high school where Jews were a comfortable minority. His great aspiration from the age of eleven had been to become a starting member of the high school football team. In his senior year he achieved his goal: he was named a starting halfback. He recalled that the opening game was on Rosh Hashanah: "I was not super-observant at that time, but all of us kids had in mind an incident that had happened some years earlier, when the most prominent Jewish baseball player in the major leagues, Hank Greenberg, played first base for the Detroit Tigers. The Tigers got into the World Series. One game was scheduled on Yom Kippur and Greenberg refused to play. This made a profound impression on us. Here was all-American Hank Greenberg, who yet had this sense of pride of being a Jew. So I too refused to play. Despite many pleadings and entreaties from my coach—couldn't I get a special dispensation from a rabbi?—I remained adamant" (interview). The fact that Greenberg had played on Rosh Hashanah and hit two home runs against the Boston Red Sox got lost in the excitement over a national figure identifying himself publicly as a Jew ten days later on Yom Kippur.[4]

Alter's parents were "tradition-minded, non-orthodox" Jews. His father always worked on Saturdays, but his mother kept a kosher kitchen. The family belonged to a Conservative synagogue and went to services frequently. They observed the Jewish holidays and the Sabbath without heeding "too many of the prohibitions, except food prohibitions." Both parents, but especially Alter's mother, encouraged Jewish learning. Alter went to afternoon Hebrew school, though rather grudgingly, feeling it to be "a terrible imposition. I was not learning very much. By the time of my bar mitzvah, I could read the words [of my Torah portion] by rote and maybe I had a vocabulary of about one hundred Hebrew words" (interview). In the year of Alter's bar mitzvah, 1948, his junior high school began offering a Hebrew class that met twice a week in the afternoon. Alter decided to attend it for a year to please his mother, but he got caught up in the excitement of mastering the subject. He met students from other parts of Albany who had gone to a better Hebrew school and knew more than he did. Alter began to compete with them. In 1949 a new teacher arrived who had just finished his Ph.D. in Semitics at London University. "He started telling us about primeval Semitic roots and things of that kind. It seemed to me much more exciting than what we were doing in junior high school. Within two or three years I acquired a very good knowledge of the formal elements of Hebrew and not a bad vocabulary" (interview). In 1951, when Alter was sixteen, he went for the first time to a Hebrew summer camp in Wisconsin.

The ideal of a Hebrew-speaking culture in America, nurtured in Hebrew summer camps, first blossomed in America between the two world wars. But, as Alan Mintz demonstrated, it was an elite enterprise from its inception. Lack of interest in creating a mass readership for the cultural productions of *Tarbut Ivrit* (Hebrew culture)—its poems, novels, and essays—doomed the movement. Its very existence, however, had a ripple effect, which in an environment as hostile to foreign languages as American society eventually created the anomaly of the afternoon Hebrew school. What Jewish parents on their way to acculturation in the first decades of the twentieth century expected when they sent their children to afternoon Jewish instruction was that they "acquire, by rote, the minimum tokens of ritual literacy: how to recite the *qiddush,* the *qaddish,* and the *haftarah.* Or, on the Reform end of the spectrum, parents wanted children to be taught (in English, of course) the basic tenets of the Jewish religion." [5]

Around World War I, Alan Mintz explained, young men and women committed to Hebrew as an integral part of Jewish identity appeared on the scene. They spread out over the country and as teachers and principals turned Jewish Sunday schools into afternoon Hebrew schools. The curriculum of these newfangled institutions centered on the study of the Hebrew texts of Torah and *siddur* (prayerbook) and on the acquisition of the language, taught by the "Hebrew-in-Hebrew" method.[6] The success of the Hebrew schools was minimal at best, because their watered-down version of *Tarbut Ivrit* was not tied to an ideology that could capture the imagination of American Jewish youngsters who thought longingly of the football field and baseball diamond while spelling out Abraham's binding of Isaac.

After the end of World War II, however, as the fighting in Palestine for a Jewish state intensified and survivors of the Shoah were looking for a new place to live, American Jews warmed to the idea of Zionism. The Hebrew school curriculum began to make more cultural sense, and parents were ready to send their children to Hebrew-speaking summer camps. By 1948 there were three different kinds of camps that had adopted Hebrew as their "official" language. Massad, sponsored by Hanoar Haivri in 1941, was strongly Zionist. In fact, its founding director, Shlomo Shulsinger, declared that "the Zionist idea should be the backbone of all cultural work [and] the Halutz [settler] spirit be emphasized and a nucleus for Aliyah [immigration to Israel] be prepared at camp."[7] Yavneh, established in 1944 by Boston's Hebrew Teachers College as its summer school and camp, had a program of formal studies conducted by experienced teachers. Ramah, which opened in Wisconsin in 1947 under the supervision of the Teachers Institute of the Jewish Theological Seminary, was geared to the needs of the Conservative movement and attracted campers almost exclusively from the time-intensive Conservative afternoon schools. The governing ideal of these camps was to immerse student campers in a completely Hebrew environment and, as Alan Mintz pointed out, to present the language "not as an academic task but, in imitation of the society being built in Israel, as a living medium in all aspects of life." As Walter Ackerman observed, "the ideal of Hebrew as the only language spoken in camp by everyone and on all occasions was rarely achieved." Massad, which was most strongly Zionist, did best, followed by studious Yavneh; while Ramah, which was more concerned with nurturing a life-style "conditioned by religious sensitivity and social consciousness," lagged behind in its commitment to Hebrew.[8]

Robert Alter, who attended Ramah in 1951, discovered within a few weeks that he could "speak Hebrew fluently, with errors, but fluently. From then on, Hebrew became rather a main priority in my life." In fact, Hebrew gained rapidly in significance for Alter as the most promising vehicle for a mature Jewish cultural identity. In a 1968 article on the "painful condition of the American Hebrew teachers colleges," written in Alter's first year as professor of Hebrew and comparative literature at Berkeley, he declared:

I cannot believe that any Jewish culture, whether religious or secular, that subsists entirely or even primarily in translation, can provide lasting or meaningful continuity with the Jewish past. . . . Hebrew does remain the one, indispensable key to three thousand years of Jewish experience. . . . I would contend that we have little prospect for surviving as a distinctive community unless there are appreciable numbers of Jews—however strong their linguistic loyalty to English—who are capable of reading the Bible in its original language, who understand the Hebrew of the prayerbook and of rabbinic law and legend, and for whom the reborn language of Israel, if not always fully intelligible, is at least not a foreign tongue. . . . We should aspire in our . . . situation to a Jewish intelligentsia . . . that will have, as a matter of course, some precise textual knowledge of the classic Hebrew sources from which the rich and troubling confusions of modern Jewish identity derive.[9]

Between Alter's call in 1968 for a Jewish intelligentsia literate in Hebrew and his first exposure to Hebrew as a spoken language in 1951 lay long years of an intense literary education. Alter had been by no means certain what he wanted to do. He enrolled at Columbia College in 1953 because some of his best friends from summer camp went there. Another reason was that "six blocks away from Columbia there was the Jewish Theological Seminary [JTS]. I definitely wanted—not necessarily for professional reasons, but just in principle—to continue my Jewish education on a college level. The Seminary College of Jewish Studies essentially offered a Jewish liberal arts program. All lectures were in Hebrew and courses, some good, some not so good, covered the spectrum from Bible and Talmud to Jewish history, medieval and modern Hebrew literature. I learned a very good abstract and analytic vocabulary; so partly for that I went two evenings a week and Sunday afternoon while I was at Columbia" (interview).

The kinds of people who went to JTS, and the materials they studied there, were familiar to Alter, while in the literary seminars at Columbia College he felt initially very much like the proverbial young man from the provinces. "Especially in the English department there were certain anglophile *raffiné* types for whom Lionel Trilling might have been the model. Among the students there was a healthy sprinkling of such types as prep school products, who always wore tweed jackets and ties and chino pants and scuffed white buck shoes. They slightly baffled and daunted me in my first year. I remember meeting people whom I had never encountered in my circles in Albany who had read writers I had never heard of and who made these complicated remarks in class discussion, discriminating between the early and middle Dylan Thomas. But actually, I discovered after a few months that any gap between my reading background and literary sophistication and theirs was being closed, and so my defensiveness on that front dissolved" (interview).

Alter's defensiveness was also eased by the observation that not all Columbia students were *raffinés*. The college was still partly a commuter school, as in the days of Marcus and Podhoretz, and students arrived by subway on Morningside Heights, carrying their lunches in brown paper bags. "There were a lot of scruffy types, people from the Jewish lower middle class and from working-class families, who were on their way to medical school and so forth. One did not necessarily feel that one had to become like Lionel Trilling in order to make it in the world. Norman Podhoretz wrote in his first autobiographical work that the longest journey in the world was the journey from Brooklyn to Manhattan; and he felt it very strongly. Maybe it was a little easier for me because, although the center of my parents' social life, and I suppose mine as well, was Jewish, my whole upbringing was much more American" (interview).

During his years in college, the two crowds in which Alter moved, the Columbia literati and the amateurs of Hebrew letters, led their separate but equal existences in Alter's mind. They never intersected unless Alter made a conscious effort to import elements of one world into the other. Thrilled by his discovery of the New Critical method of close reading at Columbia, Alter attempted to apply it in a class at JTS to the poetry of Chaim Nachman Bialik. He found, much to his dismay, that the two institutions were farther apart than a few city blocks along Broadway.

> I remember vividly when, in my first year at Columbia, after a heady session of refining out the good from the great (or so it seemed) in Baudelaire through painstaking *explication de texte,* I suggested in an evening class at the Jewish Theological Seminary that a certain image in Bialik was incongruous with its poetic context. The teacher, a Hebrew poet himself, who must have known most of the Bialik corpus by heart since his own Russian boyhood, responded with uncomprehending shock —he stared at me for a moment, shook his head in disbelief, then simply proceeded with the class. Though I was of course much annoyed at the time by what seemed to me an unreasonable failure to speak to a legitimate critical issue, I can see now that the teacher's reaction was perfectly consistent with his own cultural premises. Bialik's poetry, after all, was not for him a neutral object to be evaluated, but a kind of sacred text, a

triumphant demonstration of the eternal power of Hebrew creativity, ultimately, almost a way of life. The attitude proper to such a text was not critical cogitation but allegiance.[10]

Similar worship of Great Poets was of course not unknown at Columbia, and there Alter willingly participated in the appropriate rites. In the 1950s, T. S. Eliot electrified the minds of Columbia's emerging literati, just as Bialik had inflamed the hearts of the early Zionists. "In my immediate undergraduate circle," Alter recalled, "we actually made an impromptu ritual out of *The Waste Land,* for a brief period, reading the whole poem aloud every year on an evening in the first week of April —a celebration through performance not readily conceivable for any other modern poet" (interview). To that generation Eliot was still the quintessential modern poet; precocious *raffinés* from the city and the provinces were equally in raptures over the sheer difficulty of Eliot's allusive poems. "More substantively," however, Alter wrote, "the sardonic edginess and the brooding spiritual gloom of Eliot's poetry spoke movingly to a late adolescent's sense of squirming discomfort with himself and anxiety about the world, and were seized on as the authoritative statement about living in the modern world. This explains in part why bits and pieces of his poetry were so *memorable* in the literal sense. I can still recall sitting in classes in Hamilton Hall, repeating to myself, convinced I had discovered an ultimate expression of my own condition: 'I should have been a pair of ragged claws / Scuttling across the floors of silent seas.' "[11]

Surprisingly, Alter seems not to have been bothered then by the "general dysfunction of humanistic values operating in [Eliot's] work," most notably manifested in his anti-Semitism, which Alter described very clearly some fifteen years later.[12] The world of JTS was too far removed from Columbia to check Alter's intellectual intoxication. Occasionally, however, Alter would bring elements of his Jewish life to bear on his Columbia work. In 1957 a missionary impulse propelled him to write a senior class essay for Frederick Dupee comparing Kafka and Agnon. The center of Alter's interest at JTS was Hebrew literature, which he considered on a par with the works he studied at Columbia. He thought it increasingly absurd to keep his two loves separate. "I thought Yeats, whom I was then reading for the first time, was a great poet; but so was Bialik. I wanted to tell the world more about Bialik" (interview). Sensibly, he began with Agnon, who could be made familiar to his teachers through comparison with Kafka.

Alter showed his essay to Lionel Trilling, with whom he was studying during his senior year. Trilling said the piece was very interesting and sent Alter downtown to see his former student Norman Podhoretz, who was then assistant editor at *Commentary*. Like Steven Marcus and Podhoretz himself in the days of Elliot Cohen, Alter made his way from Morningside Heights to *Commentary*'s editorial offices with a recommendation from Trilling in his pocket. He could not know that the offices were in a state of disarray. The sudden death of Robert Warshow two years earlier, in the spring of 1955, had thrown Cohen, who was still the chief editor, into an incapacitating depression. "I have never known a death so intensely and openly grieved," Trilling wrote. "No one was inclined, in the modern way, to 'accept' it. No one was reasonable or philosophical about it." [13] In Cohen's absence the magazine was run by Martin and Clement Greenberg who had their own ideas. Podhoretz struggled to make sure that Cohen's editorial style was preserved as much as possible.

Podhoretz asked Alter whether he wanted to write a general piece on Agnon for the magazine. He did. "I worked at it very conscientiously for a month," Alter remembers, "and then sent it down to Podhoretz. After a while I got it back from him. He had invested a lot of time in rewriting the piece, but in the end he was voted down by his fellow editors, who felt it was not publishable. In retrospect, I am glad because I think it was a good undergraduate essay but nothing more than that" (interview). Podhoretz sent an encouraging cover letter in which he said that, although he disagreed with the other editors, he felt Alter had not persuaded anybody that Agnon was more than a writer of parochial interest. "That hit a raw nerve," Alter recalled. "I thought, these assimilated Jews down at *Commentary* don't have an understanding of what real Jewish culture is" (interview).

In the fall of 1957, Alter arrived at Harvard to begin graduate studies in English. He realized quickly that at Harvard he was playing on a different kind of turf from Columbia. "Among the undergraduates with whom I came in contact, but also among my fellow graduate students, I suddenly noticed this powerful feeling: we are at Harvard and no one can compare to us; there was this sense of old families sending their sons to Harvard and so forth. This put me off a great deal, as did the whiffs I got of the ethos of the gentleman-scholar" (interview). Alter decided to pursue his own course. "Coming from a family of very modest means —we never belonged to clubs, we never went on vacation—I had a strong feeling: well, that's me and I am not going to begin to behave differently, dress differently, drop different references in my speech. This may have been an exaggerated reaction to whatever at Harvard put me off. It also made me feel more patriotic toward Columbia. My reaction was largely to remain a loner in graduate school. I do not mean to say that I was isolated and alienated and haunted and lonely. I simply stayed by myself" (interview).

Alter shared an apartment with a friend from Columbia whom he knew from Hebrew summer camp. They kept a kosher kitchen and even studied Talmud together for a year. That alone would not have insulated Alter from the Harvard ambience; but at the time, from his mid-to late twenties, Alter was passing through a religious phase. The observance of the Sabbath and the holidays brought his life-style into the rhythm of Harvard's Jewish student organization (Hillel) and caused him to be out of sync with the literature departments. Moreover, in 1958, Ben-Zion Gold, whom Alter had vaguely known as a rabbinical candidate at JTS, came to Harvard Hillel as its Conservative rabbi. Gold was born in Radom, Poland, and studied at a yeshiva there. He survived persecution and internment by the Nazis and came to America after the war. Gold was a treasure trove of detailed knowledge about the bristling life in Poland's prewar yeshivot, and he spoke with passion about the subversive impact of modern Yiddish literature on the cramped, restless minds of the Talmud students. It is perhaps one of the lost opportunities in American literary criticism that Alter did not explore what Gold knew about Yiddish literature. But they had many substantive conversations about Hebrew literature, in which Gold was also interested. Nevertheless, the two men could not bridge the immense divide that in the late 1950s separated a fundamentally optimistic all-American Jew and a scarred survivor, burdened with the culture of Europe's dead Jews.

Even after the Eichmann trial in Jerusalem in 1961 led to a cautious rapprochement between old-world and new-world Diaspora Jews, Alter never made the destruction of the Jews his topic.[14] Rather, his impulse remained forward-looking (if that can be said of a literary historian), focused on Hebrew as the unfolding, productive element in Jewish culture. He was concerned with the literary past only insofar as it was the indispensable matrix of the secular intellectual culture of Jewish modernity.

As the split between Alter's Jewish self and his mainstream academic self intensified at Harvard, he worked hard to bring the two together under the rubric of comparative literature. The tenets of the New Criticism urged him to look at a poem without considering the context of its creation. Alter was then still preoccupied with the observation that the things that excited him about Yeats, linguistic ingenuity, metaphors, allusions, and the recreation of myth in poetry were the same ones that thrilled him in Bialik, and Reuben Brower at Harvard reinforced Alter's New Critical approach to poetry. But while at Harvard, Alter also came under the influence of Erich Auerbach, who combined close attention to a literary text with a profound sense of evolving historical context. Eventually Alter decided to write a dissertation with Harry Levin, then the preeminent figure in comparative literature and a scholar who combined close reading with an evaluation of a work's literary and cultural context.

Alter listed Hebrew literature as his minor field, but nobody at Harvard taught modern Hebrew literature. He went to see Isadore Twersky, the descendant of a distinguished line of Hasidic rabbis and an outstanding scholar of Maimonides. Twersky had been a student of Harry Wolfson, Harvard's first instructor in Jewish philosophy (appointed in 1915), and had succeeded him as Nathan Littauer Professor of Hebrew Literature and Philosophy. Before agreeing to sponsor Alter in comparative literature, Twersky put him to the test, asking him to write an interpretation of a Hebrew poem in Hebrew. Alter composed four pages in fancy Hebrew about Saul Tchernichovsky's *Ayit! Ayit al harayikh* ("Eagle! Eagle Over Your Mountains") and so duly convinced Twersky that he knew the language.

Although Alter had chosen to go into comparative literature because he wanted to do something with Hebrew as well as English, his dissertation, completed in 1962, did not reflect that desire. *Rogue's Progress: Studies in the Picaresque Novel* came straight out of the school and interests of Harry Levin. It is a no-frills examination of a novelistic subgenre that was published by Harvard University Press in 1964. Levin, whom Alter perceived as a "tense person and not easy to get to know" (interview), liked the liveliness of Alter's style, and despite the "correct" and distanced relationship he maintained with his graduate student, proved enormously helpful and supportive. He furnished Alter with a strong recommendation, which probably secured for Alter, who had gotten married in 1961, an instructorship in the English department at Columbia University. In 1965, Alter was promoted to assistant professor.

Columbia was not interested in Alter's command of Hebrew, literary or mundane, but saw him as an eighteenth-century scholar. Alter spent a good deal of his creative energy over the next twenty years on the literature of the academic mainstream, the great European novels of the last three hundred years. Yet the literary features that held his interest, the arguments he developed, and the methods by which he proved them —in all of which Alter owed a great deal to Harry Levin—gave direction to what he was eventually going to do with Hebrew literature.

Rogue's Progress, which Alter readied for publication during his first year at Columbia, covered a smooth, undisturbing canon: *Lazarillo de Tormes*, Le Sage's *Gil Blas*, Defoe's *Moll Flanders*, Smollett's *Roderick Ransom*, and Fielding's *Tom Jones*, before surveying the heirs of the picaresque tradition: Stendhal's *Le Rouge et le Noir*, Thackeray's *Barry Lyndon*, Mark Twain's *Huckleberry Finn*, Thomas Mann's *Felix Krull*, Joyce Cary's *Horse's Mouth*, and Saul Bellow's *Augie March*. What was missing was a hint of the truly upsetting, modern picaresque, comprising works like Mendele Moykher Sforim's *Travels of Benjamin the Third* or Kafka's *Amerika*, which bring back the subversive force and satiric power of the original *Lazarillo*. The European Jewish picaresque revives the angry questioning of God's justice that the eighteenth century had flattened into a reasonable indictment of society. In 1964, however, Alter was not yet ready to rock the boat of tradition too hard by bringing on board too many scary Jews. But what had to come down, he felt, was the idol of the Great Tradition as conceived by F. R. Leavis. In his next book Alter exposed its clay feet.

"Fielding's attitudes," Leavis had pronounced in *The Great Tradition*, "and his concerns with human nature, are simply not such as to produce an effect of anything but monotony (on a mind, that is, demanding more than external action) when exhibited at the length of an 'epic in prose.' " With a shrug Leavis summed up his assessment: "Life isn't long enough to permit one's giving much time to Fielding." [15] Alter concealed his annoyance with Leavis behind a general statement: "What happens too often is that critical intelligence is seduced by the shapeliness of the definitions it has inherited or conceived, and as a result it fails to respond adequately to works that cannot be accommodated to the definitions, those very exceptions which, in the proper sense, prove the rule—put it to the test" (*FN* vii). Alter's book *Fielding and the Nature of the Novel* (1968) did not attempt to test but to explode the rules. It lunged in two directions. In a shrewd and funny first chapter, Alter demolished the critical tradition from Samuel Johnson to F. R. Leavis and Frank Kermode that had dismissed Fielding. Then, in a second move, he made it clear that he was using Fielding only as an exemplary figure to arrive at a broader genre definition for the novel.

Fielding, Alter argued, "is virtually left out of the realm of the English novel by some critics largely because his writing does not correspond to a number of tacitly shared, more or less unquestioned assumptions about the nature and purpose of fiction and the fictional treatment of moral experience" (*FN* 7). Alter proposed an enlarged definition of the novel that would accommodate not only the mimetic intent of the Richardson-Defoe-Eliot tradition but also the tradition of literary self-reflexiveness from Fielding to Nabokov that attempted to transfigure the world through style. Alter's reason for urging a less confining genre definition for the novel may have surprised many of his readers: "If one's notion of the novel is derived primarily from figures like Richardson and Defoe, it becomes difficult to encompass critically achievements like that of the great Hebrew novelist S. Y. Agnon, who writes about the aweful dislocations and dissonances of the twentieth century in a beautifully crafted Hebrew that is basically medieval, occasionally even biblical" (*FN* 189). A critical encompassing of Agnon was probably not very high on the list of priorities for readers of a book on Fielding. However, Alter's argument testified to the extent to which Jews were now certain of their uncontested integration into literary academe; and Alter's unselfconsciousness about his reference to Agnon asserted that he considered the Jewish literary tradition on a par with the best of European culture. It is through matter-of-fact observations like Alter's that the expansion of the Western canon to include the Jews was transformed from a demand into a reality.

Alter was determined to construct a broader base of evidence for his new genre definition. In 1975 he published *Partial Magic: The Novel as Self-Conscious Genre*. One of Alter's friends half-jokingly suggested that he call the book "The Other Great Tradition" since it presented a tradition of his own, which ran from Cervantes through Sterne, Diderot, Balzac's *Lost Illusions,* Thackeray's *Vanity Fair,* and Melville's *Confidence Man,* to Nabokov and the postmodernists beyond. What distinguished these authors and their novels in Alter's view was the fact that they "raised fictional self-consciousness to a distinctive generic trend." [16] He would call the genre variously self-reflexive or self-conscious, taking his cue once more from Harry Levin, who had declared, "All novels are self-conscious, from Don Quixote to the newest *nouveau roman*" (quoted in *PM* viii). Alter's explicit goal was to provide a corrective to a critical tradition that seemed to him stiff and outmoded. He deplored the "lamentable lack of critical appreciation for the kind of novel that expresses its seriousness through playfulness, that is acutely aware of itself as a mere structure of words even as it tries to go beyond words to the experiences words seek to indicate" (*PM* ix).

20. Robert Alter. *Photograph by Dan Alter.*

While he was writing *Partial Magic,* Alter's interest shifted from the artistry of the self-reflexive genre to the "realist enterprise," which, he felt, "has been enormously complicated and qualified by the writer's awareness that fictions are never real things, that literary realism is a tantalizing contradiction in terms." He was intrigued by the question of how language and reality, experience and the telling of experience, relate to each other. What came into view and took on new luster was the work of Harry Levin, especially *The Gates of Horn,*which Alter acknowledged to be "the best general study of the realist tradition." Levin had established the preeminence of the French novel in the development of realism, and Alter asserted that "France's leading role in the creation of the great age of fiction calls for some reflection" (*PM* 89).

Alter's reflections took the form of a critical biography of Stendhal, on which he worked together with his second wife, Carol Cosman. *A Lion for Love,* which appeared in 1979, sought "to give some concrete sense of how the major fiction emerged from the experience of the author." Alter remained true to his old passion for language, offering "some close analysis of how in details of style and technique Stendhal managed to create a form of the novel so distinctively his own." [17]

Five years later, in 1984, when Alter put together a collection of his essays, the formulation but not the substance of his critical enterprise had changed slightly. In the preface to *Motives for Fiction,* Alter named as his overall concern "the problem of the representation of reality in fiction." But the volume's true objective was to counter the rise of literary theory, which threatened to put critics out of business. At the end of the lead essay, "Mimesis and the Motive for Fiction," first published in 1978, Alter pleaded for a reading of fiction unencumbered by theory:

> We seem now . . . to run some danger of being directed by the theorists to read in a way that real readers, on land or sea, have never read. If one insists on seeing all novels as congeries of semiotic systems intricately functioning in a pure state of self-referentiality, one loses the fine edge of responsiveness to the urgent human predicaments that novels seek to articulate. The greatness of the genre, both in its realist and in its self-conscious modes, has been to present us . . . lives that might seem like our lives, minds like our minds, desires like our own desires. That has been what most novelists quite clearly have tried to accomplish in their writing, and that is what still makes the reading of novels for most people, intellectuals included, one of the perennially absorbing activities of modern culture. [18]

Six years later, in the preface to *Motives for Fiction,* Alter's support of the naïve reader became a touch defensive. He could sense that his traditionalist views were being set aside by the Young Turks of theory, but at forty-nine Alter was not ready to accept the obsolescence of his literary concepts and arguments. His literary taste, however, had changed in the twenty years since he had first championed the novel as a self-conscious genre. Alter's emerging preference for reality over style came through clearly in his 1987 review of Cynthia Ozick's *Messiah of Stockholm* and Philip Roth's *Counterlife.* While Alter conceded that Ozick was "one of the most gifted stylists now writing in this country," he called her novel "too cerebral" and claimed that it was "rooted not in experience but in reading and cogitation about reading." Roth's novel, by contrast, he considered striking because of "the sense it repeatedly conveys of experience shrewdly observed and deeply felt." [19]

The adequate representation of everyday experience in literary language had become important to Alter. He responded less favorably to literary art as stylistic tour de force, to metaphoric razzle-dazzle, to Bloomian *agon* or anxiety of influence. Reading was Alter's foremost source of intellectual pleasure; and pleasure was not to be had from the mental gymnastics of postmodern stylists, but from the artful and surprising representation of the familiar. In *The Pleasures of Reading in an Ideological Age* (1989) Alter based his opposition to theory on the experience of delight and enjoyment while reading. In Alter's view the elucidation of literary texts from a definite ideological position served a moral purpose extraneous to them. Instead Alter urged an engaged explication of the "intrinsic operations of literature"—language, character, style, allusion, structure, perspective, and meaning—and argued that there were "more interesting and more important things for a critic to do than merely to expose fashionable absurdities."[20] *The Pleasures of Reading* was a highly personal attempt to distill three decades of intensive reading into a description of how literature cast its spell upon readers. Alter called his undertaking a "coalescing at a second stage" (interview), because he began to bring together his knowledge of several national literatures, which were then still leading separate but equal existences in Alter's mental household. He integrated them now by identifying those common elements that made him tingle with pleasure. In fact, *The Pleasures of Reading* is a learned, sometimes ingenious explanation of Alter's old discovery that what excited him in Yeats also thrilled him in Bialik.[21]

Alter explained that he took most of his illustrations for *The Pleasures of Reading* from English and American authors "in order to avoid the difficulties of dealing with translations." Yet the Hebrew Bible is a strong presence, perhaps because the King James Version is an English book, but most certainly also because Alter's discovery of the Hebrew Bible as a *literary* text revived his passion for close reading and literary analysis just as his interest in the novel as a self-conscious genre was flagging. To understand how this discovery came about, one needs to look into Alter's other literary life.

As a doctoral candidate at Harvard, Alter spent the academic year 1959–60 as an unmatriculated student at the Hebrew University in Jerusalem. He took a few courses on Hebrew literature and a course on Dostoevsky's *Brothers Karamazov* with Lea Goldberg, an accomplished Hebrew poet (*DI* 91–101). While in Israel, in the spring of 1960, Alter noticed that Norman Podhoretz had become the editor of *Commentary*. He wrote to Podhoretz, thanking him for his encouraging letter three years earlier and offering to write something for him now. Podhoretz accepted. Upon his return from Israel, Alter completed a new article on Agnon, which appeared in *Commentary* in August 1961. Thus began Alter's long association with the magazine. Alter skillfully turned his first assignment, a review of recently published prayerbooks of the Orthodox and Conservative movements, into a commentary on the futility of modernizing translations of ancient and medieval Hebrew texts.[22]

In 1962, Alter moved from Cambridge back to New York City to start teaching at Columbia. Everybody who was anybody on the English faculty of the college was writing for literary magazines, and so Alter was very interested in continuing his association with *Commentary* while writing straight academic studies on the European literary tradition. In the winter of 1961, Alter published a discussion of S. Yizhar's controversial novel *The Days of Ziklag* in the quarterly *Judaism*. The article demonstrated not only Alter's familiarity with Hebrew and its nascent modern fiction but also his intimacy with the Israeli scene and its ideological debates. Since there was nobody in the literary circles connected to Columbia who could match that achievement, it made Alter indispensable to *Commentary* and to the world of the literary magazines.

During the next fifteen years Alter contributed on average one long article on Israeli fiction a year to *Commentary* until, in 1978, a new crop of writers appeared to whom the topic could be entrusted.[23] However, as the magazine became politically more conservative and Israel's best writers moved further to the left, *Commentary* gradually ceased to be interested in Hebrew fiction. Taken together, Alter's pieces form a fascinating history of Israeli literature captured at the very moment of its emergence. It is a testimony to Alter's sound judgment that he was rarely misled by colorful gadflies, nor did he waver in his aesthetic allegiances or waffle in his politics.

His first essay responding to the contemporary Israeli scene was something of an exception. Yizhar's novel *The Days of Ziklag* (1958), which was set during the War of Independence, caused a great stir in Israel. Touted before publication as the great Israeli war epic, the novel turned out to comprise 1,143 closely printed pages of interior monologue and stream of consciousness about a seven-day struggle for Ziklag, a hill in the Negev. By fragmenting experienced time, Yizhar drained the novel of all dramatic excitement and thus brought out the anti-heroic side of warfare—boredom, stagnation, anonymity. He also undermined Zionist ideology, which is based on a linear historical narrative linking Jews in ancient and modern Palestine. Yizhar's fragmentation of time rattled the ideological foundations on which the still-embattled Jewish state rested.

Predictably, the older generation of Israelis, who thought of Ziklag as the city David used as his center of operations, were furious at Yizhar for distorting the image of Israel's freedom fighters and for betraying the memories of those fallen in the war. The younger Israeli intellectuals, many of whom had fought in the war and thought of Ziklag as Elevation Point 244, supported Yizhar and hailed his novel as a great achievement. Alter clearly sided with the young:

> It is a hopeful sign that one of the major spokesmen for Israel's younger generation turns out, in the final analysis, to have deep pacifist sensibilities. Secular Zionism's assigning of ultimate value to national existence in itself was bound to carry with it the danger of making moral values subordinate to the highest good of the preservation of the state. Yizhar and the members of his generation found themselves faced with this problem very concretely when the Israeli-Arab War put them in the position of having to take human lives in the name of the "Homeland," . . . a word . . . that says everything and says nothing. (*AT* 222)

Yizhar, who was a member of the Knesset representing Mapam, then the ruling party, performed in his writing the valuable service of "deflating much that called for deflating in Zionist ideology" (*AT* 224). Therefore, Alter concluded, "one may hope for a time when prevailing thought in Israel will come to a more realistic appraisal of the purpose and justification for the Jewish state" (*AT* 225). Alter's desire for an Israel above all moral reproach reflected the idealism of a very young man, which was shared by many American Jews, rather than an awareness of the actions necessary to assure the survival of a Jewish state in the Middle East. As Alter matured, he realized that literary criticism was not the place to advise a people on what it should or should not do.

In 1962, Alter turned his review of an anthology of Israeli fiction into a discussion of the differences between the fiction of the older, European-minded Israeli writers and that of the younger, Israel-centered generation. Two years later he examined the romantic–nationalist misreadings of Bialik and Tchernichovsky that annoyed him because they prevented readers from seeing through to the poets' true artistic achievement. In other articles he analyzed the ubiquity and importance of poetry in Israel as a vehicle for a sophisticated Hebrew (1965), explained the gradual emergence of the Shoah as a topic in Israeli fiction (1966), and illuminated the evolution of literary realism in Hebrew and the linguistic challenges that writers from Abraham Mapu to S. Yizhar had encountered in their endeavor to portray daily life in a language that had not accompanied its people into modernity (1966).[24] By the time Alter slowed his output twelve years later, he had provided American readers with a comprehensive survey of modern Hebrew literature and its problems.

Commentary also asked Alter to assess the Jewish literary scene at home. In 1965, Podhoretz engaged him to write a quarterly column on matters of Jewish culture. Alter examined the American Jewish scene and did not like what he saw.[25] He praised Saul Bellow as a writer but did not think of him as a Jewish writer, despite Bellow's ability to use Jewishness as an artistic resource (*AT* 37). He was critical of Bernard Malamud's intention to use Jewishness as an "ethical symbol" (*AT* 117); and he was down on the so-called American Jewish literary renaissance because it created "a new sentimental literary myth of the Jew" (*AT* 38). In his provocative debut as columnist, Alter observed that

> the American writer of Jewish descent finds himself utilizing Jewish experience of which he is largely ignorant, and so the Jewish skeletons of his characters are fleshed out with American fantasies about Jews. The result is a kind of double sentimental myth: the Jew emerges from this fiction as an imaginary creature embodying both what Americans would like to think about Jews and what American Jewish intellectuals would like to think about themselves. (*AT* 39)

Among Alter's most productive villains was Leslie Fiedler, whom he called an "ideologue of the new sentimental myth" (*AT* 39). Alter managed to put up with Fiedler's novel *Back to China* (1965) and its "fashionable archetype" of the Jew as Christ (*AT* 40), but his patience gave out when he came across Fiedler's archetypal interpretation of the biblical Joseph story in *Partisan Review.* Fiedler depicted "the Jew's characteristic cultural role as a vendor of dreams and an interpreter of dreams to the world, that is, as poet and therapist" (*AT* 19). Alter's put-down was as elegant as it was diplomatic, without losing any of its bite:

> Fiedler is more subtle and inventive than most mythopoeic critics in his articulation of archetypes, but he clearly shares with the medieval Midrash an indifference to historical perspective which allows him to speak of the varied literary productions of far-flung times and places as one eternal

system, and he is thoroughly midrashic in his readiness to establish through the merest hint of an association a "real" connection between things. (*AT* 20–21)

Alter was too unpolemical a person to criticize American Jewish writers and intellectuals less obliquely for their ignorance of Jewish literary sources. He was content to state that "the influence of traditional Jewish experience on American writers like Bellow and Malamud is for the most part peculiarly tangential" and to warn Jewish readers not to look in the fiction of the American Jewish renaissance "for an authentication of their own existence" (*AT* 10).

No one at Columbia College disagreed openly with Alter. Yet he got the impression that there was a certain uneasiness about his "split-level activity. . . . They felt I should be doing straight English literature. To be writing about Hebrew literature, and about people like Malamud and Philip Roth, was some kind of parochial diversion. It reflected perhaps a generational difference that people were uneasy because I was not doing the polite Anglophilic thing that Trilling, say, had done" (interview). When Alter's first collection of essays on modern Jewish literature appeared in 1969, two years after he had left Columbia, he asked his publisher, E. P. Dutton, to send a copy of the book to Trilling. "Eventually they sent me a little postcard they had got from Trilling, thanking whoever it was who sent him the book and saying something along the lines of: I will be interested in looking into it, although I must say that just looking at the topic I feel certain twinges of the depression which I generally get when I think about books on Jewish subjects" (interview). Columbia had become a good place for Jews who wished to become American critics, but the intellectual interests of the Columbia literati encompassed very few of Alter's fundamental commitments. "In a discussion . . . with someone who has no special concern for either the fact or the quality of Israel's existence," Alter wrote, "for whom, say, Israel and Indonesia are matters of equal interest—I feel cut off from any deep rapport because the involvements by which in part I define my own humanity do not exist for him." [26]

For the fall of 1967, Alter accepted a joint appointment as associate professor in Hebrew and comparative literature at the University of California at Berkeley. As he was driving across the country in early June of 1967, he heard on the radio that fighting had erupted in the Middle East. "I shared the driving with a student from the Midwest," Alter recalled, "who could not have cared less while I was desperately listening to the five-minute newsflashes on the hour. On the first day there were all these reports out of Arab countries that Haifa was in flames and Jerusalem had been razed. I felt an enormous sense of relief when the accurate news came through" (interview). The Six Day War strongly reinforced Alter's solidarity with Israel. His commitment became even firmer when within a day or two of his arrival on campus, Alter was seeing student papers in free-distribution boxes "with headlines like 'Zionist Running Dog of American Imperialism Strikes Free Arab People.' I knew then that I was in a different place; and I started getting involved in political polemics" (interview).

Alter began to understand the necessity of Israel's recourse to force and the "naivete and spiritual arrogance [underlying] the assumption that the Jews have a unique role as guides to the conscience of mankind" and are therefore expected to behave with the utmost "moral nobility." This expectation was in line with the sentimental myth of the Jew as Christ, fostered by American Jewish writers in works like Malamud's *Assistant* or Fiedler's *Back to China.*"Israel's very presence among the nations," Alter wrote, "is an affirmation that the Jews are not symbols, witnesses, ghostly emissaries of some obscure [moral or spiritual] mission, but men like other men who need to occupy physical space in a real world."[27]

Among the many articles Alter wrote in the late 1960s and the first half of the 1970s supporting a tough Israel (Alter's position softened in the second half of the 1970s and throughout the 1980s, as many of his Israeli friends were moving toward the Peace Now movement), the most scathing of them analyzed the reactions of American intellectuals toward the Israel-Arab wars of 1967 and 1973. Baffled by I. F. Stone's article in the August 3, 1967, issue of the *New York Review of Books,* in which Stone "felt 'honor-bound,' as a Jew emotionally tied to the birth of Israel, to devote most of his account to the Arab side," Alter wondered why Israel's victory was such a "profoundly unsettling experience" for many Jewish intellectuals, but at the time was not able to answer his question conclusively. He observed, however, that Jewish academics were not unhappy with the image of a bellicose Israel because "it fits so neatly into a popular New Left mythology of world politics in which the nations are divided into sinister superpowers and innocent, freedom-loving peoples of the Third World." A petition titled "A Call for Respect and Humanity in the Middle East Crisis," signed by Jews, Arabs, and Christians, Alter found particularly instructive:

Let me say at once that the two broad aspirations of the petition are ones to which I feel any intelligent supporter of Israel ought to subscribe unhesitatingly: a call for compassion and material aid for the Arab refugees, and an appeal to the member states of the UN to put aside cold-war intrigues and act for the welfare of the peoples of the Middle East. More questionable is the call to the Israeli government to respect the Islamic shrines under its control, because of the gratuitous and misleading implication that Israel has ever done, or intended to do, anything else. The really peculiar note, however, of the petition is struck in its affirmation that it has been made "on behalf of the peoples of the Third World" by individuals who "identify intimately and respectfully with their traditions and creative goals." One wonders why a Noam Chomsky or a Jerrold Katz, beyond the call of humanitarianism, need identify intimately and respectfully with the traditions of Egypt, Syria, Saudi Arabia, and Kuwait, except for the naive assumption that all the petty dictators and minor-league Machiavels of the Afro-Asian nations somehow represent the progressive force in world politics and culture. But then Jews have been performing this kind of self-abasing mental backbend ever since they first took up the cause of world revolution a century ago: it has always been Jewish nationalism that has been denounced by Jews as a force of reaction.

To the Jewish signatories of the petition and to the Jewish intellectuals who felt they needed to identify with Israel's adversaries on moral grounds, Alter called out: "If modern Jewish history has one lesson to teach, from the early Enlighteners and assimilationists to the good Jewish Marxists murdered by Stalin, it is that a lofty universalism with no roots in national identity exists only in the fervid imagination of the refugees from the ghettos, and that one must belong to a particular part of mankind before embracing the whole of it." [28]

One year later, in October 1968, Alter outlined the connections between the New Left and Arab rhetoric about Israel as an imperialist and colonialist power, and between the anti-Zionist rhetoric of Arab states and the anti-Semitic propaganda of Nazi Germany. [29] Five years later, on the occasion of a speech by Father Daniel Berrigan to the Association of Arab University Graduates delivered six days after the end of the Yom Kippur War, Alter exposed the ideological links between peace activism, anti-Zionist demagoguery, and theological anti-Semitism. The sum of his observations about the historical ignorance and soft moral fiber of American intellectuals was not encouraging: "In the climate of prevalent political opinion in America . . . it is much more inviting for a dissident spirit to savor its superiority vis-à-vis the Jews than vis-à-vis the Arabs."[30]

Meanwhile, however, Alter was building up a graduate studies program in Hebrew literature at Berkeley that could be accessed through the departments of Near Eastern Studies and Comparative Literature. The latter had been founded in 1966 by Alain Renoir, the son of the director Jean Renoir and grandson of the painter August Renoir. Alain Renoir was a medievalist who devised for Berkeley what Alter called "the most aggressively traditionalist program in comparative literature in the country. At a time when departments of literature at other American universities were abandoning literary history as an antiquated concept in favor of more free-wheeling theoretical approaches to the corpus of literary texts . . . , comparative literature at Berkeley was founded on the belief in the importance of literary history and of following the gradual evolution of particular literary traditions."[31] Not only did Renoir stress the importance of classical literature at the very moment when Greeks and Romans were being debunked by the progressives, Renoir's vision encompassed a comprehensive picture of literature that included not only European but Asian literatures as well. Renoir naturally thought of Hebrew literature and offered Alter a tenured position in 1967.

Renoir's notion of the scope desirable for a comparative literature department provided an excellent conceptual framework for a coherent program in Hebrew literature at a time when the only other model in the United States was Arnold Band's program at UCLA. Jewish Studies programs were just beginning to be established in American universities.[32] Alter's curriculum proceeded in two directions: "a 'vertical' axis, which goes back through three millennia of Hebrew expression, and which, because of the subtly and intensely recapitulative dynamic of literary discourse, can scarcely be slighted; and a 'horizontal' axis, which runs through the sundry methods of analysis and theoretical consideration that constitute literary studies as a formal discipline."[33] This meant that graduate students in Hebrew literature had to prepare for their examinations a large variety of texts, "beginning with Genesis and running through the rabbinic and medieval period to the Haskalah and the later nineteenth and twentieth centuries." In addition, they had to study rabbinic hermeneutics, medieval exegesis, and modern *explication de texte*. "You can't read Mendele [Moykher Sforim]," Alter argued, "you can't make sense of his language or the inventive play of his allusions without knowing Bible and Talmud and liturgy and Midrash—and without some awareness of the Yiddish in which his major achievements were first cast. But because Mendele's work is not only Hebrew but also artful fiction, you can't read him, you can't make sense of his artifices of narration and his fictional structures, without knowing a good deal about the dynamics of narrative." [34]

This regimen represented for Alter an ideal combination of tradition and modernity. While the program had its point of departure in Renoir's advocacy of the diachronic and synchronic study of literature, it was shaped by Alter's vision of the pluralism of Jewish culture. In one regard, however, Alter never took the linguistic requirements in his program as far as Arnold Band did at UCLA. Band insisted on "two examinations in Yiddish: one in the ability to read a critical article (for the M.A.) and the other designed to demonstrate the ability to analyze both Yiddish prose and poetry of the modern period." [35] In recent years, most Berkeley doctoral students in Hebrew literature have also done extensive work in Yiddish, thanks to Alter's colleague Chana Kronfeld, who is equally interested in Yiddish and Hebrew modernism.

What Alter came to call the "multiplicity or polyphonality" of Jewish tradition (interview) had always been evident to him. Yet how heterogeneous the Jews and their traditions really were became clear to him only through Gershom Scholem's work on Jewish mysticism, particularly his two volumes on Sabbatai Zevi. In 1967, Alter observed:

> The general effect of Scholem's pioneering research into Sabbatianism is to turn inside out many of our preconceptions of what is Jewish and what is not. If we think of Jews as tough-minded rationalists, wryly ironic realists, Scholem shows us a whole people emotionally caught up in the most fanatic faith, men and women alike wildly dancing, rolling on the ground, foaming at the mouth, uttering prophecies. If we think of Jews as people living within tightly drawn lines of legal restriction and self-imposed restraint, Scholem shows us Jews casting off all bonds, entering as they thought, into a new world of unlimited freedom where, according to the Sabbatian maxim, "the abrogation of the Torah is its true fulfillment." (AT 66)

The astonishing world Scholem opened to Alter made him impatient with all monolithic views of Judaism. And if Trilling's insistence on discrimination and knowledge of individual circumstances had not yet had its effect on Alter, Scholem's research drove home the importance of specific historic knowledge and the necessity to debunk sentimental myths about the "Hebrew mind" as a "set of collective mental attributes

. . . operating in unbroken continuity from the Bible to modern Israel."
When Jean Soler, a former cultural attaché to the French embassy in
Israel, proposed a new theory of kashrut in his article "The Dietary
Prohibitions of the Hebrews" (1979), Alter was stung by the narrowness
of Soler's views of Jewish thought, presented a more flexible theory of
kashrut, and admonished that "what should be avoided at all costs is
to reintroduce ethnic stereotypes into serious intellectual discourse by
constructing in the name of semiotic analysis a monolithic Hebrew mind
that dominates the actions of Jews from Leviticus to the Likud."[36]

On similar grounds, Alter disagreed with what he erroneously understood to be Cynthia Ozick's concept of Judaism; he considered it too
static, too exclusive, and too close to the notion of a "normative Judaism" proposed by George Foote Moore in the early twentieth century
and thoroughly discredited by Scholem (interview). For Alter, Judaism
is a culture in flux that nevertheless has remained continuous with itself:

> The clearest instance, I think, is the set of changes that starts about a
> century or a century and a half before the Christian era and goes on for
> the next two or three centuries, where you have a crystallization of
> Judaism which is radically different from the previous Judaism and yet
> defines itself as direct and legitimate heir to Judaism. I think that it is clear
> that Isaiah would not have recognized himself in the school of Rabbi
> Akiba and so forth. One can observe that very phenomenon by tracing
> the development of the Hebrew language. There is a fundamental change
> in all the structures and the vocabulary of the Hebrew language of the
> rabbis, which remains continuous with biblical Hebrew but is very differ-
> ent. My argument is that in the nineteenth and twentieth centuries at
> least part of Judaism—or maybe I should say Jewry—has undergone a
> similar profound set of changes while nevertheless maintaining a sense of
> continuity. I am unhappy with Cynthia Ozick's assumption that change
> cannot be legitimate, that change cancels out continuity. We can observe
> in Jewish history that this is not necessarily so. (interview)

Alter demonstrated his point in a short, riveting book, *The Invention
of Hebrew Prose* (1988), in which he traced the gradual forging of Hebrew
into a language capable of the intricate mimetic art of European literary
realism. Attaining that capacity, Alter explained, "was not just an aesthetic pursuit but a programmatic renegotiation of the terms of Jewish
collective identity."[37] Poems had always been written in Hebrew, but
they were ultimately aesthetic exercises. Novels, by contrast, especially
in the age of Dickens, Balzac, and Tolstoy, aimed at creating an illusion

of reality. And to do so in Hebrew, Alter pointed out, had been a difficult if not impossible task in the nineteenth century:

> To write a novel in Hebrew . . . was to constitute a whole world in a language not actually spoken in the real-life equivalent of that world, yet treated by the writer as if it were really spoken, as if a persuasive illusion of reality could be conveyed through a purely literary language. It was . . . to enter deeply into the mind-set of European culture with a thoroughness not characteristic of premodern Hebrew literature, it was to invent a new secular Hebrew cultural identity as if it were somehow, uncannily, native to the European sphere. (*IHP* 5)

Alter delineated how this was achieved by focusing on language as a mimetic tool in the fiction of Mendele Moykher Sforim, Uri Nissan Gnessin, and David Fogel. They, and writers like Yosef Haim Brenner and Micha Yosef Berdichevsky, enabled their readers to imagine the world in Hebrew. Alter compared their efforts to make "Hebrew think in a radically new way" under the impact of European modernity to "what the rabbis, two millennia earlier, under the pressures of Aramaic, Greek, Latin, and a transformed social-political world, had done with biblical Hebrew; and what, a thousand years later, in very different directions, the great medieval poets and the Jewish philosophers or their Hebrew translators did, under the pressures of Arabic language and literature and Greek thought." (*IHP* 94). The glue that held all these worlds together was "the uncanny binding force of the [Hebrew] language as a medium of cultural identity" (*IHP* 94). That this force had lost nothing of its effectiveness, but continued to integrate the past into the present, was due in part to the linguistic ingenuity of the early Hebrew novelists. At the end of their exertions stood the realization of a quixotic vision: the creation of a secular literature out of a still sacred language (*IHP* 11).

What a radically secular Jewish culture could be at the height of its intellectual refinement was the subject of Alter's next book. In *Necessary Angels: Tradition and Modernity in Kafka, Benjamin and Scholem* (1991), Alter not only thought through the productive tension between tradition and modernity in Jewish culture, he also pulled together materials that so far had led an orphaned existence in his own intellectual economy: his preoccupation with Scholem as radical revisionist, Scholem's friendship with Walter Benjamin, the importance of Kafka to both of them, and the Kafka-Agnon nexus, which had been perceived by both Scholem and Benjamin and had been among Alter's earliest literary interests.

The dust jacket to *Necessary Angels,* designed by Lisa Clark, was a stroke of genius. It showed a detail from Paul Gauguin's painting *The Vision after the Sermon.* Two figures, one bearded, one winged, both barefoot and in loose garments, are locked in a fight. The primary colors —yellow and blue, and even the red of the background—are the domain of the blond angel, who has gained the upper hand in the struggle, whereas Jacob, in black caftan and skullcap, is doubled over and seems almost vanquished. This episode from Genesis (32: 24–30) is the primal biblical scene of man asserting himself over the divine. The theme of Alter's book, the ascendancy of the secular over the divine, elucidated precisely that assertion and its consequences for Jewish culture. But the jacket illustration further suggested (through Jacob, who remains in the angel's grip) that no matter how strongly secular Jewish culture attempted to wriggle out of the confining grasp of its religious tradition, as long as it remains a literary culture it is inescapably tied to the strongest literary text in Western culture: the Hebrew Bible. Secular Jewish culture of the kind that mattered to Scholem and Benjamin shared in the dubious blessing Jacob received when he had finally overcome God's messenger. He was given the name "Israel"—contender with God.

Thus the project for which Alter has become best known, the analysis and interpretation of the Hebrew Bible as a coherent anthology of vastly different literary texts by methods previously reserved for secular prose and poetry, seemed not only an obvious but a necessary and timely enterprise. It was an act of secularization on Alter's part, which paralleled in the realm of criticism the quixotic endeavor of the early modern Hebrew writers: it brought the sacred into the secular world and thereby assured its continuity.

The daunting project started casually, in 1971, with an invitation to Alter from the Department of Religion at Stanford University to present an informal colloquium on the literary study of the Hebrew Bible. Some years later, "on an impulse," Alter took out his notes for the colloquium and developed them into an essay for *Commentary* entitled "A Literary Approach to the Bible." It appeared in the December 1975 issue. The response to it was overwhelming and encouraged Alter to go on. Around the same time he received complaints from students of modern Hebrew literature "that the only graduate courses in Bible offered at Berkeley were exclusively devoted to a close philological and historical scrutiny of the Book of Leviticus." Alter combined the students' interest with his own and, inspired by the pioneering work of Meir Sternberg and

Menakhem Perry on the poetics of biblical narrative, offered his first seminar on biblical narrative in 1977 and on biblical poetry in 1978.[38]

Three books soon resulted from Alter's studies: *The Art of Biblical Narrative* (1981), *The Art of Biblical Poetry* (1985), and *The Literary Guide to the Bible* (1987), coedited with Frank Kermode. The last book was reviewed in *the New York Review of Books* by Harold Bloom, who was then undertaking his own reading of the Hebrew Bible, *The Book of J* (1990). To Bloom's invention of a female J writer, Alter responded in *The World of Biblical Literature* (1992). Bloom had based his re-creation of the J writer on a translation of Genesis and parts of Exodus by the American poet David Rosenberg, a decision that Alter called "catastrophic." And while Alter "disagreed profoundly" with the imaginative contraptions of the Promethean Bloom, he conceded that *The Book of J* had at least the merit of having stirred up the anthill.[39]

In the wake of Bloom's *Book of J*, Alter found himself compelled to reconceive a text he thought he knew intimately. He embarked on his own translation of Genesis, to be accompanied by a brief literary commentary. "For years," Alter wrote, "I have been very unhappy with existing English translations, all of which in different ways do considerable violence to the literary values of the Hebrew and are variously inept as English narrative prose. This project is a kind of experiment for me, to see whether there is some way to create an English for the Hebrew Bible that is stylized and dignified but also idiomatic and reproduces at least some of the important stylistic effects of the Hebrew."[40]

When Alter completed his work in the fall of 1995, Everett Fox had just published his translation of the Five Books of Moses. Fox, a professor of Judaica at Clark University who had begun work on his translation twenty-seven years before, attempted to capture in English the linguistic and poetic qualities of the Hebrew original. Although Alter deeply appreciated Fox's effort to preserve what Alter called "the Hebrewness of Hebrew," Alter was unhappy with Fox's English style. "I am deeply convinced," Alter wrote, "that every good translation must express a simultaneous love affair with the language of the original and the language into which the translation is made. Fox's signal limitation is his monogamous attachment to the Hebrew, often at the cost of the English."[41] In his own version of Genesis, published in the fall of 1996, Alter rendered the biblical text in a cadenced English prose that corresponded to the rhythm of the Hebrew original. Alter's resourceful English reflected the stylistic variations of the original. Alter made shrewd use of archaisms since he saw "no good reason to render biblical Hebrew as contemporary English, either lexically or syntactically." [42]

Alter's translation project had a certain logic to it. It was inevitable that a scholar would eventually want to arrive at the beginning, in the way T. S. Eliot's lyric subject in *Four Quarters* wished to arrive in East Coker (and the poet himself arrived in England and at the baptismal fountain of the Anglican Church), and Pound found his way to Italy, and Joyce reworked the story of Ulysses with a Jewish hero, whose ancestral culture predates that of the Greeks. It seems that the author of so many books on Jewish modernity also needed to return to the inception of Jewish culture. But the Hebrew Bible is also the fountainhead of English literary culture. Through William Tyndale's translation and even more so through the Authorized Version of 1611, the Hebrew Bible became an English book whose literary style and moral authority reverberate through all of American and English literature. It is perhaps through his own attempts at an aesthetically pleasing and Jewishly informed English version of Genesis that Alter best managed to bring together the many aspects of his complex and productive career as an academic scholar of English and Hebrew letters and as a literary and cultural critic whose mission was the education of the general reader.

Alter was unusual in that he combined the best of what his two antithetical teachers Harry Levin and Lionel Trilling had to offer— scrupulous scholarship funneled into academic books on European literature and a sense of obligation to write on literary issues in their cultural and political context for readers of intellectual magazines. To his teachers' legacies Alter added his own commitment to the Jewish literary tradition to create an oeuvre that was unimaginable when Trilling and Levin attended college. It expressed Alter's identity as a Jewish member of an Anglophone culture who was in full possession of his family's and his nation's literary tradition.

Although Alter spent six years on translating the first book of the Hebrew Bible, he never wavered in his commitment to the "indispensability of Hebrew." [43] Alter's insistence on the importance of Hebrew for the shaping and maintenance of Jewish identity in America found vocal support in an unexpected quarter. In an essay entitled "The Hebrew Imperative," Ruth Wisse, a professor of Yiddish literature at Harvard University, pointed out that "Judaism in English lacks the dimension of historical time, without which there is no Jewish people." Moreover, direct "access to the sources has always been a key to status within Jewish life," since those who can read the Torah in Hebrew "are rightly recognized by those who cannot as more 'authentically' Jewish." Jews without Hebrew, Wisse argued, "remain forever marginal, unable to become full participants in prayer and study." More deleterious still are the effects of Jewish illiteracy on the young. Wisse claimed that

a Jewish child who is obliged to master a section of the Torah in Hebrew by the end of the first grade in his Sunday or afternoon religious school will know exactly what distinguishes him from his non-Jewish neighbors: the ability to read the Torah in Hebrew by the end of first grade. But more often, the school this child attends will require no such effort of mastery, but will rely instead on a curriculum based on the teaching of "values." Thus the typical American Jewish child will learn that Jews are particularly concerned for the welfare of other human beings, for trees and for animals, and for whatever else is deemed ethically important at the moment. The intelligent child will also learn to dismiss this unwelcome and presumptuous effort to separate him artificially from his Gentile fellow-Americans, who are patently no less kind and no less sensitive than he.[44]

But why ought Jews to insist on a distinction as dubious in practical value as access to the Torah in Hebrew? For Wisse, the point is that the acquisition of a language that is also the language of an independent, internationally recognized state increases one's interest in, and possibly solidarity with, that state. How far one should go in one's solidarity, however, is an issue on which Alter and Wisse do not see eye to eye. Wisse's unequivocal commitment to a strong Israel is partly the result of her analysis of the fatal mistakes made by the intellectual elite of Yiddish culture.

10

The Lessons of Yiddish Culture: Ruth R. Wisse

Europe

TO SAY THAT RUTH ROSKIES WISSE, Harvard's first professor of Yiddish literature, was born in Czernowitz in 1936 is to indicate right away an extraordinary fate in an ordinary beginning. For much of its life, Czernowitz has been a provincial town. Today, Chernovtsy is part of Ukraine; but between 1918 and 1940, and again from 1941 to 1944, Cernauti belonged to Romania, which annexed the province of Bukovina (along with Bessarabia and Transylvania) when the Austro-Hungarian Empire fell apart at the end of World War I. The Habsburg monarchy too had acquired the Bukovina through annexation (from Moldavia, a principality of Romania) in 1775, declaring the province an Austrian duchy and Czernowitz its capital.

The Jews were not much liked by the Austrian military administration (1774–87), but the Rescript of Toleration, signed by Emperor Joseph II in 1782, improved their legal status and eased their distressed social situation. The same ruler's *Juden Patent* of 1789 became the basis of the constitution of the Czernowitz Jewish community. The short-lived revolt of 1848 in Vienna failed to emancipate the Jews; but the administrative reform of 1849, during which the Bukovina was split off from Galicia and elevated to a crown land, strengthened the standing of the Jews. German speakers made up one-third of the region's population, but the majority of the people, particularly in the countryside, continued to speak Romanian and Ukrainian.

The December Constitution of 1867 finally granted Jews full civil

304

rights within the Habsburg Empire and established them as an autonomous *Kultusgemeinde* (religious and cultural community). In the spring of that same year, the Romanian minister of the interior, Ion Bratianu, ordered the expulsion of Romanian Jews from their villages and the banishment of noncitizens from the country. As refugees flocked into Czernowitz, the establishment of a protective legal and administrative framework became as important as the creation of a social and intellectual Jewish infrastructure similar to that in other cities of the Habsburg Empire. Jewish institutions to take care of the sick and the needy, of orphans, widows, and students, and to bury the dead existed in some form in all Jewish communities; but those in Czernowitz were modeled on the organizations of Austrian Jewry.

Ties to Vienna were strengthened further when in 1879 the Alliance Israélite of Vienna established its center for the crown land of Bukovina in Czernowitz. These ties explain why such a large portion of the city's Jews—certainly its professionals, artists, and intellectuals—spoke German in a provincial town tucked away in the far-eastern corner of the Habsburg Empire, where the closest neighbors were Ukrainians, Moldavians, Romanians, Hungarians, Slovaks, and Poles. Curiously enough, the Jews not only became a cultural outpost but a supporting pillar of the crumbling Habsburg monarchy. In 1875, Franz Joseph University opened its doors in Czernowitz. The language of instruction was German (until 1921, when the university was reorganized into a Romanian institution), and Jewish professors were as welcome as Jewish students, who made up about one-third of the student body. In fact, the first speaker at the inauguration ceremony was a Jewish student, Edward Reiß, who would eventually serve as the city's mayor (1905–7).

German remained the language of the Czernowitz Jews, especially of the financial upper crust and the educated classes, even after the annexation of the Bukovina by Romania after World War I. This fact did not endear the Jews to the government in Bucharest, nor did it bring them any closer to the rural populace, whose sentiments were strongly anti-Austrian. Israel Chalfen, a biographer of the Czernowitz-born poet Paul Celan, claims that even after Czernowitz had officially become a Romanian town, it remained "eine jüdische Stadt deutscher Sprache," a Jewish city of German language.[1] In the late 1920s, Jews made up one-third of the city's 150,000 inhabitants. They lived all over town, but the center of Czernowitz was dominated by business signs engraved with Jewish names announcing that shops and offices were owned by Jewish craftsmen and artisans, merchants and businessmen, lawyers and doctors. Yiddish too was a strong presence in Czernowitz. The three German Jewish dailies competed with a number of Yiddish newspapers, and occasionally even Hebrew magazines and journals were to be had. The first international, interparty conference to deal with problems of linguistic standardization in Yiddish, as well as with the role of Yiddish in Jewish life, was held in Czernowitz from August 30 to September 4, 1908.

Strangely enough, the idea of a world conference on Yiddish was proposed by a German-speaking Jew from Vienna, Nathan Birnbaum, who had learned Yiddish for ideological reasons and for its utility in reaching the Jewish masses. Disillusioned with Theodor Herzl's Zionism (a term coined by Birnbaum in his journal *Selbstemanzipation)* because of the Zionists' disregard for the Diaspora, Birnbaum gradually endorsed the concept of an "interterritorial nation, comprising and integrating all existing Jewish groups which had a cultural life of their own." Such an independent cultural life was most evident among the Yiddish-speaking Jews of Eastern Europe. Hence Yiddish became a cornerstone in Birnbaum's theories of Jewish cultural autonomy. The first step was to gain recognition for Yiddish as a language in its own right after centuries of dismissal as a jargon by German-speaking Jews. Having proclaimed, in 1906 and 1907, the important cultural value of Yiddish in his own weekly, *Neue Zeitung,* Birnbaum was ready to take action. In 1908 he moved to Czernowitz, where he edited the Yiddish papers *Dos folk* and *Vokhen-blatt* (1908–11) and helped organize the Czernowitz language conference.

The convention was attended or commented upon by everybody who was anybody in Yiddish letters. The seventy delegates to the conference, who included Jews of all ideological stripes, from Zionist Hebraists to militant Bundists, were supposed to discuss a ten-point agenda that included Yiddish spelling, grammar, and lexicon (especially foreign and new words), a Yiddish dictionary, Jewish youth and the Yiddish language (that is, the danger of assimilation), the Yiddish press, the Yiddish theater, the economic status of Yiddish writers and actors, and the recognition of Yiddish as a language. The last point, closest to Birnbaum's heart, dominated the discussion of the delegates. After a long debate a compromise was worked out between the delegates who espoused Hebrew as the only Jewish national language and the delegates who considered Yiddish the living Jewish language and Hebrew the language of prayer and the past. The assembly proclaimed Yiddish as *a* (not *the*) national language of the Jews and demanded its political, cultural, and social equality with other languages.[2]

This resolution left the conference participants free to take any stand on Hebrew they wanted, while it launched "Yiddishism," as David Roskies was to write, "as a secular movement aspiring towards national autonomy in Eastern Europe." A note of caution was introduced by I. L. Peretz, the main speaker at the conference, who was certainly the most celebrated Yiddish writer after Mendele Moykher Sforim and Sholem Aleichem, both of whom had declined to participate. He came and delivered an optimistic but, as Wisse pointed out, less than enthusiastic keynote address:

> Much as he wanted Yiddish to become the national language of the Jews, he felt that it still lacked some of the requirements to substantiate that title. He objected to the exaggerated claims the organizers were making for Yiddish, and to their practical agenda. . . . Peretz felt that Yiddish could never serve as the national language of the Jews unless the Tanakh, the complete Hebrew Bible, were available in excellent Yiddish translation. . . . His tempered embrace of Yiddish . . . earned him the suspicion of the younger ideologues. Hebraists accused him of betraying the Jewish national future while Yiddishists accused him of chauvinism, conservatism, and religious backsliding.[3]

At the time of the Czernowitz language conference, the parents of Ruth Wisse and David Roskies were two-and three-year-old children growing up in educated, financially successful families in Bialystok (Poland) and Vilna (Lithuania), respectively. In the two decades following the conference, the center of an intellectual preoccupation with Yiddish shifted from Czernowitz to Vilna, where in 1925 a thirty-one-year-old Marburg-trained philologist by the name of Max Weinreich established the Yiddish Scientific Institute *(yidisher visnshaftlekher institut),* better known by its acronym, YIVO. Wisse's parents met at Vilna's Stephen Báthory University and married in 1929. Three years later, they settled in Czernowitz with the first two of their five children—not out of love for that complicated city, now under Romanian sovereignty, but because professional opportunity had dictated the move.

Wisse's father, Leo (Leibl) Roskies, had earned a master's degree in chemical engineering and gone to work for a Jew who owned a rubber factory in Krosno (southern Poland). Shortly thereafter Romania stopped importing rubber in an effort to develop its own industry, and Roskies's employer sent his twenty-seven-year-old junior engineer to Czernowitz to build a rubber factory to service northern Romania. Roskies completed this task within a year and stayed to supervise the new plant. He was so successful that King Carol of Romania gave him a gold medal, an award that would become of the utmost importance a few years later.

As general manager and part owner of Romania's largest rubber factory, Caurum, Roskies prospered financially, but his own and his wife's relationship to their wealth remained complicated and uneasy. Shortly after their immigration to Romania, their second child, an exceptionally beautiful girl, died of pneumonia. Wisse speculated that this event reinforced her parents' discomfort about their new prosperity: "The moment of their greatest triumph was always associated with the loss of this beloved child as well as with the fact that they had become wealthy at one of the most problematic times in history."[4] Leo Roskies and his wife were very much aware of the political developments in Germany, Russia, and Romania, and of the impact these developments might have on their lives because they were Jews. Roskies, who belonged to a group called Massada, "a mildly Zionist organization, really more like a cultural club, for Jewish professionals and their wives,"[5] made speeches about the need for Jews to get out of Europe; but he took no such steps himself. "The myth in my family," Wisse explained, "is that my father would have gone to Palestine if it had not been for my mother, who liked comfort too much. However, my own view of family dynamics is different, more complicated. Ambivalences often express themselves by attributing to one spouse the mixed feelings of both" (interview). Meanwhile, the children were educated in the multilingual fashion of Czernowitz. Benjamin, born in 1931, was soon old enough to be sent to a Romanian school. He became fluent in the country's language. His sister Ruth, by contrast, born in 1936, had a German governess, a Jewish woman by the name of Peppi, and so acquired German as her mother tongue. Her parents spoke Yiddish between themselves. But among friends they probably attempted German or spoke Polish and Russian when that was more convenient.

Throughout the 1930s the Roskies household continued to operate with a certain nonchalance and selflessness—concern for the welfare of others being a greater priority for Leo Roskies than concern for one's own privileged self—while the snare was slowly tightened around the

Jews of Romania. By the mid-1930s, Jewish banks began to have problems getting credit from the big Romanian banks. Heavy taxes were
levied on Jewish businesses, and they were prohibited from importing
raw materials and goods.[6] The economic prospects for Jews in Romania
looked grim. During Passover of 1939, Leo's father, David Roskies, a
blind man of sharp intelligence, gathered the family around his seder
table in Bialystok. He was a successful textile merchant who understood
that productivity was no protection for Jews. David Roskies instructed
his family to escape to safety. "Grandfather told the assembled family
members that they must set out for Canada to buy a textile factory, and
thus transplant their business to the new continent. He directed his
second son [there were four in all] and eldest grandson to leave immediately after the holidays; such was his authority that they did, buying a
mill in the Province of Quebec where unemployment and anti-Semitism
were both at a peak (ours being one of the very few cases in which the
exigency of the former phenomenon would outweigh the virulence of
the latter)."[7] Barely six months later, German troops occupied Bialystok
for one week (September 15–22) and then transferred the city to Soviet
Russia. Less than two years later, however, having broken the nonaggression pact with Stalin and declared war on Russia, the Germans returned
to Bialystok for a second occupation that lasted from June 27, 1941, to
July 27, 1944. During that time the Germans murdered the fifty thousand Jews of Bialystok. The ghetto to which the Jews were confined on
August 1, 1941, was liquidated two years later, on August 16, 1943.[8]
David Roskies and his daughter Perele, who had stayed behind with her
family to assist her blind father, perished.

Leo Roskies did not attend his father's last seder in unoccupied Bialystok because his two children, Benjamin and Ruth, were sick with
scarlet fever. There is little doubt, however, that Leo too had been urged
by his father to leave Europe, and in the spring of 1940, he prepared his
family's departure. He went to Bucharest to procure the necessary papers. One of the problems was that as a native of Bialystok, Roskies had
only Polish papers, which would have doomed the travelers. Combining
verbal and monetary persuasion, he obtained exit visas on the strength
of the medal he had received from King Carol and on the condition of
never returning. The arrangements for the travel papers had taken two
months. When the signal for departure arrived by telephone from Bucharest, the family in Czernowitz packed up a few belongings in great
haste and left their home within two hours on June 22, 1940.[9] They fled

not so much from the Germans as from the approaching Russian army and from the retreating Romanian regiments, who murdered many Jews, particularly in northern Bukovina and Moldavia.[10]

Roskies and his wife and children traveled as stateless persons by train to Bucharest, where they stayed for a few weeks before continuing to Athens and from there by boat to Lisbon. The Portuguese capital was then one of the major points of transit to the Americas. Despite the obstinacy of the American consul, the family managed to obtain transit visas through New York and sailed from Lisbon on the second day of Rosh Hashanah 1940. They were four of the 626 Jews admitted to Canada that year.[11]

Family

In Montreal, Leo Roskies went to work in the textile factory that his older brothers, Shiye, Isaac, and Enoch, had set up in Huntington, Quebec, sixty miles south of Montreal. He would have preferred to remain in the field he loved, but the Canadian rubber industry was not yet hiring Jews. Leo Roskies was an idealist, who enjoyed doing things for other people. It was painful for him to have lost his professional independence, not only because it hurt his self-esteem to be reduced to a small shareholder in the family business but also because it curtailed what he might do for others. Although under his management the mill turned a profit and there were no strikes, Roskies never felt successful enough. "My father was a very complicated man, who tried to suppress his sadness." Wisse recalled "Photographs show my father as a very happy man. However, I remember most vividly that one day we were sitting in the living room and he declared himself to be a failure. He said, 'I am sorry that I am a failure.' I think my father blamed himself for many things, including his father's death, including his inability to save more lives, including his inability to become in Canada what he had been in Czernowitz" (interview). His "failure" was real only to him; to an outside observer Leo Roskies and his family appeared to prosper. Two more children, Eva and David, were born during the 1940s and grew up in close proximity to—yet worlds apart from—their European-born siblings.

The oldest child, Benjamin, had just turned nine when his family fled Europe. In Montreal he was immediately sent to an English school. As his sister Ruth was to write years later, "the burden of adaptation fell heaviest on him, as it always does on immigrant children who are well past cuteness but too young to have learned the social defenses of adults. Placed in a strange grade five, reduced to an unfamiliar language, he was most acutely embarrassed by the external sign of his estrangement—the Romanian schoolboy knickers that made him clownishly conspicuous among the Canadian boys all in pants. But he was expected to swallow his humiliation. . . . When he asked one day for a pair of trousers, mother reminded him that Hitler was rounding up his naked cousins and uncles all over Europe." [12]

During their flight through Europe, Benjamin and Ruth had been instructed never to reveal anything about their home or family to strangers. When Ruth was withdrawn without explanation from the English Protestant school she and her brother initially attended, Benjamin was called into the principal's office. Of course he remembered his parents' instructions. When he later told the story of what ensued, his family would dissolve in nervous, painful laughter. "It was not healthy laughter," Ruth Wisse said, as she recounted the story.

My brother plays dumb.
 "Where is your sister?"
 "I don't know."
 "Is she sick?"
 "I don't know."
 "Will she be coming back to school?"
 "I don't know."
 "When you wake up in the morning, is your sister at home with you?"
 "I don't know."

The nightmare never let him out of its grip. [13]

Benjamin Roskies grew up an intensely intellectual, warm, and pensive man, devoid of ferocity but full of passion. Wisse described him as "an idealist without portfolio." For a year, after the founding of the state of Israel, his Zionist group met in his parents' living room to plan a trip to the new Jewish state, "a holy mission of their own rich imagination." Ruth was caught up in the excitement.

They were so fervent, so glamorous. Their collective departure [in 1949 on the *S.S. Tabinta*] was the boldest thing I had ever known. I kept beside my bed a snapshot of my brother in a trenchcoat, against the rail of the ship, and turning toward it each morning the way pious Jews turn eastward in prayer, I pledged my own ascent. It was a curse to be five years

younger than their eighteen, unable to master the terms of discussion or
to join in defending the homeland.[14]

What most distinguished Ruth from Benjamin was fervor of the kind
Wisse expressed in this passage and in many of her essays. Being only
four years old at the time of their flight, Wisse had not been deprived of
the capacity for optimism. The difference emerged most clearly in the
way the two siblings responded to the Passover Haggadah. In Europe,
Masha and Leo Roskies had not made their own seders; but once they
reached Montreal they decided to do so in order to celebrate their exodus
into freedom. "There must have been a terrible desperation about it,"
Wisse wrote, because years later, when she asked her mother about that
first seder she prepared in 1941, "she was too agitated to respond and later
explained that my questioning had dug open a pit before her eyes." It is
pits, the burning pits of Eastern Europe, that fire Wisse's response to the
Haggadah. Reflecting on one of its poems, Wisse wrote,

Our ancestors, those who were neither killed nor cowed, saved themselves through a blast of rage. Today we follow their example, verbally.
The natural place to commemorate the European massacre occurs right
before the *shfoykh khamoskho:*

> Pour out Thy wrath upon the nations that know Thee not,
> And upon the kingdoms that call not upon Thy name.
> For they have devoured Jacob,
> And laid waste his habitation.
> Pour out Thine indignation upon them.
> And let the fierceness of Thine anger overtake them.
> Thou wilt pursue them in anger, and destroy them
> From under the heavens of the Lord!

The custom of reciting these verses . . . originated after the Crusades of
the 11th and 12th centuries when Christian Europe made the first of
several attempts to cleanse itself of Jews. . . . Before emitting their eloquent howl, Jews customarily flung open the doors of their houses. . . .
[W]e are well placed historically to appreciate the charged fury of our
medieval forefathers. . . . My brother-in-law can cite relevant psychoanalytic writings testifying to the sources of depression in stifled anger. For
myself, I need that outburst and the rush of cold air through the open
door as much as I once needed my mother's love and my father's approval.
I want those who hunt the Jews to be hunted down themselves, wiped
from under the heavens of the Lord. I feel ashamed not at the demand

for retribution, but at how little Jews have done to bring their destroyers
to trial.

Wisse's anger is directed outward, and therefore optimistic, affirmative, insistent on life in the present, or, as she once wrote of her mother,
"dedicated to the defeat of death." [15] Not all family members had her
energy and healing capacity for anger. Although the family had escaped
death, its long shadow pursued them in the form of depression. Her
older brother especially could not shake it off; eventually it engulfed him
entirely, and he hastened the end of his life. Benjamin's desire to die,
which Wisse attributes to the mental stress caused by the family's displacement and the gruesome destruction of the European Jews, may
hold an important key to Wisse's later readings of Jewish literature and
her political views. It may explain why she came to prefer wrath over
contemplation, and physical strength over moral perseverance in defeat. [16]
Wisse struggled for years to accept her brother's deliberate death. She
was furious at being abandoned by him and blamed herself for not
having been able to prevent his death. In 1989 she confessed, "I have
not yet made my peace with him for hastening the end of his life at the
age of forty-three and would drag him from the grave by his grassy hair
if I could. Apart from my parents, he was the most important influence
on my life." [17]

Benjamin is indeed an unacknowledged presence in much of Wisse's
later work, invisibly conducting the traffic of her ideas, as he had conducted his family's singing around the seder table. At the time of his
death in 1974, Wisse was just beginning to come into her own as
an intellectual. To her brother, who was becoming politically more
conservative because he thought left-wing radicalism frightening, she
had always been a radical. [18] But in the early 1970s, Wisse began to
rethink her views in the way Norman Podhoretz had begun to reconsider his political position in the late 1960s. [19] And as she closed in on
her brother's views, she became possessed by the desire to tell him that
she now understood his thinking. Since this was impossible, her political
writings included his presence and spoke sometimes as if in his behalf.
While in her literary critical work Wisse explored the origins of the
topos of moral perseverance as a strategy of defensive accommodation,
she demonstrated in her political essays that it was an inadequate response. Urging Jews to think about how absurd it was to turn the hatred
of others for them into self-reproach and encouraging them to become
active on their own behalf, Wisse argued that goodness was a necessary

but not a sufficient condition for survival. Concern for the preservation of one's moral integrity was a response to adversity that blamed the self and let the destroyers get away with murder. If Benjamin had indeed been serious about his conservative position, he would soon have recognized the need to exchange his baton if not for a bayonet, then at least for a sturdier stick.

Although Wisse may not have been a radical in the political sense of the New York Intellectuals, she was determined to go her own way. "I almost compulsively like to go against the grain," she said. "I have to stop myself these days because it is not the way I enjoy functioning any longer; but in those days it was enough for me to see everyone going in one direction to move in the other" (interview). In this, Wisse was clearly her mother's daughter. It was Masha Welczer Roskies who invented an original life for her family upon their arrival in Montreal by marching into the opposite direction of where Canada's financially successful Jewish immigrant families were going.

Masha Roskies made a crucial decision when the family settled in Montreal. She ruled that the language spoken at home was to be Yiddish. Through her storytelling she also rerouted the family tradition from Czernowitz to Vilna, because Vilna was her "bedrock of memory."[20] Her youngest son, David, born in Montreal in 1948, remembered that his "mother's monologues were never in the here and now, the present was only a springboard for her to reminisce about the past; the real world was Vilna. And all stories, all roads, led back to Vilna" (DR). Wisse concurred that her mother's identification "was with Jewish Vilna, which to her was a community under siege." Vilna served as transit center and asylum for Jewish refugees from the surrounding villages during World War I, when Masha Welczer, born in 1906, was growing up. Whether Poles or Germans occupied the city, as the front shifted back and forth, made no difference to the Jews, since both occupiers requisitioned food and property from Jews and conscripted them into forced labor. In the course of the Bolshevik Revolution in Russia, Vilna was flooded with Jews fleeing from pogroms and civil war, severely taxing the resources of the city's Jewish community. After the armistice in western Europe, the struggle for Vilna continued between Lithuanians and Poles, and Jews were again subjected to Polish aggression. On April 21, 1919, two days after the Poles had taken back the city, Polish troops beat, tortured, and killed eighty Jews. In July 1920, the district of Vilna officially became part of the Polish Republic.[21]

While Jewish Vilna may have supplied Masha Welczer with her

motto, "life is a battlefield," her ties to Vilna were strengthened by the hardships of those years. During the 1920s, Masha Welczer was caught up in the excitement of Vilna's dynamic literary and artistic circles; and their language was Yiddish. Not only did the majority of Jews speak Yiddish, but Vilna was, as Israel Klausner put it, "a world center for Yiddish culture." It boasted a Yiddish morning and evening newspaper; political, literary, educational, and scientific journals; a historical and ethnographic society; a museum and archives; a newly founded institute for Jewish research (YIVO); energetic circles of scholars, writers, and poets *(Yung Vilne);* and a sophisticated musical scene and intense theater life, to which Masha Welczer found herself particularly attracted.[22] David Roskies told the story that when his mother was engaged to be married to his father in 1929, her future mother-in-law, Hodel Ney Roskies, exacted only two promises from her: that she would keep a kosher home and that she would not associate any longer with Yiddish actors. "Apparently she consented, and then promptly violated both promises throughout the rest of her married life" (DR). It was this life that Masha Welczer packed away when she followed her husband to Krosno in 1930 and to Czernowitz in 1932 and unpacked in Montreal in the fall of 1940 to create an extraordinary home.

Montreal

Masha Roskies found herself thrown into the upscale society of Westmount, which reminded her painfully of the follies of her Russifying siblings in Vilna. What her sisters-in-law represented—upward mobility and Anglicization—was not what Masha Roskies aspired to. After a year in Westmount, she moved her family to the opposite end of the city, literally on the other side of the hill, where the majority of Montreal's Jews had settled. Encouraged by the city's pattern of ethnic self-segregation, the Jews not only cultivated their own language, Yiddish, but established an extensive and intricate network of social, educational, cultural, and artistic institutions. Rather than playing second fiddle to her sisters-in-law, Masha Roskies settled her family in a middle-class neighborhood of Outremont. A few years later, in 1950, the family moved again, this time into their permanent home on Pagnuelo Street in a hilly section of Outremont "where French Canadians lived and a fair amount of Jews; not our kind of Jews, but Jews who were on the way up in the world" (DR). David Roskies remembered their home as a "big brick house, with thirteen rooms, sun-porch, breakfast room, very large living room, grand piano, fancy furniture, and many, many, many paintings. This was in the early 1950s, when the majority of Jews in Montreal were either working class or just barely beginning to show signs of upward mobility" (DR).

In this environment Masha Roskies refined the vision of herself that she had already begun to act upon in Westmount. She hosted a Yiddish literary salon and sponsored Jewish artists—poets like Melech Ravitch, whom she engaged as a tutor for Benjamin and later for Ruth, painters like Alexander Bercovitch, who would come to the house to give lessons to the older children, and Yiddish theater folk like Chayele Grober of the Yiddish Theater Group (Yiteg). "The gatherings were quite fancy affairs," David Roskies recalled. "Yiddish culture was always something that we looked up to and that we aspired to be part of. It was not a mere vestige of some distant immigrant past; it was highbrow culture" (DR). Among the habitués of these evenings were the educators Shimshon Dunsky and Shloyme Wiseman, directors of the Yidishe Folk Shule; Mordechai Husid, editor of the Yiddish paper *Kanader Odler;* the poets Melech Ravitch and Rochel Korn; the novelist Chava Rosenfarb; and many other local writers and lovers of literature.[23]

Small wonder then, that most of Wisse's early schooling was in Yiddish. She had lost all knowledge of German during the family's traumatic flight and now acquired Yiddish and, later, English as her primary languages. The Yiddish she heard spoken at home was refined and genteel. "Yiddish as a vulgar street language was something that we had absolutely no exposure to," David Roskies said. His sister concurred, "In our home, words for sex, sexual organs, and bodily functions grow rusty behind comfortable euphemisms, and if we know them at all, it is from Weinreich's *Modern English-Yiddish, Yiddish-English Dictionary.*"[24]

Once installed in Outremont, Benjamin and Ruth as well as the *keneder kinder,* Eva and David, were sent to a Zionist-Labor school, the Yidishe Folk Shule. There were other options: the communist Morris Winchevsky school, the socialist Avraham Reisin school, the Labor-Zionist Peretz school (where Hebrew played a smaller part in the curriculum than in the Folk Shule), the Zionist-traditionalist Talmud Torah, and the Zionist orthodox school of Adath Israel.[25] The Roskies children and the Folk Shule were a good match. "The *folkshule* was our second home," Wisse recalled. "The Yiddish of our family, even to the Lithuanian pronunciation, was the language of most of my teachers; the atmosphere of warmth (or overbearing concern), the single-minded emphasis on intellectual prowess, were entirely familiar." In terms of observance, "the school was again like our home: respectful of tradition but secular." One took the High Holidays, Rosh Hashanah and Yom Kippur, in stride and got through Shavuot and Sukkot as best one could. Hanukkah, Purim, and Passover, by contrast, were happily celebrated since they could easily be thought of as national holidays, calling for the observance of many customs and rituals and few prayers. For the all-important holiday of Passover, Wisse reported, "we studied the [*shfoykh khamoskho*], pleading with God to pour out His wrath on the nations that knew Him not, but omitting the *hallel*, offering Him no praise for His efforts." The students noticed the discrepancies between orthodox Jewish practice and their own, but, as Wisse observed, "we understood that our departures represented a forward move to modernity, from faith, that is, to secularism." [26]

What the school truly cared about were the pivotal events in Jewish history. In those years they were happening before everybody's eyes:

> At a school assembly the principal explained the extermination of European Jewry: if each of you children were to take an empty notebook and write on every line of every page the name of a child, and if we were then to collect from this whole auditorium all your notebooks, the names would still not equal the number of Jewish children killed by the Germans. My notebook came alive with horror . . . and if I were to tear out half the pages! Cheat on the spaces at the top and bottom! But my guilt was assured because I could never make it less.

Steeped in the misery of the European Jews, the students followed "with feverish intensity" the struggle for the state of Israel, "smarting with the guilt of our absence." [27] A year after the founding of the new state in May 1948, Wisse graduated from the Folk Shule, and as her older brother left for volunteer work in Israel, she was about to enter a world very unlike home.

In 1949, Wisse began to attend an English-speaking Protestant high school. [28] Although her class was composed of the top-ranking students, school held no intellectual excitement for her. She got involved in drama, sports, student government—anything to relieve the boredom of classes. "I even got myself appointed mascot of the boys' basketball team because I had discovered that they left school once a week at two o'clock to go play another high school" (interview). Her great love was talk, argument, debate. "My model was the five rabbis [mentioned in the Haggadah], who according to the legend, tell about the departure from

Egypt all night long, until their disciples come to them and say, 'Masters, the time has come to read the morning *shema.*' For years I pictured myself as a participant in that all-night session where the talk would be so stimulating that dawn would catch us unawares. . . . Throughout my teens and far beyond, I took the discussion of life to be its essential part. . . . Edmund Wilson [was] then my ideal intellectual. . . ." [29]

Wisse enrolled at McGill University in 1953. But its English department turned out to be a great disappointment. "It was flat; there were one or two good teachers. But the rest taught literature as it if was sawdust" (interview). In her sophomore year Wisse discovered among the faculty the poet Louis Dudek, who in 1951 had returned from an extended stay in New York City. Dudek, born in Montreal in 1918 to Polish parents, graduated from McGill in 1939 and, after a brief stint in advertising, moved to New York City, where he started graduate work in English literature at Columbia University in the fall of 1943. He held a lectureship in English at City College from 1946 to 1951 and then decided to return to Montreal.

The writing of poetry, rather than literary criticism, had been Dudek's primary interest in New York. Dudek's poems of this period reflected his great admiration for Ezra Pound, whom he assisted during Pound's confinement at St. Elizabeth's Hospital.[30] The other great influence on Dudek was Lionel Trilling, whose adviser, Emory E. Neff, also directed Dudek's dissertation. Trilling's influence surfaced in a course Dudek offered at McGill, called "Great Writings of European Literature," which he taught in the format of Columbia's Great Books course. Wisse took this course, a two-year sequence, and described it as the sum total of her intellectual life at McGill. "It was indescribably exciting. We were expected to read the great works of European literature, some thirty-six books, at an enormous pace—*A la recherche du temps perdu, Ulysses, Crime and Punishment, War and Peace,* each in about one week" (interview). What attracted Wisse to Dudek was his passionate Europeanism. Only later did she realize that Dudek's imaginative immersion in Europe was his way of assimilating, and that he believed he was facilitating the process of assimilation for his Jewish students by not allowing the word *Jew* into the classroom. Dudek thought that "he was going to make [it] easier for us [to enter Western Civilization] by not burdening us Jews with the onus of Judaism." [31] Similarly, Dudek thought of his own descent as an impediment to his immersion in Europe's high culture. "He had completely squelched his Polish background. In the two years of his course, he never taught a Polish writer. He taught Manzoni and Céline and André Gide but no Polish author. He assimilated with a degree of dedication that went far beyond anything I had ever seen in Jews, because in Montreal Jews did not assimilate. They could not" (interview).

Wisse graduated with honors from McGill in 1957 and on the eve of graduation got married, which she wanted "more than anything" (interview). As a student she had spent most of her time working on the *McGill Daily*, whose features editor she was in 1957. A year earlier she had received a scholarship from the Canadian Women's Press Club and thereby had gotten to know a lot of women who worked in the Montreal Women's Press Club. They recommended her for a job as press officer at the Canadian Jewish Congress, which she got. She put out a newspaper for the organization for two years, and it was not until she arranged for the Canadian tour of the poet Abraham Sutzkever that extraordinary things began to happen again.

The Vilna Intellectuals

Wisse called Abraham Sutzkever's life "a microcosm of modern Jewry." [32] He was born in 1913 in Smorgón, an industrial town southwest of Vilna. During World War I, when the Russian army ordered the Jews of Smorgón to leave within twenty-four hours, the Sutzkevers moved to Omsk, in western Siberia. There Sutzkever's father died at the age of thirty. In 1920, Sutzkever's mother, Reine, returned west with her two children and settled in Vilna. Sutzkever was soon swept up in the burgeoning Yiddish culture of Vilna. He joined the Vilna Jewish scouts organization, the Bee, which promoted secular Yiddish culture and the love of nature. In the Vilna of that era, Benjamin Harshav wrote, "there was an aristocratic conception of the purity of language and elitist literature, of Yiddish as a part of world literature, measuring its achievements by the highest criteria." [33]

In the 1930s, when Sutzkever was writing poetry pervaded by a pantheistic admiration of nature, he became associated with an exciting group of writers and painters known as *Yung Vilne*, which included Shmerke Kaczerginsky, Leyzer Wolf, Peretz Miransky, Elchonon Vogler, Shimshon Kahan, Chaim Grade, and the painters Ben-Zion Michtom and Rosa Sutzkever (no relation). When German troops marched into Vilna on June 24, 1941, Sutzkever went into hiding in a crawl space in his mother's tiny apartment in the suburb of Snipishok. There he continued to write poetry, which, he believed, kept him alive. The imperative of survival became identical with the necessity of writing poetry. Each word had to be selected with the greatest care: "Tread over words as over a minefield; one false step, one false move, and the words you have been stringing together on your veins all your life will be torn to pieces together with you." [34] For Sutzkever everything hung on the precision of each Yiddish word. "In the face of so much degradation," Wisse was to explain, "Sutzkever's passion for the exactitude of every word and every syllable is the highest restorative measure of dignity." [35]

In September 1941, Sutzkever was apprehended by the Lithuanians —to be shot. After a mock execution during which he was forced to dig his own grave, he was marched into the newly established ghetto (*SPP* 17). Two years later, in September 1943, shortly after the Germans began the total liquidation of the ghetto, Sutzkever and his wife Freydke escaped through the sewers and broke through to a Byelorussian partisan group that operated in the forests and swamps around Lake Narocz. When German spies reached them in the swamp, the Sutzkevers hid deep in the freezing water. In March 1944, the Anti-Fascist Committee of the USSR decided to airlift Sutzkever from German-occupied territory to Moscow. His poetic summons to cultural and physical resistance had made him a symbol of heroism. More specifically, his rescue was due to the fact that during the last months of the Vilna ghetto, Sutzkever had some of his poems smuggled to the partisans in the forests surrounding Vilna. From there, his long poem *Kol Nidre* made its way to Moscow, where it created an enormous impression. For the first time Russian (Jewish) intellectuals were made aware of the full extent and exorbitant cruelty of the Final Solution. Ilya Ehrenburg, whose columns in *Pravda* were read even at the front, compared *Kol Nidre* to a Greek tragedy (*BP* 16; *SPP* 20). In a very physical sense, then, Sutzkever and his wife owed their survival to the quality of the poet's work.

In 1946, Sutzkever testified at the Nuremberg trials on behalf of Russian Jewry, and a year later he and his wife entered Palestine as illegal immigrants. In 1948 he became editor of a distinguished Yiddish literary quarterly, *Di goldene keyt,* in which he brought together what remained of Yiddish culture in western and eastern Europe, the Americas, and Israel. It was this man who came to visit Canada in 1959.

Wisse encountered Sutzkever before she had read and studied his verse. His tour through Canada was "triumphant" (interview), and Wisse was enthralled. "When he started to read his poems at these public evenings, I was overwhelmed." What impressed itself on Wisse went beyond the stunning effect of Sutzkever's poems, which linked the listener's aesthetic pleasure in the poet's carefully crafted Yiddish to Sutzkever's

21. Ruth Wisse with the poet Abraham Sutzkever in 1959. *Photograph by Hertz Grossbard.*

harrowing personal experiences. She began to understand that resistance even to staggering adversity was indeed possible. Sutzkever's power over Wisse's fiery imagination cannot be exaggerated. Here was a man who had been a witness to the central events of Jewish history in the twentieth century. He combined in his person everything Wisse had been taught to value at home and in school: commitment to the Jewish people, moral rectitude, aesthetic sensibility, and physical courage.

Sutzkever noticed her responsiveness to his work and one day asked her, "Why don't you study Yiddish?" Wisse laughed and replied, "And what would I do? Teach Sholem Aleichem?" This was the turning point. "When those words issued from my mouth, I looked at him in horror. I could not believe that I had said that. Sutzkever was of course insulted. If anyone was in a position to know that Yiddish literature was worth studying, it was I. So many Yiddish writers had passed through our house, which was filled with Yiddish books. I had studied Yiddish literature in *mitlshule* and knew that I enjoyed it at least as much as English literature." But it was the stuff of home; and familiarity bred contempt. Also, "there had never been anything like it in the university; and the contempt was automatic" (interview). The next day, in a spontaneous act of penitence, Wisse called up Columbia University, which had a fledgling Yiddish program. She went down for an interview and was told that she could start graduate work in the middle of the year, in January 1960. When Wisse arrived, she found herself in the presence of two other Vilna intellectuals, Max and Uriel Weinreich.

Max Weinreich, director of YIVO's research and training division, taught Yiddish language, literature, and folklore at the City College of New York, while his son Uriel, a professor of linguistics at Columbia University, had just been appointed there to a professorship in Yiddish language, literature, and culture. As persons and scholars, the two Weinreichs assured a modicum of continuity between the Vilna YIVO and the one in New York. By a stroke of good luck, Max Weinreich and his fourteen-year-old son Uriel had left Vilna in the summer of 1939 to attend a linguistics conference in Brussels. The outbreak of war prevented their return home. They continued on to New York, where they were joined in 1940 by Max's wife, Regina Szabad, and their second son, Gabriel. Max Weinreich declared that the American branch of YIVO should take over the function of the mother institute in Vilna for the duration of the war. He could not foresee the destruction of Vilna's Jews and their cultural institutions. After the war the recovery of books and papers was a very slow and difficult process.[36]

Even more important than books, however, were young scholars. Both Weinreichs worked hard at attracting students to the field, a nearly impossible task at a time when the bright, literary minds from Yiddish-speaking homes flocked to the lectures of Lionel Trilling, Harry Levin, and M. H. Abrams in the United States, or F. R. Leavis at Cambridge University. Uriel Weinreich wrote an academic textbook, *College Yiddish: An Introduction to the Yiddish Language and to Jewish Life and Culture* (1949), which is still widely used. At the time of his death, in 1967, he had just completed his *Modern English-Yiddish, Yiddish-English Dictionary.* Unlike the dictionary of Alexander Harkavy (1891), which had been written "mainly for people knowing Yiddish and aiming at a mastery of English," Weinreich, aware that times had changed, designed his own dictionary "in the main for persons who have a firm grounding in English and at least a rudimentary command of Yiddish and are eager to broaden their mastery of Yiddish vocabulary and phraseology."[37] Ruth Wisse and David Roskies used Weinreich's dictionary to find words that had been taboo at home.

College Yiddish too, became indispensable. "Although I grew up in a Yiddish-speaking home and studied in a [Yiddish] day school," David

Roskies recalled, "I knew no grammar. I remember vividly that one of my greatest discoveries [at age fifteen] was a sentence in the second lesson [of *College Yiddish*] where Weinreich writes: 'In Yiddish every preposition requires the dative.' . . . I had never understood when to use *di, der, dos,* or *dem.* I simply never knew the rule, and there it was put so simply: a preposition is followed by the dative. All one needed to know was the grammatical gender rule and—done!" Roskies memorized the gender of all Yiddish nouns and learned to speak Yiddish properly just in time for a fateful meeting with Max Weinreich, who was out to recruit students his own way. When Roskies was introduced to the great man at a Yiddish gathering, Weinreich said to him simply, "Friend Roskies, Yiddish scholarship needs you!" Roskies was nonplussed: "Me a sixteen-year-old *pisherl,* who dreamt of becoming a film director, if not more? But Weinreich spotted something in me. . . . He had a premonition that he could sit down with me and transform me into a respectable person. Weinreich believed in the necessity of creating an elite of Yiddish scholars." [38] Roskies joined their ranks.

When Ruth Wisse arrived at Columbia in January 1960, she was welcomed with open arms. She considered it her great good fortune that Uriel Weinreich was on sabbatical and was replaced for the spring term by his father. Max Weinreich became one of her most significant and beloved teachers. A few years earlier he had finally been able to resume research on his vast reconstructive project, the *Geshikhte fun der yidisher shprakh* (1973), which he completed shortly before his death. The terms and premises of his prewar studies, however, had changed. No longer did he conceive of Yiddish as a language that gradually emancipated itself from German; rather, he now defined Yiddish as a "fusion language" that consisted of several components, one of which was German. Moreover, he now saw Yiddish as a language that reflected the life of the Jewish people—a collective expression of what Jews thought, felt, and did. Weinreich called Yiddish "the language of *derekh haShas,*" the language that comprised and reflected the cultural and ethical world of the Talmud. [39] Thus, to preserve the language was to preserve not only Jewish culture but the Jewish people.

Weinreich's notion of the close interrelation between language and culture would surface ten years later in Wisse's dissertation and then throughout her literary, cultural, and political writings. In an article on the success of anti-Semitism as an ideology, she pointed out the culturally ingrained reluctance of Jews to resort to violence—a reluctance that produced a "perpetual political imbalance" between Jews and their foes.

One of her examples of Jewish restraint was taken from the Yiddish language: "Max Weinreich . . . once traced for me the following history of the Yiddish term *hargenen,* 'to kill.' Enjoying no active use among the Jews of Europe, the term gradually acquired the weaker meaning of 'strike' or 'beat,' while to signify real killing one said *derhargenen,* employing a prefix for an action seen through to its end. But this strong term, too, came to mean no more than 'beat,' or 'rough up,' and for killing one resorted to *derhargenen oyf toyt*—to kill to death." [40] The reluctance of Jews to resort to force or violence in the same measure as it was turned loose on them is a permanent source of pain for readers of classical Yiddish literature. There was no Jewish response in kind to physical terror in Eastern Europe; and Wisse would become fully aware of that in the mid-1960s.

At Columbia, Wisse deliberately faced the most deadly manifestation of the "perpetual political imbalance." While studying with both Uriel Weinreich and Salo W. Baron in the fall of 1960, she decided to do her master's thesis for the comparative literature department on Sutzkever's *Green Aquarium,* a series of prose poems written in 1953 and 1954. The first sections invoke the Vilna ghetto in the last stages of its destruction; a transition poem about a grandmother escaping from the slaughter into the woods brings into focus the precarious survival of fugitives in the forests; and the last sections "recall the ruins of the ghetto, a massive graveyard that was once a civilization" (*GA* xii–xiii).

Sutzkever's prose poems pressed on Wisse two fundamental realizations that reinforced the horrifying reality of the Shoah. The first realization was underscored by Wisse's encounters with Sutzkever and the two Weinreichs: "[W]hat went into the ghetto was a fully formed culture that had just ripened. Sutzkever was among the first Yiddish writers who had been educated at least partially in Yiddish. . . . [C]aught up in the ghetto was the first generation of writers raised on Yiddish literature, and the first such generation would also be the last" (interview).

The second realization emerged directly from the "disjunction between the beauty of the poems and the horror of the situation." The first thing to concede was that "if a poet managed to live through it, he was still a poet; he would remain who he was." Sutzkever's ability to continue to make verse while hiding under intolerable conditions challenged the suggestion that poetry and the Holocaust are antithetical concepts. For the fact is that a poet remains a poet, even in the ghetto, and, moreover, may believe, as Sutzkever did, that "what can most keep him alive is his poetry" (interview). The central metaphor of this belief was presented at the outset of *Green Aquarium:* "One day during the time of the slaughter I sat writing in a dingy little room. It was as if the Angel of Poetry had confided to me—'The choice lies in your own hands. If your song inspires me, I shall protect you with a flaming sword. If not, don't complain . . . and my conscience will remain clear' " (*GA* xviii).

Only those poems that satisfied the highest aesthetic standard would do. Wisse explained Sutzkever's position:

> Everyone realizes that the Nazis destroyed moral standards along with their victims. Any human being who wanted to maintain a prewar moral standard would be killed in a minute.[41] . . . But nothing could destroy an aesthetic standard because it is entirely independent of a moral standard. This often strikes us as regrettable. It is regrettable, for example, that talent is not always given to moral people. But the autonomy of aesthetic standards became a comfort during the war. The person who knew what a good poem was and who was working in his mind to forge that poem, could keep on with that activity, because it had nothing whatever to do with what was going on around him. In that sense the poet really did resemble a mystic. Sutzkever, it seems, can only be understood within the realm of religion. (interview)

What worked for the poet also benefited Wisse as a critic trying to come to grips with Sutzkever's ghetto poems.

> It came down to an aesthetic sense, or an independent sense of language and presentation that one carried into this material. As long as one *read* about these situations, as long as they were contained within the realm of literature and one was compelled to ask is [the presentation] good, is it bad, [one was safe]. It allowed me to work on the poems and yet to be emotionally—not free, but freer. I guess the experience of working on this body of poetry was in some ways analogous to the poet's own work on them. (interview)

The stringent aesthetic standard held up by the poet was henceforth applied by his critic to all literature. Difficult as it was to read Holocaust material that satisfied the highest aesthetic demands, if the material fell short, "if the sentiment was false, one could hardly even credit what it was that one was reading" (interview). Sutzkever articulated the danger of falseness in the initial admonition to the poet in *Green Aquarium:*

Your teeth are bars of bone. Behind them in a crystal cell, your words in chains. Remember the advice of one older than you: the guilty ones, who dropped poisoned pearls into your goblet—let them go free. In gratitude for your bounty they will build your immortality; but the others, the innocent, who trill falsely like nightingales over a grave—to them be unsparing! Hang them, become their executioner! Because no sooner do you let them out of your mouth or your pen than they become ghosts. (*GA* xiii)

Wisse took this to mean that the unpleasant, "the 'guilty words' are the less dangerous. They whose malevolence is obvious, whose aggression is plain, may be allowed into the text. But the words that pretend to sweetness when their subject is actually the grave should be mercilessly throttled" (*GA* xiv).

Her demanding standard regarding both the aesthetic perfection of literary form and the toughness and integrity of sentiment made Wisse one of the fiercest reviewers of Jewish literature, particularly when its subject was the Shoah. It was less dangerous to the uncompromised survival of the Jewish people to point out the authors' errors of judgment and to risk making one's voice unwelcome than to let false literary outpourings continue unadmonished.[42]

The day Wisse received her master's degree from Columbia in the spring of 1961, she felt disoriented and bleak. She had no clear idea for what purpose she had done her thesis on Sutzkever, and the gloom evoked by the historical context of the poems was not easy to shake off. But she soon began to see that the imperative was to live in the present and that it was time to go home to Montreal and to have children. "I felt that very strongly," she recalled. Her three children were born in 1962, 1965, and 1969. During those years she also tried to move toward a goal she had conceived for herself: to become a teacher of Yiddish literature in the Jewish Teachers Seminary in Montreal. Her plan was to rid Yiddish literature of the geriatric notions attached to it,[43] and to teach it precisely in the way English literature was being taught by the likes of Richard Chase and Frederick Dupee, with whom she had studied at Columbia. It was not only possible but absolutely necessary to apply to Yiddish poetry and prose the high literary standards and interpretive methods that were being applied to English fiction. But when she tried to get accreditation either through Sir George Williams College or in conjunction with an adult education program at McGill University for the courses she had set up in a kind of open university at the

Montreal YMHA, she was stonewalled. She understood that she would have to get academic credentials. Without a doctorate she would not be able to teach at the level she desired and would always remain "a backdoor entry instead of a frontdoor applicant" (interview).

Yiddish Literary Scholarship and Its Political Lessons

Throughout the 1960s, Wisse prepared scholarly articles in Yiddish on Yiddish literature in which she tried "to satisfy Max Weinreich and his idea of a scholar." The results were a bit stiff, unlike her English essays. One of the Yiddish articles, however, announced the interests and direction of Wisse's mature work. She had been alerted (either by Max Weinreich or possibly by the poet Melech Ravitch, her Montreal tutor and the curator of the Yidishe Folks-Bibliotek) that a sheaf of manuscripts by Mendele Moykher Sforim was to be found in the Montreal Jewish Public Library. So she went looking for them and found that the writer Reuben Brainin had once borrowed some manuscripts from Miss N. Abramovitch in Odessa and never returned them. "The real treasure among the [manuscript] fragments," she declared, "is a previously unknown variant of Mendele's second drama *The Conscription* [*Der priziv*]." Wisse analyzed the differences between the published version of 1884 and the much earlier manuscript variant (c. 1870) and concluded that the increasing hardships inflicted on the Jews in Czarist Russia, culminating in a wave of pogroms that swept through Eastern Europe in 1881 and 1882, softened Mendele's satiric attacks on his fellow Jews.[44]

But Wisse's occasional Yiddish articles did not yet add up to sustained scholarship, because she was working in an academic vacuum. There was no Jewish Studies program at McGill in the mid-1960s when Wisse decided to go back to school. In 1965 she enrolled as a doctoral candidate in the English department. She had originally planned to investigate "whether there could be Yiddish humor after Sholem Aleichem" and chosen Uriel Weinreich as her adviser. But his illness and death in 1967 at the age of forty-two meant that she had to find a new adviser and topic. She returned to McGill's English department, which had then barely started its doctoral program. The only conceivable person with whom she could work was Louis Dudek. Because of his passion for all literatures, he was willing to read whatever Wisse gave him trusting that all would come out well in the end. Since the thesis had to be accepted by an English department, it had to include English-language material.

Wisse came up with a clever solution to her dilemma—she would focus on one figure, the schlemiel, a character in Yiddish folklore and fiction, whose literary counterparts were the fools of European fiction. She would outline the schlemiel's development in the Yiddish culture of Eastern Europe and examine his continuity in the recent slew of American Jewish novels. This device allowed her not only to write half her dissertation on Yiddish fiction and the other half on a Yiddish theme in American fiction, but also to assess the differences between the Jewish cultures of Eastern Europe and North America.

While a dissertation entitled *The Schlemihl as Hero in Yiddish and American Fiction* (1969), published as *The Schlemiel as Modern Hero* (1971), may look at first glance like a Jewish version of Robert Alter's dissertation on the rogue in English literature, Wisse's findings were not academic, but profoundly influenced her assessment of the contemporary political and cultural realities. Her book was a radical investigation into a fundamental mode of Jewish behavior that for centuries had allowed Gentiles to humiliate, oppress, exploit, and murder Jews without any retaliation. What called for explanation was the structure of the Jewish nonresponse to adversity and its origins in Jewish culture.

What Wisse discovered was astonishing. In response to Gentile aggression, Jewish culture had produced the figure of the schlemiel, a character of extraordinary self-control, wit, and verbal ingenuity, who was incapable of double-talk and cunning, and was possessed by the idea that man was created to be a moral being, a *mentsh*. In the brutal world of Darwin, Marx, and anti-Semitism, such a man had to be a fool. Yet his adventures provoke "our recognition that in an insane world, the fool may be the only morally sane man" (*SMH* 4). Wisse opened her book with a joke that illuminated that particular feature of the schlemiel: "Sometime during World War I, a Jew lost his way along the Austro-Hungarian frontier. Wandering through the woods late at night, he was suddenly arrested by the challenge of a border-guard: 'Halt, or I'll shoot!' The Jew blinked into the beam of the searchlight and said: 'What's the matter with you? Are you crazy? Can't you see that this is a human being?' " (*SMH* 3).

Wisse focused on the numerous facets of the schlemiel in the history of Yiddish literature and revealed how such writers as Mendele Moykher Sforim, Sholem Aleichem, and Isaac Bashevis Singer had used the character "as a metaphor for European Jewry" (*SMH* 4). Wisse used Saul Bellow's famous translation of Singer's "Gimpel the Fool" (first printed in *Partisan Review* in 1953) to make the transition from Eastern Europe to North America, from the Pale of Settlement across the abyss of the Shoah to a privileged diaspora culture. It took some explaining, however, to account for the surfacing of the schlemiel in America. For how could a character who transformed his physical defeats into intellectual or moral victories become a success in a country where "nothing nicer could be said of a man [than] that 'He's got horse sense' " (*SMH* 74)? And Wisse argued that the schlemiel figure would have been almost unintelligible to American readers before the heroism of World War II had worn off and America began to experience itself as a "loser" in the ensuing Cold War. "Schlemiel humor, which makes hardship into laughter through recourse to the irrational and absurd, would have been as unpalatable to earlier generations of Americans as gefilte fish, a similar device for camouflaging rotten leavings as a delicacy" (*SMH* 74). In subsequent chapters, Wisse proceeded to analyze Saul Bellow's *Herzog* (1964) and Malamud's *Pictures of Fidelman* (1969) as American reworkings of the type, before she turned, with a certain relief, to Philip Roth's *Portnoy's Complaint* (1969) and Norman Podhoretz's *Making It* (1967) as the long overdue unmakings of the character. "Philip Roth passionately pleads against the schlemiel inheritance for its crippling effect on the psyche. Podhoretz calmly, though with no less passion, sets himself against the schlemiel inheritance for its crippling effect on the polity" (*SMH* 122).

The lessons that came into view at the end of Wisse's study were obvious: to ensure the safety of what remained of the Jewish people it was necessary to shake off the schlemiel inheritance, to move the Jewish polity from passivity to action and from pride in moral perseverance in defeat to seeing the appropriateness of using physical strength on one's own behalf. During the 1970s, but with new vigor after her brother succumbed to his depression, Wisse accepted these lessons as her cultural and political mission. If she had been unable to save her brother, she would now try to watch out for the Jewish people. She knew enough about the mental strategies of the Jews to counteract them and so perhaps to bring about a change of mind.

The brilliance of Wisse's first book lay in the fact that she had managed to isolate in the wealth of largely nineteenth-century material four distinct techniques Jews employed to respond to adversity. In later articles and lectures on Yiddish literature, Wisse substantiated her findings.[45] What bothered her was not so much that the Jews in nineteenth-century Eastern Europe and the Yiddish immigrant literati on New York's Lower East Side had had recourse to these strategies of defensive accommodation but that, especially after the Yom Kippur War of 1973, she was beginning to see the same techniques employed in the contemporary political discourse of assimilated American Jewish intellectuals.

Her first book had homed in on the question of whether the literary tradition of the schlemiel could continue beyond the destruction of its Eastern European matrix. It continued in Isaac Bashevis Singer's "Gimpel the Fool," and it was no accident that the story had found its first English home in *Partisan Review,* a magazine not known for its courage on Jewish issues. Singer's protagonist, teased, tortured, and disdained by his fellow townsmen, thinks that the reason people call him a fool lies in his easy gullibility. But Gimpel insists that he is no fool but has chosen credulity over cynicism, for "What is the good of *not* believing? Today it's your wife you don't believe in; tomorrow it's God Himself you won't take stock in." What is the point of responding to meanness with meanness if you can't look yourself in the face afterwards? His refusal to respond in kind to what is done to him makes him a fool in the eyes of the world. "Gimpel is fully conscious of the distinction between the figure he cuts in the world and his own self-conception," but he insists that the esteem of his neighbors is not worth the sacrifice of his integrity. And so "Gimpel is prepared to walk into eternity in pursuit of personal goodness" (*SMH* 61–69).

For Wisse there was little doubt that the willing gullibility of the Jews, their cultural ideal of moral decency as well as the "techniques of denial and avoidance, sublimation and rationalization" (*SMH* 66), had made the slaughter of the Jews one of the easiest large-scale killing operations to set in motion and execute. The great significance of the life and work of Abraham Sutzkever for Wisse lay exactly in the fact that his poetry could be read as an imperative to reshape a culture of self-defeating moral sophistication. His poem "The Leaden Plates of Romm's Printing Works," Wisse explained, "commemorates the night when the [Vilna] Jewish underground broke into the greatest Jewish publishing house in Eastern Europe and recast the rows of type into bullets: the best of diaspora culture must be refashioned in weaponry, and Jews must learn to read a new language of steel" (*BP* 16). With the founding of the state of Israel, the remnant of the Jewish people gained a new lease on life. Wisse's book ended on a hopeful note because in the wake of Israel's victory in the Six Day War of June 1967, which presented to the eyes of the world a new kind of Jew—men and women who would really use the bullets cast by these heirs of the Vilna Jewish underground—even

American Jews seemed to take heart. In the work of Philip Roth and Norman Podhoretz she saw signs of resistance to schlemiel culture.

In subsequent years, however, Wisse observed with increasing consternation how the old diaspora techniques of dealing with adversity resurfaced among American Jews. The short respite between the summer of 1967 and the fall of 1973, when Israel was at the peak of its strength and—not at all coincidentally, Wisse claimed—at the peak of its popularity, was followed by difficult times that undermined the self-confidence of American Jews. The 1973 Yom Kippur War and its frustrating aftermath coincided with the onset of a sophisticated Arab campaign to discredit a militarily undefeated Israel in the arena of international politics. In Wisse's assessment these efforts culminated in 1975 with the passage of UN Resolution 3379, equating Zionism with racism. Furthermore, the 1982 military campaign in Lebanon and the prolonged occupation of the West Bank and the Gaza strip profoundly disturbed American Jews because in their sources of information they found these events reinterpreted in ways that transformed Israel "from a land of promise to a 'tragic mistake,' from the victim of aggression to the perpetrator of aggression." [46] Shocked to find Israel accused of imperialist aggression against peace-loving peoples, and to hear themselves called nationalists and chauvinists as supporters of Israel, liberally inclined Jews backed away from their unquestioning support of the Jewish state.

In article after article, beginning in September 1978, Wisse analyzed the attitudes of American Jews toward Israel and found that all of the schlemiel's techniques of dealing with adversity were well and alive. Most popular were moral exceptionalism, once favored by I. L. Peretz, and the mode of turning outside aggression into internal argument. "The growing disaffection of American Jews from Israel," Wisse wrote in 1988, "follows a general law of modern Jewish policies: intra-Jewish argument rises in proportion to anti-Jewish aggressivity, particularly from sources deemed to be progressive." That American Jews would recommend nonresponse to aggression as a strategy to maintain their moral superiority was perhaps surprising, not only because it required thinking their opponents' ethics inferior to their own, but also because one might have thought that by 1980, American Jews had adopted some of the "horse sense" of their country. This did not appear to be the case. In response to an article critical of the "American Friends of 'Peace Now,' " Wisse received a letter from one of their supporters which concluded: "The Palestinian charter by which the PLO sets its course does not demand much morally. The Israeli declaration of independence

does, and we are only trying to see that Israel lives up to its ideals. . . ."
Wisse pointed out that the writer's "casual expression ('does not demand
much morally') is the objective correlative of his level of concern for the
consequences of the PLO's moral laxity. Being first and foremost a
moralist, he is less interested in Israel's right to live than in Israel's right
to live in the world to come." Wisse was disappointed that American
Jews, who had to some degree benefited from the "process of Jewish
normalization in the world" initiated by the founding of an internationally accredited Jewish state, became the more liberal and the more dov-
ish, the greater the pressure on Israel, a tendency that she summed up as
"the desire to dissociate oneself from a people under attack by advertising
one's own goodness." [47]

Wisse did not emerge as a political writer until the late 1970s. By that
time she had established herself as an eminent Yiddish scholar and a
critic of American Jewish literature. Having received her doctorate in
English literature from McGill University in 1969, Wisse was appointed
to an assistant professorship in the newly created Jewish Studies department there. She spent the academic year 1971–72 in Israel, where she
taught in the Yiddish departments of both Tel Aviv University and the
Hebrew University in Jerusalem. The year after she returned to Montreal the first of her editions of Yiddish literature in English appeared, *A
Shtetl and Other Novellas* (1973). The book had grown out of her teaching experience and was designed to alleviate "the scarcity of Yiddish
literary materials," but also to document the wide range of Yiddish
literary modes.

Other editions followed. Wisse began to work with Irving Howe,
who since the death of his long-time coeditor, Eliezer Greenberg, had
been looking for a new collaborator. Together they published *The Best
of Sholom Aleichem* (1979), which presented a bleaker Sholem Aleichem
than the humorist American audiences loved. In 1987 the ambitious,
bilingual *Penguin Book of Modern Yiddish Verse* appeared, coedited by
Howe, Wisse, and Khone Shmeruk.[48] Its impressive roster of translators
included Irving Feldman, Hillel Halkin, John Hollander, Irving Howe,
Cynthia Ozick, and Adrienne Rich. The strictly chronological arrangement of the poets by date of birth rather than by country seemed to
argue that "the homeland of Yiddish poetry is where the Jewish people
makes its home," and that the ties of the poets to each other as Yiddish
writers were stronger than their bonds to the national cultures and the
milieux in which they actually lived. But, as Wisse described in a lecture,
the decision in favor of strict chronology had been a pragmatic rather

than an ideological one. It had the additional advantage of bringing the book to a close with the work of Abraham Sutzkever, who, as a poet and in his function as editor of *Di goldene keyt,* was "the moving force of modern Yiddish poetry." Instead of ending on an elegiac note, "Sutzkever's poetry would conclude the book at its artistic peak, and he would figure as its anchor."[49]

Wisse's interest in Sutzkever had led her to the poetry of *Yung Vilne,* and later to its very different precursor in America, *Di Yunge.* Her research on the American circle of Yiddish poets culminated in a book about the New York poets Mani Leib and Moishe Leib Halpern, *A Little Love in Big Manhattan* (1988), that combined literary analysis and cultural history. Although both poets wrote exclusively in Yiddish, Wisse took care to make her book appealing to English readers as part of her "modest attempt to return to modern Jews part of their lost inheritance and, more important, to locate for American Yiddish poets their rightful place in the American canon."[50]

A dozen years earlier, in 1976, when Wisse had made her fiery entry onto the New York literary scene with an article in *Commentary* on new American Jewish writing, *Di Yunge* had served to illustrate the distance between Yiddish and American Jewish culture, between a literature in a Jewish language that forced its writers to burrow ever deeper into Jewish history and a literature that longed to be "centrally Jewish" without leaving the linguistic turf of Christian culture. The poets of *Di Yunge,* Wisse wrote in 1976, were "purists whose single-minded drive for a richer Yiddish poetry flaunted all the national forms of allegiance." Their intense focus on self-expression forced them, willy-nilly, to concentrate on their medium of expression, which was the Yiddish language. As a result they "created an ever-expanding Yiddish cultural base and a program of internal exploration." Moreover, their poetic program reinforced their ties to Jewish culture in paradoxical ways: "Insistent on absolute personal freedom, on the autonomy of art and the artist, they were forced back into the roots of the language—inseparable from the roots of the culture—for the sake of those very aesthetic principles that were to have freed them from national concerns."[51] The cultural programs of the new particularist American Jewish writers, who wanted to create, as Cynthia Ozick put it, "an indigenously Jewish culture in the English language," Wisse thought absurd. With verve Wisse set out to dismantle theories such as Ozick's (later abandoned by the author herself as unfeasible).[52] With her essay on the follies of American Jewish writers began Wisse's long and happy association with *Commentary,* which she called "the most admirable magazine on issues that matter to me" (interview).

For Wisse, as for Alter, the primary source of authenticity, and thus of creative strength, for Jewish writers working in the diaspora as well as for critics of Jewish literature was a good command of Jewish languages. The English works even of "Herman Wouk and Cynthia Ozick, two very different writers who are alike in being extraordinarily cultivated Jews," Wisse argued, cannot give substance to their readers' Jewishness. Their novels may "organize our feelings and perhaps point us in a direction," but they ought not to be mistaken for the "authentic works of Jewish law and faith from which (again, in very different ways) they derive their themes." For access to these works Hebrew was necessary; hence the minimum requirement for Jewish literacy was knowledge of Hebrew. "An *ideal* of Jewish cultural literacy would have to include Yiddish as well as Hebrew, Aramaic for Talmud study, and, depending on intellectual ambition, any of eighteen or so Jewish languages that preserve folkways and lore from earliest times to the present. But Hebrew," Wisse argued in unison with Alter, "always the main artery of a self-renewing Jewish tradition, is the indispensable thread that binds all Jewish languages to their biblical source." [53]

In 1992, when Wisse was appointed to a chair in Yiddish literature at Harvard University, the first of its kind at that institution, she also assumed the responsibility of building up a graduate program in Yiddish. She requires literacy in Hebrew of all its serious students "since the beginnings of Yiddish literature are inextricably linked to Hebrew and so much of the secondary literature in the field is now being written in Hebrew" (interview).

Harvard had been a bit slow to catch on to an astonishing development: the integration of Yiddish literary studies into American academe. By 1992, many of the leading universities (Columbia, Yale, Jewish Theological Seminary, the University of California, the University of Michigan, Ohio State University, the University of Texas at Austin, and some others) already offered courses in Yiddish language and literature. [54] Nevertheless, Harvard's choice for its first chair in Yiddish literature, which is affiliated with the Department of Comparative Literature and with the Department of Near Eastern Languages and Civilizations, was as surprising as it was refreshing, since it did not conform to the kinds of hirings one had come to expect from either department. As a fairly traditional, nonfeminist literary scholar unintrigued by the intricacies of literary theory and opposed to the pieties of political correctness, Wisse

22. Ruth Wisse at Harvard University in 1992. *Photograph by Laura Wulf. Courtesy of Harvard University Office of News and Public Affairs.*

was an odd addition to a department that comprised avant-garde women scholars such as the narratologist Dorrit Cohn, the feminist critic Susan Rubin Suleiman, and the poststructuralist scholar Barbara Johnson. As a fairly nonobservant, secular woman, who combined the pursuit of literary scholarship with the life of an outspoken cultural and political essayist, she was a novelty, if not a revolution, in the crusty, scholarship-oriented, and self-absorbed Department of Near Eastern Languages and Civilizations that was devoted to the buried arcana of past Middle Eastern cultures.

In Wisse, moreover, Harvard hired someone who joined its very small band of publicly identified, politically conservative and articulate Jews. Had the university's attitude toward the Jews really changed fundamentally since the arrival of Harry Levin on campus in 1929? What is one to make of the facts that the money for Wisse's chair came from a Jewish donor outside the university but that her appointment was supported by Sacvan Bercovitch, Harvard's American literature guru, who made his home in the English department, once closed to Jews? The two facts seem to place Jews in very different spheres of the University—at the margin and at the center.

The Politics of Hiring Jews: From Levin to Wisse

Within the history of the integration of Jews into literary academe, the appointment of Ruth Wisse to a chair in Yiddish and comparative literature at Harvard University takes on the symbolic function of a commencement exercise. It indicates both closure and new beginning. Wisse's tenure at Harvard marks the end of a process that began there in 1722, with the conversion to Christianity and subsequent hiring to an instructorship in Hebrew language of an Italian Jew by the name of Judah Monis. Although by 1900 conversion was no longer a prerequisite for the employment of Jews in the humanities, genteel discomfort with committed Jews as teachers in English departments was noticeable until at least the late 1950s.

The hiring of Jews in the humanities at Harvard proceeded along two distinct tracks. Until the late 1970s, Jewish scholars working on Jewish philosophy, intellectual history, or literary history were considered exotic ornaments who might adorn a university but were hardly central to its educational mission.[55] Hence they were relegated, literally and figuratively, to the margins of the institution. By contrast, assimilated Jewish literary scholars working on mainstream literatures were rewarded for having given up all particularity with a place in departments that constitute the center of the university. In the early 1980s, a middle ground was beginning to emerge that allowed for the recognition of the Jewish intellectual and literary tradition as important to the Western humanities. At Harvard, that ground was defined by the appointment of Ruth Wisse.

Harvard's first instructor in Jewish philosophy, Harry A. Wolfson, was a brilliant immigrant from the world of the Lithuanian yeshivot. He arrived at Harvard as a freshman in 1908 and never left. Having received his Ph.D. in 1915, Wolfson was hired to an instructorship that was to be renewed annually after the university made sure that his salary would be funded by outside donors. A decade later, in 1925, when Wolfson was serving his second term as assistant professor, "he was notified," his student Lewis Feuer reported, "that his appointment, unless he could secure permanent outside funding, would be a terminal one."[56] A Jewish Harvard alumnus, Lucius N. Littauer (class of 1878), was willing to help out. He endowed a chair in Jewish literature and philosophy in honor of his father, Nathan, who had begun his business career peddling notions in upstate New York. As Paul Ritterband and Harold Wechsler explain:

> Littauer agreed to provide a full professor's salary of $6,000 for three years, to be followed by a $150,000 endowment. Harvard would promote Wolfson to the rank of full professor in the Semitics and philosophy departments, beginning October 1, 1925. Wishing to distinguish his chair from Harvard's long tradition in Christian Hebraica, Littauer twice stipulated that the incumbent be "well versed in Biblical and post-Biblical Hebrew, as well as in Jewish thought and philosophy." [57]

When Wolfson retired in 1965, he was succeeded as Nathan Littauer professor by his student Isadore Twersky, who turned away from Wolfson's preoccupation with the place of Jewish philosophy within the development of European philosophy and toward research in medieval Jewish intellectual history, especially Jewish rationalism.

Despite Wolfson's joint appointment to philosophy and Semitics (subsequently the Department of Near Eastern Languages and Civilizations) he and Twersky pursued their scholarship in splendid isolation on the margins of campus. Wolfson, who never married, quite literally led an eccentric existence. Burrowed into his study in the bowels of Widener Library, or holed up, when the library was closed, in his room in Divinity Hall, Wolfson spun out tome after tome on the philosophies of the three major monotheistic religions. Twersky, an authority on the writings of Maimonides and a man of more focused interests than his mentor, was perhaps a more conventional academic than Wolfson, but at the same time he was even more unusual. Twersky was married to Atara, the daughter of Rav Joseph Baer Soloveitchik, a Talmud scholar, spiritual leader, and descendant of the greatest intellectual dynasty of Jewish Lithuania, yet Twersky was himself the scion of a distinguished line of rabbis from Talna, a shtetl near Chernobyl. Twersky assumed the responsibilities that came to him through the lineages by marriage and descent when he took on, as rebbe, the spiritual and intellectual leadership of a small congregation of observant Jews who transformed his Victorian home in Brookline, Massachusetts, into the Talner shul. [58]

In that setting the fact that Rabbi Twersky was Professor Twersky at Harvard was irrelevant. There were few niches in Boston (certainly none in its large, secular, intellectually aggressive Jewish population) where Harvard was of so little import as at the Talner shul. Harvard's marginalization there was in some measure a function of Twersky's seriousness about his rabbinic role. Although the Soloveitchik tradition encourages secular intellectual inquiry, even secular methods of study and interpretation, Twersky deliberately diminished his academic persona when he was officiating as rabbi at the Talner shul. At the same time, however, he took Harvard and the Jewish presence there seriously indeed. For decades Twersky administered the notoriously rigorous graduate program in Jewish intellectual history, which was sought out by men who had already been ordained as rabbis. In 1970, Harvard established a second professorship in Hebrew and Jewish history, and in 1975, urged by Twersky, it launched a fund drive to build a Center for Jewish Studies, which opened in 1978 under Twersky's directorship. Tucked away in the Semitic Museum on Divinity Avenue, which is also the home of the Department of Near Eastern Languages and Civilizations, and populated exclusively by male faculty, many of whom were also observant Jews, the center led a largely self-contained existence on the fringe of Harvard until the arrival of Ruth Wisse. As a secular, politically engaged woman scholar, she broke both the tradition of Jewish self-segregation and Harvard's tendency to marginalize its committed Jews. So far the two trends had effectively combined to deaden the impact the Center of Jewish Studies might have had on Harvard's increasing number of Jewish students. Coming, as most of them did, from secular and assimilated homes, the students were all too ready to consider Jewish scholarship a matter of antiquity, like the study of Greek and Latin, and quite properly at home in a museum. The quip circulating on campus that, for Twersky, Jewish history ended in the eighteenth century overstated the case but had a point, since Twersky held, as his student Allan Nadler put it, that "without at least basic training in classical Jewish and rabbinical texts, no aspect of Jewish history, thought or culture could properly be mastered." [59]

Wisse concurred. Even for Yiddish studies an adequate command of Hebrew and Aramaic, assuring access to traditional Jewish texts, was indispensable. Nevertheless, Wisse's gave Jewish studies at Harvard a new direction. For centuries, Yiddish had been regarded as a second-class language, used by the uneducated and illiterate as an all-purpose tongue, and by the religious to distinguish between the realm of the sacred (study and worship conducted in Hebrew) and the profane. In America, certainly, Yiddish was for the most part thought of as a vernacular, used by working-class immigrants and radicals. The Yiddish aesthetes were a tiny, isolated minority of language worshipers. For most Jews, Yiddish was something one abandoned on the way up. It was, as Wisse put it, "perceived to be the most expendable part of Jewishness." [60] Although, as in any language, the gradual refinement of Yiddish is coextensive with its literary history, beginning in the sixteenth century with Elye Bokher's *Bove bukh,* recognition of Yiddish as a language of high culture came only in this century. As outlined earlier, the path to recognition led from Czernowitz (and the language conference in 1908) to Vilna (and the founding of YIVO in 1925), through the upheaval of the Holocaust, to the belated acceptance of Yiddish as a subject of serious academic labor in the United States, Canada, and Israel. Wisse's appointment at Harvard conferred upon Yiddish academic nobility and completed the process of recognition.

The pressure to emancipate Yiddish from the scorn of the social and scholarly Jewish elite rarely came from within Jewish studies—especially not at Harvard, where Wolfson railed against his mother tongue.[61] Rather, it was the successful integration of Jews into American society and their concomitant abandonment of Yiddish that created first a certain nostalgic and then a scholarly interest in the language and its literature. With successful integration came greater social and psychological security; then, curiosity about one's "roots;" and finally an anxiety to preserve what one had never known, hence the interest of some Jewish donors in promoting Yiddish studies.

It is important to note, however, that Wisse's appointment was also made to Comparative Literature. Such an appointment signaled that Yiddish was neither a dead language, like Latin or Akkadian, nor exclusively Jewish. Rather, Yiddish was regarded as a living modern language, like German, French, or Japanese, with an extensive literature that could be studied with detachment by anyone. Comparative literature at Harvard had been Harry Levin's postwar creation. And it is within the tradition of Jewish hirings in the humanities that Levin represents that Wisse's appointment must also be seen. Harvard's committed Jews on the fringe had always been outbalanced by its assimilated Jews in the center.

Beginning with Judah Monis, but increasingly under the enlightened presidency of Charles William Eliot, Harvard has always hired Jewish scholars willing to participate in the intellectual enterprises considered central to American culture or all humanity, as it were, at the price of giving up all particular allegiance to their "tribe" or "race." Frank W. Taussig (economics) was hired in 1882, Adolphe Cohn, a Frenchman, was instructing Harvardians in his language by 1884, Charles Gross (history) was hired in 1888, Hugo Münsterberg (philosophy) was brought over from Germany in 1892, and Leo Wiener (Slavic languages) arrived at Harvard in 1896. One of the pockets of resistance to the employment of Jewish faculty, however, was English literature. In the mid-1920s, Jews were still talked out of pursuing graduate work in English, and in the mid-1930s, Theodore Silverstein, a gifted medievalist who for years had assisted John Livingston Lowes (originally a Chaucerian himself), was let go.

Although the hiring of Harvard's first Jewish instructor in English literature in the fall of 1939 was due to the fluke of a faculty member going blind over the summer, Jewish students were gradually finding jobs in English departments in the late 1930s. The rate of appointments accelerated after America's entry into the Second World War, and by the late 1950s they were being hired in droves. By and large, these instructors continued in the trend established earlier in the humanities: the price of admission was assimilation. However, many of these young men (rarely women) were still very close to the immigrant past—most of them were only one generation removed—and hence to join the American intellectual enterprise was an exciting and challenging adventure. Assimilation created an opportunity to do what one enjoyed; it allowed one to overcome the obstacles that had disenfranchised the Jews in Europe and caused their emigration, and to prove oneself a worthy member of American society. We have seen how these cultural pressures played themselves out in the cases of Harry Levin, M. H. Abrams, and Daniel Aaron. Of course, early Jewish professors of English rarely reflected on what they were doing as members of a group—as Jews on their way into the bastion of American high culture. They did not even recognize that they were part of a group, and yet collectively their work reflects an extraordinary outpouring of goodwill and gratitude toward America.

This outpouring continued beyond the hiatus of World War II and included an increasingly audible chorus of critical voices. But, as Sacvan Bercovitch argued in his analysis of the American jeremiad, the more one criticizes reality, the more one reaffirms the ideal of which one sees reality fall short. The critical voices raised by Jews, especially in the era of the civil rights struggle and the Vietnam War, demonstrated how deeply Jews cared that America live up to its promise. This idealism was shared by most of the Jews hired by English departments until the late 1970s. They were a self-selected group of secular, liberal intellectuals who kept a safe distance from all forms of particularism—religious, ethnic, nationalist—unless such particularism benefited the empowerment of disenfranchised groups, such as women, blacks, Hispanics, homosexuals, and so forth. By the late 1960s, Jews were no longer thought of as disenfranchised but were considered, especially in their own assessment, to be fully integrated into all power structures, and hence part of the American establishment. The term *minority literature,* for instance, which became fashionable during the 1980s, is not understood unlike its precursor *ethnic literature,* to include the literary productions of American Jews. Yet the professional activities of a large majority of Jews employed in English departments indicated that they felt it to be their duty to make sure that America did not renege on its promise of equal opportunity for all.

This development can be clearly observed at Harvard. In its hirings to tenure, the school has always been fairly cautious, preferring to confirm established trends rather than set new ones. Twenty-two years elapsed between the arrival of the first Jewish instructor in English in 1939 and the hiring of the second Jewish professor. And just as it had been Charles Feidelson, Yale's first (and for a long time only) Jewish instructor in English, who was sent to show Lionel Trilling around campus when he came up from Columbia to give a talk at Yale in the early 1950s, so it was Harry Levin who was sent to Columbus, Ohio, in the spring of 1961 to look over Morton Bloomfield as a replacement for the retiring medievalist Francis Peabody Magoun. Bloomfield, a native of Montreal and Levin's junior by one year, had recently returned to ritual observance in order to provide his children with a Jewish education.[62] It was somewhat ironic, then, and a sign of the changing social attitudes in English departments that Magoun (Harvard class of 1916, Ph.D. 1923), a decorated combat pilot in World War I, an admirer of all things military, and a pillar of A. Lawrence Lowell's Old Harvard, was succeeded by a modest, low-key Jewish scholar.

Although Bloomfield led a ritually observant Jewish life in Cambridge and was active in Harvard's Hillel organization, his Jewish commitments remained a private matter and did not surface in his scholarship, except possibly as an awareness of the culture's ability to victimize and to inflict injury through exclusion.[63] With him the Harvard tendency to choose profoundly secular and assimilated Jews continued, as it did in the appointment of the Emerson scholar Joel Porte to a faculty position in 1969. In 1971, Daniel Aaron returned to Harvard from Smith College, having been wooed by the English department for two years. In 1981, Marjorie Garber, a Shakespeare scholar from Yale, became the first tenured Jewish woman in Warren House. Competitively intellectual, aggressively secular, and feminist rather than feminine, Garber deliberately fashioned herself as a scholar in precise counterdistinction to what she had experienced as a materialistic, hypocritical, nonintellectual culture while growing up in a wealthy Jewish suburb on Long Island in the 1940s and 1950s. It is really with Garber's later work, her books on transvestism (1992) and bisexuality (1995), published after three books on Shakespeare, that English literary studies at Harvard were modernized with a vengeance. Reviewing one of Garber's books, Frank Kermode suggested that "anyone seeking a sign of the academic times" might reflect on how improbable it was that any one of Garber's precursors at Harvard, Shakespeare scholars such as George Kittredge, Alfred Harbage, and Harry Levin would approve "the content, style or purpose of 'Vice Versa: Bisexuality and the Eroticism of Everyday Life.' "

> [S]he cares nothing for *gravitas*. She devours books the character of which Kittredge couldn't even have imagined, and makes copious scholarly reference to magazines . . . of decidedly specialized interest ("bi-journals" designed for "bi-lesbians" . . .). Without a qualm she watches, indeed takes part in, the kind of talk show in which people confide intimate secrets to raucously salacious strangers. Any movie that even hints at bisexuality is accorded the same measure of analytic attention as Shakespeare's sonnets.[64]

Despite Kermode's alarm at the obliteration of distinctions that helped structure if not define literary academe as we knew it—distinctions between high and low discourse; between oral and written, popular and artistic, vulgar and refined genres; between what ought and what ought not to be aired in public—there really was no reason to panic. Garber did in her decade what Levin had done in his, when he had shocked Warren House by including the "moderns," Proust, Joyce, and Mann, in the Harvard curriculum. Garber, too, simply included the previously excluded, in her case the visual media, the lowbrow, and the sexually eccentric. These were important elements in the theater of Shakespeare's time, and Garber's preoccupation with them could in fact be understood as an extension of her academic interest to include the present. (Just as literary critics long to practice the craft they study and have thus far produced some bafflingly bad novels, so drama scholars, understandably, yearn to participate in the theater of the day.)

Garber effectively changed the direction of Shakespeare studies at Harvard and retired the literary school of Harbage and Levin (just as

Levin had helped to retire the philology of Kittredge). The expansion of literary studies into cultural studies was in step with (perhaps even a step behind) the cultural developments outside academe. What Garber did for the Harvard tradition of Shakespeare studies, Sacvan Bercovitch did for the tradition of American studies. Bercovitch came to the Harvard English department from Columbia in 1983 as its sixth Jewish appointment.

Setting himself in opposition to the Puritan studies of Barrett Wendell, Kenneth Murdock, and Perry Miller, he revised their concept of America so fundamentally that he had scholars up in arms. "Bercovitch has come not to honor Miller but [to] bury him," one critic complained, who undertook a long analysis of Bercovitch's work to ask "whether Bercovitch's history is the kind of history we need." [65] Bercovitch did not stop at Puritan scholarship but extended his revision to nineteenth-century American studies, including the work of F. O. Matthiessen that no one had yet dared to touch. After his suicide Matthiessen had ascended to the status of a martyred saint, enshrined by his disciples and progressive scholars as victim of a homophobic America moving grimly to the right. Bercovitch, however, demonstrated how deeply (albeit inadvertently) complicit Matthiessen had been in the fashioning of a fundamentally affirmative view of America. Bercovitch argued that far from offering a sharp critique of American ideology from the perspective of a Christian, socialist, and socially marginalized gay man, "Matthiessen's revisionism was rooted, consciously or not, in the ideals of the early and mid-nineteenth century," and that "in some basic sense . . . it was the country's rediscovered writers who set the terms for what was to become the framework for rediscovering the country's literary past: the question of the American-ness of American literature." [66]

Although suspected of radical political sympathies—a suspicion that Bercovitch's namesakes, Sacco and Vanzetti, all too easily invited—Bercovitch had not set out to revise the work of his Americanist precursors because he had a political ax to grind.[67] Rather, Bercovitch's peculiar and radically new analysis of the meaning of America and, by extension, of American studies is the result of his eccentric perspective on the United States as a Canadian immigrant of Russian-Jewish descent.[68] His sophisticated consensus model of American culture was a clever way to remain true to his descent (to his marginal perspective and left-wing sympathies) while he was pursing his intellectual and professional integration into America. Harvard must have known what it was getting when it hired Bercovitch: the parameters of his revision had been firmly established with the publication of his second book, *The American Jeremiad* (1978), five years before Bercovitch came to Harvard (whereas Garber's "transgressive criticism," was devised while she was a tenured professor there). What Bercovitch's appointment indicates is a certain willingness on the part of the university to move from caution and conservatism to a calculated risk-taking by putting its money on a safe (because already ensconced) avant-garde.

Within the context of Jewish hirings to tenure in the Harvard English department, the arrival of Bercovitch after Harry Levin (1939), Morton Bloomfield (1961), Joel Porte (1969), Daniel Aaron (1971), and Marjorie Garber (1981) is somewhat special but not altogether out of the ordinary. Like his precursors, Bercovitch was unequivocally secular, and at first glance it seemed that Jewishness surfaced in his scholarship only in the most muted ways.[69]

Morton Bloomfield once suggested that "the field a person chooses reflects some inner need."[70] Accordingly, Levin's mastery of Europe's literary high culture in the 1920s and 1930s, which was then, partly through the mediation of T. S. Eliot, also America's high culture, was undertaken in unconscious compensation for his parents' exclusion from both; Garber's move into an intellectually aggressive and socially transgressive scholarship was made, by her own admission, in deliberate counterdistinction to the narrow interests and repressive social attitudes of the "Jewish mercantile class" in which she grew up;[71] Bloomfield's patiently acquired expertise in medieval Christian theology can be understood as an attempt to make sense of a religiously and culturally divided Canada that was united in its allegiance to Christianity. In the same vein, Bercovitch's rereading of Puritan literature began as the deliberate accumulation of knowledge about a country he "knew virtually nothing about," as a discovery of America from scratch, which turned into "a scholar's journey into the American Self." As Bercovitch himself pointed out, his investigations "express both a developing sense of the culture and a certain process of acculturation" (*RA* 1).

At first glance, then, Bercovitch seems to fit the bill of the assimilated Jewish literary scholar at the center of Harvard's educational mission. The thrust of his work is inclusive and, like Garber's, encourages the shift from literary to cultural studies. A closer look, however, reveals that unlike his Jewish precursors, Bercovitch resisted complete assimilation. Yet his resistance does not necessarily indicate a negative assessment of America, as some of Bercovitch's critics like to believe. Rather, it has to do with his having come to the United States as an adult, having lived in other countries, and having found something valuable and worthy of preservation in his descent culture. The paradox, of course, is that Bercovitch exemplifies the American Dream, the rise from immigrant poverty to fame and financial success. The means of Bercovitch's American ascent was, again quite paradoxically, that he had managed "to channel [his] resistance to the culture into a way of interpreting it" (*RA* 1). And insiders found the outsider's discovery and analysis of America's vision of itself compelling.

Although Bercovitch claimed that "the shock of discovery proved a continuing barrier to Americanization" (*RA* 1), there is another way of looking at his intellectual development. What allowed him to acculturate but not assimilate—to preserve an inner, utterly private space that sheltered his psychological and emotional attachments to his descent culture —was the fact that America became the object of his professional attention. The act of rational scrutiny creates distance; for if you want to look at an object to perceive its shape and structure, you need to hold it away from you. To put it differently: for Bercovitch, America was a matter of the cortex, whereas the recollection of the idealist, left-wing Yiddish culture of his Montreal childhood evoked responses from the limbic system.

A professor of American literature with a deep inner pocket of cultural resistance was a new phenomenon in the Harvard English department, and a phenomenon with consequences. One of them was that Bercovitch extended the concept of inclusion to the culture of the Jews. Until the late 1980s, liberal inclusiveness (or canon revision) had been curiously selective: It excluded Jews as Jews. While it was considered progressive to study the literatures of African or Native Americans and so to contribute to their cultural (and, presumably, political) empowerment, it was considered somehow backward and parochial to study the literature of the Jews and to argue for their inclusion. Bercovitch, however, participated in panel discussions on Jewish literature and desisted from teaching on the High Holidays (when his students reminded him that they were coming up). When the question of a chair in Yiddish studies at Harvard arose, he advocated that the appointment be made not at the fringe but at the center of the college, not to the Department of Near Eastern Languages and Civilizations but to the Department of Comparative Literature. The donor, Martin Peretz, publisher of the *New Republic,* had already stipulated that the new chair in Yiddish literature was "not to be put in a little corner" but located in a department at the center of the university.[72] When the issue of Wisse's conservative politics was raised in the ad hoc committee, Bercovitch was asked what he thought, since he was taken to represent the views of the political left. "Her politics are not a problem," he said. In the end, Wisse was appointed jointly to Near Eastern Languages and Civilizations and to Comparative Literature.[73] Soon thereafter she replaced Isadore Twersky as director of Harvard's Center for Jewish Studies.

Wisse's appointment, then, caps the development of Jewish hirings both at Harvard's former fringe and at its former center, in Jewish studies and English literature. Her professional career may even signal an opening up of the two fields toward each other. Since her arrival in 1992, the Jewish studies program at Harvard has been revitalized. This is in some measure due to Wisse's secularism, her extension of textual into cultural studies, her active engagement in current political affairs, and her involvement in the world of American intellectual magazines like *Commentary* and the *New Republic;* but it is also due to her personal warmth, her tolerance of other points of view, and her scrupulous separation of scholarship and politics in the classroom.[74] Wisse's scholarship, especially her work on American Yiddish literature, expanded the notion of America as it had been conceived some sixty years earlier by Harvard's Americanists. Wisse's enlarging of America from the detached vantage point of a former Canadian citizen with deep roots in Eastern Europe coincided with a revision of "America" under way in Harvard's English department in the work of Sacvan Bercovitch. It is hardly surprising, then, that the chief proponent and driving force behind the reconceptualization of America supported her appointment. The happy congruence of their views regarding the inclusion of Jewish culture into America's intellectual pursuits, despite vast political differences, had something to do with the two scholars' intense commitment to the past formed during their childhoods in the Yiddish-speaking world of Montreal.

An examination of Bercovitch's life and work leads us back to Harry Levin, Daniel Aaron, and Leo Marx. Considering Bercovitch's scholarship in the light of his Americanist precursors illuminates sharply the extent to which an unacculturated Jewish perspective can produce a radically different vision of America. Bercovitch effectively abolished the notion of marginality by declaring "America" a constant process of practical enlargement and rhetorical renewal that subverts all resistance into co-optation, including that of its most fervent critics.

11

The Meaning of America:
Sacvan Bercovitch

The Effects of Empathy

WHATEVER ONE MIGHT HOPE FOR in literary scholarship—thorough research, ingenious arguments, clear prose, critical projects of broad scope and immediate relevance, and a sound dose of common sense—can be found in the work of Sacvan Bercovitch. Yet its most compelling and peculiar quality is the author's strong empathy for his subjects, particularly for those fighting a losing battle. Nowhere else in the critical literature is Cotton Mather's repellent egotism, the unsavory mixture of self-pity and self-congratulation that pervades his diaries, so reduced to a pardonable human weakness as in Bercovitch's portrait of him as a "dispossessed leader caught between two eras, one dead, the other beyond his moral and emotional comprehension."[1] Nowhere else is Melville's despairing bitterness and difficult literary brilliance more intensely conveyed than in Bercovitch's analysis of the writer's satiric novel *Pierre, or the Ambiguities*.[2] And nowhere is Huck Finn so convincingly portrayed as a brutalized (and hence depressed and terrified) boy, haunted by his "imagination of death and disaster," as in Bercovitch's Harvard lectures on "The Myth of America." In these lectures Huck emerges as a wonderfully quick-witted yet needy child, to whom the student audience responds with a rush of protective emotion. But when Bercovitch proceeds to point out the flip side of Huck's low self-esteem—his craving to fit in, to gain respectability in a society, which the author exposes, with Huck's help, as racist, selfish, authoritarian, and god-awful all the way through, the students get angry and upset.[3]

Most literary scholars like Huck; and even Melville, angry and embittered after the unequivocal rejection of his great whale, has had his share of scholarly love. But empathy with the Puritans would strike many as a rather tall order. In Bercovitch's scholarship, however, they become complicated, brilliant, and fascinating people, whose "stubbornly archaic moral idealism" (CM 99) moves the reader and commands, if not love, at least respect. Honest esteem of the long-dead as tough players may be the source of Bercovitch's empathy. He never talks down to his subjects. They are always equals in the playing fields of the mind.

Asked about his relation to the Puritans, Bercovitch replied, "I have a lot of respect for them. I try to understand what I am studying, and perhaps the process of understanding anything is a process of gaining respect for it." This has tempted readers to think that Bercovitch is admiring or praising the Puritans, though that is not necessarily the case. "When I am teaching or studying someone's work," Bercovitch explained, "and the same is true when I am dealing with people, I think that I see the world from their point of view, which does not mean that I do not also keep a distance from it. I remain suspicious of it." [4]

In this offhand description Bercovitch comes surprisingly close to the definition of empathy as an analytical tool in clinical psychoanalysis. Empathy is a process of coming to know something or someone; it makes specific, though not necessarily conscious, use of affective responses. It is thus unlike reason, which does not depend on affective involvement. The goal of empathy as an analytic tool is understanding, not gratification. Empathy differs from sympathy in that it does not demand the sharing of emotions or emotional states; and it is different from identification, which is an automatic, unconscious mental process whereby an individual becomes like another person in some aspects. As Michael Franz Basch put it, "The identification that takes place in an empathic encounter is not with the other person per se but with what he is experiencing." Janet Hadda, a clinical psychoanalyst and Yiddish literary scholar, defines empathy as the "ability to perceive and comprehend another by responding affectively to his or her communications and reflecting upon them so as to better understand the other." At its best, empathy combines "intimate immediacy and distance or indirection." [5]

We have already encountered examples of empathic scholarship in M. H. Abrams' concept of imaginative consent, in Daniel Aaron's empathic observation of the American cultural scene, in Jules Chametzky's work on ethnic literature, and in Ruth Wisse's analyses of Yiddish fiction. In Aaron's case, however, empathy had been tempered by sharp-witted irony and in Wisse's case by sorrow over the catastrophic consequences of her subjects' foolishness. Bercovitch, too, keeps a critical distance from his subjects. But his critique of (or, as he would term it, resistance to) American authors and their characters is never personal; their integrity is never violated. His critique takes into account the larger societal circumstances in which individuals find themselves, especially the "web of ideas, practices, beliefs, and myths through which a society, any society, coheres and perpetuates itself" (*RA* 13). Since his criticism is thus ideological rather than personal (say, moral or psychological), the subject itself (author or character) remains intact and the intersubjective field between Bercovitch and his immediate object of study or teaching remains undisturbed. Since the reader or listener shares Bercovitch's point of view, by observing the critic's immersion in the feelings, experiences, and thought processes of his subjects, Bercovitch's (early) essays and lectures evoke strongly empathic responses in his audiences. One's heart and mind go out to the Puritans as they take on the contours of real people.

There is another, perhaps better, way of describing this peculiar quality of Bercovitch's scholarship. In a wonderfully learned yet irreverent essay about the *gaon* (the traditional Jewish scholar-genius) in today's literary academe, the poet Elisa New, herself a Jewish professor of English literature, observed: "What has always distinguished Bercovitch's style, at least for me, is its uncanny intimacy, 'the past,' as Emily Dickinson has it, 'set down before the soul and lighted with a match.' [Perry] Miller chronicled the grand movements of the Puritan Mind; Bercovitch writes like a consort of its secret life. When a prose style renders its subject beloved, [and] the text [responds], as if quickening to the ministrations of intellect, to being known, then we may wonder if the *gaon* has been here."[6]

Empathy was as much a personal quality of Bercovitch's as it was a quality of the culture in which he grew up. Around 1965, Bercovitch began translating Yiddish literature into English. The immediate occasion was an exhibit of his sister Sylvia's illustrations for a group of ballads by Itsik Manger. The work involved in translating Yiddish— in capturing its cultural, emotional, and psychological dimensions— appealed to Bercovitch; and although he claims not to be a "natural translator," he has continued to render Yiddish poetry and prose into English. Characteristically understating his ability, Bercovitch explained that natural translators do their work with speed and ease, and obtained very good results, whereas "I have to labor. I have to get into the world of the other person. I don't have the instant empathy [John] Hollander has. I like the idea of translating, and I like doing it. But I find it hard."[7]

Translating indeed requires empathy. As Leonard Wolf, one of the most experienced translators of Yiddish poetry, pointed out, this is especially true for the poems of Itsik Manger. "In theory," Wolf explained, "a translator should be nearly as familiar with his original as its author, which ought to mean that he or she can choose comfortably among all the options available to render the clear sense, the form, and the tone of his text." In the case of Manger's prankish, artistically sophisticated yet folksy ballads, Wolf claimed, "the translator who is reasonably equipped to read Yiddish can recreate the clear sense fairly easily. Neither Manger's diction nor his manner presents the sorts of difficulties one has, say, with Peretz Markish." What is hard "is to find, to seize, and to manipulate Manger's tone. By tone I mean of course the pitch of his voice, which conveys the speaker's attitude to the reader."[8]

Manger's work contains two distinct intersubjective fields, one extending between the poet and his characters, the other comprising the poet and his audience (including his modern translators). These fields were already quite complicated at the outset of Manger's career, when in a world as intellectually sophisticated as Jewish Czernowitz in the 1920s, Manger was on his way, as David Roskies put it, "toward resurrecting the song, the sweet sorrow, and the bohemian life-style of the hard-drinking Yiddish troubadours of old Galician glory." Yet, as Ruth Wisse pointed out, nothing could be further off the mark than to think of Manger as a simple folk poet. "Much of the humor and charm of Manger's ballads derive not from their simplicity, but from their wicked juxtaposition of cultivated European ideas and forms with the idiomatic usage of marketplace Jews and the worn coin of fairytales. . . . Paradoxically, these neo-folk poets are the most refined of all modern Yiddish literary craftsmen."[9]

Manger's relation to his literary heritage, live culture, and diverse audience became even more complex with the destruction of Yiddish life and letters at the height of his creativity. In order to perceive, to seize, and to manipulate Manger's tone, the translator needs to enter into Manger's complicated world and into his empathetic relationship with his characters. Only from within Manger's poems is it possible to understand the poet's shifting attitudes toward contemporary Yiddish culture (or what was left of it after the war). By uncovering the concealed modernity of Manger's ballads, Bercovitch's translations preserve Manger's ability to evoke empathy in the reader for his characters as well as for the entire culture that brought them forth. Among the reasons for Bercovitch's success is the fact that Manger's profound sense of cultural homelessness deeply reverberated in his translator.

The empathic relation between the uprooted Yiddish poet and the not-yet-rooted American critic can be most easily discerned in some of Bercovitch's earliest translations. Manger was born in Czernowitz in 1901 and exiled with his family in Jassy, Romania, for the duration of World War I. With the restoration of peace he returned to Czernowitz to fashion himself into a folk poet. In the Gentile societies of his time, this objective would have been fundamentally at odds with the poet's peripatetic life-style, since folk traditions were regional phenomena. But this was much less the case with Jewish culture, because it was a society, as Bercovitch was to write about the migrating Puritans, "whose defining character lay neither in its territory nor in its nationhood . . . but in its way of life, and more precisely, perhaps, in the 'webs of significance' spun out by successive generations." [10] Hence, Manger's "folk" were transportable, and in 1928 he left Czernowitz for Warsaw, where he became a much-sought-after poet, essayist, and lecturer. In 1938 he moved to Paris, a center of literary modernism and bohemian life. The German occupation in 1940 forced him to flee. His route led from Marseilles to Tunis and on to Liverpool and London, where he found refuge with Margaret Waterhouse.

There, in 1941, amid the ruins of the Blitz, Manger wrote his eerie "Ballad of the Jew Who Found a Half-Moon in the Cornfield." The ballad's plot is enchanting. A Jew is happily walking home with his goat when, having just said his evening prayers, he finds a silver half-moon, which sends him flying through the universe. But when read in the historic context of its composition, the fairy-tale plot contrasts sharply with the string of rhetorical questions that punctuate the ballad and speak directly to Manger's (and his folk's) contemporary situation: "[I]t isn't the world that's setting, is it?" "But how can you reason with the winds, when they've decided to catch a Jew on the road, a simple, ordinary Jew, and lead him a merry chase?" "Where now? What next? I've become a wanderer through space and time, a restlessness between God and man, a sad and wanton melody swinging from the horn of the moon." In 1941, however, the end of Jewish despair was not yet in sight; in fact, the worst was yet to come. In 1944, Manger learned of the death of his brother Note. "The news unhinged Manger to such a degree,"

David Roskies reported, "that he wrote an open letter to I. J. Segal and Melech Ravitch [two Yiddish poets living in Montreal] resigning not only from Yiddish literature but from the Yiddish language itself." [11]

Of course, no such thing was possible. The end of the war left Manger with an intense hatred of the Germans and a burning fury, the result of powerlessness and despair. Manger became increasingly mercurial and narcissistic. When Rokhl Auerbach, who had survived the liquidation of the Warsaw ghetto and rescued Manger's archive, came to meet Manger in London, he welcomed her with a fit of rage. [12] In 1951, the year Manger turned fifty and published his first retrospective volume, *Medresh Itsik* (his second, *Lid un balade,* followed in 1952), he set out for America. Manger settled in New York but uprooted himself again in the early 1960s to move to Israel, where he died in 1969.

Manger first came to the United States via Montreal, where he was forced to wait for a visa. He spent much of his time in the small flat of Sylvia Ary, Bercovitch's older sister, on St. Dominique Street. "He was coming every day," Ary recalled. "He was very difficult because he was an alcoholic. By then he had quarreled with everyone in Montreal." He came to St. Dominique Street to drink and talk in relative quiet. "The more he drank, the more he talked and complained," Ary said. In order to make some use of the time, she suggested that she paint his portrait. Manger shrugged. " 'Look,' he said, 'all the other artists tried to paint me. Chagall tried, Saul Lerner tried, and they said it's no use. I can't sit for a portrait.' " [13] Manger's restlessness made it impossible. But when Ary mentioned Melech Ravitch, a fixture in Montreal's Yiddish circles, and a poet with whom Manger had a running quarrel, Manger stopped pacing and stood transfixed, talking urgently about issues that mattered to no one but a handful of cultural orphans. The portrait got done. [14]

David Roskies has argued that "there is no evidence whatsoever of Manger's personal pathology in his poems." [15] But Manger's pathology was not personal. His psychic dysfunction, which an earlier age would have termed profound melancholy, was the result of deep cultural despair. His later poems reflect that despair quite accurately. They are pervaded by the poet's sense that his folk were dead, that Yiddish culture had nowhere to go. In 1941, Manger could still write, "How will it all end, you ask?" When he compiled *Medresh Itsik,* which is really a commemorative rather than a retrospective volume, the end had long since come.

Bercovitch described Manger's ballads as "combining private vision with communal experience." What Manger saw, above all, was that he had lost his Yiddish audience, which for him meant that "his life as a poet was spent." [16] Manger's vision of a Yiddish renaissance, which he had brought from Czernowitz to Warsaw and tried to realize in the world of literary modernism, did not survive World War II. As a poet, he was only going through the motions.

At this point, as Sacvan Bercovitch was to discover in his professional life, Yiddish and American culture were furthest apart. Whereas Manger's vision shattered on the hard facts of reality, Cotton Mather's vision was reinforced by adversity. Indeed, "Mather's practical misfortune became his most formidable literary asset. It not only stimulated but, in self-protection, compelled him to draw *ad extremis* upon the metaphorical" (CM 112). He became the precursor of a long line of loners who, unlike Manger, "*refused* to substitute an apocalypse of the mind for a disappointed historic expectation, and whose epic-autobiographies, accordingly, transform personal failure into social ideal" (CM 105). Nothing in contemporary Yiddish culture could prepare Bercovitch for what he called the "shock of discovery" when he realized that America was built on an extraordinary feat of the imagination. America's early intellectuals transformed factual adversity into cosmic affirmation, and "public defeat into private triumph by recourse to metaphor and myth" (CM 99). An optimism so profound that it interpreted adversity as affirmation (inspired as it was by Christianity's central emblem of a tortured corpse promising life everlasting) proved a "continuing barrier" to the Americanization of an immigrant who was steeped in the hardnosed melancholy of an uprooted Yiddish culture, as Manger expressed in his prewar "November Ballad:"

> Midnight. The lady with red umbrella leads the way; behind her, incognito, comes the old king, and then His Excellency the fool.
>
> The king trips over a beggar-child asleep on the side-walk, dreaming pyramids of hot corn-bread.
>
> The lady laughs; the fool's command pierces the night air: "One, two, three—up, up, arise!"
>
> The king puts on his red crown, the fool his red cap, and the three continue forward; the lady with red umbrella followed by king and fool, three red crowns in chase, dancing their ghost-dance.
>
> Suddenly, "Halt!" Three knives flash before them.
>
> The king, pale as death, cries "Betrayal!" and sinking to his knees, he offers his rusty crown for his life.
>
> The lady with red umbrella pleads: "I have a bed, a slender body, and a hot night . . ."

The fool's cap flames red: "I give my laughter!" he cries.

Three knives flash sharp; three angry masks confront them, mask against mask.

Bercovitch's ingeniously abbreviated prose translation of Manger's rhymed and measured ballad sharpens the undercurrent of aggression in this melancholy Walpurgisnacht.[17] The assault at the end explodes the carnival playfulness of the scene by reducing the specters to their essences: the king to his crown, the lady to her body, the fool to his laughter. The harmless madness of the beginning, where the characters bond and switch roles—the king following, the lady laughing, the fool commanding—is overthrown by the real madness of murder. Before such anger the group falls apart and evaporates into the insubstantiality of masks.

It is difficult not to read Manger's ballad as a bitter allegory of Jewish fate in Eastern Europe. In a move that confirms Wisse's argument that external threats of destruction trigger intra-Jewish aggression (as in Manger's postwar encounter with Rokhl Auerbach), we find the poet siding with the aggressors. Manger is furious at his folk for being so vulnerable to pogroms, for being of so little substance when confronted by violence.

Manger's feelings were not pretty, and Bercovitch, who grew up in touch with the underside of Yiddish life, understood them. His rendition of Manger's final stanza toughens the ballad by dropping the last line of the Yiddish original, "god gerekhter!", Manger's ironic invocation of a just God. In Bercovitch's world, God is so dead that even the traditional indictment that rhetorically questions his justice in the face of violence against his chosen people, does not make sense any more.

The surprising element in the ballad is the softly drawn figure of the beggar-child. The child alone appears to make sense. The child's dream is straightforward wish fulfillment. But the Jewish dream, as Bercovitch was to find out when he discovered America's very different vision of itself, looks backward rather than forward. The pyramid of hot corn-bread alludes to the "fleshpots of Egypt," to the time when the Jews were enslaved to labor on Pharaoh's grand tomb but "ate bread to the full" (Exodus 16:3). An American writer, by contrast, looking for a vision of bread, might have chosen the manna that a free Israel found in the desert wilderness.

The beggar-child's dream allows us to perceive the difference between post-Shoah secular Yiddish culture and American culture. The Jews shaped their present in remembrance of the past, whereas Americans used the past as a map for their future.[18] America's history was propelled by the forward sweep of redemption. The country was continually apprehending its future, since it conceived of its destiny as a promise given in the past that was now on the verge of fulfillment. Yiddish culture, by contrast, had lost its vision—along with its visionaries—to Hitler and Stalin. It became a backward-looking, commemorative culture, reduced to yearning for an enslaved past. This was the cause of Manger's postwar depression. His sorrow turned him into a bitter man. Orphaned even in a Hebrew-speaking Israel, Yiddish poetry was reduced, in Manger's words, to a "sad and wanton melody swinging from the horn of the moon."

Although Bercovitch absorbed Manger's cultural outlook as a boy in Yiddish Montreal, he was also touched by its opposite, a visionary Jewish rhetoric, which Kafka, thinking of the Zionists of his own time, wittily referred to as "grasping the last corner of the vanishing Jewish prayer shawl."[19] In Bercovitch's case the envisioned New Jerusalem was the worker's paradise on earth. The child's exposure to the rhetoric of Jewish communists, whose small immigrant enclave in Montreal was like the Puritans' settlement, "a latter-day Zion at the vanguard of history, fired by a vision that fused nostalgia and progress, prophecy and political action" (RA 6), helped to prepare the adult's empathic reconstruction of the myth of America. The rhetoric of high idealism was the domain of Bercovitch's mother. In order to understand its appeal as well as its function as an opiate, we need to have some notion of the reality of Jewish life in Ukraine just before the Bolshevik revolution.

Ukraine

The early lives of Sacvan Bercovitch's parents were cursed, as the Chinese put it, by being part of interesting times. Bryna Avrutik and Alexander Bercovitch were born and raised in Kherson, a town on the Black Sea, east of Odessa. Jews had settled there as farmers when a spell of lenient czarist politics had allowed them to do so. Before the 1917 revolution, Ukraine was a center of Jewish political, cultural, and religious life. Although the majority of the region's one-and-a-half million Jews lived in the cities of Odessa, Ekaterinoslav, Berdichev, Kharkov, and Kiev, the countryside was studded with Jewish shtetls, sunk in unbelievable poverty. While Ukraine is arguably the birthplace of modern Yiddish literature, it is also the locale of almost continuous, singularly gruesome violence against Jews, dating back at least as far as the massacres perpetrated by Bogdan Khmielnitsky in 1648.

The childhood and adolescence of Jews born in Ukraine in the 1890s (Bryna was born in 1894, Alexander in 1891) was marked by the constant threat of aggression against Jews. With a four-day rampage against the Jews in Odessa in May 1871, modern persecution began. The pogrom signaled that despite promises to the contrary, Jews could not hope for protection from government authorities.[20] As a child Alexander Bercovitch had recurring nightmares about a big fire that had broken out during a pogrom in Kherson in 1896.[21]

From 1911 to 1913, the arrest, indictment, and trial of Mendel Beilis for ritual murder of a Christian child sent a new wave of pogroms through Russia's Jewish communities. World War I increased the suffering of Jews. Germany's eastern front transformed the Pale of Settlement into a bloody battlefield. Despite the fact that half a million Jews, ten percent of Russia's Jewish population, served in the czarist army, the Jews were accused of being spies, cowards, and deserters. The German general Erich von Ludendorff did not help matters with his professions of friendship for the oppressed Jews in the German-occupied territories. While he repealed the czar's anti-Jewish legislation, thereby confirming Russian suspicions that the Jews were in cahoots with the enemy, German commanders ruthlessly looted Jewish homes for foodstuffs and precious metals. The impending end of the war brought no relief from persecution. In 1917, the growing Ukrainian nationalist movement caused immediate concern. Because of the Ukrainians' long record of anti-Jewish violence, the Jews hesitated to endorse Ukrainian independence from Russia. The result was a series of anti-Jewish riots in the fall of 1917, followed by another in the spring of 1918 to celebrate the proclamation of the Ukrainian People's Republic.

The withdrawal of German troops at the end of World War I, writes Nora Levin, "plunged the Ukraine into unparalleled anarchy; mass killings of Jews started as soon as Ukrainian and Soviet forces clashed."[22] The unfolding events defy description. Between 1918 and 1921, when the Red Army managed to establish firm control over Ukraine, an estimated seven hundred Jewish communities were devastated by pogroms; 50,000 to 60,000 Jews were killed; 100,000 were maimed or died of their wounds; some 200,000 children were orphaned. In the chaos of the civil war, the Red Army and the Bolshevik cause offered the only protection.

The Red Army was not made up of angels. Most of the Cossacks in Semyon Budenny's First Cavalry, made famous by Isaac Babel's *Red Cavalry* stories, had previously served in the anti-Bolshevik volunteer army of General Anton Denikin, which descended upon Ukraine in June 1919. By November, Denikin's troops had participated in 213 pogroms. That month, the First Cavalry was formed as part of the Red Army's effort to harness Cossack forces for its own cause and to siphon them away from the Whites. But as Babel noted, it did not really matter on what side the Cossacks were riding. "What sort of person is our Cossack?" Babel asked in his diary on 21 July 1920. "Many-layered: looting, reckless daring, professionalism, revolutionary spirit, bestial cruelty." In Kremenchug in 1920 some Jews recognized Cossacks from the pogroms the year before, when they had come to harass the town as Denikin's men.[23]

The difference was that the Red Army command condemned the assaults and disarmed the guilty regiments. In October 1920, Mikhail Kalinin, the president of the Soviet Union, spoke out publicly against the violence and demanded that the Red Army fight a class war and not a national war. The advances of the Bolsheviks only released more aggression in the local population; and it was not until the Soviet forces had consolidated their power, and Ukraine was reoccupied, that the Jews began to enjoy some measure of security. To young Jews in particular, the Red Army looked very attractive. Nora Levin writes:

> The frightfulness of the pogroms more than anything else forced Jews to look to the Bolsheviks, and especially to the Red Army, as their only refuge. On one occasion, the entire Jewish population of a town of 4,000 Jews trooped after a retiring Bolshevik regiment. Obviously, this had important political implications, although many Jews mentally divorced the Red Army from the Communist party and government. A special recruitment section of the Red Army was set up to enlist Jewish youth. They were welcomed, but it was realized that "many enter the Red Army partially out of hatred for the White pogromists" and a desire for revenge. Even those who opposed bolshevism on ideological grounds supported the Red Army. According to an eyewitness, "Jewish youth leave the shtetlach and run to Kiev—to enter the Red Army. They are not Bolsheviks at all . . . but they go into the Red Army because one can die with rifle in hand." (*JSU* 43–44)

What the Red Army offered was a way out of the maddening passivity that accepted persecution as a hard fact of life. It provided young Jews with the illusion of having a choice of whether to live or die, and with a rhetoric that integrated Jews into a humanity undivided by race and religion.

Among the Jewish youths who flocked to the Red Army was Bryna Avrutik. She was the youngest of nine children. Her mother, who had entered into an arranged marriage at the age of thirteen or fourteen with a groom barely older than herself, had developed into a tough realist. She was more sharp-tongued and skeptical than her gentle, kind-hearted husband, who made a living as a *melamed,* a Jewish elementary-school teacher. Neither of them had the energy to restrain or reason with their grown daughter, who was inflamed by the idea of creating a new world. Bryna joined the Red Army in 1917 to defend the Revolution. She was equipped with a rifle and sent to the front in Poland, where she was wounded in 1919. In the hospital she was infected with typhus. Barely recovered, she took a leave from the army and made her way home in the summer of 1920. Her head shaved, her left arm in a sling, and wearing a man's greatcoat, she knocked at her mother's door. The older woman opened, looked at her daughter, and, as Bryna recalled thirty years later, "recoiled in horror from the emaciated body and the woebegone face. 'No, it's not Bryna: it's not my child!' " Later, sitting by the boiling samovar in a calmer mood, she asked her daughter: "Is this what your Revolution does to people?" Unfazed, Bryna replied with a speech that opened with a wonderful reversal of the central verses in the Book of Ruth, "My revolution is also your revolution, mama. It's the revolution of all hard-working people. In a year—and another year —the revolution, like a mighty fire, will engulf the whole world. You say 'wounds, suffering, bloodshed,' but, mama, you know how hard it is to give birth to a child. How much harder it is for a whole new world to be born. Yes, mama, we will create a new, good, beautiful world. No more war, no more hunger, no more prisons. Mankind will be free and happy—in the near future." [24]

This scene was emblematic of the generational rift in Russian Jewry at the time. The mother, who was probably born in the late 1860s, argued that human nature (at least, concerning the Jews) would not change, and that it was useless for Jews to run with the new slogans since these were only icing concealing the same old cake. The daughter disagreed: surely, pogroms were the result not of human nature but of oppressive social conditions that could be rectified by stamping out greed, redistributing wealth, and empowering the disenfranchised. Once communism supplanted egotism, and universal brotherhood superseded national separatism, all human suffering, including that of the Jews, would disappear. Bolshevik rhetoric seemed to speak so precisely to the Jewish situation that it is easy to see why young Jews, not yet committed to a set of ideals (Zionism, for instance) fell for it.[25]

Bryna's future husband, Alexander Bercovitch, did not. His way out of the poverty and harassment was to espouse not the ideals of a united humanity, but its opposite: radical subjectivity. He was the first surviving son of a shoemaker, traditionally one of the poorest craftsmen in a Jewish town. As a seven-year-old child he was apprenticed to a bookbinder, who beat him regularly, intensifying the child's nightmares and causing him to stammer. After a short time, Alexander ran away. Two years later, he discovered painting. "Through a grill in the wall of a Kherson monastery, he saw the monks engaged in the painting of icons. The monks saw him watching, hour after hour, day after day. After a while they asked him to run errands, and allowed him inside the walls for longer and longer periods at a time. They were amused by the little Jewish boy's fascination with icons, and he became their mascot. Finally they gave him paint and a few words of instruction. Thus began an informal and irregular apprenticeship that lasted for nearly six years."[26] By 1906, at the age of fifteen, Alexander had acquired a local reputation as an artist and some 200 rubles from the sale of his work. Studying at the St. Petersburg Academy, which had become Alexander's dream, was out of the question because of the residence restrictions imposed on Jews. Alexander invested his savings and a grant from benefactors in Kherson in a trip to Palestine in 1907 to study art at the newly established Bezalel Academy of Art and Design in Jerusalem. After three happy years, Alexander returned to Kherson, where he exhibited for the first time. Lured by the explosion of creativity in the artistic circles of Russia's large cities, Alexander risked moving to St. Petersburg in 1910. He enrolled at the Bakst-Dobujinsky school, the same school at which Marc Chagall had studied briefly the year before, and worked with Leon Bakst on stage sets for the Russian Ballet, including Diaghilev's production of *Scheherazade*. In 1911 a Nathan Strauss scholarship allowed Alexander to continue his studies with Franz Stuck in Munich. Stuck, a realistic painter who had developed a taste for symbolism and allegory, had been sought out earlier by Vassily Kandinsky and Paul Klee, artists on the move to surrealism and abstract art.[27] The outbreak of War I, however, forced Alexander to return to Russia, where he was immediately conscripted. Unable to endure the mindless brutality and herd existence of army life, he deserted and hid out in the house of the Avrutik family.

During the last year of the war, Alexander Bercovitch lived in Odessa because Bryna had thrown him out of her parents' house when she discovered that he was carrying on an affair with her best friend. While Bryna joined the Red Army, Alexander painted stage sets for the Odessa Opera and married a young woman from Kherson who was studying music at the Odessa Conservatory. Their son was born in April 1920. Poverty forced the couple to return to Kherson, where they lived with Alexander's parents. By the fall their need was so great that Alexander left for Moscow to find work. He was soon employed by Habima, a Hebrew theater affiliated with the Moscow Art Theater, and sent for his wife Baila. But fearing the long journey and the hard Moscow winter, Baila remained in Kherson and did not see her husband again.[28] He divorced her in 1921.

Although the Russian people suffered immense hardship in the aftermath of the Bolshevik Revolution, the early 1920s were an extraordinary period for Russian artists. It was in the circles of Moscow's avant-garde theater that Alexander Bercovitch met Bryna Avrutik again. She had been demobilized from the army and had come to Moscow to study theater under Vsevolod Meyerhold, whose political commitments matched Bryna's views.[29] Bryna and Alexander set up house together but did not get married because Bryna considered the ceremony a bourgeois relic.

In the famine years of 1921 and 1922, the couple was kept from starving by Bryna's four brothers who had emigrated to New York and Montreal and sent parcels of food. By 1924 the couple had settled in Turkestan, where Alexander was teaching in an art school and Bryna took care of their two daughters, Sara (later Sylvia) born in Moscow in 1923, and Ninel, born in Ashkhabad in 1924 and named after Lenin (spelled backwards) in accordance with Bryna's idealist beliefs and the fashion of the time.[30] Yet Bryna's unbroken belief in the utopia of the worker's paradise and the rightness of the Communist party brought the comparative idyll in which the couple now lived—a rented white house complete with cat, dog, and green backyard—to an abrupt end. Robert Adams reported that

> Bercovitch, who liked to tell stories in spite of his stammer, decided one night to regale Bryna and their friends with tales of intrigue. He had discovered that the school at which he taught was a centre of White Russian conspiracy. Without any political commitment himself, he found nothing but amusement in the whispered conversations of his colleagues,

full of codewords and nostalgia. Bercovitch and the guests were amused: Bryna was horrified. Without consulting Bercovitch, she hurried to the Education Commissariat and denounced the school as a nest of counter-revolutionaries. What she did not know, and found out only later, was that the personnel of the Commissariat were involved in the plotting. Within weeks, Bercovitch was summarily dismissed, without explanation.

It was only then that Bryna realised that her only evidence was hearsay, that Ashkhabad was a long way from Moscow, and that there was in fact no one to whom they could appeal. They were unemployed and without even the possibility of earning an income. They also had two young children and were living in a famine area. As their situation grew desperate, Bryna wrote to her brothers in Montreal.[31]

The answer arrived promptly, in the form of a family ticket for steamship passage from Riga to Montreal. In order to qualify for a family visa, however, the couple had to get married. This was one of the easier concessions to the world of hard facts. In the spring of 1926, Bryna and Alexander Bercovitch and their two daughters embarked on the long journey from Turkestan to Canada.

Montreal

Sacvan Bercovitch's parents were well into their thirties when they arrived in Montreal as mature yet highly idealistic adults. Their ideals and their strategies for coping with adversity were set, making them less flexible than younger immigrants in adjusting to life in Canada. They also believed that they would return to the Soviet Union as soon as the chaos had sorted itself out. What bound Bryna and Alexander to each other was a belief in the religion of art. Yet each of them would remain confined to a rather small cultural enclave, an émigré variant of their circles in Russia.

Bryna adjusted more easily than her husband, since she found a compatible community among the left-wing Jewish exiles in Montreal, while Alexander remained, as his son put it, a "very isolated person," deeply unhappy with his exile in an artistic backwater and contemptuous of most of his Canadian fellow painters. Nevertheless, he got in touch with the small band of Montreal Jewish artists, many of whom were immigrants like himself, and managed to have one of his watercolors accepted into the 1927 Spring Exhibition of the Art Association of Montreal.

Although Alexander would eventually build an interesting and varied career as an artist,[32] painting murals for synagogues, churches, and movie theaters, and producing impressionist landscapes, naturalist cityscapes, and expressionist stage sets for Yiddish and left-wing theater groups, it was not until the early 1930s that he gained a modicum of recognition and was able to sell some of his work. In fact, it was an impending catastrophe that launched his career as an artist. In April 1933, when the family was about to be evicted from their modest apartment at 4480 de Bullion Street, Bercovitch called the Baron de Hirsch Institute, operating in Montreal under the umbrella of the Federation of Jewish Philanthropies. The director of its welfare department sent a young social worker, Regina Shoolman, to investigate the family's situation. As luck would have it, Shoolman was an art student at McGill University; she had studied at the Sorbonne and had a good background in art history. When she stepped into the apartment and saw the canvases stacked along the walls, she got very excited. She persuaded Sidney Carter to mount in his gallery a month-long exhibition of Bercovitch's work and made sure that the press wrote about her discovery.[33]

Carter's show was Bercovitch's first solo exhibition in a commercial gallery. The reviews were mixed, as was the reception of his work throughout his lifetime. The ambivalence, especially of French Canadian reviewers, toward Jewish artists did not help matters. One critic, for instance, complained that his "Western mentality" could not always understand the "crudeness" and the "clashes" of Bercovitch's colors. Yet he found himself sufficiently attracted to the "Slavo-Oriental works" of Jewish painters to deplore their Canadianizing tendencies. When he observed these trends in Bercovitch's output, he discounted the paintings as "pretty rather than original." While alien styles merely offended Western sensibilities, assimilationist tendencies were positively dangerous, since they threatened Canada's shaky national identity. The critic expressed his discomfort in a terse formulation of the double bind in which Jews found themselves in North America: "Bercovitch shows a rare degree of adaptiveness—in this he must be Semitic."[34] Three years later, in 1937, the same critic was still caught between admiration and discomfort. Reviewing the Montreal Spring Exhibit, he wrote about Bercovitch's portrait *My Son*: "Not at all pretty, Daddy's little Jewish boy. Better yet, he is caught in a pure moment of fear at seeing himself sketched. Bercovitch's *My Son* is so close to nature that it is still seething with emotion free of second thoughts."[35]

Although Bercovitch did paint portraits of his family, he was not at all a family man. He needed large chunks of time in open space away

23. Sacvan Bercovitch with his father, the painter Alexander Bercovitch, c. 1943. *Courtesy of Sacvan Bercovitch.*

from confinement and obligations. "He was a terrible father and husband," his son commented. The cramped living quarters filled with tension got on his nerves, and Bryna's three solicitous brothers, who were very protective of their sister, irritated him. In January 1927, Bercovitch left his family in a great storm of emotion. It was only after he returned to his wife six years later and the couple went through a second honeymoon that their son Sacvan was born, in October 1933. The family stayed together through nine years of unrelenting poverty and emotional upheaval, until Alexander Bercovitch finally moved out in the summer of 1942.

During all those years, whether her husband lived with her or not, it was Bryna who carried the burden of responsibility for the children, a task for which she was singularly ill-prepared and ill-suited. "She was an abstract person," her son recalled, "full of big words like Truth and Beauty and the Future of the Working Class." While Bryna's recourse to high rhetoric softened the brutal impact of hard facts by integrating them into a world view, wherein salvation was always close at hand, it also prevented her from seeing those facts clearly and stifled any effort she might otherwise have made to develop a practical strategy to deal

with adversity head-on. Her profound detachment is well illustrated by
an incident recalled by her older daughter: "When I was in kindergarten,
the teacher spoke to us about God. I went home and told my mother
what I had learned. She said to me, you should stand up and say there is
no God. So the next day I went back, put up my hand, while my heart
was beating fast, and said, 'There is no God.' Incredulous, the teacher
asked, 'Who told you that?' And I replied, 'My mother.' So they called
her in and as a result I was expelled. That was the first move. From that
time on I went to different schools, because we were always moving"
(SA).

Upon arriving in Montreal in 1926, the family had moved in with
Bryna's brother Yankel, a blacksmith and the father of seven children,
whose wife had died in childbirth the year before. When Alexander
stormed out of the house, leaving his family without any means of
support, Bryna became a teacher in her brother Nachman's Sholem
Aleichem shule, a Yiddish afternoon school. She made about five dollars
a week and got a room at the school. And since the school, a shoestring
operation that barely recouped its costs from the students' tuition, was
always moving, so was the family.

Far from being lonely and depressed, Bryna was constantly among
people. Before the Moscow purge trials of 1936 to 1938, the family's
social life was closely linked to the Communist movement, which encouraged all sorts of artistic and cultural activities, especially music and
theater. Sylvia Ary recalled that when she was about eight years old, she
was asked to memorize a line and to recite it at a meeting: "a klol af
aykh, ir merder fun Sacco un Vanzetti!" ("A curse on you, you murder-
ers of Sacco and Vanzetti!") With the onset of the Moscow trials, which
purged the Soviet Communist party of old Bolsheviks and resulted in
the arrest, exile, and execution of many Jewish cultural and political
leaders, Bryna began to distance herself from the party and to focus
her attention on Yiddish culture, especially Yiddish literature. "Yiddish
became her party," her son remembered. The Yiddish writers of Montreal, who attended the soirées of the Roskies family and feasted there
on lavish spreads, also came to Bryna's home, where the fare consisted
of *tey mit milkh,* tea with milk, a euphemism for hot water and milk, but
where literary and political passions ran equally high.

Bryna Bercovitch had always been a literary person who loved reading
to her children from books and newspapers and encouraged them to
pursue their creative inclinations. Her artistic idealism was as unworldly

as her political opinions. When her son announced that he was going to be a famous writer so that he could buy her a house, she cried *ptooh!* and exclaimed that he mustn't think of these things. "When you are a writer," Sylvia Ary recalled her saying, "you must stay here, *in a shtiler velt* [in a quiet world], and do your writing. The worldly things must not interfere" (SA). This struck the boy as a strange reaction, especially since his mother, who developed rheumatoid arthritis after his birth, was always complaining about the Montreal weather and dreamed of living in a hot, dry climate. He thought, How can I get her to Arizona, if the worldly things must not interfere? [36]

Instead of wearing out, Bryna's idealism intensified over the years. What her son would later encounter in the high idealism of Puritan writing, was also true for her: adversity did not produce despair but increased hope. When asked whether disillusionment with the Soviet Union, in which she had invested so much emotion, broke her spirit, Bryna's older daughter replied that her mother's nature was to be a believer (SA). Her ability to believe in a set of ideals carried her through hard times even while it prevented her from responding to adversity in a practical way. In the end, her gift to subordinate reality to an inner vision proved to be an asset, though not for her children. Her rheumatoid arthritis rapidly compromised her ability to move about, and eventually she became confined to bed. Nevertheless, she continued to write a weekly column for the *Kanader Odler* (Canadian eagle), in which she covered a larger variety of topics with energy and imagination. In its way, her weekly column was an amazing feat—emblematic, perhaps, of a life that had always willfully denied the limitations imposed by hard facts and dissolved their crippling reality in fiery visions.

What impressed itself on her children, however, was the difference between rhetoric and reality. "I could see the gulf between her feminist ideals of being independent, of being her own woman, and reality," Sylvia Ary said. "Her ideals failed in reality, in her life with my father, because emotionally she was not independent. There was no congruence between word and reality" (SA). When the drawn-out process of the family's final breakup began in the late 1930s, the girls were old enough to create their own realities. Sylvia began dating the family's boarder at the age of sixteen and, much against her parents' wishes, eventually married him. Ninel went to work at fourteen. That left their brother Sacvan, a latecomer to the family, hanging in the air. His early sense of self was precarious.

I felt an identity with my father and mother. We spoke Yiddish at home (although I spoke English with my sisters), and my mother, who was the one at home, lived very much in a Yiddish world. But while there was a Yiddish identity, it was not connected to a group. I didn't belong anywhere. I identified with my family because there was nothing else, perhaps *because* there really was no family. There was a lot of emotion. Personal bonds were strong because everything was so heavy with hardships, heavy with extreme poverty, with extreme ill health, extreme parental confrontations. There were also deep personal ties, but they were not located anywhere; they were not connected to the normal world; they were not associated with a concrete program or establishment (Zionism, for example). I went to the Yiddish Public Library sometimes, and my sister was connected to the Yiddish theater and I was somewhat connected to that through her. But when I look back on it I see that I was extremely uprooted. The neighborhood was very mixed. Jews lived there, but mainly French, English, and Ukrainians. I tried to fit in wherever I was. It was always an immediate sort of problem: How do you get along with these people?

The boy developed a coping strategy that was the opposite of his mother's. His problem required an analytical approach. He needed to distinguish between what was said and what was meant in order to answer his key questions: Who were the people he had to deal with? And what did they want from him? In his mother's childhood these questions had been irrelevant, because pogroms were not triggered by specific Jewish behavior, as the Maskilim (Jewish intellectuals committed to the Enlightenment) had believed, but rather by the very existence of the Jews as Jews. Hence Bryna's coping strategy was not geared toward Jewish self-improvement but toward bringing the Jews into the international brotherhood of peoples. In Montreal, however, despite small pockets of resistance, the Jews were so secure that coping and adaptation ceased to be perceived as a group problem. They were now the individual's responsibility.

For Sacvan Bercovitch, getting along was always an immediate problem because he could not use any social group as a protective shield. His own family was in a constant state of disarray. The emotional chaos exacerbated the poverty and vice versa. As one visitor to their home recalled, "We were all poor, but the Bercovitch poverty was special. My father sold newspapers until he found work as a machinist in 1939 . . . but we always had enough to eat and we were well-clothed. The Bercovitch family had that terrible kind of poverty where clothes and food seemed inadequate. The atmosphere was emotionally charged, and Bercovitch and his wife seemed at daggers drawn. Perhaps it was because they had less money, fewer clothes, than anyone."[37] Hence his childhood in the Jewish slums, first on de Bullion and then St. Dominique Street, was quite unlike the childhoods in nearby St. Urbain and Napoleon Streets, described in Modercai Richler's *Apprenticeship of Duddy Kravitz* or Saul Bellow's *Herzog,* whose singular feature was intense familial, if not tribal, cohesion. "Napoleon Street, rotten, toylike, crazy and filthy, riddled, flogged with harsh weather—the bootlegger's boys reciting ancient prayers."[38] The idea of one Jewish people (the "bootlegger's boys" assembled in prayer) functions as a mechanism of cohesion that overrides the divisive reality of the filthy street. For the solitary boy on St. Dominique Street, that mechanism did not work, and he was threatening to fall through the net that had kept the Jews together.

In the early 1940s, the family was breaking apart. It was the intrusion of a stranger, the family's boarder, that by upsetting the delicate balance the family had found ended the "armed truce" the parents had concluded in the mid-1930s.[39] Sacvan Bercovitch recollected the events very clearly:

My sister Sylvia was going out with this terrible man [an immigrant from Poland who worked as a house painter]. My parents were against it. But my mother was doing exactly the wrong thing, which was to threaten her to prevent her from doing it. She enlisted my father in this cause, who actually threatened the man in the street with a knife. It did not help. My sister got married anyway [in December 1940] and moved out. Once she had gotten married, my father declared that she had excommunicated herself, but my mother said, What can I do, she is my daughter, I have to go to her. My father was so enraged about that—here he had been on her side and risked his life—that he moved out. That broke up the household, and in 1942 my sister moved back in with her husband, Solomon Ary, and her infant daughter Rokhl. My sister Ninel and I were still living there.

The first thing Ary did was to throw out Ninel. She was about seventeen and was working as a secretary. She went away for a two-week vacation, and when she came back, he told her go find another room, you cannot live here anymore. She went, and I was left. And then he decided that there was no reason for him to support me. After all, I was eating. He said my father was earning money, I am his son, let him give me the money. In other words, I should pay for room and board.

So I would go to my father's studio on Prince Arthur Street every week to get the five dollars in child support. One very cold winter day —I didn't have gloves and my hands were frozen—I remember coming into the house and I looked into my pockets and there was no five dollars. I had lost it. There was this little group meeting and he said, Well, go back and ask your father for five dollars. So I trudged all the way back and I said, he wants five dollars. And my father said, Go back and tell him that I already gave you five dollars. So I went back—this is a long walk—and I said, He is not giving me the money. And he said, Go! Go to your father and let him take care of you! So I went to my father, and said, He says I have to leave the house. So my father got an idea—a lightbulb flashed. He called up the charity institution and told them that I had been thrown out of my house and was now a charitable case, so he didn't have to pay the five dollars a week anymore. And this is how I got into foster homes.[40]

At the age of nine, the boy was sent to a foster home in one of the poor neighborhoods, and a bit later to another one in a lower-middle-class area that aspired to respectability; yet it was always clear to the child that both families did not care for the new addition to their table but needed the Jewish philanthropy money that paid for his room and board.

Since he was being moved around so much, attending his old school became a point of stability. Bercovitch went to a Protestant public school in the morning and, until the age of twelve, to a Jewish school in the afternoon. He did not continue his Jewish education beyond that age, because *mitlshule* would have cost money and he was not good enough as a student to receive a scholarship. He was too depressed to study, and school could not create in him a sense of belonging to a group. "I did not learn anything in school at all," Bercovitch recalled:

Nobody seemed to care whether I went or not. I signed my own report cards. I had no incentive to study. I found out that I could get by, by simply *telling* people, when they asked, that I had good grades. I had no particular ambitions. But I had dreams of glory. They were secret and vague and not really attached to reality. I wanted to become famous in some way, as a baseball player, say, or as a writer. But it was all very abstract. That is, my dreams of glory never had anything to do with what I *was* doing. It was not as if I was playing ball and wanted to become famous for that. Rather, I would always become somebody else. I would become—Michael Jordan; or, they would find all of Shakespeare's plays in my desk. The dreams were all the same—escape dreams, being some-one else, like Einstein, but it would not be connected to studying physics.

I never had the confidence to concentrate on anything. I did not study for school, although I had a sense that if I did study, I could do well. But I never did. I think in order to work hard at something, you need faith in yourself. My ambition was vaporous. I did not believe that I could *do* anything. There was also something else, which is hard to define: I felt I should not try to succeed. It was as though trying in the world was to betray something. I was so identified with a certain kind of misery or poverty that I felt it would be inappropriate for me to be different. I was caught in the fatalism of the poor; you don't feel that anything you do will mean anything.

In a curious way, Bercovitch's mind-set resembled that of his realistic maternal grandmother, whose down-to-earth skepticism he shared. Overwhelmed by adversity, they both witnessed the failure of the idealists and their rhetoric to change the course of events. Not only was it quite useless to carry on about the world as if it could be changed; it was equally absurd to take action, since nothing one did made the least difference. The grandmother's resigned skepticism, however, had been balanced by a strong sense of belonging to a group that valued itself, a confidence still intact in Bellow's *Herzog,* where in the midst of hideousness, "wagons, sledges, drays, the horses shuddering, the air drowned in leaden green, the dung-stained ice, trails of ashes[,] Moses and his brothers put on their caps and prayed together: 'Ma tovu ohaleha Yaacov . . .'/ 'How goodly are thy tents, O Israel.' "[41] That confidence, of belonging to a group larger than one's immediate family had eroded in Sacvan Bercovitch. Recourse to religion was out of the question; school, including Jewish school, was something to be gotten through; and the world of Yiddish culture, while most closely associated with feelings of home, was "poor and outside and incompetent and strange" (interview). The boy's "yearning for community," his longing to fit in, became intense. "The younger of my two sisters, Ninel, had a strong urge, which I shared, to be conventional. That was my dream: To be just like everybody else, to fit in, and to be liked. I wanted respectability." Years later, when Bercovitch explained to his students Huck Finn's yearning to be like Tom Sawyer, he recognized the psychological reality of Huck's longing, along with the fundamental impossibility of its fulfillment.

The reason that Huck Finn cannot conform is not his moral difference from shore society, his instinctual goodness (as Lionel Trilling would have it) compared to the selfishness and hypocrisy of "sivilized" society. (The novel's ending, which upset Leo Marx so much, implies that Huck is not morally different from shore society.) Rather, Huck compulsively lights out because respectability, when he has it, cannot satisfy the craving that arose in the time of deprivation. Hence he constantly drifts back to the state associated with home: "I got into my old rags, and my sugar-hogshead again, and was free and satisfied." [42] Bercovitch, too, would on occasion exchange respectable tweed and Oxford pinpoint for his childhood rags: "I would always assume marginality," he remembered. "And when I happened to be inside, I would drift outside all the time. When I was in New York, for example, teaching at Columbia, I would often be down at 42nd Street, walking around those areas. It's a certain world that is familiar to me. I would go to certain places for eating and drinking that felt familiar. I did not go there because I wanted to, necessarily. I just ended up there all the time. That was true even when I went to California to teach at UC–San Diego. I would always drift back to those areas. I would feel more comfortable there because what I saw my eyes were used to seeing. I would look at people in a way I had looked at them when I was growing up. I had always been outside, watching."

Saul Bellow described this phenomenon for Moses Herzog, a professor of English literature who grew up in the chaos of Napoleon Street. Herzog catches himself obsessing about childhood scenes: "To haunt the past like this—to love the dead! Moses warned himself not to yield so greatly to this temptation, this peculiar weakness of his character. He was a depressive. Depressives cannot surrender childhood—not even the pains of childhood." [43] In the end, however, an end that was much criticized at the time, Herzog, unlike Huck, is able to surrender them and to accept his imperfections as an adult.

For Bercovitch, surrendering childhood took hard work. It was certainly impossible while his parents were alive. He found himself tied by a peculiar sense of loyalty. Toward his father it expressed itself indirectly, in a single-minded interest in painting. "I used to paint all the time," Bercovitch recollects. "I stopped painting around the time my father died [in January 1951]. That was completely unconscious. But after he died, I simply found that I *disliked* painting and I stopped." A few months after his father's death, Bercovitch graduated from high school, moved back with his mother and sister and her family, and went to work as a clerk in a clothing factory. It was only when his mother's illness required hospitalization that Bercovitch felt free to leave, his sister recalled, "because she was taken care of." When she died in 1956, Bercovitch was working on a kibbutz in Israel.

24. Sacvan Bercovitch with his mother and his sister, the painter Sylvia Ary, at Hospital of Hope in 1950. *Courtesy of Sacvan Bercovitch.*

Israel

During high school, Bercovitch, who was shy and skeptical, befriended a group of students who had the air of outsiders, of kids who did not fit in. It turned out that they were members of Hashomer Hatzair (the young guard), a left-wing Zionist youth organization. "Left-wing ideas were familiar to me," Bercovitch explained, as was the group's utopianism and high rhetoric of redemption through political action. While the enthusiasm and the sense of adventure that pervaded Zionist youth organizations may have been infectious, what appealed to Bercovitch most was that the Shomrim, as the members were called, "seemed to be friendly people with principles. They seemed a secure family with a way of life that I thought was right." He joined the Shomer (guard; a colloquial abbreviation for Hashomer Hatzair) because it offered connectedness. Not only did the organization address his most immediate need of wanting to belong somewhere, it also integrated his life as a Jew into a larger historical narrative that was at once radically secular and satisfyingly redemptive. In a way, the ideology of the Shomer combined the outlooks of Bercovitch's mother and grandmother. It addressed the hard facts of Jewish suffering by proposing that the Jews give up on the Gentiles and work on their own state; and it tapped into the huge reservoir of left-wing idealism by arguing that a return to unalienated labor within socialist agricultural colonies (kibbutzim) would terminate oppression caused by exploitation and turn the Jews into exemplary members of humankind.[44] "It all seemed very romantic, exciting, brave, and idealistic," Bercovitch remembered. Moreover, the Zionists' broad historical perspective made sense of his parents' exile and offered the son a chance to undo it. Needless to say, Bercovitch did not reason these things out, but, as his sister reported, upon joining Hashomer Hatzair, "he became very conscious of being Jewish" (SA).

When Bercovitch felt free to leave Montreal after his mother's hospitalization, he wanted to go to school in the United States,—most of all in New York City. "As a kid I always saw New York as the Big City. It was where all the excitement was and where things were happening. If you thought of leaving home, it was to go to New York." Supported by the connections of the Shomer, Bercovitch enrolled at the New School for Social Research. When he got a scholarship to Reed College, he hitchhiked to Oregon.[45] But he could not focus on his studies. After a year at Reed he called his sister to announce his decision to go to Israel. When she asked him why he was leaving school, he replied, "What's the point?" (SA).

In the summer of 1954, Bercovitch found himself amid tractors, cows, and chickens on the Shomer's agricultural training farm in Hightstown, New Jersey. He liked the people there and had the sense that they liked him. He was not especially good with machinery, but he worked diligently. He felt strongly that he was on trial and succeeded. "I was redeeming myself," he recalled. After a brief period of basic training, Bercovitch was on his way to Israel. The country was then six years old, and there was still a great deal of frontier spirit.

Bercovitch was assigned to Kibbutz Nachshon, founded near the Old Road to Jerusalem at the Jordanian border just after the War of Independence. It was battle-worn territory. Nachshon had been the cover name for the Haganah's large-scale effort to reopen the road to Jerusalem during the siege of the city in the spring of 1948. When the first convoy, with eighteen hundred tons of foodstuffs, made it through the bottleneck of Bab-el-Wad and reached Jerusalem on April 5, 1948, dancing broke out in the streets. The joy was short-lived. On April 20, 1948, Abdul Khader Husseini and his men recaptured the road, and Jerusalem was again under siege. Six years into statehood, peace was tenuous at best. Arab infiltrations were frequent, and the new arrivals at Nachshon were instructed in the use of rifles and grenades. Because of its proximity to the border, the kibbutz was populated largely by young Israelis (sabras) and included only a small number of immigrants. It was a frontier community, made up of people who believed in their mission. Group cohesion was strong, morale high, and the daily routine enlivened by a daredevil spirit that induced kibbutzniks to plant vegetables in the no-man's-land, even though they were shot at.

In the early 1950s, Israel's kibbutzim were not an ideological luxury but an economic necessity. In 1952 fierce storms of opposition had been unleashed when Mapai, then the governing party, had decided that the current economic crisis could be solved only through massive importation of capital; it was therefore willing to sign a reparations agreement with West Germany. The opposing party, Mapam, argued vehemently against the agreement and suggested that the necessary capital be generated domestically by organizing large numbers of immigrants in agricultural and industrial collectives, and by socializing private capital. Mapam conveniently overlooked the widespread disaffection with practical socialism (not to mention growing disgust with Stalinism), which was reflected in its difficulty to recruit sufficient personnel for existing kibbutzim. Although the arrival of Shomrim from North and South America alleviated the problem, the reality was that in order to expand production and cultivate newly acquired state lands, even Mapam-affiliated kibbutzim had to resort to hired labor.

Nachshon turned out to be the wrong kibbutz for Bercovitch. The majority of its inhabitants were young Israelis, whose cocky self-assurance, bordering on smug self-righteousness, grated on Bercovitch, just as his skepticism and self-deprecating irony annoyed them. It was a classic instance of culture clash. "I tried very hard to fit in. But for some reason, they did not trust me. They suspected that I wouldn't stay." Their suspicion was not unfounded, since Bercovitch's Hebrew remained poor and he was compelled to communicate in English or Yiddish. In a country where language and national identity were intimately linked, Bercovitch's linguistic incompetence was read as a lack of commitment. Moreover, while English was marginally acceptable, Yiddish represented everything young Israelis wished to leave behind. "They had contempt for Yiddish," Bercovitch recalled, "because it represented the *golah* [exile] and self-deprecating humor, Jews making fun of themselves, which they hated." They felt that "seeing the humor in a situation that was awful" represented an acceptance of suffering and injustice, and they considered such acceptance evidence of "the kind of mentality that led to the concentration camps. The sabras took things very seriously."

They were dedicated, disciplined, and practical. "They liked straight talk and hard work. They were no-nonsense people. They did not read much. They respected competence and did not have much patience for people with two left hands. I understood why they didn't, but they irritated me anyway; all the more so because they were kibbutzniks, socialists, and Jews." His disappointment proved that Bercovitch had put his heart into the Jewish people, and that despite his self-ascribed skepticism, he was quite capable of idealization.

The sabras' distrust made Bercovitch all the more determined. He worked hard, graduated from shoveling manure to milking cows. In July 1956, he married an American, Gila Malmquist, who had been living in Israel since 1952. Her first husband had died of polio in 1954, leaving an infant daughter. "Gila was very well adjusted to life in the kibbutz," Bercovitch recalled. "I was very marginal. Marrying Gila meant to me that I was permanent on the kibbutz, because Gila was the sign of American permanence. The whole kibbutz thought that of all the Americans she was the one who was real. It was very clear in my mind that this marriage was the strongest commitment I could make to life in Israel." In April 1957 their son Eytan was born. But, as Huck Finn said, "it warn't no use." Two years into the experiment, Bercovitch's old way of looking at the world, dissociating rhetoric and reality, reasserted itself. He made a startling discovery: life on a kibbutz had in fact very little to do with the utopian ideals he so desperately wanted to believe in.

"One morning," Bercovitch related, "I had a revelation. I saw that after all the rhetoric about changing the world and starting a new way of life was put aside, what I was doing was being a farmer. I was milking cows. I had this vision of my whole life. I could see where I would be in forty years, and who I would be talking to, and what I would be saying and what they would be saying. And suddenly, it felt like a very small village. My revelation was that although everything people were saying about Jews finally being able to cultivate their own land, and so on, might be true, the fact was I was a farmer."

Nevertheless, Bercovitch did not want to leave. During his last year in Israel, he became very ill with asthma and was hospitalized with hepatitis. It was his wife who eventually said that she had had enough. "In a way it was easier for me [to say that we had to leave]," Gila Bercovitch explained, "because I was so established. I could see very clearly what our lives were going to be like. I remember lying in the grass and looking up at the sky with all its stars, looking at all of it and just feeling the narrowness of existence, and feeling that we had known too much when were young to have this be all. But the actual parting was still difficult, because we were deserting a community." [46]

Her husband felt similarly. "It was a way of life I wanted to believe in. I wanted to believe that people could change. I tried very hard. But there was a certain point beyond which I could not go. I could work hard for a cause and I could get excited over certain injustices, but to be a believer, that is, to believe a party, or a line, or an individual, I could not do. I could not belong to a cause. I believed in Zionism, but I could not be a Zion*ist,* for the same reason that I couldn't be a Marxist or even a Socialist. Almost in spite of myself, I could not be an *-ist.* And yet I found it very hard to leave the kibbutz. It was like leaving behind a lot of ideals. In a way, leaving the kibbutz meant recognizing that I was not going to be a believer. And that was hard."

California

In 1958, Bercovitch came back to Montreal and took a job at Steinberg's, a supermarket chain. He was quickly promoted to an executive position. The management encouraged him to go to school at night. He attended Sir George Williams College, then the adult extension of the Montreal YMCA, now Concordia University. "It was then that he began to realize that he was really talented in certain ways," Gila Bercovitch recalled. But the pursuit of talent was a luxury so remote from the urgencies of real life as to not be on the map of possibilities for Bercovitch. It was not something he thought about. He was desperate for a job that would support his wife and two small children, and he was desperate to get out of the supermarket. "I knew this was a world I would not do well in," he said. He was doing well in school and had been offered a fellowship. Hence a career in college teaching gradually came into view. "It seemed to offer a life which was fantastic to me compared to the business world. I was in a state of total ignorance about it. I don't know how to convey that. I came to graduate school without even a sense of what was in that world, but with a sense that I would just have to master whatever that world contained." [47]

25. Sacvan Bercovitch at Claremont
Graduate School in 1963. *Courtesy of
Sacvan Bercovitch.*

Since Bercovitch did not quite know what he wanted to teach, he
decided on literature. It was vaguely connected to his mother's world,
which had been full of books and literary visitors, and it seemed to him
the most interesting subject he could think of. What is more, it came
with a miraculous bonus: "I thought it was marvelous to be able to read
books and to get paid for it. In most of the world people do things they
don't like. At the beginning I could not really believe that people paid
you to read books and think. It's apparently useless, a privilege, really,
and yet, amazingly, people get paid for reading Shakespeare and Melville.
I decided that this would be a great way to earn a living."

After three years of night school, Bercovitch received his B.A. in
1961, along with the Governor General's Medal in English Studies and
a Woodrow Wilson fellowship that was good for almost any university
in the United States. "I did not know anything about graduate schools,"
Bercovitch explained. "So I sent out for pamphlets, just as you write
away to hotels for summer vacation. Claremont had the nicest pamphlet;
people seemed very happy in the photos, sitting around on green lawns
in wonderful scenery; so I went there." His wife, who was from Los

Angeles and still had family there, was glad to return to the area. Bercovitch thought "it would be good to be close by in case we needed help.
"He was then on the brink of two stunning discoveries that would
change his life—academe and America.

Bercovitch discovered academe slowly. But once he had discovered it,
he fulfilled all requirements with incredible speed. He did his graduate
class work in five semesters and left Claremont Graduate School in 1964
to accept an instructorship at Columbia University. He received his
Ph.D. from Claremont in 1965 and an appointment as assistant professor
at Brandeis University in 1966. Two years later, he moved on to the
University of California, San Diego as associate professor. He returned
to Columbia as full professor in 1970 and was promoted to an endowed
chair in 1980. Three years later, Harvard offered to make him Charles
H. Carswell Professor of English and American literature, a position he
still occupies.

Over the years Bercovitch has become aware of the links between his
migration to America and his entry into academe: "From the start," he
wrote in 1993, "the terms of discovery were interchangeably personal
and professional. What began as a graduate student's research issued in a
series of investigations that express both a developing sense of the culture
and a certain process of acculturation" (RA 1). At the same time, the
eccentric angle from which he approached academe and America, as
well as the unique style in which he first went about these discoveries,
produced an analysis of America of such startling originality and persuasiveness that a baffled academic establishment found itself utterly disarmed and without effective means to resist the transformative sweep of
Bercovitch's scholarship.

His discovery of academe, which was to him "the ultimate terra
incognita," had been cautious rather than slow. Living precariously, he
could not afford to make a mistake. "I went about it like a professional,
like an outsider. It was a matter of survival. I was scared. So I looked at
how people went through graduate school in a very objective way. I did
not think of it as, 'What am I going to write about?' I thought of it
more as, 'What do they want from me?' and I would give them what
they wanted." That meant above all a certain number of papers, which
seemed easy enough. "I thought the first paper I wrote was pretty good.
But the man who read it did not think so. I asked him how to do these
things. He suggested that I read some essays, and since he had his office
in the library, he added, they are right out there. So I went out and saw
all these books and journals, churning out hundreds of articles a month.

It was dazzling. I remember sitting all afternoon with these journals. I just sat down and thought, How do they do this? By the end of the day I had discovered the secret, which was, you take the most perverse point of view you can and you prove it with three examples. So I tried it out. The next paper I wrote was on a medieval poem, *Sir Gawain and the Green Knight*. It was taught in class as a romance and I knew what I had to do. I wrote a paper claiming that it was not a romance and I published it.[48] From then on I had the formula."

In the mid-to late 1960s, Bercovitch published on a great variety of literary subjects, including Shakespeare, Kyd, Milton, Blake, Wordsworth, Cooper, Emerson, Hawthorne, Melville, Mark Twain, Dostoevsky, and Thomas Mann. While these early essays document his easy mastery of all relevant intellectual and technical aspects of academe, from acquiring the professional lingo of criticism to finding the right outlets for his products, it was Bercovitch's analysis of American Puritan writing that revealed to him the rhetorical dynamics and narcotic properties of imaginative writing. Moreover, Puritan writing provided him with a key to the symbols and dreams of American culture, and in the end functioned as the Archimedean point from which he rather elegantly dislodged some of the canonized constructs of his academic precursors.

America

Claremont Graduate School was one of the least likely places to inspire a dissertation on Puritan typology. But Bercovitch had two incentives. The first was pragmatic: "Nobody there really knew about the Puritans," he explains, "so I could work on my own. I thought it would be faster that way." The other incentive was curiosity: "I got interested in America. I was just coming into American culture and was discovering the literature simultaneously with the national community. It seemed silly to be in America and to study English literature, which had been my plan. I decided I should find out about the Puritans, the official origins of the culture, if I wanted to understand America." He began reading the works of John Winthrop, Samuel Danforth, and Cotton Mather and was surprised to find that "they were different from the way they were pictured by the standard scholars. For example, Perry Miller claimed they were rational and theological and declined in the eighteenth century. Finished. What I found was that they were imaginative, full of dreams and rhetoric and biblical myths, which they reenacted and which continued to live on in the rhetoric of the American imagination."

Although at first glance Bercovitch's discovery seems to have conformed to the neophyte's academic formula of taking the most perverse point of view possible, his subsequent scholarship demonstrated that his notion of the Puritans had not been cooked up under the pressure of academe but had been shaped in response to an astonishing insight into the American mind. Bercovitch began to perceive the culture's tendency to dissolve hard facts in visions of the future or, as he wrote of Cotton Mather, to recast "fact into image and symbol." [49] It was an all-too-familiar strategy. But, as Bercovitch soon realized, the Puritans gave it a subtle yet effective twist: they eroded the distinction between actuality and anticipation by transforming both into myth (CM 139). That twist changed their writing from straightforward compensation into the therapeutic mythopoesis that produced the idea of America.

Setting out in pursuit of the Puritans' compelling vision of the New World, Bercovitch found himself propelled into the center of American studies as his "explication of religious types open[ed] into descriptions of national rituals, strategies of symbolic cohesion, and the paradoxes of Emersonian individualism, then and now" (RA 1). Moving outward from a single text, Cotton Mather's Magnalia Christi Americana (1702), which he used "somewhat in the Puritan manner of 'opening' a scriptural text" (PO ix), Bercovitch's exegetical vision, like his books, became ever more inclusive until it encompassed, in a true feat of gaonismo, all of America's literary history in his edition of the Cambridge History of American Literature.

Bercovitch's first essay on the Puritans appeared in 1966. It argued that Mather's Magnalia, like Virgil's Aeneid and Milton's Paradise Lost, celebrated "a great legend in the form of an epic. To be sure, Mather never says so explicitly. Sharing the Puritan distrust of all poetic modes, he adopted the role of historian." Yet Bercovitch set out to show that Mather's Magnalia needed to be read as an "important work of the figurative imagination," which "recasts fact into image and symbol, and raises the story of New England into a heroic world." Moving systematically from proofs of Mather's "familiarity with The Aeneid and Paradise Lost" to an analysis of Mather's opening lines as epic invocation, suggesting that "the New England epic surpasses as well as resembles its Latin predecessor," and on to an explication of the Magnalia's epic structure ("apparent chaos controlled by a vision that looks always beyond the present") and literary techniques (the transposition of history into "open metaphors"), Bercovitch concluded that "the *Magnalia* is a germinal work of symbolic art" whose main theme, central metaphors, and possibly even its structure, could "all be traced throughout subsequent American literature." [50]

In a series of short, focused publications, Bercovitch tried to establish precise textual evidence for his theory of the longevity of the Puritan literary imagination. In 1967 he traced the legend of the "seven-branched golden candlestick" in Hawthorne's *Marble Faun* to Mather's *Magnalia,* using the connection as an exegetical clue to Hawthorne's novel.[51] Elsewhere he examined Hawthorne's use of Puritan typology, arguing that "it has not been recognized that with his 'long absorption in Puritan writings' he understood and, for his own purposes, used their typological method throughout his fiction." [52] Compelled to leave the safe example of Hawthorne in search of further proof, Bercovitch sent feelers into the eighteenth century and suggested that one see in the *Magnalia* "not only a precursor of Benjamin Franklin's morality, but, more specifically, the pioneer in American letters of the rags to riches formula, worthy of the title of father of the New World success story." He admitted, however, that the resemblances between Franklin and Mather were "wholly accidental" and hastened to add, a bit incongruously, that "this itself underlines the more important parallel in form and outlook." [53] It was not a very satisfying line of argument. The piecemeal evidence would add up, but it was not compelling.

The way to tackle the longevity problem was not to point out little continuities here and there, but to establish the American Puritans as powerful literary minds and visionary presences whose imaginative legacy shaped America's view of itself. The opportunity came in 1972, when Bercovitch wrote a profile of Cotton Mather for a collection of essays entitled *Major Writers of Early American Literature.* His article was by far the book's longest and most unusual contribution, certainly insofar as the author turned out to be his subject's match in intellectual intensity and cultural vision. Bercovitch presented Mather, the grandson of Richard Mather and John Cotton, as a man on the brink of a new age, emotionally and psychologically bound to his forebears, deeply committed to the task for which he seemed to have been so unequivocally singled out—the leadership of the Puritan theocracy. Nevertheless, Mather was painfully aware that he was going to be a leader without a flock, a church of one, the keeper of a flame whose spiritual fire was made to look ridiculous in the brilliant illumination created by the scientific insights of the Enlightenment and the philosophic works of the Age of Reason.

In four steps Bercovitch explained Mather's strategies of coping, developed in response to the hard fact of the declining Puritan theocracy. Examining first Mather's diaries, Bercovitch finds their writer to be a man who "belonged *in toto* to the former era" (CM 98):

> His very sophistication seems from this perspective to have hardened his allegiance; in effect, it sharpened the shocks of reality that impelled him inward, toward the shelter of the imagination. The more he discovered how thoroughly his education had failed him—the further he drifted into the supersensual chaos of the Age of Reason—the closer his identification grew with the vanished theocracy which for him enshrined the true meaning of the country. It is this commitment, this visionary's No-in-thunder to the way of the world, which adds, I think, a redeeming suprapersonal dimension to Mather's outrage. More largely, it is this self-concept which welds the fragmentary entries in his "Testimony" . . . into a spiritual autobiography of remarkable coherence and extraordinary cultural import. (CM 98–99).

In the shelter of his diary, Mather invented images for himself—images of self-affirmation and heroism in the face of adversity—that helped him cope with public defeat. His most productive and soothing literary device was typological exegesis. With increasing confidence, Mather's diaries present "a procession of *figurae* which all but submerge the actual man within the metaphorical—specifically, within the dual image of John the Baptist and Christ, alternately (and in the end, simultaneously) messenger of the New Day and Man of Sorrows, the greatest of sufferers misjudged as the greatest of sinners. Through the image of John, Mather sought to recover the social role that history denied him" (CM 100).

There is nothing spectacularly remiss or overreaching in a writer's occasional recourse to the trope of *imitatio Christi;* but, as Bercovitch points out, Mather's diaries stand out "for their conscious, diversified, and transparently compensatory application of the concept" (CM 102). Augmented by a variety of other typological guises (including Adam, Job, Samson, Elijah, Moses, and David), Mather's persistent identification with the suffering Savior provides him with an "aesthetic formula through which, in the diaries, he resolved his identity crisis" (CM 111). Bercovitch then moves back to examine the first phase of Mather's

writings (1683–1700) and finds that "as in the diaries the clue to his
creative energies (as distinct from whatever psychoses we think we discern) lies in his persistent stress upon the images through which he
forged his identification with Puritan New England" (CM 107). If
the diaries became a testimonial of self-affirmation, Mather's published
writings amounted to an "impassioned affirmation of the colonial cause"
(CM 108). In the face of major social and political setbacks, such affirmation was hard to come by. But Mather's formula of reinterpretation
held, enabling him to find "solace in God's very displeasure" (CM 114).
Only a literalist despaired when faced with adversities:

> *Sub specie imaginationis,* as Mather understood them, they opened out into
> a magnificent overarching plan, one that pronounced the colonists the
> long-typed-out Israel *redivivus.* His public addresses transform the "vicious
> Body of mockers" he rails against in his letters and diaries into a belea-
> guered but "Precious *People* of God," a "people which may say before the
> Lord, as they in Isa. 63:19. Lord *We are thine,*" the blessed remnant of
> which "it was said Rev. 18:20. *Rejoice over her, thou Heaven.*" A veritable
> "cloud of witnesses," he claims, attests to his position, including the fact
> of the colony's supernatural growth into a second Paradise. How, then,
> can any thoughtful New Englander submit to pessimism? How can he
> not *"Venture his all, for this Afflicted people of God,"* how fail to "say as the
> Martyr once, *Alas That I have but one Life to loose!* 'Tis *Immanuels Land*
> that we Venture for." (CM 113)

While politically such grandiloquence seemed naïvely hyperbolical,
Bercovitch pointed out that, considered as literature, this passage from
the diaries achieved two important goals: "First, it superimposes
upon the facts of declension a corporate essence which effectually eradi-
cates the threat of reality; and secondly, it conjures up an ideal auditory
through which he can seize the present, after all, for his historiography"
(CM 113). And the latter was decidedly Mather's primary goal.

Before Bercovitch turned to Mather's most significant work, he examined the second phase of Mather's published writings (1700–1728).
If resignation was not Mather's response to adversity, neither was pure
withdrawal into the shelter of the imagination. Until the end of his life
Mather thought of himself as "prophet-watchman," urging his community to repent and to do good. Elaborating on his earlier observations
about Mather's influence on Franklin, Bercovitch now sketched two
distinct intellectual traditions inspired by Mather's essays on ethical and

religious improvement: the humanitarian-scientific outlook of Franklin and Jefferson, and the metascientific, counterrationalist view of Edwards and Emerson. Although Bercovitch showed persuasively that Mather's ethical essays reached beyond the Puritan world and became important documents "in the continuity of the culture" (CM 123), it was really Mather's historiography that was the crucial element in the evolution of American self-perception.

Hence he concluded his profile of Mather with an analysis of the Puritan's "largest and greatest book," *Magnalia Christi Americana*. Mather's "literary *summa* of the New England Way" (CM 148) provided Bercovitch with an occasion to present a preliminary summary of his investigations into America's cultural secret. One of the clues to the country's confoundingly strong cultural cohesion in the face of overwhelming social and ethnic fragmentation lay buried in the *Magnalia*. Mather's obstinate refusal to let the hard facts of the theocracy's social and political decline obliterate his forebears' vision of New England's special destiny, the Holy Commonwealth's perpetual progress toward the realization of Paradise, resulted in his construction of a "monument" or testimonial to "the mighty acts of Christ in America." Mather's *Ecclesiastical History of New England* (the *Magnalia*'s subtitle) translated fact into story. "Whether New England may live any where else or no," Mather declared, "it must live in our History." Mather's imaginative revision unified the country in a grand spiritual design that was always on the verge of fulfillment, and established "an inviolable corporate identity for America" (CM 137–139).

That corporate identity was the center of Bercovitch's interest, and he wanted to find out how Mather had made it up. Building upon his early findings, Bercovitch moved from Mather's indebtedness to the epics of Virgil and Milton to his idiosyncratic biographical method, an "aesthetic interweaving of hagiography and historiography" (CM 141) that culminated in the concept of the representative man. "This approach to biography," Bercovitch wrote, "which extols the individual not as an exceptional being, not even as an individual, but *as the community*, as a circle encompassing the country's wonders, principles, and practices, would seem to preview Emerson's notion of representative men and Whitman's personalism" (CM 144).

In the direction indicated by the words "would seem to preview" lay Bercovitch's future research. For the moment he was content to conclude that Mather's special biographical method in the *Magnalia* allowed him to "redeploy hagiography, martyrology, and ecclesiastical history for his own epic purposes" (CM 144). These purposes were clear enough: the preservation of his legacy in the only realm where it would be inviolable. "Built as a monument *against* realities, founded upon myth and fortified by hermeneutics-become-symbolism, the *Magnalia* survives as a testament to its author's ability to incorporate New England, the world, and time itself within the image-making imagination" (CM 147).

In the early 1970s, then, as Bercovitch was beginning to understand how America's mission had been invented by a small group of immigrants in the seventeenth century, and to have a sense of how their invention manifested itself in his own apocalyptic time, which saw America at war in Vietnam,[54] he found out that his insights were radically different from the views then circulating in academe. He had always known that his reading of Puritan literature was incompatible with the interpretations propounded by the doyen of Puritan studies, Perry Miller. His "basic disagreements" with the Harvard school of Puritan scholarship, which, besides Miller, included Barrett Wendell and Kenneth Murdock, lay in the area of aesthetics. Bercovitch had articulated his dissent most succinctly in his first essay on Mather's *Magnalia*. While in his eyes, Mather's ecclesiastical history was an "important work of the figural imagination,"

> Puritan scholars have discussed it either as a "historical *omnium gatherum*" or, in terms of church tradition, as the *magnum opus* of New England jeremiads. Their view, which assumes the strict subordination of literature to theology throughout the period, has in general stunted a proper literary appreciation of early colonial writing; in particular, their approach is inadequate for the *Magnalia*. Mather's arguments here are not, as they would have it, "theology clothed in metaphor." His arguments *are* metaphor. Written in defiance of "an evil Generation," not for it, the *Magnalia* recasts fact into image and symbol, and raises the story of New England into a heroic world, in which, as Hawthorne recognized, "true events and real personages move before the reader with the dreamy aspect which they wore in Cotton Mather's singular mind."[55]

The problem with pushing (which is different from pursuing) this line of inquiry too aggressively in the early 1970s was ethical rather than scholarly. It was a problem of *derekh erets,* of proper behavior toward another human being. Perry Miller had died in 1963, and Kenneth Murdock, still at work on a scholarly edition of the *Magnalia* for Harvard

University Press (published posthumously in 1977), was at the end of his career. In their own time, Murdock (b. 1895) and Miller (b. 1905), along with their elder colleague in the Harvard history department, Samuel Eliot Morison, had themselves launched a reinterpretation of American Puritanism, which they had come to see as a significant intellectual force in American history. In the early 1970s, their time had passed, and a younger group of scholars was voicing its dissent. But Bercovitch did not think it seemly to join in their clamor. When the opportunity presented itself in 1974 to articulate his overall assessment of American Puritanism, and so to place his 1972 findings on Mather in a larger context, Bercovitch was quite gentle in his critique of his predecessors' work, especially Miller's. He muted his dissent, Bercovitch noted elsewhere, because he was "unwilling to join in the patricidal totem feast following Miller's death, when a swarm of social and literary historians rushed to pick apart the corpus of his work" (*AJ* xv).

But muting one's dissent does not mean suppressing it entirely. Bercovitch had organized a group of younger scholars to contribute articles to a collection programmatically entitled *The American Puritan Imagination: Essays in Revaluation* (1974). In the introduction, one of the best thumbnail sketches of the Puritans as literary intellectuals, Bercovitch conveyed not only the main elements of his new approach but also—and this indicated his new awareness that he was becoming a player in an area that had its own tradition and anxieties—how his revaluation of the Puritans related to the evolving field of American studies. This meant largely the types of scholarship exemplified by Miller, Matthiessen, and the myth and symbol school, which included, among others, Henry Nash Smith, Leo Marx, and Charles Feidelson. Bercovitch treaded cautiously but firmly.

Instead of spelling out the limitations of Miller's view of the Puritans, Bercovitch simply pointed out that the discovery of Edward Taylor's manuscripts in the late 1930s presented a real problem. "Miller's view of the New England mind had precluded a poet of real stature, and here, suddenly thrust upon us, was the most talented and impassioned American poet before the mid-nineteenth century." For Matthiessen's aesthetic appreciation of New England creativity, by contrast, a "good poet fallen among the Puritans, and unable to repress his calling"[56] would have posed no difficulty at all. With the rise of the New Criticism, aesthetic appreciation gained firmer ground in academe, and throughout the 1940s literary scholarship remained polarized between formalism and various kinds of historicism. With the rise of American studies in the early 1950s, the two approaches began to merge.

It was here that Bercovitch saw a chance for opening the narrow concerns of literary studies to a wider "cultural perspective." American studies, Bercovitch argued, "offered, if not a methodology, then at least a rationale for broadening the definition of art from the unique, extraordinary product to the cultural pattern or artifact" (*API* 4). Cultural patterns—more specifically, the ideological texture of American culture —were the focal point of Bercovitch's attempt to figure out America's inner dynamics, that is, its terms of identity and cohesion. Literature was the royal road into the country's mind. "Literature was really a way for me to make sense of the world," Bercovitch recalled. But it all depended on what one was looking for in the literature of a country and how one went about one's discoveries.

One of the directions of inquiry Bercovitch thought promising was the analysis of the "crucial role of myth in shaping American history and historiography," to be undertaken in various humanistic disciplines, including psychology, anthropology, sociology, and of course literary studies. Bercovitch explained that "our consciousness of myth has helped us respond to the tremendous imaginative energy imparted by the Great Migration. Most of the basic elements of the Dream are there: the divine purpose behind America's 'discovery', the teleological distinction of the New World from the Old, the sense of history as ascending ineluctably towards the American paradise. Something of all this has long been recognized, but from a hostile or alien point of view" (*API* 6).

It was the *mode* of inquiry Bercovitch had to change. "To speak as enlightened historians of the 'Puritan myth' is one thing," Bercovitch maintained, "to enter symbiotically into its modes of expression is something quite different" (*API* 6). It was the latter course Bercovitch intended to pursue, since the former "has served all too often as a vehicle of self-congratulation, reinforcing our own myths of progress at the expense of our appreciation of the Puritans' " (*API* 6). Here, then, in Bercovitch's proposal of an empathic reading that would serve "perforce to heighten our respect for the dynamics of Puritan thought" (*API* 6), is the exact point where the immigrant's stance—his theory that he would get to know the country fastest from inside out, through a willing suspension of his own beliefs—is beginning to turn into a method of scholarly inquiry. In his concise introduction to *The American Puritan Imagination,* Bercovitch suggested how such a symbiotic entry should be carried out and what it might achieve:

26. Sacvan Bercovitch as a professor at Columbia University in 1977. *Photograph by
Bernard Gotfryd.*

In following the development, for instance, of the metaphors of garden
and exodus, or errand and trial (on sea, in the settlements, in the heart),
we come to feel the visionary force that sustained the venture. What we
learn thereby pertains to every aspect of the culture. It has taught us—it
promises to teach us a great deal more—about how the settlers adjusted
to the new environment, about the nature of their generational crises,
about the tensions that ultimately eroded the theocracy. It also reveals, I
believe, that the Puritan legacy to subsequent American culture lies not
in theology or logic or social institutions, but in the realm of imagination.
(*API* 6–7)

As these lines went to press, Bercovitch still owed the readers of his
scholarship (an increasing flock) a large-scale demonstration of his
method and full proof of his claim that the Puritans had invented what
we mean by "America." He discharged both obligations shortly after-

wards in two books, *The Puritan Origins of the American Self* (1975) and
The American Jeremiad (1978). These studies were feats of *gaonismo*. The
gaon does not have to start out as *ilui*, or child genius. The *gaon* whose
insights last proves himself in adulthood. The Vilna Gaon delivered his
first homilies at age five, but wrote his enduring works—seventy-odd
volumes roaming far beyond the sacred canon to encompass geometry,
astronomy, and medicine—as an adult. "Known to study with his feet
in cold water so as not to doze over his books," Elisa New wrote, "it is
said that he only slept three hours a night. Lengthening his human
allotment of time by increasing its usage per hour, the Vilna Gaon while
still a young man had drilled through more texts than his elders could
imagine, and by middle age had formulated new readings of everything."[57] As with the Vilna Gaon, so with Bercovitch, whose books drill
in recondite places and transgress marked-off domains. In the process
Bercovitch became not only a discoverer of cultural secrets, but also, as
New put it, "a happy immigrant in any textual space and, by implication,
a disrespecter of enclave or bailiwick."[58] The *gaon* exhibits both revolutionary penchant and quick adaptability to any given circumstance.

Transformation in the process of acquisition, or revolutionary reconstruction, is the paradox that characterizes Bercovitch's two monographs.
In *The Puritan Origins of the American Self,* Bercovitch delivered exactly
what the title announced: a reconstruction of the long foreground to
Emerson's ideal of the representative American. The central aspect of
the Puritan legacy, Bercovitch argued, was "the rhetoric of American
identity." He chose as his point of departure Cotton Mather's life of
John Winthrop in the *Magnalia*. Its title, "Nehemias Americanus" (the
American Nehemiah), opened a Pandora's box of *figurae*. As author and
guardian of New England's ecclesiastical history and hence prophet of
Christ's mighty deeds in America, Mather relates to Winthrop, the leader
of the Puritan exodus into the Promised Land, as Winthrop relates to
Nehemiah, the prophet who led the Israelites out of Babylonian captivity to Jerusalem. Nehemiah was seen as a type of the Messiah of the
Second Coming, just as the Puritan errand into the wilderness "was an
emblem of Christ's hastening deliverance of mankind."[59] When the idea
of specific national election is added to the Puritans' view of themselves
as a type of Israel, God's chosen people, an idea that endowed their
colony (and by extension New England and "America") with the status
of visible sainthood, then the difference between adjective and noun in
Mather's title collapses:

The rhetorical directions of "Nehemias" and "Americanus" converge because the terms come not only to equal but to define each other; Nehemiah's role in sacred history by way of America, America's holy commonwealth by way of Nehemiah. Together they embody the meaning of the errand. The colony at large is the American Nehemiah of the Reformation, as the Reformation is the Nehemiah of the universal church, and as America is the Nehemiah among the nations of the world. And of all this John Winthrop is representative. The source of his heroism is internal; its substance lies in the myth of the New World enterprise, much as the hero of *Leaves of Grass* realizes himself by demonstrating that "the United States are themselves the greatest poem." [60]

Looking back on the Puritans' peculiar auto-bio-hagio-soterio-historiography, it seemed to Bercovitch inevitable that it should be the concept of "America" that distinguished the myth of the Massachusetts Bay settlers. Summing up his observations, he explained:

> More than any other aspect of their thought, the settlers' understanding of themselves as Americans made sense of their experience as Puritans and as New Englanders. The process has something of the circular logic of all compensatory mythical self-projections. It begins by raising an imaginative defense against what seems a formidable external threat, and ends by using that defense as evidence that the threat does not "really" exist, despite "appearances." . . . The New England Puritans, who had a double threat to deal with, extended the rhetoric of self-justification to the myth of a *national* selfhood. According to their circular logic, the country's christic image certified the theocracy's role in redemptive history and this in turn was confirmed by the composite figure of the "true" American. In effect, they provided a mode of spiritual biography which could survive not only the failure of Puritanism but the subsequent revision of New England as the United States. [61]

The writers Bercovitch had in mind were, above all, the major figures of the American Renaissance: Emerson, Thoreau, Hawthorne, Melville, and Whitman, for whom, as for Cotton Mather, the "way out of private despair is the affirmation of a national selfhood which allows the individual to create himself in the image of America even as he spiritualizes America into a metaphor for the journey of the soul." [62] Thus Thoreau's sojourn at Walden Pond can become an autobiography of the exemplary self as "the only true America" (*PO* 174).

On the last pages of his study, Bercovitch presented an outline of American (literary) history as a series of disparate developments fostered by the Puritan vision of America's special destiny.

> The same Puritan myth, differently adapted, encouraged Edwards to equate conversion, national commerce, and the treasures of a renovated earth, Franklin to record his rise to wealth as a moral vindication of the new nation, Cooper to submerge the historical drama of the frontier in the heroics of *American* nature, Thoreau to declare self-reliance an economic model of "the only true America," Horatio Alger to extol conformity as an act of supreme individualism, and Melville, in *Moby-Dick,* to create an epic hero who represents in extremis both the claims of Romantic isolation and the thrust of industrial capitalism. And if that fusion of opposites could exacerbate the differences between history and the dream —if it could issue in the bleak deadpan of *Huckleberry Finn,* or the nihilism of *Pierre, The Education of Henry Adams,* and *The Great Gatsby*—it more broadly sustained the unbounded hope and omnivorous egoism of Emerson's "imperial self." (*PO* 185–86)

In Bercovitch's assessment Emerson was the crucial link "in the continuity of our culture from the Puritan through the Romantic periods."[63] Like Mather's "Nehemias Americanus," Emerson's "auto-American-biography" intertwined personal and national identity and alleviated some of the same pressures felt by the earlier prophet of the American self. "The Emersonian triad is American nature, the American self, and American destiny, a triple tautology designed to obviate the anxieties both of self-consciousness and of the recalcitrant world" (*PO* 178).

The Puritan Origins of the American Self seemed to be essentially a book about the Puritans' view of the self, their notion of the individual's role in history, and the intertwining of secular and sacred history in their idea of national election, capped by an analysis of the interplay of these three elements in Mather's *Magnalia.* The book's last chapter, however, which shifted to Emerson, examined the process by which "Puritan themes, tensions, and literary strategies were assimilated into American Romanticism" (*PO* x) and made clear that the detailed explication of the Puritans' rhetoric and imagination had not been an end in itself, but served as evidence in Bercovitch's still evolving reassessment of American culture. His goal was as simple as it was grand: to understand what "America" was really all about and "to trace the sources of our obsessive concern with the meaning of America" (*PO* ix). His mode of discovery was empathy or, as he called it, symbiotic entry; hence his need to use

Puritan terminology. And what he discovered was "the development of a distinctive symbolic mode" (*PO* ix) that elevated "America" from hard fact to an emblem of redemption that united the country rhetorically.

The publication of *The American Jeremiad* three years later substantiated Bercovitch's empathic reconstruction of American culture. Whereas his first study had examined a concept, the Puritan notion of the individual and its recasting as American self, the second study focused on a rhetorical strategy, the jeremiad or public exhortation, and its function "as a ritual mode of social coherence" (*API* 15). As in the earlier study, the author's mind-boggling discovery was that mere language, imaginatively employed, had the power to determine the perception of hard facts. In 1978, Bercovitch's amazement at the effectiveness of America's delusion still had not worn off. Recalling his first exploration of the jeremiad in 1970, he described its effect on him:

> Indeed, what first attracted me to the study of the jeremiad was my astonishment, as a Canadian immigrant, at learning about the prophetic history of America. Not of North America, for the prophecies stopped short at the Canadian and Mexican borders, but of a country that, despite its arbitrary territorial limits, could read its destiny in its landscape, and a population that, despite its bewildering mixture of race and creed, could believe in something called an American mission, and could invest that patent fiction with all the emotional, spiritual, and intellectual appeal of a religious quest. I felt then like Sancho Panza in a land of Don Quixotes. (*AJ* 11)

By the late 1970s that feeling of level-headed wonder had not yet changed very much and so *The American Jeremiad* was designed to push Sancho Panza's account of Don Quixote's adventures a little further. While *Puritan Origins* focused almost exclusively on the analysis of Puritan texts, the second study "sought to establish connections between rhetoric and history." The hard facts that gave rise to the rhetoric were coming into view. In part, this was a natural consequence of the topic under discussion, since one can hardly make sense of the American jeremiad as "a ritual designed to join social criticism to spiritual renewal" (*AJ* xi) without some awareness of the social ills the Jeremiahs were criticizing. But Bercovitch's greater attention to the hard facts of American history was also due to his insight that rhetoric is most effective when it responds adequately to the hard facts that trouble the audience. "To argue (as I do) that the jeremiad has played a major role in fashioning the myth of America is to define it at once in literary and in historical terms. Myth may clothe history as fiction, but it persuades in proportion to its capacity to help people act in history. Ultimately, its effectiveness derives from its functional relationship to facts" (*AJ* xi).

The facts Bercovitch brought into view were "the steady (if often violent) growth of middle-class American culture" in the course of America's enlargement "from agrarian society through urbanization, the transportation revolution, credit economy, industrialization, corporate enterprise, and expansionist finance" (*AJ* xii). Nevertheless, Bercovitch's emphasis was still on the rhetorical response to these facts. "My argument," he explained, "concerns an *ideological* consensus—not a quantitatively measured 'social reality,' but a series of (equally 'real') rituals of socialization, and a comprehensive, officially endorsed cultural myth that became entrenched in New England and subsequently spread across the Western territories and the South" (*AJ* xii). The study began with an analysis of the Puritan jeremiad and moved on to the adaptations of Puritan rhetoric in the eighteenth and nineteenth centuries, emphasizing "the establishment of the jeremiad as a national ritual during the Federalist and Jacksonian eras" (*AJ* xv).

The book's most important sections, however, turned out to be its first chapter and epilogue, where Bercovitch tackled head-on the two major figures in postwar American studies, Perry Miller and F. O. Matthiessen, unlikely yet tyrannical fathers both. An explicit clarification of his differences with Miller had been long in coming, and fifteen years after Miller's death Bercovitch made his introductory analysis of the jeremiad the occasion to "take issue rather directly with Perry Miller" (*AJ* xv).[64] As always, when utmost precision and clarity were important to him, Bercovitch focused on a single phrase whose conceptual centrality and far-ranging implications he would gradually reveal. In this case, Bercovitch chose a phrase from the title of Samuel Danforth's great election-day address of 1670, "A Brief Recognition of New England's Errand into the Wilderness," which had also provided the title for one of Miller's most famous essays. Calling his introductory chapter programmatically "The Puritan Errand Reassessed," Bercovitch rehearsed Miller's interpretation of Danforth's jeremiad and then pitted his own views against it. In Miller's perception, Bercovitch argued,

> the New England sermons embody a cyclical view of history: the futile, recurrent rise and fall of nations that sustained the traditional jeremiad. But the rhetoric itself suggests something different. It posits a movement

from promise to experience—from the ideal of community to the short-comings of community life—and thence forward, with prophetic assurance, toward a resolution that incorporates (as it transforms) both the promise and the condemnation. The dynamic of the errand, that is, involves a use of ambiguity which is not divisive but progressive—or more accurately, progressive because it denies divisiveness—and which is therefore impervious to the reversals of history, since the very meaning of progress is inherent in the rhetoric itself. (*AJ* 16–17)

The gist of Bercovitch's dissent, lucidly presented in one paragraph of summing up, became the nidus around which a new school of Americanists accreted. Bercovitch wrote:

[T]he fact of the theocracy's decline is incontrovertible. But we need not interpret it as Miller does. His "Errand into the Wilderness" is a hail and farewell to the Puritan vision. Danforth's *Errand into the Wilderness* attests to the orthodoxy's refusal to abandon the vision, and the fact is that the vision survived—from colony to province, and from province to nation. The fact is, furthermore, that it survived through a mode of ambiguity that denied the contradiction between history and rhetoric—or rather translated this into a discrepancy between appearance and promise that nourished the imagination, inspired ever grander flights of self-justification, and so continued to provide a source of social cohesion and continuity. In fact, that is, the New England orthodoxy succeeded, precisely through their commitment to the Puritan ideal, in transmitting a myth that remained central to the culture long after the theocracy had faded and New England itself had lost its national influence. (*AJ* 17).

What Bercovitch captured here is the rise of the "symbol of America" as the "triumphant issue of early New England rhetoric and a long-ripened ritual of socialization" (*AJ* 176). In the epilogue to his study, Bercovitch examined the use of that symbol by the major figures of the American Renaissance. Inadvertently, rather than by design, the epilogue added up to a persuasive argument that ran exactly counter to the one Matthiessen had proposed in *American Renaissance*. Instead of double consciousness, ambivalence, and various literary and cultural dichotomies, Bercovitch stressed the extraordinary ideological cohesion of America's preeminent literary intellectuals and the ways in which they saw themselves as prophets of "America." Taking his cue from Emerson's jeremiad, "The Fortunes of the Republic," Bercovitch concluded:

> To be American for our classic writers was by definition to be radical—
> to turn against the past, to defy the status quo and become an agent of
> change. And at the same time to be radical as an American was to
> transmute the revolutionary impulse in some basic sense: by spiritualizing
> it (as in *Walden*), by diffusing or deflecting it (as in *Leaves of Grass*), by
> translating it into a choice between blasphemy and regeneration (as in
> *Moby-Dick*), or most generally by accommodating it to society (as in "The
> Fortune of the Republic"). In every case, "America" resolved a conflict
> of values by reconciling personal, national, and cultural ideals. (*AJ* 203)

What Bercovitch was beginning to suggest here is that American
literature, perceived in the work of Matthiessen as a literature of subversion and dissent, was not simply "antagonistic" but in complex ways
also "culturally representative." Hence it was necessary to reconceive
"America's 'subversive literary tradition' as an insistent engagement with
society, rather than a recurrent flight from it" (*RA* 363).

The reconceptualization of American literature along these lines was
carried out by a new crop of Americanists. Their collective revision is
most accessibly documented in two volumes of critical essays, organized
in part by Bercovitch and published in 1986. Their programmatic titles
reveal their source of inspiration. *Ideology and Classic American Literature*,
edited by Bercovitch and Myra Jehlen, demonstrated the "emergence of
ideological literary criticism as an approach in its own right." In her
introduction to the volume, Jehlen saw in that emergence a "special
coincidence between a sense that 'social context' was both illuminating
and problematical in the study of literature and the development of an
analytical method that rendered ideology as an interpretive method,
indeed a linguistic, construction in many ways analogous to literature
itself." [65] Elsewhere, Bercovitch defined "ideological criticism" as a
"form of historical diagnosis which requires an appreciation of ideology
from within, in its full imaginative and emotional appeal" (*RA* 362). In
the course of twenty years, Bercovitch's old empathic approach had
acquired some very sophisticated packaging.

The other volume, titled *Reconstructing American Literary History* and
edited by Bercovitch alone, was piously dedicated "to the memory of
F. O. Matthiessen and Perry Miller" but announced its thrust unequivocally in the first sentence of the preface: "The need for a new American
literary history seems clear and unexceptionable." [66] Clear, because "a lot
had happened, critically and creatively, since Robert Spiller and his
colleagues issued their monumental *Literary History of the United States*

(1948)," and unexceptionable, because the call for constant renewal was in the American grain. "Each age must write its own books," Emerson had declared, "or rather, each generation for the next succeeding. The books of an older period will not fit this" (quoted in RALH vii).

Bercovitch agreed with Emerson, at least in the area of academe where he had gotten so perfectly into the American swing of things. He had figured out America's cultural secrets and reconfigured "America" in the process. "A terrifying and strange America is revealed in these remarkable essays," Richard Sennett wrote about Bercovitch's next book.[67] Yet what Bercovitch uncovered was simply the inventedness of America. The idea of America was driven by the powerful desire to dissolve facts in visions; it was a myth created to facilitate man's actions in history. What Bercovitch laid bare was the extreme urgency with which the myth of a redemptive America, of a promise always on the verge of fulfillment, was created and passed on. That urgency revealed something about mankind's desperate need to delude itself—be it about the reality of the world or about the reality of human motives (about the greed propelling the westward expansion for example). In that respect Bercovitch's discoveries revealed something terrifying and strange about all human beings, not just Americans: their inability and unwillingness to look squarely at the facts. But the shock and surprise at this was all on the side of his American readers. Bercovitch, for one, had known about the human need for self-deception, about flights into rhetoric and recourse to myth, since childhood. The discovery *he* made and that astonished him no end concerned the myth itself. The myth of a re-demptive, eternally new America was not terrifying at all. On the con-trary, it was wonderfully comforting and optimistic, and that of course accounted for its popularity and success. "Amerika, du hast es besser," Goethe had said, if only for the reason that Americans, God's special people, were living in the awareness of a divine promise on the verge of fulfillment.

Bercovitch had presented substantial evidence for the inventedness of "America"—its continuing persuasiveness as myth and its political function as symbol—and had not only demonstrated a new analytical method but also taken a leadership role in the ideological reexamination of American literary history. What remained for him to do in the pros-perous, forward-looking 1980s was to edit reprints of seminal primary texts of American literary history, to review and reassess critically his own scholarship, and to dare write books for the "next succeeding" generation.[68] For the next generation of Americans, Bercovitch prepared

27. Sacvan Bercovitch at Harvard University in 1991. *Photographer unknown.*

a new edition of the *Cambridge History of American Literature,* a monumental work in eight volumes, the first volume of which appeared in 1994.[69] And for the next generation of Americanists, a rather different kettle of fish, he produced two different summations of his own scholarship.

The first of these to be published was a reading of *The Scarlet Letter.* It was hailed as a "statement of the new principles of American cultural studies,"[70] a description that was even more applicable to Bercovitch's subsequent publication. *The Office of the Scarlet Letter* (1991) had begun as a series of lectures for the University of Massachusetts, whereas *The Rites of Assent* (1993) was composed of previously published essays. Bercovitch had revised the lectures and the essays to form a running argument that reflected his increasingly sophisticated reading of America. Both volumes were clearly not addressed to general readers but to a new generation of Americanists, for whom they outlined new directions of inquiry.

The Rites of Assent was a commencement of sorts. It combined closure (in the sense of knowing that something had been achieved) and retro-spection with a vision of the future and hope of good things to come ("a rich harvest in due time," *RA* 376). The retrospective was personal as well professional, and one of the book's strengths was that Bercovitch was beginning to explore what he called "the reciprocity between the personal and the professional" (*RA* 1). The book's punning title, com-plemented by its subtitle *Transformations in the Symbolic Construction of America*, hints, in the manner of a private joke, at the way in which professional discovery translated into personal ascent. Considered purely in terms of scholarship, the book presented one more time Bercovitch's vision of America as a rhetorical construct, beginning with the Puritans and ending with a passionate manifesto (first published in 1986) about a new direction for American studies.

What Bercovitch demanded of the next generation in his manifesto was a heightened awareness of ideology as a problem in literary and historical analysis, which might issue in an "attempt to understand its limits and to assess the nature and meaning of one's involvement" (*RA* 356–357). It was in this manifesto, incidentally, that Bercovitch took issue most directly with Matthiessen. He pointed out that Matthiessen had articulated his views when it was "assumed that American literary history transcended ideology" (*RA* 357), and yet Matthiessen himself had been ideologically committed in complicated ways that had shaped his perception of his subject. As Bercovitch cautiously put it, critics like Matthiessen, who understood the major writings of the American Renaissance as a literature of radical dissent "may have had their own special interests for identifying (so as to identify with) an antagonist yet representative American literature" (*RA* 365). But what Bercovitch's ideological criticism of the past thirty years had made clear was that the assumption of an American radicalism was highly questionable. It was either a tautology or a contradiction in terms, but it was definitely a concept of dubious validity in the way Matthiessen perceived it to apply to the writers of the American Renaissance. "We must consider an altogether different possibility," Bercovitch suggested; namely, "that the country's major writers were not subversive at all, or that they were radical in a representative way that *reaffirmed* the culture, rather than undermining it" (*RA* 365).

What Bercovitch hinted at here was the power of ideology to trans-form dissent into consent. This he had identified as the rhetorical thrust of American literature from the Puritan jeremiad to *The Scarlet Letter* and beyond. Just two years earlier, Bercovitch had read Hawthorne's novel as "a story of socialization in which the point of socialization is not to conform but to consent."[71] He had argued that, ideologically considered, the novel's most significant event was Hester's decision to come home to America. Her return was the moment when the scarlet letter did "its office" (*RA* 194). *The Rites of Assent* brought together a full retrospective of Bercovitch's work from his earliest analysis of Mather's *Magnalia* to his most recent essay on Emerson, which was also his most conscious effort to Americanize himself.[72] Taken together, the essays add up to a sustained argument about the function of ideology in American culture, spelled out on the very last pages of the book. Bercovitch's observations there sum up his insights acquired during his long journey from the slums of Montreal, through various utopias, to a chair in American studies at Harvard University, a seat of learning founded by Puritan visionaries:

> [U]topianism has served [in America] as elsewhere to diffuse or deflect dissent, or actually to transmute it into a vehicle of socialization. Indeed, it is not too much to see this as ideology's chief weapon. Ideology represses alternative or oppositional forms when these arise. But it seeks first of all to preempt them, and it does so most effectively by *drawing out* protest, by actively *encouraging* the contrast between utopia and the status quo. The method is as old as ideology itself. Any form of protest, utopian or other, threatens society most fundamentally when it calls into question the claims of that society to represent things as they ought to be (by divine right, natural law, the dictates of holy scripture, the forms of reason). Fundamental protest, that is, involves a historicist, relativistic perspective on the claims of ideology. And the immemorial response of ideology, what we might call its instinctive defense, has been to redefine protest in terms of the system, as a complaint about shortcomings from its ideals, or deviations from its myths of self and community. Thus the very act of identifying malfunction becomes an appeal for cohesion. (*RA* 366).

In short, there is "no escape from ideology" (*RA* 356) and no effective mode of dissent other than to confront ideology head-on as a hermeneutic problem. This was the path Bercovitch had taken; he had channeled his "resistance to the culture into a way of interpreting it" (*RA* 1). Bercovitch was of course much too smart not to see that in not resisting his academic ascent, his dissent had become a forum for consent and hence a tool of (academic) cohesion. What made *Rites of Assent* a remarkable book was precisely that it explored the tension between professional stance (assent) and personal fate (ascent), a tension wittily captured in the title's pun and underscored by the autobiographical frame Bercovitch provided in the introduction for his ideological reading of America. While in academic terms *Rites of Assent* presented the summa of Bercovitch's resistance to the culture, the book took sharp critical measure of his own personal acculturation and rise to preeminence in American academe. The dedication of *Rites of Ascent* to Bercovitch's parents, Bryna and Alexander, and his sons, Eytan and Sascha, looks back and then forward. Between these terminuses lay the author's journey into the American self, whose intellectual repercussions the book documented.

Harvard University

About the emotional repercussions of his assent, Bercovitch had always been remarkably silent, possibly because his stellar academic (and social) ascent, in what appeared to be a picture-perfect realization of the American dream, had no emotional repercussions. "What counts for me," Bercovitch explained, "is personal, not institutional. And Yiddish is the most personal of worlds." Here, then, in Bercovitch's recollection of and allegiance to a past heavy with pain and emotion, lay the center of his resistance to his American success. His acculturation, perceived by him as a way of channeling his resistance to American culture into a way of interpreting it, had been a purely intellectual exercise performed by the cortex. In the limbic system, the seat of the emotions in an older part of the brain, Bercovitch had stored his recollections of the Yiddish world of his childhood. The functions of cortex and limbic system are not reciprocal, they are antithetical. For Bercovitch the private (or inner) world, which gives emotional meaning to persons and events, was completely dissociated from the professional (outer) world.

While Bercovitch was busy surviving in the outside world, making sure he had enough money to support his family, the inner world continued to exist as the outside world's psychological antithesis. "The one thing I kept through all the shifts," Bercovitch explained a bit ruefully, "was the Yiddish connection, although I never did anything with it. I translated some things, but only under a lot of pressure. It was a sort of private world which had nothing to do with the outside world I was adjusting to. One world I associated with getting along, and I never felt at home in it. The other world was private and had to do with emotion and with suffering, with my psychological balance and with my sense of security (or insecurity)." To that private world which regulates self-esteem and determines the emotional significance of people and events, Bercovitch granted outsiders very little access.

It was because of the complete dissociation of inner (personal) and outer (professional) worlds that Bercovitch's ascent, his American success story, had no emotional repercussions. Asked in 1988 what the Harvard chair and the editorship of the *Cambridge History of American Literature* meant to him, Bercovitch replied, "On some important inner level, all these things don't mean anything to me." But he added, "Maybe they are starting to, because they have to. I *am* in Cambridge, I *am* at Harvard, I *am* in academia. I do belong to a certain profession and a way of life. And the point is that I have to have all that because that's really all there is for me now. If I don't have that, I have nothing. That is what I discovered. I don't have Yiddish, and I don't have Montreal; I don't have tradition. I don't have Emersonian self-reliance. Marginality is nothing. It may sound romantic, but it amounts to nothing."

Bercovitch's unsentimental attitude toward marginality combined with his childhood urge to "belong somewhere" to reduce his conscious resistance to his academic ascent. Every university where he accepted a job—Columbia (1964, 1970), Brandeis (1966), the University of California, San Diego (1968), Harvard (1983)—also held out the promise of community. Here, then, one might indeed speak of a strong reciprocity between the personal and the professional, between an inner need to belong and the acquisition of outer trappings. Bercovitch responded most intensely to Brandeis, because being so young, the school needed to invent itself as it went along. "It was a small-college atmosphere, very ingrown, but very excitable," Bercovitch recalled. "There was a sense that the school was growing or could set its own standards. Or that, because it was new, it would be different. The students were interesting *people,* not just good students; they would *be* various things. And the Jewish aspect of the school was very powerful. I really loved the years at Brandeis. I did my best teaching there."

In 1968, Bercovitch received an Award for Excellency in Teaching from Brandeis, along with an offer of tenure. But he decided to leave. His stepdaughter Aliza had recently died of leukemia at Boston's Children's Hospital, and his wife wanted to return to California. So Bercovitch accepted a job at the University of California, San Diego. "And that was a mistake," Bercovitch remembered. "It was a terrible place for me. The university had bought up a lot of good people who were taking advantage of the university. They had come because of the enormous salaries which enabled them to buy houses and to do their work. They were not really teaching. They were cheating the public education system. At the other extreme Ronald Reagan was governor of California, and San Diego was the Mecca of the John Birch Society. It was a crazy place, filled with all these far-left radicals, who were milking the people of California, and these rabid right-wingers, who were always denouncing them. It was just too much."

Herbert Marcuse, who had retired from Brandeis and been hired by San Diego, was an exception, Bercovitch observed, "because he had an old-fashioned, German-professional respect for learning. In 1968 he was denounced as elitist by the radicals there because he objected when they came to class without shoes." Bercovitch was sympathetic to the students; but, trained to look at the hard facts, he was not fooled by their rhetoric. "I felt the students were justified in a lot of things. Some of their demands about the curriculum were right. But I never objected to their objecting, because, generally, they were angry because the faculty did not support them on the war. The Vietnam War was the real issue. I don't think the protest was a matter of high idealism on the part of the students. What was idealism in it was good. But a large part of their protest had to do with the fact that they did not want to get killed in Vietnam. And they were right. They wanted the support of the faculty; they wanted the university to shield them from the war. But the university kept out because of its policy of not interfering in politics. The university was wrong, I think, and the students were basically right, though not particularly high-minded."

Nevertheless, Bercovitch was glad to get back to New York City and to Columbia. In the city's unsettling diversity and the university's aggressive chaos, Bercovitch felt very much at home. "At Columbia it didn't make any difference whether you were inside or not, there was no inside. This also meant that there was room for lots of different types. There could be people like Steven Marcus and Edward Said and the Renaissance scholar Joseph Mazzeo and—me. And people would just assume that there were different ways of doing things. It was very hard to be strange at Columbia, because there were so many acceptable possibilities to be. Whereas at Harvard, there is a certain pattern of doing things. You don't *have* to fit in, but if you don't, you are strange in some ways—not bad, just strange."

Yet when Harvard invited Bercovitch to join its faculty, he was intrigued by the kind of community it had to offer. "I always had a yearning for community—maybe that's why I went to the kibbutz,"

Bercovitch explained, "and perhaps that was part of the attraction of Harvard: it was like going to a kibbutz." Comparing the academic communities at Columbia and Harvard, Bercovitch observed about the former, "it was very dispersed, because New York City had too much gravity. To be in a group at Columbia had limited significance as a form of identity. It *was* a group identity, but when you left the campus and walked down Broadway, it was over. Whereas in Cambridge, at Harvard, you were always there, even when you lived in a distant suburb."

Perhaps moving from New York to Cambridge, exchanging a cosmopolis for an academic enclave, social entropy for a tight-knit community, and Columbia's open aggressiveness for Harvard's smooth professionalism meant for Bercovitch the start of a new life, it certainly meant leaving behind a whole set of experiments in living on the open road, in Whitman's America, and retreating to an Emersonian Brook Farm of the mind, a "genteel kibbutz" of thinkers.[73]

Yet at the same time the move to Harvard also meant coming into an inheritance. One might argue that Bercovitch finally acceded institutionally to Perry Miller's office, having filled his role intellectually for over a decade. Miller had been dead for twenty years when Bercovitch appeared in Warren House in 1983; and it had been fifty years exactly since Miller, at the age of twenty-eight, had published his first book, *Orthodoxy in Massachusetts,* thrown down the gauntlet before the academic establishment ("I have treated in a somewhat cavalier fashion certain of the most cherished conventions of current historiography"),[74] and been promptly appointed to a Harvard professorship. What Miller and Bercovitch both acceded to was America's tradition of dissent. Bercovitch became a beneficiary of precisely the rhetorical mode he had so painstakingly spelled out: the transformation of dissent into a basis for consent. America has always co-opted its dissenters through limited access to power on the condition that they regard the country's shortcomings as regrettable but temporary deviations from the ideals held dear by the dissenters as representative Americans. In this fashion, the subversive energy of dissent was not only defused, but dissent itself, as Bercovitch wrote, was redefined "as an affirmation of cultural values" (*RA* 367).

Was Bercovitch, then, simply another non-Protestant and thus more radical version of Miller or Matthiessen, whose dissenting scholarship became within their lifetimes the accepted and established view of things? That seems to be the case. But there is at least one significant difference between 1933, the year Harry Levin graduated, and 1983, the year Bercovitch acceded to Perry Miller's somewhat tarnished throne, and that difference was real. It lay in Harvard's attitude toward the Jews. Although Levin had always emphasized that he did not feel in the least discriminated against, inclusion and exclusion at Harvard had always been signaled with great subtlety. It was one of Levin's great achievements that he ignored, like the gentleman he was, Harvard's snobbery, and proceeded with his life and scholarship. In time, Harvard, like most other American institutions got over its anti-Jewish prejudice. When Bercovitch arrived to teach the literature of those who had once advocated the conversion of the Jews, nobody batted an eyelash that a member of the Old Covenant should speak competently about the vision of the New Israelites. On the contrary, Bercovitch's Jewishness became an asset of sorts in the eyes of a new generation of (self-)consciously Jewish graduate students.

In his own eyes, Jewishness, as it grew out of his childhood in the poorest Yiddish-speaking neighborhood of Montreal, was, for better or worse, the nucleus of his self. On the one hand, it was, as a legacy of high-mindedness, a source of empathy with Harvard's founders, which Bercovitch delineated with characteristic simplicity: "Although the Puritans were very alien to me, there was also something familiar about them: They were idealists, they were going to set up a kibbutz." On the other hand, as a legacy of social experience, it proved to be a barrier against complete assimilation, which is not to say that comfortable integration was impossible. "I'll never be part of it," Bercovitch said about the Harvard community, "but I can know that I am inside. My soul will never be Harvard, but I think that before I can live properly, I need to get a sense of belonging somewhere."

Not surprisingly, Bercovitch, who like Huck Finn could never submit for long to a belief or follow a party line, described his relation to America as similarly distanced. "I should say I am an American, just in the way as I should say I am at Harvard, because I am. I am as much an American as probably twenty percent of the country. And I know a lot about America. But I don't feel it. Maybe I can come to feel it."

Not "feeling" American is an ephemeral problem that disappears within one generation. If the life stories in this book are any indication, Bercovitch's second son, born in Cambridge in 1992, though named after his grandfather Alexander, who was born in the Ukraine in 1891, will be a regular American kid. The distance traveled between Alexander and Alexander spans a century and half the globe. It is a journey from vision to vision, from the poor man's dream of sufficient subsistence to the dream of the Emersonian young man realizing his full potential. The former is captured in the second stanza of Itsik Manger's "November Ballad," the latter in Bercovitch's narrative of the myth of America.

It seems fitting to end this chapter by recalling the two visions, the beginning and the end of Bercovitch's journey. In the streets of Montreal, Bercovitch started out, like Manger's beggar-child, with the conventional dreams born of need that can bring down foolish aspirations:

> The king trips
> over a disheveled beggar-child
> asleep on the autumnal asphalt
> dreaming of a sack, sun and wind
> a stream of milk,
> running and running,
> and the blossoming forth
> of a hot pyramid of corn-bread.[75]

What Bercovitch discovered in his pursuit of happiness was an opportunity to explore his potential. His journey toward an American self landed him in the pit of a large amphitheater at Harvard University, where he lectures, as Emerson did before him, to a carefully chosen audience of students about the dreams, visions, and ideals of their country. Each year, at the end of the lecture series, three hundred students rise to their feet and erupt into a modern-day ovation—clapping, hooting, hollering, whistling—that lasts for many minutes. As pandemonium breaks loose, the professor slips out the back door and runs up the long staircase, escaping from the myth he created as much as from his fans, and emerging into the bright New England sunshine and the world of hard facts where he has made his home.

Here is part of the narrative Bercovitch has left behind in his students' ears, almost precisely one hundred and fifty years after Emerson shocked his Harvard audience with a series of lectures delivered in 1837 and 1838:

> Emerson and Whitman represent the high euphoric moment of the American myth. They constitute an explosion of the possibility of the America of the dream in the mid-nineteenth century. I want to begin by recalling for you the terms of the myth, because it is a very striking myth, a myth unlike any other—not because it is better, or truer, but because it was formed in the modern world for a country which did not exist. In fact, it was an attempt to make a country exist in the same way that the

Declaration of Independence or the Constitution were verbal attempts at making a country come into existence. It was as though a group of people had decided that by writing it all down, they could make it come into being. It involves an enormous arrogance and self-confidence and faith in the word. The American mythical declaration of independence has the same high euphoria about it, a belief in human possibility.

Other myths are made to commemorate or to celebrate—to commemorate a place or a people, to celebrate a language or certain heroes. America had a conspicuous absence of people, language, or place; and the work of myth was to make a virtue of absence. What's good about absence? It's simple. All you have to do is look at America in the early nineteenth century. It was a country, according to the myth, with no history, a country with no people. This world was new. It was *our* opportunity. That's how you make a virtue of absence regarding space; and absence could be applied to time as well: America is the land of the future. Time does not exist. But if you create a myth for a country based on the future, the future is yours. And you can attach to the future a new set of values, built on absence: the absence of class, the absence of barriers, the absence of limits, the absence of restraint. And so you have the beginning of an American myth, built on freedom of religion, freedom of choice, freedom of place, freedom to become what you want to become—all of this built on absence.

These are the terms Emerson inherited, and he gave them a coherent set of values, a set of moral imperatives, and a hero. What does an absent hero look like? Well, he is young. He represents the one man, his goals are open-ended, his time is yet-to-be, his place is America, his field of action is the frontier of potential, and his mode of action is perpetual resistance.

Here is one of the moral imperatives—heroic action through perpetual resistance—drawn from an essay you are familiar with, "Self-Reliance": Do your thing! Fight on your own terms! Go your own, absolute road! Let hell blaze all it chooses! Trust yourself! There is your field of action, your mode of heroics, and the hero even has a name. His name is YOU —you at your most promising, you as potential representative of the true America.

That true America, which you, the potential hero, embody, if you only turn the right way, that America is a reflection of certain cultural norms, the norms of expansion, of individualism, and of mobility. Such norms, raised to a certain imaginative pitch, may actually become a threat to society. The norms emanate from the culture, but the idea of resistance is a gesture against conformity. The idea of the Self, as Emerson urges you to a Self, is a gesture against mere social identity. Society is everywhere conspiring against YOU. Once you believe that, you are on your way to becoming a true Emersonian. And it involves you in a conflict with society, because the ideal American always stands in some sort of opposition to the real America, in the same way that your ideal Self (with a capital S) always, by definition, stands at the other side of the frontier of who you are right now.

So we come to an important law of myth. First I want to remind you of what I said earlier: A myth is a story that translates the values of the culture from the specific to the universal (for example, God loves democracy), and from the universal to the specific (for example, the world needs the American way), and then back again. It is a process of transvaluation, in which the values *inside* the myth can become volatile: they can go in either direction, in many directions.

America as a symbol has many meanings. It represents the idea of individualism, it represents an actual society, and it represents things to come. A myth can electrify language. It can bring with it a volatility between levels of meaning and categories of thought, which lead to a moment of Emersonian resistance. That is the law of myth I spoke of: a myth is a story whose symbols are so charged, so volatile, that they can challenge or undermine the social values they were meant to celebrate. You set out to celebrate a certain culture, celebrate individualism, celebrate the absence of place, of time, and then, in the course of the celebration, the language is so charged that it can turn against the structures it was designed to celebrate. To repeat, Emerson's doctrine of the divine right of the individual is meant to confirm the American way, but it is a confirmation that sets you at odds with the system, it makes you uneasy about society. The power of the ideal is so electric that it can challenge the social norms that the ideal is meant to defend. That's the reason for the shock at Harvard in 1837, when Emerson delivered his Phi Beta Kappa address at Harvard.[76]

The shock was worse in July 1838, when Emerson delivered to the senior class at Harvard what became known as the "Divinity School Address." He was subsequently accused of infidelity and atheism and banned from speaking again at Harvard for thirty years. Bercovitch, however, returns every spring to explain to his compatriots what exactly Emerson had had in mind for America and how it was working itself out.

Epilogue:
The Idols of the Tribe

The Tribe: A Retrospective

AT THE END OF THE TWENTIETH CENTURY, Jewish scholars are an integral part of literary academe. The spotlight is now on other groups —African Americans, Native Americans, homosexuals, Chicanos—demanding their slice of the academic pie. The moment of the Jews has passed, partly because their integration is complete and partly because unlike the integration of women or African Americans, for example, it never became a politicized demand. And with good reason: if Jews had agitated for their inclusion into academe in proportion to their representation in the population at the time when that sort of thing became possible and fashionable, they would have had to give jobs back.

In 1969, 7.4 percent of all faculty teaching in English departments identified themselves as Jews, and the number was rising steadily. In other departments the proportion of Jewish academics was even higher, especially at Ivy League schools, where 18 percent of professors in their fifties and 25 percent of professors under fifty were Jewish, all of whom had entered academe after World War II.[1] In 1968, Jews comprised 2.94 percent of the population.[2] For them the late 1960s were magic years. They were swept up in a wave of creative exuberance and carried to the apex of cultural self-confidence. The bitter attacks on Philip Roth's novel *Portnoy's Complaint* (1969) as a *shande far di goyim,* an embarrassment before the Gentiles, seem to indicate the opposite, but these attacks came from the older Jewish establishment, while the young reveled in Roth's irreverence. In literary academe, too, the Jews felt secure enough to begin shaking its foundations in works of high-spirited originality such as Stanley Fish's 1967 book on John Milton, *Surprised by Sin*. The journal that printed the up-and-coming literary movers and shakers, many of whom were Jewish, was *New Literary History,* founded by Ralph Cohen in 1969.

The most exciting and significant episodes in the history of Jewish literary scholars unfolded in the three decades on either side of 1969. The earliest phase of integration culminated in the breakthrough year 1939, when Lionel Trilling and Harry Levin were appointed to jobs at Columbia and Harvard, respectively. A phase of consolidation followed, during which the first generation of Jewish literary scholars published their first major works. They produced an abundance of astonishing books, beginning with Levin's *James Joyce* (1941) and Richard Ellmann's *Yeats* (1948), which were followed in rapid succession by Trilling's *Liberal Imagination* (1950), Daniel Aaron's *Men of Good Hope* (1951), Morton Bloomfield's *Seven Deadly Sins* (1952), Levin's *Overreacher: A Study of Christopher Marlowe* (1952), M. H. Abrams's *Mirror and the Lamp* (1953), Charles Feidelson's *Symbolism and American Literature* (1953), Charles Muscatine's *Chaucer and the French Tradition* (1957), Ellmann's *James Joyce* (1959), Leslie Fiedler's *Love and Death in the American Novel* (1960), Aaron's *Writers on the Left* (1963), Leo Marx's *Machine in the Garden* (1964), and Alan Trachtenberg's *Brooklyn Bridge: Fact and Symbol* (1965).

It is striking how oblivious to the difficult foreign and domestic situation these books seem to be. They are the products of a safe and happy white middle class, where men go off to work while women cheerfully chauffeur the children. They are books by men who have no serious quarrel with the world—hence their (now refreshing) lack of rancor; their playfulness, energy, and earnest devotion to literary scholarship. By the mid-1960s a new kind of book was beginning to appear, betraying an increasing restlessness with the intellectual status quo. At first books like Harold Bloom's *Blake's Apocalypse* (1963), Geoffrey Hartman's *Wordsworth's Poetry* (1964), Stanley Fish's *Surprised by Sin* (1967), and Barbara Herrnstein Smith's *Poetic Closure* (1968) expressed dissatisfaction only with the established views of certain poets and literary forms. But as the 1960s segued into the 1970s, these books were joined by others critical of the social status quo. Scholars turned their attention to the literatures of women, African Americans, and other long-neglected groups, practicing in their own world the inclusion at which they saw society fail.

As literary criticism opened itself to questions of identity politics, it also became vulnerable to power struggles, fierceness, resentment, and pettiness. What began in high idealism ended in sharp arguments over how big a slice of the academic pie each group was entitled to. Like the Habsburg empire, the realm of literary criticism disintegrated into numerous nation-states often holed up in little departments of their own.[3] One of the benefits of this reethnicization was the creation of Jewish Studies departments and the publication of the first significant books on Jewish literature by major presses, among them Allen Guttmann's *Jewish Writer in America* (1971), Ruth Wisse's *Schlemiel as Modern Hero* (1971), Lawrence Langer's *Holocaust and the Literary Imagination* (1975), Robert Alter's *Defenses of the Imagination: Jewish Writers and Modern Historical Crisis* (1977).

What held the critical enterprise together for a little longer were the theoretical and methodological revolutions occurring in the works of the French poststructuralists and their American followers. The intense interest in literary theory that dominated American campuses in the 1970s and 1980s created a sufficiently large center of gravity to conceal the fact that literary critics were no longer engaged in a common undertaking. Since the literary theorists were rarely plagued by questions of identity politics, their cerebral enterprise created the illusion of a democratic critical community. But because of the deliberate complexity and difficulty of the language and methods they employed, they formed an exclusive club comparable to that formed by the white male scholars of the 1950s.

It was in the area of literary theory that many of the outstanding second-generation Jewish literary scholars were particularly active, producing their seminal works between the mid-1960s and the mid-1970s. Fish, Bloom, and Hartman, for instance, sharpened their theoretical claims and methodologies in such books, respectively, as *Self-Consuming Artifacts* (1972), *The Anxiety of Influence* (1975), and *The Fate of Reading* (1975). When Fish's radical collection of essays, *Is There a Text in This Class? The Authority of Interpretive Communities,* appeared in 1980, cleverly dedicated to his parents, it seemed indeed as if the first and second generation of literary scholars no longer shared the same interpretive universe. Yet the public disagreement of Abrams and Fish notwithstanding, the two generations were still very much connected—namely, in the pages of *New Literary History: A Journal of Theory and Interpretation.* It was due to the special genius of its editor, Ralph Cohen, that *NLH* captured the moment of transition between old and new concerns in literary criticism. Its editorial board was composed largely of traditional

literary historians, among them Bloomfield, Ellmann, and Earl Wasser-
man, but its pages featured experimental articles, many of them by
Jewish authors, including Jonas Barish, Harold Bloom, Stanley Fish,
Geoffrey Hartman, E. D. Hirsch, Stephen Orgel, and Barbara Herrnstein
Smith.

Clearly, the mid-1960s to mid-1970s, when the second generation of
Jewish literary scholars either pursued literary criticism in the service of
social justice or followed new avenues of theoretical inquiry, were peak
years in the history of Jewish literary scholars in terms of originality,
intellectual sophistication, and energetic engagement with social problems. While the first generation of Jewish literary scholars was still writing significant books and the second generation was at the height of
fame and influence, a still younger set of Jewish scholars emerged in
print around 1980, whose ideas had been shaped by the social revolution
of the late 1960s and the political and theoretical ferment of the early
1970s. Such books as Sandra Gilbert and Susan Gubar's *Madwoman in the
Attic* (1979), Stephen Greenblatt's *Renaissance Self-Fashioning* (1980), and
Jane Gallop's *Daughter's Seduction: Feminism and Psychoanalysis* (1982) very
quickly reduced the authors' immediate academic precursors from
Young Turks to old fogies, with the exception of Fish, who in the
mid-1970s moved on from phenomenological to poststructuralist modes
of thinking and would keep updating his theories and subjects throughout the 1980s and 1990s.[4]

How traditional the views and values of second-generation Jewish
critics had been after all was nowhere more evident than in the opening
words of Hartman's 1973 essay "The Interpreter: A Self-Analysis":
"*Confession.* I have a superiority complex vis-à-vis other critics and an
inferiority complex vis-à-vis art." From today's perspective Hartman has
what Lawrence Lipking inimitably called a "reverence problem." When
Hartman published his essay in the fourth volume of *NLH,* he may have
felt, as Lipking put it, that "the first half was rather daring, the second a
graceful concession. Yet now the second half may cause the trouble. In
an age where many young critics cultivate a hermeneutics of suspicion,
when students often develop by learning to distrust and to struggle
against their tendency to read the text on its own terms, a feeling of awe
in the presence of art can seem critically disabling."[5]

Indifference toward the superiority claims of art, suspicion toward all
forms of reverence, and a continual questioning of established structures
and boundaries were precisely the intellectual marks of the new generation of critics. Two of the most radically innovative younger critics,

Stephen Greenblatt and Marjorie Garber, were two Jews trained at Yale when graduate instruction was still dominated by the grand old men of formalism. Although William K. Wimsatt's theory of the concrete universal—poetry as both highly general and highly particular—seemed to Greenblatt "almost irresistibly true," and Wimsatt's absolute convictions appeared to resolve all uncertainty, Greenblatt was not seduced. As a graduate student in the 1960s, he held on to uncertainty: "The best I could manage was a seminar paper that celebrated Sir Philip Sidney's narrative staging of his own confusion; 'there is no thing so certain,' Sidney wrote, 'as our continual uncertainty.' "[6] Greenblatt and his generation of Jewish scholars succeeded where the preceding generation had failed—they pulled away from the idea of art as a revered object that, within Western culture, was an outgrowth of Christianity. Their shift of focus from one centered on quasi-sacred works of art (verbal icons) toward a criticism centered on cultural artifacts, which was inspired by Marxism, poststructuralism, and a new interest in anthropology, was the most radical secularization and de-Christianization literary academe had yet experienced.

Compared to the intellectual revolution of Greenblatt's new historicism, the simultaneously emerging scholarship that centered on a social and restitutive agenda was much more conventional. It expanded the literary canon to include neglected writers but did not affect the actual consumption of literary works, as Fish's reader-response theory and Greenblatt's new historicism had done. From the mid-1980s to the mid-1990s, the publications by the third generation of Jewish literary critics, who were then firmly established in academe, were becoming more radical and self-assured. Such books as Eve Kosofsky Sedgwick's *Between Men: English Literature and Homosocial Desire* (1985), Walter Benn Michael's *Gold Standard and the Logic of Naturalism* (1987), Jane Gallop's *Thinking Through the Body* (1988), Greenblatt's *Learning to Curse* (1990), Joel Fineman's *Subjectivity Effect in Western Literary Tradition* (1991), Garber's *Vested Interest: Cross Dressing and Cultural Anxiety* (1992), or Shelley Fisher Fishkin's *Was Huck Finn Black? Mark Twain and African American Voices* (1993) would shape the minds of the next generation of graduate students.

What was new, but hardly surprising, in this latest, fully matured generation of Jewish literary critics was how unselfconscious they were about their Jewishness—the men usually more so than the women. If they cared at all about it, they wrote and talked about being Jewish with ease, eager to relate their social and cultural backgrounds to the critical work they did. Fish even went so far as to say in 1988, "Sure I'm Jewish. You can't understand my work unless you know I'm Jewish."[7] In the decade since then, Jewish literary critics have come fully out of the closet and even celebrated their origins in a volume edited by two Americanists, Jeffrey Rubin-Dorsky and Shelley Fisher Fishkin, *People of the Book: Thirty Scholars Reflect on their Jewish Identity* (1996). This new readiness by third-generation scholars to talk about their Jewishness is checked only by their discovery that they have very little to say about it, because beyond childhood memories—some sweet, some sour— Jewishness or Judaism plays no role in their social and intellectual lives.[8]

In this respect third-generation scholars are different not only from their successors, the youngest currently emerging generation of Jewish literary scholars, which includes Emily Budick, Evan Carton, Rael Meyerowitz, Hana Wirth-Nesher, Elisa New, Adam Z. Newton, and David Suchoff, but also from their antecedents because something funny happened to the second generation of scholars, especially those at Yale, during the 1980s: they were reawakened as Jewish intellectuals. Was the awakening triggered by Bloom's unprecedented little book *Kabbalah and Criticism* (1975)? Was it caused by the remarkable new scholarship on Jewish subjects produced by professors of English such as Lawrence Langer, Alvin Rosenfeld, and Susan Handelman? Was it brought about by the desire to move on, at the apex of power and influence, to subjects more intimately linked to the earliest construction of the self than, say, Wordsworth's poetry? Or was it simply occasioned by the astonishing number of Jews then teaching literature? Perhaps all of the above.

In 1985 at Yale, for instance, the number and quality of Jewish faculty led to a remarkable, albeit short-lived, common undertaking, the publication of *Orim*, a revival of the long-defunct *Jewish Journal at Yale*. The twenty members of its faculty advisory board were drawn from fourteen departments and included Bloom and Hartman, but also Leslie Briesman, Shoshana Felman, and John Hollander. Many of the faculty published poems, essays, and imaginative *divrei torah*, commentaries on the weekly Torah portion, in *Orim*. In 1980, Yale had inaugurated an undergraduate major in Jewish studies, and in October 1982 the Video Archive for Holocaust Testimonies opened its doors. By March 1995 the archive had collected 34,000 witness accounts and provided numerous scholars with research material.

At the heart of Yale's Jewish literary enterprise stood two of its most complex and charismatic professors, Harold Bloom and Geoffrey Hartman. Both men had begun their academic careers in Romantic studies and landed their first jobs at Yale in 1955 as the second Jews (after Charles Feidelson) to join its English department. Like their personalities, their intellectual Jewish interests could not have been more different. Bloom, having famously bemoaned the belatedness of American Jewry, the weakness of its poetry in English, and the rapid falling away in America from the "text-obsessiveness" that in his view had held all significant diaspora Jewries together, increasingly turned his attention to the great revisionists of normative Jewish thought. After introducing Kafka, Freud, and Gershom Scholem as members of a new group of Jewish intellectuals who recognized themselves as products of a rupture with tradition,[9] Bloom tackled the most challenging revisionist writer of all, the "great original J," author of the oldest layer of text in Genesis, Exodus, and Numbers, inventor of a literary character called Yahweh, a writer of staggering originality whom Bloom reinvented in *The Book of J* as a female member of the intellectual elite at or near the court of Solomon's son and successor. Bloom was not interested in J as a storyteller, prophet, or moralist; he was after the "other side of J: uncanny, tricky, sublime, ironic, a visionary of incommensurates, and so the direct ancestor of Kafka, and of any writer, Jewish or Gentile, condemned to write in Kafka's mode." What fascinated Bloom in J was what he had been after in his first books on Shelley and Blake and what he thought Milton had captured in Satan—a mind on fire, an intellectual force of such power that it must reshape all established structures. In Bloom's view such originality was the ultimate "antithetical element that all normative traditions . . . have been unable to assimilate, have ignored, or repressed or evaded."[10]

Hartman's Jewish work was less obviously linked than Bloom's to his earlier work on Romantic poetry. Evan Carton speculates that the "emergence of poststructuralism helped prompt and shape Hartman's . . . expression of Jewishness." This is evident in Hartman's razor-sharp yet playful interpretations of biblical texts.[11] Carton, taking his cue from Hartman's 1971 preface to his 1964 book on Wordsworth, argues that Hartman's revision of his earlier view of the poet indicates his receptivity for poststructuralist theory and that "for Hartman, romanticism, deconstruction, and Judaism begin to converge at this time around a commitment to textuality and a shared resistance to ontotheological essentialism."[12] But Hartman, unlike Bloom, had a visceral connection to the Jewish people and to his own Jewish self because he had been touched, albeit lightly, by the deadly wings of the Holocaust. In March 1939, at the age of nine, he escaped from Germany on a children's transport to England. In 1981, Hartman became a cofounder of the Fortunoff Archive for Holocaust Testimonies and since then has on numerous occasions brought the Holocaust before the eyes of America's intellectuals. How the Holocaust and French poststructuralist theory and American (Jewish) academe connect is a complex matter that is only now being explored by younger researchers.[13]

Although books by second-generation Jewish literary scholars such as Bloom's *Western Canon* (1994), Guttmann's *Erotic in Sport* (1996), or Hartman's *Longest Shadow* (1996) still find a sizable general and academic readership, these are not the books that keep graduate students up at night and swell the footnotes of their papers. In an ever-tightening marketplace, the shrewdest of the academic hopefuls bother only with the works of the hip, the fashionable, and the powerful, among whom there are a staggering number of third-generation literary scholars. Sexy books such as Fish's *There Is No Such Thing as Free Speech and It's a Good Thing Too* (1994), Gallop's *Feminist Accused of Sexual Harassment* (1997), Garber's *Vice Versa: Bisexuality in Everyday Life* (1995), Gubar's *Race-changes: White Skin, Black Face in American Culture* (1997), as well as less faddish works such as Marjorie Perloff's *Wittgenstein's Ladder: Poetic Language and the Strangeness of the Ordinary* (1996) and Gilman's *Franz Kafka, the Jewish Patient* (1995) dominate literary academe at century's end. Third-generation Jewish literary scholars occupy positions of power as presidents of the Modern Language Association and members of its Executive Council, as directors of university presses and as editors of literary histories and anthologies marketed as standard textbooks, and as organizers of retrospectives.[14]

One such retrospective was the fiftieth anniversary session of the English Institute in 1991. It attempted to honor past achievements, to take stock of the changes in the Institute's membership and programs, and to proclaim the current tenets of literary academe. Inadvertently it provided a marvelous occasion to review the integration of Jewish scholars, to assess the significance of their contributions, and to gauge the ideals of the third generation.

The Idols: The English Institute in 1991

The English Institute, founded in 1939, was to be, in Carleton Brown's words, "simply an assemblage of persons interested in the serious study of English and American language and literature." For a few days at the end of every summer, its participants preferred, according to

Robert E. Spiller, to "appraise some of the ways, means, and ends of scholarship . . . rather than to report on specific research in progress." From the start, the names of women and Jews appear among the registrants and with increasing frequency among the panelists and keynote speakers.[15] A good example is the Institute's third session, in 1941, which mingled in its program the names of Sculley Bradley, Cleanth Brooks, Madeleine Doran, Arthur Friedman, Erwin Panofsky, Frederick Pottle, Lionel Trilling, and René Wellek. Among the twenty speakers were one woman, two émigrés (one of whom was Jewish), and four American Jews.

During the 1950s the Institute was a bit less diverse and avant-garde than in its first decade. The program for 1959, for example, featured some Jews, but no women or minorities. Of the 271 registrants, 92 were women, 32 were possibly Jews (men), and 39 belonged to religious orders (25 women, 14 men). The strong presence of nuns and Jesuits reflects academe's preoccupation then with the ties between literature and religion, which had also been a topic at the 1957 Institute meeting. The annual for that year, titled *Literature and Belief,* was edited not by a Jesuit but by a secular Jew, M. H. Abrams.

In 1991 people of the cloth had disappeared from the audience of the English Institute, and so had the sprinkling of high-school teachers and the large contingent of instructors from the small provincial colleges who had been the staple registrants during the Institute's early decades. Longfellow Hall at Radcliffe College in Cambridge, where the Institute has been held under the stewardship of Marjorie Garber for the past several years, was filled with the current bigwigs from top schools, with admirers and disciples conversant in their works, with true believers (from some smaller schools) in academe's intellectual progress toward the minimization of oppression in the world, and a handful of Harvard graduate students who could attend the conference for fifteen dollars and a subway token.

The major panel, entitled "The Institutions of English" and chaired by Susan Gubar and Jonathan Kamholtz, was dedicated to the work of retrospection; the other two panels pursued the Institute's regular business of presenting significant reflections on the state of scholarship.[16] The nine speakers chosen to represent the institutions of English were (in the order of their appearance on the program): Alvin Kernan, Leslie Fiedler, Geoffrey Hartman, Stanley Fish, Jane Gallop, Edward Said, Houston A. Baker, Eve Kosofsky Sedgwick, and Gerald Graff—seven men, two women; one WASP, one African American, one Palestinian, six Jews; a modern traditionalist, an old-fashioned canon buster, a Yale critic, a theorist, a feminist, a postcolonialist, an Afro-Americanist, a gay/lesbian theorist, a politico-cultural analyst. The first three clearly represented the Institute's past, the last five its present, and two of the five, Baker and Sedgwick, possibly its future. Stanley Fish occupied the middle ground. The first three had been chosen for the roles they had played in shaping literary studies, the other six because they followed literary academe's current ethos and had "demonstrated their commitment to critical, theoretical, or pedagogic projects grounded in public and ethical responsiveness." [17] Such responsiveness was primarily discharged by empowering the oppressed (women, blacks, homosexuals, the colonized, the disabled, and so forth). Hence Christian, Zionist, (neo)conservative, or other hegemonic and inegalitarian points of view were not represented. The suffering of the Jews, which had led to the establishment of the state of Israel, customarily attacked as imperialist and dehumanizing by Said, was obliquely acknowledged by inviting Hartman, whose personal and intellectual ties to the Holocaust and Israel were well known.

The difference between program, performance, and printed record was due precisely to the organizers' efforts to seek "contributors who acknowledge their civic roles." Said could not attend because his obligations to his community of descent, the Palestinians, overrode his promises to his community of consent (American academe), or, as the dutifully awed organizers put it, "his public role as spokesperson for the Palestinian cause required him to be out of the country on short notice." Identification with the culture of descent also created a problem in including in the printed record Baker's marvelously light and funny but ultimately scathing talk "Afro-American Studies and the English Imaginary," because Baker performed his talk on the failure of academe to meet the needs of African Americans by switching easily between standard English, Black English vernacular, and the rhythmic lingo of rap. The code switching enacted the tension Baker perceived between his fated and his acquired identity. In his "obligatory courtesies," while the audience was hiccuping with giggles, Baker slipped in a chilling remark. To be included as part of this session of the Institute, Baker said, "makes me feel rather like Frederick Douglass when he returned to the South as a free and titled man to visit his former master. It is both pleasingly terrifying and deeply moving, so Douglass, to join the company of Kernan, Fiedler, Fish, Gallop, Sedgwick, Graff, and the *différence* of Said." There was no evidence that audience or panelists, so attuned to literary subtleties, found the implied comparison of themselves to slave masters in any way unnerving.

In the printed record Baker's performance was replaced by the elegant and nuanced essay of Henry Louis Gates, Jr., about his relationship with the infinitely complicated James Baldwin, and about Baldwin's loss of skepticism and critical independence when, fearing to be relieved of the "burden of representation," he succumbed to the ideologues of Black Power. For Said's paper two essays were substituted: Jonathan Goldberg's virtuoso critique of the ostracism of sodomy, which, by way of a vulgar homophobic pun conceived during the 1990 Gulf War ("Saddamize"), also turned into a veiled critique of America's military action in Kuwait; and John Brenkman's essay on multiculturalism, which declared that what critics needed to understand, to practice, and to enable was the "transfer between the plurality of cultural vocabularies and the necessarily shared discourse of political decision-making." [18]

The scheduled panelists said more or less what the audience expected them to say. A deep chasm gaped between the old fogies who bemoaned the decline of literacy—of literary skills in America at large and of literary sophistication in academe—and the Young Turks who celebrated the passing of literary studies into cultural studies and the fading (or meltdown) of the critic's mind into the communal body. The chasm was deepest, perhaps, between Geoffrey Hartman (b. 1929) and Jane Gallop (b. 1952). Hartman's subtle but pointed essay was a defense of academe's literary mission, which he defined as a "quality of attention derived from the study of poetry and fiction." He was pleased with the expansion experienced by literary studies during the past fifty years but professed himself disturbed that "while so much energy goes into expanding the reading list, we forget that it is skilled reading that expands it." He was outright critical of including texts for social and restitutive reasons. "A social choice criterion," Hartman argued, "may ultimately have a narrowing effect on knowledge. It can be justified provisionally if it helps to motivate learning about a heritage that has been suppressed or neglected." But what needed to follow was a "qualitative reading" of all those cultural texts, because to "pass from acknowledgment to knowledge is the hard thing." [19] Hartman's view, shared by critics like Aaron, Abrams, and Levin, that the intellect was an equalizing force, was based in Enlightenment thought. It assumed that knowledge was liberating and that the intellectual penetration of any cultural text led to an enlightened understanding of all humankind as created equal and endowed with the right to life, liberty, and the pursuit of happiness.

Such idealism was anathema to Jane Gallop, who decried *literary* studies not only as elitist but as counterproductive in bringing about social change. "When feminist criticism devotes itself to geniuses like [Emily] Dickinson and [Julia] Kristeva," Gallop argued, "it contradicts feminism by preferring the woman who is different from and better than other women." The major achievement of current feminist criticism, she said, "has been the inclusion of 'black outsiders.' " She thought the discovery by classical feminists that women "produce high culture" to be destructively elitist but declared it permissible as a crutch because "in an academy which takes itself and is taken by the larger society as a purveyor of a culture that is better, it is of significant effect to associate that highness, however we might also and at the same time want to call it into question, with representatives of inferiorized groups, for example women and people of color." [20]

The debate between Hartman and Gallop as a debate between Jews is old and was last played out in nineteenth-century Russia between Jewish reformers (Maskilim) and revolutionaries. Traditional Jews were the losers on either side. [21] On this particular occasion, however, the differences were dissolved in laughter when in his talk Stanley Fish held up a mirror to the audience. For half an hour Fish transformed some three hundred troubled literati and (multi)culturati into a bunch of honorary Jews giddy with laughter at their own foolishness, which marked them as the last saints in capitalist America.

For years Fish had been irked by the attitude academics had toward themselves and their work. "What is wrong with the academy," he had said in 1988, "is precisely what the academy prizes most, which is that it rejects business ethics. What is most despicable about the academy is that it is badly run, inefficient, and, worse than that, insufficiently sensitive to human needs" (interview). And this was what Fish was prepared to tell the assembled crème of literary academe. In fact, the author of ground-breaking books on seventeenth-century literature as well as on literary and legal theory presented himself as the ultimate nonacademic and as the product of an American-Jewish milieu whose materialism he deliberately and cheerfully retained.

Stanley Fish

Fish's father came to America as a child from a village near Kraków. As an adolescent he went to work for an uncle who was a plumber in Providence, Rhode Island. He married in 1930 at the age of twenty-two, and in 1938, Stanley Eugene Fish was born as the first of four children. When America entered World War II, Fish's father was drafted to work in the Rhode Island shipyards. After the war he started his own business together with another man, fixing toilets and drains. He added a contracting business and in 1948 got his first big job, working on a synagogue in the good part of town.

The Fishes lived on the other side of the tracks. Stanley grew up on a small street that had a bar on each corner. Coming home from school, he was frequently beaten up by Irish and black kids, and when the family moved to a more affluent part of Providence, by Protestants. At the age of six or seven he started Hebrew school in his grandfather's Orthodox shul. He became a bar mitzvah there because his grandfather would not set foot in his father's Conservative synagogue. Fish remembers doing the entire service "because I had a fairly good voice and was musically inclined." [22] On a few Saturdays he would go back and serve as the shul's cantor. "I liked learning how to do things," Fish recalls. "I liked learning how to do the service." Fish went to services on Friday nights and Saturday mornings until he was fifteen years old. He also attended Sunday school, partly because all his friends went and partly because he enjoyed reading Bible stories and discussing them. But the influence of Sunday school was ethical rather than literary. To this day Fish remembers his rabbi's lesson about true honesty, which he illustrated with a down-to-earth example: "When you go to a phone booth and you put in your dime and you don't make your call and then you press the change and get your dime back plus some other coins, is the money yours? I'll never forget that. Because the idea was that true honesty has nothing to do with being in a situation where people are looking at you. True honesty was a strong feeling in oneself of what the right or wrong thing to do is, independent of circumstance. That really made a huge impression on me."

Fish attributes the greatest intellectual influence to his rigorous high school, where he took French, German, and four years of Latin. "I still wear my high school ring from 1955. It cost me three dollars and fifty-two cents, and I have never taken it off." The Fishes shared a house with another Jewish family, who were musical and owned a sizable library, to which Fish had access. While Fish was rather a failure at the violin, he read voraciously. But neither he nor his parents had any particular goal in mind. "My parents clearly thought I was good at something or other, but they did not have academic aspirations for me, because Jewish families did not think in those terms in the forties.

University teaching was not thought of as an avenue toward influence, wealth and position," which were recognizable though vague ambitions. Fish recalls being troubled for an answer from the time he was twelve years old, when people asked him what he was going to be. "The scariest question in the world. I hadn't the slightest idea. I was desperate. I remember being terrified by the idea that I would not be anything." For a while he thought of being a performer—a singer, tap dancer, and pianist—but when in the eighth grade he lost the vote for "most talented" to another student, he concluded that there was no future in that.

He applied to five colleges—Harvard, Dartmouth, Amherst, Brown, and the University of Pennsylvania—but was not admitted to the first three. Not only was his academic record lackluster, he had also gotten into trouble at school because of running a gambling pool and throwing rocks through the school windows. Since he did not want to attend Brown, four blocks from home, he went to Penn. The University of Pennsylvania was then a school with a large Jewish student body from middle-class and upper-middle-class homes, "many young women recognizably charting their lives along a certain mode." It was also a school whose social structure demanded—unless one was a strong, independent character who could get on alone—that students join a fraternity. Fish was pledged by a Jewish fraternity, Alpha Pi Epsilon, and spent four pleasant years as a "typical student, somewhat indulged by my parents. I had a good allowance. I had a car and things of that kind. I wasn't an intellectual. In some strong sense I have never been an intellectual. I didn't read poetry or literature when I didn't have to, and I still don't. I was on the student newspaper because I found writing interesting. But I didn't belong to any literary or musical clubs. I didn't go to concerts or symphonies. I went to ballgames; I played a lot of basketball, I played a lot of cards."

He majored in English by accident rather than by design. "If people have been asking you for eight or nine years what you're going to do and you're desperate for an answer and somebody tells you, oh, you're pretty good at that, you begin to think, aha, I know who I am: I am a person who is pretty good at that, and then you do a little more of it." Fish was good at writing papers, but he was also very taken with Maurice O. Johnson, a scholar of eighteenth-century literature who encouraged him. "He was genteel and ironic and cool and trimly dressed. I think I wanted to be like him, which is interesting because he had married into a very patrician Philadelphia family and was extremely Christian." This was in keeping with the general feel of the English department at the University of Pennsylvania as long as A. C. Baugh dominated its affairs.

Having long wavered between law and literature, Fish eventually applied to graduate school without a clear sense of what one did there. All he knew was that future earnings would be minimal. Fish remembers being taken to lunch by Harvey Lyons, an English teacher at Penn, "who was leaving the profession to go into advertising because, among other things, his wife was tired of living on a small salary." Lyons tried to discourage Fish by asking him how much he thought he was going to make. "But I knew the answer to that question, which was then about $42,000 a year." Fish decided to go to Yale, without knowing very much about the school itself, because they offered him the most money.

A week before starting at Yale, Fish got married to a Jewish girl from New Rochelle, New York, who came from a family very much like her husband's. To his surprise, Fish discovered

> after the first few weeks of both graduate school and marriage that my wife and her mother thought that the decision to pursue literary studies was quixotic and would soon be abandoned in favor of something else. I found out in the first year of a marriage that was to last for twenty-one years that my wife strongly disapproved of what I had chosen to do. We had long arguments that first year in which she was urging me to quit. And since at the end of each week I felt wholly inadequate to my classes, the idea of quitting was not so far from my mind. In fact, I thought of quitting every Friday afternoon when I had two back-to-back classes in which I regularly felt humiliated, not by the professors, one of whom was W. K. Wimsatt, but by my fellow students, all of whom were truly literary intellectuals. They lived and breathed literature. They fell asleep reading Virgil. They knew Portuguese epics. I had gotten into fights with Portuguese in Providence. So I continually felt inadequate. It was the beginning of my feeling that whatever culture *they* came from—they being the rest of my colleagues—I came from some other culture. This feeling intensified by the time I got my first job.

Fish finished graduate school in three years. His dissertation (1962) on John Skelton's poetry, which he wrote at the age of twenty-three in three months and three days, is still a standard work. Yale wanted to place Fish at the University of Illinois as an instructor, but Fish's wife would not hear of it. "She was a New York girl; she wasn't going to live just anywhere. She said, you get a job in New York or San Francisco or else forget it." So Fish applied for a job at the University of California,

Berkeley, and he got it. In the summer of 1962 he and his wife trekked across country in his Porsche.

It was at Berkeley that Fish began to understand what he had discerned only vaguely at Yale, which was that "the culture I had entered was a culture that was at least rhetorically opposed to material goods; whereas the culture I had come from was fixated on material goods."

Some Jewish youths of my generation entered literary academe as an act of rebellion against their parents, but I had no such thoughts. As far as I was concerned those values were fine. I liked nice cars, big houses, jewelry, good clothes, great food, and I still do. It was in graduate school, driving first a Mercedes and then a Porsche and spending weekends in jazz clubs and restaurants in New York City, that I first dimly sensed what I realized more clearly over the years, that the literary academic is uneasy with the signs of material success and is involved in the production and nourishing of guilt and shame across a series of issues. Guilt and shame are two emotions that I have very little to do with and am not interested in cultivating. I have never been able to understand to this day why so many of my literary colleagues at least profess and in some ways practice an ethic of denial, a wish to be in some way pure, free of material goods, living the life of the mind. What is interesting about the new commitment in literary studies to the historical and political is that it is not at all different from the old commitment to the life of the mind because it too is opposed to all that is thought of as the unworthy trappings of everyday American life. The opposition used to be between the material, the carnal, and the life of the mind. The current commitment to the political is just as religious and spiritual in a way as the old commitment to the life of the mind, and in that sense allies itself to a Christian tradition that elevates the purity of the spirit and a certain kind of asceticism.

When I first entered academic life at Berkeley in 1962 this took the curious form of certain prescriptions as to what you thought and what you did, what clothes you wore and what cars you drove. Everybody I knew drove Volkswagens until a certain day in 1973 or 1974, when they all sold their Volkswagens and bought Volvos, which is the same thing. I drove Porsches and Alfa Romeos. For women muted earth tones and general understatement were de rigueur, and for men patches on the jackets and clothes from various imitations of Brooks Brothers. It came home to me what the difference was between them and me when on my first Thanksgiving vacation at Berkeley, all of my colleagues went off to sleep on the ground somewhere, that is, they went camping, while my wife and I went to a golf and tennis resort in Palm Springs, California. When people heard about that they went crazy; they had never known anybody who did that. I realized then that I had entered a culture that asked you to cultivate a genteel poverty even when you didn't have to and that demanded a certain set of political attitudes and a certain kind of disdain for all people whose sensibilities were not as refined as yours. Academic literary culture derives straight from T. S. Eliot, whose anti-Semitism is so palpable.

I was (and am) not interested in being refined, especially not since I discovered fairly early on that one of the consequences was that the people in literary academe were the least well treated in a material way. Let's say you visit a campus. In addition to all the shiny new buildings there will be one section of campus where the old Quonset huts left over from World War II are being used. You can bet the English department is there. Or you go to a campus and find the oldest building where the water doesn't run, they could never put in air conditioning because the ducts weren't right, the windows don't open and the stairs bow—that's where the English department is. I found that my colleagues not only were downtrodden in the sense that they were abysmally paid, they were also often working under less advantageous conditions in terms of teaching loads, office space, and secretarial services than members of other departments. Not only was this true, but it was worn as a badge of virtue. It was a sign of their superiority.

The worst thing anyone could call you within that culture—the adjective most opprobrious to bestow—was "vulgar" in the sense of coarse, crass. I remember when we had one of our first dinner parties and I invited the man who would later be my best friend at Berkeley, Stephen Booth, a scholar of Shakespeare, a brilliant and very funny man. He walked into our apartment which was not furnished in late-graduate-school style but had all shiny up-to-date then modern Danish stuff, and which I hadn't rented in some quaint run-down house but in one of the new spiffy buildings with drapes and that sort of thing—he walked around, looked at me and said, "False values!" In terms of the academy I had then, and have to this day, false values. I love glitter, I love ostentation, I love excess. I own five automobiles.

And this is what Fish had come to tell his colleagues at the English Institute: their downtroddenness, their feelings of guilt and shame, and their political commitments were a lie to themselves. As his emblem Fish used the Volvos academics started buying in the mid-1970s. Those ugly luxury cars prized for their super-safety, Fish declared, "provided a solution to a new dilemma facing academics—how to enjoy the benefits of increasing affluence while at the same time maintaining the proper attitude of disdain towards the goods affluence brings. In the context of this dilemma, the ugliness of the Volvo becomes its most attractive feature, for it allows those who own one to plead innocent to the charge of really wanting it." From this Fish deduced the rule of thumb that "whenever [academics] either want something or get something [they] manage it in such a way as to deny or disguise its material pleasures."[23]

Fish criticized the "sloppiness, discourtesy, indifference, and inefficiency" cultivated by literary academics as "signs of an admirable disdain for the mere surfaces of things, a disdain that is itself a sign of a dedication to higher, if invisible, values."[24] While the audience roared with laughter, Fish concluded his talk with a series of aphorisms exposing the smug saintliness of literary academe:

- In the academy, the lower the act, the higher the principle invoked to justify it. . . .
- Academics like to keep their eyes on the far horizon with the result that everything in the near horizon gets sacrificed. . . .
- Academics like to feel morally culpable especially in relation to those who would give anything to be in their place. . . .
- Academics like to feel morally superior, which they manage by feeling morally culpable.[25]

The volleys of laughter that greeted every new turn of Fish's harangue were not unexpected. Fish could be certain that his talk would amuse rather than upset. The laughter arose from many sources. It was partly the mirth of children in a fun house who know that the distorted figures in the mirrors are not real; partly amusement at the antics of a court jester whose truth-telling need not be taken seriously; and partly, especially among younger listeners, the embarrassed, defensive laughter of those caught in the act. At first it seemed to me as a member of the audience that Fish's satiric vision of the anointed had cut so close to the quick that the only defense left to his audience was to treat his talk as a Jewish joke (the kind that glorifies one's own defeat as a moral victory).

On second thought, however, the laughter seemed indicative of the many changes that have transformed the critical profession since Norman Podhoretz first presented an analysis very similar to Fish's in his 1967 book *Making It*. The reaction then among the prominent New York literati, most of whom had no secure source of income, was outrage at the insinuation that literary critics perpetuated and celebrated their powerlessness as a moral victory. In 1991 the reaction of the tenured scholars was amusement. They were right to be amused because the academicization of literary criticism (beginning with Lionel Trilling) ended the powerlessness of literary critics. As teachers and writers, and protected by tenure and the first amendment, they are poised to exert as much power in academe, politics, and the marketplace as literary critics are ever likely to exert.

One is inclined to attribute the difference in reaction between 1967 and 1991 to complacency and a decline in the critics' moral seriousness. But this is not the case: the literary critics of the 1990s are, if anything, even more serious than their precursors about the political relevance and transformative power of their pursuits. In fact, Fish himself, who began his career without far-reaching plans, eventually came to believe in his mission since, as he explained, "You cannot strike a pose repeatedly without becoming the pose that you struck" (interview).

There was an element of disingenuousness in his talk: the conditions he described were now true only for toiling graduate students and possibly for ardent believers in political correctness. In the early 1960s, Fish's talk would have been daring and original, but delivered in 1991 it was superannuated and had lost its sting, because a sizable number of the academics in his audience—among them, Fish himself—had become powerful players in their respective institutions.[26] And since Fish could be sure that they would be amused, his talk was not daring but a joke from the start.

Fish and Podhoretz had made their observations about the saintliness of literary intellectuals and their professed disdain for material comforts around the same time, during the late 1950s and early 1960s. It seems no coincidence that the two men came from very similar backgrounds. They were the cherished sons of fairly secular Jewish families who were completely at ease with their descent, their milieu, and their Jewish commitment. What Fish and Podhoretz essentially intended to criticize were the last vestiges of Christianity in high culture. They shocked their audiences (Fish's being limited then to colleagues and department chairs whom he approached for raises) by playing one stereotype against another. Against the spirituality and disinterestedness of the monkish literary scholar they pitched the crass materialism of the Jews that seventy years earlier had irritated Santayana in his Jewish fellow student Loeser. In the 1960s, T. S. Eliot, who thought the Jews impervious to spiritual salvation, was still a powerful presence in literary circles; hence the specter of the materialist Jew raised by Podhoretz caused deep embarrassment that expressed itself in anger. But with the rise of yuppie culture during the 1980s, money made its way into academe as status symbol and accepted indicator of power. Thus Fish ran little risk when he exposed himself in 1991 as a man in love with material comforts. The stereotype of the materialist Jew had long vanished.

Although Fish's talk was largely based on observations made in the 1950s and 1960s, his current views were reflected in the claim that his aphorisms summed up a "curious history in which already enfranchised academics, largely male, gazed with envy and strangely mediated desire at the disenfranchised, first at Jews, then at women, then at blacks, and then at Native Americans, and now at gays and Arabs."[27] Fish's historic summary is wrong in that his first example does not fit in with the others. The integration of the Jews into American literary academe occurred unobtrusively, case by case, each individual being held up to the highest standards of academic performance. Unlike the integration of women, African Americans, and other minorities, the integration of the Jews proceeded along meritocratic principles and was unaccompanied by political pressure and demands for proportional representation. The history Fish has in mind began in the late 1960s, when the integration of Jews was almost completed. In fact, it was the Jews (rather than the male WASPs whom Fish seems to be thinking of) who were at the forefront of opening literary academe to "others"—to women and African Americans in particular.

Why does Fish revise history at a moment of ostensible and ostentatious truth-telling? Because in the age of quotas the clear, unaided success of Jews in academe, first as students and then as faculty (replicated by Asian immigrants in recent years), is a bit of an embarrassment to defenders of affirmative action like Fish. It also seemed less patronizing if Fish spoke as a member of a group that had been victimized by the same hegemonic Euro-, phallo-, and logocentric forces now impeding the progress of the social groups clamoring for empowerment. And there may be yet another reason. Ruth Wisse pointed out that the Jews can't stand victory unless they are among the defeated, because defeat preserves saintliness. Jews are uneasy as victors.

Jews in academe have yet to come to grips with their rise to institutional power. Perhaps they will have an easier time of it if they realize that their integration into literary academe, unlike that of any other group, was accompanied by the almost complete loss of their cultural heritage and concomitant communal self-esteem. The success of the Jews in American literary academe, paralleled in so many other niches of Jewish history, is an equivocal victory at best—a triumph of the independent, generous mind committed to the betterment of humanity, paid for in large part with the loss of specific cultural knowledge, group cohesion, and the self-confidence derived from being intellectually and emotionally anchored in a long, distinguished past that nourishes one's younger American self.

NOTES

INDEX

Notes

Introduction

1. Harry Levin, letter to the author, July 8, 1989.

2. Harry Levin, letter to the author, October 5, 1989.

3. George Santayana, letter to William James, Easter 1900. Quoted in John McCormick, *George Santayana: A Biography* (New York: Knopf, 1987), 88.

4. William Safire, "News About Jews," *New York Times,* July 17, 1995: A13

5. A. R. Gurney, Jr., *Entertaining Strangers* (Garden City, N.Y.: Doubleday, 1977), 34.

1. The Yard from Santayana to T.S. Eliot

1. Santayana to Smith, Rome, October 11, 1938; quoted in John McCormick, *George Santayana: A Biography* (New York: Knopf, 1987), 377. I am indebted to McCormick's excellent study for many biographical details.

2. George Santayana, *Persons and Places: The Background of My Life* (New York: Scribner's, 1944), 224–225. Further references to this edition are cited in the text as *PP.*

3. Santayana to Wheelock, November 12, 1944; quoted in McCormick, *Santayana,* 366. As the publication of the critical edition of *Person and Places* by MIT Press in 1986 revealed, Wheelock managed nevertheless to suppress a number of offensive passages. See the reviews of the critical edition by Joel Porte, "Santayana's Masquerade," *Raritan* 7 (Fall 1987): 129–147; and Daniel Aaron, "Pilgrim's Progress," *New Republic* 200 (May 18, 1987): 28–33.

4. George Santayana, *The Last Puritan: A Memoir in the Form of a Novel* (New York: Scribner's, 1936). For reasons of contemporaneity, my references are to the first edition rather than to the critical edition, George Santayana, *The Last Puritan: A Memoir in the Form of a Novel,* ed. Herman J. Saatkamp, Jr., and William G. Holzberger, with an introduction by Irving Singer (Cambridge: MIT Press, 1994).

5. Santayana to Abbott, May 20, 1887; quoted in McCormick, *Santayana,* 58. About Santayana's financial generosity in later years cf. McCormick, *Santayana,* 370–374.

6. Quoted in Ernest Samuels, *Bernard Berenson: The Making of a Connoisseur* (Cambridge: Belknap Press of Harvard University Press, 1979), 189.

7. Samuels, *Berenson* (1979), 26, 32.

8. Gerald Graff, *Professing Literature: An Institutional History* (Chicago: University of Chicago Press, 1987), 87.

9. George Santayana, *Persons and Places: Fragments of Autobiography,* ed. William G. Holzberger and Herman J. Saatkamp, Jr. (Cambridge: MIT Press, 1986), 405. This edition combines the three autobiographical volumes Santayana published separately. *Persons and Places* (1944) was followed by *The Middle Span* (1945) and *My Host the World* (1953). The MIT edition restores some unpalatable passages suppressed in the edition prepared by Wheelock in 1944. References to the critical edition of *Persons and Places* are cited in the text as *PPce.*

10. Berenson's sentences are quoted in Samuels, *Berenson* (1979), 26. Van Wyck Brooks, *An Autobiography* (New York: E. P. Dutton, 1965), 107, 111. On the abolition of compulsory chapel see Samuel Eliot Morison, *Three Centuries of Harvard, 1636–1936* (Cambridge: Belknap Press of Harvard University Press, 1936), 366–367.

11. Samuels, *Berenson* (1979), 35; Morison, *Three Centuries of Harvard,* 352.

12. Samuels, *Berenson* (1979), 35. Hilliard Goldfarb, *The Isabella Stewart Gardner Museum: A Companion Guide and History* (New Haven: Yale University Press, 1995). On the scandalous Mrs. Gardner see also Douglass Shand-Tucci, *The Art of Scandal: The Life and Times of Isabella Stewart Gardner* (New York: HarperCollins, 1997), and Daniel Aaron, "Belle du Jour," *New Republic* 218 (February 2, 1998): 3–40.

13. Samuels, *Berenson* (1979), 127. Ernest Samuels, *Bernard Berenson: The Making of a Legend* (Cambridge: Belknap Press of Harvard University Press, 1987), 573–574.

14. Samuels, *Berenson* (1979), 32, 37–38.

15. But Berenson did retain a family feeling for Jews, as is evident from a note written late in his life: "How easy and warm the atmosphere between born Jews like Isaiah Berlin, Lewis Namier, myself, Bela Horowitz, when we drop the mask of being goyim and return to Yiddish reminiscences, and Yiddish stories and witticisms." Quoted in Samuels, *Berenson* (1987), 525. Berenson's wife, Mary Costelloe, sister of Logan Pearsall Smith, was not Jewish. She came from a Pennsylvania Quaker family. Berenson's three sisters also married into Boston's Gentile elite. One sister became the wife of Ralph Barton Perry, who taught in the Harvard philosophy department; another sister married the clergyman Lyman Abbott. See A. A. Roback, "Bernard Berenson, Art Connoisseur, on Yiddish Literature," *Yiddish* 2 (Fall 1975): 10. Chapman's portrait of Norton is taken from John Jay Chapman, *Memories and Milestones* (New York: Moffat, Yard and Company, 1915), 135.

16. Henry Adams, *The Education of Henry Adams* (1907; reprint, Boston: Houghton Mifflin 1961), 56. The identity of Harvard class and social class in that period is perhaps best illustrated by this anecdote: "William James's final examination consisted of a single question put to him by Oliver Wendell Holmes. 'If you can answer that,' Holmes informed the successful applicant, 'you can answer anything! Now tell me about your family and how things are at home.' " Richard Norton Smith, *The Harvard Century: The Making of a University to a Nation* (New York: Simon and Schuster, 1986), 37.

17. Adams to Cameron on February 14, 1904. *The Letters of Henry Adams,* vol. 5

1899–1905, ed. J. C. Levenson et al. (Cambridge: Belknap Press of Harvard University Press, 1988), 550. The preceding quotation is from Adams's January 28, 1901, letter to Cameron, *Letters of Henry Adams,* 5: 189.

18. J. C. Levenson, "The Etiology of Israel Adams: The Onset, Waning, and Relevance of Henry Adams's Anti-Semitism." *New Literary History* 25 (Summer 1994): 569–600.

19. Morison, *Three Centuries of Harvard,* 342, 330; Smith, *Harvard Century,* 28.

20. Smith, *Harvard Century,* 43, see also 34–35; Morison, *Three Centuries of Harvard,* 352–353.

21. Morison, *Three Centuries of Harvard,* 327, 330.

22. Henry James, *Charles William Eliot: President of Harvard University, 1869–1909,* vol. 2 (Boston: Houghton Mifflin, 1930), 176. The author is the son of the philosopher William James.

23. Chapman, *Memories and Milestones,* 135

24. The figures are taken from Marcia Graham Synnott's superb book *The Half-Opened Door: Discrimination and Admissions at Harvard, Yale, and Princeton, 1900–1970* (Westport, Conn.: Greenwood, 1979), 39–40; and from Henry Rosovsky, "From Periphery to Center," in Nitza Rosovsky, *The Jewish Experience at Harvard and Radcliffe,* An Introduction to an Exhibition by the Harvard Semitic Museum (Cambridge: Distributed by Harvard University Press, 1986), 10–11, 55.

25. Quoted in Smith, *Harvard Century,* 49; about Walter Lippmann's fate at Harvard, see Ronald Steel, "Walter Lippmann's Harvard," in Rosovsky, *Jewish Experience at Harvard and Radcliffe,* 72–75. About the world of the clubs, see Cleveland Amory, *The Proper Bostonians* (New York: Dutton, 1947), chap. 13, "Harvard and Its Clubs." On the presence of African Americans at Harvard, see *Varieties of Black Experience at Harvard: An Anthology,* ed. Werner Sollors, Thomas A. Underwood, and Caldwell Titcomb (Cambridge: Harvard University, Department of Afro-American Studies, 1986); for figures on Harvard's diversified student body, see Synnott, *Half-Opened Door,* 39–40.

26. Stuart Sherman, in his biting essay "Professor Kittredge and the Teaching of English" (1913), reprinted in Sherman, *Shaping Men and Women: Essays on Literature and Life,* ed. Jacob Zeitlin (Garden City, N.Y.: Doubleday, 1928), 69.

27. Twenty-fifth Anniversary Report (Report VII) of the Secretary of the Class of 1884 of Harvard College (Harvard University Archives), 92. See also Graff, *Professing Literature,* 65–67, 82–83; Clyde Kenneth Hyder, *George Lyman Kittredge: Teacher and Scholar* (Lawrence: University of Kansas Press, 1962), 28; and the articles by Steven S. Jones on Francis Child, John S. Coolidge on Lewis Gates, Myron Simon on Bliss Perry, and Fritz Fleischmann on Barrett Wendell in *Dictionary of Literary Biography,* vol. 64: *American Literary Critics and Scholars, 1850–1880;* and *Dictionary of Literary Biography,* vol. 71: *American Literary Critics and Scholars, 1880–1900* (Detroit: Gale, 1988).

28. Bliss Perry, *And Gladly Teach: Reminiscences* (Boston: Houghton Mifflin, 1935), 243.

29. Brooks, *Autobiography,* 107, 101; Morison, *Three Centuries of Harvard,* 437.

30. On the transformation of the Harvard philosophy department, see Bruce Kuklick, *The Rise of American Philosophy, Cambridge, Massachusetts, 1860–1930* (New Haven: Yale University Press, 1977), chap. 21, "The Crisis of 1912–1920." On Royce, see Bruce Kuklick, *Josiah Royce: An Intellectual Biography* (Indianapolis: Hackett, 1985),

236–237; on Münsterberg, see also Phyllis Keller, *States of Belonging: German American Intellectuals and the First World War* (Cambridge: Harvard University Press, 1979), 68–118.

31. John McCormick in *Santayana* quotes Eliot's comment ("soporific") on Santayana's lectures (99, 416). He also calls attention to Eliot's larger debt to Santayana (416–417), and in a note (569n) refers to some useful articles on the Santayana-Eliot relationship. The discovery of Santayana's use of the term "correlative object" was made B. R. McElderry, Jr., "Santayana and T. S. Eliot's 'Objective Correlative,' " *Boston University Studies in English* 3 (1957); 179–181. The emphasis in the quoted text is McElderry's. Cf. also Irving Singer, "The World of George Santayana," *Hudson Review* 7 (Autumn 1954), 356–372.

32. Peter Ackroyd, *T. S. Eliot* (London: Hamish Hamilton, 1984), 37.

33. Barrett Wendell, *A Literary History of America,* 7th ed. (New York: Scribner's, 1914), 356. On Wendell's anti-black bias see Werner Sollors, "A Critique of Pure Pluralism," in *Reconstructing American Literary History,* ed. Sacvan Bercovitch, Harvard English Studies 13 (Cambridge: Harvard University Press, 1986), 250–279. What Daniel Aaron calls Norton's "impulsive heterodoxy" led him to promote "the cause of education for blacks" (Gerald Graff, *Professing Literature,* 83); but Aaron points out that "in the fifties [Norton] did not strenuously object to slavery as an institution and took for granted the 'facts' of Negro racial inferiority; at the same time, he found slavery, Southern style, distasteful." Daniel Aaron, *The Unwritten War: American Writers and the Civil War* (New York: Oxford University Press, 1973), 26. The argument that exclusive ideologies leading to discrimination do not issue "from primarily irrational, subjective impulses but rather from a very real competition for status and prestige" was advanced by John Higham in his outstanding article "Social Discrimination Against Jews in America, 1830–1930," *Publications of the American Jewish Historical Society* 47 (September 1957): 1–33.

34. McCormick, *Santayana,* 416.

35. More was deeply taken with Babbitt. He wrote to his sister Alice on April 14, 1894: "I see so many men toiling in science and erudition, and only one or two have I seen who wore his learning with grace. Babbitt is one [of] these few, Norton is another." Quoted in Arthur H. Dakin, *Paul Elmer More* (Princeton: Princeton University Press, 1960), 48.

36. T. S. Eliot, "Tradition and the Individual Talent," in *Selected Essays, 1917–1932* (New York: Harcourt, Brace and Company, 1932), 10. Irving Babbitt's quotation is taken from *Literature and the American College: Essays in Defense of the Humanities* (1908; reprint, Washington: National Humanities Institute, 1986), 129. For biographical information I am indebted to Thomas R. Nevin, *Irving Babbitt: An Intellectual Study* (Chapel Hill: University of North Carolina Press, 1984). Interesting accounts of Babbitt as a teacher are found in Van Wyck Brooks, *Autobiography,* 122–126, and in Frederick Manchester and Odell Shepard, eds., *Irving Babbitt: Man and Teacher* (New York: Putnam's, 1941).

37. Babbitt, *Literature and the American College,* 109–111. Babbitt's argument that colleges existed for the creation of a social elite was still echoed (albeit in updated form) by his friend Paul Elmer More twenty years later. On February 23, 1930, More wrote to Christian Gauss: "I simply cannot understand how anyone conversant with what is going on over the country can fail to see that the present policy of Harvard and Yale and

Princeton is suicidal. Their attempt to compete with these great state universities [such as the University of California, Berkeley] on a common ground means that ultimately they will lose their national position and sink to mere local institutions. Their only possible means of maintaining their position is by keeping themselves radically different from the state universities; and the only practical way of doing that is by keeping up a cultural standard that will attract the finer and better men from everywhere." Quoted in Dakin, *Paul Elmer More,* 280–281.

38. Quoted in Harold Wechsler, *The Qualified Student: A History of Selective Admission in America* (New York: Wiley, 1977), 160–161.

39. *The Letters of T. S. Eliot,* vol. 1: 1898–1922, ed. Valerie Eliot (New York: Harcourt Brace Jovanovich, 1988), 92. See also Santayana, *PPce,* 393.

40. The quotations are taken from Babbitt, *Literature and the American College,* 108, 73–77. Babbitt's closest ally in the pursuit and defense of humanism, Paul Elmer More, did not subscribe to Babbitt's "moral atheism." In the late 1920s, as humanism drifted to the political right, More succumbed to Anglo-Catholicism. To More, however, we owe the best description of what Babbitt believed. On April 1, 1930, More wrote to Robert Shafer: "His personal conception of religion is virtually Buddhist, leaving no place for belief in a personal deity or immortality of the soul or for purpose in the world (though it does leave room for ethical purpose to escape the world); and all this he veils under such terms as 'higher immediacy.' " On September 9, 1932, More informed Marcus Selden Goldman that Babbitt "holds that we are immediately conscious of a higher will, 'the ethical will' or the *'frein vital,'* which to us appears as a check upon the natural will and as acting only negatively in respect of our lower, impulsive will. . . . He holds that we are immediately and inexpressibly conscious that this higher will is at once ours, our essential self, and not ours, something super-personal. This is pretty pure Hinduism, the sort of philosophy which I myself got out of the Upanishads, and which Babbitt clarified by his study of Buddhism. It runs, as I see it now, into an impossible transcendental monism, and *The Catholic Faith* [1931] is my public retraction of what can be read in some of my earlier books." Quoted in Dakin, *Paul Elmer More,* 282–283, 319n.

41. T. S. Eliot, in *Irving Babbitt,* ed. Manchester and Shepard, 104. George R. Elliott's early study "T. S. Eliot and Irving Babbitt" *American Review* (September 1936): 442–454, is mainly a defense of Babbitt against Eliot's criticism of him. John D. Margolis examines Babbitt's importance for Eliot's notion of classicism in the first chapter of *T. S. Eliot's Intellectual Development, 1922–1939* (Chicago: University of Chicago Press, 1972). An unsurpassed source for older material on T. S. Eliot is Robert H. Canary, *T. S. Eliot: The Poet and His Critics* (Chicago: American Library Association, 1982).

42. Lyndall Gordon, *Eliot's Early Years* (New York: Noonday Press of Farrar, Straus, and Giroux, 1977), 71; on Eliot's early religiosity see p. 58. The influence of T. E. Hulme on Eliot was first pointed out by F. O. Matthiessen in *The Achievement of T. S. Eliot: An Essay on the Nature of Poetry* (Boston: Houghton Mifflin, 1935), particularly in the extensive notes to his chapter on the objective correlative. See also Ronald Schuchard, "Eliot and Hulme in 1916: Toward a Revaluation of Eliot's Critical and Spiritual Development," *PMLA* (October 1973): 1083–1094.

43. T. S. Eliot, *After Strange Gods: A Primer of Modern Heresy* (New York: Harcourt, Brace and Company, 1934), 15; replacement of terms, 22. T. S. Eliot, "To Criticize the Critic" (1961), reprinted in *To Criticize the Critic and Other Writings* (London: Faber and Faber, 1965), 17.

44. T. S. Eliot, *Selected Essays, 1917–1932,* 383–392. Dakin's *Paul Elmer More* illuminates the religious development of Babbitt's old friend. More, who had once shared a "twin loneliness" (273) with Babbitt as humanists in America, had thoughts quite similar to those of Eliot, with whom he was on very friendly terms. "More and more I am driven to feel," More wrote on March 28, 1929, "that . . . the effort to revive humanism without [religion] is perfectly hopeless. . . . But there is a huge difficulty. There can be no valid religion without believing something, without dogma" (271). On September 7, 1929, More reflected: "The religion I was seeking as a background and stay of humanism was somewhat of the vague, eclectic, contentless kind [Allen Tate] criticises [in the *Criterion* of July 1929]. I have come to see that time is a necessary element in religion, that it must be historical" (276). And on April 1, 1930, More summed up: "As for myself, I have changed. . . . To me the choice is between non-religion and dogmatic religion; the middle ground of religiosity I spurn. And the final issue for dogmatic religion lies between the theism of Christianity and the moral atheism (thoroughly dogmatic in its way, despite Babbitt's protests to the contrary) of the Buddhist. I choose the former. I believe in the Church, but not in an *absolute* Church." Quoted in Dakin, *Paul Elmer More,* 283–284.

45. Eliot, *To Criticize the Critic,* 15; T. S. Eliot, in *Irving Babbitt,* ed. Manchester and Shepard, 103.

46. Cynthia Ozick, "T. S. Eliot at 101," in *Fame and Folly: Essays* (New York: Knopf, 1996), 17–18. Ackroyd, *T. S. Eliot,* 41; cf. also James Torrens, "Charles Maurras and Eliot's 'New Life'," *PMLA* (March 1974): 312–322, and Kenneth Asher, *T. S. Eliot and Ideology* (Cambridge: Cambridge University Press, 1994).

47. The issue of influence and indebtedness is very complicated. As Louis Menand pointed out, Babbitt "was greatly influenced by a book called *Le Romantism français* (1907), by Pierre Lasserre. *Le Romantism français* is an attack on French cultural decadence, which Lasserre blamed on nineteenth-century Romanticism and the cult of the individual, and, in particular, on Rousseau; and it is a recommendation for a return to the spirit of classicism. Much of the book had first appeared in the *Revue de l'action française,* of which Lasserre was the editor; for the attack on Romanticism, conceived in those terms, was one aspect of the 'counter-revolutionary' program of the leader of the Action Française, Charles Maurras. . . . Babbitt admired Lasserre's critique of Romanticism . . . although he regretted the extremism of the political movement the book was associated with. He helped to persuade Eliot to take his year abroad, and he encouraged him, when he got to Paris, to get a copy of Maurras's own attack on French cultural decadence, *L'Avenir de l'intelligence* (1905). Eliot took the advice; he bought the book in 1911, and it became one of the touchstones of his thought." Louis Menand, "Eliot and the Jews," review of *T. S. Eliot, Anti-Semitism, and Literary Form,* by Anthony Julius, *New York Review of Books* 43 (June 6, 1996): 37.

48. T. S. Eliot, in Manchester and Shepard, eds., *Irving Babbitt,* 103.

49. Eliot, *After Strange Gods,* 10, 12, 17.

50. Eliot, *After Strange Gods,* 10, 18–20, 22.

51. By contrast, Paul Elmer More, who also took Eliot's route to Anglo-Catholicism, perceived clearly the split between Eliot's early poetry and his later cultural theories. On August 11, 1929, More wrote to Austin Warren: "Two things are to be remembered in judging [Eliot's] work. In the first place some time between *The Waste Land* and *For Lancelot Andrewes* he underwent a kind of conversion, due largely I believe to the

influence of Maurras and the Action Française. And in the second place, he seems to cherish the theory—very heretical in my eyes—that ethics and aesthetics are to be kept rigorously separate. I remember that last summer [1928], after reading his *Andrewes* with its prefatial program of classicism, royalism . . . , and Anglo-Catholicism, I asked him whether, when he returned to verse, he would write the same sort of stuff that he once called poetry, or whether he had seen a new light. His answer was: 'I am absolutely unconverted.' The situation is complicated by the fact that many of his most ardent followers were won by his verse and are very dubious about his later critical views. This he knows, and I think he feels himself in an embarrassing strait." Quoted in Dakin, *Paul Elmer More*, 269n. George Steiner, letter to the *Listener*, April 29, 1971, quoted in Christopher Ricks's very peculiar book *T. S. Eliot and Prejudice* (London: Faber and Faber, 1988), 28. The quotation from "Tradition and the Individual Talent" is taken from Eliot, *Selected Essays, 1917–1932*, 4.

52. Quoted in McCormick, *Santayana*, 416.

53. Eliot, *After Strange Gods*, 42.

54. Santayana, *The Genteel Tradition at Bay* (New York: Scribner's, 1931), 56. See also Robert Dawidoff, *The Genteel Tradition and the Sacred Rage: High Culture vs. Democracy in Adams, James, and Santayana* (Chapel Hill: University of North Carolina Press, 1992).

2. Portrait of a Scholar as a Young Man: Harry Levin

1. On Levin's transition from Minneapolis to Cambridge, see Harry Levin, "A View from Within," in John Lydenberg, ed., *Political Activism and the Academic Conscience: The Harvard Experience, 1936–1941*. (Geneva, N.Y.: Hobart and William Smith Colleges, 1977), 1. Harry Levin, "Memoirs of a Scholar: Perry Miller" (1964), reprinted in Levin, *Grounds for Comparison* (Cambridge: Harvard University Press, 1972), 155. Harry Levin's self-description is taken from the extensive marginal notes penciled on the manuscript of a draft of this chapter in October 1991. I will refer to these "marginal notes" throughout this chapter.

2. Carey McWilliams, "Minneapolis: The Curious Twins," *Common Ground* 7 (Fall 1946): 61. Allen Grossman, conversation with the author, Waltham, Massachusetts, December 14, 1987.

3. Harry Levin, letter to the author, July 22, 1989. Biographical information about Harry Levin's life before his arrival at Harvard is hard to come by. My reconstruction is based on the few autobiographical remarks Levin made in various essays (cited in the course of this chapter); on two long conversations with Levin, one in his library study at Harvard on December 15, 1987, the other at his Cambridge home on October 19, 1989; on a letter he sent (in answer to a list of questions) from his summer home on Cape Cod on July 22, 1989; and on the marginal notes. Harold Bloom, *The American Religion: The Emergence of the Post-Christian Nation* (New York: Simon and Schuster, 1992), 132.

4. Quoted in Charles I. Cooper, "The Jews of Minneapolis and Their Christian Neighbors," *Jewish Social Studies* 8 (January 1946): 32.

5. Albert I. Gordon, *Jews in Transition* (Minneapolis: University of Minnesota Press, 1949), 46; Selden Menefee, *Assignment: U.S.A.* (New York: Reynal and Hitchcock, 1943), 101–102. Knowledge of Isadore Levin's nickname I owe to a conversation with Eric Solomon in San Francisco, December 29, 1991.

6. Harry Levin, "A Personal Retrospect," in *Grounds for Comparison,* 8–9.

7. Abbott Lawrence Lowell, *Facts and Visions: Twenty-four Baccalaureate Sermons,* ed. Henry Aaron Yeomans (Cambridge: Harvard University Press, 1944), 138–144.

8. Lowell to Moore on October 3, 1922, Lowell Papers, 1922–1925, folder 8, "Jews," Harvard University Archives. I am much indebted to Marcia Graham Synnott's excellent exposition of Eliot's and Lowell's views on immigration in *The Half-Opened Door: Discrimination and Admissions at Harvard, Yale, and Princeton, 1900–1970* (Westport, Conn.: Greenwood, 1979), 34–37.

9. Quoted in Henry Aaron Yeomans, *Abbott Lawrence Lowell, 1856–1943* (Cambridge: Harvard University Press, 1948), 166.

10. Quoted in Yeomans, *Abbott Lawrence Lowell,* 169; on the exclusion of African Americans, cf. Yeomans, ibid., 175–177, and Synnott, *Half-Opened Door,* 49–51. During a press conference on June 4, 1993, Lani Guinier said about her father Ewart G. Guinier that he "was denied financial aid at Harvard College in 1929 on the grounds that one black student had already received a full scholarship; and he was not allowed to live in a dormitory on the grounds that no black student had resided there with the exception of a relative of a United States Senator" (broadcast on *All Things Considered,* National Public Radio, June 4, 1993). Ewart G. Guinier graduated in 1933. Thirty-six years later he became the first chairman of Harvard's newly established Afro-American Studies department. See Werner Sollors, Caldwell Titcomb, and Thomas A. Underwood, eds., *Blacks at Harvard: A Documentary History of African American Experience at Harvard and Radcliffe* (New York: New York University Press, 1993), 7.

11. Murdock to A. Chester Hanford on March 20, 1933, Dean of Harvard College Correspondence File (DHCCF), 1927–1933, A. C. Hanford, folder 115, Harvard University Archives; on the Houses as a social device for a moral purpose, cf. Yeomans, *Abbott Lawrence Lowell,* 189.

12. "Suggested Procedure for Assignment to Houses," March 20, 1934, DHCCF, 1933–1957, box House Plan—Houses (to 1938), folder Houses 1933–1934, Harvard University Archives.

13. Synnott, *Half-Opened Door,* 114. A more detailed table is reprinted by Synnott on p. 116. The group of "selected private schools" changed slightly over time. At the core were five Episcopal boarding schools: St. George's, St. Paul's, St. Mark's, Groton, and Middlesex, the so-called "St. Grotlesex." They were followed by Brooks, Milton, Noble and Greenough, and Pomfret. Later additions were Belmont Hill, Gunnery, Hill, Kent, and, for California's cream, Santa Barbara. In the 1940s, Dearfield and Hotchkiss were added. Andover and Exeter formed a separate group, because together they sent about one hundred students to Harvard every year. See Synnott, *Half-Opened Door,* 112, 114. On the superior academic achievements of Jews at Harvard and on the class stratification of learning and leisure, see also Seymour Martin Lipset and David Riesman, *Education and Politics at Harvard* (New York: McGraw-Hill, 1975), 145–150, 152–153.

14. At the very same time, restricting the admission of Jews to American colleges was also discussed in public. The *Nation* ran an article on anti-Semitism at Columbia and New York University that sparked a very lively debate in subsequent issues. An outspoken letter to the editor by W. L. Whittlesey summed up the popular objections to Jews: "Sir: The Jew problem in colleges is the farmer's stock problem: grade cattle or scrub cattle? Too many Jews are dirty, noisy, selfish, arrogant or cringing, below par physically, untidy, and in general damn bad citizens. They will not do what is right even

by their own. They oppress, cheat, lie, exploit, and will destroy anything to get a profit now. Look over New York city and see for your own purblind self. Some of my best friends are Jews but not of the usual sort. If the Jew can win to our best, it is his and welcome, but he must not degrade and defile that best to his own greasy level of low personal gain. A condition analogous to that of the New York city parks is not a proper goal for our colleges. Christ was a Jew and told a lot of the truth about them. Read it." *Nation* 115 (July 12, 1922): 46. Lowell wrote about the "Jew problem" to Kittredge on June 3, 1922, in Lowell Papers, 1919–1922, folder 1056, "Jews," Harvard University Archives.

15. The quotations in this paragraph are from the following sources: Hocking to Lowell on May 18, 1922; Lowell to Marvin on June 10, 1922; Lowell to Hocking on May 19, 1922; Lowell to Tucker on May 20, 1922, in Lowell Papers, 1919–1922, folder 1056, "Jews", Harvard University Archives. Hocking to Frankfurter on July 17, 1922, Felix Frankfurter Papers, Harvard Law School Library, box 191, folder 19. The best published account of the quota discussion is that presented in Synnott's *The Half-Opened Door*. Penny Hollander Feldman's 1975 dissertation, later published as *Recruiting an Elite: Admission to Harvard College* (New York: Garland, 1988) deals mainly with the effects of affirmative action in the 1960s and 1970s. She writes: "Today, although academic standards far higher than those employed in earlier years function as an important determinant of selection, the strict merit principle is still rejected by Harvard for social and institutional reasons. The same practices which were instituted in the 1920s and 1930s to exclude academically qualified applicants are used in the 1960s and 1970s to include applicants who could not be admitted on the basis of academic credentials alone" (8). For a discussion of this reversal, see Alan Dershowitz and Laura Hanft, "Affirmative Action and the Harvard College Diversity-Discretion Model: Paradigm or Pretext?" *Cardozo Law Review* 1 (Fall 1979): 379–424. About Hocking's pervasive anti-Jewish bias, I was informed by his former student Lewis Feuer in a conversation in Waban, Massachusetts, on September 24, 1992.

16. Documents quoted in Synnott, *Half-Opened Door*, 65, 66, 58, 69. The two petitions are kept in the Lowell Papers, 1919–1922, folder 1056, "Jews", Harvard University Archives.

17. Document quoted in Synnott, *Half-Opened Door*, 110; all figures are cited in the same work on pages 107 and 115; cf. also Lipset and Riesman, *Education and Politics at Harvard,* 179.

18. Harry Levin, conversation with the author, October 19, 1989. On J. L. Coolidge, see Morison, *Three Centuries of Harvard,* 378, 457, 478; and Synnott, *Half-Opened Door,* 117–118, and Levin's marginal notes.

19. Levin, marginal notes; about leaving Minneapolis see Levin, *Grounds for Comparison,* 6. About "Harvard indifference" I learned in my conversation with Levin on October 19, 1989; see also "Delmore Schwartz's Gift," in Harry Levin, *Memories of the Moderns* (New York: New Directions, 1980), 161. The phenomenon of "Harvard indifferentism" or "Harvard indifference" as an undergraduate attitude is also mentioned in Bliss Perry's 1935 memoir *And Gladly Teach* (233), and in Timothy Fuller's mystery *Harvard Has a Homicide* (Boston: Little, Brown, 1936), 38.

20. T. S. Eliot, "Tradition and the Individual Talent", reprinted in T. S. Eliot, *Selected Essays, 1917–1932* (New York: Harcourt, Brace, 1932), 4.

21. Levin, "A View from Within," 2.

22. Levin, conversation with the author, October 19, 1989; Levin, *Grounds for Comparison,* 6

23. Harry Levin, "The Private Life of F. O. Matthiessen," in *Memories of the Moderns,* 228.

24. Levin, *Memories of the Moderns,* 227. For Matthiessen's comments see *Rat and the Devil: Journal Letters of F. O. Matthiessen and Russell Cheney,* ed. Louis Hyde (1978; reprint, Boston: Alyson Publications, 1988), 258. The assessment of his visit to Matthiessen is found in Levin's marginal notes.

25. Joseph Summers and U. T. Miller Summers, "Matthiessen, Francis Otto," in *Dictionary of American Biography,* supplement 4, 1946–1950 (New York: Scribner's, 1974), 559.

26. Hyde, ed., *Rat and the Devil,* 47, 47–48.

27. William E. Cain, *F. O. Matthiessen and the Politics of Criticism* (Madison: University of Wisconsin Press, 1988), 57. Matthiessen's comment on Babbitt appears in *From the Heart of Europe* (New York: Oxford University Press, 1947), 74.

28. Eliot wrote, "The element of enjoyment is enlarged into appreciation, which brings a more intellectual addition to the original intensity of feeling." T. S. Eliot, *The Use of Poetry and the Use of Criticism: Studies in the Relation of Criticism to Poetry in England* (London: Faber and Faber, 1933), 19; On Whitmann as dissertation topic, see Cain, *F. O. Matthiessen,* 47–48. For a dissenting view of Matthiessen's reading of Whitman, see David Bergman, "F. O. Matthiessen: The Critic as Homosexual," *Raritan* 9 (Spring 1990): 62–82.

29. Hyde, ed., *Rat and the Devil,* 156, 215.

30. Hyde, ed., *Rat and the Devil,* 156. Whether Matthiessen was indeed successful in combining his political concerns and aesthetic views is still a matter of dispute. William Cain in *F. O. Matthiessen and the Politics of Criticism* denies it, while Frederic Stern affirms it in *F. O. Matthiessen: Christian Socialist as Critic* (Chapel Hill: University of North Carolina Press, 1981). Levin, "A View from Within," 1; on Levin's view of the past, see Levin, *The Power of Blackness: Hawthorne, Poe, Melville* (1958; reprint, Athens: Ohio University Press, 1980), vi–vii.

31. John Rackliffe, "Notes for a Character Study," in *F. O. Matthiessen: A Collective Portrait,* ed. Paul M. Sweezy and Leo Huberman, (New York: Henry Schuman, 1950), 86. Lionel Trilling, "Manners, Morals, and the Novel," in Trilling, *The Liberal Imagination: Essays on Literature and Society* (New York: Viking, 1950), 209. Levin wrote "I felt at home in [*sic*] Harvard from the beginning. Tutorial and the house system helped me fit in." Levin, letter to the author, July 22, 1989.

32. Levin, conversation with the author, October 19, 1989.

33. Harry Levin, *The Broken Column: A Study in Romantic Hellenism* (Cambridge: Harvard University Press, 1931), 13, 17, 30.

34. Levin, *Broken Column,* 69. For Babbitt's comment on French, see William F. Giese, in *Irving Babbitt,* ed Manchester and Shepard, 4.

35. Nevin, *Irving Babbitt,* 28; Harry Levin, "Irving Babbitt and the Teaching of Literature," in Levin, *Refractions: Essays in Comparative Literature* (New York: Oxford University Press, 1966), 328. Dazzling examples of controlled abundance are Levin's 1950 essay "The Tradition of Tradition," reprinted in Levin, *Contexts of Criticism* (Cambridge: Harvard University Press, 1957), 55–66, and his 1968 essay "Thematics and Criticism," reprinted in *Grounds for Comparison,* 91–109; less successful perhaps is Levin's

1985 essay "From Bohemia to Academia: Writers in Universities," *Bulletin of the American Academy of Arts and Sciences* 44 (January 1991): 28–50.

36. Harry Levin, "New Frontiers in the Humanities," *Contexts of Criticism,* 8.

37. Burton Pike, "Harry Levin: An Appreciation," *Comparative Literature* 40 (Winter 1988): 33. In his essay "Leech Gathering," Levin pointed out that his interest in "thematics" was an offshoot of the comparative method: "the effects of fantasy can be studied through the progressive transformation of images or myths" (*Grounds for Comparison,* 23). In his introduction to "Thematics and Criticism," Levin explained that he tried to utilize the method of thematics in *The Power of Blackness* (1958) and *The Myth of the Golden Age in the Renaissance* (1969). See also Cándido Pérez Gállego, "El método crítico de Harry Levin," *Arbor: Ciencia, Pensiamento y Cultura* 114 (February 1983): 99–107.

38. Levin, *Refractions,* 327, 328.

39. Ibid., 330–331, 329, 324.

40. Ibid., 331, 331–332.

41. George Santayana, "The Genteel Tradition in American Philosophy" (1911), reprinted in Santayana, *Winds of Doctrine: Studies in Contemporary Opinion* (New York: Scribner's, 1926), 205.

42. Alfred Kazin, *On Native Grounds: An Interpretation of American Prose Literature* (1942; reprint, Garden City, N.Y.: Anchor-Doubleday, 1956), 225; Eliot, *After Strange Gods,* 42.

43. Levin, conversation with the author, October 19, 1989.

44. Levin, conversation with the author, October 19, 1989. Cf. Levin, *Grounds for Comparison,* 7. In his response to this chapter, Levin played down the importance of Eliot's presence and claimed that the main event of his senior year was "working up—at the last minute, because someone had dropped out—a major role in a tragedy of Sophocles put on by the Classical Club in which I was an officer (in Greek). Since that meant dropping out of classes for a fortnight, Kittredge called me a 'nuisance' for not being there to recite when he called on me in his Beowulf course. When I apologized and explained, he characteristically said: 'Well, I've heard worse excuses.' " Levin, marginal.

45. Ozick, "Eliot at 101," *Fame and Folly,* 5–6.

46. Sylvia Rothchild, "Was Assimilation a Mistake? Interview with Leslie Fiedler," *Jewish Advocate* (Boston), September 13–19, 1991: 4; Irving Howe, "An Exercise in Memory. Eliot and the Jews: A Personal Confession," *New Republic* 204 (March 11, 1991): 31

47. Levin, *Grounds for Comparison,* 7; Levin, conversation with the author, October 19, 1989; Howe, "An Exercise in Memory," 31.

48. Matthiessen, *The Achievement of T. S. Eliot: An Essay on the Nature of Poetry,* 3d ed. (New York: Oxford University Press, 1958), 135; Levin, *Grounds for Comparison,* 7. Eliot's bias against the Jews did not preclude friendly relations with them. At the time of Eliot's cautious sponsorship of Levin he was also engaged in a warm correspondence with the philosopher Horace M. Kallen; cf. Ranen Omer, " 'It is I Who Have Been Defending a Religion Called Judaism': The T. S. Eliot and Horace M. Kallen Correspondence," *Texas Studies in Literature and Language* 39 (Winter 1997): 321–356.

49. Smith, *Harvard Century,* 97; Lowell, quoted in Yeomans, *Abbott Lawrence Lowell,* 531; Levin, *Grounds for Comparison,* 9.

50. Harry Levin, "Appendix: A Letter to F. O. Matthiessen (About T. S. Eliot)," in Levin, *Memories of the Moderns,* 232; Levin, conversation with the author, October 19, 1989.

51. Matthiessen, *Achievement of T. S. Eliot,* 59, 153 n. 9, viii, 19. Paul Elmer More to Austin Warren on August 11, 1929, quoted in Dakin, *Paul Elmer More,* 269 (see also chap. 1, n. 56).

52. Matthiessen, *Achievement of T. S. Eliot,* 106, 59. William Cain, *F. O. Matthiessen and the Politics of Criticism,* 89, 66.

53. Matthiessen, *Achievement of T. S. Eliot,* 100–101, 99.

54. Matthiessen, *Achievement of T. S. Eliot,* 111, 109. This approach to Eliot's poetry was most recently used by Anthony Julius in *T. S. Eliot, Anti-Semitism, and Literary Form* (Cambridge: Cambridge University Press, 1995).

55. Howe, "An Exercise in Memory," 29. Levin, *Memories of the Moderns,* 247.

56. Levin, *Memories of the Moderns,* 239, 235, 234.

57. Levin, *Memories of the Moderns,* 244, 245, 242, 246, 238–239.

58. Levin, conversation with the author, October 19, 1989. When I asked Prof. Silverstein about his time at Harvard, he replied with a brief note: "The difficulty was my timing; I came at a moment when Harvard was still a New England college and before it became the great national institution which it subsequently announced itself to be. I was of course too innocent to understand these matters. Fortunately I finally came to another great institution, where anti-Semitism doesn't exist—but then we are not stylish out here." Letter to the author, March 12, 1992. Silverstein got a job at the University of Chicago, where he established himself as a superb medievalist known for his meticulous editions. His students perceived him as a man with "a great sense of style about him. One had the sense of someone who was almost British and of someone who believed in the English tradition." He was known to say to his students that "this line of study separates the scholar from the shoe salesman." Conversation with Dan Isaac, San Francisco, December 29, 1991.

59. Elena Zarudnaya Levin reports that for one week her husband could not make up his mind whether or not to accept the appointment. He was then at work on a study of French Realism. Confronted with the choice between a job at the institution he loved and finishing a book, he felt that his entire career was at stake. "He was very tormented. He did not know what decision to make. For one week he thrashed around, because he wanted to finish his book on the French Realists." In the end his pragmatism prevailed; he took the job, and the study of the French Realists, which became *The Gates of Horn,* was not published until 1963. Conversation with Elena Z. Levin, Cambridge, Massachusetts, March 17, 1995.

60. James Atlas, *Delmore Schwartz: The Life of an American Poet* (New York: Farrar Straus Giroux, 1977), 164, 163. Levin, *Memories of the Moderns,* 159.

61. Levin, *Memories of the Moderns,* 163–164. Delmore Schwartz, *The World Is a Wedding* (Norfolk, Conn.: New Directions, 1948), 31. About the relationship between Schwartz and Levin, see the entries in Elizabeth Pollet, ed., *Portrait of Delmore: Journals and Notes of Delmore Schwartz: 1939–1959* (New York: Farrar Straus Giroux, 1986), and Atlas, *Delmore Schwartz,* 193–197.

62. Recollection by Elena Z. Levin in a conversation with the author, March 17, 1995. James Laughlin sent the card to Harry Levin; it is now lost in Levin's papers.

However, Laughlin confirmed the content of the card in a letter to the Spanish literary scholar José-Antonio Gurpegui.

63. On April 8, 1940, Laughlin wrote to Levin about a second card he had from Joyce:

> I have just had a card from Joyce in which he says: "many thanks for having sent me the book with Prof. Levin's article. Please convey to the writer my thanks also for his kindly and painstaking study of my book. In the opinions of all those to whom I have shown it this article, beginning with the title, is the most striking one that has appeared so far."
>
> I thought you would be pleased with that, as I was. And I hope it may help inspire you to undertake the book on Joyce in our makers of Modern Literature Series. I really feel that you could whack that on the head.

64. Matthiessen, *Achievement of T. S. Eliot,* 11. Levin, "Putting Pound Together," *New York Review of Books* 36 (November 9, 1989): 45–47.

65. Nadine Gordimer, "Three in a Bed," *New Republic* 206 (November 18, 1991): 36; interview with Stephen Orgel, Cambridge, Massachusett, March 3, 1991; interview with Stepen Greenblatt, Cambridge, Massachusetts, December 13, 1991.

66. Levin, *Memories of the Moderns,* 165; Atlas, *Delmore Schwartz,* 163; Levin, *Grounds for Comparison,* 4, 19; Levin, marginal notes.

67. Levin, *Power of Blackness;* 3.

68. Elena Z. Levin, conversation with the author, May 19, 1995, about Levin's mindset at the time of the Guggenheim fellowship.

69. Cynthia Ozick, "The Responsibility of Intellectuals," unpublished paper presented at "What Has Neoconservatism Wrought: A Conference on the 50th Anniversary of *Commentary,*" Harvard University, February 27, 1995. The Forster quotations are taken from Ozick's text.

70. John Wilmot, earl of Rochester, *A Satire Against Mankind and Other Poems,* ed. Harry Levin (Norfolk, Conn.: New Directions, 1942), 21–22. The introduction to this edition was reprinted in Levin, *Grounds for Comparison,* 207–211; quotation, 208.

71. Dorrit Cohn, interview with the author, Cambridge, Mass., April 16, 1988.

72. "Harry Levin, Literary Critic, Is Dead at 81," *New York Times,* June 1, 1994: B9.

73. Cohn, interview with the author, April 16, 1988. The other women hired to tenure in 1971 were in English, history, anthropology, and music.

74. Donald Fanger, "Remembering Harry Levin," *Harvard Magazine* 97 (January-February 1995): 79.

3. Man of Imaginative Consent: M. H. Abrams

1. Owen Johnson, *Stover at Yale* (New York: Frederick A. Stokes, 1912), 247–248.

2. Ibid., p. 68.

3. M. H. Abrams, interview with the author, Ithaca, N.Y., August 28, 1988. All biographical material is taken from this interview. In the spring of 1993, I sent Professor Abrams a draft of this chapter. He responded on June 17, 1994, with a 13-page hand-written letter that contained more information, all of which I have included in a

thorough revision of my draft. Passages from the letter are cited in the text and referred to as "letter."

4. Lewis S. Feuer, "Arthur O. Lovejoy," in *Masters: Portraits of Great Teachers,* ed. Joseph Epstein (New York: Basic Books, 1981), 120. Asked about his teachers in Romantic studies, Abrams replied: "I really did very little formal work at college in the Romantic period. I remember as an undergraduate taking a course in English Romantic Poetry from John Livingstone [*sic*] Lowes, who unfortunately was past his prime at the time, but still an eloquent and persuasive lecturer. . . . My undergraduate essay . . . obviously did get quite a lot from Lowes." Peter Schock, "An Interview with M. H. Abrams," *Iowa Journal of Literary Studies* 4 (1983): 6.

5. Abrams pointed out that "equally influential on my thinking about reading and about writing about literature, in addition to Lovejoy and Richards, was R. S. Crane (at the University of Chicago, and twice a visiting professor during my earlier years at Cornell). I did not study with Wittgenstein at Cambridge, where he was already a legend, and did not even read more than some scattered passages in his *Tractatus.* His influence on my thinking began only with the publication of his *Philosophical Investigations,* in 1953—too late, for example, to have had any effect on my *Mirror and the Lamp"* (letter).

6. M. H. Abrams, "What's the Use of Theorizing about the Arts" (1972), in M. H. Abrams, *Doing Things with Texts: Essays in Criticism and Critical Theory* (New York: Norton, 1989), 70, 48.

7. Schock, "An Interview with M. H. Abrams," 8.

8. Abrams took issue with my phrases "Gentile culture" here and "Gentile literary tradition" elsewhere. "It was the western European literary tradition [we studied], and it never occurred to me to think of it as non-Jewish. Indeed, it was *not* non-Jewish, when you take into account the degree in which it was founded on the Hebrew Bible, borrowed concepts from Jewish theologians, and incorporated the work of Jewish writers and scholars" (letter). This is of course how we think about the Western literary tradition *after* the integration of Jews into literary academe. My point, however, is that during Abrams's formative years, in the late twenties and throughout the thirties and forties, English literature was considered a product of Christian Europe and the domain of Christian scholars. Jews were simply not in the picture, either as authors or as critics and scholars. This book is about why, when, and how that changed.

9. M. H. Abrams, "Belief and the Suspension of Disbelief," in *Literature and Belief,* ed. M. H. Abrams, English Insitute Essays 1957 (New York: Columbia University Press, 1958), 5. All further references to this essay are cited in the text as *B*.

10. M. H. Abrams, *The Mirror and the Lamp: Romantic Theory and the Critical Tradition* (New York: Oxford University Press, 1953), 4–5. Further references to this book are cited in the text as *ML.*

11. T. S. Eliot, "The Idea of a Christian Society," in T. S. Eliot, *Christianity and Culture* (New York: Harcourt Brace Jovanovich, 1968), 10.

12. M. H. Abrams, "Rationality and Imagination in Cultural History" (1976), reprinted in Abrams, *Doing Things with Texts,* 134.

13. Vincent B. Leitch, *American Literary Criticism from the Thirties to the Eighties* (New York: Columbia University Press, 1988), 279.

14. Ibid., 304.

15. Abrams, "Rationality and Imagination," 132, 126. On the Romantic positives

see M. H. Abrams, *Natural Supernaturalism: Tradition and Revolution in Romantic Literature* (New York: Norton, 1971), 427–431.

16. David Lehman, *Signs of the Times: Deconstruction and the Fall of Paul de Man* (New York: Poseidon Books, 1991), 69–71.

17. Abrams, "What's the Use of Theorizing about the Arts?" 38, 45, 48.

18. M. H. Abrams, "How to Do Things with Texts," (1979), reprinted in Abrams, *Doing Things with Texts,* 281, 285. Further references to this essay are cited in the text as H.

19. Quoted in H, 286.

20. Fish was piqued by Abrams's pointed critique, which Abrams first presented as a paper in the Lionel Trilling Seminar of 1978. Fish responded quickly to Abrams's points in the John Crowe Ransom Memorial Lecture delivered at Kenyon College in April 1979 and reprinted in his book *Is There a Text in This Class? The Authenticity of Interpretive Communities* (Cambridge: Harvard University Press, 1980).

21. M. H. Abrams, "The Language and Methods of Humanism," in *The Philosophy of the Curriculum: The Need for General Education,* ed. Sidney Hook, Paul Kurtz, and Miro Todorovich (Buffalo, N.Y.: Prometheus Books, 1975), 94–95.

4. The Lure of Literary Stwardship: Daniel Aaron

1. Daniel Aaron, interview with the author, January 13, 1988. I conducted three further formal interviews with Daniel Aaron in his office at Harvard University (June 21, 1989; June 30, 1989; April 2, 1993). I shall quote from these interviews, citing the source as "interview" without indicating its exact date in the running text. In addition, Daniel Aaron lent me the manuscript of his introduction to *American Notes: Selected Essays* (Boston: Northeastern University Press, 1994). The printed version is cited in the text as *AN,* the manuscript version as *ANms.* Aaron is currently at work on a memoir, tentatively entitled *Circlings.*

2. Arthur Crew Inman, *The Inman Diary: A Public and Private Confession,* ed. Daniel Aaron (Cambridge: Harvard University Press, 1985), 532. Further references to this book are cited in the text as *ID.*

3. Hans Kohn, *Living in a World Revolution: My Encounter With History* (New York: Trident Press, 1964), 150. Aaron knew Kohn at Smith College, where Kohn taught from 1934 to 1949.

4. T. S. Eliot, *After Strange Gods: A Primer of Modern Heresy* (New York: Harcourt, Brace, 1933), 16, 17. Steven B. Hudson in *Fragmentation and Restoration: The Tikkun Ha-Olam Theme in the Metaphysical Poetry of Abraham Regelson* (Chicago: Adams Press, 1988) points out that Regelson conceived of the ideal macrocosm as "a totality comprised of the integration of all accident into oneness while retaining differentiation. It serves as a possible solution to the problem of fragmentation" (62).

5. Thorstein Veblen, "The Intellectual Pre-Eminence of Jews in Modern Europe," (1919), reprinted in Thorstein Veblen, *Essays in Our Changing Order,* ed. Leon Ardzrooni (New York: Viking, 1934), 227–229.

6. Robert B. Heilman, letter to the author, January 10, 1993.

7. Daniel Aaron, "Trash, Classics, and the Common Reader," *Texas Humanist* 6 (May-June 1984): 41; reprinted as part of the introduction to *American Notes* (*AN* xxix–xxxi).

8. On the attitude of the University of Chicago toward Jews see Josef Dorfman, *Thorstein Veblen and His America* (New York: Viking, 1934), chap. 6; Harold Wechsler, *The Qualified Student: A History of Selective College Admission in America* (New York: Wiley, 1977), chap. 9; William H. McNeill, *Hutchins' University: A Memoir of the University of Chicago, 1929–1950* (Chicago: University of Chicago Press, 1991); Mary Ann Dzuback, *Robert M. Hutchins: Portrait of an Educator* (Chicago: University of Chicago Press, 1991); Edward Shils, ed., *Remembering the University of Chicago: Teachers, Scientists, and Scholars* (Chicago: University of Chicago Press, 1991).

9. Meyer Levin, *The Old Bunch* (1937; reprint, Secaucus, N.J.: Citadel Press, 1985), 297.

10. Howard Mumford Jones, *Howard Mumford Jones: An Autobiography* (Madison: University of Wisconsin Press, 1979), 150. Further references to this book are cited in the text as *Au*.

11. Kermit Vanderbilt, *American Literature and the Academy: The Roots, Growth, and Maturity of a Profession* (Philadelphia: University of Pennsylvania Press, 1986), 449. See also Peter Brier, *Howard Mumford Jones and the Dynamics of Liberal Humanism* (Columbia: University of Missouri Press, 1994).

12. John Lydenberg, ed., *Political Activism and the Academic Conscience. The Harvard Experience, 1936–1941* (Geneva, N.Y.: Hobart and William Smith Colleges, 1977), 14.

13. Richard Bridgman, "The American Studies of Henry Nash Smith," *American Scholar* 56 (Spring 1987): 259–268; Howard Mumford Jones, *The Theory of American Literature* (Ithaca, N.Y.: Cornell University Press, 1948), 141–142.

14. Henry Steele Commager, *The American Mind: An Interpretation of American Thought and Character Since the 1880s* (New Haven: Yale University Press, 1950), 298, 300; Vanderbilt, *American Literature and the Academy*, 302–303. Vanderbilt's section on Parrington draws on a dissertation by H. Lark Hall that has now appeared in print: *V. L. Parrington: Through the Avenue of Art* (Kent: Kent State University Press, 1994). Hall's biography presents an interesting revaluation of Parrington's very complicated relationship to Harvard University. Despite Parrington's ostensible disdain for this bastion of privilege, he faithfully kept all his Harvard notebooks. Daniel Aaron's review of Hall's biography appeared as "The Mid-American Scholar," *New Republic* 211 (September 5, 1994): 47–49.

15. Daniel Aaron and Henry Nash Smith, "Recent Works on the Social History of the United States, 1935–1939," *International Review for Social History* (1939): 499–500, 508.

16. Daniel Aaron, "Parrington Plus," review of *American Renaissance*, by F. O. Matthiessen, *Kenyon Review* 4 (Winter 1942): 102–106.

17. Granville Hicks, *Part of the Truth* (New York: Harcourt, Brace and World, 1965), 154. Further references to this book are cited in the text as *PT*.

18. Daniel Aaron, *Writers on the Left: Episodes in American Literary Communism* (New York: Harcourt, Brace and World, 1961), 357. Further references to this book are cited in the text as *WL*.

19. Daniel Aaron, "Cambridge, 1936–39," *Partisan Review* 50/51 (1984/85): 833–836. The book Aaron refers to is Emile Burns, *A Handbook of Marxism: Being a Collection of Extracts From the Writings of Marx, Engels, and the Greatest of Their Followers, Selected So As to Give to the Reader the Most Comprehensive Account of Marxism Possible Within the Limits Of a Single Volume / The Passages Being Chosen By Emile Burns, Who Has Added in*

Each Case a Bibliographic Note, & an Explanation of the Circumstances in Which the Work Was Written & Its Special Significance in the Development of Marxism: As Well As the Necessary Glossaries and Index (New York: Random House, 1935).

20. Aaron, *Writers on the Left*, 363; Aaron, "Cambridge 1936–39," 836.

21. A bibliography of Aaron's work has been appended to *American Notes* (315–326).

22. Daniel Aaron, "Henry Adams: The Public and Private View," *Hudson Review* 5 (Winter 1953): 611; Daniel Aaron, introduction to Paul Elmer More, *Shelburne Essays on American Literature*, selected and edited by Daniel Aaron (New York: Harcourt, Brace and World, 1963), 4; Daniel Aaron, "Of This Time, of That Place," *Partisan Review* 34 (Summer 1967): 480.

23. Daniel Aaron, "The Treachery of Recollection: The Inner and Outer History," *Carleton Miscellany* 6 (Summer 1965): 17. This essay was reprinted in *American Notes* (3–17); further references are to this reprint.

24. Daniel Aaron, "Writers on the Left Assessed," *Indian Journal of American Studies* 3 (June 1977): 5. This essay was first presented at the 1972 convention of the Modern Language Association.

25. Daniel Aaron, *Cincinnati, Queen City of the West, 1819–1938* (Columbus: Ohio State University Press, 1992), xxiii, 6–7. So as not to paint too rosy a picture, Aaron pointed out that pride in regional descent caused significant tension. "Most of the antagonism, if we are to rely upon contemporary evidence, could be attributed to the character and activities of the New Englanders. Southerners and westerners, for the most part, lived together harmoniously, but they both resented the overweening Yankee who clung tenaciously to the New England institutions and sought to impose them on every community" (147).

26. See, for instance, Douglas Bush's blasé attitude toward Howard Mumford Jones. Recollecting his time at Harvard, Bush wrote, "Howard Mumford Jones—who said he always used his middle name as a sort of gilding for Jones—was perhaps never entirely comfortable at Harvard. He was brought in not by a department vote but by President Conant's appointment; the president's idea may have been to infuse new vigor and largeness of outlook into a department he regarded as effete and precious. Howard had had no Harvard connection and had spent his teaching life in the South and Middle West; in some quarters he may have seemed a cultivated frontiersman." Douglas Bush, "Memories of Harvard's English Department, 1920–1960," *Sewanee Review* 89 (Fall 1981): 602.

27. Aaron, *Cincinnati*, 284–285, 286, xxiv.

28. Daniel Aaron, *Men of Good Hope: A Story of American Progressivism* (New York: Oxford University Press, 1951), xiv. All further references to this book are cited in the text as *MGH*.

29. On December 12, 1857, Parker wrote to D. A. Wasson: "Religious Emotion—religious Will I think never went further than with the Jews. But their *intellect* was sadly pinched in those narrow foreheads. They were cruel *also*—always cruel. I doubt not they did sometimes kill a Christian Baby at the Passover, or the anniversary of Haman's famous day! If it had been a Christian *Man* we should not blame them much, considering how they got treated by men who worshipped a Jew for God. They were also *lecherous*, no language on earth I think is so *rich* in terms for sexual mixing.—All Shemites are given to flesh, what *mouths* they have—full of voluptuousness, only the Negro beats them there. The African has the largest organs of generation in the world, the most

erotic heat; he is the most polygamous of men. The Negro girls of Boston are only *chaste* in the sense of being *run after*. After their first menstruation they invariably take a man—so say such who know. I think the Jews come next—their *mouths* are African." Quoted in Daniel Aaron, "Of This Time, Of That Place, 482.

30. About the power of stereotypes to accommodate contradictions see Sander Gilman, *Franz Kafka, the Jewish Patient* (New York: Routledge, 1995), 59.

31. Veblen, "The Intellectual Pre-Eminence of Jews," 227.

32. Daniel Aaron, "The Bigger They Come," *New Republic* 113 (September 24, 1945): 379–381; and "A Note on the Businessman and the Historian," *Antioch Review* 6 (Winter 1946–47): 575–584.

33. Daniel Aaron, "The Helsinki the Athletes Didn't See," *Reporter* 7 (September 2, 1952): 24–27; "The American Professor and the Soviet Cookie Pusher," *Reporter* 8 (March 31, 1953): 24–27. On Aaron's new regard for conservatism, see "Conservatism Old and New," *American Quarterly* 6 (Summer 1954): 99–110.

34. Alan Wald, introduction to Daniel Aaron, *Writers on the Left: Episodes in American Literary Communism* (New York: Columbia University Press, 1992), xxii.

35. Daniel Aaron, "The Man of Letters in American Culture," in *The American Future and the Humane Tradition: The Role of the Humanities in Higher Education,* ed. Robert Heidemann (New York: Associated Faculty Press, 1982), 68, also reprinted in *AN* 179–198. In *Upstate: Records and Recollections of Northern New York* (New York: Farrar, Straus, and Giroux, 1971), Edmund Wilson refers to a trip he undertook together with Aaron while the latter was at work on *Writers on the Left*. Aaron had asked him about people involved in radical activities in the twenties and thirties. "The whole thing seems to me so stale," Wilson noted, "that I can't imagine anybody's now wanting to write about it. . . . It seemed to me like that grisly museum of the early nineteenhundreds that I had [Aaron] visit at Niagara Falls" (188).

36. Daniel Aaron, introduction to Harvey Swados, *On the Line* (New York: Laurel Edition, 1977), 13.

37. On the sources of Jewish radicalism see Steven Cassedy, *To the Other Shore: The Russian Jewish Intellectuals Who Came to America* (Princeton: Princeton University Press, 1997). "From the Notebooks of Lionel Trilling, Part I," *Partisan Review* 50/51 (1984/85): 498. See also Alan Wald, *The New York Intellectuals: The Rise and Decline of the Anti-Stalinist Left* (Chapel Hill: University of North Carolina Press, 1987), 334–335.

38. Daniel Aaron, "Some Reflections on Communism and the Jewish Writer" (1965), in *The Ghetto and Beyond: Essays on Jewish Life in America,* ed. Peter I. Rose (New York: Random House, 1969), 253, 255, 257–258. Aaron decided to reprint this essay in the appendix to the 1992 edition of *Writers on the Left*. In a prefatory note he explained that he had played down the subject of Jewish radicals in his book because Joseph Freeman, one of Aaron's most valuable informants, vigorously denied "the preeminence of Jews in radical circles" (see also *AN* xxv). Daniel Aaron, "Richard Wright and the Communist Party," *New Letters* 38 (Winter 1971): 170–181; reprinted in *AN* 91–101.

39. One of Aaron's sisters, for instance, became a physician. She must have faced obstacles as a woman as well as a Jew. For data on Jews in medicine see Leon Sokoloff, "The Rise and Decline of the Jewish Quota in Medical School Admissions," *Bulletin of the New York Academy of Medicine* 68 (November 1992): 497–518.

40. Aaron, "Some Reflections on Communism and the Jewish Writer," 258.

41. Cf. Cassedy, *To the Other Shore,* chapters 5–9. Charles S. Liebman and Steven M. Cohen in "Jewish Liberalism Revisited," *Commentary* 102 (November 1996): 51–53, confirm implicitly Cassedy's analysis of the Gentile Russian sources of inspiration for Jewish left-wing radicalism when they point out that "there is little support for the notion that Jewish liberalism derives from an attachment to the Jewish religious tradition" (52).

42. Carleton Coon, *The Races of Europe* (New York: Macmillan, 1939), 441–442; plate 46, figure 1;

43. Ibid., 644.

44. Daniel Aaron, "The Hyphenate Writer and American Letters," *Smith College Alumnae Quarterly* (July 1964): 213; this essay was reprinted in *AN* 69–83.

45. Ibid., 214.

46. Daniel Aaron, *The Unwritten War: American Writers and the Civil War* (New York: Oxford University Press, 1973), xviii.

47. Daniel Aaron, *The Unwritten War: American Writers and the Civil War* (Madison: University of Wisconsin Press, 1987), xvi.

48. Aaron, *"Writers on the Left* Assessed," 3–4; and *WL* xviii.

5. Leaving the Yard: Leo Marx

1. See Matthiessen's letter to Russell Cheney, written April 1, 1945, *Rat and the Devil: Journal Letters of F. O. Matthiessen and Russell Cheney,* ed. Louis Hyde (1978; reprint, Boston: Alyson Publications, 1988), 341.

2. Quoted in Richard Norton Smith, *The Harvard Century: The Making of a University to a Nation* (New York: Simon and Schuster, 1986), 157.

3. The term *myth and symbol school* derives from Bruce Kuklick's influential and somewhat polemical article "Myth and Symbol in American Studies," *American Quarterly* 24 (October 1972): 435–450.

4. Leo Marx, eulogy for Henry Nash Smith (1986), unpublished manuscript. Henry Nash Smith to Daniel Aaron, June 13, 1939. Both documents in the possession of Daniel Aaron.

5. Samuel Marx, *Queen of the Ritz* (Indianapolis: Bobbs-Merrill, 1978) is a biographically sound but almost unreadable book about Blanche Rubinstein Auzello. Other biographical information from Leo Marx, interview with the author, Cambridge, Mass., May 13, 1988; further references to this interview are cited in the text.

6. Leo Marx commented: "Because of your subject the chapter inevitably suggests that Jewishness and my relation to Judaism generally played a much more central role in my life, and especially my intellectual life, than it (consciously) did. That's inevitable, I suppose, but the truth as I remember it is that during much of my life the issue has been of relatively marginal importance for me. Somehow my conscious atheist-tending convictions ought to be included . . . , and since childhood—encouraged by many people around me—I have been a commmitted believer in the universalist anti-church values of the Enlightenment. I probably represent a certain widely disseminated rationalistic assimilationist viewpoint (and experience) within my cohort of third generation American Jews. (How can you ignore my 52 year marriage to a non-Jewish woman of New England Yankee ancestry?)" Leo Marx, letter to the author, June 23, 1994.

7. Theresa Marx was kept informed by her sister Blanche about the persecution of the Jews in France.

8. David Levin, *Exemplary Elders* (Athens: University of Georgia Press, 1990), 19, 22; Perry Miller, *Errand into the Wilderness* (Cambridge: Belknap Press of Harvard University Press, 1956), vii.

9. Levin, *Exemplary Elders*, 40, 42; Miller, *Errand into the Wilderness*, 1. The complexity of Miller's attitude toward the dichotomy of mind and environment is the subject of David Hollinger, "Perry Miller and Philosophical History," *History and Theory* 7 (1968): 189–202. Hollinger argues, for instance, that for Miller the process of culture "was primarily the interaction of mind and environment." He cites Miller's remark that *The New England Mind* (1939) was not merely a study of the intellectual life of New England but "a case history of the accommodation to the American landscape of an imported and highly articulated system of ideas" (194).

10. Miller, *Errand into the Wilderness*, viii.

11. Leo Marx, "The Harvard Retrospect and the Arrested Development of American Radicalism," in *Political Activism and the Academic Conscience: The Harvard Experience, 1936–1941,* ed. John Lydenberg (Geneva, N.Y.: Hobart and Smith Colleges, 1977), 33. Further references to this book are cited in the text as *PA.*

12. Letter from Matthiessen to Daniel Aaron, June 14, 1939; letter in the possession of Daniel Aaron. By his own admission, Matthiessen was neither a Communist nor a Marxist; see Frederick Stern, *F. O. Matthiessen: Christian Socialist as Critic* (Chapel Hill: University of North Carolina Press, 1981), 17 ff.

13. Responding to this passage, Leo Marx wrote, "No one of minimal intelligence could have failed to recognize the complexity of the Miller/Matthiessen personalities and relations. Their relations were a subject of immense interest to, and constant discussion among, other faculty and students. As their mutual hostility grew, their students found themselves in a terrible bind. What I and my contemporaries were astonishingly oblivious of, however, was the insecurity and complexity of Matthiessen's situation as a closeted gay man. The extent to which we succeeded in denying, repressing or—in any case—failing to acknowledge, that situation is difficult to understand." Leo Marx, letter to the author, December 21, 1994.

14. How deeply Matthiessen's friends were upset by his suicide can be discerned in Paul M. Sweezy and Leo Huberman, eds., *F. O. Matthiessen (1902–1950): A Collective Portrait* (New York: Henry Schuman, 1950). This volume also contains Leo Marx's essay "F. O. Matthiessen: The Teacher," later reprinted in Marx's collection *The Pilot and the Passenger: Essays on Literature, Technology, and Culture* (New York: Oxford University Press, 1988), 231–239; further references to this collection are cited in the text as *PaP.* In response to my presentation of his relationship with 1930s radicalism, Leo Marx wrote: "In my talk [at the Hobart conference] I was consciously aiming to correct what I took to be the failure of many of the speakers to recognize the inherent tension between our youthful political convictions and the aspiring roles we were destined to perform in middle class American life. In your reading those feelings come out as some sort of deep personal guilt, but that is very far from my sense of the matter." Leo Marx, letter to the author, June 23, 1994.

15. Kuklick, "Myth and Symbol in American Studies," 437; John Higham, "The Cult of the 'American Consensus': Homogenizing Our History," *Commentary* 27 (February 1959): 96. When traditional American studies came again under attack twenty years

after Kuklick's original 1972 critique, Kuklick softened his earlier response to Marx. See Jeffrey Louis Decker, "Dis-Assembling the Machine in the Garden: Antihumanism and the Critique of American Studies;" Bruce Kuklick, "A Reply to Decker," *New Literary History* 23 (Spring 1992): 282–310.

16. For a discussion of Leo Marx's socialist humanism, see Günter H. Lenz, "American Studies and the Radical Tradition: From the 1930s to the 1960s," *Prospects* 12 (1987): 21–58.

17. Gene Wise, " 'Paradigm Dramas' in American Studies: A Cultural and Institutional History of the Movement," *American Quarterly* 31 (1979): 302; Miller, *Errand into the Wilderness,* viii, ix, 16.

18. Henry Nash Smith, *Virgin Land: The American West as Symbol and Myth* (New York: Vintage, 1950), v; all further references to this book are cited in the text as *VL.*

19. Miller, *Errand into the Wilderness,* 1.

20. About the relationship between Miller and Matthiessen, Marx said "they were always jealous of each other, Perry and Matty. They were like a couple of kids; and Harry [Levin] too. To this day Harry will tell you that he told Matty what the title of *American Renaissance* should be. He says he invented the title" (interview). Rivalry also characterizes the tense and intense relationship between Edward Cavan [Matthiessen] and Ivan Goldberg [Harry Levin] in May Sarton's novel *Faithful Are the Wounds* (New York: Rinehart, 1955).

21. Leo Marx, letter to the author, June 23, 1994.

22. Henry Nash Smith, "Symbol and Idea in *Virgin Land,*" in *Ideology and Classic American Literature,* ed. Sacvan Bercovitch and Myra Jehlen (Cambridge: Harvard University Press, 1986), 23.

23. Ibid., 27. Smith to Aaron, October 15, 1939. Letter in the possession of Daniel Aaron.

24. Smith, "Symbol and Idea in *Virgin Land,*" 28. I agree with Leo Marx's assessment (in his letter of June 23, 1994) that Smith, an inordinately fair-minded and generous man, was too hard on himself here.

25. Smith to Aaron on May 30, 1947, and on November 23, 1948. Both letters in the possession of Daniel Aaron.

26. Tremaine McDowell, *American Studies* (Minneapolis: University of Minnesota Press, 1948); Gayle Graham Yates, "Mary C. Turpie: A Life in American Studies," *American Studies Association Newsletter* 17 (March 1994): 1, 3. For an appreciation of Leo Marx's work at the University of Minnesota, see Elaine Tyler May, " 'Radical Roots of American Studies': Presidential Address to the American Studies Association, November 9, 1995," *American Quarterly* 48 (June 1996): 175–194.

27. Leo Marx, "Pastoralism in America," in *Ideology and Classic American Literature,* ed. Bercovitch and Jehlen, 43.

28. Lawrence Buell, "American Pastoral Ideology Reappraised," *American Literary History* 1 (Spring 1989): 4

29. Leo Marx, "The American Scholar Today," *Commentary* 32 (July 1961): 52.

30. Marx, "Pastoralism in America," 38.

31. Ibid., 59

32. Buell, "American Pastoral Ideology Reappraised," 4.

33. Marx, "Pastoralism in America," 38, 40.

34. "Science [Brooks Adams thought] only permitted man to 'control without un-

derstanding.' It hastened the process of disintegration since 'an education of conservation was contrary to the instinct of greed which dominated the democratic mind, and compelled it to insist on the pillage of the public by the private man.' " Daniel Aaron, *Men of Good Hope,* 265.

35. Aaron, Levin, and Marx married non-Jews. About the cultural void of his world, Marx said, "There was something sad about these people, my aunts and uncles on both sides. They gave up a great deal; they gave up [Jewish] culture; and what took its place was a very thin sort of American [preoccupation]: career, ambition, and so on. Their values seemed to me not very admirable, not very rich. Even as a child I was constantly offended by the crudely materialistic values of these people. The topic of conversation was always money and things and making it. Jewishness was the richest part of their cultural heritage. When they gave that up, what was left was not very interesting. They had nothing to put in its place except universal bourgeois values, and they are not all that great. It just seemed that they were very deprived people" (interview).

36. Alfred Kazin, *New York Jew* (New York: Vintage, 1978), 348–359.

37. The texts at issue here are Trilling's and Eliot's introductions to *Huckleberry Finn,* written in 1948 and 1950, respectively.

38. A notable exception was the medievalist Morton Bloomfield (1913–1987), the second tenured Jewish professor in the Harvard English department after Harry Levin. He came to Harvard from Ohio State University in Columbus in 1961.

6. The Meaning of Freedom: Allen Guttmann

1. Leo Marx, "Mr. Eliot, Mr. Trilling, and *Huckleberry Finn,*" (1953), reprinted in *The Pilot and the Passenger: Essays on Literature, Technology, and Culture in the United States* (New York: Oxford University Press, 1988); on the extraordinary influence of Leo Marx's essay on subsequent criticism of *Huckleberry Finn,* see Peter Shaw, "The Genteel Fate of *Huckleberry Finn,*" *Partisan Review* 60 (1993): 434–449.

2. Allen Guttmann, interview with the author in Amherst, Mass., April 24, 1988. Further references to this interview, augmented by Guttmann's letter to the author, May 24, 1994, are cited in the text.

3. Allen Guttmann, *The Wound in the Heart: America and the Spanish Civil War* (New York: Free Press, 1962), v; all further references to this book are cited in the text as *W.*

4. Guttmann's quotation is taken from Lionel Trilling's *Liberal Imagination* (1950). Daniel Aaron, too, concurred with Trilling: "I have always believed that a healthy political philosophy has to have a recognition and appreciation of conservative opposition" (Aaron, interview, April 2, 1993).

5. Allen Guttmann, *The Conservative Tradition in America* (New York: Oxford University Press, 1967), 11; all further references to this book are cited in the text as *CT.*

6. When Huck rejoins Jim on the raft after they had gotten separated in the fog, he pretends that he never left the raft and tells Jim that he dreamed that Huck had gotten lost. Jim is almost convinced but then discovers debris left on the raft from the night's bad weather. He calls Huck's bluff and scolds him for making fun of him. " 'En all you wuz thinkin 'bout wuz how you could make a fool uv ole Jim wid a lie. Dat truck dah is *trash;* en trash is what people is dat puts dirt on de head er dey fren's en makes 'em ashamed.' . . . It was fifteen minutes before I could work myself up to go and humble myself to a nigger—but I done it, and I warn't ever sorry for it afterwards, neither."

Mark Twain, *The Adventures of Huckleberry Finn* (New York: Random House, 1996), 110.

7. Allen Guttmann, "Jewish Radicals, Jewish Writers," *American Scholar* 32 (Autumn 1963): 563, 569.

8. Ibid., 566–567.

9. Ibid., 575.

10. Emmanuel Levinas, "Assimilation Today" (1954), reprinted in Emmanuel Levinas, *Difficult Freedom: Essays on Judaism* (Baltimore: Johns Hopkins University Press, 1990), 257.

11. Allen Guttmann, *The Jewish Writer in America: Assimilation and Crisis of Identity* (New York: Oxford University Press, 1971), 227. Further references to this book are cited in the text as *JW.*

12. In May 1994, Allen Guttmann commented on an early draft of this chapter. The second phrase is one of Guttmann's editorial comments.

13. Ludwig Lewisohn, *The Island Within* (New York: Harper and Brothers, 1928), 277–278; Klingenstein, *Jews in the American Academy,* 50.

14. Allen Guttmann, *From Ritual to Record: The Nature of Modern Sports* (New York: Columbia University Press, 1978), 158. Subsequently Guttmann edited, together with James A. Sappenfeld, Washington Irving's *Life of Washington* (Boston: Twayne, 1982), and then continued to write more books on sports. They are to date: *The Games Must Go On: Avery Brundage and the Olympic Movement* (New York: Columbia University Press, 1984); *Sports Spectators* (New York: Columbia University Press, 1986); *A Whole New Ball Game: An Interpretation of American Sports* (Chapel Hill: University of North Carolina Press, 1988); *Women's Sports: A History* (New York: Columbia University Press, 1991); *The Olympics: A History of Modern Games* (Urbana: University of Illinois Press, 1992), *Games and Empires: Modern Sports and Cultural Imperialism* (New York: Columbia University Press, 1994), *The Erotic in Sports* (New York: Columbia University Press, 1996).

7. A Jew from Brooklyn: Jules Chametzky

1. Jules Chametzky, *Our Decentralized Literature: Cultural Mediation in Selected Jewish and Southern Writers* (Amherst: University of Massachusetts Press, 1986), 56; further references to this collection of essays are cited in the text as *OD.*

2. Jules Chametzky, editorial comment penciled on a draft of this chapter in May 1994.

3. Jules Chametzky, interview with the author, Amherst, Mass., April 24, 1988; and conversation with the author, May 25, 1993. On the Woodbine colony see Joseph Brandes, *Immigrants to Freedom: The Jewish Communities in Rural New Jersey Since 1882* (Philadelphia: University of Pennsylvania Press, 1971), 69–72, 216–222; Samuel Joseph, *History of the Baron de Hirsch Fund: The Americanization of the Jewish Immigrant* (Philadelphia: Jewish Publication Society, 1935); Ellen Eisenberg, *Jewish Agricultural Colonies in New Jersey, 1882–1920* (Syracuse, N.Y.: Syracuse University Press, 1995), 129–133.

4. Irving Howe with Kenneth Libo, *World of Our Fathers* (New York: Simon and Schuster, 1976), 347, 524.

5. Jules Chametzky, "The Fate of American Jews," *Dialectical Anthropology* 8 (October 1983): 28.

6. Chametzky's experience is reminiscent of Irving Howe's discovery of poverty as a teenager: "The realization of what it meant to be poor I had first to discover through reading about poverty; the sense of my own deprivation grew keen after I learned about the troubles of people I did not know." Irving Howe, *A Margin of Hope: An Intellectual Autobiography* (New York: Harcourt Brace Jovanovich, 1982), 8–9. Alan Dershowitz, by contrast, who grew up Orthodox and attended Yeshiva University High School during the 1950s, learned of his own social status in graduate school: "Indeed, it was not until I met my Yale classmates that I realized I was relatively poor! In my working-class neighborhood of Brooklyn I was middle class." Dershowitz, *Chutzpah* (Boston: Little, Brown, 1991), 48–49.

7. Dershowitz, *Chutzpah,* 45.

8. Gene Bluestein, letter to the author, July 1, 1994.

9. Aaron, *Writers on the Left* (1992), 425

10. Aaron, *Writers on the Left* (1992), 420; Howe, *A Margin of Hope,* 8.

11. Nora Levin, *The Jews in the Soviet Union Since 1917: Paradox of Survival,* vol. 2 (London: I. B. Tauris, 1988), 518. Further references to this work are cited in the text as *JSU.*

12. Carl T. Rowan, "Two 'U' Teachers Called Reds at Capital Subversive Hearing," *Minneapolis Morning Tribune,* January 14, 1954: 1, 7, 12.

13. During the 1940s the anti-Semitism prevalent in Minneapolis was amply described by Selden Menefee (1943), Carey McWilliams (1946), Charles J. Cooper (1946), and Albert I. Gordon (1949). Cf. chap. 2, nn. 2, 4, and 5. Anti-Semitism was *not* mentioned in the Minneapolis section of Lincoln Steffens's *Shame of the Cities* (1904), a book Chametzky erroneously ascribed to Carey McWilliams in "My Chinese Problem —And Ours: A Memoir of the Fifties," *Carleton Miscellany* 9 (Spring 1968): 60. Although McWilliams is the author of *A Mask for Privilege: Antisemitism in America* (Boston: Little, Brown, 1948), that book has no section on Minneapolis.

14. David Suchoff, "Jewish Identity and the Left: Lionel Trilling, Stephen Greenblatt and Subversion in American Cultural Criticism," (paper presented at the convention of American Studies Association, Boston, Mass., November 7, 1993). See also Suchoff, "The Rosenberg Case and the New York Intellectuals," in *Secret Agents: The Rosenberg Case, McCarthyism and Fifties America,* ed. Marjorie Garber and Rebecca L. Walkowitz, (New York: Routledge, 1995), 155–169.

15. Jules Chametzky, "The Rites of Passage," *Kansas Magazine* (1957): 89–94; quotations, 90, 91. The magazine is now called *Kansas Quarterly.*

16. Glass cups in which the burning of alcohol had created a vacuum were applied to the skin of a sick person in order to suck out the bad humors causing the illness; this was considered an improvement over the application of leeches.

17. Delmore Schwartz, "Adventure in America," review of *The Adventures of Augie March,* by Saul Bellow, *Partisan Review* 21 (1954): 112; James Atlas, *Delmore Schwartz: The Life of an American Poet* (New York: Farrar, Straus, and Giroux, 1977), 207, 209, 308–309; Saul Bellow, *Humboldt's Gift* (1975; reprint, New York: Avon, 1976), 129. Also of interest is Alexander Bloom, *Prodigal Sons: The New York Intellectuals and Their World* (New York: Oxford University Press, 1986), 290–293.

18. Letter in the possession of Daniel Aaron.

19. Jules Chametzky, "Jewish and Other Studies in Germany: Mainstreaming the Marginal," in ed. Brigitte Georgi-Findlay and Heinz Ickstadt., *America Seen From Out-*

side: Topics, Models, and Achievements of American Studies in the Federal Republic of Germany, Materialien 26, Berlin: John F. Kennedy-Institut für Nordamerikastudien, 1990), 97; Richard Bridgman, "The American Studies of Henry Nash Smith," *American Scholar* 56 (Spring 1987): 261.

20. Jules Chametzky and Sidney Kaplan, eds., *Black and White in America: An Anthology from "The Massachusetts Review"* (Amherst: University of Massachusetts Press, 1969); Jules Chametzky, ed., *A Tribute to Baldwin: Black Writers Redefine the Struggle,* Proceedings of a conference at the University of Massachusetts at Amherst, April 22–23, 1988 (Amherst: Institute for Advanced Studies; distributed by University of Massachusetts Press, 1989).

21. Leslie Fiedler, *Being Busted* (New York: Stein and Day, 1969), 59, 60.

22. Seymour Martin Lipset and Everett Carll Ladd, Jr., "Jewish Academics in the United States: Their Achievements, Culture and Politics," *American Jewish Yearbook* 72 (1971): 89–128.

23. Guttmann, "Jewish Radicals, Jewish Writers," 563.

24. Werner Sollors, *Amiri Baraka/LeRoi Jones: The Quest for a 'Populist' Modernism* (New York: Columbia University Press, 1978). Sollors left Berlin in 1977 for a job at Columbia University, where he continued his research on African American literature and broadened his scope to include other ethnic litertures. He then began his investigation of the nature and history of cultural pluralism that resulted in his important study *Beyond Ethnicity: Consent and Descent in American Culture* (New York: Oxford University Press, 1986). From Columbia, Sollors went on to Harvard, where he taught in the English department and chaired Afro-American Studies until he was succeeded by Henry Louis Gates, Jr.

25. Lawrence Langer, interview with the author, Boston May 17, 1988.

26. Lawrence Langer, *The Holocaust and the Literary Imagination* (New Haven: Yale University Press, 1975), xi.

27. Ibid., xii.

28. Lawrence Langer, *Holocaust Testimonies: The Ruins of Memory* (New Haven: Yale University Press, 1991), xiv. Langer's ground-breaking essays were published in *Admitting the Holocaust: Collected Essays* (New York: Oxford University Press, 1995).

8. Refractions of Lionel Trilling

1. "Under Forty: A Symposium on American Literature and the Younger Generation of American Jews," *Contemporary Jewish Record* 7 (February 1944): 15.

2. Eugene Goodheart, interview with the author, Cambridge, Mass., March 17, 1989.

3. John Hollander, interview with the author, New Haven, Conn., January 15, 1991.

4. At least 19 percent of Harvard freshmen enrolling in the class of 1946 were Jewish. Between 1950 and 1970 the percentage of Jewish students at Harvard and Columbia would be well in the 20 percent bracket, averaging about 25 percent during the two decades. The percentage of commuters at Harvard dropped steadily: from 16.5 percent in 1942—43 to 15 percent for the class of 1951, to 11 percent in 1955—56. "Recognizing their need for a fuller collegiate experience," Marcia Synnott wrote, "the Phillips Brooks House Association, a social service organization open to all Harvard

students, . . . urged that the university provide a building for commuters, which would be managed by an undergraduate organization and maintained by a $10 annual membership fee." The Harvard Corporation consented, and the first floor of Dudley Hall opened in September 1935. Synnott explained that Dudley Hall fulfilled two important roles: it integrated commuters into the college community, and it worked toward "overcoming race prejudice" in those who worked with the commuters on the house committee. Dudley Hall tended to have a high (although steadily decreasing) percentage of Jews (about 66 percent in 1936–37; about 22 percent in 1942). Marcia Graham Synnott, *The Half-Opened Door: Discrimination and Admissions at Harvard, Yale, and Princeton, 1900–1970* (Westport, Conn.: Greenwood Press, 1979), 112, 119–120, 206, 209–210. Norman Podhoretz, interview with the author, New York City, September 27, 1993.

5. Elsewhere I have described in some detail Trilling's career at Columbia, his intellectual development, and his efforts to balance the Jewish legacy of his childhood, adolescence, and student days with the social style of his professional life. Susanne Klingenstein, *Jews in the American Academy, 1900–1940: The Dynamics of Intellectual Assimilation* (New Haven: Yale University Press, 1991), 137–198.

6. Lionel Trilling, *The Liberal Imagination: Essays on Literature and Society* (New York: Viking, 1950), 11. Further references to this work are cited in the text as *LI*. "Thematics" was a term Harry Levin used for one of his scholarly pursuits (delineating literary themes), as in "Thematics and Criticism," in *The Disciplines of Criticism: Essays in Literary Theory, Interpretation, and History,* ed. Peter Demetz, Thomas Greene, and Loury Nelson, Jr. (New Haven: Yale University Press, 1968), 125–145.

7. Diana Trilling, *The Beginning of the Journey: The Marriage of Diana and Lionel Trilling* (New York: Harcourt, Brace and Co., 1993), 162; further references to this work are cited in the text as *BJ.*

8. "From the Notebooks of Lionel Trilling, Part I." *Partisan Review* 50/51 (1984/85): 514; Trilling's emphases. Further references to this work are cited in the text as *N1.*

9. Gerald Graff, *Professing Literature: An Institutional History* (Chicago: University of Chicago Press, 1987), 182–226. Harry Levin, "The Tradition of Tradition," *Hopkins Review* 4 (Spring 1951): 5–14.

10. Steven Marcus, interview with the author, New York City, December 2, 1988.

11. Trilling's scathing assessment of Parrington in "Reality in America" remained the dominant view for forty years. It was not until Russell J. Reising's article "Reconstructing Parrington," *American Quarterly* 41 (March 1989): 155–164, that Parrington's contributions to American literary criticism were reconsidered. Reising sees him as an originator of new trends, as does H. Lark Hall, whose biography *V. L. Parrington: Through the Avenue of Art* (Kent, Ohio: Kent State University Press, 1994), is written as a refutation of Trilling's assessment.

12. It would take another twenty years until Dreiser's inadequacies were being dealt with critically, and yet another twenty years until Dreiser could be examined with critical neutrality. Superbly enlightening on this issue are two reviews by Daniel Aaron of Dreiser biographies: "The Unbuttoned Titan," review of *Dreiser,* by W. A. Swanberg, *Reporter* (3 June 1965): 37–39, and "Brother Theodore," review of *Theodore Dreiser: An American Journey, 1908–1945,* volume 2, by Richard Lingeman, *New Republic* 203 (November 17, 1990): 34–37, 40.

13. Lionel Trilling, contribution to "The State of American Writing, 1948: Seven Questions," *Partisan Review* 15 (August 1948): 889.

14. Lionel Trilling, contribution to "The Situation in American Writing," *Partisan Review* 6 (Fall 1939): 111.

15. Cynthia Ozick, *Art and Ardor* (New York: Dutton, 1984), 74.

16. Cynthia Ozick, letter to the author, August 30, 1990.

17. Cynthia Ozick, letter to the author, March 2, 1989; conversation with the author in New Rochelle, New York, September 27, 1993; "Forster as Homosexual," *Commentary* 52 (December 1971): 81–85. This controversial review of Forster's novel *Maurice* provoked angry letters from readers, to which Ozick replied five months later with an essay on "Forster as Moralist." Incidentally, she began her response to her readers' comments by quoting the opening sentence of Trilling's book on Forster (*Commentary* 53 [May 1972]: 36, 40, 42). Both essays were reprinted in Ozick's collection *Art and Ardor*, 61–79.

18. "Culture and the Present Moment: A Round-Table Discussion," *Commentary* 58 (December 1974): 31. Further references to this work are cited in the text as *CPM*.

19. Norman Podhoretz, *Breaking Ranks: A Political Memoir* (New York: Harper and Row, 1979), 297. Further references to this work are cited in the text as *BR*.

20. Cynthia Ozick, "We Are the Crazy Lady and Other Feisty Feminist Fables" (1972), in *Woman as Writer*, ed. Jeannette Webber and Joan Grumman (Boston: Houghton Mifflin, 1978), 105.

21. Cynthia Ozick, letter to the author, July 20, 1988.

22. Lionel Trilling, *The Last Decade: Essays and Reviews, 1965–1975,* ed. Diana Trilling (New York: Harcourt Brace Jovanovich, 1981), 227. Further references to this work are cited in the text as *LD*.

23. "From the Notebooks of Lionel Trilling, Part II." *Partisan Review* 54 (1987): 10. Further references to this work are cited in the text as *N2*.

24. Ozick, "We Are the Crazy Lady," 105

25. Ozick, "We Are the Crazy Lady," 106. Today, Ozick feels uneasy about her essay. She wrote, "given the vulgarization and trivialization and reductionism of current so-called 'feminism'—I feel worse than ever about being associated with any assault on so distinguished a cultural figure as Lionel Trilling." Cynthia Ozick, letter to the author, June 16, 1994. For a description of the atmosphere women encountered at Columbia University in the early 1950s, see Susan Kress, *Carolyn G. Heilbrun: Feminist in a Tenured Position* (Charlottesville: University Press of Virginia, 1997), 44–47 and for Trilling's relation to female graduate students, see pp. 49–50.

26. Cynthia Ozick, interview with Tom Teicholz, *Paris Review* 29 (Spring 1987): 170.

27. Cynthia Ozick, letter to the author, March 21, 1989.

28. As Jewish intellectuals became assured of their integration into academe and American society, they relocated Freud in the context of his time. Among the most important recent works are Emanuel Rice, *Freud and Moses: The Long Journey Home* (Albany: State University of New York Press, 1990); Yosef Hayim Yerushalmi, *Freud's Moses: Judaism Terminable and Interminable* (New Haven: Yale University Press, 1991); Sander L. Gilman, *Freud, Race, and Gender* (Princeton: Princeton University Press, 1993), and *The Case of Sigmund Freud: Medicine and Identity at the Fin de Siècle* (Baltimore: Johns Hopkins University Press, 1993); and Moshe Gresser, *Dual Allegiance: Freud as a Modern Jew* (Albany: State University of New York Press, 1994).

29. Norman Podhoretz, *Making It* (New York: Harper Colophon Books, 1967), 110. All further references to this memoir are cited in the text as *MI*.

30. Henry David Thoreau, *Walden, or Life in the Woods* (New York: Library of America, 1985), 395.

31. Norman Podhoretz, *The Bloody Crossroads: Where Literature and Politics Meet* (New York: Simon and Schuster, 1986), 79. Further references to this collection are cited in the text as *BC*.

32. Terry Eagleton, *Theory of Literature* (Oxford: Blackwell, 1983), 33.

33. Norman Podhoretz, "The Arnoldian Function in American Criticism," review of *The Liberal Imagination,* by Lionel Trilling, *Scrutiny* 18 (June 1951): 61.

34. Lionel Trilling, "The Leavis-Snow Controversy," in *Beyond Culture: Essays on Literature and Learning* (New York: Harcourt Brace Jovanovich, 1965), 131.

35. Alan Wald, *The New York Intellectuals: The Rise and Decline of the Anti-Stalinist Left From the 1930s to the 1980s* (Chapel Hill: University of North Carolina Press, 1987), 31–33; Dan A. Oren, *Joining the Club: A History of Jews and Yale* (New Haven: Yale University Press, 1985), 102; Mark Krupnick, "The Menorah Journal Group and the Origins of Modern Jewish-American Radicalism," *Studies in American Jewish Literature* 5 (Winter 1979): 58.

36. Robert Alter, "Epitaph for a Jewish Magazine," *Commentary* 39 (May 1965): 52.

37. Lionel Trilling, "On the Death of a Friend," *Commentary* 29 (February 1960): 93.

38. Ibid., 94. On Cohen's vision for *Commentary,* see Steven J. Zipperstein, *"Commentary* and American Jewish Culture in the 1940s and 1950s," *Jewish Social Studies* 3, no. 2 (1997): 18–28. On Podhoretz's vision for *Commentary,* see Ruth R. Wisse, "The Maturing of *Commentary* and the Jewish Intellectual," *Jewish Social Studies* 3, no. 2 (1997): 29–41.

39. Norman Podhoretz, "My Negro Problem—and Ours," in *Doings and Undoings: The Fifties and After in American Writing* (New York: Farrar, Straus, and Giroux, 1964); quotations, pp. 354–55, 362–63. The essay was reprinted with a 1993 postscript by Podhoretz in *Blacks and Jews: Alliances and Arguments* ed. Paul Berman (New York: Delacorte Press, 1994), 76–96.

40. Marcus, interview with the author, December 2, 1988. Further references to this interview are cited in the text.

41. Lionel Trilling, "The Dickens of Our Day" (1952), in *A Gathering of Fugitives* (Boston: Beacon Press, 1956), 41.

42. Ibid., 44, 42.

43. Lionel Trilling, *"Little Dorrit,"* in *The Opposing Self,* 44. Steven Marcus said, "Trilling was really a big influence there, because he too thought that Dickens was the greatest novelist" (interview).

44. Steven Marcus, *Dickens: From Pickwick to Dombey* (New York: Basic Books, 1965), 11. Further references to this work are cited in the text as *D.*

45. Ruth R. Wisse, *The Schlemiel as Modern Hero* (Chicago: University of Chicago Press, 1971), 95.

46. In an interview Norman Podhoretz described the career of his father, who came to New York from Galicia in 1912. "He went to work in a butcher shop in Brooklyn which was owned by his uncle. He was a kid and worked at some sort of menial position. He had a series of jobs, not exactly in the garment center. I remember he worked in

some sort of hat factory very briefly; and then he tried with another cousin to go into business. They opened a butcher store in Harlem, which was then a Jewish neighborhood. It failed after a brief time. It was shortly thereafter that he went to work as a milkman, which was what he did until he became ill, which was many years later. He had a heart attack and his health was generally bad. There was always one thing or another wrong with it. And when he was finally fired for all the right purposes from his job as a milkman . . . he worked as a messenger for a company. . . . He was quite broken. There was a small period in my parents' life when they opened up what was then called a commission bakery. I guess it was in my late teens and twenties. They would buy stuff from a nearby bakery and sell on commission. They put in their savings of a few thousand dollars—I mean this is really penny-anty stuff—and opened this store for which both worked endless hours and eked out barely enough to live on. That lasted for six or seven years. Then they lost their lease. The landlord wanted the store for something else. So that went out of business. But for most of his working life, my father was a milkman with a horse and wagon." Podhoretz, interview with the author, September 27, 1993.

47. Diana Trilling, "Lionel Trilling, A Jew at Columbia," *Commentary* 67 (March 1979): 46

48. Eagleton, *Theory of Literature*, 35–36; Francis Mulhern, *The Moment of "Scrutiny"* (London: NLB, 1979), 25.

49. Noel Annan, "Bloomsbury and the Leavises," in *Virginia Woolf and Bloomsbury: A Centenary Celebration*, ed. Jane Marcus (London: Macmillan, 1987), 33.

50. Ibid., 33. Cf. also Ian MacKillop, *F. R. Leavis: A Life in Criticism* (London: Allen Lane, 1995), and G. Singh, *F. R. Leavis: A Literary Biography* (London: Duckworth, 1995).

51. Mulhern, *Moment of "Scrutiny,"* 34.

52. Trilling, "Leavis-Snow Controversy," 130.

53. Alice Green Fredman, interview with the author, New York City, April 11, 1989.

54. Morris Dickstein, interview with the author, New York City, February 10, 1989.

55. Steven Marcus, *Engels, Manchester, and the Working Class* (1974; reprint, New York: Norton, 1985), ix.

56. Steven Marcus, *The Other Victorians: A Study of Sexuality and Pornography in Mid-Nineteenth Century England* (New York: Basic Books, 1966), x.

57. Most recently this was the subject of a book by Robin Tolmach Lakoff and James C. Coyne, *Father Knows Best: The Use and Abuse of Power in Freud's Case of Dora* (New York: Teachers College Press, 1993).

58. Steven Marcus, "Lionel Trilling, 1905–1975," in *Art, Politics, and Will: Essays in Honor of Lionel Trilling,* ed. Quentin Anderson, Stephen Donadio, Steven Marcus, (New York: Basic Books, 1977), 270.

59. Alice Green Fredman, interview.

60. Lionel Trilling, preface to *The Opposing Self: Nine Essays in Criticism* (New York: Harcourt Brace Jovanovich, 1979).

61. Trilling wrote: "It is the despair of those who having committed themselves to culture, have surrendered the life of surprise and elevation, of impulse, pleasure, and imagination." *The Opposing Self,* preface; see also Diana Trilling, BJ 372, 373.

62. Carolyn G. Heilbrun, *Reinventing Womanhood* (New York: Norton, 1979), 53, 55. Further references to this source are cited in the text as *RW.*

63. Anne Matthews, "Rage in a Tenured Position," *New York Times Magazine,* November 8, 1992: 72. Since this chapter was written, two books on Heilbrun have appeared: Julia B. Boken, *Carolyn G. Heilbrun* (New York: Twayne, 1996) and Kress, *Carolyn G. Heilbrun.* Kress, in particular, has unearthed a wealth of facts and documents pertaining to Heilbrun's time at Wellesley College, and she offers some excellent observations about Heilbrun's uncomfortable relation to herself as a Jew.

64. Susan Kress, in her astute exposition of Heilbrun's relation to Trilling, calls attention to Heilbrun's outright attack on Trilling in Heilbrun's 1972 review of James Dickey's novel *Deliverance* for the *Saturday Review;* see Kress, *Carolyn G. Heilbrun,* 99–101.

65. Lionel Trilling, "The Situation of the American Intellectual at the Present Time," *Gathering of Fugitives,* 68.

66. Kress, *Carolyn G. Heilbrun,* 60–61.

67. Alice Green Fredman, interview with the author, New York City, April 11, 1989.

68. Heilbrun, *Writinq a Woman's Life* (New York: Norton, 1988), 114. About the relationship between Carolyn Heilbrun, Amanda Cross, and Kate Fansler, see Carmen Birkle, " 'To Create a Space for Myself': Carolyn Heilbrun a.k.a. Amanda Cross and the Detective Novel," *Amerikastudien/American Studies* 39, no. 4 (1994): 525–535.

69. Marjorie Nicolson, "The Professor and the Detective," in *The Art of the Mystery Story: A Collection of Critical Essays,* ed. Howard Haycraft (New York: Simon and Schuster, 1946), 124.

70. Amanda Cross, *Poetic Justice* (1970; reprint, New York: Avon, 1979), 13. Further references to this work are cited in the text as *PJ.*

71. A less charitable interpretation of the murder was suggested by J. M. Purcell in "The 'Amanda Cross' Case: Sociologizing the U.S. Academic Mystery," *Armchair Detective* 13 (Winter 1980). Purcell pointed out that "for complex symbolic reasons involving both academe and the New York Jewish-intellectual community, Columbia's Lionel Trilling quite naturally and inevitably became the symbolic target of the [1968] 'riot' and the center of the most intellectually serious confrontation of the rebels with the faculty and administration." The mystery begins with Trilling's eviction from his office. Purcell argued that in the *early* 1960s it would have been "witty and even professionally daring for a writer on the Columbia faculty" to make "Trilling" a murderer. Purcell then criticized Heilbrun for waiting until "it would be modish to make such a fictional attack on Trilling" (39). In Purcell's view this made Heilbrun an accomplice to the students' rebellion and to their symbolic patricide.

72. Kress, *Carolyn G. Heilbrun,* 132.

73. Carolyn G. Heilbrun, "The Politics of Mind: Women, Tradition, and the University," *Hamlet's Mother and Other Women* (New York: Ballantine, 1990), 253.

74. Robert Alter, "The Revolt Against Tradition: Readers, Writers, and Critics," contribution to "The Changing Culture of the University: A Symposium," *Partisan Review* 58 (1991): 283.

75. Robert Alter, "The Jew Who Didn't Get Away: On the Possibility of an American Jewish Culture," *Judaism* 31 (Summer 1982): 275.

9. Unfolding Hebrew Prose Robert Alter

1. Alter's essay was reprinted as "S. Y. Agnon: The Alphabet of Holiness," in his collection *After the Tradition: Essays on Modern Jewish Writing* (New York: Dutton, 1969), 131–150. Further references to this collection are cited in the text as *AT.*

2. Robert Alter, "The Jew Who Didn't Get Away: On the Possibility of an American Jewish Culture," *Judaism* 31 (Summer 1982): 275.

3. Robert Alter, interview with the author, Berkeley, Calif., October 21, 1988. All biographical information is taken from this interview.

4. Hank Greenberg, *The Story of My Life,* ed. Ira Berkow (New York: Times Books, 1989), 59–62; John M. Carlisle, "2 Homers on Rosh Hashana Prick Hank's Conscience," *Detroit News,* September 11, 1934: 1.

5. Alan Mintz, ed., *Hebrew in America: Perspectives and Prospects* (Detroit: Wayne State University Press, 1993), 14, 17. Robert Alter, "Teaching Jewish Teachers," *Commentary* 46 (July 1968): 61.

6. Mintz, introduction to *Hebrew in America,* 17.

7. Shlomo Shulsinger, "Hebrew Camping—Five Years of Massad (1941–1945)," *Jewish Education* 17 (June 1946): 16–22; quoted in Walter Ackerman's excellent article "A World Apart: Hebrew Teachers Colleges and Hebrew-Speaking Camps," in *Hebrew in America,* ed. Mintz, 116.

8. Mintz, introduction to *Hebrew in America,* 18; Walter Ackerman, "A World Apart," 116–117.

9. Alter, "Teaching Jewish Teachers," 60, 61, 62.

10. Alter, "Teaching Jewish Teachers," 63. Alter wrote about the romantic nationalist appreciation of Bialik in "The Kidnapping of Bialik and Tchernichovsky," *Midstream* 10 (June 1964): 27–35; reprinted in *AT* 226–240. Alter's point in the essay is that the Bialik celebrated by Hebraist ideologues, who focus on the national content of Bialik's poetry, prevents readers in Israel and abroad not only from apprehending a more disturbing, ambivalent, and perhaps truly modern poet, but from seeing Bialik's literary qualities as a poet at all.

11. Robert Alter, "What Was T. S. Eliot?" *Commentary* 87 (March 1989): 31.

12. Robert Alter, "Eliot, Lawrence, and the Jews," *Commentary* 50 (October 1970): 81–86; the quotation is from page 85. The article was reprinted in Alter's essay collection *Defenses of the Imagination: Jewish Writers and Historical Crisis* (Philadelphia: Jewish Publication Society of America 1977). Further references to this collection are cited in the text as *DI.*

13. Lionel Trilling, "The Mind of Robert Warshow," *Commentary* 31 (June 1961): 501.

14. Alter rarely wrote about the Shoah. He did not doubt the "importance of a deepened and more detailed historical understanding of the Nazi effort to destroy the Jewish people." What made him apprehensive was that "serious distortions of the Holocaust itself and, what is worse, of Jewish life occur when the Holocaust is commercialized, politicized, theologized, or academicized—all of which processes seem to be occurring today in varying degree and manner." Robert Alter, "Deformations of the Holocaust," *Commentary* 71 (February 1981): 49, reprinted as "Vistas of Annihilation," in *Hebrew and Modernity* (Bloomington: Indiana University Press, 1994), 104–119; re-

sponses to this essay appeared in *Commentary* 71 (June 1981): 2–12. Among Alter's essays touching on the Shoah are "The Novels of Elie Wiesel," *Haddassah Magazine* (April 1966), reprinted in *AT* 151–160; "Confronting the Holocaust: Three Israeli Novels," *Commentary* 41 (March 1966), reprinted in *AT* 163–180; "A Poet of the Holocaust [Uri Zvi Greenberg]," *Commentary* 56 (November 1973), reprinted in *DI* 103–118; review of *The War Against the Jews* by Lucy Dawidowicz, *Commentary* 59 (June 1975): 72–74.

15. Quoted from Leavis, *The Great Tradition,* in Robert Alter, *Fielding and the Nature of the Novel* (Cambridge: Harvard University Press, 1968), 2–3. Further references to this work are cited in the text as *FN.*

16. Robert Alter, *Partial Magic: The Novel as Self-Conscious Genre* (Berkeley: University of California Press, 1975), xii.

17. Robert Alter, with Carol Cosman, *A Lion for Love: A Critical Biography of Stendhal* (1979; reprint, Cambridge: Harvard University Press, 1986), xii.

18. Robert Alter, *Motives for Fiction* (Cambridge: Harvard University Press, 1984), 21. On Alter's unhappiness with the course of contemporary theory, see also Alter, "The Decline and Fall of Literary Criticism," *Commentary* 77 (March 1984): 50–56.

19. Robert Alter, "Defenders of the Faith," *Commentary* 84 (July 1987): 53, 54. Alter also reviewed Roth's *Counterlife* in the *New Republic* 196 (February 2 1987): 36–38.

20. Robert Alter, *The Pleasures of Reading in an Ideological* Age (New York: Simon and Schuster, 1989), 9, 14.

21. In his review of Alter's book, Denis Donoghue called attention to the terminology of pleasure, which, he argued, had not yet recovered from the experience of being appropriated by Roland Barthes in *The Pleasures of the Text.* Denis Donoghue, "The Joy of Texts," *New Republic* 200 (June 26, 1989): 36. Alter's defense of the pleasures of reading against the academic preoccupation with theory was vindicated when one of the most prominent literary theorists publicly confessed that while touting theory in his classes and publications, he had been indulging himself secretly in the "pleasures of reading." See Frank Lentricchia, "Last Will and Testament of an Ex-Literary Critic," *Lingua Franca* 6 (September/October 1996): 59–67. The Association of Literary Scholars and Critics, founded in 1994 to promote a new engagement with literature and presided over by Alter in 1996–97, gloatingly printed a long excerpt from Lentricchia's confession in their fall 1996 *Newsletter.*

22. Robert Alter, "The New Prayer Books," *Commentary* 32 (November 1961): 456–460.

23. In the January 1978 issue, Alan Mintz published an article entitled "New Israeli Writing," clearly stepping into the old shoes of Robert Alter, who was then getting ready to abandon them for a new pair. Alter's June 1969 article for *Commentary,* entitled "New Israeli Fiction," was reprinted as "Fiction in a Stage of Siege," (*DI* 213–231).

24. Most of Alter's essays on modern Hebrew literature were reprinted in three of his essay collections, *After the Tradition* (1969), *Defenses of the Imagination* (1977), and *Hebrew and Modernity* (1994).

25. Alter's most important early essays on American Jewish literature are: "The Stature of Saul Bellow," *Midstream* 10 (December 1964): 3–15; "Sentimentalizing the Jews," *Commentary* 40 (September 1965): 71–75; "Malamud as a Jewish Writer," *Commentary* 42 (September 1966): 71–76; "Jewish Dreams and Nightmares," *Commentary* 45 (January 1968): 48–54.

26. Alter, "The Jewish Community and the Jewish Condition," *Commentary* 47 (February 1969): 56.

27. Robert Alter, "Israel and the Intellectuals," *Commentary* 44 (October 1967): 50, 51.

28. Alter, "Israel and the Intellectuals," 51, 49, 46.

29. Robert Alter, "Rhetoric and the Arab Mind," *Commentary* 46 (October 1968): 61–65.

30. Robert Alter, "Berrigan's Diatribe," *Commentary* 57 (February 1974): 73.

31. Robert Alter, "Graduate Training in Hebrew Literature," in *New Humanities and Academic Disciplines: The Case of Jewish Studies,* ed. Jacob Neusner (Madison: University of Wisconsin Press, 1984), 82.

32. Alter, "Graduate Training in Hebrew Literature," 82; Robert Alter, "What Jewish Studies Can Do," *Commentary* 58 (October 1974): 71–76. Cf. also Alan Mintz, ed., *Hebrew in America;* Harold Wechsler, Paul Ritterband, eds., *Jewish Learning in American Universities: The First Century* (Bloomington: Indiana University Press, 1994); Deborah Dash Moore, "On the Necessity and Impossibility of Being a Jew in the Academy," *Cross Current* 43 (Winter 1993/94): 503–516.

33. Alter, "Graduate Training in Hebrew Literature," 81.

34. Ibid., 93–94.

35. Arnold Band, "Graduate Education in Modern Hebrew Literature," in *New Humanities and Academic Disciplines,* ed. Neusner, 102.

36. Robert Alter, "A New Theory of Kashrut," *Commentary* 68 (August 1979): 48, 49, 52.

37. Robert Alter, *The Invention of Hebrew Prose: Modern Fiction and the Language of Realism* (Seattle: University of Washington Press, 1988), 3; further references to this book are cited in the text as *IHP.* Alter's essay on "Agnon's Psychological Realism (*Hebrew and Modernity* 134–153) continued his thoughts on the invention of Hebrew prose. An interesting review by Jeffrey M. Green, presenting an Israeli perspective on Alter's *Invention of Hebrew Prose,* appeared in the *Jerusalem Post International Edition,* December 31, 1988: 16.

38. Robert Alter, *The Art of Biblical Narrative* (New York: Basic Books, 1981), xi; Alter, "Graduate Training in Hebrew Literature," 85–86.

39. Robert Alter and Frank Kermode, eds., *The Literary Guide to the Bible* (Cambridge: Harvard University Press, 1987), and David Rosenberg, ed., *Congregation: Contemporary Writers Read the Jewish Bible* (San Diego: Harcourt Brace Jovanovich, 1987), in which Bloom released his first trial balloons on the J writer, appeared at exactly the same time and were reviewed side by side on the front page of the *New York Times Book Review* on December 20, 1987. Bloom reviewed Alter and Kermode's *Literary Guide* in the *New York Review of Books* 35 (March 31, 1988): 23–25, complaining that "Fokkelman, and Alter and Kermode in printing Fokkelman, simply disregard the major narrative authorial voice of Genesis and Exodus, J or the Yahwist" (23). Alter, in turn, reviewed Bloom's *The Book of J* in *Commentary* 90 (November 1990), in an essay Alter reprinted as "The Quest for the Author" in *The World of Biblical Literature* (New York: Basic Books, 1992), 153–169; the quotations in the text are taken from pages x and 155. The academic industry that since the early 1980s has sprung up around the literary interpretation of the Bible has been assessed in Jason P. Rosenblatt and Joseph C.

Sitterson, Jr., *"Not in Heaven": Coherence and Complexity in Biblical Narrative,* Indiana Studies in Biblical Literature, ed. Herbert Marks and Robert Polzin (Bloomington: Indiana University Press, 1991).

40. Robert Alter, letter to the author, September 9, 1994.

41. "In the Beginning Was the Word—and They've Been Arguing About It Ever Since," *New York Times Magazine,* October 22, 1995: 66.

42. Robert Alter, "Beyond King James," *Commentary* 102 (September 1996): 62. Alter provided an extensive analysis of the difficulties translators of Genesis face in his introduction to *Genesis: Translation and Commentary* (New York: Norton, 1996), ix– xlvii.

43. Alter, letter to the author, December 27, 1994.

44. Ruth Wisse, "The Hebrew Imperative," *Commentary* 89 (June 1990): 37.

10. The Lessons of Yiddish Culture: Ruth R. Wisse

1. Israel Chalfen, *Paul Celan: Eine Biographie seiner Jugend* (Frankfurt: Insel Verlag, 1979), 19. An English translation by Maximilian Bleyleben appeared as Israel Chalfen, *Paul Celan: A Biography of His Youth* (New York: Persea Books, 1991). Chalfen estimates the population of Czernowitz in the early 1920s at 110,000 (of whom 50,000 were Jews). But I follow the figures quoted in "Czernowitz," *Jüdisches Lexikon* (1927; reprint, Königstein: Jüdischer Verlag im Athenäum Verlag, 1982), 1455–1458. See also "Czernowitz," in *Jewish Encyclopedia* (New York: Funk and Wagnall, 1906), 4: 407–408; "Rumania," in *Encyclopedia Judaica* (Jerusalem: Keter, 1971), 14: 386–416; William O. McCragg, Jr., *A History of the Habsburg Jews, 1670–1918* (Bloomington: Indiana University Press, 1988).

2. Cf. Sol Liptzin, "Czernowitz Yiddish Language Conference," in *Encyclopedia Judaica* (Jerusalem: Keter, 1972), 5:1211–1212.

3. Ruth R. Wisse, *I. L. Peretz and the Making of Modern Culture* (Seattle: University of Washington Press, 1991), 95, 97; David Roskies, "The Emancipation of Yiddish," *Prooftexts* 1 (January 1981): 29–30. See also "Birnbaum, Nathan," in *Encyclopedia Judaica,* 4: 1040–1042, and Joshua A. Fishman, "Attracting a Following to High-Culture Functions for a Language of Everyday Life: The Role of the Tshernovits Language Conference in the 'Rise of Yiddish,' " in *Never Say Die! A Thousand Years of Yiddish in Jewish Life and Letters,* ed. Joshua A. Fishman (The Hague: Mouton, 1981), 366–394.

4. Ruth R. Wisse, interview with the author, Cambridge, Mass., April 28, 1993; a second interview was conducted in Cambridge on July 18, 1994.

5. Ruth R. Wisse, "Between Passovers," *Commentary* 88 (December 1989): 42.

6. Cf. Theodor Lavi, "Rumania," *Encyclopedia Judaica,* 14: 396.

7. Wisse, "Between Passovers," 42.

8. Nathan M. Gelber, "Bialystok," *Encyclopedia Judaica,* 4: 805–807. See also Bronia Klibanski, "Bialystok—Holocaust Period," *Encyclopedia Judaica,* 4: 807–810.

9. Ruth R. Wisse, "What My Father Knew," *Commentary* 99 (April 1995): 44.

10. Cf. Lavi, "Rumania," *Encyclopedia Judaica,* 14: 399–400. What happened to the Jews of Romania who did not make it to safety can be gathered from Siegfried Jagendorf, *Jagendorf's Foundry: A Memoir of the Romanian Holocaust, 1941–1944,* edited with commentary by Aron Hirt-Manheimer (New York: HarperCollins, 1991).

11. Ruth R. Wisse, "A Golus Education," *Moment* 2 (January 1977): 26; Wisse,

"What My Father Knew," 44–45. The figure given by Irving Abella is much lower. See Irving Abella, *A Coat of Many Colours: Two Centuries of Jewish Life in Canada* (Toronto: Lester and Orpen Dennys, 1990), 207; and Irving Abella and Harold Troper *None Is Too Many: Canada and the Jews of Europe, 1933–1948* (Toronto: Lester and Orpen Dennys, 1982).

12. Wisse, "A Golus Education," 26.

13. Ibid., 26; Wisse also recounted the story in her interview with me. I conflated both sources.

14. Ruth R. Wisse, *If I Am Not For Myself . . . : The Liberal Betrayal of the Jews* (New York: Free Press, 1992), 2–3. "Pledged my own ascent" means that Wisse pledged that she too would go to Israel. Since the temple once stood on a hill in Jerusalem, Jews think of going to Israel as going *up* (to Mount Zion).

15. Ruth R. Wisse, "The Most Beautiful Woman in Vilna," *Commentary* 71 (June 1981): 38. The passages about Passover and the Haggadah are taken from Wisse, "Between Passovers," 42, 46.

16. This is Sacvan Bercovitch's formulation. In a 1971 review of an anthology of Yiddish poetry, he wrote: "The most powerful of these poems are affirmations, in the sense not of victory or resolution or even struggle (in any neo-Faustian connotation), but of the necessity of moral perseverance in defeat." Sacvan Bercovitch, "Wine from a Broken Vessel," review of *A Treasury of Yiddish Poetry,* edited by Irving Howe and Eliezer Greenberg, *Judaism* 20 (1971): 240.

17. Wisse, "Between Passovers," 44.

18. About Wisse's radicalism see Ruth R. Wisse, "My Life Without Leonard Cohen," *Commentary* 100 (October 1995): 27–33.

19. "As it happens," Wisse wrote in 1997, "I can fix the exact moment when I—a reader of *Commentary* since my teens—was shocked to attention by an item in the magazine unlike anything I had ever read." In July 1970, Podhoretz commented in a new editorial column on the debacle of America's war in Vietnam. "By setting Vietnam within the context of U.S. history and the history of human civilization, he was saying that revulsion against a mistaken or misfought war cannot become an excuse for ideological pacifism; that despite its ugliness and inefficiency, the reality of war remains the final safeguard of freedom. His column had the sour taste of unpalatable truth, and I can remember how unfeeling I found it for the very reason that it struck me as so true. Its truth struck me particularly as a Jew. All that separated the doomed uprising in the ghettos of Poland from Israel's victory against the combined Arab forces in 1967 was this unpalatable truth, that 'to die young in a war is one of the possible ways for moral beings to die, and not necessarily the worst.' " Ruth R. Wisse, "The Maturing of *Commentary* and of the Jewish Intellectual," *Jewish Social Studies* 3, no. 2 (1997): 35–36.

20. David Roskies, interview with the author, New York City, February 5, 1992. When my tape was stolen, Roskies reconstructed the interview on February 17, 1992, narrating the story of his family and his own intellectual development. References to this narrative are cited in the text as DR. David Roskies is a professor of Jewish literature at the Jewish Theological Seminary in New York City.

21. Lucy S. Dawidowicz, *From That Place and Time: A Memoir, 1938–1947* (New York: Norton, 1989), 48. In 1921, some 47,000 Jews were living in Vilna (36 percent of the population). Ten years later the figure had risen to 55,000 (28 percent). Cf. Israel Klausner, "Vilna," *Encyclopedia Judaica,* 16: 147.

22. Klausner, "Vilna," *Encyclopedia Judaica,* 16: 147. On the ubiquity of Yiddish in Vilna, see Dawidowicz, *From That Place and Time,* 102.

23. Masha Roskies made sure that the local writers she supported were also read. Invitations to the literary soirées on Pagnuelo Street, Wisse wrote, "required the purchase of a recent book by a local writer, selections from which the author would read as the evening's entertainment." Wisse, "What My Father Knew," 47. There is no adequate history of the Montreal Jewish community; some information on representative figures can be found in Chaim Spilberg and Yaacov Zipper, eds., *Kanader yidisher zamlbukh* (Montreal: Natsyonales yidishes komitet baym kanader yidishen, kongres, 1982), and in Ira Robinson, Pierre Anctil, and Mervin Butovsky, eds., *An Everyday Miracle: Yiddish Culture in Montreal*(Montreal: Véhicule Press, 1990).

24. Wisse, "Hurra! Hurra!" *Moment* (December 1975): 23.

25. Wisse, "A Golus Education," 27; see also David Roskies, "A Hebrew-Yiddish Utopia in Montreal: Ideology in Bilingual Education," in *Hebrew in America: Perspectives and Prospects,* ed. Alan Mintz (Detroit: Wayne State University Press, 1993), 155–167.

26. Wisse, "A Golus Education," 27.

27. Ibid., 26–28, 62.

28. On the importance of English for the Jews of Quebec, see also Irvin Cotter and Ruth R. Wisse, "Quebec's Jews: Caught in the Middle," *Commentary* 64 (September 1977): 55–59.

29. Wisse, "Between Passovers," 43.

30. Cf. Frank Davey, "Louis Dudek," in *Canadian Writers, 1920–1959,* ed. W. H. New, Second Series, vol. 48 of *Dictionary of Literary Biography* (Detroit: Gale Research Company, 1989), 46.

31. Ruth R. Wisse, "A Critical Look at the Jewish Condition in North America" (Speech delivered at the 53rd General Assembly of the Combined Jewish Welfare Funds, Toronto, November 14–18, 1984), 17. Wisse wrote more extensively about Dudek's course and her student life at McGill in "My Life Without Leonard Cohen."

32. Ruth R. Wisse, "The Ghetto Poems of Abraham Sutzkever," *Jewish Book Annual* 36 (1978–79), 26–36; reprinted as introduction to *Burnt Pearls: The Ghetto Poems of Abraham Sutzkever,* trans. Seymour Mayne (Oakville, Ontario: Mosaic Press, 1981), 9–18; quotation, 17. All references are to the reprint and are cited in the text as *BP.*

33. Abraham Sutzkever, *Selected Prose and Poetry* trans. Barbara and Benjamin Harshav (Berkeley: University of California Press, 1991), 14. I am indebted to Benjamin Harshav's excellent intoduction for many biographical details about Sutzkever. Further references to this edition are cited in the text as *SSP.*

34. Sutzkever, quoted in Ruth R. Wisse's introduction to Abraham Sutzkever, *Griner Akvarium* (Jerusalem: Hebrew University, 1975), xiv. Further references to this edition are cited in the text as *GA.*

35. Ruth R. Wisse, introduction to Abraham Sutzkever, *Di nevue fun shvartsaplen: dertseylungn* (Jerusalem: Magnes Press of Hebrew University, 1989), xix. Further references to this edition are cited in the text as *DN.*

36. Dawidowicz, *From That Place and Time,* 263–264. See also David E. Fishman, *Embers Plucked From the Fire: The Rescue of Jewish Cultural Treasures in Vilna* (New York: YIVO Insitute for Jewish Research, 1996).

37. Uriel Weinreich, *Modern English-Yiddish, Yiddish-English Dictionary* (1968; reprint, New York: Schocken, 1977), vii–viii.

38. Dovid-Hirsh Roskes, without title, *Yugntruf* 68–69 (December 1989–April 1990): 10, 12 (in Yiddish, my translation).

39. Ruth R. Wisse, "The Politics of Yiddish," *Commentary* 80 (July 1985): 30; David Roskies, "The Emancipation of Yiddish," 31–32. Lucy Dawidowicz, "Max Weinreich (1894–1969): The Scholarship of Yiddish," *American Jewish Yearbook 1969*, 70: 59–68; Leonard Prager, "Yiddish in the University," in *Never Say Die!* ed. Fishman, 540.

40. Wisse, *If I Am Not For Myself,* 60–61.

41. This is precisely Lawrence Langer's finding in *Holocaust Testimonies: The Ruins of Memory* (New Haven: Yale University Press, 1991).

42. In Wisse's reviews few books escaped unscathed. She would point out how works failed to achieve either integrity of sentiment or perfection of form in her reviews of *The Yeshiva*, by Chaim Grade, *Commentary* 63 (April 1977): 70–73; *Rachel, the Rabbi's Wife*, by Silvia Tennenbaum, *Commentary* 65 (June 1978): 76–78; *Zuckerman, Unbound*, by Philip Roth, *Commentary* 72 (September 1981): 56–60; *Kagan's Superfecta*, by Allen Hoffman, *Commentary* 73 (May 1982): 84–87; *The Longest War: Israel in Lebanon*, by Jacobo Timerman, *Commentary* 75 (March 1983): 73–76; *Tsili: The Story of a Life*, by Aharon Appelfeld, *Commentary* 76 (August 1983): 73–76; *Chutzpah*, by Alan Dershowitz, *Commentary* 92 (September 1991): 54–56.

43. "When I first started to teach Yiddish literature I bought myself a chic new wardrobe because I was determined to alter through my own person the geriatric associations of the language." Ruth R. Wisse, "Living With Women's Lib," *Commentary* 86 (August 1988): 45.

44. In her dissertation Wisse would argue: "The more local Jews became the whipping boy of the Czarist and local governments, the harder it was for the satirist to jibe at their—by contrast—minor imperfections. Social satire is predicated on the possibility of social reform; where no reform is possible, the purpose of satire is blunted. Social satire can serve only those who control their own destinies, and whose actions affect their fate; Mendele's instrument was inappropriate for his readers, who seemed less and less in control of theirs." Ruth R. Wisse, *The Schlemiel as Modern Hero* (Chicago: University of Chicago Press, 1971), 27–28. Further references to this study are cited in the text as *SMH*. Cf. also Rut Roskes-Vays, "Kminhag yud: an umbakanter ksaf-yad fun Mendele moykher sforim," in *For Max Weinreich on His Seventieth Birthday: Studies in Jewish Languaqe, Literature, and Society* (The Hague: Mouton, 1964), 342–341. Other Yiddish articles by Wisse include "Stil un politik bay dovid bergelson," *Yugntruf* 15–16 (December 1968): 16–20; "Vegn dovid bergelsons dertseylung 'yoysef shor,' " *Di goldene keyt* 77 (1972): 133–144.

45. See, for instance, Ruth R. Wisse, "Sholem Aleichem and the Art of Communication" (B. G. Rudolph Lecture in Judaic Studies delivered at Syracuse University in March 1979). Here Wisse argued that Sholem Aleichem's *Tevye the Dairyman* "is less an account of action than of action filtered through speech. Thus acts of interpretation and verbal mastery take precedence over the drama of actual events. . . . In Sholem Aleichem's work, Jews repeatedly 'win' the situation they were historically losing in fact." See also Ruth R. Wisse, "Two Jews Talking: A View of Modern Yiddish Literature," *Prooftexts* 3 (September 1983): 35–48; *I. L. Peretz and the Making of Modern Jewish Culture;* and "A Monument to Messianism," *Commentary* 91 (March 1991): 37–42.

46. Ruth R. Wisse, "Blaming Israel," *Commentary* 77 (Ferbruary 1984): 31; "Israel and the Intellectuals: A Failure of Nerve?" *Commentary* 85 (May 1988): 23.

47. Wisse, *If I Am Not for Myself,* 34; Ruth R. Wisse, "The Delegitimation of Israel," *Commentary* 74 (July 1982): 36; "Letters from Readers: American Jews and Israel," *Commentary* 70 (November 1980): 12, 14 Ruth R. Wisse, response to "American Jews and Israel: A Symposium," *Commentary* 85 (February 1988): 75.

Other articles in which Wisse outlined the political follies of American Jews and the desertion of Israel by the liberal community include: "The Anxious American Jew," *Commentary* 66 (September 1976): 47–50; "A Light Unto the Nations?" *Commentary* 84 (December 1987): 30–35; " 'Peace Now' and American Jews," *Commentary* 70 (August 1980): 17–22; and "No left Turn: The Case Against Jewish Liberalism," *New Republic* 200 (May 22, 1989): 23–27, responses to which appeared in the *New Republic* 200 (June 26, 1989): 2.

Wisse's articles about the political developments in Israel itself include "Israel: A House Divided?" *Commentary* 84 (September 1987): 33–38; and "Jewish Guilt and Israeli Writers," *Commentary* 87 (January 1989): 25–41.

48. Khone Shmeruk, a professor of Yiddish at the Hebrew University in Jerusalem, died in July 1997. For a profile of this remarkable and complicated man see Ruth R. Wisse, "Yiddish: Past, Perfect, Imperfect," *Commentary* (November 1997): 32–39.

49. Ruth R. Wisse, "What Shall Live and What Shall Die: The Makings of a Yiddish Anthology" Twelfth Annual Rabbi Louis Feinberg Memorial Lecture in Judaic Studies, University of Cincinnati, May 1989, 26.

50. Ruth R. Wisse, *A Little Love in Big Manhattan* (Cambridge: Harvard University Press, 1988), ix. Her other articles on Yiddish poetry include *"Di Yunge* and the Problem of Jewish Aestheticism," *Jewish Social Studies* 38 (Summer-Fall 1976): 265–276; *"Di Yunge:* Immigrants or Exiles?" *Prooftexts* 1 (January 1981): 43–61; introduction to *Voices Within the Ark: The Modern Jewish Poets,* ed. Howard Schwartz and Anthony Rudolf (New York: Pushcart Press, 1980), 236–242; "A Yiddish Poet in America," *Commentary* 70 (July 1980): 35–41.

51. Wisse, *"Di Yunge* and the Problem of Jewish Aestheticism," 269.

52. Ruth R. Wisse, "American Jewish Writing, Act II," *Commentary* 61 (June 1976): 41; responses to this article by Cynthia Ozick, Norma Rosen, and others, as well as Wisse's reply appeared in *Commentary* 62 (September 1976): 8–14.

53. Ruth R. Wisse, The Hebrew Imperative," *Commentary* 89 (June 1990): 36–38.

54. On the early integration of Yiddish studies into American universities, see Paul Ritterband and Harold Wechsler, *Jewish Learning in American Universities: The First Century* (Bloomington: Indiana University Press, 1994), 187–189; about the genealogy of early Yiddish scholars see David Roskies, "The Emancipation of Yiddish," *Prooftexts* 1 (January 1981): 28–42.

55. Cf., Robert Liberles, *Salo Wittmayer Baron: Architect of Jewish History* (New York: New York University Press, 1995).

56. Lewis S. Feuer, "Recollections of Harry Austryn Wolfson," *American Jewish Archives* 28 (April 1976): 31. For the complicated history of Wolfson's employment at Harvard between 1915 and 1925, see the excellent account in Ritterband and Wechsler, *Jewish Learning in American Universities,* 107–121.

57. Ritterband and Wechsler, *Jewish Learning in American Universities,* 120.

58. On the intellectual tradition that nourished both Soloveitchik and Wolfson, and, by extension, Twersky, see Hillel Goldberg, *Between Berlin and Slobodka: Jewish Transition Figures from Eastern Europe* (Hoboken, N.J.: KTAV, 1989), esp. chap. 3, on Wolfson

(scathing, because of Wolfson's fall from observance); and chap. 5, on Soloveitchik. On Isadore Twersky see also Ruth R. Wisse, "A Summons to Dignity," *Forward* October 17, 1997: 1, 15.

59. Allan Nadler, "Paying Tribute to a Terrifyng Teacher's Legacy," *Forward* December 26, 1997: 11.

60. Ruth R. Wisse, "Found in America," review of *I Keep Recalling: The Holocaust Poems of Jacob Glatstein,* trans. Barnett Zumoff, and *Selected Poems of Yankev Glatshteyn,* trans. and ed. Richard J. Fein, *New Republic* 213 (September 18 and 25, 1995): 52.

61. Klingenstein, *Jews in the American Academy,* 32–33.

62. Charles Feidelson, interview with the author, New Haven, Conn., May 4, 1988. As luck would have it, Levin arrived in Columbus (ostensibly to give a lecture) on the eve of Passover. Diplomatically, the Bloomfields inquired through a third party whether Levin would like to come to their seder, not knowing how he might respond to such an invitation. But Levin accepted, and as a man to whom literacy in foreign languages mattered a great deal, he was quite taken when six-year-old Micah Bloomfield recited, in Hebrew, the four questions that initiate the narration of the Haggadah. For years the Bloomfields quipped that it was really Micah who had earned his father a job at Harvard. Caroline Bloomfield, interview with the author, Cambridge, Mass., June 22, 1995.

63. See, for instance, Bloomfield's article on "The Man of Law's Tale: A Tragedy of Victimization and a Christian Comedy," *PMLA* 87 (1972): 384–90. The Harvard "Faculty Minutes" record that "Morton was deeply concerned with the moral and religious values of literature, and his appreciation of these values was personal as well as academic;" W. Jackson Bates, Michael Shinagel, James Engell, eds., *Harvard Scholars in English, 1890–1990* (Cambridge: Harvard University Press, 1991), 118. Bloomfield's initiation of the Harvard course "The Bible as English Literature" reflected the centrality of the Bible in his professional and personal life. However, his wife told me that he was always particularly pleased when at the end of his lecture course, students would come up to him and ask to which, if any, religion he belonged.

64. Frank Kermode, "Beyond Category," review of *Vice Versa: Bisexuality and Eroticism in Everyday Life,* by Marjorie Garber, *New York Times Book Review,* July 9, 1995: 6. On Garber see Susanne Klingenstein, " 'But My Daughters Can Read the Torah': Careers of Jewish Women in Literary Academe," *American Jewish History* 83 (June 1995): 269–273.

65. David Harlan, "A People Blinded from Birth: American History According to Sacvan Bercovitch," *Journal of American History* 78 (December 1991): 952. For a rejoinder to Harlan see Arne Delfs, "Anxieties of Influence: Perry Miller and Sacvan Bercovitch," *New England Quarterly* 70 (December 1997): 601–615.

66. Sacvan Bercovitch, *The Rites of Assent: Transformations in the Symbolic Construction of America* (New York: Routledge, 1993), chap. 10, "The Problem of Ideology in a Time of Dissensus," 374–375. An earlier version of this chapter was published as "The Problem of Ideology in American Literary History," *Critical Inquiry* 12 (Summer 1986): 631–653. Further references to *Rites of Assent* are cited in the text as *RA.*

67. Andrew Delbanco in *The Puritan Ordeal* (Cambridge: Harvard University Press, 1989), 217, argues that he did.

68. Delfs, "Anxieties of Influence," 613.

69. Rael Meyerowitz, a student of Bercovitch's in the late 1980s, tried to work out the relation between Bercovitch's Jewishness and his criticism; see "Jewish Critics and

American Literature: The Case of Sacvan Bercovitch," in *Cohesion and Dissent in America,* ed. Carol Colatrella and Joseph Alkana (Albany: State University of New York Press, 1994), 31–47. See also Rael Meyerowitz, *Transferring to America: Jewish Interpretations of American Dreams* (Albany: State University of New York Press, 1995), esp. chap. 5, "Identifying Rhetorics: The Acculturation of Sacvan Bercovitch." In recent years Bercovitch did some work on Jewish literature, at first cautiously at the margins of the university by chairing a session on Yiddish literature at the annual convention of the Association of Jewish Studies in December 1992, and a panel on "What is Jewish Literature: A Symposium with Israeli Writers Aharon Appelfeld and Yoav Elstein," at the Harvard College Library, March 31, 1992. But beginning in the fall of 1996 he took his renewed interest in Jewish culture to the center of the university by offering seminars on Jewish American literature.

70. Caroline Bloomfield, interview with the author, June 22, 1995.

71. Marjorie Garber, interview with the author, Cambridge, Mass., May 22, 1989.

72. Martin Peretz, interview with the author, May 6, 1996, via telephone.

73. Sacvan Bercovitch, conversation with the author, Cambridge, Mass., May 10, 1994.

74. "The only legitimate use of the first person plural pronoun in class," Wisse said, "is 'we students.' 'We Jews' or 'we anything-else' is not an appropriate category in what must be a disinterested, investigative framework. You can understand how difficult it is to maintain this position when everywhere around you these categories have been collapsed. But one is not a propagandist and the classroom is not a pulpit." Her students confirm that Wisse keeps politics out of the classroom, even in a course entitled "Literature and Politics." One of her students, Lizzy Ratner (class of 1997) said, "I went in there as an advocate of the PLO; my thesis came from . . . the opposite end of the spectrum from where she is. I never felt misunderstood or penalized for my views; I felt my views were welcome. We used to get into these big discussions outside of class, like at her house. She actually cooked dinner for us!" Quoted in Janet Tassel, "Mame-loshn at Harvard," *Harvard Magazine* 99 (July–August 1997): 40.

11. The Meaning of America: Sacvan Bercovitch

1. Sacvan Bercovitch, "Cotton Mather," in *Major Writers of Early American Literature,* ed. Everett Emerson (Madison: University of Wisconsin Press, 1972), 98. All further references to this essay are cited in the text as CM.

2. Sacvan Bercovitch, "Melville's Pierre: Eine Lektüre," in *Romantik: Literatur und Philosophie,* ed. Volker Bohn, Internationale Beiträge zur Poetik (Frankfurt: Suhrkamp Verlag, 1987), 121–156. This essay is based on a talk Bercovitch delivered at the Free University of Berlin in 1984. An expanded version was reprinted in Bercovitch, *The Rites of Assent: Transformations in the Symbolic Construction of America* (New York: Routledge, 1993), 246–306. All further references to this collection are cited in the text as *RA.*

3. "Huck is a wonderful kid. But the problem is that he has the wrong values. He is a racist, he believes in class hierarchy, and he wants respectability in the worst way. . . . He is a would-be conformist. He can't make it, but he would love to if he could. Huck Finn would love to be Tom Sawyer, if he could. And he would love to sell Jim back, if he could. And he would love to please Miss Watson, if he could. He tries to please all

the time. But he is a kind of Zelig in reverse—he can't conform. So let me repeat the problem with Huck: He is a wonderful kid, but he believes in society. . . . If Huck came here and announced what he believed in, you would find it detestable. We have to read his goodness into him. . . . We have to protect Huck from his own words [through acts of interpretation]." Sacvan Bercovitch, "The Myth of America," lecture course at Harvard University, March 16, 1988.

4. Sacvan Bercovitch, interview with the author, Cambridge, Mass., April 14, 1989. In the course of my work on this study, I conducted five extensive formal interviews with Professor Bercovitch in his Cambridge office. We talked on February 2, 1988; February 10, 1988; March 9, 1988; April 4, 1988; and April 14, 1989. A discussion of the material in this chapter was taped on November 10, 1995. All quotations in this text attributed to Bercovitch but cited without an attribution of their exact source are taken from these interviews.

5. Janet Hadda, untitled paper on the Abishag poems in Itsik Manger's *Medresh Itsik* (delivered on a panel, "Rereading *Medresh Itsik*," chaired by Sacvan Bercovitch, at the annual convention of the Association for Jewish Studies, Boston, December 16, 1991).

6. Elisa New, "The Gaon in the Academy" (paper delivered on a panel, "Taking Stock: Jewish Literary Scholarship in the American Academy," at the annual convention of the Modern Language Association in San Francisco, December 29, 1991).

7. Sacvan Bercovitch, interview with the author, Cambridge, Mass., March 9, 1988. Bercovitch translated poems by Itsik Manger and stories by Yaacov Zipper, Solomon Ary, and Sholem Aleichem. His rendition of Sholem Aleichem's stories "The Pot" and "The Krushniker Delegation" appeared in *The Best of Sholom Aleichem*, ed. Irving Howe and Ruth Wisse (Washington: New Republic Books, 1979), 71–81, 232–244.

8. Leonard Wolf, untitled paper on translating *Medresh Itsik* (delivered at the Association for Jewish Studies, Boston, December 16, 1991). On empathy as a tool in the translation of Yiddish poetry, see also Cynthia Ozick, "A Translator's Monologue," in *Metaphor and Memory* (New York: Knopf, 1989), 199–207.

9. Ruth Wisse, "Introduction to Book II" in *Voices Within the Ark: The Modern Jewish Poets,* ed. Howard Schwartz and Anthony Rudolf (New York: Pushcart, 1980), 241. David G. Roskies, "The Last of the Purim Players: Itzik Manger," *Prooftexts* 13 (September 1993): 216. An expanded version of this essay was published in David G. Roskies, *Bridge of Longing: The Lost Art of Yiddish Storytelling* (Cambridge: Harvard University Press, 1995). See also Ruth Wisse, "Itsik Manger: Poet of the Jewish Folk," *Jewish Heritage* 12 (Spring 1970): 27–37.

10. Sacvan Bercovitch, *The American Jeremiad* (Madison: University of Wisconsin Press, 1978), xiv. All further references to this book are cited in the text as *AJ.*

11. Roskies, "Last of the Purim Players," 229. Itsik Manger, "The Ballad of the Jew Who Found a Half-Moon in a Cornfield," trans. Sacvan Bercovitch, *Moment* 3 (1978): 45.

12. Roskies, "Last of the Purim Players," 230.

13. Sylvia Ary, interview with the author, Montreal, Quebec, September 17, 1994. Further references to this interview are cited in the text as SA.

14. This portrait, *Manger with Cigarette,* is on display in the Manger Archive at the Jewish National and University Library, Jerusalem. About Manger's quarrel with Ravitch, see Roskies, "The Last of the Purim Players," 233 n. 27.

15. Roskies, "Last of the Purim Players," 230.

16. Ibid., 231. Bercovitch, introductory note to "Ballads of Itzik Manger," *Moment* 3 (1978): 44.

17. Bercovitch shortened the ballad so that the translated text could be displayed alongside his sister's illustration. Manger's ballad, which has twelve stanzas of varying length, meter, and rhyme, first appeared in his volume *Lamtern in vint: lid un balade* (Warsaw: Turem, 1933), 83–85, and was reprinted in *Lid un balade* (New York: Itsik-manger-komitet, 1952), 169–171.

18. About the shaping of Cotton Mather's American vision, Bercovitch wrote, "The meaning of the present (and the future) is accessible only through memory, since that action has already been fulfilled. Mather's myth comes to us from the inevitable future. It reshapes the past into a foreshadowing of greater things to come, a developing drama where meaning is accessible only through anticipation." *The Puritan Origins of the American Self* (New Haven: Yale University Press, 1975), 133. All further references to this book are cited in the text as *PO*.

19. "[Ich] habe nicht den letzten Zipfel des davonfliegenden jüdischen Gebetsmantels noch gefangen wie die Zionisten." Franz Kafka, "Die acht Oktavhefte," *Hochzeitsvorbereitungen auf dem Lande und andere Prosa aus dem Nachlaß, Gesammelte Werke;* ed. Max Brod (1935; reprint, Frankfurt: Fischer, 1989), 89.

20. Ruth Wisse, "The Jewish Intellectual and the Jews: The Case of *Di kliatshe* (The Mare) by Mendele Mocher Sforim" (Daniel E. Koshland Memorial lecture, San Francisco, March 24, 1992), 16.

21. Robert Adams, *The Life and Work of Alexander Bercovitch, Artist* (Montreal: Editions Marlowe, 1988), 13.

22. Nora Levin, *The Jews in the Soviet Union Since 1917: Paradox of Survival* (London: I. B. Tauris, 1990), 40; see also 28–29. Further references to this work are cited in the text as *JSU*. For information on the Jews in the Ukraine in this section of the book, I am deeply indebted to Nora Levin's study.

23. Levin, *Jews in the Soviet Union Since 1917*, 42–43. Isaac Babel, *1920 Diary*, ed. Carol J. Avins (New Haven: Yale University Press, 1995), 28, 64, xxiii.

24. Bryna Bercovitch, "Reflections," *Kanader Odler*, December 21, 1949 (in Yiddish). A translation of this article by Sylvia Ary, from which these quotations are taken, was reprinted as appendix 2 in Adams, *Life and Work of Alexander Bercovitch*, 117. The biographical information in this section is a conflation of material presented by Adams, additional stories told by Sylvia Ary (September 17, 1994) and Sacvan Bercovitch (November 10, 1995), and information pieced together from reading the columns Bryna Bercovitch wrote for the *Kanader Odler* between 1945 and 1950.

25. See also Ruth Wisse's less charitable view in her review essay "By Their Own Hands," *New Republic* 216 (February 3, 1997): 34–43.

26. Adams, *Life and Work of Alexander Bercovitch*, 13.

27. Ibid., 14–15; Edwin Becker, *Franz von Stuck, 1863–1928: Eros and Pathos* (Seattle: University of Washington Press, 1988).

28. Baila V'Dovetz and her son Kalmushe (a.k.a. Kalman Barkov) ended up in Israel, where Kalmushe fought in the War of Independence. He was deafened by a premature explosion while dynamiting a British installation. "On August 19, 1949, while driving a tractor on his kibbutz Givaot Zeid, he did not hear the malfunction of the engine and was crushed to death when the machine overturned." Adams, *Life and Work of Alexander Bercovitch*, 108.

29. Adams, *Life and Work of Alexander Bercovitch,* 17; see also Edward Braun, *Meyerhold: Revolution in Theatre* (London: Methuen, 1995); and Robert Leach, *Revolutionary Theatre* (London: Routledge, 1994). At this point the stories circulating in the Bercovitch family differ widely. About Bryna's coming to Moscow, Sacvan Bercovitch reports that after Bryna had thrown Alexander out of the house in 1917, "the next thing she heard was that he was living in Odessa, was married and had a child. And then the next thing she heard was contained in a letter to her, saying: If you don't come right away and save me I am going to throw myself off the bridge. So she went to Moscow." Sacvan Bercovitch, conversation with the author, November 10, 1995.

30. There are two different accounts of the family's move to Turkestan. Sacvan Bercovitch reports that in 1922 Bryna, who was working for the Communist Party, was assigned to Turkestan as a party member, "to tell these poor people about the truth of Communism. My father went along because he thought he might be able to get a job there. He was getting into trouble with party officials in Moscow because he was a very ironic, apolitical person. They took the job and went to Turkestan." Very soon after their arrival, Alexander returned to Moscow, leaving Bryna in Ashkabad, and rejoined her only when she was about to emigrate to Canada. In Robert Adams's and Sylvia Ary's version, it was Alexander who applied for a job in Turkestan, but found upon his arrival there that the art school where he was supposed to teach existed only on paper. Starving, he sent a letter to Bryna, who had remained in Moscow, that if she did not send such money or food as the Montreal parcels would allow her, he would throw himself into the nearest river (an empty threat in the desert of Turkestan). Bryna, who had found work in a state-run nursery, subsidized Alexander with what she could spare, and when the art school had become a reality and Alexander drew a regular salary, Bryna "accepted his offer of reconciliation and a fresh start and took the train to Ashkabad." Adams, *Life and Work of Alexander Bercovitch,* 21–24, and Sylvia Ary, conversation with the author, September 17, 1994.

31. Adams, *Life and Work of Alexander Bercovitch,* 28.

32. Sacvan Bercovitch does not quite concur in this assessment: "He certainly was convinced that he was an artist, and he was a bit of a snob about it, looking down on the other artists in Montreal and Canada. But I don't think he had enough confidence in himself to develop. I think he stopped developing at a certain point. Canada was very hard for him. He began to make paintings more and more to sell. He challenged himself less and less as an artist. He found it easy to paint and he painted a lot; he was very dedicated to it. But many of the paintings just came too easily to him; they were too repetitive" (conversation with the author, November 10, 1995). The most comprehensive study of Bercovitch's development as a painter is Adams, *The Life and Work of Alexander Bercovitch.*

33. Adams, *Life and Work of Alexander Bercovitch,* 62. Adams also reprints a facsimile of the article in the *Montreal Daily Herald* (April 7, 1933: 3, 9), entitled "Eviction of Artist Brings Recognition" (65). See also Charles C. Hill, *Canadian Painting in the Thirties* (Ottawa: National Gallery of Ottawa, 1975), 130.

34. Reynald [E. R. Bertrand, pseud.], "Contradictions des Vingt-Huit," *La Presse,* January 4, 1934: 11. An English translation appears as appendix 5 in Adams, *Life and Work of Alexander Bercovitch,* 123.

35. French text quoted in Esther Trépanier, *Peintres Juifs et Modernité[/]Jewish Painters and Modernity, Montreal 1930–1945* (Montréal: Centre Sadye-Bronfman, 1987), 77.

36. Sacvan Bercovitch, conversation with the author, November 10, 1995.

37. Rose Mamelak Johnstone, quoted in Adams, *Life and Work of Alexander Berco-vitch*, 88.

38. Saul Bellow, *Herzog* (New York: Viking, 1964), 140.

39. Adams, *Life and Work of Alexander Bercovitch*, 98.

40. Sacvan Bercovitch, conversation with the author, November 10, 1995.

41. Bellow, *Herzog*, 140.

42. Mark Twain, *The Adventures of Huckleberry Finn*, comprehensive edition (New York: Random House, 1996), 4.

43. Bellow, *Herzog*, 143.

44. Hashomer Hatzair, which together with Achdut Haavoda (a left-wing splinter of Mapai) constituted Mapam in 1948, advocated a binational (Arab-Jewish) state rather than an exclusively Jewish state in Palestine. Nadav Safran, *Israel, the Embattled Ally* (Cambridge: Belknap Press of Harvard University Press, 1981), 142–143; Haim Hillel Ben-Sasson, ed., *A History of the Jewish People* (Cambridge: Harvard University Press, 1976), 1055.

45. When he heard one of his Shomer friends speak glowingly about Reed College, he thought it might be a nice idea to go to college for a year before starting work on a kibbutz in Israel. "So I wrote away to Reed College. They asked for transcripts and an essay. The essay proved to be important because I certainly did not get good grades in high school. They answered right away, saying we have received your documents and your chances for getting in are—and they would check off a box: high, low, whatever. In my letter they had checked off the lowest box. So I forgot about it, thinking, well, why should I be able to go to college. I was preparing to go to the Shomrim's training farm and moved out of the place where I had lived. I went back a few months later to pick up a pair of forgotten shoes, and there was a letter waiting for me from Reed, offering me a scholarship. So I hitchhiked to Oregon because I had no money, got a job in a motel, working every other night, and attended Reed College for one year." Sacvan Bercovitch, conversation with the author, November 10, 1995.

46. Gila Bercovitch, interview with the author, New York City, April 18, 1994. Gila Bercovitch died in 1997. For her obituary see *New York Times* October 25, 1997: B16.

47. Sacvan Bercovitch, conversation with the author, November 10, 1995.

48. Sacvan Bercovitch, "Romance and Anti-Romance in *Sir Gawain and the Green Knight*," *Philological Quarterly* 46 (1965): 30–37.

49. Sacvan Bercovitch, "New England Epic: Cotton Mather's *Magnalia Christi Americana*," *ELH* [English Literary History] 33 (September 1966): 338.

50. Ibid., 337–338, 340, 350.

51. Sacvan Bercovitch, "Hilda's 'Seven-Branched Allegory': An Echo from Cotton Mather in *The Marble Faun*," *Early American Literature* 2 (Summer 1966): 5–6. Bercovitch delineated the significance of the golden candlestick as a metaphor in American Puritan writing in his essay "New England Epic" (341 n. 5).

52. Sacvan Bercovitch, "Endicott's Breastplate: Symbolism and Typology in 'Endicott and the Red Cross,' " *Studies in Short Fiction* 4 (Summer 1967): 291.

53. Sacvan Bercovitch, " 'Delightful Examples of Surprising Prosperity': Cotton Mather and the American Success Story," *English Studies* 51 (1970): 40–43.

54. Having prefaced his section on Cotton Mather's diaries with a quotation from Norman Mailer's novel *The Armies of the Night* ("Once History inhabits a crazy house,

egotism may be the last tool left to History"), Bercovitch commented: "This is not the place to speculate on the cultural continuities that underlie such continuities in imaginative strategy [i.e., transforming personal failure into social ideal]. It must suffice to recall our recurrent crisis of national identity, and the recurrent emergence of Jeremiahs seeking to set the crazy house of history in order by invoking the idea of America and finding instead 'rich compensation' for an untoward political reality in the self-contained, all-encompassing, exemplary American self" (CM 105).

55. Bercovitch, "New England Epic," 337–338.

56. Sacvan Bercovitch, introduction to *The American Puritan Imagination: Essays in Revaluation,* ed. Sacvan Bercovitch (New York: Cambridge University Press, 1974), 2. Further references to this essay are cited in the text as *API*.

57. New, "Gaon in the Academy."

58. Ibid.

59. Sacvan Bercovitch, " 'Nehemias Americanus': Cotton Mather and the Concept of the Representative American," *Early American Literature* 8 (Winter 1974): 228–229.

60. Ibid., 232.

61. Ibid., 233.

62. Ibid., 234

63. Bercovitch, " 'Nehemias Americanus,' " 222.

64. The complicated relationship between Miller and Bercovitch has occasioned a slew of articles and polemics which were reviewed and evaluated in Arne Delfs, "Anxieties of Influence: Perry Miller and Sacvan Bercovitch," *New England Quarterly* 70 (December 1997): 601–615. Donald Weber in "Historicizing the Errand," *American Literary History* 2 (1990): 101–118 broadened the debate by comparing Andrew Delbanco's perspective on the Puritans to that of Miller and Bercovitch.

65. Sacvan Bercovitch and Myra Jehlen, eds., *Ideology and Classic American Literature* (New York: Cambridge University Press, 1986), 5.

66. Sacvan Bercovitch, ed., *Reconstructing American Literary History* (Cambridge: Harvard University Press, 1986), vii. All further references to this volume are cited in the text as *RAHL*. Five years later, when multiculturalism had asserted itself as a force in literary academe, another 'reconstructive' volume appeared, edited by Philip Fisher and entitled *The New American Studies* (Berkeley: University of California Press, 1991), in which the contributors were billed as "a new generation of Americanists deal[ing] a fatal blow to the idea of a unified American culture" (press advertisement). In a discussion of the book at Harvard's Center for Literary and Cultural Studies in the fall of 1991, Bercovitch remarked wryly about the hard facts underlying the new movement: "Multiculturalism is a professional academic mode that allows people to enter the marketplace. It involves a set of identities, American-Jewish, American-Irish, African American, and so forth, that is geared toward a certain marketplace. What is really important is punching through the rhetoric, and getting at the political mechanism generating the rhetoric."

67. Richard Sennett, on the back cover of *Rites of Assent.*

68. Bercovitch edited two sets of reprints, 70 volumes in all. They are *American Puritanism: The Seventeenth Century* (New York: AMS Press, 1983), 27 volumes with brief descriptions and a general introduction by Sacvan Bercovitch; and *The Millennium in America: From the Puritan Migration to the Civil War* (New York: AMS Press, 1983), 43 volumes with brief descriptions and a general introduction by Sacvan Bercovitch.

69. "Cambridge University Press allowed me to do what I wanted," Bercovitch explained. "So I thought it would be interesting to do a history that was not a summation of knowledge but was written by young scholars who would be disagreeing with each other and who had irreconcilable points of view. I chose scholars who were representative of what was going on in the field. I thought, let this be a history of this generation. Since no history is for eternity but speaks to what is going on at the time, let this be a real statement. There was only one practical constraint. I wanted the writers to have tenure. Since I was dependent on them, I wanted at least the security that they would have a job and stay there. And so my criterion was between tenure and forty-five." Interview with the author, Cambridge, Mass., April 4, 1988.

70. Eric Sundquist, on the dust jacket of *The Office of the Scarlet Letter* (Baltimore: Johns Hopkins University Press, 1991).

71. Bercovitch, *Office of the Scarlet Letter,* xiii.

72. In a conversation with the author on November 10, 1995, Bercovitch explained: "The last essay I wrote [for *Rites of Assent*] was the Emerson essay. In a way it's my effort—the biggest effort I've ever made—to compromise with actually calling myself something of an Emersonian. It's the essay in which I do the most to try to Americanize myself in a conscious way. I was trying to see how far I could go in adapting to this mode. It was really an attempt to see what it would be like to accept this world, to stop fighting it, and to integrate. It was an attempt to see what the possibilities for me would be, what part of Emerson I would pick up, if I were to become an Emersonian." Question: "But you aren't one." Answer: "I can't be. It's not in my nature." Question: "Why is that?" Answer: "I distrust individuals. I can't follow a person. People are human and I see all sorts of problems."

73. Gila Bercovitch did not wish to move from New York City to Cambridge, Massachusetts. She had created a life of her own in the city, which she wanted to continue. Their marriage ended in divorce in 1983. Bercovitch remarried and started a new family.

74. Perry Miller, *Orthodoxy in Massachusetts, 1630–1650: A Genetic Study* (Cambridge: Harvard University Press, 1933), xi.

75. Itsik Manger, "November balade," in *Lamtern un vint,* 83; my translation.

76. Bercovitch is referring to Emerson's essay "The American Scholar," delivered before the Phi Beta Kappa Society in Cambridge on August 31, 1837; Sacvan Bercovitch, "The Myth of America," lecture course at Harvard University, session on Emerson and Whitman, February 29, 1988.

Epilogue: Idols of the Tribe

1. Seymour Martin Lipset and Everett Carll Ladd, Jr., "Jewish Academics in the United States: Their Achievements, Culture and Politics," *American Jewish Yearbook* 72 (1971): 92–93.

2. Alvin Chenkin, "Jewish Population in the United States," *American Jewish Yearbook* 70 (1969): 265.

3. At Harvard this fragmentation was reversed recently with the creation of the Barker Center, which brings together under one roof different humanities departments, among them English Literature, Afro-American Studies, and Women's Studies.

4. In fact, Fish (b. 1938) is nine years younger than Hartman and five years older

than Greenblatt. Having written important works while still in his twenties, Fish arrived on the academic scene a decade earlier than his contemporaries.

5. Lawrence Lipking, "Competitive Reading: The New Academic Sport," *New Republic* 201 (October 2, 1989): 30.

6. Stephen Greenblatt, *Learning to Curse: Essays in Early Modern Culture* (New York: Routledge, 1990), 1. On Marjorie Garber's development, see Susanne Klingenstein, " 'But My Daughters Can Read the Torah': Careers of Jewish Women in Literary Academe," *American Jewish History* 83 (June 1995), 247–286.

7. Stanley Fish, interview with the author, Cambridge, Mass., August 27, 1988. Further references to this interview are cited in the text as interview.

8. The exceptions to this rule, scholars such as Sander Gilman or Ruth Klüger, do not usually work in English departments.

9. Harold Bloom, *The Strong Light of the Canonical: Kafka, Freud and Scholem as Revisionists of Jewish Culture and Thought,* The City College Papers, no. 20 (New York: City College, 1987), 41.

10. Harold Bloom, *The Book of J* (New York: Grove Weidenfeld, 1990), 9, 13; Bloom, *Ruin the Sacred Truths: Poetry and Belief from the Bible to the Present* (Cambridge: Harvard University Press, 1989), 22; see also Bloom, "Free and Broken Tablets: The Cultural Prospects of American Jewry," in *Agon: Towards a Theory of Revisionism* (New York: Oxford University Press, 1982), 318–329; Bloom, "The Sorrows of American-Jewish Poetry," *Commentary* 53 (March 1972): 69–74.

11. Geoffrey Hartman, "The Struggle for the Text," in *Midrash and Literature,* ed. Geoffrey Hartman and Sanford Budick (New Haven: Yale University Press, 1986), 3–18; Geoffrey Hartman, "Ki Tissa," *Orim* 2 (Fall 1986): 126–127.

12. Evan Carton, "The Holocaust, French Poststructuralist Theory, and the American Literary Academy" (paper delivered at the annual convention of the Association of Jewish Studies, Boston, December 17, 1996).

13. Evan Carton, a professor of English at the University of Texas at Austin, very kindly let me see his yet unpublished manuscript " 'Nous sommes tous les Juifs allemands': The Holocaust, French Poststructuralist Theory, and the American Literary Academy." Geoffrey Hartman recently collected some of his essays on the Holocaust in *The Longest Shadow: In the Aftermath of the Holocaust* (Bloomington: Indiana University Press, 1996).

14. Between 1984 and 1995 six out of twelve MLA presidents were Jewish. Between 1981 and 1995, 21 of the 73 members of the MLA's Executive Council were Jewish. Among the most important textbooks are *The Norton Anthology of Literature by Women,* ed. Sandra Gilbert and Susan Gubar (New York: Norton, 1985); *The Norton Shakespeare,* ed. Stephen Greenblatt (New York: Norton, 1997); and *The Oxford Mark Twain,* ed. Shelley Fisher Fishkin (New York: Oxford University Press, 1997).

15. *English Institute Annual 1939* (New York: Columbia University Press, 1940), v, 1. At the second meeting in 1940, at least 28 out of 105 registrants were women. The number of Jews is harder to assess from the list of names; my guess is that the figure is very low (perhaps between 6 and 10 individuals).

16. The printed record of the Institute unfortunately no longer includes the actual program. One panel, chaired by Susan Stewart, was called "Representing Practices" and featured John Brenkman on "Multiculturalism and Criticism," Jonathan Goldberg on "Sodomitries," and Henry Susman on "Versions of the Literary Grandiose"; the other

panel, chaired by Michael McKeon, was called "Historicizing Lyric Poetry" and presented papers by Richard L. Halpern on " 'Sacred Poems and Private Ejaculations': The Domain of Early Modern Lyric," Douglas Lane Patey on " 'Aesthetics' and the Rise of Lyric in the Eighteenth Century," and Clifford H. Siskin on "The Lyricization of Labor."

17. Susan Gubar and Jonathan Kamholtz, eds., *English Inside and Out: The Places of Literary Criticism* (Routledge: New York, 1993), 3.

18. Ibid., 89.

19. Ibid., 43, 42, 38.

20. Ibid., 65, 64, 66.

21. Cf. Ruth Wisse, "By Their Own Hands," *New Republic* 216 (February 3, 1997): 34–43. Culling her information from a questionnaire Gallop had filled out Susan Gubar wrote, "Jane Gallop believes that Jewishness bequeathed a ' "negative" identity' of being 'set apart from a larger culture.' Her sense of herself as 'an internal alien within American (Christian) culture'—'being proudly not-Christian'—has 'analogies in my theoretical positions and in my implicit definition of woman as proudly not a man.' " Gubar, "Eating the Bread of Affliction: Judaism and Feminist Criticism," in *People of the Book: Thirty Jewish Scholars Reflect on Their Jewish Identity,* ed. Jeffrey Rubin-Dorsky and Shelley Fisher Fishkin (Madison: University of Wisconsin Press, 1996), 26.

22. All quotations in this section are taken from my interview with Stanely Fish unless otherwise indicated.

23. Stanley Fish, "The Unbearable Ugliness of Volvos," in *English Inside and Out,* ed. Gubar and Kamholtz, 102–103.

24. Ibid., 105.

25. Ibid., 106.

26. Cf. David R. Shumway, "The Star System in Literary Studies," *PMLA* 112 (January 1997): 85–100.

27. Fish, "The Unbearable Ugliness of Volvos," 106.

Index